Follow Your

INTERESTS TO FIND THE RIGHT COLLEGE

ART/ARCHITECTURE
BUSINESS
INTERNATIONAL RELATIONS
EQUESTRIAN
COMMUNICATIONS
ENVIRONMENTAL STUDIES
STUDY ABROAD
MUSIC

JANET MARTHERS, MA
PAUL MARTHERS, EdD

Follow Your Interests to Find the Right College
Copyright © 2016 Janet and Paul Marthers. All rights reserved. No part of this book may be reproduced or retransmitted in any form or by any means without the written permission of the publisher.

Cover design by Margot Ecke, Smokey Road Press.

Published by Wheatmark®
1760 East River Road, Suite 145, Tucson, Arizona 85718 USA
www.wheatmark.com

ISBN: 978-1-62787-262-1 (paperback)
ISBN: 978-1-62787-263-8 (ebook)
LCCN: 2015933878

rev201602

CONTENTS

PART II: AREAS OF STUDY

INTRODUCTION

Think of this book as a type of buying guide. Most buying guides help the shopper become educated about product choices, turning that shopper into an educated consumer able to navigate the myriad product options offered. Buying guides tend to emphasize that the shopper is in charge of the transaction. So it seems odd to us that many college guides cast the shopper in the position of supplicant and focus on strategies for communicating and negotiating with the sales department (the admissions and financial-aid offices) rather than on understanding the actual quality of the product (the focus of the college and its academic offerings). Our guidebook takes a different approach because it is grounded in the fundamental belief that the shopper (the prospective college student) is in charge. Our book steps beyond the well-trod path of handicapping admissions chances to explain the products (the range of college options), including the features and potential benefits of making particular choices. The goal of our book is to educate readers about the diversity of institutions and academic programs available to them.

There are many different kinds of colleges. Getting into the right one for you requires knowing as much as possible about the options available across the higher education landscape. This book attempts to provide direction to anyone confronting the seemingly endless array of choices and removes some of the confusion surrounding the college search process. When we began writing, our goal was to produce a book that would match the way most students go about their college search. Countless research studies (by organizations such as the ACT and the Higher Education Research Institute at UCLA) show that prospective students tend to organize their college search around a particular academic program of interest, and from that starting point they seek to find the best place to study. Taking a cue from those insights, we crafted this fact-driven and accessible discussion of leading academic programs and types of colleges and titled it *Follow Your Interests to Find the Right College*.

Follow Your Interests to Find the Right College is a reference book for prospective college students, their parents, college guidance counselors, and career advisers. We believe that this book will be indispensable for students searching for college options that best match their needs. Our book will help readers gain a clear understanding of the vast array of study options available in the United States, Canada, and at selected English-speaking universities in the rest of the world. This book's focus on academic programs and types of colleges mirrors the way students approach their college search. Taking the investigate-your-interests-first, figure-out-your-admissions-chances-later approach makes our book a new type of college guide, one filled with information that no other book is providing in one place. In this way, *Follow Your Interests to Find the Right College* fills a void in the college guide universe.

Most college guides focus on admissions strategy or provide encyclopedic listings and summary descriptions of colleges. This is a different kind of book, one focused on the range and types of academic opportunities and college options. Our book presents information not found in other guidebooks, such as the range of study opportunities beyond the United States—with chapters describing universities in Canada, Great Britain, continental Europe, Asia, Australia, and New Zealand. The opening chapters provide explanations of college groupings (such as liberal arts colleges, state universities, and science and technology institutions—to name just a few examples). Part two of the book covers specialized academic options, such as where to study for a degree in architecture, business, environmental studies, equine science, fashion design, hospitality, international relations, journalism, musical theater, nursing, expedited entry into medical school, and more. Along the way, our book provides lists and subjective rankings of colleges and universities, as a sorting mechanism rather than as the definitive word on institutional quality. Colleges and programs are placed onto lists when it seems necessary to help prospective students distinguish among a sea of competing (and sometimes confusing) options. All rankings in this book are based on a critical examination of hundreds of assessments of academic and institutional quality as well as consultation with experts, such as deans and professors.

So often the college search process is daunting because students and parents do not know where to look for or how to ask for what they want. Beyond illuminating the options available, this book explains and demystifies processes, terms, and programs, such as applying to service academies, art portfolios, auditions, ROTC, and admissions for home-schooled students. This book also brings lesser-known college options out of obscurity. Knowing about less publicized alternatives (such as public liberal arts colleges, colleges with learning-difference programs, honors colleges at state universities, colleges for aviation, Hispanic-serving institutions, and historically black colleges and universities) will help students determine which options are best suited for them. We believe that when students and their families know what is being offered and how to access the information they need, enthusiasm for the many exciting future paths available will replace the anxiety that can accompany the college search process. One of our goals in writing this book was to make the journey of college selection a more illuminating, affirming, and (dare we say?) enjoyable experience for the entire family. We want our readers to become better-educated consumers of college information. We want them to chart out their short and long-term career plans with confidence.

In our opinion, the college-selection process should be primarily about the student following her or his academic and personal interests to find a suitable school. Unfortunately, many college guides focus too much on the admissions office (potentially) rejecting the student. While our book does not intend to sugarcoat the reality of competitive college admissions, we wrote it to point out two key realities often lost in the frenzy to get into the so-called best college:

1. There are hundreds of excellent (and potentially transforming) college options available.

2. Admissions selectivity should not be the chief factor that drives the college search.

At one point when we were exploring publishing options, a representative from a large press (who hadn't even bothered to read our book) suggested that most of the information in it could be found on college-finder websites and in college rankings guides. We strongly disagree, and think our readers deserve more thoughtfully researched information. Take rankings guides and websites. When we examined such supposedly authoritative resources, more often than not, we found listings of top programs where the "highly ranked" college or university did not even offer an undergraduate major in that particular academic area. In some cases, the rankings were based on the reputed quality of the graduate program in the field. In other cases, the highly ranked program was an undergraduate minor, not a major. That last point begs the question of how a limited program, such as a minor, can stand out when stacked up against major programs. Aren't majors inherently more extensive than minors? In just about every such case, it appeared that the program was highly ranked due to its location at a prestigious university assumed to be outstanding at everything. We question that kind of simplistic reasoning and believe that our readers should, too.

What about college-finder web tools, where students fill out their interests, hit enter, and get a list of schools to investigate? Don't such tools work as well as this book? Caveat emptor (that is, let the buyer beware). Anyone who has ever used college-finder web tools has learned that they are extremely limited. At best, such tools give students a mere list of college names. But those lists can be fraught with the kind of errors described in the previous paragraph. Search tools that produce a list of colleges generally have not been built on the extensive research we did in gathering, synthesizing, and analyzing vast quantities of anecdotal and numerical data that we have distilled into what, we hope, are insightful descriptions and authoritative lists. Using college-finder web tools can bring to mind a new twist on the old computer programming adage "garbage in, garbage out," resulting in high expectations going in and flawed information coming out. Those using college-finder web tools would do well to check the resulting list against the more detailed information found in our book. We are confident that our approach will prove more useful.

So, to our readers, we say, let others rely on inferior methods while you use our book to refine your search for the degree program and school that will best meet your needs. We think that after reading this book, you will emerge believing—as we do—that there are many excellent colleges and programs out there. Let others believe the hype and anxiety generated by all the college-admissions strategy books that aid and abet the myth that only a limited number of excellent college choices exist. That myth of scarcity serves those strategy guides quite well.

If everyone believes that the most highly sought after colleges are self-evidently the best for all, then, of course, there will be great demand for any book that purports to unlock the secrets known only to those with inside knowledge of highly selective admissions.

Because the myth of scarcity is so daunting, so powerful, and so potentially paralyzing, we think unpacking it is a worthwhile exercise. The myth of scarcity goes something like this. Clearly, there are twenty-five to fifty colleges and universities that *everyone* recognizes as the best. Going to one of those colleges is not just a mark of achievement and cachet, but a head start on, if not a guarantee of, future success in life and work. Those twenty-five to fifty best colleges are getting more selective each year, so knowing strategies for how to get admitted to one of those colleges is crucial. Admittedly, it is clear that in this era of admission rates below ten percent at the most selective colleges, predicting who will be admitted to such colleges seems next to impossible. What is less clear is whether it makes sense for students to let the myth of scarcity, and the accompanying anxiety it foments, drive their college search.

Let's take a close look at the premises underlying the myth of college admission scarcity. First of all, among the supposed top twenty-five to fifty colleges, while there is excellence, there is also great uniformity in the majors and programs offered. Yes, the so-called top twenty-five to fifty colleges are outstanding places to prepare for business school, law school, and medical school. But very few of them offer undergraduate majors in areas such as architecture, journalism and communications, nursing, pharmacy, or teaching. Many of them lack depth and strength in areas such as engineering, environmental studies, fine arts, and performing arts. As a result, students who fixate on the top twenty-five to fifty name-brand colleges end up cutting themselves off from many specialized programs that can lead to rewarding careers. A great number of the interesting academic programs highlighted in our book—in chapters related to the arts, business, creative writing, health professions, hospitality, public policy, video game design, and so on—do not have very selective admissions. There are many good options out there at all ranges of admissions selectivity. In our opinion, abundance, rather than scarcity, describes the higher education opportunities available to students. If the readers of our book emerge with just one conclusion about the college search process, we hope it will be the reality of abundance, not the myth of scarcity.

The following chapters jump right into descriptions of different types of colleges and specialized academic programs. We invite you to take your own individual journey through this book. Because we do not expect many readers to start at the beginning of the first chapter and read to the end of the last chapter, we created a very detailed table of contents. We expect that many readers will start with the sections that describe the academic area or college type that is of greatest interest to them. Other readers, perhaps guidance counselors who view this as a resource book, may be more likely to read the book in a linear way. Whichever type of reader you are and however you proceed through this book, the aim throughout is to help you.

Part 1

TYPES OF COLLEGES

LIBERAL ARTS COLLEGES

The term *liberal arts college* can confuse people because it invites the false impression that a liberal arts college education is restricted solely to the study of arts and humanities subjects. In reality, liberal arts colleges provide their students with a broad-based education that encompasses the arts, social sciences, humanities, *and* sciences. A number of features—when combined—makes the liberal arts college experience distinctive and even inspires some alumni to think of it as the ultimate form of undergraduate education.

At the educational core of most liberal arts colleges are small classes, teaching-oriented professors, and a classroom experience that is highly personalized and interactive. Liberal arts colleges make it their mission to help students develop certain habits of mind—including, but not limited to, independent thinking, critical reasoning and analysis, and clear and persuasive writing and speaking—that will serve students well for the rest of their lives. Liberal arts colleges provide an education less focused on producing graduates with technical competence (or training) in a specialty. Instead, a liberal arts education seeks to prepare students for virtually any type of future work or further education. Liberal arts college graduates who have achieved success (and the list is long and impressive) often attribute that success to the learning skills they picked up studying subjects like history, foreign languages, literature, mathematics, physics, psychology, and sociology.

Students best fitted to a liberal arts college (LAC) are those attracted to the idea that their college education might not prepare them to do one particular specialty but will instead prepare them to learn how to do virtually anything. The benefits of the less specialized LAC approach to education show up in both direct and indirect ways. An example has to do with font styles on computers. When technology entrepreneur Steve Jobs studied at Reed College, he took a calligraphy class that was not directly related to computers or physics (his major there). That calligraphy class later had a profound impact on Jobs when he was designing the fonts for the company he cofounded: Apple Computer. Jobs's study of calligraphy at Reed gave him an understanding of typography and different artistic styles that he later applied when developing user-friendly and visually appealing technology at Apple. Choice and variety of font type soon became a central part of the computer user's experience. Addressing the Stanford University class of 2005, Jobs relayed his profound appreciation for his liberal arts experience and directly credited calligraphy at Reed as his inspiration for making Apple devices distinctive in their design.

In the very same speech, however, Jobs claimed that his decision to drop out of Reed was necessitated by the high cost of tuition that his working-class parents could not afford. Indeed, the price tag for a private LAC is usually far higher than the amount charged by the typical large public university. Still, sticker prices, like appearances, can be deceiving. The reality is that most people do not actually pay the full sticker price for their LAC education because many of the best-endowed liberal arts colleges have the resources to provide generous financial aid. Compared with many public universities—where scholarship aid can be scarce—the actual cost of some liberal arts colleges can be equal or lower. For that reason, cost should not be a prohibitive factor in considering LACs. Over 75 percent of the students at many liberal arts colleges (Grinnell College in Iowa and Macalester College in Minnesota, to name just two examples) are getting scholarship aid packages.

Often scholarship aid reduces the cost to well below half of the sticker price. Numerous other LACs, such as Amherst, Davidson, Oberlin, Pomona, Swarthmore, and Wellesley, provide scholarship-only, no-loan packages for low-income students.

LIBERAL ARTS COLLEGES VERSUS LARGE UNIVERSITIES

The defining difference between liberal arts colleges and research universities is that LACs are generally small (under 5,000 students) and do not have significant numbers of graduate students. The classic liberal arts college has an enrollment under 2,500 students (95 to 100 percent of whom are undergraduates) learning in small, interactive classes. Research universities are usually large and comprised of different academic schools that serve both undergraduate and graduate students. At universities where the student population exceeds ten thousand, freshmen and sophomores typically find themselves in large lecture classes where a professor is assisted by graduate students who grade papers and lead the discussion sections. At large universities, many of the senior faculty members (especially the notables) tend to interact primarily with the graduate students.

Due to their small size and singular focus on undergraduates, liberal arts colleges generally foster an environment where students feel bonded to the whole place—much like how residents of small towns know and experience the whole town, not just a particular neighborhood. Universities, by contrast, can feel more like cities, where students bond to particular neighborhoods. This is because universities often consist of multiple schools that can feel like autonomous divisions. An example of this is Boston University whose nearly thirty thousand students identify themselves by the three-letter abbreviations for the particular college they attend—for example, COM for communications, SED for education, and SMG for management. A student can attend such a university without ever stepping into certain buildings because those facilities are for specialized research or academic programs divergent from their interests. This phenomenon is far less common at LACs.

The small size of the typical LAC enables its students to feel like the proverbial big fish in a small pond. Attention from and collaboration with faculty can nurture academic growth and help LAC students develop increased intellectual and social confidence. The small LAC environment also fosters an ethos of participation. Students get involved rather than watch from the sidelines. Leadership positions are easier to get and organizations are easier to join because there are fewer students competing for coveted spots on the newspaper staff, student senate, debate team, or editorial board of the literary magazine. At larger universities, there will undoubtedly be a bigger constellation of academic, athletic, and professorial stars that collectively might shine brighter than those in the LAC universe, but to the typical student, those university stars may seem like distant planets rarely glimpsed.

Liberal arts colleges are based on the notion that the undergraduate years should provide the educational foundation for later specialization. For the student with a variety of interests who is reluctant to choose one as a specialty, the liberal arts college ethos of generalist over specialist provides a comfortable educational fit. Liberal arts college students get to specialize (through their chosen major) and get a broad-based education through the academic distribution requirements that introduce them to disciplines ranging from anthropology and art history to math, psychology, and physics. As a result, the liberal arts graduate often feels prepared to take a number of different career paths. For example, biology students required to take half of their courses beyond the sciences (a typical requirement at liberal arts colleges) may graduate prepared for medical school and graduate school in biology but also for careers in business or international relations, or even entry into law school.

Liberal arts colleges generally do not offer vocation-specific majors such as interior design or pharmacy. Instead, to be an interior designer, a liberal arts college student might major in art or art history and then go on to graduate study in architecture or interior design at a large university or at a specialized art school. To be a pharmacist, a liberal arts college student might major in biology or chemistry as an undergraduate and then go on to get a doctorate from a professional pharmacy school. In fact, certain fields, such as architecture, interior design, and pharmacy are packed with successful practitioners who went to a liberal arts college for an undergraduate degree followed by specialized study for a graduate degree. Students who leave high school with numerous interests in disparate areas might be better off avoiding specialized undergraduate degree programs (that can narrow options) and instead selecting the liberal arts route toward more general preparation for a variety of career paths.

LIBERAL ARTS LUMINARIES

The evidence that a liberal arts college education can provide a path to success appears in the countless examples of prominent attorneys, business owners, executives, physicians, professors, and writers—even some famous names—who attended a LAC. Liberal arts colleges prepare students for future careers by providing a kind of intellectual tool kit: critical thinking, clear and analytical writing, and in-depth research skills. Frequently, liberal arts college graduates cite how the thinking, writing, and research skills they acquired in college helped them adapt to and master the professional and academic challenges they faced after graduation. Below is a selection of well-known LAC graduates:

➤ WELL-KNOWN LIBERAL ARTS GRADUATES

Madeleine Albright, former secretary of state (Wellesley)

Kofi Annan, former secretary general of the UN (Macalester)

Joseph Barnette, former CEO of Bank One (Wabash)

Dave Barry, humor columnist (Haverford)

Gloria Borger, journalist (Colgate)

Margaret Wise Brown, children's book author (Hollins)

Ken Burns, filmmaker (Hampshire)

Steve Carrell, actor (Denison)

Thomas Chappell, cofounder of Tom's of Maine (Trinity—Connecticut)

Ben Cherington, general manager, Boston Red Sox (Amherst)

Julia Child, chef (Smith)

Hillary Clinton, former senator and secretary of state (Wellesley)

Harlan Coben, novelist (Amherst)

John Cornyn, US senator (Trinity—Texas)

Harry Coover, inventor of Super Glue (Hobart and William Smith)

Wes Craven, horror film director (Wheaton—Illinois)

→

► WELL-KNOWN LIBERAL ARTS GRADUATES (CONT.)

Beth Daniel, Hall of Fame golfer (Furman)

Lena Dunham, actress and filmmaker (Oberlin)

Marian Wright Edelman, founder of Children's Defense Fund (Spelman)

Rahm Emanuel, mayor of Chicago (Sarah Lawrence)

Eve Ensler, *Vagina Monologues* creator (Middlebury)

Drew Gilpin Faust, first female president of Harvard (Bryn Mawr)

Jennifer Garner, actress (Denison)

Doris Kearns Goodwin, historian (Colby)

Jerry Greenfield, cofounder of Ben and Jerry's (Oberlin)

Bryant Gumbel, television journalist (Bates)

Michael C. Hall, actor (Earlham)

Mary Hart, television host (Augustana—South Dakota)

Woody Harrelson, actor (Hanover)

Reed Hastings, Netflix founder (Bowdoin)

Ed Helms, actor (Oberlin)

Katharine Hepburn, actress (Bryn Mawr)

Harry Hopkins, architect of the New Deal's WPA (Grinnell)

Zora Neale Hurston, writer (Barnard)

Abigail Johnson, president of Fidelity Investments (Hobart and William Smith)

Herb Kelleher, founder of Southwest Airlines (Wesleyan)

Barbara Kingsolver, writer (DePauw)

Jon Krakauer, writer (Hampshire)

Peter Krause, actor (Gustavus Adolphus)

Frances Moore Lappe, hunger activist (Earlham)

Spike Lee, film director (Morehouse)

Patrick Leahy, US senator (St. Michael's)

Dennis Lehane, writer (Eckerd)

Marv Levy, Hall of Fame NFL coach (Coe)

Keith Lockhart, conductor, Boston Pops (Furman)

Hunter Lovins, founder of Natural Capitalism (Pitzer)

Joe Maddon, manager, Chicago Cubs (Lafayette)

Chris Matthews, journalist (Holy Cross)

James Michener, author (Swarthmore)

Jim Mora Sr., former NFL coach (Occidental)

Viggo Mortensen, actor (St. Lawrence)

Paul Newman, actor (Kenyon)

Robert Noyce, cofounder of Intel (Grinnell)

Diana Nyad, distance swimmer (Lake Forest)

Lupita Nyong'o, actress (Hampshire)

Lute Olson, NCAA champion basketball coach (Augsburg)

Ron Paul, congressman/presidential candidate (Gettysburg)

Frances Perkins, first female cabinet member (Mount Holyoke)

Sylvia Plath, writer (Smith)

Roy Plunkett, inventor of Teflon (Manchester)

Herb Ritts, photographer (Bard)

Pat Robertson, televangelist and Regent University founder (Washington and Lee)

Gene Robinson, first openly gay Episcopal bishop (Sewanee)

Fred Rogers, creator and host of *Mister Rogers' Neighborhood* (Rollins)

Philip Roth, author (Bucknell)

Pleasant Rowland, creator of American Girl dolls (Wells)

Ken Salazar, former US senator and interior secretary (Colorado College)

Peter Schickele, composer as fictional PDQ Bach (Swarthmore)

Ellen Browning Scripps, philanthropist (Knox)

B. F. Skinner, behavioral psychology theorist (Hamilton)

Stephen Sondheim, composer (Williams)

George Steinbrenner, legendary owner of the New York Yankees (Williams)

Gloria Steinem, pioneering feminist (Smith)

Sufjan Stevens, singer (Hope)

Martha Stewart, retail magnate (Barnard)

Meryl Streep, actress (Vassar)

Matt Taibbi, journalist (Bard)

Donna Tartt, writer (Bennington)

Rich Templeton, CEO of Texas Instruments (Union)

Twyla Tharp, dancer/choreographer (Barnard)

Clarence Thomas, US Supreme Court justice (Holy Cross)

Stephen Updegraff, LASIK surgery pioneer (Eckerd)

Tom Vilsack, US secretary of agriculture (Hamilton)

David Viniar, CFO of Goldman Sachs (Union)

Alice Walker, writer (Sarah Lawrence)

Joss Whedon, film and television producer (Wesleyan)

George Will, columnist (Trinity—Connecticut)

Frederick Wilson, former CEO of Saks Fifth Avenue (Wabash)

Tom Wolfe, writer (Washington and Lee)

Nina Zagat, cofounder of Zagat survey (Vassar)

STUDYING ENGINEERING OR BUSINESS AT LIBERAL ARTS COLLEGES

There are a handful of LACs—such as Lafayette, Swarthmore, Trinity, and Washington and Lee—that offer engineering as a major. At liberal arts colleges, engineering is usually taught in an interdisciplinary fashion that stresses broad applications. Unlike the more specialized approach found at tech school and research universities, LAC engineering puts more emphasis on teaching design and problem solving than on graduating licensed professional engineers. That may be why numerous LAC engineering graduates find their way into business, patent law, and medicine. Another route to engineering for a liberal arts college student is through one of the 3-2 programs (listed in the tech school chapter) that link a LAC to an engineering school. The following LACs offer engineering as a major:

- Bucknell University
- Lafayette College
- Smith College
- Swarthmore College
- Trinity College (CT)
- Trinity University (TX)
- Washington and Lee University

Business is the other preprofessional major that people get confused about when thinking of a liberal arts education. Many LACs consider business or marketing too vocational to be a sanctioned major. As a result, subject areas (such as accounting and finance) traditionally found in the business major at the typical large university can show up in economics department course listings at LACs. At many liberal arts colleges, the business and economics departments are interchangeable or interconnected—meaning, students looking to major in business will very likely find a reasonable facsimile in the economics department. Regardless of their major, LAC students aspiring toward careers in business come away with critical thinking skills (a staple of the liberal arts tool kit). Additionally, admissions officials at the highest-rated MBA programs often say that they are wary of applicants who majored in business as undergraduates. Many prestige MBA programs prefer economics or other social science majors—especially those from elite liberal arts institutions.

Some LACs, however, have a separate business major that resembles programs found at large universities. But there are usually a few key differences. One is the small class atmosphere of the liberal arts college, which permits an emphasis on group projects. The other difference stems from the seeming allergy liberal arts colleges have to specialization and vocationalism. Students majoring in business at LACs are typically required to take a core curriculum laden with arts and humanities that is intended to shape them into broadly educated future captains of industry. Taking a core curriculum of courses outside business increases the likelihood that LAC business graduates will have a global awareness, acquired through exposure to foreign languages and diverse cultural perspectives. Listed below are LACs that have either a clearly defined business or management major or a concentration embedded in the economics department. A fuller discussion is found in the chapter on business.

- Beloit College
- Berea College
- Bucknell University
- Claremont McKenna College
- Colorado College
- Cornell College (Iowa)

- Drew University
- Franklin and Marshall College
- Furman University
- Goucher College
- Morehouse College
- Muhlenberg University
- University of Puget Sound
- Rhodes College
- University of Richmond
- Skidmore College
- Washington College (Maryland)
- Washington and Jefferson College
- Washington and Lee University
- Willamette University
- College of Wooster

The existence of business and engineering majors at LACs can reassure students and parents who worry about employment prospects for liberal arts graduates. Indeed, LAC graduates can be fodder for the many clichéd jokes that stress, and often exaggerate, the supposed economic disadvantages of majors like art history and philosophy. The economy is not always initially welcoming to classics, history, and sociology majors seeking entry-level employment. Still, it could be that the coffee-shop barista or bike messenger with a degree in a liberal arts subject is busy (in off hours) writing the next big novel, preparing to start her own business enterprise, or applying to medical or law school.

STUDYING SCIENCE AND DOING RESEARCH AT LIBERAL ARTS COLLEGES

Another misconception plaguing liberal arts colleges relates to science and technology. People wonder if liberal arts colleges offer majors in the sciences and if they prepare students for medical school. As a result, many liberal arts colleges feel compelled to create special brochures highlighting their science departments. Studying science at a LAC is usually a hands-on experience, involving access to sophisticated instrumentation normally restricted to graduate students at larger universities and providing opportunities to serve as research apprentices to faculty. A close look reveals that LACs offer numerous interesting specialized science majors, such as neuroscience (Allegheny College and Oberlin College); biochemistry (Bowdoin College, Occidental College, and Trinity College); marine science (Eckerd College); astrophysics (Ohio Wesleyan University); earth and environmental sciences (Wesleyan University); cognitive science (Carleton College and Vassar College); geology (Colby College, Colgate University, Earlham College, and Pomona College); and interdisciplinary, science-inclusive programs like prairie studies at Grinnell College and ethnobotany at Connecticut College.

An impressive number of pioneers in science and technology studied at liberal arts colleges. Liberal arts college graduates have invented new processes and fields, such as semiconductors (Robert Noyce, a Grinnell graduate who founded Intel), virtual universities (John Sperling, a Reed graduate who started the University of Phoenix), aluminum (Charles Martin Hall, an Oberlin graduate whose discovery led to Alcoa Aluminum), and the German measles vaccine (Harry Martin Meyer Jr., a graduate of Hendrix). B. F. Skinner, a graduate of a liberal arts college

(Hamilton), established the field of behavioral psychology. Stephen Jay Gould, a graduate of another liberal arts college (Antioch), revolutionized the field of paleontology. Another standout example (and symbol) of the power liberal arts colleges wield in the world of science and technology is the Millikan tower, the architectural focal point of the California Institute of Technology campus: it memorializes Robert Millikan, a Nobel Prize–winning physicist who graduated from Oberlin with a degree in classics—before earning a PhD in physics at Columbia University. The following liberal arts colleges count Nobel Prize–winning scientists among their alumni:

- Amherst College
- Augsburg College
- Augustana College (IL)
- Berea College
- DePauw University
- Earlham College
- Furman University
- Gettysburg College
- Grinnell College
- Hamilton College
- Haverford College
- College of the Holy Cross
- Juniata College
- Lafayette College
- Lawrence University
- Manchester University
- Oberlin College
- Ohio Wesleyan University
- Rollins College
- Swarthmore College
- Washington and Lee University
- Whitman College
- College of Wooster
- Union College

In the spirit of imitation being the highest form of flattery, several science and technology institutions keen on crafting an education for the next generation of engineers and technology innovators have put a spotlight on the importance of not neglecting liberal arts courses. The F. W. Olin College of Engineering—founded in 1997 to create the engineer of the future—places liberal arts courses on one side of its curricular triangle. Similarly, Harvey Mudd College claims that its distinctive advantage against competitors like Caltech and MIT is its liberal arts–inclusive science and engineering curriculum.

Research, whether it occurs in a biology class or a psychology course, is a core skill taught at liberal arts colleges. Liberal arts colleges exist to teach students how to acquire knowledge independently, how to analyze data, how to construct a cogent argument, how to spot and refute specious reasoning, how to articulate ideas, how to ask penetrating questions, how to initiate research, how to find gaps in the existing experimental literature, and how to spot the issues that will need to be addressed in the future. In fact, built into the curriculum at most liberal arts colleges is the opportunity (sometimes even a requirement) for students to conduct guided research as early as their sophomore or junior year. Numerous studies show the disproportionate prominence of small liberal arts colleges as per capita sources of future PhDs (Bryn Mawr, Carleton, Oberlin, Reed, and Swarthmore rank in the top ten), which validates the strong research training LAC students receive.

Due to the collaborative learning and guided research that marks undergraduate life at small liberal arts colleges, students often experience an unforeseen academic and personal transformation. For example, when a student works on a thesis at a liberal arts college such as Reed (where a thesis is required for graduation), the thesis student becomes expert on a topic, eventually knowing more about it than his or her thesis adviser/professor. That inversion of expertise, where the teacher guides the student along the path of scholarship to a point where the student is teaching the teacher about what she or he has discovered, leads to an academic confidence unknown to students whose majors (or double majors) are a mere collection of required courses. Reed's required thesis also has an entrepreneurial component because the thesis student manages the process of creation and discovery from start to finish, to the point of delivering a tangible product (a hardbound thesis) that becomes part of Reed's permanent library collection, available to future students and faculty at Reed as well as through online and interlibrary loan consortiums.

FACILITIES AT LIBERAL ARTS COLLEGES: IT'S ALL ABOUT ACCESS

A defining strength of liberal arts colleges is the extent to which resources are allocated to create a campus environment that best meets undergraduate student needs. There are often extensive (at no additional fee) career, health, counseling, tutoring, learning disability, and other services at liberal arts colleges that can profoundly enhance a student's success both during and after college. For example, at many LACs, alumni can get assistance from the career services office throughout their lives. Small liberal arts colleges are less likely to cap the number of psychological counseling sessions a student can have per semester. Also, students at LACs generally have far greater access to the fitness and recreation facilities. A large university may have stunning athletic facilities but if they are almost always reserved for the athletes on teams, those facilities are a mirage to the student who simply wants to play a game of pickup basketball.

Because scholarship athletes and graduate students are rare at most liberal arts colleges, a sense of access and equality prevails on LAC campuses. Accessibility to the gym, specialized laboratory equipment, library stacks, photo dark room, and every other amenity of a campus is the hallmark of the LAC. The professors, administration, and facilities are all there to serve undergraduate students and provide them with the best education possible. There are fewer agendas, such as high demands on professors to publish and secure research grants, leaving more time for professors to focus on individual student needs.

When it comes to selecting a college, students tend to get what they pay for. A higher-priced LAC will spend much more on each student than will a lower-priced public university. When a liberal arts college has a large endowment, it generally means that it can take very good care of its students, thus providing what could be considered the best education money can buy. Typically, LACs use their endowment income and annual alumni donations to subsidize (often heavily) the full cost of the student experience. Per student expenditures on classroom instruction, co-curricular opportunities, and special programs such as study abroad and internships are much higher (sometimes double the tuition charge) at many small liberal arts colleges. The higher per student investment made by the typical LAC translates into the greater access (described above) to campus facilities, student services, and professors. While severe economic downturns can negatively impact college endowments, the richest LACs still spend lavishly (compared to everyone else) on their students.

Below is a list of colleges that have significant resources relative to their size. Visits to these campuses will reveal impressive facilities and programs.

- Amherst College
- Berea College
- Bowdoin College
- Claremont McKenna College
- Grinnell College
- Middlebury College+
- Pomona College
- Oberlin College*#
- University of Richmond
- Smith College*
- Swarthmore College
- Vassar College*
- Wellesley College
- Williams College*

Another distinguishing feature of the LAC experience is the sole focus on undergraduates. For example, Scripps College, one of the Claremont Colleges in California, enrolls a thousand students, all of whom are undergraduate women. Haverford College in suburban Philadelphia is similarly small (1,185 students) and also just for undergraduates. At both Haverford and Scripps, nearly 100 percent of the students are eighteen to twenty-four years old. The residential and close-knit nature of the Scripps and Haverford experience is representative of liberal arts colleges in general. There are graduate students in liberal arts or teacher training programs at some liberal arts colleges, such as Colgate, Reed, and Skidmore, but those graduate students number under one hundred, attend part-time, and do not live on campus.

For all of their specialness, liberal arts colleges can strike some prospective students as communities that exist in some sort of hermetically sealed bubble. Indeed, the strong sense of campus community and interconnectedness can make a LAC feel a lot like a family (for better) or a cult (for worse). In their strong efforts to support the individual growth of each of their students, small liberal arts colleges can run the risk of creating a culture that looks from the outside like an experience only appreciated and understood by the initiated. Overall, such sentiments merely signal that the small liberal arts college experience (just like the large university experience or the tech school experience) is not for everyone. When the fit is right, LACs tend to create in their graduates a strong belief that they had a life-transforming experience that could not have occurred anywhere else. Such feelings often translate into great loyalty toward the alma mater. For example, the highest alumni donation rates are found at small liberal arts colleges, such as Centre in Kentucky and Williams in Massachusetts.

*includes an art collection valued at $500 million to $1 billion
#includes nearly five hundred pianos, most of them Steinways
+owns and operates the Monterey Institute for International Studies

LIBERAL ARTS COLLEGES WITH CITY LOCATIONS

For some students, attending a LAC located in a city is a very attractive option. While city schools can be great choices, it is wise to consider nonurban options as well. Certain campuses in relatively remote locations are a constant hub of excitement that can successfully satisfy the artistic and intellectual stimulation needs of even the most sophisticated city dweller. Those seemingly out-of-the-way campuses often bend over backward to import world-renowned performers and speakers and may even have world-class art museums and music or theater programs right on campus. Still, for some students those amenities may not be enough to quench the need for a location in or near a city. For those students who prefer high rises over open fields, we have compiled a list of LACs located in or near major cities.

- Agnes Scott (Atlanta)
- Barnard (NYC)
- Lewis and Clark (Portland, OR)
- Macalester (St. Paul, MN)
- Mills (Oakland)
- Morehouse (Atlanta)
- Occidental (Los Angeles)
- Oglethorpe (Atlanta)
- University of Puget Sound (Tacoma)
- Reed (Portland, OR)
- Spelman (Atlanta)
- Rhodes (Memphis)
- University of Richmond
- Trinity University (San Antonio)

LIBERAL ARTS COLLEGES FOR FUTURE ACADEMICS

An area where small liberal arts colleges really shine is their relative strength at preparing students to go on to PhD programs. One way to measure the quality of an undergraduate academic program is to chart its success at getting students into doctoral programs at the top-ranked research universities. Aspiring professors and researchers might want to look closely at how many graduates of small liberal arts colleges populate the faculty ranks at colleges and the research ranks within prestigious institutes. Reed College, a leader when it comes to alumni with PhDs, publishes a comprehensive list of academic disciplines and the top undergraduate schools represented in the per capita enrollment numbers of the respective PhD programs. Consistently, LAC graduates stand out in the per capita PhD attainment studies. The LACs listed below have perennially sent more graduates (per capita) onto doctoral programs than many schools twenty times their size.

- Amherst
- Bryn Mawr
- Carleton
- Earlham
- Grinnell
- Harvey Mudd
- Haverford
- Hendrix
- Oberlin
- Pomona
- Reed
- St. John's
- Spelman
- Swarthmore
- Wabash
- Wesleyan

SPORTS AT LIBERAL ARTS COLLEGES

Most LACs operate NCAA Division III athletic programs. In basic terms, this means the college cannot award a scholarship for athletic talent. It also means that less of the college's revenue is dependent on sports. In Division I, heaps of money can pile into the coffers of the high-profile sports like football and basketball. Think basketball at Duke, football at Michigan, and hockey at North Dakota. Division I athletes represent the top of the talent pool in college sports. Division III operates on a smaller scale. Division III LACs tend to attract scholar-athletes in the truest sense of the term: students who are scholars first and athletes second. Only a rare Division III athlete harbors realistic dreams of playing at the professional level.

In many ways, however, the Division III athlete has a better situation than the Division I athlete. Typically, Division I athletes must make sports their main priority. For the Division I athlete, the entire college experience is tightly bound up in the team and one's identity as an athlete, whereas the Division III athlete has the opportunity to achieve a more balanced life. Playing at the Division III level certainly requires a serious commitment, but there is an understanding that sports participation is just one aspect of the student's college experience. Students who enjoy a sport but don't intend to go to the Olympics or become professionals usually have a great time playing on a Division III team. To have a chance to play in college, the aspiring Division III athlete still must register for the NCAA clearinghouse as a high school student and contact college coaches to express interest. Although athletic scholarships are not offered in Division III schools, having a coach actively recruiting a student can have a favorable impact in the admissions process.

Among the LACs, there are a few that buck the Division III trend and compete on the Division I level. Or, in certain cases, there are LACs that are mostly Division III but support one or two Division I teams. Here is a list of those schools.

- Colorado College (hockey, soccer)
- Colgate
- Davidson
- University of Richmond
- Union (hockey)
- Lafayette
- Bucknell
- St. Lawrence (hockey)
- Holy Cross
- Wofford

There are a number of liberal arts colleges where sports are central to the student culture. At these colleges, well over half of the students participate in varsity or intramural sports. The number of teams at these schools can exceed more than forty—a surprisingly high number for colleges such as Amherst or Williams, where the student population is less than two thousand. Recruited athletes are a key constituency at these colleges, which means that the admissions offices work closely with coaches to make sure that teams remain competitive. All things equal, applicants who are talented athletes (and good students) may draw more interest from a sports-intensive college than they might at a slightly less selective and less sports-intensive college. The following is a list of LACs where sports are central.

- Amherst College
- Bates College
- Bowdoin College
- Colby College
- Colgate University

- College of the Holy Cross
- Colorado College
- Connecticut College
- Davidson College
- Denison University
- Hamilton College
- Haverford College
- Hobart and William Smith Colleges

- Kenyon College
- Lake Forest College
- Middlebury College
- St. Lawrence University
- Trinity College
- Union College
- Washington and Lee University
- Williams College

LIBERAL ARTS COLLEGES SORTED INTO TIERS OF QUALITY

Below is a list of the best-known LAC's, separated into five tiers of perceived quality. The tier groupings are based on an aggregation of the most respected rankings and extensive research that consisted of consultations with experts, such as faculty, deans, and guidance counselors; and an examination of financial data to determine institutional strength and stability. Many of the colleges on this list represent enduring quality, while others stand out as up-and-comers that are making strides forward.

TIER 1
Amherst, Barnard, Bowdoin, Carleton, Davidson, Grinnell, Haverford, Oberlin, Pomona, Swarthmore, Vassar, Wellesley, Wesleyan, Williams

TIER 2
Bates, Bryn Mawr, Bucknell, Claremont McKenna, Colby, Colgate, Colorado, Hamilton, Kenyon, Macalester, Occidental, Reed, Scripps, Smith, Trinity (CT), Washington and Lee

TIER 3
Bard, Berea, Connecticut, Denison, DePauw, Dickinson, Earlham, Franklin and Marshall, Furman, Gettysburg, Hampshire, Holy Cross, Lafayette, Morehouse, Mount Holyoke, New College (FL), Pitzer, Richmond, St. Olaf, Sarah Lawrence, Sewanee, Skidmore, Spelman, Union, Wheaton (MA), Whitman

TIER 4
Agnes Scott, Allegheny, Beloit, Centre, Coe, College of the Atlantic, Cornell (Iowa), Goucher, Hendrix, Hobart and William Smith, Illinois Wesleyan, Juniata, Kalamazoo, Knox, Lewis and Clark, McDaniel, Millsaps, Muhlenberg, Puget Sound, Rhodes, St. John's (MD and NM), St. Lawrence, St. Mary's (MD), Southwestern, Trinity U (TX), Ursinus, Wabash, Washington (MD), Wheaton (IL), Wofford, Willamette, Wooster

TIER 5
Albion, Augsburg, Augustana (both IL and SD), Austin, Bennington, Berry, Calvin, Drew, Goshen, Gustavus Adolphus, Hampden-Sydney, Hanover, Hillsdale, Hollins, Hope, Lake Forest, Linfield, Manchester, Mills, Monmouth, Oglethorpe, Ohio Wesleyan, Principia, Randolph Macon, Ripon, St. Anselm, St. Benedict, St. John's (MN), St. Mary's (IN), St. Michael's, Stonehill, Susquehanna, Transylvania, Washington and Jefferson, Whittier

If the approach to learning and the scale of the community at liberal arts colleges sounds appealing, taking that path will open a student to a relatively small but impressive population of people who have benefitted from an experience founded on educating and developing one student at a time.

PUBLIC UNIVERSITIES AND PUBLIC LIBERAL ARTS COLLEGES

In just about every corner of the United States, students grow up viewing the local public flagship university as the model for college. Whether it is due to football games on television or logos on sweatshirts, children in Georgia grow up dreaming of attending the University of Georgia or Georgia Tech. In Michigan, it's Michigan or Michigan State, in North Carolina it's the University of North Carolina at Chapel Hill or NC State in Raleigh, in Ohio it's Ohio State, and in Washington you belong if you are a Husky (University of Washington) or a Cougar (Washington State University). The flagship university is often the dominant institution in the hearts and minds of people who live in the state, and going there is a mark of achievement as well as a strong signal of local pride. Indeed, graduates of the flagship public university can so dominate professional networks in many states that it can be more advantageous to get a degree there than from an Ivy League university or some other prestigious but faraway place, such as Georgetown or Stanford.

Virtually every ranking or membership roster of the best universities in the United States lists a significant number of state flagships. For example, thirty-four of the sixty-two members of the prestigious Association of American Universities (AAU) are US state universities, while two others are Canadian public universities (McGill and Toronto). A handful of state flagships are frequently grouped among the very best research universities in the world. Those institutions are the University of California, Berkeley; UCLA, Georgia Tech, the University of Michigan, the University of North Carolina at Chapel Hill, the University of Texas at Austin, the University of Virginia, and the College of William and Mary.

➤ PUBLIC MEMBERS OF THE ASSOCIATION OF AMERICAN UNIVERSITIES (AAU)

Georgia Institute of Technology

Indiana University

Iowa State University

Michigan State University

Ohio State University

Penn State University

Purdue University

Rutgers, the State University of New Jersey

Stony Brook University—State University of New York (SUNY)

Texas A&M University

University of Arizona

University at Buffalo—SUNY

University of California, Berkeley

University of California, Davis

University of California, Irvine

University of California, Los Angeles (UCLA)

University of California, San Diego

University of California, Santa Barbara

University of Colorado Boulder

University of Florida

University of Illinois at Urbana-Champaign

University of Iowa

University of Kansas

University of Maryland, College Park

University of Michigan

University of Minnesota

University of Missouri at Columbia

University of North Carolina at Chapel Hill

University of Oregon

University of Pittsburgh

University of Texas at Austin

University of Virginia

University of Washington

University of Wisconsin at Madison

Flagship public universities have the same great strength and chief weakness: size. State flagships are attractive to students because they are like small cities unto themselves, offering courses, majors, and degrees in just about every area. Flagships also offer the opportunity to participate in activities, such as athletics, performing arts, and student government, on a very large stage. State flagships make students feel like the famous line from the song "New York, New York": "If you can make it here, you can make it anywhere." On the other hand, the large size of state flagships means that students can easily get lost in crowds.

Getting lost in the crowd has a dimension beyond large class sizes and long lines. Some students get lost in the crowd simply by following their high-school peer group to the state flagship. Making such a choice has its advantages and disadvantages. On the plus side, the student arrives at college with a core group of friends, thus ensuring that a big place feels familiar from day one. On the minus side, going to college with a pack of high-school friends may restrict opportunities to connect with the larger community of people on campus. In such cases, the student may go away to college but not truly get away from the familiar. Still, for others, staying close to home for college, career, and lifetime—and having a degree from the local flagship—is the preferred choice.

LEADING PUBLIC UNIVERSITIES IN THE USA

When national and international rankings, expert opinions of deans and faculty members, and perceptions of the college guidance community get aggregated, a consensus emerges as to which are the leading public colleges and universities in the United States. The alphabetical list below reflects both expert and popular opinion. The opinions of the experts and the rankings aside, students should not assume that the eight highly regarded universities listed first are any better than the schools named on the larger list of great choices appearing further below.

University of California at Berkeley
University of California at Los Angeles
Georgia Institute of Technology
University of Michigan
University of North Carolina at Chapel Hill
University of Texas at Austin
University of Virginia
College of William and Mary

OTHER TERRIFIC CHOICES TO CONSIDER:

Northeast: University at Albany (SUNY), Binghamton University (SUNY), University at Buffalo (SUNY), University of Connecticut, University of Delaware, SUNY-Geneseo, Hunter College (CUNY), University of University of Maryland (College Park), Massachusetts at Amherst, University of New Hampshire, the College of New Jersey, Penn State University, University of Pittsburgh, Rutgers University, Stony Brook University (SUNY), SUNY College of Environmental Science and Forestry, SUNY-Purchase, Temple University, University of Vermont.

Midwest: University of Cincinnati, University of Illinois at Urbana-Champaign, Indiana University, Iowa State University of Iowa, Kansas State University, University of Kansas, Miami University (Ohio), Michigan State University, Michigan Technological University, University of Minnesota, Missouri University of Science and

Technology, University of Missouri, University of Nebraska, Purdue University, Ohio State University, Ohio University, Truman State University, University of Wisconsin at Madison.

South: University of Alabama at Birmingham, University of Alabama at Tuscaloosa, Auburn University, College of Charleston, University of Florida, Florida State University, University of Georgia, James Madison University, Louisiana State University, University of Kentucky, North Carolina State University, University of South Carolina, University of Tennessee, Virginia Commonwealth University, Virginia Polytechnic and State University.

Southwest: Arizona State University, University of Arizona, University of Houston, Texas A&M University, Texas Tech University.

West: California Polytechnic State University at San Luis Obispo, University of California at Davis, University of California at Irvine, University of California at San Diego, University of California at Santa Barbara, University of California at Santa Cruz, Colorado School of Mines, Colorado State University, University of Colorado, Humboldt State University, Montana State University, University of Montana, Oregon State University, University of Oregon, Portland State University, San Diego State University, University of Utah, Washington State University, University of Washington, Western Washington University.

PUBLIC UNIVERSITY HONORS PROGRAMS

Over the last quarter century, honors programs have proliferated at public universities. State flagship institutions, such as the University of Connecticut, have established honors programs to attract talented students. Increasingly, students choose public honors programs over private universities and colleges. Typically, public university honors programs receive generous funding to function like a small college embedded within a large university. Students selected to participate in honors programs are usually guaranteed smaller classes and special academic opportunities not available to the mass of undergraduates at universities such as Maryland and Minnesota, where the population surpasses thirty-five thousand students. Public university honors programs are marked by personal attention and special access to senior faculty members, honors community activities, and unique opportunities for housing, study abroad, and internships.

Most public university honors programs have two entry points. A select group of freshman applicants is invited to the honors program at the point of admission. Later entry can occur for students with strong freshman and sophomore grades at the university. In addition to university-wide honors programs, many institutions have school or department-based honors tracks.

Perhaps the most attractive feature of a public university honors program, in comparison to private institutions, is the price differential. For residents of the state, attending the public university honors college can provide the equivalent of a high-quality private university education at a much lower price. Entry to most honors programs also comes with a generous scholarship. The following are examples of the many public university honors programs at state universities of all sizes and prestige levels.

University of Arizona. By sponsoring several clubs and organizations and providing special residence halls, the UA Honors College creates a sense of community affiliation for its students. Students interested in leadership can join the Honors Student Council. There is an Honors Players group for students interested in drama. An Honors Mentor Association helps guide students through their first year at UA. And the Honors College Ambassadors assist in recruiting future students. Yuma Hall (listed on the National Register of Historic Places) houses 184 students, while a complex of five connected buildings (Arbol de la Vida) features green design, including smart and sustainable technologies. Typically, honors students have taken nine to twelve Advanced Placement (AP)/ International Baccalaureate (IB) classes in high school, earned a 3.8/4.0 grade point average, and achieved at least a 1350 (critical reading [CR] plus math [M]) on the Scholastic Aptitude Test (SAT) or 30 on the American College Test [ACT].

Arizona State University. The Barrett Honors College at ASU helps personalize the largest university in the United States (seventy-two thousand students). Barrett Honors College has a $12 million endowment that underwrites special programs and projects, such as undergraduate research, study abroad, internships, community service, and seminar-style classes enriched by visitors such as former Supreme Court Justice Sandra Day O'Connor. Roughly half of the 3,500 students enrolled in Barrett Honors College live in a nine-acre residential community that has a dining hall. The one hundred special seminar classes offered at Barrett are capped at twenty-five students. Barrett students may undertake an honors thesis or a creative project,

the findings of which get presented at an honors symposium. Barrett Honors College students represent the apex of academic quality at ASU and are more likely than other Sun Devils to go on to top-ranked graduate and professional schools. Getting admitted to Barrett requires at least a top 10 percent ranking in high school, ACT scores approaching 30, or SAT (CR plus M) scores over 1300.

Binghamton University (SUNY). The Scholars Program at Binghamton is very small and distinct from the honors programs operated by individual academic departments. Each year Binghamton enrolls up to forty freshmen in the Scholars Program. While there are no GPA or ACT/SAT cutoffs for selection, the students in the Scholars Program are Binghamton's most outstanding applicants, ones who exhibit excellence in academics, extracurricular pursuits, and leadership activities. Scholars Program courses emphasize collaborative learning and start students on a path toward undergraduate research with faculty mentors. Scholars get priority for course registration and live in residential communities that provide shared learning and cocurricular experiences. Through the small classes, mentored research, and living/learning activities, Scholars Program students at Binghamton are primed for departmental honors and competition for prestigious postgraduate fellowships.

University at Buffalo (SUNY). The thousand Honors College students at Buffalo get priority registration for courses, an honors notation on their transcript, personalized advising, a faculty mentor, and preferred on-campus housing. The UB Honors College provides guidance for students seeking prestigious postgraduate fellowships, such as the Goldwater, Marshall, and Rhodes. There are funds for honors research and creative activities, study abroad, thesis assistance, and presentations at national conferences.

Honors College students are also eligible for the Early Assurance Programs operated by UB's medical and pharmacy schools. Competitive UB Honors College applicants need at least a 93/100 unweighted high school grade average and SATs of 1300 (CR plus M) or 29 on the ACT.

University of California at Los Angeles (UCLA). The Honors Program at UCLA is limited to students in the College of Letters and Science (CLS). CLS Honors Program students have flexibility in selecting courses, choosing a major, and participating in honors seminars. Honors classes are small, interdisciplinary, and interactive. Honors Program counselors provide personalized advising—something not always expected at a large school of twenty-six thousand undergraduates. Students who complete the program get honors notated on their transcript and an Honors College diploma. In addition to special scholarships ($1,000 to 4,000) for Honors Program students, there are summer research stipends available. A select group of students can become Honors Fellows who serve as mentors and assist in the operation of the program. Students selected for UCLA's Honors Program generally rank in the top 3 percent of their high school classes and have SAT section scores in the 650+ range or an ACT composite above 31.

University of California at San Diego. Students can enter the Warren Honors College straight from high school, as transfer students, or as continuing students who have achieved outstanding academic records at UCSD. Special opportunities available to honors students include an undergraduate research program, a faculty speaker series, and monthly community-building cultural, educational, and social events. Honors students who have participated in undergraduate research have the opportunity to enter their research papers in competition for the Addison Award. UCSD honors students tend to have high

school GPAs of 3.8/4.0, 700s on SAT sections, or at least a 31 on the ACT.

University of Colorado. The top 10 percent of students admitted to CU's colleges/schools of arts and sciences, architecture and planning, journalism and mass communication, and music get invited into an honors program. The determination of top 10 percent varies by college/school but tends to be based on a strong high school GPA and high scores on the ACT or SAT. CU's College of Engineering selects its honors students based on their high school records and test scores but also looks for evidence that the applicant cares about learning and is eager to engage in research. The Leeds School of Business at Colorado selects 140 freshmen each year for a residential academic program that provides personal faculty advising, student mentors, and honors seminar classes. Because honors courses at Colorado are limited to fifteen students, they are interactive and personal. Honors students at Colorado have their own journal for publishing creative and academic work. Admission to the Honors Program at CU often comes with a generous scholarship.

University of Connecticut. UConn's Honors Program provides its 1,552 students with challenging courses, a personalized collegiate environment, a residential community, and opportunities for internships, research experiences, and study abroad programs in places like the Netherlands, South Africa, and an archaeological field school in Armenia. Honors students can also serve as interns for one of Connecticut's US representatives. Funds support summer on-campus research projects as well as travel to conferences to present research findings. The Honors Program also provides numerous events and mentoring programs that encourage competition for prestigious awards such as the Goldwater, Marshall, Rhodes, and Truman scholarships. Honors students tend to rank in the top 5 percent of their high school class and have SAT scores approaching 1400 (CR plus M).

University of Delaware. The Honors Program at the University of Delaware provides a challenging interdisciplinary curriculum, a special residential living/learning environment, and small classes designed to foster intellectual engagement. Incoming students live together through the Freshman Honors Housing program, which is designed to create community affiliation. Honors students tend to have a high school GPA of 3.8 to 4.0 and scores of 2010 to 2170 on the SAT. A majority of Delaware's 1,800 honors students receive merit scholarships. Graduates of the program receive an Honors Degree.

University of Florida. The UF Honors Program is for students with a passion for academic and extracurricular pursuits. There are two ways to get into the UF Honors Program: by invitation, at the point of admission, or by petition before or right after enrolling. The 2,800 honors students at UF have special opportunities to collaborate with faculty on research projects, do an honors thesis, work closely with an academic adviser, and have an internship experience. Honors courses are limited to twenty-five students, and an honors residence hall sleeps six hundred. Students in UF's Honors Program typically have stellar academic credentials (33 ACT, 2070 SAT, 4.0 GPA) and receive the best merit scholarships available.

University of Georgia. The Honors Program at Georgia goes a long way toward personalizing a large public university. Honors classes average seventeen to twenty students and are taught by leading faculty. Up to 250 first-year honors students can live in a residence hall (staffed with an advising office) set aside for the program. The 2,350 students in the program can pursue honors internships in New York, Savannah, and Washington, DC. Stipends from the Honors International Scholars Program fund study abroad or undergraduate research. Honors students at Georgia can gain entry into combined bachelor's/master's degree programs. Many students in Georgia's Honors Program receive very generous scholarship support for four years. The Foundation Fellowship, for example, covers full tuition and provides an additional $9,000 stipend for Georgia residents and $15,700 for nonresidents. To be competitive, students should have GPAs approaching 4.0 and SATs (CR plus M) around 1500.

Georgia Institute of Technology. The special Honors Program courses at Georgia Tech are limited to twenty students, focus on interdisciplinary topics, and emphasize critical thinking. Students in the program also get to take small sections of introductory core courses and live in an honors residence hall. Admission to the Georgia Tech Honors Program requires a stellar high school record, including high scores on the ACT or SAT. Many honors students at Georgia Tech receive generous scholarships.

Indiana University. Many of the 4,200 students in Indiana's Hutton Honors College feel they have the best of both worlds: small liberal arts college academics coupled with research university resources. The seminar classes offered by Hutton Honors College typically enroll twenty-two or fewer students and are interdisciplinary and global in nature. A variety of programs build community. For example, Hutton has its own dean and its own building, which gives students a home base for classes, advising, study sessions, and special events, like lectures by distinguished visitors such as Nobel laureate and former Secretary of Energy Steven Chu. Special funds provide students with grants to engage in internships, thesis research, creative activities, volunteer service, and overseas travel. Graduates of Hutton receive an honors notation on their diploma. Hutton students also have the option to live in an honors residential community. A high percentage of Hutton students receive merit scholarships ranging from $1,000 to $6,000 per year. Incoming student credentials average 31 (ACT), 1350 (CR plus M) SAT, and 3.85/4.0 GPA.

University of Illinois. At Illinois there are three honors programs. The Campus Honors Program, which is small and selective, includes students (called Chancellor's Scholars) from every college and school. Each college at Illinois has its own honors program comprised of students called James Scholars. The third way to achieve honors at Illinois is through sophomore-year entry into individual departmental honors programs. In addition to needing an extraordinary record of past academic achievement, honors students at Illinois are selected based on evidence of creativity, motivation to excel, intellectual curiosity, and leadership potential. Regardless of the program, honors participation at Illinois is for high-ability, high-achieving students who have a special interest in intellectual adventure and professional growth. Through small classes that average twenty, honors students at Illinois form collaborative relationships with faculty and fellow students. Illinois honors students also enjoy priority registration for classes, graduate student status in the libraries, and the opportunity to form a close community through special extracurricular and study abroad programs to places such as the Galapagos Islands and South Africa.

University of Kansas. The Kansas Honors Program fosters an active and collaborative learning environment for its 1,500 students. Classes in the Kansas Honors Program average fifteen to twenty students and emphasize active participation. Honors study at Kansas is geared toward developing skill in critical thinking, independent analysis, and written and spoken expression. The Kansas Honors Program encourages independent research, study abroad, and community service. Honors students at Kansas get priority enrollment in courses and can live on special honors floors. The Kansas Honors Program also has its own building with classrooms, conference rooms, meeting and study areas, and a kitchen. Many honors students receive scholarships; incoming credentials average 3.75/4.0 (GPA), 30 (ACT), and 1320 (SAT—CR plus M).

Louisiana State University. Through its Honors College, LSU offers a dynamic learning community that functions like a small neighborhood within a large campus. The LSU Honors College neighborhood includes French House, the Laville Residential Hall, and the 459 Dining Hall—all located within easy walking distance of classroom buildings, the student union, and the recreation center. Honors College advisers help students design a customized path through LSU—with a unifying emphasis on stimulating academics, community service, study abroad, internships/research projects, and a senior thesis. A special program called Louisiana Service and Leadership (LASAL) develops future leaders who will use their education to improve the Bayou State. LASAL participants take a sequence of courses on Louisiana history and politics and complete an internship with a government or service organization. The Honors College also sponsors study abroad trips to destinations such as South Africa. LSU Honors College graduates get a notation on their diploma. Selection for honors (and an accompanying merit scholarship) requires a 3.5/4.0 GPA, 30 ACT, or 1330 (CR plus M) SAT.

University of Maryland. Through its Honors

College, Maryland seeks to create a small college atmosphere that has the advantages of a large research university. The Honors College at Maryland (enrolling three thousand students) touts its excellent students, small seminar-style classes, and superb faculty—including three Nobel laureates. The approximately 130 honors seminars offered are interdisciplinary courses taught by faculty interested in mentoring undergraduates. Maryland honors students frequently pursue undergraduate research, internships, or the federal semester—an academic program on Capitol Hill. Community building is an important goal of the two residence halls set aside for Maryland's Honors College. Each year a special Honors College Convocation celebrates the program's students, faculty, and staff. Through the Gemstone Program, a select number of honors students participate in multidisciplinary research projects. Banneker/ Key Scholarships provide full or partial tuition for numerous honors students. Honors College graduates receive a notation on their transcripts and diploma.

University of Massachusetts. The approximately 3,800 students in the Commonwealth Honors College (CHC) at UMass begin their studies with a seminar class called Ideas That Changed the World. The shared experience of taking the Ideas seminar orients students to the mission of CHC, which is to offer an intellectually challenging curriculum, create a community of scholars, and prepare future leaders. Averaging nineteen students, the classes offered by CHC provide global and interdisciplinary perspectives and emphasize active learning. The residential academic program (RAP) creates learning communities organized around a theme. Through the RAP, groups of honors students who live in the same residence hall take classes together. An undergraduate research conference brings together student researchers from UMass and

other Massachusetts public colleges and universities. The Citizen Scholars program integrates community experiences into classroom discussions and assignments. Students take an active role in governing the CHC through a student advisory board. CHC students also have special opportunities for leadership training, service learning, study abroad, and entrepreneurial activities. The cost of attending CHC is often subsidized by merit scholarships.

Miami University of Ohio. The 1,600 students in Miami's Honors Program take challenging honors courses and work closely with an adviser to create their own academic plan. They also live in a special honors residence hall. Other benefits of the program include monetary support for research, creative projects, and study abroad as well as priority class registration and an honors notation on the transcript. Miami provides ample scholarship support for Honors Program students. Gaining admission requires a high school GPA near 4.0, an ACT of 30 or higher, or SATs (CR plus M) of at least 1330.

University of Michigan. Once students are admitted into Michigan's College of Literature, Science, and Arts (LSA), they have the option to apply to its Honors Program. Applicants need to show a strong desire to participate in a vigorous intellectual community. The LSA Honors Program enables roughly two thousand students to pursue their intellectual interests as deeply and as fully as they wish. LSA honors students get intensive faculty contact and advising, access to special honors courses, and the opportunity to live in honors housing. A program called Ideas in Honors pairs freshmen with seniors who lead minicourses. Community building occurs through special activities and trips. Preparation for the senior thesis project occurs through the Summer Fellows Program, which provides research opportunities for LSA honors students.

Michigan State University. The Honors College at Michigan State is built around dynamic, small, seminar-style classes that promote interactive learning. The 2,700 students in the Honors College are given great flexibility in fulfilling university-wide course requirements and bypassing restrictions. Honors College students may take courses that are designated for majors only, courses that are set aside for juniors or seniors, graduate-level classes, or work with a professor to make a class an honors course. After their freshman year, Honors College students get first priority when registering for courses. Special programs exist for Honors College students to do research, independent study, or thesis projects. MSU's Honors College builds community through six residence halls with floors for honors students and through a student-operated programming board that coordinates co-curricular activities and mentors new honors students. Honors College students have the opportunity to get to know their professors through fireside chat dinners hosted at faculty homes. An advising office assists students applying for prestigious international and national postgraduate fellowships. Numerous Honors College students receive scholarships, ranging from $2,300 to $18,000 per year.

University of Minnesota. Minnesota's Honors Program is for high-achieving students who want to create their own academic path. Students take honors courses with some of the most distinguished faculty at Minnesota, and the program fosters a close-knit community through an honors student association and honors floors in Middlebrook Hall. Advisers work closely with students to guide them through an honors curriculum that emphasizes interdisciplinary learning and prepares them to complete an honors thesis. In addition to individual academic advisers, there are advising offices available to point Honors Program students toward scholarship opportunities and prestigious postgraduate fellowships. Numerous Honors Program students have received Goldwater Fellowships and Udall Scholarships. Minnesota's Honors Program also provides support to enable its students to study abroad or spend summers doing research, internships, or community service projects.

University of Mississippi. Barksdale Honors College at Ole Miss has its own four-story building in a central campus location as well as two floors in residence halls for its eight hundred students. The Honors College building includes classrooms, a computer lab, study rooms, a lounge, and a kitchen—all specially set aside for Barksdale students. Freshmen entering Barksdale get priority registration for their classes and the opportunity to participate in Freshmen Ventures, a program where students travel across America to learn about its different regions. Funds are available for community service trips, study abroad, internships, research projects, or humanitarian efforts. Through an agreement with the law school at Ole Miss, juniors in the Honors College can explore law by taking courses normally open only to law students. Honors scholarships that provide $8,000 per year for four years are offered to a limited number of new entrants to Barksdale. Average incoming student credentials are 3.87/4.0 GPA, 30 ACT, and 1340 SAT (CR plus M).

University of North Carolina. The Honors Program at UNC–Chapel Hill is separate from the Morehead Scholars program, which provides full scholarships and other benefits to recipients. Most of the 1,200 Honors students at Carolina get scholarships (of varying amounts), but such awards are not automatic. There are more than a hundred honors courses, with an average class size of twenty-two. Scholars can live in special residential learning communities and have mentored research experiences. Study abroad programs take honors students to institutions in Cape Town, London, Rome, and Singapore. The Burch Field Research Seminars provide individualized study adventures, which in recent years have included an internship with NASA, an investigation of climate change in the Philippines, and a research project on jazz in Cuba. Students are selected for UNC's Honors Program based on the strength of their high school record, essays, recommendations, and standardized test scores.

Ohio State University. At Ohio State, students have the opportunity to participate in an academic Honors Program or a co-curricular Scholars Program. The Honors Program offers more than five hundred honors course sections, faculty-guided research, study abroad programs (in Athens, London, and Nicaragua), an honors diploma, and an honors residence hall. Honors students get two advisers, one from the program and one from their major department. Out-of-classroom experiences are at the core of the fourteen different Scholars Programs at Ohio State. Students in Scholars Programs take group trips, including explorations of other countries, and participate in theme-based activities and workshops. Environment and Natural Resources Scholars, for example, go on camping retreats, take winter hikes, explore Lake Erie, and do community service. All participants in the Scholars Program must live in Scholars housing that attempts to build a strong sense of community, develop peer networks, and provide opportunities to get involved in residence hall governance.

University of Oregon. Oregon's Robert D. Clark Honors College is a small liberal arts college-type oasis of approximately seven hundred students (from every school and major) within a large state university that enrolls twenty-four thousand students. Students in Clark Honors College experience small classes and significant amounts of interaction with faculty. The Clark

Honors College curriculum emphasizes interdisciplinary study and faculty-supervised research projects. Clark Honors College students proceed through a sequence of courses geared toward teaching the research skills they will need for a senior thesis. Dedicated to the Clark Honors College are two residence halls, a classroom building, a library, and twelve faculty members—all of which combine to create a close community. A majority of Clark Honors College students receive attractive scholarship packages. Average SATs for Clark Honors College entrants are 1340.

Oregon State University. The University Honors College (UHC) at Oregon State is a rare honors program that grants its own degrees. UHC students graduate with an honors baccalaureate diploma after they complete a required senior thesis project. Courses in the UHC generally have fewer than twenty-five students and are taught by professors, not graduate students. UHC has special funds to support environmental research, travel to conferences, thesis-related expenses, study abroad, internships, service learning projects, group trips, and work supervised by faculty members. Students in the incoming UHC classes tend to have achieved a 3.96/4.0 GPA or a 2050 on the SAT or a 31 on the ACT.

Penn State University. With 1,800 students and 250-plus honors courses, the Schreyer Honors College at Penn State seeks to give students a global perspective on learning. Schreyer was established with a $30 million endowment fund that enables opportunities for leadership, career exploration, and independent research. Schreyer provides funding for summer internships, international travel, service learning projects, and honors thesis research. Schreyer students get priority registration for classes and have the option to be part of a living and learning community in two residence halls located in the heart of the Penn State campus. Each graduate of Schreyer receives the Scholars Medal, a symbol of excellence recognizing scholarly achievement, integrity of purpose, and intellectual curiosity. Schreyer students receive a $4,000 scholarship that is renewable for eight semesters. Selection into Schreyer requires a stellar high school record and outstanding test scores—ACT of 32 or SAT of 1960–2160.

University of Pittsburgh. The University Honors College (UHC) at Pittsburgh is for intellectually curious, self-motivated, and academically adventurous students. UHC students take the most challenging courses available in their areas of interest and get advising and instruction from faculty mentors. UHC's emphasis on academic excellence and intellectual curiosity has resulted in its students winning four Rhodes Scholarships and one Marshall Scholarship. A number of special programs build bonds within UHC—such as a lecture series and reading groups. Freshman can live in residential communities organized around the honors experience. Honors students can conduct summer research under the Breckenridge Fellowship program. Admission into UHC requires outstanding high school grades and standardized test scores. Students not admitted to UHC straight from high school can qualify by earning a 3.25 GPA or higher in classes at Pittsburgh.

Purdue University. The six hundred students in Purdue's University Honors Program (UHP) spend their freshman year in a learning community. There are a number of other special programs offered to UHP students including advising for graduate and professional school entry, opportunities to work closely with faculty on research projects, and study abroad programs in places such as Quebec, Venice, and Transylvania. Admission into UHP requires an outstanding high school record and excellent

standardized test scores. Honors students tend to receive Purdue's most generous scholarships. There are also honors programs operated by the colleges of agriculture, engineering, liberal arts, and science. Entry to those programs depends on the student's academic record while enrolled at Purdue.

Rutgers University. At Rutgers (the State University of New Jersey), students can pursue honors study by school or by department. The departmental route involves taking an honors track of courses and then completing an honors thesis project. Following the departmental honors track is something students do after enrolling at Rutgers. The honors programs run by individual schools are the ones that students are invited to join from high school—based on outstanding grades and test scores. At Rutgers, the four schools operating honors programs are Arts and Sciences; Engineering; Environmental and Biological Sciences; and Pharmacy. Honors students are encouraged to live in an honors housing community organized around passion for learning. Other features of the Rutgers honors programs include opportunities to work closely with a professor on a research project, options to have internships or on-the-job co-op experiences, access to a network of advisers, and connections to other honors students through a peer mentoring program.

University of South Carolina. The Honors College at South Carolina provides an individualized education for roughly 1,300 students, including one-on-one advising, classes averaging fourteen students, and an honors residence. The numerous special co-curricular programs sponsored by the Honors College include summer travel classes and study abroad programs in countries such as England and India. There are special scholarships for Honors College students. Entry into the Honors College requires outstanding high school grades and test scores (ACT of 31–33 or SAT CR plus M of 1335–1460).

University of Texas. The Plan II Honors Program at Texas traces its roots back to 1935. Through an interdisciplinary curriculum, Plan II attempts to provide an education without boundaries. Selection into Plan II requires not just a strong high school record (top 10 percent)—including exceptional standardized test scores (SAT of 2090–2270)—but also a lively spirit of intellectual adventure, a genuine desire for a broad-based education, and a capacity for imagination and originality. The seven hundred students in Plan II pursue a special curriculum designed to provide intellectual depth, collaborative learning experiences, research opportunities, and a senior thesis project. Through its special courses and helpful advisers, Plan II makes a large university of more than fifty thousand students feel smaller and more personal. Joyner Suite, the campus hub for honors students at Texas, includes a reading room, browsing library, and seminar rooms where visiting writers give readings and lectures. There are also travel grants for study abroad, such as classes at the American Institute for Roman Culture in Rome, ecobiology research in Costa Rica, and medical ethics study in Amsterdam.

University of Vermont. Students in the Honors College at UVM are given priority for class registration, have opportunities for directed research with faculty members, and get graduate student status in the libraries. The Honors College at UVM functions like a small college with its own residence hall, which includes apartments for live-in faculty members, classrooms, and multipurpose rooms for meetings, lectures, and dinners. UVM tries to create a sense of community among its eight hundred honors students through special lectures and symposia as well as through cultural trips to cities such as Boston

and Montreal. Students enter the Honors College either by invitation as incoming freshman (based on a stellar high school record and test scores) or during the sophomore year, based on academic performance at UVM.

University of Virginia. Virginia has three honors programs in addition to its prestigious Jefferson Scholars program that covers tuition, fees, room, board, and supplies and offers myriad academic and extracurricular opportunities to the recipients. The College Science Scholars Program provides opportunities to work closely with research faculty members. College Science Scholars who maintain a GPA of at least 3.4/4.0 are guaranteed admission into a five-year master's program in science, engineering, or education. The Echols Scholars Program, designed to give Arts and Sciences students the flexibility to build a curriculum around their interests, includes the option to declare an interdisciplinary major. Echols Scholars have priority when registering for classes, their own common living environment in a residence hall, and access to an extensive advising network dedicated to their success. The top 5 percent of students in Virginia's School of Engineering and Applied Science get selected to a program (Rodman Scholars) that works to develop future leaders in science and technology. Rodman Scholars share housing in a residential community with the Echols Scholars, get priority registration for courses, and have access to undergraduate research opportunities. A large number of the College Science, Echols, and Rodman students receive scholarships.

Virginia Polytechnic and State University. Students in the University Honors program at Virginia Tech get an enriched academic and residential experience. UH students can take one-on-one tutorials with top faculty members, devise independent study projects around a topic of interest, and undertake research during the academic year or in summers. After their first semester, UH students get priority registration for classes. The Honors Residential College provides a living/learning atmosphere built around intensive advising and close contact with professors and includes classrooms, a faculty apartment, a library, study lounges, living rooms, a theater, and a fitness area. A program called Presidential Global Scholars gives selected students the opportunity to spend a semester living and studying in the Swiss Alps. The UH program also gears students to be competitive candidates for prestigious graduate school awards, such as the Rhodes and Marshall scholarships. Selection into University Honors requires outstanding high school grades (3.8/4.0) and test scores (ACT of 30 or SAT CR plus M of 1380).

University of Washington. The Honors Program at Washington celebrates diversity, fosters leadership, encourages lifelong learning, and stimulates student interest in research and community service projects. The honors core curriculum at UW is interdisciplinary with an international perspective. Honors classes tend to operate in a seminar style that encourages active learning and close interaction with professors. The 1,500 students in the UW Honors Program have numerous special opportunities, such as funding for travel abroad, an honors computer lab, honors peer mentors, honors faculty advisers, and residence hall floors set aside for them. There are numerous scholarships available for UW honors students, including awards covering full tuition for residents and nonresidents of Washington. Selection into the UW Honors Program requires an outstanding high school record (3.92/4.0) and test scores (ACT of 31 or SAT of 2070).

University of Wisconsin. The primary honors program at the University of Wisconsin's flagship campus in Madison is operated by the College of Letters & Science. The L&S Honors Program (enrolling 1,600 students) is for students who want to be active learners, engaging in service and leadership experiences beyond the classroom. With its discussion-oriented classes and opportunities for research collaborations with faculty, the L&S Honors Program is Wisconsin's answer to the small liberal arts college experience. Special programs and opportunities available include First Year Interest Groups that help create an honors community, the Sophomore Apprenticeship that provides funded summer research opportunities, and an Honors Student Organization that sponsors co-curricular learning experiences and professional development activities. Seniors can conduct original research through an honors thesis project. Honors graduates have their achievement noted on their transcript and their diploma. Coming from a university widely recognized as one of the best in the world, Wisconsin Honors Program graduates have a leg up on admission to top graduate and professional schools.

PUBLIC LIBERAL ARTS COLLEGES

At first glance, the idea of a public liberal arts college sounds like a contradiction in terms. After all, aren't public universities inexpensive partly because they offer a less-than-personal education to the masses? For example, how personal can public universities, such as Ohio State and the University of Florida, be if they have total student enrollments larger than fifty thousand? Private liberal arts colleges, by contrast, are small and highly personal institutions, such as Bowdoin, Grinnell, and Whitman, where total student populations do not exceed two thousand and where the education resembles a boutique shop, not a big-box store. The currency at the private liberal arts college is the small classes taught by faculty whose priority is teaching and mentoring undergraduates. But private liberal arts colleges are expensive due to the labor-intensive nature of the education they provide: costs to attend them typically approach $60,000 per year. Recognizing that not all state universities have to be large, research-oriented, and less-than-personal, the public university sector over the last two decades has transformed some of its branch campuses into institutions that look and feel in their day-to-day operations similar to small liberal arts colleges. The emergence of the public liberal arts college has given students an additional high-quality option, while at the same time reinvigorating existing institutions.

In some cases, such as at the College of William and Mary, the long-standing emphasis has been on teaching undergraduate students. The College of William and Mary does have graduate and professional programs (including an excellent law school), but like the smaller members of the Ivy League (Brown and Dartmouth), it is best known as an undergraduate-centered arts and sciences institution. William and Mary cedes a focus on research to its larger public cousins in the state, most notably the University of Virginia and Virginia Polytechnic and State University. William and Mary is arguably a special case, which may explain why it frequently gets mistaken for a private college. Its founding in 1693 occurred nearly two hundred years before the Morrill Act of 1862 that established land-grant public universities. Perhaps because William and Mary originated in the era when all colleges were private and focused on teaching the traditional liberal arts and sciences to those who would become clergy, educators, or

statesmen, it, throughout its history, has more closely resembled a small private liberal arts college than a large state university. In many respects, William and Mary has been the model public liberal arts college for others to emulate as this category of institutions has developed and expanded.

THE COLLEGE OF WILLIAM AND MARY—WILLIAMSBURG, VIRGINIA

8,437 students (6,299 undergraduates)

Suburban campus

Student-faculty ratio of twelve to one

Schools: arts and sciences, business, education, law, marine science

33 percent admitted

Middle 50 percent on SAT: 1270–1470

Notable alumni: Three US presidents (Thomas Jefferson, James Monroe, John Tyler), Henry Clay (statesman), Robert Gates (US defense secretary), Glenn Close (actress), Jon Stewart (*The Daily Show*), Perry Ellis (fashion designer), Christina Romer (former chair of President Obama's Council of Economic Advisers)

Unlike William and Mary, most public liberal arts colleges and universities were once lesser-known branch campuses of state university systems. Many of these newly incarnated public liberal arts jewels were in their former lives less selective, teacher-training campuses languishing in the shadows of the long-established flagships in their states. One representative example is the College of New Jersey (formerly Trenton State College). The campus at the College of New Jersey has a lovely pond and a collection of collegiate red brick buildings with Georgian elements. It is a campus that invites not outlandish comparisons to Dartmouth, Wake Forest, and William and Mary. Geneseo College (SUNY) also looks more like William and Mary in its campus design than the utilitarian SUNY flagships at Albany, Binghamton, Buffalo, and Stony Brook. Under their public liberal arts reincarnations, institutions such as the Massachusetts College of the Liberal Arts (formerly North Adams State College) and Truman State University (formerly Northeast Missouri State University) have grown in stature, popularity, and admissions selectivity. They also have carved out their own niche identities regionally and in some cases nationally.

The advent of the public liberal arts college has given students an alternative to the flagship state university. Establishing other public university models has, for example, enabled the University of Minnesota at Morris and Indiana University of Pennsylvania to emerge as attractive alternatives to the larger flagships in those states. The situation is similar for UNC–Asheville in North Carolina, Keene State College in New Hampshire, the College of Charleston in South Carolina, Evergreen State in Washington, Saint Mary's College of Maryland, and Truman State in Missouri.

A few states have multiple small-to-medium-sized universities with an arts and sciences focus and campus atmosphere that more closely parallels small private colleges than huge public universities. Joining the College of New Jersey in the Garden State are Ramapo College, Richard Stockton College, and Rowan University. In addition to William and Mary, Virginia offers James Madison University and the University of Mary Washington. California has the University of California branches at Merced and Santa Cruz. Merced has fewer than 6,500 students but plans to grow to 20,000 students to resemble its larger University of California counterparts. For now Merced looks and feels like a public liberal arts college. At nearly 20,000 students, UC–Santa Cruz is larger than the typical public liberal arts college. But what gives Santa Cruz a legitimate claim to membership in the public liberal arts category is the decentralized and distributed nature of its campus. Santa Cruz has ten residential colleges to which students belong. Santa Cruz's campus was intentionally planned to reflect the foundational residential element of the small liberal arts college environment rather than the research university model. New York, in addition to Geneseo, has Binghamton, which also vies with Albany, Buffalo, and Stony Brook to be the state's research flagship. Like Santa Cruz, Binghamton is a hybrid of public liberal arts college and flagship state university. Arguably, Binghamton is too large (nearly 20,000 students) to be a classic public liberal arts college, yet there is an undergraduate academic emphasis and culture at Binghamton that aligns it with public liberal arts institutions.

The institutions on the list below are widely considered to be the most prestigious and best-known examples of the public liberal arts college/university species. Each has a significant population of students living on campus, and each draws more out-of-state students to its campus than the typical branch campus in a public university system.

THE EVERGREEN STATE COLLEGE— OLYMPIA, WASHINGTON

4,509 students (4,193 undergraduates)

Special academic program: Students enroll in an interdisciplinary program rather than a sequence of courses. Evergreen prides itself on innovative academics, collaborative learning, and narrative-style evaluations (no letter grades).

Examples of self-directed student programs: American stories; animal behavior and zoology; creativity and constraint; food, health, and sustainability; music, math, and motion; order and chaos; sustainable design; temperate rain forests

97 percent admitted

SAT and ACT: not used

Notable alumni: Matt Groening (creator of *The Simpsons*), Michael Richards (actor—Kramer on *Seinfeld*), Steve Thomas (host of *This Old House*), Carrie Brownstein (*Portlandia*), Kathleen Hanna (lead singer for Bikini Kill and Le Tigre)

FORT LEWIS COLLEGE—DURANGO, COLORADO

3,789 students (all undergraduates)

Arts, humanities, and social sciences; business administration; natural and behavioral sciences

Special opportunities: programs in adventure education, mountain studies, Native American and indigenous studies, and Southwest studies

Fort Lewis strives to be a top public liberal arts college in the West

68 percent admitted

Middle 50 percent on SAT: 925–1195; ACT: 19–24

SUNY-GENESEO—GENESEO, NEW YORK

5,347 students (5,249 undergraduates)

Arts and sciences, accounting, education, business, communication, and speech pathology

53 percent admitted

Middle 50 percent on SAT: 1180–1340; ACT: 26–29

Notable alumni: J. T., "the Brick," Fox Sports radio host; Glen Gordon Caron (TV producer—*Medium* and *Moonlighting*); Greg "Opie" Hughes of radio's *Opie and Anthony*

INDIANA UNIVERSITY OF PENNSYL-VANIA—INDIANA, PENNSYLVANIA

14,728 students (12,471 undergraduates)

Business and information technology; education and educational technology; fine arts; health and human services; humanities and social sciences; natural sciences and mathematics

Special opportunities: Robert E. Cook Honors College

90 percent admitted

Middle 50 percent on SAT: 890–1050; ACT: 17–22

Notable alumni: Chad Hurley (YouTube cofounder and CEO), Jim Haslett (former NFL player and current coach), Jeff Burk (author and producer of the *Magazine of Bizarro Fiction*)

KEENE STATE COLLEGE—KEENE, NEW HAMPSHIRE

5,340 students (4,987 undergraduates)

Arts and humanities; professional and graduate studies; sciences and social sciences; and Division of Continuing Education

82 percent admitted

Middle 50 percent on SAT: 870–1080

UNIVERSITY OF MARY WASHINGTON—FREDERICKSBURG, VIRGINIA

4,831 students (4,383 undergraduates)

Arts and sciences; business; and education

Forty major options

Special features: honor system

81 percent admitted

Middle 50 percent on SAT: 1030–1190; ACT: 22–27

Average high school GPA: 3.54

Notable alumni: Judy Muller (ABC News), Judge Reinhold (actor)

MASSACHUSETTS COLLEGE OF THE LIBERAL ARTS—NORTH ADAMS, MASSACHUSETTS

2,219 students (1,782 undergraduates)

Fifty major options

Average SAT (CR plus M): 1022

Average high school GPA: 3.14

67 percent admitted

Special programs: tuition reduction for residents of CT, NH, NY, RI, and southern Vermont who major in arts management, athletic training, or English/communications

Notable alumni: Anton Stout (fantasy novelist)

UNIVERSITY OF MINNESOTA AT MORRIS—MORRIS, MINNESOTA

1,700 students (all undergraduates)

Thirty majors, including teaching licensure in fifteen areas

Students can design their own major.

Student-faculty ratio of thirteen to one; average class size of sixteen

Special features: tuition, fees, plus room and board is the same for residents and nonresidents.

58 percent admitted

Average ACT: 25

NEW COLLEGE OF FLORIDA—SARA-SOTA, FLORIDA

832 students (all undergraduates)

Student-faculty ratio of ten to one; average class size of seventeen

Liberal arts curriculum with minimal required courses

Narrative evaluations take precedence over letter grades.

Average SAT: 1304; GPA: 3.98

69 percent admitted

Notable alumni: David Allen (*Getting Things Done* time management method), Lincoln Diaz-Ballart (US representative, Florida).

THE COLLEGE OF NEW JERSEY—TRENTON, NEW JERSEY

6,964 students (6,205 undergraduates)

Student-faculty ratio of thirteen to one; average class size of twenty-one

Arts and communication; business; culture and society; education; engineering; nursing, health, and exercise science; science

43 percent admitted

Average SAT: 1228

Notable alumni: Holly Black (author of the *Spiderwick Chronicles*), Jim Florio (former governor of New Jersey), Tom McCarthy (Phillies play-by-play announcer)

UNIVERSITY OF NORTH CAROLINA AT ASHEVILLE—ASHEVILLE, NORTH CAROLINA

3,609 students (3,574 undergraduates)

Thirty major options

Average class size of eighteen students

Special features: honors program

69 percent admitted

Average SAT: 1197

Notable alumni: Sarah Addison Allen (writer), Wiley Cash (writer)

ST. MARY'S COLLEGE OF MARYLAND—ST. MARY'S, MARYLAND

1,879 students (primarily undergraduate)

Student-faculty ratio of ten to one

Arts and sciences focus: twenty-four majors, twenty-seven minors

Special opportunities: St. Mary's is the honors college for the state of Maryland;

Center for the Study of Democracy, Nitze Scholars Program, student-designed major

Middle 50 percent on SAT: 1110–1320

73 percent admitted

TRUMAN STATE COLLEGE—KIRKSVILLE, MISSOURI

5,990 students (5,700 undergraduates)

Student-faculty ratio of sixteen to one

Arts and letters; business; health sciences and education; science and mathematics; social and cultural studies; interdisciplinary studies and liberal studies programs

Middle 50 percent on SAT: 1080–1330; ACT: 25–30

72 percent admitted

Notable alumni: Jenna Fischer (actress), Ken Norton (boxer), Rhonda Vincent (bluegrass musician), Gregg Williams (NFL coach)

► COUNCIL OF PUBLIC LIBERAL ARTS COLLEGES (COPLAC)

A growing number of institutions have been moving to stake their claim to public liberal arts territory. Most of the institutions listed above belong to the Council of Public Liberal Arts Colleges (COPLAC), which according to its mission statement works to champion "the cause of liberal arts education of superior quality in the public sector." Listed and in a few cases profiled below are some emerging members of COPLAC that might be of interest to students and parents who are looking not just for alternatives to large flagship state universities but for alternatives to the more selective public liberal arts colleges. We have labeled these institutions as emerging public liberal arts colleges because each is less residential and more local in character than the more established group highlighted above.

- Georgia College and State University
- Henderson State University (Arkansas)
- University of Illinois at Springfield
- University of Maine at Farmington
- Midwestern State University (Texas)
- University of Montevallo (Alabama)
- Ramapo College of New Jersey
- University of Science and Arts of Oklahoma
- Shepherd University (West Virginia)
- Sonoma State University (California)
- Southern Oregon University
- University of Virginia College at Wise
- University of Wisconsin at Superior

UNIVERSITY OF MONTEVALLO— MONTEVALLO, ALABAMA

3,006 students (2,620 undergraduates)

Seventy-five major options

Arts and sciences; business; education; fine arts

Special features: bike share program in partnership with the city of Montevallo

Middle 50 percent on ACT: 20–26

67 percent admitted

Notable alumni: Polly Holliday (actress), Rebecca Luker (Broadway actress)

SOUTHERN OREGON UNIVERSITY— ASHLAND, OREGON

6,203 students (4,490 undergraduates)

One hundred academic programs; thirty-five major options

Special features: Ashland is home to the world-renowned Oregon Shakespeare Festival.

Average SAT: 1012; ACT: 22

92 percent admitted

Notable alumni: Ty Burrell (actor), Joel David Moore (actor)

UNIVERSITY OF VIRGINIA AT WISE— WISE, VIRGINIA

2,067 students (all undergraduate)

Thirty major options

Student-faculty ratio of thirteen to one

Average high school GPA: 3.34/4.0

Average SAT: 1090

75 percent admitted

There are some other state colleges and universities that in certain ways resemble small to medium-sized arts and sciences institutions. These are not institutions designated by an organization such as COPLAC, but each offers a distinctive and increasingly popular alternative to the flagship university in its state. Some are hybrids of the flagship state university and the public liberal arts university. Others are former commuter or regional colleges that have integrated aspects of the public liberal arts brand into the academic and co-curricular experience for students. All of the institutions listed and profiled below are smaller and more undergraduate-centric than the public flagships in their states.

- University of California at Merced
- University of California at Santa Cruz
- Castleton State College (Vermont)
- Humboldt State University (California)
- James Madison University (Virginia)
- SUNY-Fredonia
- SUNY New Paltz
- Northern Arizona University
- Stockton University (New Jersey)
- Western Washington University
- Rowan University (New Jersey)

UNIVERSITY OF CALIFORNIA AT MERCED

6,268 students (5,884 undergraduates)

Engineering; natural sciences; social sciences, humanities, and the arts

Planned: School of Management, School of Medicine

Nineteen undergraduate academic programs; emphasis on interdisciplinary learning

Student-faculty ratio of twenty to one

98 percent of students are California residents (70 percent students of color)

64 percent admitted

Average high school GPA: 3.61/4.0

Average ACT: 24; SAT: 1098

HUMBOLDT STATE UNIVERSITY— ARCATA, CALIFORNIA

8,485 students (7,962 undergraduates)

Forty-nine undergraduate academic programs

Arts, humanities, and social sciences; natural resources and sciences

Excellent environmental programs, strong institutional commitment to sustainability

Middle 50 percent on ACT: 18–24; SAT: 990–1140

Average high school GPA: 3.15/4.0

76 percent admitted

Notable alumni: Raymond Carver (writer), Kenneth Fisher (financial writer and CEO of Fisher Investments), Stephen Hillenburg (creator of *SpongeBob SquarePants*)

JAMES MADISON UNIVERSITY— HARRISONBURG, VIRGINIA

20,855 students (19,144 undergraduates)

Sixty-nine degree programs

Standout programs in business, music, musical theater, and theater

Middle 50 percent on SAT: 1060–1220; 23–27

66 percent admitted

Notable alumni: LeRoi Moore and Butch Taylor, both of the Dave Matthews Band, and National Football League players Gary Clark and Charles Haley

THE IVY LEAGUE

ORIGINS OF THE TERM *IVY LEAGUE*

Ivy League is a phrase that is simultaneously well-known and mysterious. *Ivy League* most commonly connotes academic excellence and admissions exclusivity. The Ivy League, from its historic evolution to its current iterations, comprises a prominent group of colleges that are often considered the best (or among the best) in the world. Still, people sometimes forget that the Ivy League is a designation, not a particular college. Each of the eight Ivy League schools has its own distinctive history, traditions, academic offerings, and campus atmosphere. For students intrigued by the Ivy mystique, we recommend examining each of these eight famous schools to determine whether any of them seem like a good fit.

The eight schools in the Ivy League are Brown University, Columbia University, Cornell University, Dartmouth College, Harvard University, the University of Pennsylvania, Princeton University, and Yale University. While these schools have existed for a long time (the oldest, Harvard, since 1636 and the youngest, Cornell, since 1865), the Ivy League, as an organized collection of institutions, has only been an official group since 1954. When the Ivy League was formally organized (following two decades of discussion), the goal was to coordinate intercollegiate athletic competition so that a group of prestigious schools could play in a league whose members had similar policies for recruiting athletes, particularly an agreement prohibiting athletic scholarships. To this day, the eight schools maintain what is known as the Ivy League Index for determining if an athlete meets certain academic requirements for admissions viability.

When sports writers in the 1930s first bandied about the term *Ivy League*, there was not yet a clear sense of exactly which schools they meant. A handful of universities, called the Big Three (Harvard, Yale, and Princeton), were always in the Ivy discussions, but there was some fluidity about the others. As far back as 1852, the schools that now comprise the Ivy League became athletic rivals, when Harvard and Yale held a boat race on New Hampshire's Lake Winnipesaukee. In 1902, the Eastern Intercollegiate Basketball League formed (involving Harvard, Yale, Columbia, Cornell, and Princeton—later joined by Dartmouth, Pennsylvania, and Brown) to establish a set of rules and regulations for the newly emerging sport. In 1916, a presidential agreement between Harvard, Yale, and Princeton established rules for their football teams. By 1945, the eight schools now in the Ivy League had signed an agreement reiterating the student athlete standards of 1916 and stipulating that scholarships would not be awarded for athletic performance. When the Ivy League was formed in 1954, the standards for admitting athletes established in 1945 were expanded to include all sports. By 1956, the Ivy League had become an official league organized around agreed-upon rules, with schools competing primarily against each other but also continuing to schedule games against long-standing regional rivals such as Colgate (for Cornell) and Lehigh (for Princeton).

While athletic competition led to the formation of the Ivy League, many other social and historical factors brought the eight schools together. Starting with Harvard (America's oldest college), the Ivy League represents a collection of old and distinguished institutions of higher learning. Seven of the nine oldest colleges in the United States are in the Ivy League: Harvard (1636), Yale (1701), Penn (1740), Princeton (1746), Columbia (1754), Brown (1764), and Dartmouth (1769). All of the member schools are located in America's oldest settled region (the Northeast), and by the time of the official formation of the Ivy League, those eight schools had established themselves as preferred choices for educating the country's social elite. Collectively, the Ivy League has a long history of producing graduates who have gone on to achieve success in the worlds of finance, politics, education, the arts, philanthropy, and science. Because of its success at producing leaders and moguls, an Ivy League education is seen by many as the proverbial ticket to success in life.

In previous generations, the Ivy League sometimes used controversial means to mark its exclusivity. For example, in the 1930s, the Ivy establishment feared that a growing wave of Jewish applicants from public high schools would change the character of the universities and take away spaces that they felt belonged to more traditional candidates from the exclusive feeder preparatory academies of the Northeast. As a result, several Ivy League schools changed their admission policies to make it more difficult for less preferred groups to supplant the traditional white Anglo-Saxon Protestant (WASP) majority, whose fathers had graduated from the Ivy League. The anti-Semitic admissions policies used to cap the number of Jews enrolling in the Ivy League (see Jerome Karabel's *The Chosen: The Hidden History of Admission and Exclusion at Harvard, Yale and Princeton*) were adapted from the procedures used to limit entry to exclusive private clubs, lending credence to the popular conception of the Ivy League as a private club. Those same exclusionary admissions policies (ironically) provided a template for the subjective, holistic admissions processes used at highly selective colleges today. The discriminatory admissions policies enacted in the 1930s moved the Ivy League beyond general entrance exams and toward viewing the applicant as a whole person rather than primarily as a student. While the Jewish quotas enacted in the 1930s have

long been abolished, the Ivy League's approach to selecting applicants based on more than just their academic merits remains intact—in an effort to construct a class that meets institutional priorities for diversity, athletics, academic and artistic specialties, legacy, and other identified areas of interest.

Entry into the Ivy League no longer fits stereotypes from a bygone era. No longer must one be a WASP male from a select group of prep schools collectively known as St. Grottlesex (Groton, Middlesex, St. George's, St. Mark's, and St. Paul's—founded in the mid-nineteenth to the early twentieth century in the image of the famous British public schools, such as Eton, Charterhouse, Harrow, Rugby, Shrewsbury, Westminster—that attracted the sons of the WASP elite) or from a handful of other schools (Andover, Choate, Deerfield, Exeter, Hill, Hotchkiss, Milton, Lawrenceville, Pomfret, and Taft) that sent disproportionate numbers of their students to the Ivy League for many years. Beginning in the 1960s, Ivy League schools widened their recruiting focus to include every region of the United States and the rest of the world. It is not uncommon to find Ivy League admissions officers looking for students at rural Indian reservations or making school visits in remote regions where only the local public universities recruit. This broader recruiting has resulted in more applications and lower admission rates at Ivy League schools.

Prior to the 1930s, there was (arguably) a bit more predictability to Ivy League admissions, as applicants who performed the best on the entrance exam and had the backing of their elite prep schools were admitted. But when applicants from public and less-established prep schools began to outperform the favorite sons of the elite prep schools on the entrance exam, it became clear that more factors would need to be considered. Even after the discriminatory Jewish quotas were abandoned and admission standards and requirements evolved, they remained, like the Ivy League itself, widely known and mysterious at the same time. For example, it is a given that Ivy League schools expect applicants to have an excellent academic record. But that alone does not guarantee admission. What else is needed for admission is more of a mystery. Today, as record numbers of students apply and the admission rates to the Ivy schools range from 5 percent to 15 percent, the selection process can seem almost random—one 4.0 student with 2400 on the SAT is rejected, and another is accepted.

For those fortunate to gain entry to the Ivy League, extraordinary resources and opportunities await. Each school has its own distinctive history and culture that makes the experience very special. Still, the enduring club-like aspect of the Ivy League causes some people to thrive and makes others uncomfortable. Indeed, admission to the Ivy League is arguably akin to an invitation to join an exclusive club, one with eight clubhouses, each of which will now be described in more detail.

HARVARD, YALE, PRINCETON

HARVARD UNIVERSITY

Harvard students and alumni sometimes refer to their alma mater with false modesty as a "little college in Cambridge." Calling Harvard a "little college in Cambridge" is a coy (bordering on nausea-inducing) way to downplay that the person has attended one of the most well-known and impressive schools in the world. Memo to Harvard people: those you might deem the hoi polloi actually like you less when you pretend to minimize the wonderful opportunity you had to study at America's oldest and wealthiest college. Since 1636 when Harvard first started training young clergymen, the university has attracted bright young people and brilliant faculty to its campus. With an endowment exceeding $36 billion, Harvard is able to provide students and faculty with superior resources and the assurance that their school will be successful well into the future.

Harvard has an extensive array of academic programs, including world-famous graduate and professional schools for business, government, law, and medicine. On the undergraduate side, the most popular majors are economics, government,

history, and sociology. But all programs at Harvard, even those that gather tumbleweeds in terms of popularity, are highly regarded and well funded. Although it may seem crass to keep mentioning Harvard's wealth, that vast wealth is a huge factor that cannot be ignored in explaining why Harvard can attract some of the best students and faculty in the world. Harvard's wealth makes it possible for the university to provide excellent research facilities and attractive salaries to faculty. The wealth also helps maintain the extraordinary Harvard campus that has become a tourist stop for people eager to glimpse one of the world's most storied cathedrals of learning.

The Harvard faculty, as mentioned, is one of the most impressive in the world. Prominent names aren't everything, but Harvard has a constellation of stars, such as Henry Louis Gates, the preeminent scholar of African American history and culture; Lisa Randall, the leading expert on particle physics and cosmology; and Amartya Sen, the Nobel Prize–winning economist best known for his work on famine's causes and potential solutions. Critics of Harvard assert that undergraduate classes are too often taught by graduate students rather than tenured or tenure-track faculty. But Harvard insists that nearly 100 percent of its faculty teach undergraduate classes. With an enviable teacher-student ratio of one to seven, Harvard can resemble a smaller liberal arts college in terms of faculty access. For example, about 80 percent of undergraduate classes have fewer than twenty students—impressive for a school of approximately 6,650 undergraduates.

Having such a huge endowment translates into very generous financial aid. Harvard can easily afford to be need blind, which means that admissions decisions are made without regard to the applicant's financial situation. If admitted, Harvard promises to meet 100 percent of demonstrated need. Harvard is one of the few colleges in the United States where financial-aid packages do not include loans. Grants (which do not need to be repaid), a campus job (through work-study), and other scholarships make up the Harvard financial-aid package. Families earning less than $65,000 a year do not pay anything outright for a Harvard education. To those who qualify, Harvard awards approximately $172 million in need-based aid annually. As a result, no prospective student should rule out Harvard on sticker price alone.

Harvard's large endowment also comes in handy when maintaining its extensive campus. The 210-acre Cambridge campus is the heart of the undergraduate experience, with freshman required to live along the famed Harvard Yard and nearly all upperclassmen living in one of twelve residential houses, each with its own dining hall, library, and advising and other services. Another 359 acres of facilities, including the Harvard Business School (HBS) campus and football stadium, are located across the Charles River in the Allston section of Boston. The HBS campus is easily accessible via a pedestrian bridge over the Charles River. At an additional 22-acre site in Boston, Harvard operates its medical, dental and public health schools.

Harvard and Yale have had an intense, long-standing rivalry, so it is ironic that a Yale graduate (Edward Harkness, class of 1897) helped establish the residential college system that Harvard undergraduates enjoy today. An $11 million gift from Harkness in 1928 paid for the creation of what Harvard calls the house system, where proctors, tutors, and faculty live in the self-contained residences—enabling consistent and close interaction with students. Since the 1930s, Harvard houses have been an integral part of undergraduate life. Reminiscent of the residential system at Oxford and Cambridge, each house sponsors special academic and social events and engenders fierce student loyalty. Soon after Harvard pioneered the house system, Harkness made a gift to his alma mater to establish a similar system at Yale.

Beyond the residential colleges, Harvard has countless extracurricular traditions that stretch back centuries. The Hasty Pudding Club (founded in 1770) is considered the oldest collegiate social club in the United States. The *Harvard Lampoon* (founded in 1876) is the longest continuously published humor magazine in the world. In addition to these storied organizations, Harvard offers thousands of other clubs and activities, including the *Harvard Crimson* newspaper.

One of the most significant advantages of a Harvard education is the networking opportunities with fellow alumni. Plus, Harvard is a name that everyone knows and respects. Some of the famous people who attended Harvard as undergraduates are listed on the next page.

➤ ATTENDED HARVARD AS UNDERGRADUATES

John Adams (1755)—president of the United States

James Agee (1932)—novelist, screenwriter

Ben Bernanke (1975)—former chairman of the Federal Reserve Bank

Leonard Bernstein (1939)—composer, conductor

Benazir Bhutto (1973)—first female prime minister of Pakistan

E. E. Cummings (1915)—poet

Jared Diamond (1958)—biologist, author of *Guns, Germs and Steel*

W. E. B. Du Bois (1890)—civil rights leader, African American scholar

T. S. Eliot (1909)—poet

Ralph Waldo Emerson (1821)—author

Al Franken (1973)—senator, comedian

Amy Goodman (1984)—founder, *Democracy Now!*

Al Gore (1969)—environmentalist, former US vice president

John Hancock (1754)—president of Continental Congress

Philip Johnson (1930)—architect

Helen Keller (1904)—trailblazer for the blind and deaf

John F. Kennedy (1940)—president of the United States

Robert F. Kennedy (1948)—US attorney general, senator

Henry Kissinger (1950)—US secretary of state, National Security Advisor

Yo-Yo Ma (1976)—cellist

Norman Mailer (1943)—author

Soledad O'Brien (1987)—television host

J. Robert Oppenheimer (1925)—physicist, "father of the atomic bomb"

George Plimpton (1948)—author, journalist, actor

Natalie Portman (2003)—actress

Franklin Delano Roosevelt (1904)—president of the United States

Theodore Roosevelt (1880)—president of the United States

Whit Stillman (1973)—filmmaker

Henry David Thoreau (1837)—philosopher, author

John Updike (1954)—author

YALE UNIVERSITY

In many ways, Yale has imprinted the image of the classic collegiate experience in the collective American mind. Arguably more than Harvard, Yale has come to stand for a platonic ideal of what college should be. Perhaps the relative isolation of Yale in New Haven, Connecticut, a city of highs and lows that has long had a complicated relationship with the university, causes Yalies to turn inward and create a campus experience not quite replicated (due to the readily available distractions of Cambridge and Boston) at Harvard. Since its early beginnings in 1701, Yalies have been making their marks, first on their campus, and then on the world.

About a hundred years ago, a fictional character named Dink Stover (in Owen Johnson's 1912 novel, *Stover at Yale*) graduated from the Lawrenceville School and entered Yale. Stover in many ways represents the classic Yalie: smart, athletic, honorable (but not too pious), and aware of the importance of making lasting connections (through secret societies, an athletic team, or a residential college) at school. Nowadays, a wider variety of students attend Yale and a fuller array of student organizations exist, but campus life is not completely removed from the days of Dink Stover. Every time Handsome Dan the bulldog parades onto the football field (a tradition dating back to 1889) to mark the spirited annual Yale versus Harvard football game, the atmosphere bears more than a passing resemblance to the Dink Stover era. The stuffed body of the original Handsome Dan (the first of sixteen) is on display at Yale's famed Payne Whitney gym, serving as a macabre celebration of the first live mascot in US college history.

Stuffed Victorian-era bulldogs aside, Yale has a long history of academic excellence amid a well-rounded college experience. Certainly, the Yale experience is about what you study, but it is also about the relationships you develop along the way. Academically, Yale offers a wide variety of programs and boasts an impressive student-faculty ratio of five to one for its approximately 5,310 undergraduates. A shopping period at the beginning of each term encourages students to check out multiple courses that are of interest before committing to a schedule during registration. Still, more than a third of each Yale class chooses to major in political science, history, or economics. The popularity of the aforementioned majors should not suggest that Yale's other departments are of lesser quality. Yale, in fact, has world-class departments of art history, classics, English, and psychology. The nearly 100 percent retention rate indicates that students are satisfied with all of the academic departments at Yale.

Like Harvard, Yale has residential colleges that took their current form in the early 1930s, thanks to the largesse of Edward Harkness. Within higher education, the Yale residential colleges are often held up as a model and have been copied (in one form or another) on many campuses. Each of Yale's twelve residential colleges functions like a self-contained small school led by a dean and a master, both of whom are professors who live and eat in the college. Each college's dean is its academic leader, while the master is the college's presiding administrative officer. Yale has extensive plans for two new residential colleges to be built in what's known as the Science Hill area of campus in an effort to increase enrollment and provide better access to services, but for now the residential colleges are Berkeley College, Branford College, Calhoun College, Davenport College, Ezra Stiles College, Jonathan Edwards College, Morse College, Pierson College, Saybrook College, Silliman College, Timothy Dwight College, and Trumbull College. Students are assigned to a residential college as freshmen and stay with that college for all four years at Yale, building allegiances and friendships that last a lifetime.

When not in class, Yale students are involved in countless activities. Many people have an awareness of the secret societies at Yale, such as Skull and Bones (whose members have included Presidents George H. W. and George W. Bush and Secretary of State John Kerry) to the point where calling them secret seems inaccurate. The number of students in secret societies at Yale is relatively small, but they do add an element of intrigue to campus life. Yale also has a Greek system. But in far greater numbers, Yalies involve themselves with a cappella singing groups and the heated and intricate rush, audition, and selection process to join them. Securing a spot in one of Yale's a cappella groups involves an elaborate wooing of singers through auditions, concerts, meals, singing desserts, and parties, culminating with tap night, whereupon those selected for a cappella royalty are notified and asked to run around campus with their group. Yale's a cappella groups—many of which have existed for nearly a century—often travel the world and engender life-long friendships, making an invitation to join one a big deal. The following groups participate in Yale's a cappella rush.

- New Blue (women)
- Proof of the Pudding (women)
- Something Extra (women)
- Whim and Rhythm (senior women)
- Alley Cats (men)
- Baker's Dozen (men)
- Duke's Men (men)
- Society of Orpheus and Bacchus (men)
- Spizwinks (men)
- Whiffenpoofs (senior men; oldest, most prestigious of the groups)
- Living Water (coed)
- Mixed Company (coed)
- Out of the Blue (coed)
- Red, Hot and Blue (coed)
- Shades (coed)

Members of a cappella groups and other student leaders at Yale have used Mory's clubhouse as a meeting spot for about 150 years. Mory's has been a social outpost for generations of Yalies and has been particularly popular with a cappella groups as a concert venue. The energy and buzz during a typical meal at Mory's can make a student feel like New Haven is the center of the universe. Given the accomplishments of the Yalies listed below, arguably it is.

➤ YALIES

Angela Basset (1980)—actress

George H. W. Bush (1948)—president of the United States

George W. Bush (1968)—president of the United States

Walter Camp (1880)—father of American football

Anderson Cooper (1989)—CNN anchor

Jodie Foster (1985)—actress

Thomas Gallaudet (1805)—educator for the deaf

Nathan Hale (1773)—America's first spy

John Hersey (1936)—author

Amy Klobuchar (1982)—senator

Paul Krugman (1971)—Nobel-winning economist and *New York Times* columnist

Sinclair Lewis (1908)—author

Robert McNeil Jr. (1936)—developed Tylenol and founded McNeil Laboratories

Samuel F. B. Morse (1810)—invented Morse code

Cole Porter (1913)—composer

Eero Saarinen (1934)—architect who designed St. Louis Gateway Arch

Sargent Shriver (1938)—developer and first head of Peace Corps

Frederick W. Smith (1966)—founder and CEO of FedEx

Benjamin Spock (1925)—child psychologist, pediatrician

Garry Trudeau (1970)—creator of *Doonesbury* comic

Sam Waterston (1961)—actor, known for *Law and Order*

Eleazar Wheelock (1733)—founder of Dartmouth College

Eli Whitney (1792)—invented the cotton gin

Thornton Wilder (1920)—author of *Our Town*

Bob Woodward (1965)—journalist

PRINCETON UNIVERSITY

Princeton University's beginnings trace back to 1746 when a group of Presbyterians founded the College of New Jersey. The fourth oldest college in the United States, Princeton was originally located in Newark. Under the presidency of Aaron Burr Sr., the College of New Jersey moved to donated land in Princeton in 1756, whereupon construction of Nassau Hall——then the largest stone building in the original thirteen colonies—began. The College of New Jersey started with roughly seventy students and two teachers but by the time the school expanded its offerings in 1896, its name was changed to Princeton University in honor of the town it called home.

One of Princeton's proudest traditions has ignominious roots. During the second part of the nineteenth century, cheating was rampant on campus. Students took great pride in outfoxing their professors though elaborate trickery during exams. Turning in one's peers for cheating was verboten, and the problem escalated to its height in the 1890s. In a welcome turn of events, the students suggested that an honor code be developed to allow them to take their exams without proctors. The honor code, familiar in southern prep schools but less common in the Northeast, was established by students in 1893 to rid Princeton of the cheating culture. Ever since, the honor code has been an effective policy at Princeton. That Princeton's honor code is a southern import is more than a curious historical footnote.

While its northern peers, Brown, Columbia, Harvard, and Yale were considered dangerously entrenched in the godless North, Princeton became a popular college choice for sons of the South looking for options beyond the University of North Carolina and the University of Virginia. For much of its time as a men's college, Princeton was referred to as the South's Ivy League university. Thus, it is not surprising that the notions of honor associated with southern gentility found their way to the Princeton campus.

In 1855, a fire broke out in Nassau Hall, leading students to turn to boardinghouses in Princeton for their meals. By the 1890s, official eating clubs began to spring up as sources for meals and social events. Since then, the eating clubs have become a unique part of Princeton culture, helping differentiate it from other schools in the Ivy League. While Princeton is overwhelmingly residential (98 percent of students live on campus), over 70 percent of upperclassmen choose to join an eating club for meals and social connections. For a non-Princetonian, there is understandable confusion about the eating clubs. But knowing the role of the eating clubs is crucial for getting a sense of the Princeton experience. Currently, there are eleven eating clubs. Some of the clubs require "bickering" (campaigning or rushing) to get in, whereas others determine entry based on a combination sign-up and lottery system. For the non-bicker clubs, if there is space when students apply, they are allowed to join. Each eating club has its own facilities for serving food and drinks and providing entertainment. In addition to the more formal activities, students use their club as a study or hang-out space. Eating clubs cost more than traditional board plans. But Princeton covers the additional costs of membership through generous financial-aid adjustments, so that socioeconomic factors do not keep students from joining a club. Although the clubs all have distinctive reputations that can change from decade to decade, what follows is a thumbnail breakdown of each.

Ivy. Generally considered the most established and exclusive club, Ivy is a bicker club characterized by a sophisticated crowd. Some students say it has an old-money vibe.

Cottage. Cottage's elaborate facility is grand or gaudy, depending on one's perspective. Members include many athletes, particularly football players. Some students consider this the club for southern old money. Cottage is a highly desirable bicker club.

Tiger Inn. Tiger Inn is a blend of *Animal House* and the Ivy club. Generally considered Princeton's rowdiest club, TI (as some call it) is home to many athletes, particularly wrestlers and water-polo players. Students say that TI's food ranks below other clubs because much of the budget is spent on beverages and entertainment. TI is a bicker club.

Cap and Gown. Heavily populated by athletes, this club is often considered more laid back and very friendly to students of color, who typically do not join eating clubs as frequently as do white students. This is a bicker club.

Tower. Often considered the least socially elite of the bicker clubs, Tower is popular with intellectuals and Triangle Club (theater) people. Sometimes considered a little nerdy, Tower is loved for its signature cider.

Terrace. Considered somewhat alternative, Terrace is known for live music. Students say this club has a reputation for drugs and poor food. There is a curious stuffy/scruffy overlap between the Ivy and Terrace crowds.

Cloister. Sometimes called the club of floaters and boaters because of the large number of swimmers and rowers who are members, Cloister is known as a fun club populated by people "hosed" (rejected) by bickers.

Colonial. Colonial is distinctive for its beautiful facility, popularity among Asian students, and impressive array of beers on tap.

Charter. Charter is popular with engineers due to its proximity to the engineering quad. Regarded as nerdy, Charter has a gorgeous facility and has experienced a surge of popularity in recent years.

Quad. Known for attracting freshmen to its dance floor, Quad is also popular with African American students.

Cannon Dial Elm. This relatively new club emerged from the merger of three defunct clubs. CDE utilizes the renovated Cannon Club facility and is a bicker club.

Beyond the eating clubs, Princeton students come together to experience excellent academic opportunities. For its 5,000 undergraduates and 2,500 graduate students, Princeton offers a remarkable student-faculty ratio of six to one. A standout aspect of the curriculum is that all undergraduates must write a senior thesis. This is not a deterrent and may actually be a motivation for the thousands of students vying for admissions to Princeton, which typically accepts fewer than 10 percent of its freshman applicants. About 60 percent of Princeton students receive financial aid, with an average grant approaching $50,000. Princeton is in the enviable position of only awarding grants (not loans) in its aid packages, meaning that students are not responsible for paying back any loans after graduation. This is a far cry from the Princeton of the 1930s that offered minimal financial aid and had admission rates of 70 to 80 percent.

Academically, Princeton has much to offer. It has a comprehensive selection of arts and science majors as well as an engineering program. Engineering is elected as a major by about one-sixth of Princeton students, but other popular majors include politics, economics, and history. The public policy and international affairs program at the Woodrow Wilson School (WWS) is Princeton's only selective major and is limited to ninety students per class. Within the WWS, there are approximately twenty centers that focus on specific public policy issues, enabling students to participate in efforts to find solutions to pressing challenges. The Program in Global Health and Health Policy (GHP) and the Bendheim-Thoman Center for Research on Child Well-Being (CRCW), for example, involve undergraduates in their research.

Another exciting opportunity available to Princeton students is the Atelier Program. Developed by author and Princeton Professor Toni Morrison, the Atelier Program brings together innovators in different fields to work out artistic visions together. The merging of perspectives that occurs in Atelier leads to exciting collaborations and new ideas. For example, a renowned poet when paired with an emergent sculptor may create something that neither would be able to achieve independently. Sometimes even the students who have applied for the classes (but have not been selected) also get to participate in the resulting creative project. One Atelier project resulted in students participating in the Trenton Mural Arts Project.

Regardless of their major or eating club, graduates of Princeton are a fanatically devoted bunch. Numerous traditions, such as elaborately decorated class jackets, build close networks among Princetonians. When surveyed, nearly 100 percent of Princeton seniors say they will be returning for reunions and other alumni events. There is a lot of Tiger pride and this helps Princeton's endowment grow. The high level of alumni devotion in turn provides current and future Princetonians with an abundance of opportunities and resources unheard of at most colleges. The following successful and notable individuals earned their undergraduate degree from Princeton.

➤ NOTABLE PRINCETON UNDERGRADUATES

Samuel Alito (1974)—Supreme Court justice

Jeff Bezos (1986)—founder of Amazon.com

Bill Bradley (1965)—former US senator and pro basketball player

Aaron Burr (1772)—US vice president who shot and killed Alexander Hamilton in a duel

Ethan Coen (1979)—part of the Coen Brothers filmmaking duo

Jason Garrett (1989)—head coach, Dallas Cowboys

Charlie Gibson (1965)—broadcast journalist

Andrea Jung (1979)—first female CEO of Avon Products

Elena Kagen (1981)—Supreme Court justice

John Katzman (1981)—founder of *Princeton Review*

Peter Lewis (1955)—CEO of Progressive Insurance

James Madison (1771)—president of the United States

Ralph Nader (1955)—political activist, Green Party presidential candidate

Queen Noor of Jordan (1974)

Michelle Obama (1985)—First Lady of the United States

David Remnick (1981)—editor, the *New Yorker*

Eric Schlosser (1982)—journalist who wrote *Fast Food Nation*

Brooke Shields (1987)—actress

Sonia Sotomayor (1976)—Supreme Court justice

Adlai Stevenson (1922)—US vice president

James Stewart (1932)—actor

Katrina vanden Heuvel (1981)—editor, the *Nation*

Robert Venturi (1947)—noted architect

Meg Whitman (1977)—CEO of Hewlett Packard, former CEO of eBay

Woodrow Wilson (1879)—president of the United States

BROWN, COLUMBIA, CORNELL, DARTMOUTH, AND PENN

BROWN UNIVERSITY

Founded in 1764 by northern Baptists, Brown resides in a city (Providence) that in its founding years was the site of religious freedoms not tolerated in New England's Puritan colonies. Today, Providence's relatively progressive historical roots can be seen in Brown's commitment to liberal thought, relatively open curriculum, and emphasis on inclusive community.

Prior to the 1970s, Brown was known at some elite prep schools as "the doormat of the Ivy League." Although it still rivaled the best colleges in the country, Brown, when compared to its Ivy League counterparts, was regarded as less prominent and desirable. In 1970 everything changed for Brown when the university accepted a student-submitted proposal for a new curriculum. The Brown Curriculum jettisoned all academic core requirements for undergraduates. Students subsequently fully owned their academic experience, only taking classes of interest to them or ones required for their chosen concentration (as majors are called at Brown). The opportunity to select courses free of restrictive core requirements, which resonated with the post-1960s zeitgeist, immediately made Brown extremely popular and as a result much more difficult for admission. In the minds of many, the self-directed education at Brown represents intellectual nirvana. But to its tradition-bound critics, the Brown curriculum represents a way to coast to an Ivy League degree.

The defining idea behind Brown's curriculum is to free students to follow their intellectual passions. Without the burden of required, chore-like core courses, so goes the thinking (and proselytizing) at Brown, students can delve deeper into their chosen concentration. After (presumably) taking a rigorous set of classes in high school, Brown students are trusted to guide their own education at college. The lack of D and F grades on transcripts also encourages Brown students to take classes outside of their comfort zone without fearing how a low grade might impact their overall GPA.

Yes, you read that last sentence correctly. No bad grades appear on Brown transcripts, meaning Brown students can take courses without fear that flunking one will besmirch their prestigious Ivy League degree. Students get this freedom to follow their academic bliss on a charming urban campus of approximately 6,100 undergraduates in a city known for great restaurants and close proximity to Boston and Newport. Could this college be too good to be true? For the approximately 91.5 percent of applicants rejected by the Brown Admissions Office each year, sadly, it is. By far, the toughest thing about Brown is getting admitted. The perception that Brown is both academic playground and prestigious school has made it one of the most selective colleges in the world. Those with long memories know that after John F. Kennedy Jr. graced its halls in the late 1970s, Brown became the cool-kid college within the Ivy League and has not surrendered that identity since. Due to this cachet, Brown consistently attracts celebrities, their offspring, and wealthy foreigners.

Brown's undergraduate academic program offers a solid representation of the standard college fare as well as some more exotic concentrations such as archeology and Egyptology. At Brown there is also greater willingness than at other Ivy League schools to treat student-created concentrations as viable study pathways. This creates limitless academic options for students to exercise their intellectual creativity. Recently a dual degree was created with Brown's neighbor, the Rhode Island School of Design, enabling students to earn both a BA and BFA in five years. Another excellent opportunity is Brown's Program in Liberal Medical Education (PLME) that combines applying to college and medical school. High school students chosen for the astronomically selective PLME are admitted to an eight-year course of study leading to a Brown undergraduate degree as well as an MD from the Alpert Medical School.

The student body at Brown is predominantly a liberal, urban crowd, but all types of people thrive on campus. Anecdotal reports suggest an overwhelming majority of Brown students are happy with their college experience, although there seem to be more complaints about housing than at some other Ivies. There is a small but active Greek scene and a plethora of theme housing—providing a sense of community around areas such as the environment, faith, culture, technology, and global awareness. Among the lucky few who attended Brown are the illustrious alumni listed below.

➤ WELL-KNOWN BROWN ALUMNI

Chris Berman (1977)—ESPN host

Lisa Birnbach (1978)—author of *The Official Preppy Handbook* and *True Prep*

Julie Bowen (1991)—actress

John Seely Brown (1962)—invented SpellCheck

Dana Buchman (1973)—fashion designer

Mary Chapin Carpenter (1981)—country singer/songwriter

Lincoln Chaffee (1975)—former governor and senator (Rhode Island)

Ira Glass (1982)—host, producer, PBS's *This American Life*

Todd Haynes (1985)—filmmaker

Charles Evans Hughes (1881)—served as chief justice of the US Supreme Court

John F. Kennedy Jr. (1983)—lawyer, journalist

John Krasinski (2001)—actor

Laura Linney (1986)—actress

Lois Lowry (1958)—children's and young adult author

Horace Mann (1819)—considered father of American public school education

Joe Paterno (1950)—legendary Penn State football coach

Marilynne Robinson (1966)—Pulitzer Prize–winning author

Tom First and Tom Scott (both 1989)—cofounders of Nantucket Nectars

John Sculley (1961)—former CEO of Apple and Pepsi

Duncan Sheik (1992)—pop singer, Broadway composer

Thomas J. Watson (1937)—legendary CEO and president of IBM

COLUMBIA UNIVERSITY

America's fifth oldest college, Columbia, has been a significant part of the US educational landscape since it was founded in 1754 in New York City as King's College. Currently, most of Columbia's 6,000 undergraduates and 23,000 additional graduate, full-time professional, and part-time students occupy the Morningside Heights campus (on Manhattan's Upper West Side), which was designed and built as a classical academic village in 1896. Manhattan provides a dynamic backdrop for Columbia students, but what some might consider an exciting location others might find distracting and scary. Clearly, many people hold the former opinion, as Columbia has experienced a consistent and steep rise in applications over the past two decades, to the point where it now accepts only 7 to 10 percent of applicants to the College of Arts and Sciences and 13 to 15 percent to the Fu Foundation School of Applied Science and Engineering. Columbia can afford to be picky, as its yield (students who accept the admission offer) is quite high at 60 percent.

Besides its Big Apple location, students are drawn to Columbia for its many academic offerings and exceptional education. For example, Columbia is a recognized leader in academic areas, such as anthropology, East Asian studies, economics, English and comparative literature, sociology, and urban studies. In addition to the resources available at Columbia, students can take classes, pursue interdisciplinary programs, and participate in organizations at Barnard College, the women's college that operates alongside Columbia.

A distinguishing aspect of Columbia is its required core curriculum, which was first developed in 1919 as a way to broaden academic horizons, inspire students to grapple with the major questions of human existence, and develop critical thinking and writing skills. Required core classes cover contemporary civilization, humanities (both art and music), foreign language, science, writing, and global/international studies. The Columbia core curriculum is well-known, and while variations of it exist at other colleges, Columbia is considered an originator and an innovator.

Long before the existence of fraternities, sports teams, and most extracurricular clubs, a central locus of campus social life was the college literary society. Columbia's Philolexian Society, founded in 1802, is one of the nation's oldest such societies still in existence. (Note: the University of Pennsylvania argues that their Philomathean Society is the oldest college literary society because it has continuously operated since 1813, whereas there was a period when Columbia's Philolexian Society was inactive.) Originally serving as a debate and oratory club, Columbia's Philolexian Society (which counts among its alumni Jacques Barzun, Allen Ginsburg, Joyce Kilmer, and Thomas Merton) has evolved over time to include other activities. A particularly fun event is the Joyce Kilmer Memorial Bad Poetry Contest, the winner of which is crowned poet laureate. Wordsmith contests are par for the course at Columbia, which also administers the Pulitzer Prize. Of course, other clubs proliferate on campus, but the Philolexian Society is an example of how something special from Columbia's earliest days is still popular with students today. Another event unique to Columbia occurs just before winter break, when there is a festive lighting of the trees on the quad and students dressed as Continental Army soldiers bring a Yule log to John Jay Hall while everyone sings carols. Afterward, there are readings of 1798 graduate Clement Moore's classic poem "A Visit from St. Nicholas" and 1859 graduate Francis Pharcellus Church's famous editorial, "Yes, Virginia, There Is a Santa Claus."

Beyond yuletide merriment, Columbia is a busy, sophisticated place where students are tenaciously smart, driven, and success oriented. The most popular majors at Columbia are, in descending order: political science, economics, history, English, psychology, industrial management systems for engineering and operations research, biomedical engineering, mechanical engineering, and anthropology. A host of research centers expose students to multiple academic opportunities, some of which were actually pioneered at Columbia. Interested in anthropology? It was first developed as an academic discipline by Columbia faculty member Franz Boas. The modern study of genetic research also got its start at Columbia under Thomas Hart Morgan. Columbia's location enhances several centers and special programs. For example, the Columbia Center for Jazz Studies is a great resource complemented by a city filled with musicians. With a $6.5 billion endowment,

Columbia can sustain a wide variety of programs that benefit students and also have an impact on the intellectual and social development of communities beyond its campus.

In addition to its main Morningside Heights campus, Columbia operates a satellite outpost in Paris and two world-renowned research sites north of New York City: Nevis Laboratories in Irvington, New York, has (since 1947) served as a major center for high-energy experimental particle and nuclear physics, and Lamont Doherty Earth Observatory in Palisades, New York, has (since 1949) charted global climate change, earthquakes, volcanoes, nonrenewable resources, and environmental hazards. Listed below are prominent Columbia undergraduates.

➤ PROMINENT COLUMBIA UNDERGRADUATES

Isaac Asimov (1939)—science fiction author

Paul Auster (1969)—author

Pat Boone (1957)—singer

Annie Duke (1987)—professional poker player

Art Garfunkel (1965)—singer/songwriter

Lou Gehrig (1925)—baseball player

Alan Ginsberg (1949)—beat poet (fellow Columbian Jack Kerouac dropped out)

Maggie Gyllenhaal (1999)—actress

Armand Hammer (1919)—president of Occidental Petroleum and Arm and Hammer

Oscar Hammerstein II (1916)—Broadway lyricist; *Oklahoma!*, *Sound of Music*

Jim Jarmusch (1975)—filmmaker

John Jay (1764)—coauthor of *Federalist Papers*, first chief justice of Supreme Court

Alfred Knopf (1912)—publisher

Jerzy Kosinski (1965)—National Book Award–winning novelist

Robert Kraft (1963)—owner of the New England Patriots

Tony Kushner (1978)—Pulitzer Prize–winning playwright

Robert Merton (1966)—Nobel Prize–winning economist

Barack Obama (1983)—president of the United States

Claire Shipman (1986)—television reporter

George Stephanopoulos (1982)—Clinton administration staffer, political commentator

Arthur Ochs Sulzberger Sr. (1951)—former publisher of the *New York Times*

Marcellus Wiley—ESPN host and former NFL player

Herman Wouk (1934)—author

CORNELL UNIVERSITY

In many ways Cornell is a bit of an outlier in the Ivy League due to its size, age, location, and blend of private and public academic programs. Cornell's structure varies from the other Ivies. A

unique relationship with the state of New York makes Cornell a private-public hybrid. Back when Ezra Cornell donated land for the campus, he sought the creation of a school where one could study anything. This included emergent areas such as agriculture and veterinary science. The result is a school more similar to the all-encompassing land-grant universities and the great public flagship campuses, such as the University of Michigan. Like many of those schools, Cornell embraced coeducation in the nineteenth century and has a commitment to serving its home state through such efforts as the Cornell Cooperative Extension Program, which teaches people in New York about gardening, farming, and sustainability.

It might seem paradoxical for a university to be both private and public. In Cornell's case, it is helpful to understand how the public-private dynamic impacts students. Cornell, which enrolls fourteen thousand undergraduates and eight thousand graduate students, is broken down into individual colleges and schools, each containing multiple academic majors. Students applying to Cornell simultaneously apply to the university and to one of its seven undergraduate colleges/schools. Certain academic units at Cornell, called endowed colleges, are private and have the same base tuition for everyone. Other academic units—agriculture and life sciences, human ecology, and industrial and labor relations—are public land-grant schools affiliated with the state of New York, meaning that for New York residents the base tuition rate at those schools is a much lower in-state fee. Nonresidents of New York pay the same private tuition rate, no matter if they apply to Cornell's private endowed schools or to its public land-grant schools. The following example further illustrates the tuition difference, irrespective of financial aid and room and board charges.

2015–16 tuition for Cornell's endowed (private) schools:

    Non–New York resident: $49,116
    New York resident: $49,116

2015–16 tuition for Cornell land-grant schools:

    Non–New York resident: $49,116
    New York resident: $32,976

There are many extraordinary programs within Cornell's land-grant schools including fashion design, business (known as applied economics and management), and nutritional science. Within the land-grant colleges, there is a focus on programs that can benefit the economy of New York State. While the reduced tuition rate is an excellent benefit for New Yorkers, it is not advisable to fake an interest in viticulture (winemaking) or landscape architecture just to get into Cornell with reduced tuition. The admissions folks at Cornell are pretty wise about those sorts of shenanigans, and it is unfair for the applicants who have genuine interest in the land-grant schools to be denied access because of subterfuge.

Cornell is big enough that there are nuanced options for what might be a single major elsewhere. For example, at a lot of colleges, there is one program in biology. At Cornell, the options related to biology are far broader. Students have a proverbial academic candy store of choices, such as agricultural science; animal science; biology and society; biological engineering; biological science; chemical biology; ecology and evolutionary biology; entomology; food science; human biology, health, and society; molecular biology; neurobiology; nutritional science; and plant science.

The range of academic offerings available at Cornell is extraordinary. While most major public universities offer a similar variety of programs, the key differentiator at Cornell, besides its Ivy League imprimatur, is its vast financial resources. Cornell's $6 billion endowment ensures that every program has the professors and facilities it needs to pursue excellence. The other core resource at Cornell is its students. Arguably, Cornell's extremely competitive 14 percent admission rate creates a student body that collectively brings a higher level of academic octane than found at many other similarly structured schools. The high-achieving peer group creates a classroom environment that fosters intellectual growth, guided discovery, and professional training.

Although Cornell has medical and graduate campuses in New York City and Qatar (and approximately five hundred undergraduates studying abroad each semester), the Ithaca campus and its adjoining Collegetown neighborhood are at the center of the undergraduate Big Red experience. Often referred to as "centrally isolated," Ithaca is snowy and remote, especially when compared to every Ivy League campus except Dartmouth. Despite its remoteness, Ithaca is generally considered a lively town with breathtaking views of Cayuga Lake, numerous gorges, and a people's republic vibe. Ithaca is home to the famed Moosewood vegetarian restaurant and numerous bars. In addition, Cornell's campus social life—through private house parties and the many fraternities and sororities—is vigorous.

Due to the sheer size of Cornell, there are many activities for students. Intercollegiate and intramural athletics are extensive, with football, hockey, and lacrosse serving as sports of note. Cornell hockey games are a huge draw. There are also hundreds of academic groups and clubs, such as a cappella groups, that provide a Big Red take on activities found on other campuses. Some more uniquely Cornellian activities include getting ice cream at the campus dairy bar, diving into gorges (be very careful!), and crafting elaborate snow sculptures of male genitalia (really).

Descriptions of the authentic Cornell experience show a definite tendency toward activities that involve alcohol and ice, be it on the ground or in a drinking glass. Alcohol-centricity is further enhanced through the popular Greek system that officially involves roughly one-third of the students and informally many more. While the Greek societies provide organized activities such as community service, they are viewed by students as a key campus social hub. Perhaps Adolph Coors (1908) and Joseph Coors (1939) were inspired by their time at Cornell to make brewing beer their life's work. In addition to Greek events, there is an emphasis on visiting the numerous bars in town and hiding bottles of liquor on Libe Slope (the steep hill in front of the Uris Library) to dig up during the thaw.

While many Cornell students ward off the freezing weather and sheer physical vastness of campus with the illusion of warmth created by imbibing alcohol, there are certainly those who do not drink. The incorporation of drinking events in the school's social fabric is significant enough, however, that prospective students need to approach Cornell aware that school spirit there is heavily fueled by spirits. Prospective students also need to recognize that the steepness of the Ithaca terrain, harsh and long winters, and spread-out campus make Cornell an environment best suited to the hale and hearty. Cornell has been the undergraduate home for many notable people, exemplified by the following list:

➤ PROMINENT CORNELL UNDERGRADUATES

Robert C. Baker (1943)—invented chicken nuggets

Joyce Brothers (1947)—author, psychologist, media personality

Adolph Coors (1908) and Joseph Coors (1939)—founders of Coors Brewing

Ann Coulter (1984)—conservative pundit

Ken Dryden (1969)—NHL Hall of Fame goalie, former member of Canadian Parliament

David Edgerton (1947) and James McLamore (1947)—cofounders of Burger King

Frank Gannett (1898)—founded largest US newspaper publishing company

Ruth Bader Ginsburg (1954)—Supreme Court justice

Jeff Hawkins (1979)—invented Palm Pilot

Henry Heimlich (1941)—invented Heimlich maneuver

Bill Maher (1978)—comedian/satirist

> **PROMINENT CORNELL UNDERGRADUATES** *(CONT.)*

Keith Olbermann (1979)—journalist, sportscaster

Christopher Reeve (1974)—actor, quadriplegic activist

Janet Reno (1960)—former US attorney general

Daniel Elmer Salmon (1872)—first

DVM in United States, namesake of Salmonella bacteria

Andrew Ross Sorkin (1999)—journalist, author of *Too Big to Fail*

M. Carey Thomas (1877)—famed president of Bryn Mawr College

Jay Walker (1977)—founder of Priceline.com

Lauren Weisberger (1999)—author, *The Devil Wears Prada*

Peter Yarrow (1959)—folksinger and member of Peter, Paul and Mary

DARTMOUTH COLLEGE

Since its founding in 1769 by Congregationalists in the White Mountains of New Hampshire, Dartmouth has been, as its motto (*Vox clamantis in deserto*) states, "a voice crying out in the wilderness." While the advent of planes, trains, and automobiles has made getting to Dartmouth easier, it is still the most rural campus in the Ivy League. Dartmouth takes full advantage of this ready access to nature and the outdoors. For example, incoming freshman are encouraged to sign up for orientation trips as an opportunity to get to know fellow students. Trips include biking, hiking, camping, canoeing, and climbing in the wilds of New Hampshire. The less athletic options include community service with hiking or organic farming with canoeing. Many of the trips occur on Dartmouth's 27,000-acre wilderness area in northern New Hampshire. Trips are optional, but students whose skin crawls at the thought of pitching a tent in the woods and cooking over a campfire will likely feel like aliens within the outdoorsy culture that characterizes Dartmouth.

The 4,100 undergraduates and 1,700 graduate students at Dartmouth are enthusiastic about their Big Green experience. Many more students would love to have the Dartmouth experience, but fewer than 10 percent of applicants are offered admission. High achievers abound. Typically, more than 90 percent of admitted students were in the top 10 percent of their high school class. Once admitted, about 53 percent of students receive financial aid, and roughly 33 percent identify as students of color. Popular majors include economics, government, biology, English, history, psychological and brain science, and engineering.

One paradoxical aspect of Dartmouth is that its students are simultaneously geographically isolated and globally connected. Due in large part to the D-Plan (a creative way of offering study options within a year-round academic calendar), Dartmouth leads the Ivy League in the percentage of students studying abroad. About two-thirds of Dartmouth students take advantage of the extraordinary study abroad options available, in large part because the structure of the D-Plan makes it possible to have more than one experience abroad. The range of opportunities to study, take service trips, and have internships in other countries is particularly impressive at Dartmouth. Perhaps fitting for a school with such a high study-abroad rate, Dartmouth has the only geography department in the Ivy League. Dartmouth also offers instruction in an impressive number of languages including Arabic, Chinese, French, German, Hebrew, Italian, Japanese, Korean Portuguese, Spanish and Russian.

Dartmouth's D-Plan can also help students get a head start on their careers. Because

Dartmouth requires students to spend at least one summer quarter on campus, students have the flexibility to take a non-summer quarter off to pursue an internship. Unlike students competing with the throngs of peers seeking limited summer internships, students on the D-plan can apply for internships in the fall, winter, or spring, when there are fewer applicants. For those who stay on campus to take classes, the summer quarter is often considered a favorite time at Dartmouth. Even though Dartmouth's student-teacher ratio is already low (eight to one), summer is a great time to experience Dartmouth with fewer students (which means smaller classes) and warmer weather.

Dartmouth's commitment to global engagement often takes an altruistic bent. For example, engineering majors, a group who, at most schools, typically have a harder time going abroad due to curriculum constraints, have a phenomenal opportunity to participate in Dartmouth's Humanitarian Engineering Leadership Project (HELP). A recent HELP project sponsored in conjunction with Vermont's Green Mountain Roasters enabled students to develop a stove fueled by coffee husks (a by-product of coffee production) for use in Africa. After developing the stove in a Dartmouth engineering design course, students went to Africa to work with graduate students at the University of Dar es Salaam to demonstrate its use. The stove had to be reworked due to differences in moisture content in coffee husks stored in Africa, but the design revisions, the establishment of distribution centers, and the evaluation of the stove's viability all became part of an instructional and international venture run by Dartmouth students.

Socially, Dartmouth is one of those work hard, play hard schools, where athletes and former athletes with large amounts of stamina feel right at home. There is a strong Greek culture (about 40 percent of the students) with sixteen fraternities and nine sororities. Even students not officially in a fraternity or sorority are engaged in aspects of Greek life due to the large shadow it casts on the student social scene—a presence reinforced by the lingering lore of the famous movie *Animal House*, which allegedly drew on Dartmouth for inspiration. No discussion of Dartmouth is complete without mention of its famous conservative newspaper, the *Dartmouth Review*. Since its founding in 1980, the *Dartmouth Review* (whose staffers have included the conservative writer Dinesh D'Souza and right-wing talk-show host Laura Ingraham) has inspired hundreds of other similar papers on college campuses across the country. While not every Dartmouth student is conservative, the *Dartmouth Review* has made the school a media darling of Fox News and right-wing talk radio.

For students who like snow, camping, outdoor recreation, drinking beer, and Greek life, Dartmouth is a great choice. For students for whom the thought of wearing polar fleece for months on end while trudging across campus to a keg party triggers feelings of despair, Dartmouth probably isn't the best fit, no matter how stellar its academic offerings may be. Dartmouth, due to its smaller size and remote location, has a more insular environment than most of the Ivy League. For some, this makes for a wonderfully familial feeling. For others, it spells cabin-fever isolation. Yes, students primarily interested in the arts and culture can find outlets at Dartmouth, but it is important to recognize that most creative areas are at the margins of the dominant extracurricular and social culture that has developed at Dartmouth due to its history and location. That said, students ready to grab some GORP (unfamiliarity with GORP—a trail mix with M&M candies thrown in for extra excitement—is perhaps a sign that Dartmouth is not a fit) and begin hiking through the White Mountains will be following in the snowshoe-clad footsteps of the notable alumni listed on the next page.

➤ NOTABLE DARTMOUTH ALUMNI

Connie Britton (1989)—actress

Louise Erdich (1976)—writer

Theodor Seuss Geisel (1925)—author (a.k.a. Dr. Seuss)

Timothy Geithner (1983)—former US treasury secretary

Louis Gerstner (1963)—former CEO of IBM

Kirsten Gillibrand (1988)— US senator

Jeffrey Immelt (1978)—CEO of General Electric

Mindy Kaling (2001)—actress

Edward Norton Lorenz (1938)—discovered chaos theory

John Humphrey Noyes (1830)—founder of utopian Oneida community

Henry (Hank) Paulson (1968)—former CEO of Goldman Sachs and US treasury secretary

Charles Alfred Pillsbury (1863)—founder of Pillsbury Co.

Shonda Rhimes (1991)—writer, director, producer—*Grey's Anatomy* and *Scandal*

Nelson Rockefeller (1930)—served as US vice president, NY governor

Bob Smith (1902)—cofounder of Alcoholics Anonymous

Jake Tapper (1991)—political reporter and talk-show host for CNN

UNIVERSITY OF PENNSYLVANIA

The City of Brotherly Love (Philadelphia) is a city of American firsts. Philadelphia was America's first capital city, the city where the first bank opened, the first daily newspaper was established, the first piano was built, and where the first lemon meringue pie was baked. Thus, it should come as no surprise that Philadelphia is also home to the first institution in America to call itself a university: the University of Pennsylvania. Penn traces its beginnings to 1740, when famed Philadelphia resident Ben Franklin began to promote the college. In 1755, the fledgling school received a charter as the College of Philadelphia and subsequently graduated its first class in 1757. By 1765 the College of Philadelphia had created the first American medical school, and by 1779 it had become the first American college to be called a university—primarily due to its medical school and graduate research programs. Today, Penn continues this tradition of groundbreaking education at the west Philadelphia campus it has occupied since 1872. Even though Penn has a strong tradition of graduate and professional school excellence, the undergraduate experience has a tremendous amount to offer students whose qualifications meet the high admissions standards.

Like Cornell, Penn has a collection of schools within the university. Most of its undergraduates are enrolled in arts and sciences (6,417); the rest are divided among engineering and applied sciences (1,616), the Wharton School of Business (2,085), and nursing (578). Penn is particularly receptive to interdisciplinary studies, so some students may find their academic programs are structured through more than one school. One popular interdisciplinary academic option, the Huntsman Program in International Studies and Business, links Penn's College of Arts and Sciences to its Wharton School of Business.

Wharton is one of the more famous schools at Penn. The degree to which a student can specialize at Wharton surpasses the options offered at many much larger universities. For example, Wharton offers more than twenty undergraduate business- and finance-related concentrations, including accounting; actuarial science; business and public policy; entrepreneurial management; environment and risk management; finance; global analysis/ multinational management; health-care management; human resource and organizational management; individualized majors; insurance and risk management; legal studies and business ethics; management; managing electronic commerce;

marketing; marketing and communication; marketing and operations management; operations and information management; real estate; retailing; social impact and responsibility; and statistics. There are also several opportunities for undergraduates to earn joint degrees through Wharton and another program at Penn. Examples of dual degrees (in addition to the Huntsman Program) include the Fisher Program in Management and Technology (BSE/BAS), nursing and health-care management (BSN/BS Econ), and life science and management (BS).

Penn's Philadelphia location is home to several Fortune 500 companies and other potential employers for Wharton students. The increasingly vibrant University City neighborhood surrounding Penn provides an excellent source of research and internship opportunities for Wharton and non-Wharton students alike. Unlike some private urban universities, Penn has cultivated a close and mutually beneficial relationship with its home city. Through its campus expansion and neighborhood redevelopment efforts, Penn has shown an unusually strong commitment to the vitality of Philadelphia.

Up until the 1990s, Penn's west Philly location had long been considered a dangerous place to go to college. For the past two decades, Penn has invested considerable resources into making the area surrounding campus safe and student friendly. Numerous thriving shops, restaurants, and hotels adjacent to the campus enhance daily life at Penn. Beyond the immediate business district, Penn has transformed what was once urban blight into a massive green space and sports facility to share with Philadelphians. Opened in September 2011, Penn Park is a prime example of urban renewal. Penn took an abandoned post office distribution center and an adjacent fourteen acres of decaying parking lot and transformed it (while still preserving the historical integrity of the postal building) into a multiuse athletic area, complete with walking trails and eco-friendly initiatives. The resulting Penn Park has become a recreational resource for students and comes on the heels of several multimillion-dollar improvements made to athletic facilities. The commitment to quality of life on the campus and its surroundings has made Penn a national model for other urban universities.

The university's recent commitments to community and quality of life are significant because Penn sometimes has the reputation for attracting only type-A, pre-professional students fixated on the bottom line. The extraordinary effort to create a beautiful center for outdoor recreation and repose sends a strong message to the world that Penn is about the whole person, not just the accumulation of accolades and achievements en route to a high-paying job on Wall Street. Of course, Penn attracts a highly competitive applicant pool of which fewer than 12 percent are admitted. Nearly 100 percent of admitted students are in the top 10 percent of their high school class. And yes, many do end up working on Wall Street. The following are successful (and in some cases famous) Penn graduates.

► SUCCESSFUL PENN GRADUATES

Elizabeth Banks (1996)—actress

William Brennan (1928)—US Supreme Court justice

Tory Burch (1988)—fashion designer

Jean Chatzky (1986)—financial journalist

Noam Chomsky (1949)—activist, linguist

Richard Clarke (1972)—author, expert on terrorism

Whitney Cummings (2004)—actress

Zane Grey (1896)—writer of western novels

Andrea Kremer (1980)—ESPN reporter

John Legend (1999)—singer/songwriter

Andrea Mitchell (1967)—journalist

William S. Paley (1922)—founder of CBS network

→

► SUCCESSFUL PENN GRADUATES (CONT.)

Maury Povich (1962)—journalist, television host

Ed Rendell (1965)—former governor of Pennsylvania

Lisa Scottoline (1981)—author

Joseph Segal (1951)—founder of QVC and Franklin Mint

Arlen Specter (1951)—former US senator (Pennsylvania)

Donald Trump (1968)—entrepreneur

Dick Wolf (1969)—producer, creator of *Law and Order*

William Carlos Williams (1906)—poet

THE MANY CLAIMS ON THE IVY BRAND

Lest the Ivy League get all the attention, it is worth noting that there are several other schools that more than adequately hold their own with the finest universities in the world. Some might ask what about Berkeley, Caltech, the University of Chicago, Duke, Johns Hopkins, Michigan, MIT, Northwestern, Rice, Stanford, and Virginia? And for that matter why not extend the Ivy-facsimile list to other excellent schools, such as Emory, Georgetown, Notre Dame, NYU, UCLA, Vanderbilt, and Washington University? Over the years, a number of near-Ivy categories have emerged. There are the **Catholic Ivies**: Boston College, Georgetown, and Notre Dame. There are the **Public Ivies**: Berkeley, Michigan, North Carolina, Texas, UCLA, Virginia, William and Mary, and Wisconsin. There are the **Tech Ivies**: Caltech, Carnegie Mellon, Georgia Tech, and MIT. And there are the **Small-College Ivies**: Amherst, Pomona, Swarthmore, Wellesley, and Williams.

STANFORD, CHICAGO, AND MIT

Among the many Ivy-facsimile schools, Stanford University, the University of Chicago, and the Massachusetts Institute of Technology seem (to us at least) to be able to make the best claims that they are as good as, if not better than, the Ivy League. Differences in founding origins, educational focus, and geographic locations kept these three outstanding schools out of the Ivy League for athletics, but they have proven themselves to be institutions worthy of top-tier recognition when lists of the world's best universities are compiled. Stanford University, for example, surpasses most of the Ivy League in terms of endowment, ratings of academic programs, and admissions selectivity. MIT is widely considered the best school in the world for the study of science and engineering. And the University of Chicago is quite often referred to as America's most intellectual college.

STANFORD UNIVERSITY

After their son Leland Jr. died in 1884 from typhoid at the age of fifteen, Leland and Jane Stanford honored their only child's intellectual curiosity by founding a university (in 1885) bearing his name and designed to serve "the children of California." Stanford has evolved into a major research institution that serves 7,000 undergraduates and 8,900 graduate students from all over the world. With an enviable $17 billion endowment and a student-teacher ratio of five to one, Stanford is able to provide unsurpassed resources to its students.

The vast Palo Alto campus, designed in part by Frederick Law Olmstead, provides a striking visual contrast to the Ivies. Stanford's mission style and Italianate architecture create an ambiance quite different from the red-brick buildings and cobblestone footpaths of Harvard Yard or the brown and gray collegiate gothic edifices of Princeton and Yale. Participating in the Pacific 12 sports conference, comprised largely of public universities (such as Arizona, Oregon, and UCLA), puts Stanford in a different athletic orbit from the Ivy League. The national television exposure Pac-12 athletes receive makes Ivy League games seem quaint by comparison. The combination of geographic distance from the East Coast, different athletic rivalries, relative youth as an institution, and mild sunny climate makes Stanford its own unique place. The academic quality, cachet, and caliber of students who attend Stanford equals (and some would say surpasses) the schools in the Ivy League. With particular strength in engineering, economics, and computer science, plus an unmistakable tech-oriented entrepreneurial vibe, Stanford is an appealing alternative to the Ivy League, particularly for the winter adverse.

➤ NOTABLE STANFORD UNDERGRADUATE ALUMNI

Ray Dolby (1957)—invented noise reduction system

Michael Drake (1974)—president, Ohio State University

Dianne Feinstein (1955)—senator

Edith Head (1920)—Hollywood costume designer

Taylor Howard (1955)—invented home satellite dish

Richard Levin (1968)—former president, Yale University

Rachel Maddow (1994)—political commentator

Allen Newell (1949)—pioneered artificial intelligence

Sandra Day O'Connor (1950)—first female US Supreme Court justice

UNIVERSITY OF CHICAGO

According to an oft-cited jibe, the University of Chicago is where fun goes to die. Those who love that image proudly point to Chicago's reputation as America's most intellectual college. Those who do not are quick to point out that Chicago, over the past two decades, has been moving more toward the mainstream collegiate ideal epitomized by the Ivy League. Something fun (or at least appealing) must be occurring at Chicago because freshman applications have topped the thirty-thousand mark, and getting admitted has never been more difficult. Those lucky enough to get admitted tend to stay, as exemplified by an impressive 98 percent freshman to sophomore retention rate. Granted, Chicago is not known as a social or athletic powerhouse, but it more than makes up for that in intellectual vigor and academic opportunity. Perhaps no other American university is so strongly identified as a place for the mind as U of C. Long a bastion for independent thinkers, Chicago is a viable alternative to the Ivy League, particularly if intellectual growth and academic experiences trump other expectations for undergraduate life.

Founded in 1890 and located in Chicago's Hyde Park neighborhood, the U of C campus includes land that once housed the 1893 Columbian Exposition and has an imposing gothic grandeur, complete with multitudes of gargoyles. Indeed, Chicago is a place where visitors, after stepping onto its campus quads, would half expect to find actual ivory towers looming overhead. In addition to being the place where the fictional Indiana Jones went to school, there are a number of actual Chicago alumni (listed below) who have shaped the world.

➤ NOTABLE CHICAGO ALUMNI

David Brooks (1983)—*New York Times* columnist

Ana Marie Cox (1994)—*Wonkette* web blog founder

Philip Glass (1956)—composer

Katharine Graham (1938)—head of *Washington Post* for over two decades

Eliot Ness (1925)—*The Untouchables* fame

Carl Sagan (1954)—astronomer, cosmologist

Bernard Sanders (1964)—senator

Nate Silver (2000)—statistician, *Five Thirty Eight* founder

MASSACHUSETTS INSTITUTE OF TECHNOLOGY

Being Harvard's Ivy adjacent neighbor could have been deflating for many schools. But MIT has carved out its own niche down the street in Cambridge, Massachusettes. MIT has science and technology offerings that are envied the world over. There is also an endearing blend of excellence and quirkiness about MIT that makes it the exemplar of technological education. Beyond the world-class faculty and academic resources, there is (as the tech-school chapter explains) an odd sense of fun at MIT, making it particularly appealing for independent thinkers, technology trailblazers, and future inventors. For example, MIT proudly generates power through an on-campus nuclear reactor, and through the tradition called hacking, MIT students engage in clever pranks and explore the institute's unauthorized spaces. MIT students can also vie on the Charles River for a coveted certificate in pirating.

To ease into MIT's rigorous academic program, there is a generous pass-no record grading system for the first semester of the freshman year. In their second semester at MIT, students earn A, B, C, or No Record grades. The goal of the unusual freshman-year grading system at MIT is to encourage students to dive into the rigorous academic culture sans fear of failure and grade-driven course selection. Once inside the institute, most MIT students would not trade their resources for an Ivy experience.

➤ NOTABLE MIT UNDERGRADUATE ALUMNI

John Dorrance (1895)—invented condensed soup, headed Campbell Soup Co.

Charles (1957) and David (1962) Koch—own largest private company in United States

Herbert Kalmus (1904)—invented Technicolor

I. M. Pei (1940)—architect who designed the Louvre

Generoso Pope (1946)—founder and owner of the *National Enquirer*

Larry Summers (1975)—former president of Harvard, adviser to Presidents Clinton and Obama

SERVICE ACADEMIES AND ROTC

Popular images of military academies tend to start with the oldest and the best known of them: the United States Military Academy in West Point, New York (founded in 1802), and the United States Naval Academy in Annapolis, Maryland (founded in 1845). Although the federal service academies are part of the US military, technically the term *military academy* refers just to West Point. Of the five federal service academies, only West Point has *military academy* in its name. From their first day at Annapolis, West Point, the Air Force Academy, the Coast Guard Academy, and the Merchant Marine Academy, students are considered to be on active duty in the US armed forces. Four of the five federal service academies are attached to branches of the US military, while the United States Merchant Marine Academy is part of the US Department of Transportation. West Point, Annapolis, and the Air Force Academy each enroll approximately 4,500 students. The Coast Guard Academy (1,000 students) and the Merchant Marine Academy (900 students) are considerably smaller.

United States Air Force Academy—Colorado Springs, Colorado

United States Coast Guard Academy—New London, Connecticut

United States Merchant Marine Academy—Kings Point, New York

United States Military Academy—West Point, New York

United States Naval Academy—Annapolis, Maryland

Students at federal service academies have their full education funded by the government. Funding includes monthly stipends to pay for books, supplies, and uniforms. In return for getting a free education, students are obligated to complete a minimum number of years on reserve or active duty for one of the military branches of the United States. Service obligations vary by academy but usually consist of at least five years beyond graduation. Service academy students awarded prestigious postgraduate scholarships, such as Rhodes, Churchill, Marshall, or Truman, are allowed to complete their studies before fulfilling their service obligation.

Getting admitted to a federal service academy is no easy task. Acceptance rates tend to be around 10 to 15 percent. With the exception of the Coast Guard Academy, applicants to the federal service academies must get nominated by high-level officials, such as members of Congress or the president or vice president of the United States. Merchant Marine Academy applicants can only be nominated by senators or US representatives. Applicants to the Coast Guard Academy apply through a direct process more like the typical application to a selective university. For all but the Coast Guard Academy, there is a state-by-state nomination quota (parallel to the size of a state's congressional delegation) for each service academy.

If you do not personally know your senator or regularly hang out with your Congressperson, do not panic. Although done by politicians, the nomination process for entering a service academy is not political. Applicants do not need to know their member of Congress to be nominated. Congressmen typically nominate ten students per academy, and the nomination requirements are set by their offices. To get nominated, applicants must submit an application, including essays and letters of recommendation, and complete an interview. The nomination procedure supplements the forms, transcripts, standardized test results, and physical examinations required by the actual service academies. Members of Congress may make two types of nominations: competitive nominations and principal nominations. Competitive nominees are reviewed by the academies to determine qualifications. When a Congressman makes a principal nomination, as long as the service academy judges the applicant to be academically, medically, and physically qualified that applicant will be admitted, even if there are other more qualified applicants.

ESSENTIAL INFORMATION FOR SERVICE ACADEMY APPLICANTS

Applying for a nomination from your senators or congressional representative can be a time-consuming and competitive process. Before getting started, the information below can help a student put forth a strong, organized application.

- Presidential nominations are reserved for children of career military personnel.

- Applicants can seek out multiple sources to secure a nomination. For example, a student can appeal to both senators for a nomination. Because getting a nomination can be competitive, seeking it from more than one source is a smart move.

- A student has from January of his or her junior year in high school to November of his or her senior year to apply for a nomination. Students can also submit an application (for a nomination) after finishing high school.

- On the application for a nomination, students are asked to rank (in order of preference) the service academies they would like to attend. Students should only list the academies they would consider attending.

- Nominations go to the academies by mid-December. Academies make appointments from late December through May.

- If a student is not nominated or appointed, he or she may apply again.

Some applicants to the federal service academies get turned down but simultaneously referred to a military high school for further preparation. Among the numerous schools where students can go to shore up their credentials are prep schools on the campuses of the Air Force Academy and West Point as well as the Naval Academy Preparatory School (NAPS) in Newport, Rhode Island. To gain admission to Annapolis, students at NAPS must pass their classes with a minimum GPA of 2.0/4.0 and pass a fitness assessment. Merchant marine applicants referred for a preparatory year end up either at NAPS or at the New Mexico Military Institute in Roswell. Coast Guard prep referrals study at Marion Military Institute in Alabama or at the New Mexico Military Institute. In addition, each year a small number of rejected West Point applicants receive scholarships from the West Point Association of Graduates (WPAOG) to attend civilian universities or military junior colleges for one year. WPAOG scholarship recipients who earn acceptable grades in their interim year are then welcomed into West Point. The five military junior colleges listed below (at which students participate in army ROTC) have become popular stops for the WPAOG scholarship holders en route to West Point.

Georgia Military College—Milledgeville, Georgia

Marion Military Institute—Marion, Alabama

New Mexico Military Institute—Roswell, New Mexico

Valley Forge Military Academy and College—Wayne, Pennsylvania

Wentworth Military Academy and College—Lexington, Missouri

Lesser known than the five tuition-free federal service academies are the state-affiliated service academies—such as the Citadel and Virginia Military Institute, the large cadet corps that give public universities, such as Texas A&M and Virginia Tech, a discernible military identity—and private military-oriented institutions, such as Norwich University in Vermont. Even lesser known are the half-dozen state-supported maritime colleges and universities. Students at state maritime academies graduate with training from the US Merchant Marines and have the option to become commissioned reserve officers in the US Navy, Coast Guard, or Marine Corps. Six states, all of which have coast lines facing or bordering other countries, operate maritime academies.

California Maritime Academy—Vallejo, California

Great Lakes Maritime Academy—Traverse City, Michigan (part of Northwestern Michigan College)

Maine Maritime Academy—Castine, Maine

Massachusetts Maritime Academy—Buzzards Bay, Massachusetts

State University of New York Maritime College—Throggs Neck, New York

Texas Maritime Academy—Galveston, Texas (part of Texas A&M University)

FEDERAL SERVICE ACADEMIES

UNITED STATES MILITARY ACADEMY—WEST POINT, NEW YORK

Fifty miles north of New York City, the United States Military Academy (USMA) occupies sixteen thousand acres astride the Hudson River in West Point, New York. The entire USMA campus is classified as a national landmark. Frequently referred to as West Point, the USMA enrolls 4,400 students (known as cadets) who are trained for lives of leadership. Generations of military leaders—from Grant and Lee to Eisenhower, MacArthur, and Patton—have walked the long gray line as new graduates of West Point. An oft-heard expression at West Point is "much of the history we teach is made by the people we taught." West Point also takes pride in the countless graduates who have achieved success in business, law, medicine, politics, science, and sports.

The education at West Point blends academic, physical, and military training. During the forty-seven-month-long cadet program, the West Point curriculum emphasizes STEM subjects alongside the ethical, spiritual, and social values that it believes mark successful leaders. At the core of West Point life is the Cadet Honor Code, which states that "a cadet will not lie, cheat, steal, or tolerate those who do." West Point's ethical code is also expressed in its motto: Duty, Honor, Country. The shared values, the challenges, and the common elements in the cadet experience (for example, all cadets must live on campus and eat breakfast and lunch together on weekdays) help build enduring bonds and a close community.

Each summer roughly 1,200 new cadets enter West Point. College for West Point students begins that summer with cadet basic training—colloquially known as "Beast Barracks." During cadet basic training, all plebes must memorize a book referred to as the "plebe bible" or "the manual of plebe knowledge," called *Bugle Notes*. *Bugle Notes* contains a collection of anecdotes, facts, poems, songs, and lore about the USMA. Plebes must be ready at all times to answer questions posed by cadets in the upper classes about information contained in *Bugle Notes*.

With a student-faculty ratio of eight to one, classes averaging fewer than eighteen students, and individual student progress monitored through daily homework assignments, West Point is more like a personalized small college than an impersonal large university. All cadets complete a core of twenty-six courses, including a sequence in engineering, a course in information technology, and courses in chemistry, constitutional law, economics, English, foreign language, geography, history, international relations, leadership, math, philosophy, physics, political science, and psychology. Following completion of the core, cadets may choose from forty different major options offered by West Point's thirteen academic departments: behavioral sciences and leadership; chemistry and life science; civil and mechanical engineering; electrical engineering and computer science; English and philosophy; foreign languages; geography and environmental engineering; history; law; mathematical sciences; physics; social sciences; and systems engineering.

At graduation, West Point cadets receive a BS degree and are commissioned as second lieutenants in the United States Army. A cadet's rank in class determines his or her army branch and initial officer assignment. Rank is based 55 percent on academic performance, 30 percent on military leadership performance, and 15 percent on physical fitness and athletic performance.

Class designations at West Point have their own peculiar nomenclature. Cadet classes are referred to as fourth class (first years), third class (second years), second class (third years), and first class (seniors). The colloquial names are plebes for the fourth class, yearlings or yuks for the third class, cows for the second class, and firsties for the first class.

The requirements West Point cadets must complete are not limited to the academic and the military. To fulfill physical activity requirements, all cadets participate in an intercollegiate, club, or intramural sport each semester and must pass the army physical-fitness test twice each year. Rigorous physical training, so goes the West Point belief, ensures a cadet's mental and physical fitness. The West Point experience is year-round. Fall and spring are for academic courses and physical training, while summers consist of intensified military training. During the summer between the first and second year, cadets undergo field training at nearby Camp Buckner. In their following two summers, cadets serve in active army units around the world.

West Point is not for everyone. Success there requires the intellectual capacity and the physical stamina to thrive in a rigorous forty-seven-month-long leadership development program. Students are drawn to West Point by its tradition of excellence and reputation as a training ground for America's leadership elite. But students are also drawn to West Point for an extraordinary education and experience that occurs free of charge.

Admission to West Point is extremely competitive and based on a candidate's academic, physical, and leadership potential. Applicants must be medically qualified (as determined by a physical examination) and have been nominated by an approved source, such as a member of Congress. In addition to presenting excellent academic, physical, and leadership credentials, there are some basic restrictions: applicants must be at least seventeen years of age but not twenty-three years old as of July 1 of the year of entry to the academy, and applicants must also be unmarried with no legal obligation to support children. Typically, just 10 to 15 percent of applicants are admitted. Successful candidates tend to rank in the top 20 percent of their high school class. The middle 50 percent on the SAT hovers between 1100 and 1360 (critical reading [CR] plus math [M]).

West Point cadets also come from a variety of ethnic and cultural heritages (just over 20 percent are students of color) and comprise as diverse a mix of socioeconomic backgrounds as can be found on any college campus in the United States. For nearly forty years, West Point has admitted women; they now comprise roughly 15 percent of the student body. An additional fifteen to twenty entering cadets come from beyond the United States under the sponsorship of their home nation.

Some notable West Point alumni include Edwin "Buzz" Aldrin (second man to walk on moon); Marshall Carter (chairman of the New York Stock Exchange); Wesley Clark (former NATO commander and presidential candidate); Michael Collins (operated command module during first moon mission); Jefferson Davis (president of the Confederacy); Dwight D. Eisenhower (US president); Ulysses S. Grant (US president); Mike Krzyzewski, a.k.a. Coach K (Duke University men's basketball coach); Robert E. Lee (Civil War Confederate general); Douglas McArthur (WWII and Korean War general); Norman Schwarzkopf (commanded US forces in Operation Desert Storm); and William Tecumseh Sherman (Civil War general).

UNITED STATES NAVAL ACADEMY— ANNAPOLIS, MARYLAND

Forty-five minutes from the nation's capital, the United States Naval Academy sits on the Chesapeake Bay in the beautiful and historic town of Annapolis, Maryland. The naval academy's 4,400 students, referred to as midshipmen, become ensigns in the navy or second lieutenants in the Marine Corps at graduation. Like their counterparts at the other service academies, midshipmen at the naval academy are designated according to their class year as fourth class or plebes (first year), third class (second year), second class (third year), and first class (fourth or senior year). Freedoms for midshipmen increase as graduation approaches. Second-class midshipmen train the plebes under the supervision of the first class (firsties), get to drive their own cars (but not park them on campus), and can enter or exit campus in civilian attire on weekends. First-class students (firsties) can park their cars on campus and have greater liberties than the other three classes.

Daily life at the naval academy abides by the Honor Concept, which stresses integrity, fairness, and truth. Living honorably means no lying, cheating, or stealing. When a midshipman witnesses an honor violation, she or he may report it or confront the violator without making a report to academy officials.

The academic program at the naval academy requires all midshipmen to complete a core curriculum and a major. There are twenty-two majors leading to the BS degree in the following fields: Arabic; chemistry; Chinese; computer science; economics; engineering (aerospace, computer, electrical, general, mechanical, naval, ocean, and systems); English; general science; history; information technology; mathematics; oceanography; physics; political science; and quantitative economics. Participation in competitive athletics is mandatory, either on an intercollegiate team or through club or intramural sports. There are numerous extracurricular activities available beyond athletics. For example, musical performance groups abound, including a drum and bugle corps, glee club, gospel choir, and bagpipe band. Class rank is based on academic performance, military leadership, and participation in competitive athletics.

Each year roughly 1,300 students enter the academy by embarking on an experience called plebe summer, a rigorous program consisting of basic training and indoctrination into the ways and traditions of the naval academy. The plebe summer and plebe year are designed to transition the student from civilian to officer. All midshipmen at the naval academy pledge to serve their country for five years after graduation. The formal act of making the pledge occurs at the beginning of year two at the academy. Making the pledge is known as signing the two for seven. Midshipmen selected as pilots are required to serve for eight to eleven years. Midshipmen chosen to be flight officers must serve for six to eight years.

Tuition plus room and board is fully funded for all midshipmen at the naval academy. Midshipmen also receive a monthly stipend to pay for books, uniforms, and other necessary items. If a student resigns or is expelled from the naval academy within the first two years, that student incurs no military obligation. If a student leaves Annapolis after year two but before graduation, the student has two choices: (1) serve on active duty for two to four years, or (2) reimburse the US government for the investment made in the student (at least $150,000).

Applicants to the naval academy must secure a nomination from either a member of the US Congress, the vice president, or president of the United States. Candidates must also apply directly to the academy—sending a high school transcript, application forms, personal references, and results of personality and standardized tests. Candidates additionally have to pass a fitness test and a medical exam that includes a visual acuity test. Candidates must be at least seventeen years old but not more than twenty-three years old, unmarried without children, and of good moral character. Appointments without a nomination are available for children of active military personnel as well as for children of military servicemen (or women) who were killed in action, rendered 100 percent disabled, prisoners of war, or missing in action. Each year the naval academy also selects a small number of international students from allied countries or other US-friendly nations.

Notable naval academy alumni include Jimmy Carter (US president), Robert Heinlein (science fiction writer), John McCain (US senator), Oliver North (infamous for his involvement in the Iran Contra affair, radio and TV program host), Ross Perot (computer industry billionaire and former presidential candidate), Hyman Rickover (father of the nuclear navy), David "the Admiral" Robinson (NBA championship winner), Alan Shepard (first US astronaut in space), and Roger Staubach (Heisman Trophy winner and Super Bowl champion).

UNITED STATES AIR FORCE ACADEMY— COLORADO SPRINGS, COLORADO

Perched 7,258 feet above sea level, the eighteen-thousand-acre Air Force Academy campus is just north of Colorado Springs. The approximately 4,500 students at the Air Force Academy live and learn in an environment where the core values are "integrity first, service before self, and excellence in all we do." The Air Force Academy experience is rooted in what are referred to as the four pillars of excellence: military training, academics, athletics, and character development. As they prepare to be future officers, air force cadets complete a program that combines rigorous military training, an extensive core curriculum, and vigorous physical activity.

Roughly 60 percent of the courses air force cadets take en route to the BS degree are mandated by the core curriculum, which takes nearly two years to fulfill. The core curriculum includes courses in basic sciences, engineering, humanities, social sciences, and military studies. Academics at the Air Force Academy are focused heavily on science and engineering. Humanities and social science courses are available, but even the 55 percent of cadets who major in nontechnical subjects are expected to graduate ready to manage complex air, space, and cyber systems.

There are four academic divisions at the Air Force Academy: basic sciences, general engineering, humanities, and social sciences. The following twenty-four majors are offered: behavioral sciences; biology; chemistry; computer science; economics; engineering (aeronautical, astronautical, civil, computer, electrical, environmental, mechanical, systems); engineering mechanics; English; foreign area studies; geospatial science; history; legal studies; management; mathematics; meteorology; military strategic studies; operations research; physics; political science; space operations; and systems engineering management.

All cadets must participate in athletics. Each semester, cadets must compete in intramural athletics unless they are members of an intercollegiate team that is active that term. Required physical education classes teach skills such as swimming and water survival and introduce cadets to combative sports (such as boxing, wrestling, and judo) that build confidence and develop controlled aggression. Every semester, cadets must pass two fitness tests. When cadets fail a fitness test, they must undergo reconditioning until they pass. Repeated failure may lead to dismissal from the academy.

Each summer 1,400 students admitted to the Air Force Academy show up on the Colorado Springs campus for six weeks of Basic Cadet Training (BCT). BCT, known as "Beast," is led by the first-class (fourth year) and second-class (third year) cadets. BCT comprises a rigorous six-week period of physical training and initiation into the customs and courtesies of military academy life—such as proper wear and care of uniforms and the rudiments of drill, ceremony,

and field encampment. When BCT is completed, the basic cadets take the academy's honor oath and are accepted as full-fledged cadets. During each of their subsequent summers, cadets undergo military training in settings where they are fully deployed. Typical summer programs include combat survival, parachute, and glider training.

Making it through the initial year at the academy (called fourth-class year and regarded as the most challenging one) is no small accomplishment. In addition to full course loads, fourth-class cadets are expected to learn prodigious amounts of information about the US military and the Air Force Academy. At any time, fourth-class cadets may be quizzed on military or air force matters. When quizzed by their cadet elders, fourth-class cadets are expected to respond correctly and respectfully (according to academy rules of decorum). Fourth-class cadets also have their movements and freedoms severely restricted. For example, they can only cross the cadet area by following approved routes, such as staying on the marble strips of the terrazzo. Fourth-class year ends with Recognition, a physically and mentally demanding several-day event, which, when completed, results in relaxing of year one's stringent rules.

Applicants to the Air Force Academy are evaluated on academic achievement, demonstrated leadership, athletic experience and ability, and character. Eligible applicants are US citizens, unmarried (with no dependents), at least seventeen years of age (but not yet twenty-three years old), of good moral character, and able to meet high leadership, academic, physical, and medical standards. Physical and medical readiness is determined by a fitness test and a thorough medical examination. Applicants must secure a congressional nomination, unless one of their parents is career military personnel, a disabled veteran, a Medal of Honor recipient, or a veteran who was killed in action.

Some notable Air Force Academy alumni include Charles Phillips (president of Oracle Corporation), Gregg Popovich (coach of the San Antonio Spurs), Chesley Sullenberger (pilot who safely landed US Airways flight 1549 in the Hudson River), Robert Thomas (former CEO of Nissan Motor Corporation); also, thirty-eight Air Force Academy graduates have been US astronauts.

UNITED STATES COAST GUARD ACADEMY—NEW LONDON, CONNECTICUT

Compared to Annapolis, West Point, and the Air Force Academy, the United States Coast Guard Academy is a small institution. With fewer than a thousand students, the Coast Guard Academy's riverside campus resembles that of a small New England liberal arts college. The Coast Guard Academy (CGA) is an undergraduate institution that assesses students holistically on the dimensions of academics, physical fitness, character, and leadership. At all times, cadets must adhere to the Honor Concept emblazoned in the foyer of the academy's largest building (Chase Hall): "Who lives here reveres honor, honors duty."

In addition to completing a major, cadets take a core curriculum of science and professional development courses as well as courses in ethics, leadership, organizational behavior, and nautical science (such as ship handling, piloting, voyage planning, and deck seamanship). The CGA offers eight majors leading to the BS degree: engineering (civil, mechanical, and electrical); naval architecture and marine engineering; operations research and computer analysis; marine and environmental sciences; government; and management. Cadets may also take courses at Connecticut College, which is located across the street. Coast Guard cadets must additionally spend, on average, two hours per day in athletic activities, either on varsity teams, club teams, or in other sports pursuits, such as intramurals. Sailing is a central activity at the Coast Guard Academy. Using the academy's 150 vessels, students compete on offshore sailing and dinghy sailing teams.

New entrants to the CGA start in July with a basic training program called Swab Summer, an intense regimen designed to prepare new cadets for the rigors of their first year at the academy. Classes at the Coast Guard Academy are not referred to as freshman through senior but as fourth class (first year), third class (second year), second class (third year), and first class (senior year). After Swab Summer, cadets spend their summers training aboard Coast Guard cutters or on smaller boats in roles such as helmsman, lookout, quartermaster of the watch, or engineering watch. By the arrival of their first-class summer, cadets are ready to train as junior officers aboard an operational cutter.

The cadet corps at the CGA is a self-directed organization that follows a typical military chain of command. First-class cadets lead the whole corps. Second-class cadets lead Swab Summer training. Third-class cadets mentor the fourth-class cadets. Each class has its own company commander. At the very top, the highest-ranking cadet at the CGA is called the regimental commander. From the point they complete Swab Summer, cadets are active duty, officers-in-training who must wear uniforms at all times as they train to become Coast Guard officers (usually engineering or deck watch officers) after graduation.

Outside the academy's library are historic chain links that were used during the Revolutionary War to prevent ships from sailing up the Hudson River to attack West Point. During the annual fall homecoming football game, fourth-class students must hide the chain from second-class students until halftime. Doing this successfully results in a reward.

Admission to the Coast Guard Academy is extremely competitive. In typical years, 2,500 prospective cadets apply, 400 are selected, and 280 enroll. Admission is based solely on merit and does not require a congressional nomination. The CGA is the only federal service academy that does not require a nomination. Cadets are fully funded (tuition, room, and board) by the US government and receive a monthly stipend that covers the cost of books, uniforms, and other necessities. In exchange for a fully funded education, cadets must serve five years of active duty after graduation.

Some notable alumni include Thad Allen (commander of the federal response to the Deepwater Horizon oil spill), Daniel Burbank and Bruce Melnick (space shuttle astronauts), G. William Miller (former chairman of the Federal Reserve and US treasury secretary), and Sandra Stosz (first woman to be superintendent of the Coast Guard Academy).

UNITED STATES MERCHANT MARINE ACADEMY—KINGS POINT, NEW YORK

The United States Merchant Marine Academy (USMMA) is a small, specialized training institution located just outside New York City on Long Island Sound. Although it is a federal service academy, the Merchant Marine Academy is anomalous. The four other federal service academies are operated through the US Department of Defense, while the USMMA is under the auspices of the US Department of Transportation (as part of the US Maritime Administration). The 910 students at the USMMA take a specialized curriculum that includes marine engineering, international law, maritime law, customs, navigation, personnel management, and ship administration. Midshipmen there train to serve as officers in the US Merchant Marine, in other branches of the military, or in the transportation industry. As officers, USMMA graduates frequently operate large and complex ships.

Like their counterparts at the other academies, USMMA graduates pay back the federal government's investment in them by fulfilling a service obligation. But unlike the other academies, USMMA graduates are allowed to fulfill their service obligations by selecting from a number of possible options. Merchant Marine Academy graduates may work as officers on US merchant vessels, as civilians in the maritime industry, or as active-duty officers in any branch of the armed services (for at least five years)— as long as they maintain their merchant marine officer's license (issued by the US Coast Guard) for a period of at least six years and stay active as a military reservist for at least eight years.

Merchant Marine Academy first-year students are known as plebes. They enter the USMMA in July for a two-and-a-half week indoctrination period called indoc. Run by upperclassmen (with oversight by officers), indoc is a high-stress period of physical training, marching, and other activities designed to introduce plebes to life at the USMMA. Once indoc is completed, plebes officially become midshipmen. In their sophomore and junior years, USMMA midshipmen work as cadets on American merchant ships. Typically, midshipmen are paired two to a ship: one deck cadet and one engineering cadet. While serving as part of a ship's crew, midshipmen get hands-on experience and exposure to numerous foreign ports. It is not uncommon for midshipmen to log three hundred days as a ship cadet and travel to fifteen to twenty different countries. Because merchant marine students spend so much time at sea, the student experience encompasses the whole year.

Academic life at the Merchant Marine Academy does not begin until the fall semester. Soon after commencing their studies, midshipmen choose either the track in marine transportation or the track in marine engineering. Transportation students concentrate on cargo handling, ship navigation, and maritime law.

Engineering students study ship operational systems and engines. Of the six BS degree majors available, three are referred to as deck majors, and three are called engine majors. The deck majors are marine transportation; logistics and intermodal transportation; and maritime operations and technology. Engine majors are marine engineering, marine engineering systems, and marine engineering and shipyard management.

USMMA graduates tend to go in one of three directions. A third of the new graduates end up in the United States Merchant Marine as officers on ships involved in transportation and trade. Another third go into maritime industry jobs in commercial shipping, marine engineering, maritime law, maritime insurance, or defense contracting. The final third enter the military as active-duty commissioned officers for the navy, marines, coast guard, army, or air force.

Prospective applicants to the USMMA need a congressional nomination, a strong high school GPA, high SAT or ACT scores, an essay, and three letters of recommendation. Applicants must also pass a Department of Defense Medical Examination Review Board physical and take the candidate fitness assessment. The full cost of tuition, room and board, and books and supplies is funded by the US Department of Transportation's Maritime Administration.

Some notable alumni include Andrew Card (former White House chief of staff), Mike Kelly (space shuttle pilot), Robert Kiyosaki (author of the *Rich Dad, Poor Dad* books), and Skip Prosser (former men's basketball coach at Wake Forest).

STATE MILITARY ACADEMIES

THE CITADEL—CHARLESTON, SOUTH CAROLINA

The Citadel has been featured prominently in the novels of alumnus Pat Conroy; for example, *The Lords of Discipline* was made into a movie in 1983. A place where high standards, duty, and honor are taken seriously, the Citadel prides itself on educating the whole person—mind, body, and spirit. As at the federal military academies, the Citadel blends challenging academic programs with a structured, disciplined military environment, where physical fitness and moral and ethical principles are paramount.

The Citadel has a bit of a dual identity. Among its 3,300 students, 2,100 are full-time undergraduates and cadets. Of the remaining 1,200 students, 100 are active duty veterans in evening study and 1,100 are graduate students (most of whom are civilians) in master's programs. The Citadel is coeducational, but nominally so, with just 7 percent women among the corps of cadets. Although The Citadel is best known for its cadet corps, only one-third of its students accept military commissions following graduation.

Honor is the most cherished principle at the Citadel. Cadets are governed by an honor code that simply states: "A cadet does not lie, cheat, or steal, nor tolerate those who do." The honor code encompasses all aspects of cadet life. The Citadel seeks to prepare leaders who give selfless service to others and have the discipline to persevere when facing challenges. According to the Citadel, a leader

> Believes in an optimistic view for the future; motivates others to achieve; demonstrates loyalty; respects the rights of others; sets a good example; pursues excellence in all endeavors; treats others with concern and civility; demonstrates the courage to

act responsibly; possesses uncompromising integrity; is devoted to duty and honor.

Through the Citadel's five schools (business, education, engineering, humanities and social sciences, and science and mathematics), there are sixteen majors offered. More than half of the cadets major in business. Other popular majors include criminal justice/law enforcement (14 percent), education (9 percent), physical education (9 percent), and psychology (8 percent).

As part of the Citadel's physical-fitness requirements, cadets must meet height and weight requirements and pass a physical training (PT) test each semester. Sit-ups, push-ups, and a two-mile run are key components of PT. All cadets must also complete at least four physical education courses, two of which are activity based.

Eligibility for admission requires a high school diploma or GED, a physical exam, and medical approval by the Citadel's surgeon. Applicants must be at least seventeen years old but not twenty-three or married. Roughly 60 percent of applicants are admitted. Most Citadel enrollees ranked in the top half of their high school class, achieved at least a B-plus average, and scored between 960 and 1180 on the SAT (CR plus M) or over 20 on the ACT.

The Citadel has one comprehensive charge that encompasses tuition, room and board, athletic fees, books and supplies, uniforms, laundry, and dry cleaning. Living on campus is strongly encouraged for cadets, and undergraduate students are guaranteed housing and room and board for all four years. Annual charges for South Carolina residents are approximately $26,500. Nonresidents pay roughly $46,000. The first year at the Citadel costs $4,000 to $5,000 more than subsequent years. Nearly 80 percent of students at the Citadel receive scholarships. Approximately twenty-five first-year cadets receive full scholarships. All applicants are automatically considered for scholarships.

Notable Citadel alumni include Pat Conroy (writer), Greg Davis (former NFL placekicker), Ernest Hollings (former US senator from South Carolina), Paul Maguire (ESPN announcer, former NFL player), Livonia "Stump" Mitchell (former NFL running back), and Robert Wackenhut (founder of world's largest security firm).

VIRGINIA MILITARY INSTITUTE— LEXINGTON, VIRGINIA

Virginia Military Institute (VMI) is a small, specialized state college located in the Blue Ridge Mountains. The VMI campus abuts the campus of Washington and Lee University, which makes both institutions feel larger. Although enrolled at a public institution supported by Virginia, the 1,500 cadets at VMI come from forty-five states and eleven foreign countries. All VMI cadets participate in ROTC, either with the air force, army, marines, or navy. At graduation VMI cadets get to choose whether they will accept a military commission. In most years, just over half do.

With a student-teacher ratio of eleven to one, VMI's classes resemble the small, interactive classes found at liberal arts colleges. All students complete a core curriculum organized around the theme of the Nucleus of Effective Citizenship and Leadership. After completing their core requirements, VMI students have fourteen major choices available in arts, engineering, humanities, sciences, and social sciences en route to their BA or BS degree.

Like all military academies, VMI is mentally and physically demanding. VMI puts its students through a rigorous four-year program that combines intellectual and character development with military and physical training. Students learn to control their behavior while getting pushed to their physical and emotional limits. Courage, valor, leadership, and service are core values underlying VMI's commitment to producing graduates prepared to serve the nation as citizen-soldiers. Twice each semester, cadets take the VMI Fitness Test (VFT), which involves a 1.5-mile run, sit-ups, and pull-ups. Students who fail the VFT receive remedial training and dietary counseling. The collective first-year class, referred to as a "rat mess," begins its indoctrination to life at VMI with Cadre Week. During Cadre Week, the "rat mess" starts rigorous physical training, learns lessons on the history of VMI, gets a rat haircut, and undergoes an overall immersion into the requirements and regimens of cadet life. By the completion of Cadre Week, the "rat mess" has been transformed into a "rat line" of official VMI fourth-class cadets.

Admission to VMI follows a two-step process. First, the admission office reviews the candidate's application to determine academically eligibility. Competitive candidates have completed four years of English and mathematics and three years of laboratory sciences, social studies, and foreign languages. Typically, more than half of VMI's incoming students have ranked in the top 25 percent of their high school class and their average high school GPA has been 3.47 on a 4.0 scale. The middle 50 percent range on the SAT is usually 1040 to 1230 (CR plus M), and the middle 50 percent on the ACT is 22 to 27. Readiness for VMI is also assessed through a review of an applicant's optional essay, extracurricular activities, and character recommendations. Applicants must be at least sixteen years old but not more than twenty-two years old, unmarried, and not a parent. If deemed academically eligible by VMI's admissions committee, an applicant gets a conditional appointment, which gets changed to an official appointment once the candidate passes VMI's fitness and medical examinations.

VMI is not free. Tuition, room, board, and fees total roughly $24,000 for Virginia residents. Nonresidents pay almost twice as much: $46,000. Slightly fewer than 50 percent of students receive financial aid. A limited number of Virginia residents get State Cadet Scholarships, awarded to exceptional students who need significant financial assistance. State Cadets do not have to pay tuition or room and board, but they must pay all other charges, such as the auxiliary fee ($4,940) and the quartermaster charge ($3,080).

Some notable VMI alumni include Josiah Bunting (writer and former head of the Lawrenceville School and president of Hampden Sydney College), Harry Byrd (former US senator from Virginia), Harold Easterly (former president of the US Golf Association), Benjamin Franklin Ficklin (helped found the Pony Express), George Marshall (WWII general), Bobby Ross (former NFL and college football coach), and Fred Willard (comedian, actor).

WOMEN AT MILITARY ACADEMIES

Women have been admitted to service academies for more than two decades, but the gender ratio and the overall atmosphere at the federal service academies still skews heavily male. The male/female imbalance is even more pronounced at state-supported military academies, such as the Citadel and Virginia Military Academy, both of which put up vehement public fights against efforts to admit women. The service academies may be coeducational, but the women who attend them will tell you that they are still masculine places, holding tight to time-honored traditions developed during their past days as all-male institutions.

MARITIME ACADEMIES

California Maritime Academy—Vallejo, California. 850 students attend Cal Maritime, the smallest school in the California State University (CSU) system. Cal Maritime students operate a five-hundred-foot training ship—essentially a floating classroom where students get a hands-on education while out in the ocean. The applied nature of the learning that occurs in Cal Maritime's specialized academic programs results in graduates having the highest job placement rates in the CSU system. The six majors offered at Cal Maritime are for students interested in marine, international, and engineering careers: marine engineering, business administration, global studies and maritime affairs, mechanical engineering, marine engineering technology, and marine transportation. In addition to sailing around the globe, students at Cal Maritime can go on school-sponsored study abroad trips.

Great Lakes Maritime Academy—Traverse City, Michigan. A division of Northwestern Michigan College, Great Lakes Maritime is the only freshwater maritime academy in the United States. It is also the only maritime academy in the United States that offers licensing for marine vessels on both the Great Lakes and the oceans. Using a 224-foot former navy vessel as a training ship, GLMA has programs to prepare maritime engineers and mates or pilots. Through a partnership with Ferris State University, GLMA students earn a bachelor's degree in business administration while acquiring maritime credentials (either as a maritime deck officer or as a maritime engineering officer). Engineering cadets at GLMA are prepared for US Coast Guard licensing as a third assistant engineer.

Maine Maritime Academy—Castine, Maine. MMA has nine hundred students on its coastal campus located nearly three hours north of Portland. Students at Maine Maritime can pursue associate, bachelor's, and master's degrees in marine engineering, marine systems, power engineering, marine transportation, international business, marine biology, and marine science. A five-year program combines training in small-vessel operations with the study of marine biology and marine science. International business program students can stay at MMA for an additional year to pursue a MS degree. Through cooperative work experiences with seventy-five partner companies, special leadership training programs, and placements on training, research, and recreation vessels, MMA students are well prepared for jobs—exemplified by an annual placement rate that surpasses 90 percent. Students at MMA have the option to join the navy or marine ROTC.

Massachusetts Maritime Academy—Buzzards Bay, Massachusetts. Located on Cape Cod, Mass Maritime trains 1,050 students in maritime-related fields. All residential students at Mass Maritime belong to the regiment of cadets. Although students at Mass Maritime are not required to follow their cadet service with military service, many become officers in the US Merchant Marine. Mass Maritime offers BS degree programs in marine transportation, marine engineering, marine safety and environmental protection, facilities and environmental engineering, international maritime business, and emergency management. Marine transportation and marine engineering students get trained to become deck officers and ship operators, utilizing the Academy's 540-foot steamship during the January through February sea term and going to places such as the Caribbean and the Mediterranean.

State University of New York (SUNY) Maritime College—Throggs Neck, New York. SUNY Maritime is the oldest and largest maritime college in the United States. Located on the Throggs Neck peninsula of New York City, SUNY Maritime's fifty-five-acre waterfront campus enrolls 1,850 students, 1,250 of whom belong to the regiment of cadets. SUNY Maritime offers five ROTC options as well as US Coast Guard licensing programs. Training on SUNY Maritime's 565-foot ship is a central part of student life. All students travel across the world, seeing at least twelve different countries by graduation. SUNY Maritime offers bachelor of engineering programs in electrical engineering, facilities engineering, marine engineering, mechanical engineering, and naval architecture as well as BS degree programs in international transportation and trade, marine business and commerce, marine environmental science, marine operations, marine transportation, and maritime studies. Job placement for SUNY Maritime graduates is nearly 100 percent.

Texas Maritime Academy—Galveston, Texas. Texas Maritime Academy is part of Texas A&M University's branch campus in Galveston, which enrolls 2,100 students. The four hundred students at Texas Maritime Academy form a corps of cadets focused on leadership, self-discipline, and management. Using the Texas Maritime–owned *Texas Clipper* training ship, students are trained to operate ocean-going vessels. TMA offers degree programs in marine biology, marine science, marine transportation, and marine engineering technology. Texas Maritime's curriculum prepares students to become officers in the US Merchant Marine.

COLLEGES WITH SIGNIFICANT CADET POPULATIONS

University of North Georgia—Dahlonega, Georgia. Renowned for its ROTC program, UNG is often referred to as the Military College of Georgia. Among the six thousand students at UNG are seven hundred cadets, known as the Boar's Head Brigade. With the drill field for parades and ceremonies located in the heart of the campus and three residence halls for ROTC cadets, the military aspect of UNG is hard to miss. Students do not take shortcuts through the drill field; they walk around it. On campus, reveille is played at 7:00 AM every morning, and retreat is played every day at 5:00 PM. Memorial Wall honors the UNG alumni killed in service to their country. The now dormant retreat cannon used to be fired daily. UNG's color guard team has won the national championship twice in the past fifteen years, and its Blue Ridge Rifles unit is one of the top drilling units in the country.

Norwich University—Northfield, Vermont. Norwich has the historic distinction of being the nation's oldest private military college and the birthplace of the Reserve Officers' Training Corps (ROTC). Among the 2,300 undergraduates from forty-five states and twenty foreign countries at Norwich are cadets (in all four branches of the US military) and civilians. Norwich has two types of cadets: ROTC scholarship holders committed to military service following graduation and non-ROTC scholarship cadets who have until junior year to decide if they will commit to the military. A high percentage of Norwich cadets choose civilian life after graduation. Whether cadets choose the military path or not, they are trained in a structured environment that Norwich believes is a laboratory for producing future leaders. The Norwich experience that occurs in classrooms, on athletic fields, and through campus organizations teaches students to take responsibility and aim high. With schools of architecture and art, business and management, engineering, humanities, mathematics and sciences, social sciences, and national services, Norwich offers thirty major and minor programs of study.

Texas A&M University—College Station, Texas. Up until 1965, all Texas A&M students belonged to the corps of cadets. Today, roughly two thousand of the thirty-nine thousand undergraduates at A&M belong to the Fightin' Texas Aggie Corps of Cadets. A great deal of pride and tradition accompanies membership in the aggie cadet corps at A&M. The corps has its own quad of residences on campus. Class years are marked by distinctive names, such as fish year for the first year, and seniors show their status and Aggie Corps pride by wearing special brown leather riding boots called senior boots. Aggie Corps members take ROTC courses and belong to units (represented by all the US military branches). Roughly half of all corps members continue with military service after graduation.

Notable Aggie Corps alumni are Texas Governor Rick Perry and actor Rip Torn.

Virginia Polytechnic and State University—Blacksburg, Virginia. Among the twenty-three thousand undergraduates at Virginia Tech are eight hundred who belong to the corps of cadets. Virginia Tech cadet tradition dates back to 1872. Up until 1964 membership in the corps was mandatory. Cadets live together in residence halls, march to meals in formation, receive military training through ROTC, and can minor in leadership through the Pamplin School of Business. Approximately 80 percent of cadets accept military commissions as officers following graduation. Women make up 15 percent of the cadets at Virginia Tech, and over the years the corps has been led by four female regimental commanding officers. Cadet training in year one is divided into the physically rigorous red phase, followed by the white phase focused on leadership training, and culminating in the blue phase, which marks the transition of the cadet from follower to leader.

WHAT IS ROTC?

The Reserve Officers' Training Corps (ROTC) is a military training program offered at hundreds of college campuses in the United States. ROTC started in 1862 as part of the Morrill Act that established land-grant colleges in the United States. The federal government specified that land-grant colleges should include military tactics as part of the curriculum. Throughout its 150-plus-year history, ROTC has enabled students to train to be officers in the air force, army, marines, and navy. The Coast Guard is the one major branch of the US military that does not offer ROTC.

Students interested in colleges that offer ROTC programs may apply to the US Department of Defense for air force ROTC scholarships, army ROTC scholarships, and navy ROTC Scholarships.

As the largest branch of the US military, the army offers the most ROTC scholarships. When colleges have just one ROTC unit, that unit is usually army ROTC and students are called cadets. Air force ROTC participants are also called cadets. Navy ROTC students are called midshipmen. Navy ROTC midshipmen have the option to train as officers for the marines (a branch of the navy) or the navy. Students in ROTC take courses focused on military history and training, participate in drill activities, and fulfill summer training requirements.

There are three different entry points into ROTC.

1. Apply for ROTC while applying to college as a high school senior. Prospective students apply to a branch of ROTC (using the ROTC application forms) and to colleges (using college admission application forms) that offer the student's selected ROTC branch. ROTC scholarships are portable, so students awarded ROTC scholarships select from the colleges that admit them.

2. Apply to enter ROTC as a college freshman or sophomore. Because some students withdraw from ROTC and not every ROTC unit enrolls its desired number of freshmen, there are unfilled ROTC slots at colleges. Students turned down for a ROTC scholarship in high school may (if they have earned a high college grade point average) get accepted into ROTC after their freshman year. Others may choose to apply to a ROTC unit after developing an interest in the military as a freshman or sophomore. A strong GPA is a basic requirement, as is passage of a physical-fitness test. Students seeking to enter ROTC while in college, rather than out of high school, need to consult their campus ROTC unit to determine the eligibility requirements and the extent to which scholarship aid is offered.

3. Apply for a ROTC scholarship as an enlisted serviceman seeking to go to college. The prior-service ROTC entry option is one that encourages military service personnel (who have not attended or finished college) to attend college and simultaneously train to be an officer.

In general, the military service branches in the United States are most interested in having officers who are trained in the technical subject areas. For that reason, ROTC scholarship recipients typically intend to major in STEM fields. In addition to their major, ROTC students must complete a certain number of military science courses prescribed by the branch of the service and the unit to which they belong. At midsize and large universities, ROTC units and courses tend to be offered on the campus. Many small-college ROTC programs are offered in cooperation with a nearby university, and some colleges and universities in the same city field ROTC units from a collection of campuses. Prospective students need to check to see which colleges offer ROTC and where the units take courses and participate in military drill activities.

The scholarship support ROTC students receive from the federal government varies by service branch. Most ROTC scholarships cover full tuition for all four years. Books and fees for supplies, including uniforms, are also frequently covered by ROTC scholarships through a monthly stipend. In some cases, when a ROTC scholarship is not equal to full tuition, the college will provide a grant to close the gap. Many universities also waive room and board charges for ROTC scholarship recipients. In return for scholarship support, ROTC students agree to accept commissions as officers and serve for at least four years in the US military.

TECH SCHOOLS

Some of America's best colleges are so-called tech schools, and the students who attend them are called techies. Tech schools are known for STEM (science, technology, engineering, and math) subjects. Students interested in tech schools will not be surprised to learn that getting admitted to one requires strength in math and science, as demonstrated by grades earned in high school calculus, physics, chemistry, and biology. Most of the engineering programs at tech schools require high school calculus and physics courses, and some recommend that those courses be taken at the Advanced Placement (AP) or International Baccalaureate (IB) level. Not surprisingly, tech schools also pay close attention to SAT or ACT math scores.

Two tech schools stand out as household names: California Institute of Technology (Caltech) and Massachusetts Institute of Technology (MIT). A handful of other institutions show up on lists of prestigious tech schools, for example, Carnegie Mellon University, Case Western Reserve University, Georgia Institute of Technology (Georgia Tech), Lehigh University, and Rensselaer Polytechnic Institute (RPI). Famous tech schools, like Caltech, MIT, and Carnegie Mellon, have STEM departments that are among the best in the world and faculties chock-full of Nobel laureates. Groundbreaking discoveries, applied learning experiences, and new inventions are everyday experiences for the students at those and other tech schools.

CALTECH AND MIT: THE GEEK MYSTIQUE

MIT and Caltech command a special spot in college and university lore. While Harvard or Yale graduates are often imagined to be first-in-their-class, future leaders of corporations or the free world, it is the graduates of Caltech and MIT who are frequently given the tag genius. Just think of the movie *Good Will Hunting*. Where did the math savant played by Matt Damon decide to show his genius? MIT. Similarly, it was MIT students in *21* (based on the book *Bringing Down the House*) who used their brilliance to win big sums outsmarting the black jack dealers in Las Vegas. And what science geek is not familiar with famed Caltech professor and Nobel laureate Richard Feynman's books that make technical concepts accessible to those unfamiliar with research laboratories?

Virtually everyone has heard stories of Caltech and MIT students employing their brilliance and ingenuity to create what are called hacks, that is, clever pranks, such as putting a replica of the Apollo Lunar Module atop MIT's great dome, arranging for fans at the nationally televised 1961 Rose Bowl game to hold signs that in aggregate spelled out Caltech rather than Washington, rigging the scoreboard at the 1984 Rose Bowl matchup of Illinois versus UCLA to say Caltech 31 MIT 19, and using hydraulics to make a balloon labeled MIT sprout out of the fifty-yard line during the 1982 Harvard-Yale football game. Hacks are a big part of the geek mystique. The clever pranks occurring at Caltech and MIT signal that students there leaven the academic rigor with lighthearted and ingenious fun. The pranks also contribute to building school spirit that binds students and alumni. A few hacks have even become a permanent part of the landscape. For example, the bridge spanning Massachusetts

Avenue from Cambridge to Boston is colloquially called the Smoots Bridge because in 1962 MIT students measured one of their classmates Oliver Smoot and then marked off the length of the bridge in units called Smoots. Visitors to Boston can still chart their progress in Smoots as they cross from Boston to Cambridge.

CALIFORNIA INSTITUTE OF TECHNOLOGY—PASADENA, CALIFORNIA

2,181 students (977 undergraduates)

Student-faculty ratio of three to one

Majors in applied and computational mathematics, applied physics, astrophysics, bioengineering, biology, business economics and management, chemistry, chemical engineering, computer science, economics, electrical engineering, engineering and applied science, English, geobiology, geochemistry, geology, geophysics, history, history and philosophy of science, mathematics, mechanical engineering, philosophy, physics, planetary science, political science, independent studies program

Jet Propulsion Laboratory, Laser Interferometer, Gravitational-Wave Observatory, and Southern California Earthquake Data Center

9 percent of applicants admitted

Middle 50 percent on SAT: 2230–2240; ACT: 34–35

Notable alumni: Frank Capra (filmmaker), York Liao (inventor of liquid crystal displays), Harrison Schmitt (astronaut who walked on moon and served as US senator), William Shockley (Nobel laureate, invented the transistor)

MASSACHUSETTS INSTITUTE OF TECHNOLOGY—CAMBRIDGE, MASSACHUSETTS

11,319 students (4,512 undergraduates)

Student-faculty ratio of seven to one

Majors: architecture and planning; engineering; humanities, arts, and social sciences; management; science, health sciences, and technology (graduate only)

Draper Laboratory for Innovation in Engineering, MIT Media Lab, Wright Brothers Wind Tunnel

8 percent of applicants admitted

Middle 50 percent on SAT: 1440–1590; ACT: 33–35

Notable alumni: Robert Metcalfe (inventor of Ethernet), Ray and Tom Magliozzi (Click and Clack of *Car Talk*), Benjamin Netanyahu (prime minister of Israel), I. M. Pei (architect), Lawrence Summers (former president of Harvard and US treasury secretary)

Eighty alumni Nobel laureates

Some tech schools provide far more than STEM programs. The economics department at MIT rivals Harvard and the University of Chicago for the number of Nobel prizes its faculty have won. Carnegie Mellon has one of the nation's top programs in graphic design alongside outstanding schools of music and theater. Lehigh University has a full-fledged liberal arts college. Georgia Tech offers majors in international affairs and public policy, and RPI has a highly ranked game-design program. Lest students think that going to a tech school means forgoing the opportunity to learn a foreign language or study abroad, think again. Just about every tech school offers study abroad programs. You can study in Denmark, England, France, and Scotland through Caltech; England (Cambridge and Oxford), France, Germany, Israel, the Netherlands, Spain, and Sweden through MIT; and Australia, Denmark, Germany, Hong Kong, India, Japan, Korea, Singapore, and South Africa through RPI. Many tech schools offer three or more foreign languages. You can learn Chinese, French, German, Japanese, and Spanish at Caltech; Chinese, French, German, Japanese, and Russian at Carnegie Mellon; Chinese, French, German, Japanese, and Spanish at MIT; and German, Japanese, and Spanish at Rose Hulman.

OTHER TOP-TEN TECH SCHOOLS

GEORGIA INSTITUTE OF TECHNOLOGY—ATLANTA, GEORGIA

23,109 students (14,682 undergraduates)

Student-faculty ratio of twenty to one

Architecture, computing, engineering, liberal arts, management, sciences

Center for Music Technology, Algorithms and Randomness Center, Center for Organic Photonics and Electronics

BS degree in global economics and modern languages

Foreign languages offered: Arabic, Chinese, French, German, Japanese, Korean, Russian, Spanish

33 percent of applicants admitted

Middle 50 percent on SAT: 1440–1550; ACT: 30–33

Notable alumni: Krishna Bharat (creator of Google News), Chris Bosh (NBA player), Jeff Foxworthy (comedian), Nomar Garciaparra (former major league baseball player), Bobby Jones (Hall of Fame golfer), Kary Mullis (Nobel laureate who developed the polymerase chain reaction—PCR), Arthur Murray (dance instructor), James D. Robinson (CEO of American Express), Ken Whisenhunt (NFL coach)

RENSSELAER POLYTECHNIC INSTITUTE—TROY, NEW YORK

6,761 students (5,557 undergraduates)

Student-faculty ratio of fifteen to one

Architecture, engineering; humanities, arts, and social sciences; management; science

Archer Center for Student Leadership Development, Experimental Media and Performing Arts Center, Inventor's Studio, Lighting Research Center

Students can add a fifth year and earn a master's degree.

41 percent of applicants admitted

Middle 50 percent on SAT: 1300–1490; ACT: 27–32

Notable alumni: Marshall Brain (author of the *How Stuff Works* series), Miles Brand (led the NCAA), Bobby Farrelly (film director—*There's Something About Mary*, etc.), George Ferris (inventor of the Ferris wheel), George Low (managed NASA's Apollo 11 project), Adam Oates (NHL Hall of Famer)

Practically all tech schools offer more than just STEM courses and majors. But few come close to offering breadth in arts, humanities, and the social sciences. Three notable exceptions are Carnegie Mellon University, Case Western Reserve University, and Lehigh University. Carnegie Mellon resulted when Carnegie Institute of Technology fused with Mellon Institute of the Arts, and Case Western Reserve formed when Case Institute of Technology merged with Western Reserve University. Carnegie Mellon, Case Western, and Lehigh are more or less full-fledged arts and sciences universities. Carnegie Mellon offers some of the nation's top programs in engineering and computer science but also offers exceptional programs in creative writing, music, and theater. In addition to Case's outstanding programs in biomedical engineering and materials science are a business school, law school, medical school, and the Mandel School of Social Policy. English majors, prelaw students, and philosophy majors are as welcome at Case as future engineers. Alongside its dozen engineering programs, Lehigh offers colleges of arts and sciences, business and economics, and education.

CARNEGIE MELLON UNIVERSITY— PITTSBURGH, PENNSYLVANIA

13,285 students (6,237 undergraduates)

Student-faculty ratio of thirteen to one

Carnegie Institute of Technology, fine arts, humanities and social sciences; business; public policy and management; science; computer science

CyLab Cyber Security Center, Entertainment Technology Center, Robotics Institute, Studio for Creative Inquiry

26 percent of applicants admitted

Middle 50 percent on SAT: 1340–1530; ACT: 30–34

Notable alumni: Six Nobel laureates, including John Nash (*A Beautiful Mind*); Ted Nierenberg (Dansk International founder); Robert Dennard (inventor of dynamic random access memory [DRAM]); Scott Fahlman (creator of the emoticon); Edgar Mitchell (the sixth person to walk on the moon); Randy Pausch (*The Last Lecture*); Ted Danson (actor); Henry Mancini (composer); Mike Florio (sportscaster)

CASE WESTERN RESERVE UNIVERSITY—CLEVELAND, OHIO

10,771 students (4,911 undergraduates)

Student-faculty ratio of ten to one

Arts and sciences, engineering, management, nursing, applied social science, dental medicine, law

Great Lakes Energy Institute, Institute for Management and Engineering, Yeager Center for Electrochemical Sciences

42 percent of applicants admitted

Middle 50 percent on SAT: 1270–1480; ACT: 29–33

Notable alumni: Paul Buchheit (creator of Gmail), Herbert Henry Dow (founder of Dow Chemical), Dennis Kucinich (former US representative and presidential candidate), Polycarp Kusch (1955 Nobel Prize for determining the magnetic moment of the electron), Craig Newmark (creator of Craigslist), M. Scott Peck (self-help author), James Polshek (architect of the Clinton Presidential Library)

LEHIGH UNIVERSITY—BETHLEHEM, PENNSYLVANIA

6,961 students (4,904 undergraduates)

Student-faculty ratio of ten to one

Arts and sciences, business and economics, engineering and applied science, education (graduate/professional only)

Center for Advanced Materials and Nanotechnology, Center for Optical Technologies

All twenty-five athletic teams compete in NCAA Division I.

30 percent of applicants admitted

Middle 50 percent on SAT: 1290–1475; ACT: 29–33

Notable alumni: Lee Iacocca (former CEO of Chrysler), Roger Penske (NASCAR team owner)

With their broad range of academic programs,

Carnegie Mellon, Case, and Lehigh are outliers in the tech-school world. More often than not, tech schools provide just a handful of arts and sciences majors and courses. That's why they are called tech schools. For example, Stevens Institute of Technology does not offer foreign language courses. Typically, the arts, humanities, and social science offerings at tech schools tend to emphasize the places where those curricular areas intersect with science and technology fields. For example, the school of humanities at Illinois Institute of Technology (IIT) offers a major in the journalism of technology, science, and business as well as a major in technical communication. RPI's school of humanities, arts, and social sciences offers majors in cognitive science, communication, economics, electronic arts, games and simulation arts and sciences, and sustainability studies. At both IIT and RPI there are only a few traditional arts and science majors: psychology and political science at IIT and economics, philosophy, and psychology at RPI.

Most tech schools are quite specialized, which means that they offer their arts and sciences courses primarily to round out a technical education. Colorado School of Mines, for example, is respected for its strong programs in chemical, mining, metallurgical, and petroleum engineering. There is more than engineering at Mines (as it is nicknamed) but not much more. Mines has a division of humanities and social sciences that offers a major in economics as well as minors in a handful of areas such as international political economy, business and economics, and humanities. Those nontechnical programs are not the reason students choose Mines. Students are there to prepare for good jobs in technical fields, not to write poetry and debate the ideas of Plato. The atmosphere at specialized schools like Mines is very focused and career directed. The perceived value of the education at tech schools like Mines is the ability of its graduates to have successful and lucrative careers in industry.

COLORADO SCHOOL OF MINES—GOLDEN, COLORADO

5,673 students (4,383 undergraduates)

Student-faculty ratio of fifteen to one

Academic programs in applied science and mathematics, economics, engineering, geosciences, and resource engineering

Colorado Renewable Energy Collaboratory

Mines' slogan: Earth, Energy, Environment

36 percent of applicants admitted

Average SAT: 1320; ACT: 30

Notable alumni: John Polk Allen (inventor of Biosphere 2), Arden Bement (former director of the National Science Foundation), Derrick Jensen (environmental writer), Michelle Roark (Olympic skier)

SMALL BUT INNOVATIVE TECH SCHOOLS: OLIN AND HARVEY MUDD

Two very small tech schools—Franklin W. Olin College of Engineering and Harvey Mudd College—offer a personalized education of unsurpassed quality. The academic horsepower of the incoming freshmen at HMC and Olin rivals that of its tech school siblings in Cambridge and Pasadena, and many HMC and Olin students end up at those other two places for graduate school.

Students at Olin have just three major options: electrical and computer engineering; mechanical engineering; and an engineering major with concentration options in bioengineering, computing, materials science, and systems. Olin students get their non-STEM courses through cross registration partnerships with Babson College (which borders the Olin campus), Brandeis University, and Wellesley College. Harvey Mudd offers ten major choices: biology, biology/chemistry, chemistry, computer science, engineering, mathematics, mathematics/computer science, mathematical biology, physics, and independent program. Harvey Mudd students merely cross the street to take arts, humanities, and social science courses at the other Claremont colleges: Claremont McKenna, Pitzer, Pomona, Scripps, and Claremont Graduate University. For certain students, the smaller, more intimate scale of Mudd and Olin provides a supportive yet challenging environment in which to thrive.

FRANKLIN W. OLIN COLLEGE OF ENGINEERING—NEEDHAM, MASSACHUSETTS

350 students (all undergraduates)

Student-faculty ratio of eight to one

Academic programs in electrical and computer engineering, engineering (computing, bioengineering, materials science, and systems design), mechanical engineering

Every student receives a half-tuition scholarship.

17 percent of applicants admitted

Middle 50 percent on SAT: 1425–1565; ACT: 33–34

Notable alumni: Since Olin's first graduating class (2006), a high percentage of its alumni have gone on to graduate study—including Olin's first PhD recipient (in laser physics) from Oxford University.

HARVEY MUDD COLLEGE— CLAREMONT, CALIFORNIA

807 students (all undergraduates)

Student-faculty ratio of nine to one

Major programs in biology, chemistry, computer science, engineering, mathematics, mathematics/computer science, mathematical biology, physics, independent program

Cross registration with the other Claremont colleges

19 percent of applicants admitted

Middle 50 percent on SAT: 1400–1560; ACT: 32–35

Notable alumni: Jonathan Gay (creator of Flash software), Stan Love and George Nelson (space shuttle astronauts), Scott Stokdyk (Oscar winner for special effects)

STUDYING ARCHITECTURE AT A TECH SCHOOL

Tech schools are full of stereotype-defying surprises. One example is the large number of tech schools that offer degrees in architecture, art, or design. In fact, some of the best undergraduate architecture programs are found at tech schools. An added benefit for students who study architecture at tech schools is the opportunity to get their training alongside future civil and industrial engineers. Tech-school architecture programs often provide a design laboratory environment in which students can model their work using cutting-edge computational and digital technologies and collaborate with engineering students to determine the effectiveness of their building designs. In the real world, architects always collaborate with project engineers. Tech-school architecture programs give their students a head start in understanding that important aspect of the field. In learning how to design the buildings of the future, tech-school architecture students frequently have opportunities to integrate the latest technologies and study alongside experts in acoustics, lighting, earthquake preparedness, environmental engineering, and sustainability. The following tech schools offer architecture as a major.

- California Polytechnic State University
- Carnegie Mellon University
- Cooper Union
- Georgia Tech
- Illinois Institute of Technology
- Kettering University
- Lawrence Institute of Technology
- MIT (graduate only)
- New Jersey Institute of Technology
- Rensselaer Polytechnic Institute
- Virginia Polytechnic Institute
- Wentworth Institute of Technology

ILLINOIS INSTITUTE OF TECHNOLOGY—CHICAGO, ILLINOIS

7,898 students (3,046 undergraduates)

Student-faculty ratio of twelve to one

Engineering, architecture, science and letters, Institute of Psychology, applied technology, business, law, Institute of Design (graduate)

Majors in environmental management and sustainability; food safety and technology; landscape architecture; power engineering

Center for Digital Design and Manufacturing; Center for Strategic Competitiveness; Electric Power and Power Electronics Center; International Center for Sustainable New Cities

57 percent of applicants admitted

Average SAT: 1268; ACT: 28

Notable alumni: Valdas Adamkus (president of Lithuania), Martin Cooper (invented mobile phone), Martin Jischke (former president of Iowa State and Purdue), Art Paul (designed the Playboy rabbit-head logo), Susan Solomon (shared Nobel Prize in 2007 with Al Gore for work on global climate change)

KETTERING UNIVERSITY—FLINT, MICHIGAN

1,991 students (1,690 undergraduates)

Student-faculty ratio of thirteen to one

Programs in applied mathematics, applied physics, biochemistry, business administration, chemical engineering, chemistry, computer engineering, computer science, electrical engineering, engineering physics, industrial engineering, mechanical engineering—also offers a four-year BS/MS program. Engineering sub-specialty options include aerospace engineering, alternative energy, automotive engineering design, bioengineering applications, machine design, and plastics product design.

Kettering was formerly the General Motors Institute of Technology, providing important connections to the auto industry for co-op and job opportunities. Kettering runs strong cooperative/internship and job placement programs.

65 percent of applicants admitted

Middle 50 percent on SAT: 1120–1310; ACT: 24–28

Notable alumni: Donald Almquist (CEO of Delco Electronics), Mary Barra (CEO of General Motors), Ivan Deveson (former mayor of Melbourne Australia), Chet Huber (president of On Star Corporation), Henry Juskiewicz (CEO of Gibson Guitar Corporation)

WENTWORTH INSTITUTE OF TECHNOLOGY—BOSTON, MASSACHUSETTS

3,838 students (3,714 undergraduates)

Student-faculty ratio of seventeen to one

Architecture, design and construction management, arts and sciences, engineering and technology

Majors offered in electromechanical engineering and facility planning and management; a cooperative/internship program provides students with work experience and outstanding job preparation; cross registration for courses at the Colleges of the Fenway: Emmanuel College, Massachusetts College of Art, Massachusetts College of Pharmacy and Health Sciences, Simmons College, and Wheelock College.

58 percent of applicants admitted

Middle 50 percent on SAT: 1030–1190; ACT: 22–26

Notable alumni: David Lovering (drummer for the Pixies), Stephen Lynch (US representative, Massachusetts), Joe Lauzon (mixed martial arts professional who appeared on *The Ultimate Fighter 5*), John Volpe (former governor of Massachusetts and US secretary of transportation)

STUDYING BUSINESS AT A TECH SCHOOL

Ask most high school guidance counselors where to study undergraduate business and few will point their students toward tech schools. That is a mistake because there are excellent business programs to be found at many tech schools. One key competitive advantage tech school business programs have is their location on campuses that often serve as incubators of new product development. More so than their liberal arts counterparts, tech schools are training grounds and launching pads for the developers of the next Guitar Hero, Google, or Xbox. Business-school students at STEM institutions such as Georgia Tech and RPI have the opportunity to study alongside engineering and science students who will start the IBMs and Intels of the future. Tech-school business programs have a strong focus on getting students to develop the entrepreneurial frame of mind needed to create inventions and launch start-up companies. Tech schools also draw from their computational strength in offering business-related concentrations in areas such as actuarial science, financial engineering, information management, business systems and processes, and technology innovation and entrepreneurship. Below is a comprehensive, but not exhaustive, list of tech schools with impressive business programs.

- California Institute of Technology
- California Polytechnic State University
- Carnegie Mellon University
- Case Western Reserve University
- Clarkson University

- Colorado School of Mines
- Florida Institute of Technology
- Georgia Tech
- Illinois Institute of Technology
- Massachusettes Institute of Technology
- Michigan Technological University
- New Jersey Institute of Technology
- Rensselaer Polytechnic Institute
- Rochester Institute of Technology
- Rose Hulman Institute of Technology
- Stevens Institute of Technology
- Worcester Polytechnic Institute

CLARKSON UNIVERSITY—POTSDAM, NEW YORK

3,873 students (3,247 undergraduates)

Student-faculty ratio of thirteen to one

Arts and sciences, business, engineering

Center for Advanced Materials Processing, Center for the Environment, Center for Rehabilitation Engineering Science and Technology, Honors Program

64 percent of applicants admitted

Middle 50 percent on SAT: 1090–1290; ACT: 24–28

Notable alumni: Kent Huskins (won Stanley Cup with Anaheim Mighty Ducks in 2007), Martin Roesch (developed the Snort intrusion prevention system), Paul Tonko (US representative, New York), M. Emmet Walsh (actor)

ROSE HULMAN INSTITUTE OF TECH-NOLOGY—TERRE HAUTE, INDIANA

2,200 students (2,100 undergraduates)

Student-faculty ratio of thirteen to one

Majors in applied biology and biomedical engineering, chemical engineering, civil engineering, computer science and software engineering, economics, electrical and computer engineering, environmental engineering, mathematics, mechanical engineering, physics, and optical engineering

Rose Hulman Ventures pairs students with technology companies—providing students with hands-on experience in product development and research.

Rose Hulman promotes itself as the nation's top undergraduate engineering, science, and mathematics college.

56 percent of applicants admitted

Middle 50 percent on SAT: 1180–1420; ACT: 27–32

Notable alumni: Tim Cindric (president of Penske Racing), Marshall Goldsmith (author of management books)

STEVENS INSTITUTE OF TECHNOLOGY—HOBOKEN, NEW JERSEY

6,463 students (2,892 undergraduates)

Student-faculty ratio of ten to one

Arts and letters, engineering and science, systems and enterprises, technology management

Atlantic Center for the Innovative Design and Control of Small Ships, National Center for Secure and Resilient Maritime Commerce, cooperative work program, majors in cyber security, music and technology, naval architecture and marine engineering, and quantitative finance

44 percent of applicants admitted

Middle 50 percent on SAT: 1260–1410

Notable alumni: Alexander Calder (sculptor—inventor of the mobile), Mark Crispin (inventor of IMAP), Nate Davis (president of XM Satellite Radio)

WORCESTER POLYTECHNIC INSTITUTE—WORCESTER, MASSACHUSETTS

6,057 students (4,123 undergraduates)

Student-faculty ratio fourteen to one

Engineering and computer science, liberal arts, management, sciences

Center for Water Research, Fire Science Laboratory, Fuel Cell Center, Metal Processing Institute Ultrasound Research Lab; Wireless Innovation Laboratory

WPI's seven-week terms enable students to work and travel off-campus and still complete their work.

All WPI students must work on two real-world projects to graduate.

52 percent of applicants admitted

Middle 50 percent on SAT: 1240–1470; ACT: 28–32

Notable alumni: Robert Goddard (father of modern rocketry), Nancy Pimental (wrote for *South Park* and cohosted *Win Ben Stein's Money*), Robert Stempel (invented catalytic converter and was CEO of General Motors), John Geils (dropped out of WPI to start the J. Geils Band)

WHO ATTENDS TECH SCHOOLS?

Students for whom a tech school could be a good college choice are comfortable with a curriculum that is stacked heavily (and we mean heavily) with STEM courses. Some tech schools have few non-STEM major options—and even those majors may be technology based. Other tech schools, usually large state institutions, such as Purdue or Virginia Tech, offer a full range of liberal arts and sciences majors and do not require all students to be STEM focused. The first-year curriculum at tech schools can be unforgiving of spotty high school preparation in math and science, which is why tech schools have slightly higher attrition rates than other colleges and universities. Still, gone are the days when all introductory courses at tech schools were designed to weed out weak students. Today's tech school, while no cakewalk, is a kinder and gentler place. Another key factor that foreshadows a good student fit at a tech school is strong interest in creating new technologies and making discoveries plus strong interest in hands-on learning.

The typical tech school was once nearly all male. As recently as the late 1980s, it was common to find ratios of 85 percent men to 15 percent women at tech schools, such as Georgia Tech, Harvey Mudd, RPI, and Rose Hulman. The few women who ventured into the tech-school environment felt like pioneers entering uncharted territory. The situation has changed dramatically. Women make up 45 percent of the student population at MIT, 50 percent of the student body at Olin, and 46 percent at Harvey Mudd. But the percentage of women still falls in the 25 to 33 percent range at the tech schools that lack the full-fledged arts and sciences programs found at Carnegie Mellon, Case Western, and Lehigh. Tech schools like IIT, Rose Hulman, RPI, and WPI work extremely hard to bring their female enrollment up into the 30 to 40 percent range. This often creates a slightly favorable advantage for female applicants as admissions offices try to create a more gender-balanced class. It can also create a slightly different social dynamic than at schools with a more equal gender ratio.

➤YES, WOMEN GO TO TECH SCHOOLS

Caltech—31 percent

Cal Poly—45 percent

Carnegie Mellon—43 percent

Clarkson—28 percent

Colorado School of Mines—27 percent

Georgia Tech—33 percent

FW Olin—49 percent

Harvey Mudd—46 percent

IIT—30 percent

Kettering—18 percent

Lawrence Tech—25 percent

Lehigh—44 percent

MIT—45 percent

Michigan Tech—25 percent

Missouri Technology University—
23 percent

RPI—30 percent

Rose Hulman—22 percent

South Dakota School of Mines—23 percent

Stevens—28 percent

WPI—33 percent

HISTORICALLY BLACK COLLEGES AND UNIVERSITIES STRONG IN STEM SUBJECTS

A number of historically black colleges and universities (HBCUs) have science and technology at the core of their identity. Four institutions stand out for their storied histories as training grounds for African American engineers and scientists: Florida Agricultural and Mechanical University (Florida A&M), North Carolina Agricultural and Technical University (NC A&T), Hampton Institute, and Tuskegee University.

FLORIDA AGRICULTURAL AND MECHANICAL UNIVERSITY— TALLAHASSEE, FLORIDA

10,743 students (8,930 undergraduates)

Student-faculty ratio of seventeen to one

Arts and sciences; education; engineering sciences, technology, and agriculture; pharmacy and pharmaceutical sciences; allied health sciences; architecture; business and industry; journalism and graphic communication; nursing; law

Center for Environmental Equity and Justice, Center for Water Quality, and Environmental Sciences Institute

FAMU's School of General Studies helps undecided students choose majors and focuses on increasing graduation rates. FAMU's marching band has become a fixture at presidential inaugurations.

45 percent of applicants admitted

Average high school GPA: 3.27/4.0

Middle 50 percent on SAT: 850–1030; ACT: 18–22

Notable alumni: Julian "Cannonball" Adderly (jazz saxophonist), Althea Gibson (pathbreaking tennis player), Alcee Hastings (US representative, Florida), Pam Oliver (television sports reporter)

HAMPTON UNIVERSITY—HAMPTON, VIRGINIA

4,397 students (3,504 undergraduates)

Student-faculty ratio of ten to one

Business, engineering, journalism and communications, liberal arts, nursing, pharmacy, and science

Hampton operates an honors college and a leadership institute.

Students adhere to a code of conduct as well as a dress code.

36 percent of applicants admitted

Average high school GPA: 3.2/4.0

Middle 50 percent on SAT: 920–1090; ACT: 18–23

Notable alumni: Spencer Christian (former weatherman on *Good Morning, America*), Freeman Hrabowski (president of University of Maryland, Baltimore County). Wanda Sykes (comedian), Booker T. Washington (famous author and educator)

NORTH CAROLINA A&T UNIVERSITY—GREENSBORO, NORTH CAROLINA

10,734 students (8.923 undergraduates)

Student-faculty ratio of sixteen to one

Arts and sciences, engineering, agriculture and environmental sciences, business and economics, education, technology, graduate studies

Center for Entrepreneurship and E-Business, Transportation Institute, Waste Management Institute

NC A&T has the largest school of agriculture among HBCUs.

55 percent of applicants admitted

Average high school GPA: 3.1/4.0

Middle 50 percent on SAT: 830–990; ACT: 16–20

Notable alumni: Al Attles (former NBA player, coach, and executive), Jesse Jackson (civil rights activist), Jesse Jackson Jr. (former US representative, Illinois), Ronald McNair (first African American astronaut)

TUSKEGEE UNIVERSITY—TUSKEGEE, ALABAMA

3,156 students (2,584 undergraduates)

Student-faculty ratio of twelve to one

Agricultural, environmental, and natural sciences; business and information science; engineering, architecture, and physical sciences; liberal arts and education; veterinary medicine, nursing, and allied health

Alabama Center for Nanostructured Materials, Center for Biomedical Research, National Center for Bioethics in Research and Health Care

41 percent of applicants admitted

Average high school GPA: 3.1/4.0

Middle 50 percent on SAT: 790–1000; ACT: 17–22

Notable alumni: Ralph Ellison (writer), Tom Joyner (radio show host), Lionel Richie (singer), Keenan Ivory Wayans (actor/director)

GET A TECH-SCHOOL EDUCATION AT A BARGAIN PRICE

At many colleges, students can get a high-quality STEM education for a state university price. Highlighted below in parentheses following the name of each school is the 2015 annual cost of attendance (including tuition, room and board, fees, books, and personal/travel expenses) for in-state students.

California Polytechnic State University, San Luis Obispo ($25,467)

Colorado School of Mines ($31,417)

Clemson University ($26, 912)

Florida A&M ($20,360)

Georgia Institute of Technology ($25,752)

Iowa State University ($19,270)

Michigan Technological University ($27,056)

Missouri University of Science and Technology ($23,052)

New Jersey Institute of Technology ($34,828)

North Carolina A&T ($18,252)

Purdue University ($23,002)

South Dakota School of Mines and Technology ($19,670)

SUNY Polytechnic Institute ($19,453)

SUNY Technology Colleges: Alfred State, Canton, Cobleskill, Delhi, Farmingdale, Maritime, Morrisville State ($19,487)

Texas A&M University ($24,024)

Texas Tech University ($24,870)

Virginia Polytechnic Institute and State University ($20,711)

CALIFORNIA POLYTECHNIC STATE UNIVERSITY—SAN LUIS OBISPO

19,703 students (18,739 undergraduates)

Student-faculty ratio of nineteen to one

Agriculture, food, and environmental sciences; architecture and environmental design; business; engineering; liberal arts; science and mathematics; education

Air Pollution Training Institute, Center for Sustainability in Engineering, Environmental Biotechnology Institute, Urban Forest Ecosystems Institute, honors program

Cal Poly combines technical and professional curricula with an extensive array of major programs in the arts and humanities.

Average high school GPA: 3.9/4.0

Middle 50 percent on SAT: 1130–1320; ACT: 25–30

35 percent of applicants admitted

Notable alumni: Bobby Beathard (former NFL general manager), Chuck Liddell (ultimate fighting champion), John Madden (NFL coach and broadcaster), Ozzie Smith (MLB Hall of Fame shortstop), Burt Rutan (designed first plane to fly around the world without refueling), Weird Al Yankovic

MICHIGAN TECHNOLOGICAL UNIVERSITY—HOUGHTON, MICHIGAN

7,104 students (5,662 undergraduates)

Business and economics, engineering, forest resources and environmental science, sciences and arts, technology

Student-faculty ratio of thirteen to one

Degree programs in audio production and technology, geological engineering, pharmaceutical chemistry, sound design, surveying engineering, theater and electronic media performance, theater and entertainment technology, and wildlife ecology and management

Average high school GPA: 3.7/4.0

Middle 50 percent on ACT: 24–29; SAT: 1090–1330

78 percent of applicants admitted

Notable alumni: Melvin Calvin (Nobel laureate—Calvin Cycle), Tony Esposito (NHL Hall of Fame goaltender), Donald Saari (influential game theorist)

VIRGINIA POLYTECHNIC INSTITUTE AND STATE UNIVERSITY—BLACKSBURG, VIRGINIA

31,205 students (24,034 undergraduates)

Student-faculty ratio of sixteen to one

Agriculture and life sciences, architecture and urban studies, business, engineering, liberal arts and human sciences, natural resources, science

Operates a corporate research center.

Historically rooted in military training, Virginia Tech maintains a prominent corps of cadets.

Average high school GPA: 3.8/4.0

Middle 50 percent on SAT: 1170–1350; ACT: 25–30

70 percent of applicants admitted

Notable alumni: Ed Clark (president of Atlanta Motor Speedway), Chris Craft (architect of NASA's Mission Control), Homer Hickam (author of *Rocket Boys*, made into the movie *October Sky*), Bruce Smith (NFL Hall of Fame), Michael Vick (NFL player and infamous animal abuser).

SURPRISING MAJORS OFFERED AT TECH SCHOOLS

CALTECH: economics, English, history, political science, and philosophy

CARNEGIE MELLON: Chinese studies, creative writing, English, environmental policy, European studies, French and francophone studies, German, global studies, Hispanic studies, international relations and politics, Japanese, linguistics, music, philosophy, professional writing, Russian studies, theater

CLARKSON UNIVERSITY: Communication, history, humanities, liberal studies, physical therapy, political science

GEORGIA TECH: computational media; economics; global economics and modern languages; history, technology, and culture; international affairs; psychology; public policy

ILLINOIS INSTITUTE OF TECHNOLOGY: political science, psychology

MIT: anthropology, comparative media studies, global studies and languages, history, linguistics, literature, music, philosophy, political science, and writing

MICHIGAN TECH: anthropology, English, history, humanities, liberal arts, psychology

RIT: advertising and public relations, criminal justice, international studies, journalism, new media marketing, philosophy, political science, professional and technical communication, psychology, public policy, urban and community studies

RPI: communication; design, innovation, and society; electronic arts; electronic media arts and communication; philosophy; psychology

STEVENS INSTITUTE OF TECHNOLOGY: history, humanities, philosophy

WORCESTER POLYTECHNIC: environmental studies, international studies, professional writing, psychological science, and a humanities and arts major with concentration options in American studies, drama/theater, German studies, Hispanic studies, history, music, philosophy/religion, writing and rhetoric.

WHERE TECH SCHOOL MEETS ART SCHOOL

Some colleges are as much art and design schools as tech schools. **Cooper Union** and **Rochester Institute of Technology (RIT),** for example, combine the creative, edgy art-school atmosphere with the practical, career-focused tech-school ethos. Cooper Union operates a full-fledged fine arts school that in addition to providing BFA degree instruction in drawing, painting, photography, printmaking, and sculpture also offers courses in animation, art history, casting techniques, digital photography, digital sound art, sound design, film, graphic design, motion graphics, papermaking, typography, and the art of the book. Cooper's curriculum encompasses foreign-language instruction in Arabic, French, German, and Japanese as well as courses on African art, history of cinema, linguistics, Shakespeare, and urban archaeology.

Within its college of imaging arts and sciences, RIT has six different schools. RIT offers schools for the study of American crafts, art, design, film and animation, photographic arts and sciences, and print media. In its arts-oriented offerings, RIT rivals and even surpasses many art schools. Crafts students at RIT can work in studios for clay, glass, metal, and wood. Art students can study medical illustration. In addition to graphic design as a concentration, design students can focus on industrial design, interior design, 3-D digital graphics, and new media design and imaging. RIT photography programs include specialties in advertising photography, photojournalism, and biomedical photographic communications. Film and animation facilities at RIT support work in digital cinema and film production. Printmaking programs encompass new media publishing. Art students at RIT have the special opportunity to study in an environment that emphasizes the creative side of science and technology and the commercial opportunities for art, design, and film. RIT also has an array of language study options (American Sign Language, Arabic, Chinese, French, German, Italian, Japanese, Russian, and Spanish) that compares favorably to opportunities students find at large arts and sciences focused universities.

THE COOPER UNION FOR THE ADVANCEMENT OF SCIENCE AND ART—NEW YORK, NEW YORK

920 students (850 undergraduates)

Student-faculty ratio of nine to one

Architecture, art, engineering, faculty of humanities and social sciences (no degree programs, just courses, including language courses in Arabic, French, German, and Japanese)

All students get a half-tuition scholarship. Students must pay for books and supplies; on-campus students must pay for room and board.

Average high school GPA: 3.6/4.0

Middle 50 percent on SAT: 1220–1490: ACT: 28–33

15 percent of applicants admitted

Notable alumni: Roy DeCarava (photographer), Thomas Edison (inventor), Milton Glaser (founder of *New York Magazine* and creator of the *I Love New York* logo), Eva Hesse (sculptor), Daniel Libeskind (architect)

ROCHESTER INSTITUTE OF TECHNOLOGY—ROCHESTER, NEW YORK

18,063 students (15,006 undergraduates)

Student-faculty ratio of fourteen to one

Applied science and technology, business, computing and information sciences, engineering, imaging arts and sciences (includes the School of American Crafts), liberal arts, science

University Studies Program for undecided students; cooperative/internship programs for work experience; honors program; research centers focused on imaging, sustainability, and interdisciplinary research to solve challenges in biology, health care, and medicine. RIT offers a major in packaging science.

RIT is home of the National Technical Institute for the Deaf.

Average high school GPA: 3.7/4.0

Middle 50 percent on SAT: 1110–1320; ACT: 25–31

60 percent of applicants admitted

Notable alumni: Ralph Avery (artist), Bruce Davidson (photographer), Jacob Lodwick (founder of MTV's *College Humor*).

TOP SCHOOLS FOR COMPUTER SCIENCE

In the history of computing, tech schools such as **Caltech, Carnegie Mellon, MIT**, and **RPI** have been pioneers. Carnegie Mellon, home of one of the nation's first computer science programs, has a whole school devoted to computing—offering BS programs in computer science, computational biology, computer science and the arts, and human-computer interaction and minors in robotics, software engineering, and machine learning. The PhD program in computer science at Carnegie Mellon is often ranked at or near the top. MIT alumni helped invent Ethernet, the Internet, and computer games. The Computer Science Department at MIT (linked to the Electrical Engineering Department) frequently sits atop undergraduate program rankings. At MIT, students can pair computer science with computer engineering, electrical engineering, or computational biology. Faculty and alumni of Caltech were early innovators in the analysis of algorithms, computer textbooks, the invention of the transistor, and the establishment of technology companies such as Intel, Hotmail, and MathWorks. At Caltech students can major in computer science or applied and computational mathematics. RPI alumni helped develop IBM's Watson, the supercomputer that beat the all-time Jeopardy champion, and the video graphics chip. For computer enthusiasts, RPI offers majors in computer science, computer engineering, information technology/web science, and cognitive science.

A number of other schools are standouts in computer science. The **University of Illinois** at Urbana-Champaign, prominent for its National Center for Supercomputing Applications, has produced graduates who founded YouTube, Yelp!, SLIDE, PayPal, and Netscape. Computer science students at Illinois have three BS degree choices: computer science (including a five-year BS/MS track), math and computer science, or statistics and computer science. The **Stanford University** computer science department is perennially ranked among the best in the world. Stanford has spawned numerous computer companies like Cisco Systems, Google, Hewlett Packard, Instagram, LinkedIn, Nvidia, Sun Microsystems, Wipro, and Yahoo! Students majoring in computer science at Stanford can pursue specialized tracks in artificial intelligence, biocomputation, computer engineering, graphics, human-computer interaction, and information systems and theory. Stanford also offers computer-related majors in mathematical and computational sciences and in symbolic systems. Also on the West Coast is the highly ranked program in computer science at the **University of Washington**. Washington alumni were instrumental in developing Microsoft's MS-DOS operating system, MacPaint and Macintosh software for Apple, the CP/M operating system, and the concept of shareware. Washington offers BS and BS/MS programs in computer science and degrees in computer engineering, computational mathematical sciences, and informatics. Additional leading places to study computer science are listed below.

- University of British Columbia
- Brown University
- University of California at Berkeley
- University of California at Irvine
- University of California at Los Angeles
- University of California at San Diego
- University of Chicago

- Columbia University
- Cornell University
- F. W. Olin College of Engineering
- Georgia Institute of Technology
- Harvard University
- Harvey Mudd College
- McGill University
- University of Michigan
- University of Maryland
- Northwestern University
- University of Pennsylvania
- Princeton University
- Purdue University
- Rice University
- University of Texas
- University of Toronto
- University of Wisconsin (Madison)
- Yale University

NON-TECH INSTITUTIONS STRONG IN ENGINEERING

Students who want to study applied science and engineering, but not at a tech school, have many options. Virtually every school that calls itself a research university (including most of North America's most distinguished institutions) has a high-quality engineering school or department.

- Boston University
- Brown University
- Bucknell University
- Columbia University
- Cornell University
- Dartmouth College

- Duke University
- Harvard University
- Johns Hopkins University
- McGill University
- Michigan State University
- New York University-Polytechnic
- North Carolina State University
- Northwestern University
- Penn State University
- Princeton University
- Queen's University
- Rice University

- Stanford University
- Tufts University
- Tulane University
- University of British Columbia
- University of California at Berkeley
- University of California at Davis
- University of California at Irvine
- University of California at Los Angeles
- University of California at San Diego
- University of Florida
- University of Illinois
- University of Maryland
- University of Michigan
- University of Minnesota
- University of Notre Dame
- University of Pennsylvania
- University of Pittsburgh
- University of Rochester
- University of Southern California
- University of Texas
- University of Toronto
- University of Virginia
- University of Washington
- University of Wisconsin
- Vanderbilt University
- Washington University
- Yale University

some who helped build the Golden Gate Bridge and the Hoover Dam; devised ways to bring water to Central California's agricultural lands; and turned Silicon Valley into the world's leading technology incubator. Berkeley's engineering programs enroll nearly 3,000 undergraduates and 1,500 graduate students. Berkeley also operates nearly forty research centers, including the Lawrence Berkeley National Laboratory, the Center for Entrepreneurship and Technology, and the Berkeley Wireless Research Center.

Undergraduate engineering programs at UC–Berkeley:

- Bioengineering
- Chemical Engineering
- Civil and Environmental Engineering
- Electrical Engineering and Computer Sciences
- Industrial Engineering and Operations Research
- Materials Science and Engineering
- Mechanical Engineering
- Nuclear Engineering

Undergraduate engineering science programs at UC–Berkeley:

- Computational Engineering Science
- Engineering Mathematics and Statistics
- Engineering Physics
- Environmental Engineering Science

UNIVERSITY OF CALIFORNIA– BERKELEY—COLLEGE OF ENGINEERING

By every measure of quality, UC–Berkeley's College of Engineering ranks among the five best in the United States. Berkeley offers eight engineering options and four programs in engineering sciences. Berkeley trains its engineers to be innovators. Over the years, Berkeley has graduated more than 50,000 engineers, including

UNIVERSITY OF MICHIGAN— COLLEGE OF ENGINEERING

The College of Engineering at Michigan's flagship campus in Ann Arbor encourages its students to span disciplines to gain competencies beyond engineering. The Michigan approach integrates an entrepreneurial mind-set across the engineering curriculum, encourages international experiences, and promotes real-world problem solving in multidisciplinary teams. Michigan offers seventeen different engineering majors. One standout feature of engineering at Michigan is the opportunity to earn dual or combined degrees in art and design, business, and music. Also, Michigan's School of Music, Theater, and Dance offers a BS degree in sound engineering. Supporting the engineering college are more than forty laboratories and centers focused on areas such as air pollution monitoring, automotive research, autonomous underwater vehicles, biomedical optics, solar and thermal energy, sustainable technology, and space and environment modeling.

Undergraduate engineering programs at Michigan:

- Aerospace Engineering
- Biomedical Engineering
- Chemical Engineering
- Civil Engineering
- Computer Engineering
- Earth System Science and Engineering
- Electrical EngineeringEngineering Physics
- Industrial and Operations Engineering
- Materials Science and Engineering
- Mechanical Engineering
- Naval Architecture and Marine Engineering
- Nuclear Engineering and Radiological Sciences
- Sound Engineering
- BBA Business/BS Engineering
- Combined Degree in Art and Design and Engineering
- Combined Degree in Music and Engineering

NORTHWESTERN UNIVERSITY— MCCORMICK SCHOOL OF ENGINEERING

Northwestern seeks to educate whole-brained engineers who think and work across disciplines. All Northwestern engineering students start with two first-year courses—Engineering Design and Communications and Engineering Analysis—that introduce students to team-based, real-world design problems; develop writing and presentation skills; and emphasize the fundamentals of science that every engineer needs to master. Beyond the classroom, Northwestern offers a five-year co-op program that integrates on-the-job experience with formal academic study.

Undergraduate engineering programs at Northwestern:

- Biomedical Engineering
- Chemical Engineering
- Civil Engineering
- Computer Engineering
- Electrical Engineering
- Environmental Engineering
- Industrial Engineering
- Manufacturing and Design Engineering
- Materials Science and Engineering
- Mechanical Engineering

STANFORD UNIVERSITY—SCHOOL OF ENGINEERING

Engineering at Stanford is geared toward imagining the future. Stanford students and faculty work to push the frontiers of engineering, science, and technology and seek solutions to global problems. Stanford takes a multidimensional approach to engineering, one that has fostered the culture of entrepreneurship and new product development that brought the world start-ups such as Google and Hewlett Packard. Although Stanford has fifteen engineering and technology-related programs, the engineering school teaches students from day one that discovery exists at the intersection of disciplines. Thus, a central tenet of engineering at Stanford is the belief that the future has no walls, as exemplified by the four multidisciplinary areas Stanford engineering has identified for long-term focus: bioengineering; environment and energy; information technology; and nanoscience and nanotechnology.

One innovative aspect of Stanford's engineering school is its interdisciplinary programs. Examples include architectural design—offered by the department of civil and environmental engineering; engineering physics; and product design. An emphasis on design permeates Stanford's approach to engineering. The Stanford Design Program, for example, is world renowned for its innovative approach to weaving design into the engineering curriculum.

Undergraduate engineering programs at Stanford:

- Aeronautics and Astronautics
- Bioengineering
- Chemical Engineering
- Civil and Environmental Engineering
- Electrical Engineering
- Management Science and Engineering
- Materials Science and Engineering
- Mechanical Engineering

TUFTS UNIVERSITY—SCHOOL OF ENGINEERING

Tufts University offers the students in its engineering school a dozen different study opportunities. In addition to the traditional, specialized engineering majors geared toward professional licensure, Tufts offers less specialized majors such as engineering and architectural studies, engineering health, engineering psychology, engineering physics, and engineering science. For students looking for lessons in project leadership, Tufts provides an engineering management minor. That Tufts has dental, medical, and veterinary schools expands the study and research opportunities available to biomedical engineering students.

Undergraduate engineering programs at Tufts:

- Biomedical Engineering
- Chemical Engineering
- Civil Engineering
- Computer Engineering
- Electrical Engineering
- Environmental Engineering
- Engineering—Architectural Studies
  Engineering—Environmental Health
  Engineering Physics
  Engineering Psychology
  Engineering Science
  Mechanical Engineering

TOP-RANKED ENGINEERING PROGRAMS BY SPECIALTY

The following are alphabetically ordered lists of the ten strongest departments in selected engineering specialties. Like all rankings, there is an element of subjectivity, but even so the lists reflect the collected wisdom of the numerous rankings of undergraduate and graduate programs that can be found online and in the media, the opinions of engineering faculty and deans at highly respected institutions, and the reputations that programs command among employers. One curious discovery we made while researching and compiling these ratings was that in a number of cases, the rankings touted in various media sometimes rate schools highly in specialties that do not even exist as an undergraduate major at that university. The specialty rankings that follow went through thorough checking and rechecking to avoid such errors.

AEROSPACE/AERONAUTICAL/ASTRONAUTICAL ENGINEERING

Embry Riddle University
Georgia Institute of Technology
University of Illinois
University of Maryland
Massachusetts Institute of Technology
University of Michigan
Princeton University
Purdue University
University of Southern California
University of Texas at Austin

AGRICULTURAL/BIOLOGICAL ENGINEERING

University of California at Davis
Cornell University
University of Florida
University of Illinois
Iowa State University
North Carolina State University
Ohio State University
Penn State University
Purdue University
Texas A&M University

BIOMEDICAL/BIOSCIENCES ENGINEERING

Boston University
University of California at San Diego
Carnegie Mellon University
Georgia Institute of Technology
Duke University
Johns Hopkins University
Massachusetts Institute of Technology
University of Michigan
University of Texas at Austin
Washington University

CHEMICAL ENGINEERING

California Institute of Technology
University of California at Berkeley
University of California at Santa Barbara
University of Delaware
Massachusetts Institute of Technology
University of Minnesota
Princeton University
Stanford University
University of Texas at Austin
University of Wisconsin

CIVIL ENGINEERING

University of California at Berkeley
Cornell University
Georgia Institute of Technology
University of Illinois
Massachusetts Institute of Technology
University of Michigan
Purdue University
Stanford University
University of Texas at Austin
Virginia Polytechnic and State University

ELECTRICAL ENGINEERING

California Institute of Technology
University of California at Berkeley
Carnegie Mellon University
Cornell University
Georgia Institute of Technology
University of Illinois
Massachusetts Institute of Technology
University of Michigan
Purdue University
Stanford University

ENVIRONMENTAL ENGINEERING

University of Colorado Boulder
Cornell University
University of Florida
Georgia Institute of Technology
Johns Hopkins University
Massachusetts Institute of Technology
University of Michigan

Northwestern University
Stanford University
Yale University

INDUSTRIAL/SYSTEMS ENGINEERING

University of California at Berkeley
Georgia Institute of Technology
University of Michigan
Northwestern University
Ohio State University
Penn State University
Purdue University
Texas A&M University
Virginia Polytechnic and State University
University of Wisconsin

MATERIALS SCIENCE AND ENGINEERING

University of California at Berkeley
Carnegie Mellon University
Cornell University
University of Florida
Georgia Institute of Technology
University of Illinois
Massachusetts Institute of Technology
University of Michigan

Northwestern University
Stanford University

MECHANICAL ENGINEERING

California Institute of Technology
University of California at Berkeley
Cornell University
Georgia Institute of Technology
University of Illinois
Massachusetts Institute of Technology
University of Michigan
Purdue University
Rose Hulman Institute of Technology
Stanford University

NUCLEAR ENGINEERING

University of California at Berkeley
University of Illinois
Massachusetts Institute of Technology
University of Michigan
North Carolina State University
Penn State University
Purdue University
University of Tennessee
Texas A&M University
University of Wisconsin

UNUSUAL ENGINEERING SPECIALTIES AND WHERE TO FIND THEM

Audio Engineering. At the **University of Miami**, the College of Engineering collaborates with the Frost School of Music to offer a BS degree in audio engineering. Students acquire skill in areas such as acoustics, digital audio, production, and recording.

Ceramic Engineering. Tucked in a corner of western New York is the leading US ceramic engineering program. Over one-third of the ceramic engineers in the United States have at least one degree from **Alfred University**. The ceramic engineering major is part of the New York State College of Ceramics at Alfred University, which means that students in the program pay New York State (in-state and out-of-state) tuition rates. Because ceramics play a pivotal role in electronics, transportation, defense, and environmental technologies, Alfred ceramic engineering graduates are highly sought after by companies across the globe.

Construction Engineering. A number of engineering schools and departments offer degree programs in construction engineering. Top programs are found at **Iowa State University**, **Oregon State University,** and **Purdue University**. Graduates of Purdue's BS in Construction Engineering and Management program have had a 100 percent job placement rate for seventeen consecutive years.

Cyber Engineering. **Louisiana Tech University** offers this major, which blends together courses in computer science, electrical engineering, math, and physics.

Electronic Materials Engineering. Students at the **University of California at Davis** can major in this specialty as preparation for fields related to integrated circuit manufacturing, catalyst production, polymer synthesis, and the fabrication of bioreactive materials.

Energy Engineering. Within its Department of Energy and Mining Engineering, **Penn State University** offers concentrations in energy engineering and energy business and finance.

Entertainment Engineering and Design. Students in the Howard Hughes College of Engineering at the **University of Nevada, Las Vegas** can elect a BS track that prepares them for engineering positions in the entertainment industry and have internships along the way at places such as Cirque du Soleil.

Fire Engineering. Leading programs are found at **Worcester Polytechnic Institute**, the **University of Cincinnati**, and the **University of Maryland**. Cincinnati offers a degree program in fire and safety engineering technology and a minor in fire service technology. Maryland has a BS degree program in fire protection engineering. Worcester Polytechnic Institute's Fire Science Laboratory is a learning resource for its BS in Fire Protection Engineering program.

Glass Engineering. The nation's top program in glass engineering is at **Alfred University**. In fact, Alfred offers the only US undergraduate program in glass engineering science. Graduates of the program have plentiful job opportunities developing energy-efficient windows, fiber optics, and advanced medical devices.

Geoengineering. Students at the **University of Minnesota** can choose to major in geoengineering, a department closely related to civil engineering. Geoengineers plan and analyze tunnels and dams as well as water and waste systems.

Human-Centered Design and Engineering. Students interested in investigating how people and communities interact with technical systems can get a BS degree in this specialty at the **University of Washington** in Seattle.

Intelligent Systems Engineering. Starting in 2016, students will be able to pursue this BS degree specialty at **Indiana University.**

Mining and Materials Engineering. A number of engineering schools offer degree programs in mining engineering. With 170 undergraduates and twenty graduate students, the Department of Mining and Materials Engineering at **Virginia Tech** is one of the largest in the United States.

Nano Engineering. **University of California at San Diego** students can pursue a BS in nanoengineering. Nanoengineering BS programs are also found at **SUNY Polytechnic Institute** and **Louisiana Tech University**.

Natural Gas Engineering. Frequently, natural gas engineering is a specialty offered through petroleum engineering degree programs. But **Texas A&M at Kingsville** offers a rare standalone BS program in natural gas engineering.

Naval Architecture and Marine Engineering. Students interested in this field will want to know about the **Webb Institute** on New York's Long Island Sound. The Webb Institute is a specialized institution where all eighty-five of its students study tuition-free and major in the only program offered (naval architecture and marine engineering). Naval architecture and marine engineering are interdisciplinary fields with strong connections to civil, electrical, mechanical, and systems engineering. Naval architects and marine engineers design, build, and analyze all the systems on which floating vessels and ocean structures depend. Through Webb's Winter Work Term, students are required to work (for pay) in the marine industry. Freshmen go to work in shipyards, sophomores go to sea as cadets/observers, and juniors and seniors pursue internships in design and engineering. Demand for naval architects and marine engineers exceeds the supply, and because Webb offers a standout education, its graduates get multiple job offers and high starting salaries.

Naval Engineering. **Stevens Institute of Technology** has a standout program in naval engineering. Students in the program learn the skills needed to design, build, and maintain ships and other seafaring structures.

Ocean Engineering. Among the universities that offer degrees in ocean engineering are **MIT**, **Texas A&M**, and **Virginia Tech**. One of the more extensive ocean engineering programs is found at the **University of Rhode Island**. The Ocean Engineering Department at Rhode Island resides on its Narragansett Bay campus and offers six areas of specialization: ocean instrumentation and seafloor mapping, underwater acoustics and data analysis, marine hydrodynamics and water-wave mechanics, coastal and near-shore modeling, marine geomechanics, and coastal and offshore structures. In addition to its BS in ocean engineering program, **Virginia Tech** offers a minor in naval engineering.

Optical Science and Engineering. Students at the **University of California at Davis** and **Rose Hulman Institute of Technology** can major in this specialty. Optical science and engineering students at Davis and Rose Hulman work on developing advanced lasers, fiber optic cables,

new surgical techniques, and missile guidance systems.

Packaging Engineering. **Rutgers University** was the first US institution to offer a packaging degree in its school of engineering. Packaging engineering at Rutgers is widely seen as the leading program in the field. Graduates are highly sought after by companies, often having multiple job offers that include signing bonuses. Packaging engineering as a discipline draws heavily on chemical, industrial, materials, and mechanical engineering.

Petroleum Engineering. There are many petroleum engineering degree programs in the United States beyond the one at the **Colorado School of Mines**. Standout programs tend to be found at universities in or near the oil-rich regions of the United States. Leading petroleum engineering degree programs are found at **Louisiana State University**, **Oklahoma State University**, **University of Oklahoma**, **Penn State University**, **Texas A&M University**, **Texas Tech University**, the **University of Texas** (frequently ranked the top program in the country), the **University of Tulsa**, and the **University of Wyoming**.

Radiological Health Engineering. With its radiological health engineering major, **Texas A&M** offers a specialty that prepares students to use radiation in medical and industrial settings.

Software Engineering. Within its Department of Electrical and Computer Engineering, **McGill University** in Montreal offers a major in software engineering. The software engineering program at **Iowa State University** is an interdisciplinary major that draws upon computer science and electrical and computer engineering.

Theme Park Engineering. **California State University at Long Beach** offers this BS program to prepare students to work as engineers in amusement facilities or theme parks. The core of the program consists of courses in electrical engineering with additional work in civil and mechanical engineering.

Wood, Forest, and Paper Engineering. The Department of Forest Biomaterials at **North Carolina State University** offers BS programs in paper science and engineering and in wood products manufacturing and engineering. The **State University of New York College of Environmental Science and Forestry** (SUNY-ESF) offers BS programs in forest engineering and wood products engineering. **Oregon State University**'s College of Forestry's Wood Science and Engineering offers a standalone degree program in forest engineering, a dual major linking forest engineering to civil engineering, and a major in renewable materials.

3-2 ENGINEERING PROGRAMS

A number of liberal arts colleges and universities offer their students the opportunity to combine a BA in an arts and sciences subject with a BS in engineering. These five-year BA/BS options are called 3-2 programs because in most cases students study math or one of the sciences (often physics) for three years at their original institution and then follow with two years studying engineering at the partner university. Engineering schools at universities such as Columbia welcome 3-2 students and often send representatives to conduct information sessions at the partner liberal arts colleges. Some of the other engineering schools that operate 3-2 programs include California Institute of Technology, Case Western Reserve University, Dartmouth College, Duke University, Northwestern University, Rensselaer Polytechnic Institute, Vanderbilt University, and Washington University. **Columbia University**, for example, has approximately one hundred 3-2 partners, some of which are listed below.

- Bard College
- Barnard College
- Bates College
- Beloit College
- Bowdoin College
- Brandeis University
- Carleton College
- Claremont McKenna College
- Colgate University
- Davidson College
- Dickinson College
- Earlham College
- Elon University
- Fordham University
- Georgetown University
- Grinnell College
- Hendrix College
- Lawrence University
- Middlebury College
- Morehouse College
- Oberlin College
- Occidental College
- Pitzer College
- Providence College
- Reed College
- University of Richmond
- Sarah Lawrence College
- Spelman College
- Williams College
- College of William and Mary

Washington University in St. Louis has more than eighty affiliates for its 3-2 engineering program. Participating schools include the following:

- Allegheny College
- Bates College
- Beloit College
- Berea College
- Carleton College
- Connecticut College
- Davidson College
- Denison University
- DePauw University
- Drake University
- Franklin and Marshall College
- Grinnell College
- Hamilton College
- Kalamazoo College
- Kenyon College
- Lewis and Clark College
- Macalester College
- Oberlin College
- Pomona College
- Rhodes College
- St. Olaf College
- University of the South (Sewanee)
- Whitman College

The **California Institute of Technology** has a relatively small number of 3-2 engineering partners. Getting into the Caltech 3-2 program is more difficult than the typical 3-2 admission process, where the primary hurdle is meeting the prerequisite course requirements and securing the backing of the 3-2 advisory committee at the student's liberal arts institution. Generally, the partner engineering school will admit all or nearly all of the 3-2 candidates endorsed by the affiliate liberal arts college. Caltech, on the other hand, applies its own admission standards when reviewing recommended candidates, resulting in frequent denial decisions. So although Caltech has the following 3-2 partners, students interested in those schools should not expect that admission to the program will be automatic.

- Bowdoin College
- Bryn Mawr College
- Grinnell College
- Haverford College
- Mount Holyoke College
- Oberlin College
- Occidental College
- Ohio Wesleyan University
- Pomona College
- Reed College
- Spelman College
- Wesleyan University
- Whitman College

STUDYING ENGINEERING AT LIBERAL ARTS COLLEGES

For a less specialized approach to engineering, students may want to go the liberal arts route, where engineering departments exist alongside programs in English, history, philosophy, and religion. A handful of liberal arts colleges offer engineering as a major. Some keep the engineering program very general. For example at Smith College, Swarthmore College, Trinity College, and Trinity University, students can study engineering in programs that lead to BA or BS degrees in engineering, engineering science, or engineering arts. At Washington and Lee University, students can major in physics and engineering. At some other liberal arts colleges, the programs are more specialized. For example, Bucknell University offers BS programs in biomedical, chemical, civil, computer, electrical, environmental, and mechanical engineering. In addition to a generalized program in engineering studies, Lafayette College offers BS degree programs in chemical, civil, electrical/computer, and mechanical engineering. Similarly, Union College in Schenectady, New York, has BS programs in bioengineering, computer engineering, electrical engineering, and mechanical engineering. Compared to their counterparts at tech schools, engineering students at liberal arts colleges are more likely to take a sampling (or perhaps even a required core) of courses from the arts, humanities, and social sciences. That way the liberal arts engineering student can keep options open to other career possibilities in case interest in engineering wanes. Regardless of the type of college where they get earned, engineering degrees generally open doors to high-paying first jobs.

COLLEGES ORGANIZED AROUND GENDER, ETHNICITY, OR RACE

SINGLE-SEX COLLEGES

Most of the notable colleges in America were originally single-sex institutions. On the East Coast and in the South, in particular, men went to men's colleges, such as Amherst, Harvard, Johns Hopkins, and the University of North Carolina at Chapel Hill. Women went to women's colleges, such as Bryn Mawr, Connecticut College for Women, Hollins, and Vassar. By the mid-1970s, of the colleges just named, only Bryn Mawr and Hollins were still single sex. Across America, coeducation had taken hold. By the late 1980s, even holdouts such as Davidson and Haverford had admitted women, and Goucher and Wheaton (Massachusetts) had admitted men. Over the next two decades, Randolph Macon Women's College would admit men and become Randolph College, and Wells College would also leave the ranks of women's colleges.

Women's colleges continue to stand out as a vital and recognizable part of the landscape of higher education opportunities available to prospective students. Nearly everyone has heard of famous and prestigious women's colleges such as Smith and Wellesley. On the other hand, the men's college has nearly become a historical footnote. In the world of 2013, there are less than a handful of men's colleges left and most people cannot name any of them. Dig a little deeper and you will discover that three men's colleges stand out. Hampden-Sydney College, located in the foothills of Virginia, is steeped in the southern gentleman tradition. Morehouse College in Atlanta seeks to develop young black men into leaders. Wabash College in Indiana is a liberal arts college that has promoted itself with the slogan, Boys Will Be Boys, Men Go to Wabash. Each of these men's colleges is proud of its traditions and distinctive identity.

Hampden-Sydney, Morehouse, and Wabash, although not quite throwbacks to the past, have held to tradition and resisted the trend to coeducation at the same time that those historical bastions of masculinity, the military academies, have admitted women. All of the federal and state military academies have been coeducational for at least two decades, but at them men continue to outnumber women by a large ratio, which causes some people to think of them as de facto men's colleges. Military academies are profiled in another chapter. For now we concentrate on the last remaining true men's colleges: Hampden-Sydney, Morehouse, and Wabash.

MEN'S COLLEGES

HAMPDEN-SYDNEY COLLEGE— HAMPDEN-SYDNEY, VIRGINIA

1,105 undergraduates

Small-town campus

Student-faculty ratio of eleven to one

Most popular majors: biology, business, economics, English, history, political science, psychology

Average high school GPA: 3.4/4.0

Middle 50 percent on SAT: 1020–1220; ACT: 21–27

55 percent admitted

Notable alumni: William Henry Harrison (ninth president of the United States), Maurice Jones (Rhodes Scholar and publisher of the *Virginia Pilot*), Ed Kelley (cofounder of Jiffy Lube), Paul Trible Jr. (former US senator, president of Christopher Newport University)

MOREHOUSE COLLEGE—ATLANTA, GEORGIA

2,170 undergraduates

Urban campus

Most popular majors: biology, business administration, economics, English, political science, psychology, sociology (The Morehouse School of Medicine is a separate institution.)

Student-faculty ratio of twelve to one

Exchange programs with Claremont McKenna College, Davidson College, New York University, Pitzer College, Saint John's University, Stanford University, University of California at San Diego, Vassar College

Average high school GPA: 3.2/4.0

Middle 50 percent on SAT: 900–1100; ACT: 18–24

67 percent admitted

Notable alumni: Herman Cain (founder of Godfather's Pizza, Republican presidential candidate), Samuel L. Jackson (actor), Martin Luther King Jr., Spike Lee (filmmaker), Edwin Moses (Olympic gold medalist)

WABASH COLLEGE— CRAWFORDSVILLE, INDIANA

902 undergraduates

Small-town campus—forty-five miles from Indianapolis

Student-faculty ratio of eleven to one

Most popular majors: biology, economics, English, history, philosophy, psychology, religion

Average high school GPA: 3.7/4.0

Middle 50 percent on SAT: 1030–1250; ACT: 22–28

70 percent admitted

75 percent of alumni enter graduate school within five years of graduating.

Notable alumni: Robert Allen (former CEO of AT&T), John Bachmann (former CEO of Edward Jones), Pete Metzelaars (former NFL player)

For the time being, there is a fourth men's college: Deep Springs. Located on the border of California and Nevada, Deep Springs College has been, since 1917, a tuition-free, two-year college where twenty-six men live and work on a ranch and study a great books–centered liberal arts curriculum. In September 2011, the trustees of Deep Springs voted to admit women. Soon after that vote, Deep Springs found itself in court defending against a lawsuit challenging coeducation. Until the legal case gets resolved, Deep Springs will remain all male. We have listed Deep Springs under men's colleges due to its long heritage as one and the possibility that it may remain one.

DEEP SPRINGS COLLEGE—DYER, NEVADA

26 undergraduates

Rural ranch campus

Free tuition, room, and board

Awards associate of arts (AA) degree

Three pillars: academics, labor, self-governance

6–15 percent admitted

Middle 50 percent on SAT: 1400–1560

Graduates transfer to: Harvard (16 percent), University of Chicago (13 percent), Brown (7 percent), Yale (7 percent), rest to UC–Berkeley, Columbia, Cornell, Oxford, Stanford, and so on.

Two-thirds of alumni go to graduate school—50 percent earn doctorates.

Notable alumni: Raymond Jeanloz (MacArthur "genius grant" Fellow), Erik Mueggler (MacArthur "genius grant" Fellow)

WOMEN'S COLLEGES

Women's colleges, by contrast, are determined not to be dismissed as anachronisms. There are roughly fifty stand-alone women's colleges operating in the United States. A promotional organization, called the Women's College Coalition, exists to make the case for the necessity of single-sex higher education for young women. The Women's College Coalition maintains a website (http://www.womenscolleges.org/) that provides research findings on the benefits of women's colleges, profiles of successful women's college graduates, and web links to information on the more than fifty member colleges. That five of the seven oldest and most famous women's colleges have not become coeducational indicates that single-sex education for women is still a viable (and some would say vital) option. Of the original Seven Sister colleges (Barnard, Bryn Mawr, Mount Holyoke, Radcliffe, Smith, Wellesley, and Vassar), only Radcliffe (which was absorbed into Harvard) and Vassar are no longer women's colleges.

Before coeducation, the Seven Sister colleges defined the gold standard for women's education. The sisters came to be famous because they were the first colleges to attempt to provide women with an education of the same high quality as that offered to men by the Ivy League. Each of the original Seven Sisters has a strong claim to quality and prestige. But to see the five remaining sisters as the only excellent choices for women seeking a single-sex environment would be to take a shortsighted and geographically restricted view. In addition to the remaining five all-female sister colleges, there are at least three women's colleges located beyond the Northeast with a strong claim on being the replacements for Radcliffe and Vassar. Those three are Agnes Scott College near Atlanta, Scripps College in Greater Los Angeles, and Spelman College in Atlanta. The admissions standards and academic quality at Scripps, for example, arguably surpass remaining Seven Sister colleges, such as Mount Holyoke and Smith.

In alphabetical order, here is a list of the eight institutions that we believe are the top women's colleges in the United States.

- Agnes Scott College—Decatur, Georgia
- Barnard College—New York, New York
- Bryn Mawr College—Bryn Mawr, Pennsylvania
- Mount Holyoke College—South Hadley, Massachusetts
- Scripps College—Claremont, California
- Smith College—Northampton, Massachusetts
- Spelman College—Atlanta, Georgia
- Wellesley College—Wellesley, Massachusetts

There are a handful of women's colleges a tier below.

- Converse College—Spartanburg, South Carolina
- Hollins University—Roanoke, Virginia
- Mary Baldwin College—Staunton, Virginia
- Mills College—Oakland, California

- Saint Mary's College—Notre Dame, Indiana
- Simmons College—Boston, Massachusetts

Women's colleges make compelling arguments for the benefits of single-sex education. Research shows that students who attend all-women's colleges gain self-confidence; are more likely to pursue undergraduate study in math, science, and engineering (areas in which women are underrepresented); go on to graduate and professional study; feel encouraged to participate in class discussions; and engage in research projects under the direction of faculty mentors. Women's college graduates are disproportionately represented among achievers and path-breakers, especially when the list of notables includes women who attended now coeducational colleges (such as Vassar and Wheaton) when those institutions were for women only.

Some young women seek all the benefits of a women's college but want to live and learn in an atmosphere that feels more coordinate than separate. Historically, there were many coordinate colleges for women, often housed on (or alongside) the men's main campus; note that at these institutions, the main or original campus was always considered first and foremost a men's college. Examples included Jackson College of Tufts University, Flora Stone Mather College of Western Reserve University (now Case Western Reserve University), Pembroke College of Brown University, Kirkland College of Hamilton College, and Sophie Newcomb College of Tulane University. Over the years, these coordinate colleges got absorbed into the parent men's college. One exception is the former female counterpart to Hobart College (William Smith College): it is still recognized in the name of the coeducational Hobart and William Smith Colleges. During their era, the coordinate colleges gave women the opportunity to study in a single-sex environment while experiencing a coeducational social life. The remaining women's colleges are stand-alone institutions, like Mount Holyoke and Smith, where there are opportunities for cross registration options with neighboring coeducational colleges.

At a few women's colleges, the students have, what could be argued, is the best of both worlds: a women's college campus alongside, or embedded within, a coeducational environment. Perhaps the best example of this is Scripps College in Southern California. The Scripps campus is adjacent to four other undergraduate Claremont Colleges, each of which is a coeducational institution. The colleges in the Claremont consortium share a centrally located library and some dining facilities. Scripps students can take courses at any of the other Claremont Colleges: Claremont McKenna, Harvey Mudd, Pitzer, and Pomona. Also within walking distance of the Scripps campus are two coeducational graduate-level institutions: Claremont Graduate University and the Keck Graduate Institute for the Applied Life Sciences. Scripps students have the opportunity to experience a small women's college (nearly a thousand students) while also enjoying the university-like features of a college consortium that knits together more than six thousand students.

All-female Spelman College sits alongside all-male Morehouse College within the Atlanta University Center, a contiguous consortium of historically black institutions. The Atlanta University Center (AUC) consists of the ten thousand students at Spelman, Morehouse, Clark Atlanta University, and the Morehouse School of Medicine. Cross registration opportunities within the AUC make day-to-day life at Spelman as coeducational as its 2,290 students want it to be. Through the AUC, Spelman students have access to 3-2 engineering programs at Georgia Tech and to early entry into nursing programs at Emory University. In New York City, Barnard College is a women's college located next door to, and technically within, Columbia University. At

Barnard, having a coeducational classroom and social experience, as at Scripps and Spelman, is as easy as crossing the street.

BARNARD COLLEGE—NEW YORK, NEW YORK

2,489 undergraduates

Urban campus located contiguous to Columbia University

Most popular majors: American studies, anthropology, art history, Asian studies, economics, English, history, neuroscience, political science, psychology

Average high school GPA: 3.9/4.0

Middle 50 percent on SAT: 1240–1440; ACT: 28–32

21 percent admitted

Notable alumnae: Laurie Anderson (musician), Hortense Calisher (writer), Greta Gerwig (actress), Lauren Graham (actress), Zora Neale Hurston (writer), Jhumpa Lahiri (writer), Margaret Mead (anthropologist), Cynthia Nixon (actress), Anna Quindlen (author, columnist), Joan Rivers (comedian), Martha Stewart, Twyla Tharp (dancer/choreographer), Suzanne Vega (musician)

SCRIPPS COLLEGE—CLAREMONT, CALIFORNIA

979 undergraduates

Small-town campus located alongside Claremont McKenna College, Harvey Mudd College, Pitzer College, Pomona College, Claremont Graduate University, and Keck Graduate Institute (totaling 6,300 students)

Most popular majors: biology, English, fine arts, math, political science, psychology

Average high school GPA: 3.9/4.0

Middle 50 percent: SAT: 1260–1460; ACT: 28–33

27 percent admitted

Notable alumnae: Serena Altschul (broadcast journalist for MTV, CNN, and CBS News), Gabrielle Giffords (former US representative, Arizona)

SPELMAN COLLEGE—ATLANTA, GEORGIA

2,129 undergraduates

Urban campus located alongside Clark Atlanta University, Morehouse College, and Morehouse School of Medicine (total of 10,000 students)

Most popular majors: biology, economics, education, English, political science, psychology

Average high school GPA: 3.6/4.0

Middle 50 percent on SAT: 910–1030; ACT: 18–21

41 percent admitted

Notable alumnae: Marian Wright Edelman (founder of the Children's Defense Fund), Keshia Knight Pulliam (Rudy on *The Cosby Show*), Bernice Johnson Reagon (founder of Sweet Honey in the Rock), Shaun Robinson (co-anchor *Access Hollywood*)

At Bryn Mawr College in suburban Philadelphia, taking courses at nearby coeducational Haverford College is relatively easy but does require more than crossing the street. To help students make the two-mile trip between the campuses, a bus runs around the clock. Because Bryn Mawr and Haverford have pooled their academic resources—enabling students to major or minor in a course of study offered at the other campus—most of the classes taken by Bryn Mawr students have both women and men in them. Certain administrative offices, such as career services, are also shared by the two campuses, and Bryn Mawr's graduate division (offering master's and doctoral study options) is coeducational. Students at Bryn Mawr can also take courses at the University of Pennsylvania and Swarthmore, but the shuttle to Swarthmore takes at least twenty to thirty minutes, and getting to Penn by SEPTA train or bus can take up to an hour. Although the campuses are not geographically contiguous, as they are at Barnard, Scripps, and Spelman, the high degree of cooperation with Haverford gives the women who attend Bryn Mawr all the special benefits of a historically significant women's college while also providing ample opportunity to have something approximating a coeducational experience.

Within Massachusetts' Pioneer Valley, there are five colleges (Amherst, Hampshire, Mount Holyoke, Smith, and the University of Massachusetts—totaling twenty-five thousand students) in a consortium that enables students to take courses at any of the member campuses. A bus runs from campus to campus more or less around the clock. The Five College Consortium provides the women at Mount Holyoke and Smith opportunities to have vestiges of a coeducational academic and social experience. But unlike at Barnard, Scripps, and Spelman, where those opportunities are literally around the next corner, students at Mount Holyoke and Smith must make an effort to integrate into the Five College Consortium. For that reason, prospective students looking at Mount Holyoke and Smith need to consider the situation carefully. Unless a student has a car, getting from Mount Holyoke or Smith to the campuses of Amherst, Hampshire, and UMass involves a bus trip of eight to ten miles, which during the best weather and traffic conditions can take between thirty to forty-five minutes. Add another fifteen minutes per trip during the snowy winter months and you can see why the benefits of the Five College Consortium can be more difficult to derive for

Mount Holyoke and Smith students in comparison to the situation at Barnard, Bryn Mawr, Scripps, and Spelman. Be prepared also for the admissions offices in the Five College Consortium to oversell the ease of transit between the campuses and overstate the everyday nature of the collaborative experience. There is no doubt that the Five College Consortium provides a rich and dynamic array of opportunities to the students at each of the participating institutions. But women considering Smith and Mount Holyoke should not expect that their day-in and day-out life will closely approximate the nearly coeducational experience of attending Barnard, Scripps, Spelman, and even Bryn Mawr.

BRYN MAWR COLLEGE—BRYN MAWR, PENNSYLVANIA

1,700 students; (1,300 undergraduates)

Suburban location

Cross registration with Haverford College, University of Pennsylvania, and Swarthmore College expands courses available to five thousand.

Graduate programs are coed.

Most popular majors: anthropology, biology, economics, English, math, political science, psychology

Average high school GPA: 3.7/4.0

Middle 50 percent on SAT: 1210–1470; ACT 27–32

40 percent admitted

Notable alumnae: Drew Gilpin Faust (president of Harvard University), Hanna Holborn Gray (first woman president of the University of Chicago), Edith Hamilton (classics scholar), Katharine Hepburn (actress), Marianne Moore (poet), Alice Rivlin (first director of the Congressional Budget Office)

MOUNT HOLYOKE COLLEGE— SOUTH HADLEY, MASSACHUSETTS

2,183 undergraduates

Small-town location

Member of Five College Consortium, enabling cross registration with Amherst College, Hampshire College, University of Massachusetts, and Smith College

Most popular majors: anthropology, art history, biology, economics, English, environmental science, history, international relations, political science, psychology

The Frances Perkins Program (for women beyond the traditional college age) provides generous financial aid.

Average high school GPA: 3.7/4.0

Standardized tests are optional.

Middle 50 percent on SAT: 1210–1460; ACT: 27–31

47 percent admitted

Notable alumnae: Elaine Chao (former secretary of labor), Carol Higgins Clark (author), Emily Dickinson, Ella Grasso (first woman governor of Connecticut), Mona Sutphen (deputy White House chief of staff for President Obama), Nancy Vickers (former president of Bryn Mawr College).

SMITH COLLEGE—NORTHAMPTON, MASSACHUSETTS

3,033 students (2,606 undergraduates)

Located in one of New England's best college towns

Member of the Five College Consortium, enabling cross registration with Amherst College, Hampshire College, University of Massachusetts, and Mount Holyoke College

One thousand courses in fifty areas of study

Most popular majors: art, biology, economics, English, government, psychology

Special academic programs and resources: Botanic Garden, Center for Amazonian Literature and Culture, Clark Science Center, Picker School of Engineering, Portuguese-Brazilian Studies, Semester in Washington, Smith College Museum of Art

The Ada Comstock Program (for women beyond the traditional college age) provides generous financial aid.

Average high school GPA: 3.9/4.0

Standardized tests are optional

Middle 50 percent: SAT: 1220–1450; ACT: 28–31

43 percent admitted

Notable alumnae: Tammy Baldwin (US senator, Wisconsin), Barbara Bush, Julia Child (chef), Betty Friedan (feminist author), Molly Ivins (columnist, author), Anne Morrow Lindbergh (author, aviator), Margaret Mitchell (author of *Gone with the Wind*), Sylvia Plath (author), Gloria Steinem (feminist), Nancy Reagan, Niki Tsongas (US representative, Massachusetts)

A few other consortia and proximity arrangements might be of interest to students thinking about attending a women's college. For example, Simmons College is located in Boston within a short walk or T ride to Fenway Park, the Museum of Fine Arts, Back Bay clubs, restaurants, shopping, and nearby coeducational colleges and universities such as Berklee College of Music, Boston College, Boston University, Emerson College, Harvard University, Massachusetts Institute of Technology, and Northeastern University. In addition, Simmons is a member of the Colleges of the Fenway, a collection of institutions located side by side that, like the Atlanta University Center and the Claremont Colleges, share facilities and provide cross registration. Other members of the Colleges of the Fenway are Emmanuel College, Massachusetts College of Art and Design, Massachusetts College of Pharmacy and Health Sciences, Wentworth Institute of Technology, and Wheelock College. All combined, the Colleges of the Fenway enroll eleven thousand undergraduates and seven thousand graduate students.

In Minnesota, all-female Saint Benedict's College sits alongside all-male Saint John's University in a town aptly named Collegeville. Together Saint Benedict's and Saint John's (both Catholic institutions) provide a coordinate college experience for four thousand undergraduates. Although the women attend and get a degree from Saint Benedict's, while the men go to Saint John's, the two co-located colleges operate like a coeducational university. A not-too-dissimilar arrangement exists at Saint Mary's College of Indiana, which was the sister college when the Notre Dame was all male. Having Notre Dame as a next-door neighbor enables St. Mary's women to take classes, attend sporting events, participate in social activities, and belong to clubs and organizations simply by crossing the street to the larger campus.

Students at Wellesley College can take courses at Babson College, Brandeis University, MIT, and the Franklin W. Olin College of Engineering. Babson, Brandeis, and Olin are within five to fifteen minutes by car from the Wellesley campus. Wellesley's exchange program with MIT is aided by a bus that links the two campuses—although students should allow forty-five minutes each way and an hour or more if trying to make the trip using MBTA trains. Wellesley students can earn a certificate in engineering or sustainability at Olin, a five-year BA/MA degree in international studies through Brandeis, or a five-year BA/BS with MIT.

There is no doubt that proximity to a city can minimize the isolation that some women fear will accompany the single-sex college experience. A number of women's colleges are located in or near major metropolitan areas, which can make the surrounding city feel like an extension of the campus. Agnes Scott College in Decatur, Georgia, is a short drive from the campus of Emory University and a MARTA train ride away from Georgia Tech. The Agnes Scott curriculum includes options to earn joint degrees in engineering (BA/BS in five years) at Georgia Tech and in nursing (BA/BSN in five years) at Emory. Additionally, Agnes Scott belongs to the Atlanta Regional Council for Higher Education (ARCHE), whose twenty members range from Emory, Morehouse, Oglethorpe University, and Spelman to Georgia Tech. Agnes Scott students can take up to eighteen credits at ARCHE-member colleges in courses that are not offered at ASC. Three other women's colleges offer urban features. Mills College in Oakland is not far from the University of California at Berkeley campus. In fact, periodically Mills has housed male graduate students from Berkeley on its campus. And Trinity Washington University is not far from American University, Georgetown University, George Washington University, and Howard University.

AGNES SCOTT COLLEGE—DECATUR, GEORGIA

998 students (914 undergraduates)

Suburban location—borders Atlanta

Most popular majors: biology, creative writing, economics, English, history, international relations, psychology

Dual degrees with Georgia Tech and Emory University School of Nursing

Exchange program with Mills College, Washington semester in cooperation with American University, BA/MA in art and architecture with Washington University

Average high school GPA: 3.6/4.0

Middle 50 percent: SAT: 1090–1240; ACT: 23–27

68 percent admitted

Notable alumnae: Ila Burdette (Georgia's first female Rhodes Scholar), Katherine Harris (former US representative, Florida), Katherine "Kay" Krill (CEO of Anne Taylor), Jennifer Nettles (lead singer for Sugarland)

SAINT MARY'S COLLEGE—NOTRE DAME, INDIANA

1,479 undergraduates

Suburban campus

Most popular majors: biology, business administration, communication studies, education, history, psychology, social work

Special programs: accounting, communicative disorders, management information systems, statistical and actuarial mathematics, accelerated nursing program

Over 40 percent of students study abroad.

Two-thirds of students engage in volunteer service.

Average high school GPA: 3.7/4.0

Middle 50 percent on SAT: 1030–1240; ACT: 23–29

86 percent admitted

Notable alumnae: Catherine Hicks (actress), Anne Northrup (former US representative, Kentucky), Adriana Trigiani (author and screenwriter)

SIMMONS COLLEGE—BOSTON, MASSACHUSETTS

4,933 students(2,060 undergraduates)

Urban location—member of the Colleges of the Fenway

Most popular majors: biology, communication studies, dietetics, international relations, nursing, physical therapy, psychology

Special programs: number one ranked MBA program for women, top-rated (coeducational) master's programs in library science and social work

Average high school GPA: 3.4/4.0

Middle 50 percent on SAT: 990–1190; ACT: 23–28

49 percent admitted

Notable alumnae: Nnenna Freelon (jazz singer), Gwen Ifill (journalist, moderator of *Washington Week*), Allyson Schwartz (US representative, Pennsylvania), Suzyn Waldman (New York Yankees radio broadcaster)

WELLESLEY COLLEGE—WELLESLEY, MASSACHUSETTS

2,474 undergraduates

Suburban location—twenty minutes from Boston

Bachelor's degree programs in fifty-six departments/majors

Most popular majors: biology, English, economics, art and architecture, international relations, foreign languages, political science, psychology, neuroscience

Special facilities: Child Study Center, Davis Museum and Cultural Center, Madeleine Albright Institute for Global Affairs, Newhouse Center for the Humanities, Wellesley Centers for Women, Wellesley College Botanic Gardens, Whitin Observatory

Cross registration with Babson College, Brandeis University, Franklin W. Olin College of Engineering, and Massachusetts Institute of Technology

Member of Twelve College Exchange (includes Amherst, Dartmouth, Vassar, Williams, etc.)

Exchange programs with Mills College and Spelman College

Davis Degree Program for women beyond the traditional college age

75 percent of students do internships

Average high school GPA: 3.9/4.0

Middle 50 percent: SAT: 1310–1510; ACT: 29–33

29 percent admitted

Notable alumnae: Madeleine Albright (former US secretary of state), Hillary Clinton (former US secretary of state), Nora Ephron (author, screenwriter), Nannerl Keohane (former president of Duke University), Ali McGraw (actress), Cokie Roberts (journalist), Diane Sawyer (journalist), Linda Wertheimer (journalist)

MEN AT WOMEN'S COLLEGES

Although it may seem like a contradiction in terms, there are men enrolled in certain programs at some women's colleges. Such colleges are women's colleges at the undergraduate level but open to men for graduate and certificate programs. Mills College in Oakland is an example. Mills has roughly 1,500 students. The undergraduate population of 900 students at Mills is all women. The nearly 600 students working on certificates and graduate degrees at Mills are a coeducational group. At Smith College all 2,875 of the undergraduates are women, but men are admitted to graduate programs in teaching, fine arts, sciences, and social work. Smith's programs in social work consistently earn top rankings. Similarly, Bryn Mawr is an undergraduate college of 1,300 women, but it has men and women studying for MA, MS, and PhD degrees in the arts and sciences and social work/social policy. Hollins University in Virginia has 775 undergraduate women plus 260 men and women enrolled in MA, MAT, and MFA programs in children's book writing and illustrating, children's literature, creative writing, dance, liberal studies, playwriting, screenwriting and film studies, and teaching. At Trinity Washington University in the District of Columbia, the undergraduate college of arts and sciences is for women only, but its part-time and graduate schools of education and professional studies are both coeducational. The alma mater of former Speaker of the House Nancy Pelosi and former US Secretary of Health and Human Services Kathleen Sebelius, TWU began admitting men to its evening and weekend programs in the 1960s.

Simmons College has a distinctive history as a college that—from its founding just before the turn of the twentieth century—has placed a special emphasis on job preparation for women. Simmons is a women's college for its undergraduates (1,900) but maintains some coeducational graduate programs. With the exception of its highly ranked MBA program for women, all of Simmons's graduate programs are coeducational. The Simmons program in library and information science consistently ranks as one of the best of its kind; for many years, a MLS from Simmons was a calling card for library director positions. For example, the late William Moffett (who opened scholarly access to the Dead Sea Scrolls while he was director of the Huntington Library in San Marino, California) had a MLS from Simmons. Equally well-regarded is Simmons's graduate program in social work, which offers MSW and PhD programs and is also coeducational.

At Mary Baldwin College in Virginia's Shenandoah Mountains, there are approximately eight hundred women studying for a bachelor's degree plus roughly seventy female students in an early-entry Program for the Exceptionally Gifted (PEG). PEG students enter Mary Baldwin for collegiate study as early as after eighth grade. By the time many of their peers are moving into the second or third year of college, most PEG students have graduated or are enrolled in graduate programs. Beyond its full-time undergraduate program, Mary Baldwin has two coeducational divisions that collectively enroll around 1,500 students: the adult part-time degree program and the graduate division. Like many women's colleges, Mary Baldwin offers master's programs in education and teaching. But perhaps the most exciting graduate study option is a program focused on Shakespeare and Renaissance literature and performance. Just a block away from the Mary Baldwin campus, the American Shakespeare Center's Blackfriars Playhouse is the only authentic re-creation of Shakespeare's indoor London theater. The playhouse serves as a classroom and laboratory for Mary Baldwin's Shakespeare studies program. Other examples of colleges where women exclusively comprise the undergraduate student body, but where continuing study and/or graduate programs are coeducational, include Alverno College, a Catholic college in Milwaukee, and Brenau University in Georgia.

CONVERSE COLLEGE—SPARTANBURG, SOUTH CAROLINA

1,153 students (748 undergraduates)

Small city campus

More than thirty-five undergraduate major/minor programs

Special academic programs: accounting, art therapy, business administration, interior design, music education, music therapy

Most popular majors: art, education, English, music, psychology

Converse II Program for women who are twenty-four years of age or older

Graduate programs are coed

Average high school GPA: 3.8/4.0

Middle 50 percent on SAT: 960–1160; ACT: 21–26

52 percent admitted

Notable alumnae: Julia Mood Peterkin (winner of Pulitzer Prize in Literature), Harriet Smith O'Neill (Texas Supreme Court justice)

HOLLINS UNIVERSITY—ROANOKE, VIRGINIA

794 students (613 undergraduates)

Small city campus

Most popular majors: biology, business, communication studies, English, film, fine arts, psychology

Outstanding program in creative writing

Campuses in London and Paris

65 percent of students do internships, and 50 percent study abroad.

Graduate programs are coed.

Average high school GPA: 3.5/4.0

Middle 50 percent on SAT: 970–1220; ACT: 21–27

69 percent admitted

Notable alumnae: Margaret Wise Brown (children's book author), Ann Compton (ABC News

White House correspondent), Annie Dillard (writer), Ellen Malcolm (founder of Emily's List), Sally Mann (photographer), Lee Smith (writer)

MARY BALDWIN COLLEGE— STAUNTON, VIRGINIA

1,742 students (769 undergraduates)

Small-town campus

Most popular majors: business administration, education, history, psychology, sociology

Graduate teacher education

Special programs: master of letters (MLitt) and master of fine arts (MFA) in Shakespeare and performance, coaching and exercise leadership, health-care administration, historic preservation, leadership studies, marketing communication, Renaissance studies, social work, Spencer Center for Civic and Global Engagement

Graduate programs are coed.

Average high school GPA: 3.3/4.0

Middle 50 percent on SAT: 820–1080; ACT: 19–26

93 percent admitted

Notable alumnae: Tallulah Bankhead (actress), Anna Jarvis (founder of Mother's Day), Paula Lambert (cookbook author), Anne St. Clair Wright (historic preservationist)

MILLS COLLEGE—OAKLAND, CALIFORNIA

1,548 students (922 undergraduates)

Urban campus

Most popular majors: English; psychology; ethnic studies; political, legal, and economic analysis; studio art

Special academic programs: Book Art Program, Hellman Summer Science and Math Fellows, Institute for Civic Leadership

Average high school GPA: 3.6/4.0

Middle 50 percent: SAT: 1040–1250; ACT: 23–29

68 percent admitted

Notable alumnae: Renel Brooks-Moon (announcer for the San Francisco Giants), Trisha Brown (dancer, choreographer, MacArthur Fellow), March Fong Eu (first woman to serve as California's secretary of state), April Glaspie (former US ambassador to Iraq), Barbara Lee (US representative, California)

Below are other women's colleges for students to investigate.

- Bennett College (NC)
- Brenau University (GA)
- Cedar Crest College (PA)
- College of Notre Dame of Maryland
- College of St. Catherine (MN)
- Georgian Court University (NJ)
- Rosemont College (PA)
- Salem College (NC)
- St. Benedict's College (MN)
- St. Mary of the Woods College (MO)
- Stephens College (MO)
- Texas Women's University
- Wesleyan College (GA)
- Wheelock College (MA)

ONCE UPON A TIME, THESE WERE MEN'S COLLEGES

- Amherst College
- Boston College
- Bowdoin College
- Brown University
  (had women's division: Pembroke College)
- Claremont McKenna College
  (was Claremont Men's College)
- Colgate University
- Columbia University
- Dartmouth College
- Davidson College
- Georgetown University
- Hamilton College
- Harvard University
  (had women's division: Radcliffe College)

- Haverford College
- Johns Hopkins University
- Kenyon College
- University of Pennsylvania
- Princeton University
- Trinity College
- Tufts University
  (had women's division: Jackson College)
- Union College
- Washington and Lee University
- Wesleyan University
- Williams College
- Yale University

FORMER WOMEN'S COLLEGES

- Bennington College
- Chatham University
- Connecticut College
- Elmira College
- Goucher College
- James Madison University
- Longwood University
- University of Mary Washington
- University of North Carolina at Greensboro

- Randolph College
- Sarah Lawrence College
- St. Mary's College of Maryland
- Skidmore College
- Vassar College
- Wheaton College (MA)
- Wells College
- William Peace University
- Wilson College

HISTORICALLY BLACK COLLEGES AND UNIVERSITIES

Owing to America's unfortunate history of racial segregation, there is a group of institutions known as historically black colleges and universities (HBCUs). These schools came into existence in the nineteenth and twentieth century to provide opportunities for African Americans when established colleges, such as Duke and Princeton, did not allow them to enter as students. With the exception of some liberal arts colleges, such as Oberlin and Swarthmore, and the state universities beyond the South, such as Michigan and Wisconsin, African Americans seeking a college education in the twentieth century were largely confined to

HBCUs. During the many years of segregation before the civil rights movement, students at HBCUs developed their own traditions and established a proud legacy.

Most of the HBCUs originated in the former slave states of the South and the so-called border states. In those states, there was a two-tiered system of higher education, where white students attended well-funded flagship universities such as the University of North Carolina or the University of Virginia, while black students attended modestly funded HBCUs such as North Carolina A&T and Virginia State University. Most southern states had several HBCUs, while very few northern states had one. Northern states with HBCUs include Delaware, Ohio, and Pennsylvania.

HBCUs started out as courageous institutions, dedicated to providing access to a disenfranchised segment of the American population. From the beginning, however, HBCUs were not funded at the same level as majority-white institutions. They were often derided by racists as lesser schools for lesser beings. For as long as they have existed, most HBCUs have had an uphill battle to draw attention, funds, respect, and recognition. Through it all, HBCUs have stuck to their mission to expand access and opportunity, even as American colleges and universities have pursued affirmative action.

Among the many HBCUs several are well-known, but three stand out as national institutions: Howard University in Washington, DC; Morehouse College in Atlanta; and Spelman College in Atlanta. Howard, Morehouse, and Spelman represent well-funded, popular, high-profile HBCUs. At least three other HBCUs are names commonly cited in conversations: Hampton University in Virginia, North Carolina A&T, and Tuskegee University in Alabama. Each has a proud heritage, including many distinguished graduates who have made significant contributions to the world.

HOWARD UNIVERSITY— WASHINGTON, DC

Sometimes called the "Black Harvard," Howard University is a dynamic, full-service university of nearly eleven thousand students with twelve schools and colleges offering degrees from the bachelor's through the doctoral and professional level. Students looking for an HBCU with a sterling reputation, well-known name, large number of degree programs, and vibrant location should look no further than Howard.

Howard's location in Washington, DC, enables students to enrich their education through ready access to institutions such as the Smithsonian and National Gallery of Art as well as to federal government offices, where internship opportunities abound. Howard has graduated numerous prominent, difference-making people including Senator Edward Brooke, musician/entrepreneur Sean (P. Diddy) Combs, former New York City Mayor David Dinkins, singers Billy Eckstine and Roberta Flack, California Attorney General Kamala Harris, writer Toni Morrison, famed opera singer Jessye Norman, *Cosby Show* actress Phylicia Rashad, and former United Nations Ambassador Andrew Young.

The twelve schools and colleges at Howard encompass architecture, arts and sciences, business, communication, computer sciences, dentistry, divinity, education, engineering, health sciences, law, medicine, nursing, pharmacy, and social work. While Howard strives to achieve high quality in all of its schools, the School of Communication is particularly notable for the number of its graduates in prominent positions in the media. Examples include journalism professor and Pulitzer Prize winner Leon Dash, sportscaster Gus Johnson, Pulitzer Prize–winning reporter and editor Colbert King, ABC News reporter Vicki Mabrey, CBS News reporter Michelle Miller, actress and television personality La La Vazquez, ESPN host Stan Verrett, and CNN anchor Fredricka Whitfield. Aspiring entrants into the media world benefit from the experience they get as students working at Howard's campus-based radio and television stations.

MOREHOUSE COLLEGE—ATLANTA, GEORGIA

With 2,800 students, Morehouse College is the largest liberal arts college for men in the United States. Over nearly 150 years, Morehouse has awarded bachelor's degrees to more African American men than any other college in the United States. Morehouse was also the first HBCU to graduate a Rhodes Scholar.

There are three academic divisions at Morehouse: humanities and social sciences, science and mathematics, and business administration and economics. Morehouse is part of the Atlanta University Center, a group of contiguous schools that also includes Clark Atlanta University, Spelman College, and the Morehouse School of Medicine (which is separate from Morehouse College). Students at Morehouse have cross registration privileges with Clark Atlanta and Spelman. Through the Atlanta University Center, there are numerous engineering dual-degree partners, including the University of Florida, University of Michigan, University of Notre Dame, and Rensselaer Polytechnic Institute. At Morehouse, there is also a dual-degree program in engineering with nearby Georgia Tech.

Morehouse (as pointed out in the section on men's colleges) is a highly respected liberal arts college, known for grooming future leaders. A special 73,000-square-foot campus facility houses cocurricular and academic leadership development programs focused on international affairs, community service, public service, and business and economics. Prominent Morehouse graduates include Martin Luther King, businessman and presidential candidate Herman Cain, actor Samuel L. Jackson, filmmaker Spike Lee, Olympic gold medalist Edwin Moses, and former

US Secretary of Health and Human Services Louis Sullivan.

SPELMAN COLLEGE—ATLANTA, GEORGIA

Spelman College is one of the best small liberal arts colleges in the United States. As pointed out in the earlier section, Spelman is also one of the nation's most distinguished colleges for women. Spelman has 2,100 students (all undergraduates) from more than forty states and fifteen foreign countries. Part of the Spelman experience is membership in the Atlanta University Center (AUC), a cluster of contiguous institutions described above. Through membership in the AUC, Spelman students share facilities, cross register for classes at the member schools, and have a university experience while still attending a small college. Visitors to Spelman will notice that it stands out in the AUC for its impressive facilities.

Spelman offers BA and BS degrees in twenty-six major areas and twenty-five minor areas. With a twelve to one student-teacher ratio, Spelman classes tend toward small and highly interactive. In addition to arts and sciences majors, Spelman students can pursue degrees in education, human services, and engineering. The engineering program is a dual-degree option with partners that include Columbia, Dartmouth, University of Florida, Georgia Tech, Michigan, Notre Dame, and RPI. Prominent Spelman alumni include Children's Defense Fund founder Marian Wright Edelman and actresses Keshia Knight Pulliam and Esther Rolle.

FLORIDA AGRICULTURAL AND MECHANICAL UNIVERSITY— TALLAHASSEE, FLORIDA

Florida A&M University (FAMU), with 12,000 students, is the largest HBCU in the United States. Located atop the highest of Tallahassee's seven hills, FAMU has a 422-acre campus that has 156 buildings. FAMU shares Tallahassee and some academic programs with a fellow public university, Florida State. Students come to study at Florida A&M from across the United States and from more than seventy countries.

There are thirteen schools and colleges at Florida A&M offering bachelor's degrees in sixty-two areas, master's degrees in thirty-nine disciplines, and doctoral degrees in ten specialties. The schools, colleges, and institutes at Florida A&M span from allied health sciences, architecture, arts and sciences, business and industry, education, and environmental sciences to journalism and graphic communication, nursing, engineering science, technology, and agriculture. Florida A&M also has a law school that is located in Orlando. The most popular undergraduate majors at Florida A&M are architecture, computer information sciences, journalism, and psychology. Notable FAMU alumni include trailblazing tennis player Althea Gibson, Olympic gold medalist and NFL great "Bullet Bob" Hayes, former US Congressman Kendrick Meek, sports reporter Pam Oliver, rappers Common and Smitty, and baseball stars Andre Dawson, Marquis Grissom, and Hal McCrae.

HAMPTON UNIVERSITY—HAMPTON, VIRGINIA

One of the most storied of the HBCUs, Hampton University traces its roots back to 1861, when it began as a school for free blacks. The first classes at what became Hampton were held under an oak tree, which was also the site of the first reading of the Emancipation Proclamation in the South. That oak tree, now known as the Emancipation Oak, still stands on the Hampton campus as a symbol of its courageous and historic beginnings.

Today, Hampton is a primarily undergraduate university of 5,400 students on a 314-acre campus with 118 buildings located in Virginia's Tidewater area, which includes the cities of Newport News, Norfolk, and Virginia Beach. Students come from more than forty-five states and thirty-five nations to study in one of Hampton's twenty-seven undergraduate and thirty-three graduate and professional programs. More than 80 percent of Hampton's students are undergraduates enrolled across its schools of business, continuing studies, engineering and technology, journalism and communications, liberal arts, nursing, pharmacy, and science. Long admired for its strength in scientific and technical fields, Hampton enrolls nearly 25 percent of its students in the schools of engineering and technology, nursing, pharmacy, and science. Roughly 40 percent of Hampton's students are enrolled in the schools of business and liberal arts. Prominent alumni of Hampton include Freeman Hrabowski (president of the University of Maryland at Baltimore County) and Wanda Sykes (comedian).

NORTH CAROLINA AGRICULTURAL AND TECHNICAL STATE UNIVERSITY—GREENSBORO, NORTH CAROLINA

Founded in 1891, North Carolina Agricultural and Technical State University (NC A&T) is a historically significant place. In 1960, four A&T students brought worldwide attention to Greensboro, North Carolina, when they staged a sit-in at a Woolworth lunch counter that, like most establishments in the South at that time, refused to serve African Americans. Those students, referred to as the Greensboro Four, became civil rights pioneers whose efforts led to historic changes in the United States.

Originally an agricultural and technical school, NC A&T has expanded to encompass ten thousand students and more than 150 degree programs at the bachelor's, master's, and doctoral level. Through eight degree-granting colleges and schools, NC A&T offers 177 undergraduate programs on its 800-acre campus that includes a 600-acre farm. The emphasis at NC A&T is decidedly toward career preparation, and roughly 90 percent of students have jobs by the time they graduate. The colleges and schools at A&T span agriculture, arts and sciences, business and economics, education, engineering, environmental sciences, nanoscience and nanoengineering, nursing, and technology. Among the specialized programs offered by A&T are architectural engineering, biological engineering, landscape architecture, sport science and fitness management, geomatics, and graphic communication systems. Biological engineering students can concentrate on either bioprocess engineering or natural resources engineering. Graphic communication systems majors have three concentration options: computer-aided drafting and design, integrated Internet technologies, or printing and publishing. Geomatics is a field focused on geographic information systems, satellite positioning (particularly global positioning systems—GPS), remote sensing, surveying, and mapping.

Among HBCUs, NC A&T has the largest agriculture school and more African American engineers graduate from A&T than from any other college in the United States. NC A&T is also one of the largest producers of African American certified public accountants (CPAs). Notable graduates of NC A&T include NBA executive and former player Alvin Attles, NFL Hall of Famer Elvin Bethea, civil rights activist and former presidential candidate Jesse Jackson, Congressman Edolphus Towns, and the late astronaut Ronald McNair.

TUSKEGEE UNIVERSITY—TUSKEGEE, ALABAMA

Founded by Booker T. Washington, Tuskegee University has a distinguished history. The famous Tuskegee airmen originated on the campus, which is partly why the US Congress designated it a National Historic Site, making Tuskegee University the only college in the United States to hold that distinction. Tuskegee is the only HBCU with an accredited veterinary school, one that produces 75 percent of the world's black veterinarians. In science and engineering, Tuskegee is the number one producer of African American aerospace engineers as well as PhDs in materials science and engineering.

A relatively small university of three thousand students, Tuskegee enrolls students in degree programs spanning the bachelor's to doctoral levels. The seven colleges and schools at Tuskegee are the Brimmer College of Business and Information Science; the College of Agriculture, Environment, and Nutrition Sciences; the College of Engineering; the College of Veterinary Medicine, Nursing, and Allied Health; the Taylor School of Architecture and Construction Science; and the School of Education. Other academic units at Tuskegee include centers of excellence in advanced materials, battlefield capability enhancement, biomedical research, food and environmental systems, nanostructured materials, and plant biotechnology. Notable alumni of Tuskegee include Ralph Ellison (writer), Daniel "Chappie" James (the first African American four-star general), Tom Joyner (nationally syndicated radio host), Lionel Richie (Grammy Award–winning singer), and Keenan Ivory Wayans (actor/director).

NOTABLE HBCU ALUMNI

Erykah Badu (Grambling State); Ed Bradley (Cheyney State); Wilma Rudolph and Oprah Winfrey (Tennessee State); Cab Calloway, Gil Scott-Heron, Langston Hughes, and Thurgood Marshall (Lincoln University); Jerry Rice (Mississippi Valley State); Barbara Jordan (Texas Southern); Michael Clark Duncan, Medgar Evers, and Alex Haley (Alcorn State); W. E. B. DuBois, John Hope Franklin, and Nikki Giovanni (Fisk); Randy Jackson, Avery Johnson, and Branford Marsalis (Southern University); Rosa Parks (Alabama State); Ronald McNair and Jesse Jackson (North Carolina A&T); Rod Paige and Walter Payton (Jackson State); Louis Farrakhan and Steven A. Smith (Winston Salem State); Leonyne Price and Nancy Wilson (Central State); A. Philip Randolph (Bethune Cookman); Whitney Young (Kentucky State); Benjamin Hooks (LeMoyne-Owen); L. Douglas Wilder (Virginia Union); Ruth Simmons (Dillard); Reuben Studdard (Alabama A&M).

► COMPREHENSIVE LIST OF HBCUs

Alabama A&M University

Alabama State University

Albany State University (Georgia)

Alcorn State University (Mississippi)

Allen University (South Carolina)

Arkansas Baptist College

Benedict College (South Carolina)

Bennett College (women) (North Carolina)

Bethune-Cookman University (Florida)

Bluefield State College (West Virginia)

Bowie State University (Maryland)

Central State University (Ohio)

Cheyney University (Pennsylvania)

Claflin University (South Carolina)

Clark Atlanta University

Concordia College (Alabama)

Coppin State University (Maryland)

Delaware State University

Dillard University (Louisiana)

Edward Waters College (Florida)

Elizabeth City State University (North Carolina)

Fayetteville State University (North Carolina)

Fisk University (Tennessee)

Florida Agricultural and Mechanical University

Florida Memorial University

Fort Valley State University (Georgia)

Grambling State University (Louisiana)

Hampton University (Virginia)

Harris-Stowe State University (Missouri)

Howard University (Washington, DC)

Huston-Tillotson University (Texas)

Jackson State University (Mississippi)

Jarvis Christian College (Texas)

Johnson C. Smith University (North Carolina)

Kentucky State University

Lane College (Tennessee)

Langston University (Oklahoma)

LeMoyne-Owen College (Tennessee)

Lincoln University of Missouri

Lincoln University of Pennsylvania

Livingstone College (North Carolina)

Miles College (Alabama)

Mississippi Valley State University

Morehouse College (men) (Georgia)

Morgan State University (Maryland)

Morris College (South Carolina)

Norfolk State University (Virginia)

North Carolina Agricultural and Technical State University

North Carolina Central University

Oakwood College (Alabama)

Paine College (Georgia)

Paul Quinn College (Texas)

Philander Smith College (Arkansas)

Prairie View A&M University (Texas)

Rust College (Mississippi)

St. Augustine's College (North Carolina)

Savannah State University (Georgia)

Shaw University (North Carolina)

Southern University and A&M College (Louisiana)

Southwestern Christian College (Texas)

Spelman College (women) (Georgia)

Stillman College (Alabama)

Talladega College (Alabama)

Tennessee State University

Texas College

Texas Southern University

Tougaloo College (Mississippi)

Tuskegee University (Alabama)

University of Arkansas at Pine Bluff

University of District of Columbia

University of Maryland Eastern Shore

Virginia State University

Virginia Union University

Virginia University of Lynchburg

Voorhees College (South Carolina)

West Virginia State University

Wilberforce University (Ohio)

Wiley College (Texas)

Winston-Salem State University (North Carolina)

Xavier University of Louisiana

IF I AM NOT BLACK , IS AN HBCU RIGHT FOR ME?

One misconception of HBCUs is that they are only for African American students. Indeed, the student population at HBCUs is overwhelmingly African American; however, at many HBCUs the nonblack population ranges from 5 to 20 percent. Nonblack students who are interested in broadening their cultural experience may find a congenial environment at HBCUs. Nonblack students at HBCUs are pioneers of sorts—individuals willing to step outside their comfort zone to be a minority at college.

For many African Americans, attending a HBCU feels like home because their whole life has been lived in black neighborhoods, at black schools, and in black churches. For others, especially those from suburban and private-school environments, choosing a HBCU provides an opportunity to experience, possibly for the first time, an environment where they are in the majority. For some students, going to a HBCU allows them to come to terms with their cultural heritage by living it rather than reading about it or having to constantly educate others about it.

HISPANIC-SERVING INSTITUTIONS (HSI'S)

In recognition of the growing Latino population in the United States, the Hispanic-serving institution category exists to spotlight colleges and universities where a significant percentage of students are of Hispanic heritage. There are hundreds of colleges with the HSI designation. Among the Hispanic-serving institutions, a subset have undergraduate populations that are at least 40 percent Latino. The following is a list of colleges and universities that offer at least a bachelor's degree and enroll 40 percent or more Latino students.

- California State University at Bakersfield
- California State University at Dominguez Hills
- California State University at Los Angeles
- California State University at San Bernardino
- City University of New York–John Jay College of Criminal Justice
- City University of New York–Lehman College
- Florida International University
- Heritage University (Washington)
- University of Incarnate Word (Texas)
- New Mexico Highlands University
- New Mexico State University
- University of New Mexico
- St. Mary's University (Texas)
- St. Thomas University (Florida)
- Sul Ross University (Texas)
- Texas A&M University–Kingsville
- University of Texas at Brownsville
- University of Texas at El Paso
- University of Texas–Pan American
- University of Texas–Permian Basin
- University of Texas at San Antonio
- Western New Mexico University

In addition to their high representation at HSIs, Latino students comprise a significant segment of the population at most of the colleges (both public and private) in Arizona, California, Colorado, Florida, New Mexico, Texas, and metro New York City. Some of the public universities in metro Chicago, Oregon, and Washington have also been experiencing a growing influx of Latino students. The institutions listed below stand out for their commitment to enrolling and graduating Latino students.

- Arizona State University
- University of Arizona
- California State Polytechnic University at Pomona
- University of California at Davis
- University of California at Irvine
- University of California at Los Angeles
- University of California at Merced
- University of California at Riverside
- University of California at Santa Barbara
- University of California at Santa Cruz
- University of California at San Diego
- University of Florida
- University of Houston
- University of LaVerne
- University of Miami
- Occidental College
- Pomona College
- Rice University
- St. Edwards University
- St. John's University
- St. Mary's College of California
- San Diego State University
- University of San Diego
- San Francisco State University
- University of Southern California
- Stanford University
- Texas A&M University (College Station)
- Texas Tech University
- University of Texas at Austin
- Whittier College

NATIVE AMERICAN COLLEGES AND UNIVERSITIES

There are thirty-seven tribal colleges in the United States, most of which are located on or close to Indian reservations. The vast majority of students at tribal colleges are Native Americans and members of the particular tribe that sponsors the college. Most of the tribal colleges are community colleges that offer associate degree programs. A small number of tribal colleges (some of which are listed below) offer bachelor's degree programs and might be of interest to Native American students and others who are drawn to American Indian history and culture.

- Haskell Indian Nations University— Lawrence, Kansas
- Institute of American Indian Arts—Santa Fe, New Mexico
- College of the Menominee Nation—Keshena and Green Bay, Wisconsin

- Northwest Indian College—Bellingham, Washington
- Oglala Lakota College—Pine Ridge Reservation, South Dakota
- Salish Kootenai College—Pablo, Montana
- Sinte Gliska University—Mission, South Dakota

A number of nontribal colleges and universities have significant Native American populations. The following schools have five hundred to two thousand Native Americans in their student bodies.

- University of Alaska at Anchorage
- University of Alaska at Fairbanks
- Arizona State University
- University of Central Oklahoma
- East Central University (Oklahoma)
- University of New Mexico
- New Mexico State University
- University of North Carolina at Pembroke
- Northeastern State University (Oklahoma)
- Northern Arizona University
- University of Oklahoma
- Oklahoma State University
- Southeastern Oklahoma State University

Several other colleges and universities (in the United States and Canada) are known for programs related to Native American students and studies. Although the number of Native American students at these colleges is not as large as at the institutions listed above, each of these schools is known for its commitment to recruiting and graduating Native American students and/or for its Native American Studies program.

- University of Alberta
- University of Arizona

- University of British Columbia
- University of California at Berkeley
- University of California at Davis
- University of California at Los Angeles
- Cornell University
- Dartmouth College
- Evergreen State College
- Fort Lewis College
- Harvard University
- University of Hawaii at Manoa
- Humboldt State University
- University of Illinois
- University of Iowa
- University of Manitoba
- University of Massachusetts at Amherst
- Michigan State University
- University of Minnesota
- University of Montana
- Montana State University
- University of Nebraska at Lincoln
- University of North Carolina at Chapel Hill
- University of North Dakota
- Northland College
- Northern Michigan University
- University of South Dakota
- Stanford University
- University of Washington
- University of Western Ontario
- University of Winnipeg
- University of Wyoming

When engaged in the college selection process, some students are quick to rule out a single-sex college or a HBCU due to hearsay and stereotypes, often the result of limited or flawed information about what these schools offer. This chapter may help counter that phenomenon and allow students to understand these options before making the decision whether to investigate them further or pass them by. This chapter also gives voice to people who have attended a single-sex college or an HBCU, HSI, or tribal college and are passionate proponents of the experience. Those partisans know something that prospective students would do well to consider during their college search.

CANADIAN UNIVERSITIES

Americans tend to underestimate Canada, stereotyping it as a montage of hockey players, Mounties, and Celine Dion. Dismissing our neighbor to the north obscures the reality of a country with universities of uniformly high quality that can provide an excellent education for Americans, often at staggeringly low tuition rates when compared to private and public colleges in the United States. This chapter spotlights Canadian universities and explains why some students might want to head north of the border for their college experience.

Just about all of the major universities in Canada are public institutions. To the outside observer, Canadian universities can seem like a hybrid of British and French universities and the Big Ten universities in the United States. Consider the three most prominent universities in Quebec, for example. Laval University in Quebec City and the University of Montreal are French-speaking universities. And McGill University often seems like an English-speaking enclave in the French city of Montreal. With approximately 73,000 students, the University of Toronto, on the other hand, is a vast research university akin to the University of Michigan or Ohio State. Vancouver's University of British Columbia (with an enrollment of 48,000) likewise resembles the University of Washington and UCLA in size, scope, research emphasis, and West Coast city location. While there are smaller universities in Canada, such as Queen's (14,491 undergraduates), there are relatively few small colleges, such as British Columbia's Quest University (540 students).

Canadian colleges and universities are increasingly popular in the United States because they are a relative bargain, particularly for those not eligible for need-based financial aid. Even after factoring in the higher tuition charged to non-Canadians, the typical Canadian university is far less expensive than the typical American private college. The cost of many Canadian universities compares favorably to the out-of-state charges at US public universities—and this has been especially true when exchange rates have favored the US dollar. Although the US to Canadian exchange rate goes through periods where the Canadian dollar is of equal or greater value, the exchange tends to favor the US dollar when the US economy is not in a recession.

Many students are drawn to Canadian universities for reasons beyond affordability. Some students want to have a simulated study abroad experience without getting too far out of their cultural and geographic comfort zone. Other students are attracted to the cosmopolitan and international atmosphere of cities such as, Montreal, Toronto, Halifax, or Vancouver. Students interested in venturing north for a culturally broadening experience and a new perspective on their home country will find many intriguing options in Canada.

TUITION COMPARISON: CANADA VERSUS THE UNITED STATES

Below are the 2015 average tuition costs for freshmen at a sampling of Canadian and US universities. Keep in mind that charges for certain programs, such as commerce, engineering, or pharmacy, and charges for upper-level students (juniors and seniors) are often higher in Canada. All totals are in Canadian dollars *tuition only* (not factoring in room, board, books, travel, or the possibility that the student is receiving need-based or merit aid).

International tuition rates at selected Canadian universities (in Canadian dollars); the price may vary depending on program, and the ranges are given below.

- University of Alberta: $28,835–$29,409
- University of British Columbia: ($26,999–$42,238)
- Dalhousie University: $13,701–$19,123
- McGill University: $17,727–$39,872
- Mount Alison University: $16,420
- Queen's University: $27,412–$34,980
- Simon Fraser University: $21,614
- University of Toronto: $29,520–$43,540
- University of Victoria: $17,792–$24,849
- University of Western Ontario: $23,100-$29,200

Compare the above prices to 2015 tuition rates given below at selected US universities (in US dollars).

- University of California at Berkeley: CA resident—$13,878, nonresident—$37,902
- Johns Hopkins University: $48,710
- Massachusetts Institute of Technology: $46,400
- University of Michigan: MI resident—$13,486, nonresident—$41,906
- University of Notre Dame: $47,929
- Stanford University: $45,729
- Swarthmore College: $47,070
- University of Virginia: VA resident—$11,892, nonresident—$40,506
- University of Washington: WA resident—$12,394, nonresident—$33,513
- Yale University: $47,600

AFFORDING A CANADIAN UNIVERSITY

The students for whom Canadian universities present the greatest financial value are those who do not qualify for need-based aid and are unlikely to get much merit aid from US colleges—a group admission and financial-aid officers often refer to as "full pays." If a US family is eligible for a generous amount of need-based aid (as determined by the FAFSA and CSS Financial Aid Profile) or a student is an exceptionally strong full-pay student applying to a college that offers a merit scholarship as an enticement, then choosing an American college may be the lower cost option. For others, particularly those students not interested in attending the public universities in their home state, Canadian universities often offer the best quality for the price.

Students expecting to get scholarship aid in Canada are generally out of luck. Canadian universities offer minimal scholarship aid (known in Canadian university parlance as *bursaries*)

to US students, particularly freshmen. That said, there has been a move in recent years at several Canadian universities toward non-need, merit scholarships for international applicants. Universities offering them include University of British Columbia, McGill, Mount Allison, Queen's, Toronto, and the University of Victoria.

Students seeking need-based aid should consult US federal and state financial-aid sources. Most grant aid used to finance college in the United States is *not* available for Americans studying in Canada. For example, Pell Grants, Federally Funded Need-Based Supplement Programs (FSFOG), Perkins Loans, and the US Federal Work Study Program are all void for study at Canadian universities. Fortunately, Americans who qualify for Stafford and PLUS loans can use them at the Canadian universities recognized by the US Department of Education. Students can apply for loans through the

William D. Ford Federal Direct Loan Program administered by the Department of Education or the Federal Family Educational Loan (FFEL) from banks, credit unions, or other lenders that have been approved by the US federal student aid program.

Students seeking to determine if any aid sources are portable to Canada need to file the FAFSA form, just as they would if applying to US colleges. The FAFSA determines the family's estimated contribution and eligibility for federal sources of need-based and self-help aid. Students should also consult the higher education agency in their home state that provides information on financing college—to determine eligibility and procedures for getting PLUS loans, Stafford loans, and other forms of state-based financial aid. Also, some states, such as Minnesota, North Dakota, South Dakota, and Wisconsin, have tuition exchange reciprocity arrangements with the province of Manitoba. Although such reciprocity agreements are relatively uncommon, students should check to see if their state offers one.

Some families are eligible for tax credits while their children are in college. Sometimes tax credits can be applied when the student is studying at an approved Canadian university. Parents, or students filing as independents, may be eligible for either an American Opportunity Credit (up to $2,500 per student for four years in postsecondary school for family incomes under $180,000, or for single filer incomes under $90,000) or a Lifelong Learning Credit (up to $2,000 per tax return, available for an unlimited number of years as long as income is under $120,000 for families, or $60,000 for single filers). Of course, new tax and loan regulations may have passed since the time of this writing, so it is best to check for updates on www.finaid. gov or other reliable sources.

THE CANADIAN UNIVERSITY EXPERIENCE

While investigating Canadian universities, students must ask a key question: what do I want from the college experience? Academically, there are excellent resources north of the border, but the study path from first year to graduation can vary (compared to the United States) in significant ways. The differences begin with the application process. Rather than apply to the university as a whole, Canadian students apply to particular faculties within a university and, once admitted, generally study within that program. This more focused and no-frills approach to university study is also reflected in student life. Canadian students (in greater numbers than in the United States) attend college in or near their hometown—often living at home, commuting to school, or living off campus with friends from high school. This nonresidential aspect of Canadian universities mirrors the European university experience, where campus residence halls are rare.

At the University of Toronto, for example, only 16 percent of students live in campus housing, suggesting a larger commuter culture than at most American universities. Typically more than 75 percent of Toronto's students hail from Ontario, and approximately 16 percent come from outside Canada. The University of Alberta has a similar local draw. Nearly three-quarters (73 percent) of Alberta's thirty-nine thousand students come from the home province, with 11 percent from other Canadian provinces, and 16 percent from outside the country. At McGill, roughly 20 percent of the students are non-Canadians. While Canadian universities do actively recruit students from the United States, it is important to recognize that Canada's universities are primarily local in their character, which means that Americans are very much in the minority.

The United States certainly has large universities where a majority of students commute from home or choose to live off campus, but by and large the American system of higher education puts high emphasis on residence life in campus-owned buildings. Housing for international students and others traveling a far distance is a given at the vast majority of US colleges and universities. Also, Greek (fraternities and sororities) housing, although technically considered off campus, is often adjacent to campus. Greek housing is far more prevalent at American universities than at Canadian universities. For example, at the University of Virginia about 43 percent of students live in on-campus housing, but an additional 30 percent live in Greek houses adjacent to campus. In contrast, barely eighty to one hundred women join sororities at Toronto each year, and fraternities are not recognized by the U of T.

Another contrast with the US student experience shows up in the level of financial support given to clubs and organizations. Because Canadian universities are more about academics and less about a holistic student experience, there are generally fewer student clubs and organizations on campus. Don't get us wrong, there are many extracurricular and athletic options at Canadian universities, but universities in Canada do not invest large sums of money in big-time sports programs or in the vast number of student-run activities found at comparable US universities. For example, the University of Michigan has 999 university-sanctioned clubs and organizations as well as a highly visible Division I athletic program. By contrast, the University of Toronto has 432 student organizations and minimal emphasis on athletics. Certainly 432 options is more than enough for most students, but it is a significantly smaller number of options than at Michigan, especially

considering that Toronto's student population outnumbers Michigan's by more than 20,000.

The differences between Canadian and American universities are relatively minor compared to the contrast between the typical Canadian university and the classic American small liberal arts college. Canada does not have a small liberal arts college tradition, where the exploratory journey toward a major is a critical part of being a college student. The American liberal arts college encourages students to select a broad scope of classes in order to develop and internalize critical reading, thinking, and writing skills. Canadian universities, conversely, are structured for students who have a good idea of what they want to study from day one. Also, the typical American liberal arts college considers on-campus residential life essential to the holistic nature of its education. For example, 98 percent of Pomona College and 95 percent of Vassar College students live on campus. By contrast, Canadian universities tend to have a large off-campus population and more of a do-it-yourself approach to the student experience. Students needing a warm and fuzzy college experience will more likely get that from the signature blankets sold at the Bay than from a Canadian university.

Arguably, the Canadian university experience represents less of a limbo period between high school and adulthood. For some, the responsibility Canadian universities place in the hands of individual students to chart their own course is refreshing, especially after the confines of a structured high school. This change in emphasis can work especially well for students accustomed to navigating a major city or those ready to move beyond residence hall life at a boarding school. One case where students attending Canadian universities have to make more adult-type choices at a younger age concerns alcohol. Because fewer students live on campus or in Greek houses, and because Canada has a younger drinking age (in most provinces it is eighteen or nineteen), binge drinking at college is less a rite of passage than merely another social option.

Overall, comparing Canadian universities to American colleges is tricky because of the diversity of educational options in the United States. The most apt comparison is between a Canadian university and a large, public university in the United States (think: orange versus tangerine). For example, the University of Alberta (35,000 students) is not too dissimilar from the University of Iowa (31,000 students). Greater contrasts emerge when comparing private liberal arts colleges in the United States (such as Amherst or Reed) to large public Canadian universities, such as McGill or Queen's (think: blueberry versus coconut). Still, there are a few Canadian universities—such as Mount Allison with 2,500 students—that are undergraduate focused and similar in size to US liberal arts colleges such as Gettysburg (2,600 students), Oberlin (2,800), and Vassar (2,450). Regardless of the characteristics of the institutions, the advantages and disadvantages of each are subjectively determined by the individual student. For some students, Canadian universities may seem like four years of study abroad without having to leave the continent. For others, going to Canada may appear not much different from venturing to another state's public flagship.

Students who look closely at Canadian universities will be pleasantly surprised by the number of options available. Whether it's the stunning outdoor environment of Vancouver, the sophistication of Toronto, or the bicultural French-English magic of Montreal, the American student in Canada can have a lot of fun while earning a quality degree. Safety also tends to favor Canadian universities. Canadian municipalities typically have lower crime rates than their US counterparts—meaning that the increased autonomy accompanying student life in Canada is leavened by far less access to guns or proximity to criminal elements. There are certainly some crime-ridden areas in Canada, but the cultural and legislative emphasis tilts the country toward nonviolence—a reality that should allay some parental concerns about sending a child to a foreign country for college.

There is quality throughout the Canadian university system. But four standout institutions are acclaimed internationally for their overall excellence and are sometimes called the Canadian Ivies: University of British Columbia, McGill University, Queen's University, and the University of Toronto. A number of other universities are distinguished, although less well-known outside of Canada. This distinguished next tier includes the University of Alberta, Mount Allison University, Simon Fraser University, the University of Waterloo, and the University of Western Ontario. Like certain state universities in the United States, Alberta, Mount Allison, Simon Fraser, Waterloo, and Western Ontario are considered especially prestigious in their home regions and provinces.

GETTING INTO A CANADIAN UNIVERSITY

The freshman admission process for Canadian universities is highly numerical. While admissions decisions at the most selective US universities are made according to a holistic model, the Canadian universities base decisions overwhelmingly on the applicant's high school record and standardized test scores. Generally, applicants to Canadian universities do not have to write application essays, sit for interviews, submit recommendation letters, or try to impress admissions committees with lists of extracurricular activities. Typically, all that is required is an application data form, a high school transcript, and results of the required standardized tests. Most Canadian universities detail on their admissions websites the required high school course sequence/level and expected standardized test scores that US applicants need to be competitive for admission. Expectations and standards for US applicants are usually explained under admissions for international students. Within the international admissions site, there is usually an option to go to web pages that explain the requirements for applicants from American high schools or colleges (for transfer applicants).

Consider the University of Toronto. For US applicants, Toronto recommends an ACT composite score of at least 26 or SAT scores of at least 600 on the critical reading, math, and writing sections. Toronto prefers that applicants have taken Advanced Placement (AP), International Baccalaureate (IB), or honors level (HL) courses up through the twelfth grade. In addition, Toronto requires results of two SAT subject tests, IB exams, or AP exams. McGill and Queen's University have similar numbers-based admissions criteria. McGill likes to see SAT section scores of at least 620 or an ACT composite of at least 26. Queen's draws the qualification line at 580 for SAT sections and at 26 for the ACT composite. Recently, the University of British Columbia (UBC) became the first Canadian university to introduce a holistic review into its admissions process. As a result, UBC does not list SAT/ACT requirements. Still, UBC expects US applicants to present strong high school transcripts and competitive standardized test scores (on either the ACT or SAT). Certain programs at Canadian universities, such as architecture, fine arts, and music, may have additional application requirements, such as an audition or submission of a portfolio. When researching Canadian universities, students should check whether there are specific application requirements set by academic faculties and schools.

No matter the university destination in Canada, it is essential for American students to get a Canadian study permit (CSP) issued by Citizenship and Immigration Canada (CIC). Permits enable students to study in Canada and also work part-time on campus while enrolled. An official acceptance statement from a Canadian university is all that is needed to apply for a study permit. It is possible for students to obtain their CSP from Canadian customs officials on the day they are crossing the border en route to university. But we strongly discourage waiting until the proverbial last minute to obtain a CSP. Because it is a legal document, students are advised to take some time before packing up and leaving for Canada to get acquainted with the requirements for the CIC-issued Canadian study permit. Getting familiar with the CSP process will enable the student to take the steps necessary to make a smooth and legal entrance into Canada. No one wants to be that student who gets turned away by Canadian customs officials one day before classes start.

RANKING THE CANADIAN UNIVERSITIES

For over twenty years, Canada's weekly current affairs magazine (*Maclean's*) has produced an annual issue that ranks Canadian universities. While we are not endorsing the *Maclean's* rankings, we present them because in Canada they are widely read (and touted by universities)—just like the *US New and World Report* rankings in the United States. Below are the results of the 2015 *Maclean's* university rankings.

MEDICAL/DOCTORAL UNIVERSITY CATEGORY

1. McGill University
2. University of Toronto
3. University of British Columbia
4. Queen's University
5. University of Alberta
6. McMaster University
7. Dalhousie University
8. University of Ottawa
8. University of Western Ontario (tie)
10. Laval University
10. University of Montreal (tie)
12. University of Calgary
12. University of Manitoba (tie)
14. University of Saskatchewan
15. Sherbrooke University

COMPREHENSIVE UNIVERSITY CATEGORY

1. Simon Fraser University
2. University of Victoria
3. University of Waterloo
4. University of New Brunswick
5. University of Guelph
6. Carleton University
6. Memorial University (tie)
8. Ryerson University
8. York University (tie)
10. University of Regina
11. Concordia University
12. University of Windsor
13. Wilfrid Laurier University
14. University of Quebec at Montreal
15. Brock University

PRIMARILY UNDERGRADUATE UNIVERSITY CATEGORY

1. Mount Allison University
2. University of Northern British Columbia
3. University of Lethbridge
4. Acadia University
5. Saint Mary's University
6. Trent University
6. St. Francis Xavier University (tie)
8. Lakehead University
9. Bishop's University
10. University of Prince Edward Island
10. Laurentian University (tie)
12. University of Moncton
13. University of Ontario Institute of Technology
14. University of Winnipeg
15. St. Thomas University
16. Brandon University
17. Mount Saint Vincent University
18. Cape Breton University
19. Nipissing University

Below is the result when other rankings (including various world university reputational rankings) are aggregated.

1. University of Toronto
2. McGill University
3. University of British Columbia
4. McMaster University
5. University of Alberta
6. University of Montreal
7. Simon Fraser University
8. University of Calgary
9. University of Laval
10. University of Western Ontario
11. University of Waterloo
12. Queen's University
13. Dalhousie University
14. University of Manitoba
15. University of Ottawa

CANADIAN IVY: UBC, MCGILL, QUEEN'S, AND TORONTO

UNIVERSITY OF BRITISH COLUMBIA

UBC is a large institution. Approximately fifty-four thousand people study at UBC's two campuses: Vancouver and Okanagan. Since its opening in 2005, the Okanagan campus of the University of British Columbia, located in what is considered Canada's premier wine country, has grown to a medium-sized regional university of seven thousand students. While trekking to Canada's equivalent to the Napa Valley for college might sound appealing, it is UBC's main campus in Vancouver (founded in 1908) that is the academic home for the majority of UBC students (forty-seven thousand) and the more likely destination for Americans.

The setting of UBC's main campus in Vancouver is nothing short of stunning. UBC is on Point Grey, twenty minutes from downtown Vancouver. On the campus, there are lush forests, a botanical garden, and serene spaces that provide respite from the cosmopolitan and international city nearby. The UBC campus offers sweeping views of the North Shore Mountains, the city of Vancouver, the Burrard Inlet, and the Strait of Georgia. Although most of UBC's buildings are of the modern functional style, the beautiful setting and surroundings create a sublime sense of place appropriate for a university that is frequently hailed as one of Canada's three or four best, if not one of the top fifty in the world. And for those attracted to innovative architecture, UBC boasts many green buildings and a futuristic performing arts center that has been featured on television shows such as *Battlestar Galactica* and *Stargate Atlantis*.

Numerous academic units at UBC are renowned for their excellence. UBC's programs in economics and engineering are consistently ranked among the top twenty in the world. Engineering, for example, offers an innovative major in integrated engineering. The foreign language departments, especially Chinese and Japanese, are world leaders, and UBC is a rare institution that offers an undergraduate major in creative writing. Through numerous research centers, UBC students and faculty collaborate to make discoveries that push the boundaries of their fields. For example, UBC has an interdisciplinary institute focused on the future of the sciences, social sciences, and humanities. UBC commands further academic prestige as the home to the internationally known TRIUMF (Canada's national lab for subatomic physics), the joint operator of the Bamfield Marine Sciences Center on Vancouver Island, and for the Centre for Plant Research, which along with the campus botanical garden, houses a collection of eight thousand different plants. There is more that can be said about UBC's academic bona fides, but suffice to say that by virtually every measure, whether it is the five Nobel laureates who have taught at or graduated from UBC, or that Albert Bandura—the father of social learning theory and the most cited psychology researcher of all time—is an alumnus, it is a significant institution that commands respect around the world.

Students at UBC Vancouver have hundreds of major options. While quality abounds across all of UBC's faculties, there is particular energy surrounding environmental areas of study. The Pacific Northwest is generally known as a progressive place for environmental sustainability, and UBC has become an epicenter for innovations through its faculties of land and food systems and forestry. For example, the university farm (the only working farm in the city of Vancouver) is a multidisciplinary effort spearheaded by students that strives to be an internationally significant research center for sustainability, agriculture, food production, and conservation of land. The

UBC farm's Saturday market attracts thousands of people to the campus. In addition to the farm, the Centre for Interactive Research in Sustainability (CIRS) at UBC is housed in North America's greenest building. CIRS focuses on quick and innovative solutions to sustainability challenges facing rapidly increasing urban centers.

Most of the students at UBC live in the city of Vancouver and take public buses to campus. The university has on-campus residences for just eleven thousand students—with more dormitory spaces and construction plans on the drawing board. UBC is somewhat unusual in Canada for having eighteen Greek organizations on campus. UBC's fraternities and sororities make up the largest and most active Greek system at a Canadian university. That means American students looking for Greek life have an option north of the border on a stunning campus, in a dynamic city, at a school that commands respect across the globe.

MCGILL UNIVERSITY

Perhaps the most familiar Canadian university to Americans is McGill. Located in French-speaking Montreal, McGill is one of Canada's most prestigious universities—generally vying with the University of Toronto for the premier designation. An astounding 132 Rhodes Scholars have graduated from McGill—more than from any other university in Canada. Among McGill's alumni are eleven Nobel laureates, nine Academy Award winners, three foreign leaders, three astronauts, three Pulitzer Prize winners, and two Canadian prime ministers. McGill is one of only two Canadian universities (the other is Toronto) in the vaunted Association of American Universities (AAU). World rankings of the top universities consistently place McGill among the top twenty-five, recognizing its excellence in the arts and humanities, engineering, law, life sciences, management, natural sciences, social sciences, and technology.

Over the years, McGill has emerged as a viable option for top-tier American students looking for a somewhat exotic locale where course work is taught in English—in contrast to the other major university in town, the University of Montreal, which is French speaking. Montreal arguably feels more like Europe than perhaps any other city in North America. McGill has been particularly popular with Americans from the northeastern United States due to Montreal's proximity to the Boston to Washington corridor. These days roughly 20 percent of McGill's students are from outside Canada.

With approximately twenty-five thousand undergraduates and nine thousand graduate students, McGill is a large research university with a grand campus of limestone buildings in the Mount Royal neighborhood of Montreal. Students at McGill can select among over three hundred fields of study. Although large, McGill boasts a manageable student-faculty ratio of sixteen to one. Between its main Mount Royal campus, MacDonald campus in metro Montreal, and numerous off-campus research facilities, McGill offers extraordinary resources, including one of the top music programs (the Schulich School) in Canada. On its MacDonald campus, McGill maintains a Faculty of Agriculture and Environmental Sciences, the School of Dietetics and Human Nutrition, an Institute of Parasitology, and a School of the Environment. Near the MacDonald campus are the Morgan Arboretum and the Marshall Radar Observatory. McGill also operates a marine science center in St. Andrew's, New Brunswick; a nature reserve in the St. Lawrence Valley; and a research institute on the Caribbean island of Barbados.

While there is much to recommend McGill—in particular a degree that will be recognized and respected in every corner of the globe, US students need to go there with their eyes wide open to the contrasts with McGill's name-brand American counterparts. For starters, McGill only has campus housing for 2,700 students. Combine that statistic with another one (55 percent of the students are from the province of Quebec) and you have a college experience characterized by a majority commuter population, many of whom are still living with their parents. Freshman year at McGill can be marked by large lecture classes and little personal contact with professors. Add to that the European-style view that university is a place for classes and little else and you have the ingredients of an experience that could be jarring or alienating to some American students. Anecdotally, we have found that American students expecting to find a strong sense of campus community at McGill often transfer back to the United States to small liberal arts colleges or to universities with student populations under 7,000.

Generally the more independent and mature a student is at the time of entry, the better that student will fare at McGill. The extracurricular resources at McGill are outstanding and vast— including approximately two hundred student organizations and many more activities within the larger Montreal community. But success at McGill requires students to be proactive in seeking out academic and social opportunities. With fewer than three thousand students living on campus, entering freshmen must be prepared to find their own housing and dining arrangements. This may sound exciting to students eager to take in all that Montreal has to offer, but it could be daunting for students who have never lived on their own and are looking for a residential college experience.

The American students adventurous enough to select McGill and thrive there will get an education of unsurpassed quality and a college experience that will mark them as global citizens aware of how their home country appears to others. US students who graduate from McGill will join a long line of prominent achievers that includes the legendary composer Burt Bacharach (AMus 1948, DMus 1972); Harold Shapiro (former president of the University of Michigan and Princeton, BComm 1956); the singer Leonard Cohen (1955); and Captain Kirk himself, William Shatner (BComm 1952).

QUEEN'S UNIVERSITY

One of the oldest and most prestigious schools in Canada, Queen's offers a midsize university experience in a college town. Queen's University's lakeside setting in Kingston, Ontario, provides its approximately fifteen thousand undergraduate and nine thousand graduate students with a picturesque collegiate atmosphere. In many respects, Queen's is the Canadian university that most calls to mind an American Ivy League university. With collegiate Gothic buildings, a bell tower, and cobblestone streets, the Queen's campus also resembles, more than most Canadian universities, its older cousins in the United Kingdom and the fictional Hogwarts of the *Harry Potter* novels. For these reasons, Queen's has become popular with students at leading schools in the northeastern United States.

The focus in Kingston, Ontario, is Queen's University, and many businesses in town cater to the student population. Some students want a college bubble, and Queen's creates that with a location that is more isolated in comparison with its urban university cousins in Montreal, Toronto, and Vancouver. This is not to say that Kingston is a dull backwater town. The city of Kingston (population 123,000), located on the northern shore of Lake Ontario, is a charming backdrop and can provide a lovely home while studying at Queen's. Because of Queen's, Kingston has become a diverse, international city where students from 150 different countries coexist. Queen's attracts students who are well prepared, and due to its undergraduate-focused academic and social atmosphere, those who make the trek to Kingston and Queen's (whether coming from Boston or Singapore) do remarkably well there. Queen's typically has the highest graduation rate among Canadian universities (92 percent in 2010).

The academics at Queen's are uniformly strong. The eleven faculties at Queen's provide students with hundreds of major choices, including some not commonly found elsewhere, such as applied economics, biomedical computing, geographic information science, and Hebrew language and literature. For undergraduates, Queen's has faculties and schools of arts and science, business, education, engineering and applied science, and nursing. The largest enrollments at Queen's are found in social sciences and engineering. The program in business/commerce at Queen's is frequently ranked among the best in Canada. Queen's also has a strong program in music. For those who remain for graduate or professional education, there are top-ranked schools of law, medicine, and rehabilitation therapy.

Queen's prides itself on its global interconnectedness. The Bader International Study Centre at Herstmonceux Castle (ISC) is a unique satellite campus run by Queen's in southeast England. The fifteenth-century castle is a second Queen's campus. Students are able to spend their freshmen year (and beyond) at the castle. In addition to the Bader ISC, Queen's students can add an international dimension to their college experience through over forty-five study abroad programs. There is also a well-structured internship program (that provides sites in or near Kingston as well as in other Canadian cities and beyond) for students interested in hands-on, applied learning.

Graduates of Queen's whose names or titles may ring a bell with Americans include the former president of Princeton University, Shirley Tilghman; actors Tom Cavanagh, Wendy Crewson, and Lorne Greene; writer, Robertson Davies; CNN business reporter, Ali Velshi; and several CEOs of major companies such as AMR, Proctor & Gamble, Royal Bank of Canada, and Warner Lambert.

UNIVERSITY OF TORONTO

The University of Toronto is arguably Canada's premier university. But it is very large. Going to a university that enrolls approximately seventy-three thousand students can be daunting. Yes, there are hundreds of majors and excellent faculty but the U of T's population far exceeds that of many small cities (Burlington, Vermont, for example, population of forty-five thousand, and home of the University of Vermont). Fortunately, the University of Toronto's historic college system helps to give the place a more user-friendly scale. Like Oxford and Cambridge in England, Toronto has long embraced a small-college network that helps personalize the school and distribute services on a human scale.

Overall, the University of Toronto is a complex decentralized institution. There are distinctive schools (called faculties) for medicine, music, engineering, law, and arts and science. The majority of students enrolling from high school enter the Faculty of Arts and Science, primarily because most of the hundreds of degree programs available to undergraduates are found there. All students in the Faculty of Arts and Science are assigned to one of U of T's seven major colleges, each with a distinctive history and set of resources. The assigned college serves as the student's home base. Students applying to Toronto's Faculty of Arts and Science must apply to the seven colleges, ranking them in order of preference. Using information gleaned from admission application essays and supplemental forms, Toronto places students in individual colleges. Once assigned to a college, the student goes there for housing, orientation, registration, bill payment, financial aid, scholarships (known as bursaries), advising, and numerous other student services. Each college at Toronto also maintains its own residence halls and dining facilities. What makes this situation different from the residential colleges of Yale or Rice is that Toronto's residential colleges include a number of academic departments that further shape the culture of the college.

Faculty of Arts and Science students at Toronto may take classes throughout the campus, but the college to which the student is assigned often coincides with the student's academic interest, further reinforcing it as the student's home. Although not every major is attached to a particular college, prospective students may want to think of those that are as an overarching theme to the college. Toronto's Innis College, for example, is the academic home to cinema studies, urban studies, and writing/rhetoric— offering courses and first-year seminars from those academic areas. For a student entering Toronto with an interest in film, Innis College might be an appropriate choice because it has a concentrated group of students with similar interests. On the other hand, if a dance troupe from Haiti is coming to perform at Toronto, it would most likely be sponsored by New College, which houses the Caribbean studies program. Can someone from another college attend that performance or major in Caribbean studies? Can a student in Innis College have a complete change of heart and concentrate on biology? Yes, absolutely, because under the Toronto college system, it is permissible to take classes and graduate with a degree from academic areas beyond one's home college. Even when students choose that route, their core services still come through their home college.

A basic breakdown of Toronto's seven colleges can be helpful for someone considering the U of T because the college system helps personalize an institution with upward of seventy thousand students in a city of 2.6 million people. Students and alumni are very loyal to their colleges due to the social and academic ties formed at them. Each college has its own student government to make decisions within the college and represent students in the larger University of Toronto community. The colleges also tend to have their own newspapers, clubs, and social activities.

UNIVERSITY COLLEGE

Founded in 1853, University College (UC) enrolls roughly 4,500 undergraduates and sponsors the following academic departments: Canadian studies, drama, health studies, peace and conflict studies, and sexual diversity studies. UC offers first-year seminars called UC-ONE. A recent seminar organized around the theme Engaging Toronto offered tracks—related to academic departments housed at University College—called Citizenship in the Canadian City, Performing Toronto, Gradients of the Health and Well-Being in the Urban Mosaic, and Sex in the City. In addition to classes, students can purchase a meal plan at the eco-friendly University College dining hall and café. To eat at campus establishments beyond their assigned college, U of T students need to purchase flex dollars. Like Toronto's other residential colleges, University College has active clubs such as the University College and Athletic Society and competes in intramural athletics. Due to the community-building aspect of intramurals at a school of seventy thousand students, often the college-based sports programs are more popular than the U of T programs that compete against other universities. Notable graduates of University College include the writer Michael Ondaatje and Lorne Michaels, the creator/producer of *Saturday Night Live*.

NEW COLLEGE

The academic home of African studies, Buddhism, psychology and mental health, Caribbean studies, equity, and paradigms and archetypes, New College has approximately 4,300 students. New College is one of the few colleges with faculties outside of arts and science, such as commerce. Since 1998, New College has sponsored a special exchange program with the University of Namibia that focuses on HIV and women's issues.

INNIS COLLEGE

Innis is the academic home for cinema, urban studies, and writing/rhetoric. One of the newer colleges, Innis enrolls about 1,650 undergraduates. When Innis was founded in 1964, people considered calling it Newer College because it was developed after New College in 1962. The architecture and facilities at Innis are more modern and industrial than some of the other colleges.

TRINITY COLLEGE

The academic home for ethics; society and law; immunology; and international relations, it is also home to the Trinity Faculty of Divinity, Canada's oldest Anglican theological school. Trinity was founded in 1851 and typically has 1,700 arts and science students plus 140 divinity students. Trinity is one of the smaller colleges and boasts that the average GPA for entering students is over 90 percent. Trinity is also proud that high numbers of its graduates become Rhodes Scholars. The Trinity One program for first-year students has traditionally had two tracks, international relations and ethics, with both seminars capped at twenty-five people. Trinity College alumnus Malcolm Gladwell, author of many books, including *The Tipping Point*, graduated in 1984 with a history major.

VICTORIA COLLEGE

Tracing its origins to 1832, Victoria College is the academic home for literary studies, Renaissance studies, and semiotics and communication theory. The Victoria College campus is home to five living-learning communities that provide unique social opportunities for people to bond over issues they are passionate about. Victoria has been home to several well-known University of Toronto graduates including author Margaret Atwood, filmmaker Norman Jewison, and actor Donald Sutherland, whose memories of Victoria's formerly all-male Gates residence hall inspired certain aspects of the *Animal House* script. The more traditional ivy-covered buildings of Victoria College look very collegiate, particularly when compared to the utilitarian architecture of some of Toronto's newer colleges.

ST. MICHAEL'S COLLEGE

Founded in 1852 by Basilican Fathers, the Catholic roots of this college make it an appropriate academic home for Celtic studies, Christianity and culture, and medieval studies. St. Michael's sponsors a special program to prepare people to teach in Catholic schools throughout Ontario. St. Michael's is also home to media studies.

WOODSWORTH COLLEGE

Created in 1974, Woodsworth is Toronto's largest and newest college. Originally founded as the college for part-time students, particularly adult students studying education, Woodsworth transitioned into a college primarily for traditional-age students in 1999. Woodsworth serves approximately 6,200 students, is the academic home for criminology and employment relations, and also sponsors the International Summer Program, which annually sends 900-plus students to eighteen non-Canadian destinations.

FOUR INTRIGUING OPTIONS: MOUNT ALLISON, QUEST, VICTORIA, AND WESTERN ONTARIO

MOUNT ALLISON UNIVERSITY

Mount Allison University in Sackville, New Brunswick, is unusual by Canadian standards in that it enrolls only 2,500 students, most of whom are undergraduates. Mount Allison is reminiscent of an American liberal arts college in terms of its size and focus on undergraduates, and it is also more residential than most Canadian universities. On-campus housing is guaranteed for all freshmen and 50 percent of all students live in Mount Allison residence halls. There are forty majors and minors offered at Mount Allison. Degree programs range from bachelor of arts (BA) and bachelor of science (BS) to bachelor of fine arts (BFA) and bachelor of music (BM). Unlike traditional American liberal arts colleges that encourage a wide range of courses in an effort to obtain a more holistic education, Mt. Allison offers degree programs, such as a BS in aviation—in conjunction with Moncton Flight College—that are more career specific, and thus more like the specialized offerings at larger universities. Similarly, Mount Allison offers a preprofessional major in commerce for future business executives.

Mount Allison is a consistent leader in rankings such as *Maclean's*, *Globe and Mail*, University Report Card, and the National Survey of Student Engagement. That Mount Allison has earned fifty-two Rhodes Scholarships (an impressive number for *any* college but astounding given its small student population) is a testament to the academic quality of the school. Likewise, Mount Allison is the alma mater of several of the painters in Canada's famed Group of Seven and has an extensive Group of Seven art collection in its museum. Per capita, Mount Allison has greater financial resources than most Canadian universities. Its endowment per student is the second highest in Canada. Mount Allison also has pioneering aspects to its history. In 1875 it became the first school in the British Empire to award a BS degree to a woman.

Located approximately thirty minutes from Moncton, New Brunswick, roughly twenty minutes from an international airport, Mount Allison draws students from every Canadian province as well as from fifty different nations. Consistent with its location far from densely populated urban centers, Mount Allison has developed standout programs in environmental sustainability. Through its Department of Geography and Environment, Mount Allison operates a Coastal Wetland Institute, a marine and ocean research center, and a laboratory focused on tree-ring research. In recent years, Mount Allison students and faculty have researched the effects of climate change on the Canadian Arctic region.

QUEST UNIVERSITY

And now for something completely different from any other college in Canada: Quest University. Located an hour away from Vancouver in a stunning mountain setting, Quest is a new school taking a divergent path from most Canadian universities. Courses are limited to twenty students and Quest operates on the rather unique block plan where students take one course at a time. The block plan enables students to immerse themselves in a subject and then move on to a new academic adventure with each subsequent block. Colorado College and Cornell College (Iowa) are US colleges that follow a block plan.

Founded by a former president of University of British Columbia, Quest's reason for being is to provide a very intimate, interactive educational experience for students. The first two years at Quest are considered the liberal arts foundation, and the last two years are called the concentration, where students work in-depth on a single topic of choice. Quest, which has an enrollment of about five hundred students, graduated its first class in 2011. Most students reside on the eco-friendly Quest campus. As the school grows, enrollment will be capped at 650 students to ensure the twelve to one student-faculty ratio. One of the few private colleges in Canada, the price tag for Quest ($45,000 CDN in 2015) makes it more expensive than other Canadian schools. That said, all students, including Americans (who currently make up 33 percent of Quest's enrollment) are eligible for a number of scholarships, some of which cover full tuition.

UNIVERSITY OF VICTORIA

UVic, as the University of Victoria is often called, is a typical Canadian university in many ways. Arguably, UVic provides a representative snapshot of Canadian higher education as a whole. UVic is medium sized (twenty-two thousand students), in a moderately sized Canadian city of eighty thousand people, and generally gets solid, but not stellar, academic prestige rankings from *Maclean's*. The solid middle quality of UVic is illustrative of Canada as a nation. Some Americans might argue that the Canadian population likes to gear itself toward a healthy middle, as opposed to cultivating extreme societal highs and lows. In Canada there is a more consistent norm for the standard of living. For example, there are fewer luxury cars than in the United States but also fewer rusted-out beaters. The same goes for housing, health care, and general sensibilities. Similarly, the gulf between the best and the worst in Canadian higher education is not as large as it is in the United States. As a result, average for a Canadian university equates to above average in the US university context.

Still, there is an aspect to UVic that makes it special: its location. Nestled on the coast of Vancouver Island, the UVic campus is five minutes from the ocean. Nearby Oak Bay has a decidedly British character, evidenced by its many tearooms and Tudor-style buildings. The sixteen thousand undergraduates at UVic have access to a wide array of academic options in a bucolic campus setting complete with semi-tame rabbits dotting the manicured lawns and softening the nondescript institutional architecture. Bunnies, and related bunny-population controversies aside, the university's close proximity to downtown Victoria (considered one of Canada's most beautiful cities) provides students with social and educational opportunities beyond campus. Because Victoria is the provincial capital of British Columbia, UVic students have access to the workings of a major government center. UVic's popular co-op program facilitates student involvement with government offices and local firms. The area's tourism also brings international diversity to Victoria, making the area feel more cosmopolitan than most small cities where Canadian universities are located. Plus, the ocean-side location of the school creates a sense of peace and tranquility that can be a welcome counterbalance when the stresses of university seem overwhelming.

With a milder climate than much of Canada, the Victoria area is a popular vacation and retirement spot, known for attracting the newlywed and the nearly dead. Weather on Vancouver Island resembles that of the northern California coast from Monterey to San Francisco and is not as rainy as Vancouver. The setting and climate of Victoria lends itself to great opportunities for all sorts of sports and recreation as well as impressive ocean and climate research centers, such as the Pacific Institute for Climate Solutions and Ocean Networks Canada, which UVic operates in cooperation with the universities of Alberta, British Columbia, Calgary, and Simon Fraser University. In addition to its leading School of Earth and Ocean Sciences, UVic has strong programs in business, law, and public administration. The Gustavson School of Business, for example, offers an innovative specialization in service management. Students in the program learn about strategy, operations, marketing, technology, and human resources as they apply to service fields such as hospitality management and property management. Students get to Vancouver Island by plane or via ferry (from Seattle, Port Angeles, Washington, or Vancouver). Once there, students seem to have a very balanced, Canadian university experience.

UNIVERSITY OF WESTERN ONTARIO

Western Ontario is a bit of a sleeper in that it is a high-quality university with a relatively low profile in the United States. Students looking for the benefits associated with a city location will find it at Western, as will students looking for a campus community. Western is located in a residential neighborhood of the Ontario city of London (population 366,000) and has a pleasant (even picturesque in some corners) collegiate Gothic campus. Numerous campus buildings evoke the collegiate ideal, especially University Tower, which is the visual symbol of Western. Western's home city of London, Ontario, is midway between Toronto and Detroit. For many students in the Great Lakes area of the United States, getting to the Western Ontario campus involves a drive not much further than the trek to a nearby state's flagship university. For example, by car, London, Ontario is reachable in two and a half hours from Detroit; three to four hours from Buffalo and Rochester; five to six hours from Cleveland, Columbus, and Pittsburgh; and seven hours from Chicago.

Given its reasonable proximity to students who have grown up in the shadow of the Big Ten universities, Western is a place that more US students should consider when looking for academic quality at a reasonable price. At least in size and scope, Western resembles many Big Ten universities. The total student population at Western is thirty-five thousand, thirty thousand of which are undergraduates. Although students from Ontario are the majority, there are one hundred different countries represented at Western. As one of Canada's leading research universities, Western offers hundreds of degree programs. There is academic strength across the board at Western, but on the undergraduate level, there are certain areas, such as the social sciences and business, that are recognized as excellent well beyond the campus. Western's Don Wright School of Music is also top notch. Musical groups at Western put on more than three hundred concerts annually. Science-oriented students might be interested to know that Western's Center for Brain and Mind is on the leading edge of research in cognitive neuroscience.

Students looking for more than an academic community will find 180 different student organizations at Western. Nearly twenty thousand students belong to one or more of the extracurricular clubs. US students seeking a fraternity or sorority experience might be pleasantly surprised to find twelve Greek organizations at Western. As at most Canadian universities, residence spaces are limited at Western, with room for roughly six thousand students in on-campus living arrangements that run the gamut from single and double rooms to suite-style dormitories. Notable former students of Western include the author Alice Munro and Robert Dynes, the former president of the University of California system.

OTHER CANADIAN UNIVERSITIES WORTH CONSIDERING

Acadia University—Wolfville, Nova Scotia. Located one hundred miles northwest of Halifax, Acadia is a primarily undergraduate university of 3,500 students. Acadia has an innovative program in environmental and sustainability studies that includes concentrations in environmental advocacy, sustainable community development, innovation and entrepreneurship for sustainability, and environmental thought and practice.

University of Alberta—Edmonton, Alberta. Alberta is a comprehensive research university of thirty-nine thousand students with highly rated programs in engineering, health sciences, life sciences, social sciences, and medicine. It houses the province of Alberta's National Institute for Nanotechnology, which is one of the world's most advanced university research facilities. Sixty-eight Alberta alumni have become Rhodes Scholars.

Carleton University—Ottawa, Ontario. Reflecting its location in Canada's capital, Carleton University is known for strength in journalism, international relations, and public affairs. Carleton also offers an innovative program in sustainable and renewable energy engineering.

Dalhousie University—Halifax, Nova Scotia. Founded in 1818 and molded after Scotland's University of Edinburgh, Dalhousie is one of Canada's oldest universities. Dalhousie is consistently ranked as one of Canada's top universities and is considered the leading school in the eastern provinces of Canada. This seventeen-thousand-student university is known for excellent academic programs in business and law as well as for pathbreaking research in dentistry, medicine, health sciences, and pharmacology.

University of Guelph—Guelph, Ontario. Guelph is a comprehensive institution (enrolling twenty-one thousand students) that includes the Ontario Veterinary College and the Ontario Agricultural College. University of Guelph researchers were the first to confirm water particles on Mars.

University of Lethbridge—Lethbridge, Alberta. Lethbridge (enrollment of nine thousand) is known for strength in the sciences, especially related to water quality research. Lethbridge has one of Canada's largest collections of nineteenth- and twentieth-century American, Canadian, and European art.

Memorial University—Saint John's, Newfoundland. With over 17,500 students, Memorial is the largest university in Atlantic Canada. Memorial is known for having satisfied students (ranked sixth in Canada), strong programs in business and dietetics, and a leading center for marine research—the Marine Institute.

McMaster University—Hamilton, Ontario. McMaster is a 26,500-student research university with a medical center, Canada's largest nuclear research facility (which includes a cyclotron), and a leading health science program with research groups focused on genetics and infectious diseases. A student-centered, problem-based, interdisciplinary approach to learning developed there, known as the McMaster Model, has been adopted by universities throughout the world.

University of New Brunswick—Fredericton, New Brunswick. Founded in 1785, UNB is Canada's oldest English-speaking university. UNB is known for its Canadian Rivers Institute, strong law school, and the Institute of Biomedical Engineering.

University of Northern British Columbia—Prince George, British Columbia. An undergraduate-focused institution with 4,200 students, UNBC is known as Canada's green university.

The UNBC campus is designed to represent the northern BC landscape. UNBC aims to heat all of its buildings with wood pellets harvested from pine trees killed by the mountain pine beetle.

University of Ottawa—Ottawa, Ontario. Located in Canada's capital city not far from the Parliament buildings, the University of Ottawa (forty thousand students) has top-ranked programs in business, chemistry, and neuroscience.

University of Prince Edward Island—Charlottetown, Prince Edward Island. With an enrollment of 4,500 students, the University of Prince Edward Island is undergraduate focused. Students at UPEI can participate in co-op programs associated with the departments of business administration, computer science, dietetics, and physics. UPEI is also known for its strong emphasis on community service.

Royal Conservatory—Toronto, Canada. Affiliated with the University of Toronto until 1991, the Royal Conservatory is home to Canada's leading music school, the Glenn Gould School of Music. Former students of the Royal Conservatory include Oscar Peterson, Sarah McLachlan, Diana Krall, Bruce Cockburn, Paul Shaffer, Glenn Gould, Jon Vickers, Robert Goulet, and Angela Hewitt.

Ryerson University—Toronto, Canada. This urban university of thirty-nine thousand students was formerly known as Ryerson Polytechnic University. Focused on professional education, Ryerson is the home of Canada's largest undergraduate business school (Rogers) and the nation's first undergraduate program in biomedical engineering. Ryerson also has schools of fashion design, radio and television arts, and interior design. A large number of Ryerson students are part-timers enrolled in the continuing education division. Notable alumni of Ryerson include actress/filmmaker Nia Vardalos and actress Nina Dobrev.

Simon Fraser University—Burnaby, British Columbia. Located just outside Vancouver, Simon Fraser (thirty-five thousand students) has leading research facilities in the fields of chemistry, marine biology, and subatomic physics. The modernist design of Simon Fraser's campus has been recognized with many architecture awards. In 2009, Simon Fraser became the first Canadian university to join the NCAA.

University of Waterloo—Waterloo, Ontario. The University of Waterloo (thirty-one thousand students) is a member of the U15, which is comprised of Canada's most research-intensive universities. Waterloo stands out for its programs in computer science, engineering, and informational technology. Waterloo alumni and researchers have developed several technology companies, most notably Research in Motion (the makers of the Blackberry).

Wilfred Laurier University—Waterloo, Ontario. The other university in Waterloo, Wilfred Laurier (seventeen thousand students), also has a campus in Brantford, Ontario. Wilfred Laurier has one of Canada's strongest faculties of music. Music students at Wilfred Laurier can concentrate on contemporary music in addition to classical performance areas. The university is prominent in Canadian political circles for its Laurier Institute for the Study of Public Opinion and Policy.

York University—North York, Ontario. With fifty-three thousand students, York has two campuses near Toronto and ten faculties. York's Faculty of Fine Arts includes Ontario's largest graphic design program. The law school at York (Osgoode Hall) is often ranked the top law school in Canada. Research strengths at York include climate change, digital media, health, history, refugee studies, space sciences, sustainability studies, and vision sciences. The actress Rachel McAdams studied drama at York.

ART SCHOOL IN CANADA

For aspiring art and design students, there are a number of quality options in Canada. Perhaps the best-known Canadian art school is **OCAD University**—formerly known as Ontario College of Art and Design. Located in the art and design hub of Toronto, OCAD is Canada's oldest and largest school for art and design. OCAD enrolls more than six thousand students and offers seven bachelor of design degree programs and ten BFA programs. For students seeking to study art in Canada's largest western city (Vancouver), **Emily Carr University of Art and Design** has 1,800 full-time students and offers BFA, bachelor of design, and bachelor of media arts programs. Emily Carr is known for its innovative programs in interaction design, integrated media, animation, and social media arts. **NSCAD University** in Halifax, Nova Scotia, is Atlantic Canada's leading art school. Formerly called Nova Scotia College of Art and Design, NSCAD University has approximately one thousand students and is organized into the divisions of crafts, design, fine arts, media arts, and historical and critical studies. Majors offered at NSCAD include textiles/fashion, jewelry design and metalsmithing, intermedia, and interdisciplinary design. **Alberta College of Art and Design** (ACAD), located in the growing city of Calgary, offers eleven degree programs in fine arts and design. The 1,300 students at ACAD have study options such as fiber, glass, jewelry and metals, media arts and digital technologies, and visual communications design.

Beyond Canada's specialized art schools, there are several university art programs of note. At the **University of Windsor** (located a bridge ride over the river from Detroit) there are majors in visual arts, visual arts and communication, visual arts and visual culture, and a visual arts and the built environment program that involves a collaboration with the School of Architecture at University of Detroit Mercy. The School of the Arts at **McMaster University** has BA and BFA programs in art. BFA students at McMaster can explore areas such as book arts, foundry, lithography, integrated media, and print media. McMaster also offers a course on the environmentally responsible studio. The **University of Alberta** offers BA and BFA programs in art and design as well as a bachelor of design (BDes) degree. Students in the BDes program choose specializations in visual communications design or industrial design and can link their program of study to areas such as business and marketing, engineering, computer science, and printmaking. At **University of Western Ontario**, students can pursue a BFA in visual arts with a specialization in studio arts. All BFA students at Western complete a practicum class that simulates the creative experience of a working artist. **University of British Columbia** students can earn a BA or BFA in visual arts. There is also an option at UBC to specialize in art education. At the **University of Victoria**, BFA students can specialize in digital media arts, drawing, painting, photography, sculpture, or video art.

CANADIAN STUDIES: EXAMINING CANADA THROUGH A US LENS

There are some people for whom Canada is fascinating from an intellectual perspective.

Arguably as well, understanding Canada can increase a person's appreciation of the United

States' place in North American culture and history. Indeed, Canada has an intriguing history and culture of its own, the focus on which has become an academic discipline called Canadian studies. The academic discipline of Canadian studies varies from program to program, but generally all programs encompass economic, historical, political, geographic, and artistic issues that define Canada as a nation. For those who want to study Canada without leaving the United States, below is a list of schools that offer undergraduate opportunities in Canadian studies:

- University of Washington—Canadian Studies Center at the Henry M. Jackson School of International Studies
- University of Vermont
- Bowling Green State University (OH)
- Bridgewater State College (MA)
- Duke University
- Franklin College (IN)
- Michigan State University—the United States' oldest Canadian studies program (founded in 1958)
- State University of New York College at Plattsburgh
- St. Lawrence University (NY)
- University of California at Berkeley—study opportunities, but not a major
- University of Maine—Canadian American Center
- Wayne State University (MI)
- Western Kentucky University—online certificate program plus an opportunity to intern in the Canadian Parliament
- Western Washington University
- University of New Hampshire—minor only

COLLEGE OPTIONS AROUND THE GLOBE AND/OR ON MULTIPLE CAMPUSES

UNIVERSITIES BEYOND NORTH AMERICA

The first American colleges and universities took as their models the great universities of Europe—institutions like Oxford and Cambridge in England and Heidelberg in Germany. Across America there are reflections of European universities in the campus architecture of Princeton and Yale and in the original missions of Johns Hopkins and the University of Chicago, just to name a few examples. Generations of Americans seeking the European university experience have made sure to schedule into their undergraduate years a semester or year of study abroad at universities in England, France, Germany Ireland, Scotland, Spain, and other countries. Recently, however, a growing number of US students have chosen to take their whole undergraduate experience abroad by venturing to Europe, and other continents, to get a degree. The universities of Great Britain have been the most sought-after destinations because instruction is in English and the cultural hurdles to surmount are seen as minimal in comparison to some other parts of the world. Although most of the students leaving America for college go to countries like England and Scotland, a growing number of English-speaking universities in other countries are seeking to enroll US students. This chapter introduces students to opportunities for undergraduate study in countries beyond the United States and Canada.

Among the choices students will find as they venture beyond North America are foreign universities (where English is the primary language of instruction) and American colleges and universities located in foreign countries. Many American campuses in foreign countries are branches (or study abroad sites) of a college back in the United States. In some cases, American colleges operate degree-granting affiliates accredited by one of the recognized accrediting agencies in the United States. When investigating college options abroad, students, in our opinion, should stick to schools that are accredited because a degree has greater value and more legitimacy if a respected source has certified that its academic programs follow sound practices acknowledged as the standards in the field. Foreign universities, although not governed by American regulatory standards, also tend to answer to certifying organizations in their own country, such as an education ministry or board. The schools mentioned in this chapter are all fully accredited, real colleges, described in relation to their capacity to support the educational needs of American students.

Another issue to consider is safety. While going to college in another country offers novel and potentially perspective-broadening experiences, some countries are less safe than others. Students are advised to consider the safety of the city and country where universities of interest are located. This issue is especially critical for female, gay, lesbian, transgender, and minority students. Students who choose carefully screened study abroad options (with established support networks and transition programs for American students) tend to encounter fewer problems, even in dicey areas, than students who go it alone with minimal knowledge of the local customs and risk factors. Erring on the side of caution is a good idea. Still, there are many countries that are as safe, if not safer, than the United States.

THE UNITED KINGDOM AND UCAS

In the United Kingdom (UK)—consisting of England, Scotland, Wales, and Northern Ireland—universities manage the college admissions process using the Universities and Colleges Admissions System (UCAS). Through UCAS, students can apply to up to five universities while paying a single fee. With over three hundred university choices available, the United Kingdom (with UCAS) provides a vast opportunity for American students seeking to earn their college degree internationally. Submitting an application through UCAS is a bit different from the typical application process in the United States, but once a student gets grounded in how UCAS works, it is relatively straightforward.

For starters, students need to recognize that the typical UK bachelor's degree program is structured differently from the United States. In many UK programs (or programmes, as they spell it), a student exclusively studies or "reads" one subject or "course" and graduates in three years instead of four. That means students generally confine themselves to classes relevant to their major. UK universities tend not to have a general education core requiring students to take classes beyond their chosen field. For some, the freedom to delve deep into a particular academic discipline is pure heaven. For others, especially those who are unsure of what they might want to study in depth, the lack of a general studies requirement can feel hasty and confining. Indeed, there are UK universities that offer a four-year program allowing for a wider range of classes and elective choice, but it is imperative for students looking at UK universities to understand that a majority of the degrees offered follow the more subject-specific, three-year program.

UK students tend to organize their search around the course of study they wish to pursue first and university options second. The organization of the UCAS website reflects that difference in approaches. For example, if a student wants to study anthropology or British history, the UCAS website has a search feature that identifies which universities offer that course as a degree program. From there, students can research and consider the respective features of each program as well as the qualifications needed for entry.

UCAS POINTS

Overall, the admissions process at UK universities is more transparent than the often opaque holistic review system employed by selective colleges in the United States. UCAS relies on a relatively straightforward point (or tariff) system to review applicants. UCAS awards each applicant a number of points. Having more UCAS points improves an applicant's chances for admission to the targeted programs. The UCAS system is clear about how points are awarded to applicants based on courses taken, the applicant's essay, exam results, and other factors explained on the UCAS site. Points are portable throughout the UCAS network of universities. Although a student's points, as determined by UCAS, will be the same everywhere he or she applies, each university has a different point threshold for admission to its particular programs. An applicant's tariff (points) score may be high enough to gain admission to study academic program X at university A but not at universities B and C. Another course of study may not require as high a tariff score, so the same applicant may be able to study Y at university A, B, and C. It all varies by university and academic program.

UCAS points are usually calculated based on a series of classes and exams in the United Kingdom called A levels. American applicants typically do not take A-level exams, so for them the UCAS tariff system can substitute Advance Placement (AP) or International Baccalaureate (IB) classes. For example, IB aggregate exam results of 24 to 45 points get converted to a UCAS tariff score range of 260 to 720. The UCAS tariff system also awards higher point totals to certain IB classes as well as for the extended essay, theory of knowledge, and creativity, action, and/or service. For a detailed breakdown of how UCAS converts the IB curriculum into tariff points, prospective applicants to UK universities should take a close look at www.ucas.ac.uk/students/ucas_tariff/factsheet/ib.

Although the IB curriculum is gaining a foothold in the United States, AP courses are more frequently taught in American high schools. Applicants from the United States need to recognize that not all AP courses are considered equal in the eyes of UCAS. UCAS has a two-tier system for awarding tariff points for AP course work. What UCAS deems the A group of AP courses is worth more points than the B group of AP courses, although all AP courses are worth some points in the UCAS tariff system.

A Group courses. (Each AP exam score of 5 generates 120 points; each AP exam score of 4 generates 90 points; and each AP exam score of 3 generates 60 points.)

- Biology
- Calculus AB and BC
- Chemistry
- English literature and composition
- English language and composition
- European history
- French language
- French literature
- German
- Italian language and culture
- Latin literature
- Latin: Virgil
- Physics
- Spanish language
- Spanish literature
- US history
- World history

B Group course. (Each AP exam score of 5 generates 50 points; each AP exam score of 4 generates 35 points; each AP exam score of 3 generates 20 points.)

- Art history
- Computer science (A)
- Computer science (AB)
- Economics (micro and macro)
- Environmental science
- Government and politics (all)
- Human geography
- Psychology
- Statistics
- Studio art (all)

If a US applicant's high school curriculum is neither AP- nor IB-based, UCAS will likely need to determine another way to evaluate the applicant's transcript. If, however, an applicant's high school offers AP or IB courses, and the applicant has not elected to take those courses, chances for direct admission to a UK university are quite slim. In the United Kingdom, university-bound students take (with their A-level preparation) what equates in America to a thirteenth grade. The rough equivalent in the United States is usually offered as ten to twenty AP classes or completion of the full IB diploma.

For American students aspiring to a UK university but falling short of UCAS requirements, one option is a year in a general-education program at a sixth-form college, such as Oxford's Brooks College. Some people think of the sixth-form colleges as the British junior colleges. Typically, admission to a sixth-form college is considerably less competitive than admission to a UK university. In the sixth form, the student will take a year's worth of A-level study. Given that most UK bachelor's degree programs are three-year courses of study (with the exception of some of the Scottish universities), taking a general-studies year in the beginning (at a sixth-form college) actually makes it more like the four-year US college experience of first seeking general knowledge and then zeroing in on a major. Once armed with the necessary credentials of A-level completion, a student can apply to specific degree programs in the United Kingdom.

For the American student, attending a sixth-form college can provide an excellent transitional bridge to study in the United Kingdom. A year at a sixth-form college can familiarize American students with the study approaches and social mores of the United Kingdom as well as with the reputations and strengths of the different universities and programs of study available. Because sixth-form colleges are often located near a major university, sixth-form students can get an early sense about the larger university community. The sixth-form college experience can also provide students with a clearer sense of which UK universities are realistic options for entry. For the dedicated student, attending a sixth-form college can be excellent preparation for getting into a UK university that would not have admitted the student straight out of a US high school. Listed below are some sixth-form colleges for American students to consider.

- Brookes College (Oxford)
- Cambridge Center for Sixth Form Studies (Cambridge)
- Mander Portman Woodward (Cambridge, London, and Birmingham)

For US applicants to UK universities, the process of trying to determine the best choice (both for academics and social life) can be daunting. Beyond UCAS, the UNISTATS website is a useful resource, while another site, www.push.co.uk, offers a slightly irreverent approach to evaluating UK universities. Students seeking to understand the ranking and relative prestige of the UK universities may want to check out the Times Higher Education World University Rankings and the QS World University Rankings.

OXBRIDGE

Generally considered the most prestigious universities in the United Kingdom (if not the world), the two universities known as Oxbridge (Oxford and Cambridge) have additional application requirements. First of all, applicants can apply either to Oxford or Cambridge but not to both. An application to Cambridge or Oxford starts through UCAS and then gets passed along for an additional review handled directly at each university. Oxbridge applicants deemed truly viable are often required to have an interview. Interviews are usually held on campus, but off-campus accommodations can be made for applicants from outside the United Kingdom. Understandably, making a trip to England for the interview may not be possible, but there are a few key reasons why US applicants should seriously consider making the trip to England for the interview (if invited). For one, tutors (the Oxbridge name for professors) in the applicant's intended course of study often conduct the interview, and, second, the off-site interviewers may be less familiar with the nuances of the applicant's academic program of interest. Even though the UCAS deadline for Oxbridge applications has traditionally been October 15, it is best to apply earlier in case extra time is needed to arrange for an interview. Also, keep in mind that some courses require additional exams that may coincide with the interview.

When applying to Oxbridge or any other university within the UCAS system, applicants have the option to choose a specific college. What is labeled a college at most UK universities has more to do with social affiliation than academics. When investigating British universities, it is especially wise to research the character and history of particular colleges to determine whether Magdalen College at Oxford may be a better fit than, say, Christ Church College. Students with a strong preference for a certain college should designate that choice when applying. Some students admitted to Oxbridge get assigned a college randomly, which can be fine as long as any college will do. In cases of random assignment, applicants must be sure to confirm whether the assigned college offers their intended course of study. Most colleges have students from all courses of study, but there are exceptions, so it is worth checking this through UCAS or through the Cambridge or Oxford individual admission sites. Admission decisions at Oxbridge are typically announced in January. Decisions can be contingent on successful exam results for the remainder of senior year.

UNIVERSITY OF ST. ANDREWS

The Scottish university where Prince William met Kate Middleton has become a very popular destination for American students. Having recently celebrated its six-hundredth anniversary, St. Andrews, founded in 1413, is the third-oldest university in the English-speaking world. St. Andrews is a medium-sized school of 7,200 students (one-third from overseas) on a compact campus interwoven into its seaside namesake town of 17,000. Compared to most UK universities, St. Andrews offers more flexible degree programs and courses of study within its four faculties: arts, divinity, medicine, and science.

The strong emphasis on high-quality teaching at St. Andrews has led to its strong reputation and growing popularity beyond the United Kingdom. Typically, St. Andrews receives ten times as many applications as there are spaces available. In addition to the US students enrolling at St. Andrews directly from high school, others are there working on a joint degree program linking the university to the College of William and Mary in Virginia. Applicants from overseas can apply to St. Andrews using the Common Application, rather than going through UCAS.

THE COMMON APPLICATION IN THE UNITED KINGDOM AND EUROPE

Within the United Kingdom, there are other universities, beyond St. Andrews, that accept the Common Application as an alternative to UCAS. Students can apply to these schools via the Common Application.

- Hult International Business School
- Keele University
- King's College London
- Richmond, the American International University in London
- University of Aberdeen (Scotland)
- University of Birmingham
- University of Bristol
- University of Stirling (Scotland)

The following European universities use the Common Application:

- The American University of Paris
- The American University of Rome
- Franklin University Switzerland
- Jacobs University Bremen
- John Cabot University in Rome
- Modul University, Vienna

IRELAND

Ireland has a relatively small but appealing network of universities, several of which are located in the cosmopolitan city of Dublin. A good starting point for students looking at Ireland is the National Framework Qualification (NFQ) website (www.nfq.ie). The NFQ website can help students match their study interests to the required academic qualifications at individual universities. Most North American students will likely find themselves investigating a level seven or eight study program in Ireland, which in Irish higher education speak translates to a three-year bachelor's degree program.

In Ireland, annual college costs range from $14,700 USD to $73,000 USD (2013 data). The most expensive university options (those in the top third of the range) are specialized training programs, such as medicine (which in Ireland begins directly from high school), rather than the typical undergraduate courses of study. Ireland has experienced major financial upheaval in recent years, but it is still more affordable than many other places in Europe, such as London and Paris. General livability and high-quality educational opportunities make Ireland an appealing option for students, regardless of their personal stance on Guinness, leprechauns, and U2. Due to generous government incentives, many US companies such as Apple, Pfizer, PayPal, Twitter and Microsoft have chosen to set up their European outposts in Ireland. The resulting connectivity with American business has increased the recognition and portability of an Irish diploma back in the United States.

The largest Irish university (University College, Dublin) enrolls roughly twenty-five thousand students. But overall, Irish universities are what Americans typically label midsize universities, with student populations of seven to twelve thousand. The size of most Irish universities plays to their advantage because for many Americans, the midsize university is the ideal. For students looking for that middle-sized university, the Irish universities best set up to serve American students are listed below.

- Dublin City University
- Dublin Institute of Technology
- National University of Ireland (Galway)
- National University of Ireland (Maynooth)
- Trinity College, Dublin
- University College, Cork
- University College, Dublin
- University of Limerick

One Irish study option is targeted to Americans of Irish heritage. Through the Homecoming Study Programme, the Irish government seeks to celebrate the Irish diaspora by welcoming the children, grandchildren, and great grandchildren of Irish nationals to study in Ireland. For those who qualify, the Homecoming Study Programme offers reduced tuition at the Dublin Institute of Technology along with an opportunity to live with an Irish host family.

OTHER OPTIONS IN EUROPE

In many European countries, attending university is free. But free tuition means fewer amenities compared to the typical American college.

While European universities are recognized for their academic quality and the alumni loyalty some engender, the experience tends to be less personal. Many of Europe's universities are very large, resulting in an overall experience that is more assembly line than handcrafted. At the typical European university, the onus is on students to fight for what they need amid large populations and finite resources. Large lecture classes and minimal contact with professors tend to be the norm. Because it is expected that students will live at home or on their own, the typical European university does not have residence halls. Also, because many students attend university in their hometown, there is a larger commuter culture than at American schools. There is also a strong emphasis on specialization in a chosen field and nothing else. This occurs because by high school many European students have already selected a specific academic track. By college they are ready to specialize even further. For an American student who is already committed to a single academic area, this approach might be appealing. It might be too specific, however, for the many American high school students who are still deciding what they want to study as a specialty or major in college.

Students considering continental Europe for an undergraduate degree will find more options if they are comfortable undertaking a degree taught in another language. While there are some students ready to handle a college experience comprised of three to four years of immersion in another language, most American students investigating Europe for college will be more comfortable and successful in English-friendly settings. For that reason, this chapter focuses on institutions where English is the primary mode of instruction. In most cases, however, learning the local language is important, even if schoolwork is in English. In addition to instruction in English, many of the institutions highlighted below are unusual in another way. They are private institutions, unlike the majority of universities in Europe. Being private, many of these schools are set up to offer a smaller, more intimate academic setting than their public counterparts—characteristics that make them more American friendly than the typical European university.

American University of Paris. This school has been an option since 1962 for Francophiles and others seeking educational opportunities in the City of Light. Unlike prestigious but massive French public universities, such as the famed Sorbonne, the American University of Paris is a private school with only nine hundred undergraduates, making for a rather intimate academic setting, akin to small liberal arts colleges in the United States. With students hailing from all over the world, AUP has an international vibe while still offering the convenience of an American accredited degree. AUP offers twenty majors and thirty-five minors. While there are many interesting courses, AUP tends to be limited in the science and technology subjects. New AUP students initially live in a hostel while they decide which type of housing they prefer. Housing options include dorms, rented rooms, host families, and shared apartments. This reality of European university life scatters students around Paris, but there are opportunities to come together through sports, student government, and other activities.

Bogazici University (Turkey). Located in Istanbul and often ranked as Turkey's top university, Bogazici's ties to the United States can be traced back to its founding in 1863. More than twelve thousand students attend Bogazici, and courses in its six faculties and schools are taught in English.

Denmark and Sweden. In Denmark, a large number of academic programs are open to English-speaking students, either as exchange students or degree seekers. The Study in Denmark website (studyindenmark.dk) is a useful place for Americans to begin investigating Danish universities. In Sweden, degree study options for English speakers are more limited, but exchange opportunities are abundant. The Study in Sweden website (www.studyinsweden.se) can help American students sort through the possibilities for study abroad or degree study.

Franklin University Switzerland. Franklin University (an American-accredited college located in the picturesque Italian-speaking lakeside city of Lugano) aims to give its students a cross-cultural education that spurs them to engage the world. The 450 students at Franklin get to extend their class work through the Academic Travel Program (ATP), which consists of faculty-led, two-week trips that take students to sites around Europe. The most popular majors at Franklin are international management and international relations.

University of Freiburg. This German university of 24,000 students offers an interdisciplinary bachelor's degree program in liberal arts and sciences that is taught in English. Launched in 2012, the selective program annually enrolls a new cohort of 75-100 intellectually curious students on a campus where the noted thinkers Friedrich Hayek, Martin Heidegger, Edmund Husserl, and Herbert Marcuse once studied or taught.

Jacobs University Bremen. This school seeks to provide an engaging, innovative environment for studying science and technology. The majority of the three-year bachelor's degree programs at Jacobs focus on engineering, math, and science. But there are options—including global humanities and intercultural relations and behavior—for the less technically minded. Unlike larger German universities, Jacobs encourages campus social life through four residential colleges that serve the approximately 1,120 undergraduates.

Maastricht University. Founded in 1976, Maastricht is the youngest university in the Netherlands but it is quickly rising in prominence, as illustrated by its rapid climb in prestigious university

rankings such as London's Times Higher Education World University Rankings and the QS World University Rankings. Maastricht has been called one of the top one hundred universities in the world and one of the top fifty among universities less than fifty years old. Originally founded as a medical school, Maastricht has greatly expanded to include many other degree offerings, including sixteen undergraduate programs. At Maastricht, there is an emphasis on problem-based learning, which puts students in small tutor-led groups to solve problems and learn from the process. Of the approximately fifteen thousand students at Maastricht, about half are from outside the Netherlands. Also, because the vast majority of its classes are taught in English, Maastricht has become a host campus for several study abroad programs. American students pay higher tuition rates than their European counterparts, but after converting the 8,500 to 9,500 euro annual tuition to dollars, it rings in at $11,490 to $12,842 (2013 figures)—a cost far lower than many colleges and universities in the United States. Obviously, the euro to dollar exchange rate varies, as does the increase in tuition from year to year, but even factoring that in, Maastricht is a good value, particularly because its students usually earn their degrees in just three years.

Paris Institute of Political Studies. Known as Sciences Po, this school has a joint degree program with Columbia University's College of General Studies. Sciences Po is considered the training ground for France's leading politicians and diplomats and is widely recognized (analogous to the London School of Economics) as one of the world's top schools for the social sciences. Students in the program split their four years between France and New York City. No matter the site, courses are in English. The program begins in France and offers students three potential sites (Le Havre, Menton, and Reims), where the curriculum focuses on languages, economics, international relations, law, political science, and sociology. Graduates of the program receive BA degrees from Columbia University and Sciences Po. There is an automatic admission option for students who wish to stay on to earn a MA from Sciences Po, but admission is not similarly guaranteed to any Columbia graduate programs. Prospective students should also note that the dual degree Sciences Po program is only available through Columbia's College of General Studies, not through Columbia College or the Fu Foundation School of Engineering. Students cannot transfer from the Columbia/Sciences Po program to Columbia College or to the Fu Foundation School of Engineering.

STUDYING DOWN UNDER

Students seeking English-speaking universities beyond North America may want to look down under. In recent years, universities in Australia and New Zealand have stepped up efforts to enroll international students from Asia, Europe, and the United States as a way to increase their revenue. For many American students, the chief drawback of university down under is adapting to the different calendar. The fall semester for Australians begins in March, which means that students from the states must wait six months to begin collegiate studies. On the other hand, the wait can enable students to earn extra tuition money or explore an interest (through a truncated gap year) before going off to college.

Students looking for universities with mild climates will find Australia and New Zealand appealing as neither country is known for weather extremes. Much of Australia has weather resembling California, and much of New Zealand has weather like the Pacific Northwest. For students who are overwhelmed with joy at the thought of studying among koalas and wallabies or amid the landscape of the *Lord of the Rings* movies, there are many options to explore in Australia and New Zealand.

Prospective students can search out schools in Australia and New Zealand independently, but may find it more helpful to utilize the resources of australearn.org, a branch of the nonprofit agency, globalinksabroad.org. Australearn provides free program information and logistical support regarding university study opportunities in Australia, New Zealand, and Fiji. Many American students use Australearn to investigate study abroad programs—and indeed its parent company, Globalinksabroad.org, is primarily a study abroad service. However, because Gloabalinksabroad has already done much of the work to help students understand the procedures and documentation required, Australearn's services can also help ease the application process for students seeking a degree down under.

HIGHEST-RANKED AUSTRALIAN UNIVERSITIES

The most distinguished of Australia's universities belong to the so-called group of eight, listed below in alphabetical order.

- University of Adelaide
- Australian National University
- University of Melbourne
- Monash University
- University of New South Wales
- University of Queensland
- University of Sydney
- University of Western Australia

In addition to scoring high when Australian universities are ranked, the universities in the group of eight tend to hold higher places in the various rankings of the world's top universities. When numerous rankings are compiled and averaged, Australia's group of eight expands to ten leading universities (listed in rank order).

1) University of Melbourne

2) Australian National University (Canberra)

3) University of Sydney

4) University of Queensland (Metro Brisbane)

5) University of New South Wales (Metro Sydney)

6) Monash University (Melbourne)

7) University of Western Australia (Perth)

8) University of Adelaide

9) Macquarie University (Metro Sydney)

10) Wollongong University (New South Wales)

HIGHEST-RANKED UNIVERSITIES IN NEW ZEALAND

Eight universities in New Zealand tend to dominate the conversation. Aggregating various rankings of New Zealand's universities by quality and reputation leads to the following top-eight list.

1) University of Auckland

2) University of Otago (Dunedin)

3) University of Canterbury (Christchurch)

4) Victoria University of Wellington

5) University of Waikato (Hamilton)

6) Massey University (Palmerston North)

7) Auckland University of Technology

8) Lincoln University

OPTIONS IN AFRICA, ASIA, LATIN AMERICA, AND BEYOND

Many students from around the world hope for the opportunity to study at an American or Canadian university. This is partly because North America is fortunate to have an abundance of quality educational choices not commonly found elsewhere. That said, there are always some North American students eager to leave their continent for a college experience, particularly if there is a personal draw to a certain area. For those adventurous students, there are degree options all over the globe.

Students seeking to venture beyond study abroad to degree study will find that the landscape is changing. While it is still true that, overall, American employers and graduate school admissions committees can more readily interpret the value of an American college degree, there is growing recognition of (and comfort with) the quality of degrees offered in the United Kingdom, Europe, and some of the former British Commonwealth nations. But when students get farther afield, they may find that employers are less familiar with overseas colleges and universities and can have trouble interpreting the relative quality of the degree. Sometimes the best option is to seek out a campus (if available) with American or British roots and accreditation. Studying in a program approved by, or modeled after, an American college improves the likelihood that the degree will be understood and the credits will apply (in the case of transfer) back home. We offer this information as a caution, not as discouragement.

AFRICA

Most Americans do not seek out degrees from African schools. This is true for three basic reasons: language barriers, safety concerns, and resource gaps. Unlike Asia and Europe, Africa is a continent of varied and complex languages that are not widely taught in North American schools. Many African countries are poor and under-developed in comparison to Asia and the West. The reality of third-world conditions, pervasive levels of economic hardship, and rapidly changing levels of political stability create serious obstacles for even the most adventurous American student to surmount. Unfortunately, many countries in Africa can pose varying (and often high) levels of danger for students seeking to earn degrees or take courses. Still, taking the African continent as a whole, it is possible to find places where students from the United States can find rewarding educational opportunities. In some cases, African universities offer instruction in English, but even those schools are almost exclusively attended by locals—meaning that US students must be ready to stand out as pioneers amid a near complete lack of a non-African presence.

Many of the universities best equipped to enroll American students are in South Africa, including South Africa's two most distinguished schools: the **University of Cape Town** and the **University of Witwatersrand**. Other South African universities that American students might want to consider are **Rhodes University**, a highly residential medium-sized university of seven thousand students, or **Stellenbosch**

University, which is a popular study abroad partner with many US colleges. Beyond South Africa, American students will find opportunities at **Addis Ababa University** in Ethiopia, the **University of Botswana**, and **Egerton University** in Kenya. Historically, Edgerton was an agricultural college for white colonials, but it has since opened to all races, expanded its academic offerings, and formed a partnership with Western Michigan University.

THE MIDDLE EAST

Universities in Israel are popular study abroad sites for American students. Although many of the study in Israel programs are English friendly, it is nearly impossible to earn a degree from a university in Israel—such as Technion, Tel Aviv, Haifa, or Hebrew University—without fluency in Hebrew. Despite warfare and political upheaval in Middle Eastern countries beyond Israel, there are some viable university options for Americans seeking English-based instruction—many of them in the Arab Emirates. Still, as with Africa, students need to recognize that political stability and personal safety can vary greatly from country to country. Conservative local religious beliefs and customs—particularly in Islamic countries—must also be respected and navigated by westerners. In recent years, numerous options for degree seekers have emerged in the relatively Western-friendly Arab Emirate countries of Abu Dhabi and Qatar. Recommending the Emirates are the resources put into universities there, along with the relative safety and stability of the surroundings. Several American universities have set up campuses in the Emirates, helping lend brand quality to the education offered in the region as well as easy portability of degrees across borders.

Qatar's government started a trend by creating the Foundation for Education, Science, and Community Development in an effort to become the education center for the entire region. The foundation invited six American, one British, and one French university to set up branch campuses. While the schools are independent from one another, there is a good deal of sharing and exchange within the community. A few of the schools, such as Cornell University's medical school, are focused on graduate-level programs, so we have only included the schools that also offer undergraduate programs. In each case, these branch campuses are small, which means they offer an excellent opportunity to earn a prestigious degree in a setting that is more intimate than the larger main campuses back in the United States. The campuses in Qatar blend a small-college atmosphere with the resources of a powerhouse American research university. The American universities in Qatar that offer undergraduate degrees include **Northwestern, Virginia Commonwealth University, Carnegie Mellon, Georgetown,** and **Texas A&M**. Keep in mind that the schools only offer certain degree programs at their Qatar campus rather than the full range of majors and minors offered at their US campuses. For example, Georgetown's program is for its School of Foreign Service, and Northwestern's Qatar campus is concentrated on its Medill School of Journalism. Also, keep in mind that very few American students are enrolled at these campuses. The following schools (where instruction is primarily in English) may be worth considering.

Abu Dhabi University. Instruction at ADU is in Arabic and English. The 4,300 students come from fifty-five different countries for academic programs in arts and sciences, business, and engineering.

American University of Beirut. Of the 8,000 students at AUB, 2,000 are from outside Lebanon, and 6,400 are undergraduates. AUB offers more than 120 academic programs in areas such as architecture, arts and sciences, business, and engineering.

American University in Cairo. Among the 5,300 students at AUC, just 8 percent are from outside Egypt. Academic areas where students can earn degrees at AUC include arts and sciences, business, computer science, and engineering.

American University of Sharjah. The approximately five thousand students at AUS come from more than eighty foreign countries. Between the four colleges and schools, there are twenty-six majors offered. Instruction is in English.

IDC Hertzlia (Israel). Through IDC's International School, students from overseas can pursue BA programs in business administration, communications, government, and psychology.

Middlesex University (Dubai). Middlesex bills itself as London's first and only university campus in the United Arab Emirates. The approximately 2,500 undergraduates and graduates at Middlesex-Dubai represent more than ninety nationalities.

King Saud University (Saudi Arabia). Course instruction, except for Islamic subjects, is in English, but the overwhelming majority of the thirty-eight thousand students are Saudis.

ASIA

Due to Asia's prominence in global trade, there are increasing numbers of students seeking to study in Asia. Competition to get into Asian universities is legendary, but a growing number of schools (some of which are listed below) are offering course instruction in English.

Yale–National University Singapore. An Ivy League outpost in Singapore, Yale-NUS saw its first 150 students arrive on campus in August 2013. Those 150 students are the pioneering first class at a hybrid East-West university that expects to grow to 1,000 undergraduates. The joining of Yale and NUS is an effort to create a premier liberal arts college experience in

Asia. Students can apply to Yale-NUS using the Common Application.

University of Hong Kong. This highly respected Asian university, founded when Hong Kong was under British rule, offers instruction in English. The University of Hong Kong is a popular study abroad destination for American students. UHK enrolls roughly 10,500 undergraduates and offers a wide array of academic programs. For North American applicants, the UHK website clearly spells out the admission requirements for each degree program. UHK is selective, which means that to be viable applicants should have taken AP or IB classes. The UHK campus has several architecturally significant (and collegiate-looking) buildings that reflect its British roots.

Hong Kong University of Science and Technology. This school consistently ranks as one of the top universities in Asia.

International Christian University. This university of 2,500 undergraduates in Tokyo (founded after World War Two to promote peace) offers a wide array of majors.

Jogakkan College. This Japanese women's college has instruction in Japanese and English.

National University Singapore. Independent of its program with Yale, NUS is an option for North American students.

Ritsumeikan Asia Pacific. At this Japanese school, almost half of the 5,700 students are international students—with roughly one hundred from North America.

Sophia University Tokyo. Sophia, a popular study abroad destination for US and Canadian students, has partnerships with nearly seventy American colleges.

Waseda University. A Japanese university with some degree programs taught in English.

Yonsei University. Within this Korean university, Underwood International College is an English-speaking, liberal arts unit that enrolls one thousand students from forty-seven countries.

LATIN AMERICA

While some courses at Latin American universities are taught in English, no degree-granting colleges in Latin America base their academic program in English or have American accreditation. Because South and Central America were dominated during colonial times by Spain and Portugal, the linguistic legacy in the region is Spanish and Portuguese. As a result, students not fluent in Spanish or Portuguese are limited to experiencing Latin American universities through study abroad programs. While there are wonderful opportunities to study in Central and South America, it is best to do so in programs that are accredited and offer course credits that transfer back to North American institutions.

NORTH AMERICAN COLLEGES WITH CAMPUSES ABROAD

Many study abroad programs involve student exchange agreements or cooperative affiliations with foreign universities. But some colleges maintain facilities in other parts of the world that function as a global extension of the main campus. Most notably, New York University has become a global network university with stand-alone, degree-granting campuses in Abu Dhabi and Shanghai. Students at NYU's Washington Square campus may spend a semester studying at any of the sites in the global network. A number of other institutions (listed and in some cases profiled below) have established a presence in one or more countries. While many students utilize these sites for study abroad, others choose to spend their undergraduate years at these outposts and earn their degree entirely abroad. This list ranges from fully comprehensive degree-issuing campuses to satellite locations created expressly for term-length study abroad experiences.

University of Dallas—Rome

Emerson College—a castle in the Netherlands

University of Evansville—Hardaxton, England

Ithaca College—London Center

Loyola University Chicago—Rome Center

University of Maryland—Schwabisch Gmund (Germany)

New York University—Abu Dhabi, Berlin, Buenos Aires, Florence, Ghana, London, Madrid, Paris, Prague, Shanghai, Tel Aviv

Pepperdine University—Buenos Aires, Florence, Heidelberg, Lausanne, London, Shanghai

Queen's University (Canada)—Herstmonceux Castle in England

St. Louis University—Madrid

Savannah College of Art and Design—Hong Kong and LaCoste, France

Suffolk University—Madrid

Syracuse University—Beijing, Florence, Hong Kong, London, Madrid, Santiago (Chile), Strasbourg (France)

Temple University—Oviedo (Spain), Rome, Tokyo

Trinity College (Connecticut)—Rome

Webster University—Cha-am (Thailand), Geneva, Leiden (the Netherlands), London, Shanghai, Vienna

NYU Abu Dhabi. Perhaps the most appealing option for North Americans wanting to study in the Middle East is NYU Abu Dhabi. NYU Abu Dhabi offers twenty-two different majors and an honors college–type of experience. Small and nurturing, like an American liberal arts college, NYU Abu Dhabi combines a liberal arts college environment with major university resources. Competitive admissions and degree seekers from all over the world make this a truly international intellectual experience. Having the NYU name and accreditation behind NYU Abu Dhabi makes the degree portable and thus desirable.

NYU-Shang Hai. An attempt to bring American liberal arts education to China, NYU-Shang Hai enrolled is first class in fall 2013. Plans call for one thousand students, half from China and half from other countries.

Temple University Japan. Philadelphia's Temple University has a branch campus in Tokyo, where courses are taught in English and students do not have to speak Japanese to enroll. Several majors are offered at the Tokyo campus for degree seekers wishing to study there for four years. There is also the option to divide time between Philadelphia and Tokyo through 2-2 or 2-3 programs. The 2-2 option is an even split between the campuses, whereas the 2-3 program consists of three years in Tokyo, followed by two years in Philadelphia to finish up undergraduate course work and complete a master's degree. In Tokyo, Temple's Institute of Contemporary Asian Studies operates the Wakai Project focused on issues facing young Japanese people. For their first semester in Japan, Temple students are housed in dorms or with host families. Following that, Temple helps students secure off-campus housing.

COLLEGES WITH HIGH STUDY-ABROAD RATES AND LARGE NUMBERS OF PROGRAMS

There are generally two routes to studying abroad: (1) choosing a program offered by or affiliated with a student's home campus; (2) selecting a program not offered by or affiliated with a student's university. Under the first option, study abroad course credits get pro forma approval, either because the program is sponsored by a department or school at that university or because the program is part of a consortium affiliation or an agreed-upon university exchange. Students seeking study abroad programs whose course credits will count toward graduation are best advised to choose only those programs either offered or approved by their university. Choosing an unaffiliated study abroad program is a trickier proposition if the student wants that credit to count toward graduation. Some students may not care about credit for study abroad. For them, any and every study abroad program in the world is an open opportunity. But students expecting study abroad credits to transfer should check with their registrar or international studies office to see if a potential program of interest will be approved for credit transfer. In addition to easing course credit acceptance, another advantage of selecting a school-approved program is the greater likelihood for a seamless continuation of financial aid.

A small number of colleges require every student to have a study abroad experience before graduating—examples include Goucher College in suburban Baltimore and Soka University in Orange County, California. There are nearly fifty colleges and universities where at least half of the students have a study abroad experience. Some schools, such as Colby, Florida State, Hamilton, New York University, Northeastern, Skidmore, and Syracuse, even have significant numbers of freshmen going abroad.

The percentage of students electing to experience another country or culture before graduation is one gauge of whether a college is a good choice for students interested in study abroad. Another potentially useful measure is the perceived quality and range of study abroad options offered at a college. On the other hand, regardless of the college, some academic areas have lower study abroad rates. For example, students majoring in engineering or the sciences are less apt to study abroad. The schools (highlighted and listed below) get high marks for their study abroad programs, high percentages of students who go abroad, and their emphasis on global education.

American University. Among AU's offerings are a film production program in Prague, the Sotheby's Arts and Business Program in London, and a sustainable development program based in Nairobi, Kenya.

Boston University. BU students can explore archaeology in Guatemala, Menorca (Spain), or Quito (Ecuador); study engineering in Dresden (Germany), Dublin, Grenoble (France), Madrid, Singapore, Sydney, or Tel Aviv; study business and economics at Bocconi University in Milan or at the Copenhagen Business School; pursue internships in Auckland (New Zealand), Dublin, London, and Madrid; study the environment in Auckland (New Zealand) or Ecuador; learn acting in London; or create art in Venice.

Dartmouth College. Among the many choices at Dartmouth are a global health internship in Tanzania, exchanges with McGill University and the University of Copenhagen, engineering study in Thailand, film and media studies in Edinburgh (Scotland), and a biological sciences program that takes students to the Cayman Islands and Costa Rica.

University of Minnesota (Twin Cities). Students at Minnesota can go to Estonia, Finland, and Sweden to study wind engineering; study architecture in Argentina, Australia, or Brazil; study the environment in Bhutan; or learn Scandinavian languages in Denmark, Iceland, and Norway.

Stanford University. Among Stanford's numerous offerings are an Australian Coastal Studies semester (in collaboration with the University of Queensland's Center for Marine Studies); a program in Cape Town, South Africa, focused on emerging democracies; and a program in Kyoto centered on Japanese language, culture, and technology.

Wake Forest University. Wake Forest students can study global health in Nicaragua, conduct field studies on the Galapagos Islands, examine ecology and conservation in Tanzania, or study anthropology in Kathmandu, Nepal.

➤ OTHER STANDOUTS FOR STUDY ABROAD

Arcadia University

College of the Atlantic

Austin College

Bates College

Beloit College

Berea College

Bowdoin College

Brandeis University

Butler University

Calvin College

Carleton College

Centre College

Champlain College

Colby College

Colgate University

Colorado College

University of Colorado Boulder

Columbia University

Connecticut College

University of Dallas

University of Delaware

Denison University

University of Denver

DePauw University

Dickinson College

Duke University

Earlham College

Elon University

Emory University

University of Evansville

Florida State University

Georgetown University

George Washington University

Goshen College

Goucher College

Hamilton College

Hartwick College

University of Illinois at Urbana Champaign

Illinois Wesleyan University

Indiana University (Bloomington)

Linfield College

Loyola University Chicago

Loyola University of Maryland

Michigan State University

Kalamazoo College

Lewis and Clark College

Macalester College

Michigan State University

Middlebury College

University of Mississippi

New York University

University of North Carolina at Chapel Hill

University of Notre Dame

Oberlin College

Pepperdine University

Pomona College

Randolph-Macon College

Rhodes College

College of St. Benedict

St. John's University (Minnesota)

St. John's University (New York)

St. Lawrence University

St. Mary's College (Indiana)

St. Mary's College of Maryland

St. Olaf College

Scripps College

Skidmore College

Soka University

Syracuse University

University of Texas

Transylvania University

Tufts University

Tulane University

Union College

Vanderbilt University

University of Vermont

University of Virginia

Webster University

Whitman College

Willamette University

Wofford College

Yeshiva University

CONSORTIUM AND EXCHANGE PROGRAMS

There are a number of cooperative arrangements (listed below) that link colleges through cross registration or exchange opportunities.

THE COLLEGES OF THE FENWAY

Within walking distance of each other are Boston's Colleges of the Fenway. Collectively, the Colleges of the Fenway enroll over 12,000 students, comprise roughly 16 percent of the undergraduates attending college in Boston, and offer approximately 2,300 courses. A number of performance groups combine the talents of students at the member colleges—examples include the Colleges of the Fenway (COF) Orchestra, COF Jazz Band, COF Chorus, COF Dance Project, and COF Theater Project. Study abroad programs are operated jointly through the Global Education Opportunities Center. Intramural athletics also bring students from the member colleges together as teammates and competitors. Benefits of the consortium include cross registration for courses and opportunities to attend lectures, performances, and social events on the member campuses. The Fenway Card enables students to make purchases (including at cafes and in dining halls) at member campuses and in selected businesses in Boston.

- Emmanuel College
- Massachusetts College of Art and Design
- Massachusetts College of Pharmacy and Health Sciences
- Simmons College
- Wentworth Institute of Technology
- Wheelock College

THE CLAREMONT COLLEGES

East of Los Angeles in the Southern California town of Claremont, there are seven colleges and universities that are contiguous and connected through cross registration programs, cooperative athletic teams, and many shared services. Collectively, the Claremont Colleges enroll nearly seven thousand students and offer approximately two thousand courses. The five undergraduate institutions (often referred to as the 5Cs) combine resources in athletics to field NCAA Division III varsity teams, with Claremont McKenna, Harvey Mudd, and Scripps on one side and Pitzer and Pomona on the other. The 5Cs cooperatively run the Five College Theater Department, and Claremont McKenna, Pitzer, and Scripps operate a joint science department. Other centralized services within the Claremont Colleges include the library system, student health, campus safety, the student radio station, and campus mail.

- Claremont McKenna College
- Harvey Mudd College
- Pitzer College
- Pomona College
- Scripps College
- Claremont Graduate University
- Keck Graduate Institute of Applied Life Sciences

THE FIVE COLLEGE EXCHANGE

In the Pioneer Valley of Massachusetts, the Five College Exchange links together four liberal arts colleges and a research university. Bus service connecting the campuses in the Five College Exchange makes it possible for students to take classes, participate in clubs, attend lectures and performances, and socialize at any of the member colleges. But it is important to note that the Five College Exchange schools are not on contiguous campuses like the Claremont Colleges. Shared services and resources coordinated through the consortium include a Five College Radio station (which is the area's NPR affiliate), a Five College Center for the Study of World Languages, and a Five College Automated Library System. Through an affiliation with the Duke Marine Lab, the Five Colleges also offer a certificate program in marine sciences.

- Amherst College
- Hampshire College
- University of Massachusetts
- Mount Holyoke College
- Smith College

SUBURBAN PHILADELPHIA COLLEGES

The close partnership between Bryn Mawr and Haverford is referred to as the Bi-College rela-tionship, otherwise known as Bi-Co. The Bi-Co colleges share departments and offices (such as career services) and run bus service between two campuses located less than two miles apart. An integral part of life at Bryn Mawr and Haverford is the ease of cross registration and pursuing a major at the partner college. A Tri-College arrangement that includes Swarthmore (roughly twenty minutes away by car) enables students to attend lectures, performances, social events, and classes (schedule permitting). Getting to the Swarthmore campus is easiest by car, although public transportation is an option. Bryn Mawr, Haverford, and Swarthmore students can also take classes and participate in academic and campus life at the University of Pennsylvania, which is roughly a half hour from each campus by car and up to an hour by SEPTA train or bus.

- Bryn Mawr College
- Haverford College
- University of Pennsylvania
- Swarthmore College

THE ATLANTA UNIVERSITY CENTER

The Atlanta University Center is comprised of historically black colleges and universities that are contiguous. Similar to the Claremont Colleges, the AUC institutions collectively feel like one medium-sized university. It can be hard to tell where one member campus ends and another begins. In addition to cross registration, students at the AUC are interconnected through shared clubs, facilities, and numerous social activities. The AUC experience is a big part of the draw to each of the member institutions.

- Clark Atlanta University
- Morehouse College
- Morris Brown College
- Spelman College

BOSTON METRO WEST CONSORTIUM

Students at colleges in the Boston Metro West Consortium have cross registration privileges at member schools. The program is easiest to navigate for Babson and F. W. Olin students because their campuses are contiguous.

- Babson College
- Brandeis University
- Franklin W. Olin College of Engineering
- Wellesley College

COLUMBIA UNIVERSITY-BARNARD COLLEGE

Columbia and Barnard (a women's college) are located side by side on New York's Upper West Side. Technically, Barnard College is a unit of Columbia University, which makes Columbia courses available to Barnard students and vice versa. In addition, a number of accelerated and double degree programs enable Barnard students to earn an undergraduate or graduate degree at Columbia.

MIT-WELLESLEY

Students at MIT and Wellesley can take classes at each other's campus, and Wellesley students can opt for a five-year double degree program (BA from Wellesley/SB from MIT). Making the fourteen-mile trek between the MIT and Welles-ley campuses takes thirty minutes by car and an hour by public transportation.

Numerous colleges are members of consortia the collectively offer extensive study abroad and domestic exchange opportunities.

GREAT LAKES COLLEGE ASSOCIATION (GLCA)

The GLCA operates dozens of semester and yearlong programs in the United States and abroad. Students at any of the member colleges can choose GLCA foreign study programs in places like Dakar, Senegal; Nairobi, Kenya; and Tokyo, Japan. In the United States, the GLCA sponsors a border studies program based in Tucson, Arizona; an urban studies semester in Philadelphia; an intensive studio art semester in New York City; a humanities research program at the Newberry Library in Chicago; and a semester focused on the study of energy and the environment at Oak Ridge National Laboratory in Tennessee. There are thirteen members of the GLCA.

- Albion College
- Allegheny College
- Antioch College
- Denison University
- DePauw University
- Earlham College
- Hope College
- Kalamazoo College
- Kenyon College
- Oberlin College
- Ohio Wesleyan University
- Wabash College
- College of Wooster

ASSOCIATED COLLEGES OF THE MIDWEST (ACM)

The Associated Colleges of the Midwest (ACM) provides students at member institutions with an extensive array of domestic and study abroad programs. Study abroad destinations include Botswana, Brazil, Costa Rica, India, Italy, Japan, Mexico, Tanzania, and the United Kingdom. Within the United States, the ACM offers urban studies programs in Chicago, a humanities research program at the Newberry Library in Chicago, and an energy and environmental research program at the Oak Ridge National Laboratory in Tennessee. There are fourteen ACM member institutions.

- Beloit College
- Carleton College
- Coe College
- Colorado College
- Cornell College
- Grinnell College
- Knox College
- Lake Forest College
- Lawrence University
- Luther College
- Macalester College
- Monmouth College
- Ripon College
- Saint Olaf College

TWELVE COLLEGE EXCHANGE

The Twelve College Exchange is a group of New England colleges that operate domestic study and semester exchange programs. Examples include the Eugene O'Neill Theater Program in New London, Connecticut, and the Maritime Studies Program at Mystic Seaport in Connecticut. Students can study away for a semester at any of the member colleges.

- Amherst College
- Bowdoin College
- Connecticut College (including the National Theater Institute)
- Dartmouth College
- Mount Holyoke College
- Smith College
- Trinity College
- Vassar College
- Wellesley College
- Wesleyan University
- Wheaton College
- Williams-Mystic Seaport Program in American Maritime Studies

SPECIALIZED OFF-CAMPUS PROGRAMS IN THE UNITED STATES

Boston University. Los Angeles internship program in advertising, film, public relations, and television

Columbia College (Chicago). Hollywood campus for filmmaking students

Cornell University. The Washington, DC, Wolpe Center serves many students but has, in particular, programs for urban scholars (CUSP) and Chinese and Asian Pacific Studies (CAPS).

Dartmouth College. Earth sciences program focused on the geology of western North America that uses as its campus national parks in Arizona, California, Montana, Nevada, Utah, Wyoming, and the Canadian Rockies.

Emerson College. Entertainment industry semester in Los Angeles

Ithaca College. Semester-long internship program in Hollywood for students enrolled in Ithaca's Park School of Communications

Middlebury College. Student exchange programs with the Monterey Institute for International Studies (owned by Middlebury) in Monterey, California

New York University. Washington, DC, program focused on politics and economics

St. John's College. Students at the Annapolis, Maryland, campus can spend a semester at the Santa Fe, New Mexico, campus and vice versa.

Southern Methodist University. SMU in Taos, New Mexico program

Stanford University. Stanford-in-Washington Program focused on study and internships in government and public policy.

Syracuse University. Semester-long programs and centers in Los Angeles, New York, and Washington, DC

University of Texas at Austin. Semester in Los Angeles focused on the entertainment industry

As this chapter tries to make clear, there are multiple options for students who are (1) seeking a degree from a university beyond North America, (2) searching for a study abroad experience, or (3) interested in courses or a semester exchange at another college. For some students branching out may mean experiencing the nation's capital through a program like Stanford-in-Washington or studying for a semester at a university in Brazil. For others it might mean going abroad for the full college experience. If a foreign study adventure is a central goal, please keep two things in mind. First, only seriously consider institutions that offer credits that will transfer back to the United States in cases of an abandoned or shortened adventure. Second, pay close attention to safety issues and any cultural adaptations necessary to thrive in the particular locale of choice. With careful planning, venturing beyond the familiar to write term papers in Singapore, study coral reefs in Australia, or spend a semester at another locale in the United States will be perspective broadening and maybe even life changing.

COLLEGES WHERE FAITH MATTERS

Many students come to terms with their spiritual identity while in college. For some, selection of a college depends on finding a place that supports their religious beliefs. For students seeking colleges where religious and spiritual life is prominent, there are many options. Catholic students have choices ranging from regional institutions, such as Saint Michael's College in Vermont, to national universities, such as Georgetown University in Washington, DC. Jewish students have Brandeis University near Boston and Yeshiva University in New York. Mormon students have Brigham Young University in Provo, Utah. Protestant students have numerous options, ranging from Pepperdine University in California to Baylor University in Texas. Students drawn to Quaker principles have Earlham College in Indiana and Haverford College near Philadelphia. Students interested in Buddhism will find Naropa University in Colorado and Soka University in Southern California.

The history of higher education in the United States is rooted in religion. America's oldest university, Harvard, started out as a college for future Protestant ministers. Up to the end of the nineteenth century, most US colleges traced their missions to the religious denomination responsible for their founding. Each brand of Protestantism had multiple colleges. Episcopalians had Hobart, Kenyon, Sewanee, and Trinity (CT). Methodists had Boston University, Duke, Emory, Northwestern, Syracuse, and Vanderbilt. Lutherans had Gettysburg, Gustavus Adolphus, Muhlenberg, and St. Olaf. Presbyterians had Agnes Scott, Davidson, Lake Forest, Macalester, and Princeton. Congregationalists had Beloit, Carleton, Grinnell, Middlebury, Pomona, and Whitman. Baptists had Bates, Colby, Brown, Bucknell, Furman, and Wake Forest. Most of the Catholic universities, with the exception of Georgetown (founded in 1789), came somewhat

later, as America's Catholic immigrants acquired wealth and status. Brandeis (named for America's first Jewish Supreme Court justice) opened in 1947 as a post-Holocaust expression of pride in Judaism.

Most of the colleges founded with ties to a specific religious sect are now secular institutions. Except for the presence of a chapel along its historic college row, today's students at Wesleyan University in Connecticut would have no idea that their college was once deeply Methodist in its curriculum and campus culture. Students at the religiously pluralistic Oberlin College, where Jewish students are well represented, might be surprised to learn that their college once emphasized training Protestant missionaries. Brandeis University has a Jewish heritage, but non-Jews are welcomed and are a significant part of the population.

Faith communities exist on just about every campus in the United States. Students looking to join Christian Fellowship, Hillel, Newman Society, or Eastern religion groups have abundant options. At most colleges, the religious faith of students is attended to in the co-curricular sphere or through courses found in the department of religion. Most prospective college students, if they are religious, leave faith to the side when choosing a college and merely look for places where they will have the option to interact and worship with others of similar spiritual background and interest. For these students, faith does not drive college selection.

For another group of students, faith, because it is a prominent guiding factor in their daily life, directs their college search. It is for those students that this chapter is intended. What follows are brief descriptions and lists of colleges where Buddhist, Catholic, Jewish, and Protestant students will find a prominent religious/spiritual dimension to academic and campus life.

CATHOLIC COLLEGES

There are hundreds of Catholic colleges spread across the United States. Most of them are regional institutions that serve students in their proverbial backyard. With a few exceptions, regional Catholic colleges, such as Assumption in Massachusetts, LeMoyne in New York, and St. Anselm in New Hampshire, draw students within a 250-mile radius of campus. Other Catholic colleges, such as Dominican University in California and Immaculata University in Pennsylvania, supplement residential undergraduate programs with part-time degree programs for adults. Providing access and convenience for local students is the mission of such schools.

A handful of Catholic institutions are truly national in scope and reach. These Catholic colleges, due to academic strength, location in a vibrant metro area, or a prominent athletic team, or some combination of all three, vie for national status. America's truly national Catholic colleges are Boston College, Georgetown University, and the University of Notre Dame. Stretching back to the days of legendary football coach Knute Rockne, Notre Dame has been a household name, and not just for Catholics. Notre Dame is now America's wealthiest Catholic college, with an endowment of $9 billion, and draws students from every corner of the world. Largely owing to Heisman Trophy winner Doug Flutie's oft-televised 1984 touchdown pass to Gerard Phalen, Boston College became a national institution. No longer just for metro Boston's Catholic families, BC enrolls students from all faiths (roughly 25 percent non-Catholics) from around the world. Perhaps the most religiously pluralistic of the Catholic universities, Georgetown University has not had a priest as president for a decade. Starting in the late 1970s, the success of Georgetown's men's basketball teams focused attention on what had been a high-quality, but still regional, university. Another boost for Georgetown came when alumnus Bill Clinton (a non-Catholic) became president of the United States. Perhaps more than any other Catholic university, Georgetown is highly sought after by students at private schools that were once bastions of the moneyed Protestant elite.

Another half-dozen Catholic colleges are at the edge of becoming national institutions. Although these colleges draw students from across the country, their populations are still anchored by students from places no more than 100 to 250 miles from campus. These nearly national Catholic colleges include the College of Holy Cross, Fordham University, Marquette University, Santa Clara University, the University of San Diego, and Villanova University. A few other Catholic institutions have nationally prominent programs, such as drama at Catholic University, music and theater at DePaul University, the school of film and television at Loyola Marymount University, and study abroad programs at St. Louis University.

Historically, the Jesuits, an order founded by Saint Ignatius of Loyola, have been dedicated to education and teaching. Among Roman Catholic orders, the Jesuits (formally named the Society of Jesus) have a well-earned reputation for intellectual curiosity and progressive theology. Going back to their inception in 1534, the Jesuits have founded hundreds of schools, colleges, and universities around the world. A unifying ethos of Jesuit schools and colleges is the motto For Others. You do not have to look too far to find examples of student organizations at Jesuit institutions that are dedicated to putting the principle of Men and Women for Others into practice. As a group, Jesuit institutions (listed below) are disproportionately overrepresented among the most highly regarded Catholic colleges in the United States.

Boston College—Chestnut Hill, MA

Canisius College—Buffalo, NY

College of the Holy Cross—Worcester, MA

Creighton University—Omaha, NE

University of Detroit Mercy—Detroit, MI

Fairfield University—Fairfield, CT

Fordham University—New York, NY

Georgetown University—Washington, DC

Gonzaga University—Spokane, Washington

John Carroll University—University Heights, OH

Le Moyne College—Syracuse, NY

Loyola University Chicago—Chicago, IL

Loyola University of Maryland—Baltimore, MD

Loyola Marymount University—Los Angeles, CA

Loyola University of New Orleans—New Orleans, LA

Marquette University—Milwaukee, WI

Regis University—Denver, CO

Rockhurst University—Kansas City, MO

Saint Joseph's University—Philadelphia, PA

Saint Louis University—Saint Louis, MO

Saint Peter's College—Jersey City, NJ

University of San Francisco—San Francisco, CA

Santa Clara University—Santa Clara, CA

University of Scranton—Scranton, PA

Seattle University—Seattle, WA

Spring Hill College—Mobile, AL

Wheeling Jesuit University—Wheeling, West Virginia

Xavier University—Cincinnati, Ohio

Listed below are other Roman Catholic colleges for students to consider.

Assumption College—Worcester, MA

Barry University—Miami Shores, FL

The Catholic University of America—Washington, DC

Chaminade University—Honolulu, HI

University of Dallas—Dallas, TX

University of Dayton—Dayton, OH

DePaul University—Chicago, IL

Duquesne University—Pittsburgh, PA

Iona College—New Rochelle, NY

La Salle University—Philadelphia, PA

Manhattan College—Riverdale, NY

Merrimack College—North Andover, MA

Niagara University—Niagara Falls, NY

University of Notre Dame

University of Portland—Portland, OR

Providence College—Providence, RI

College of Saint Benedict—Saint Joseph's, MN

Saint Edward's University—Austin, TX

Saint John's University—Collegeville, MN

Saint John's University—Jamaica, NY

Saint Mary's College—Notre Dame, IN

Saint Mary's College of California—Moraga, CA

Saint Michael's College—Colchester, VT

Saint Norbert College—De Pere, WI

University of Saint Thomas—Saint Paul, MN

Salve Regina University—Newport, RI

University of San Diego—San Diego, CA

Seton Hall University—South Orange, NJ

Siena College—Loudonville, NY

Stonehill College—Easton, MA

Villanova University—Villanova, PA

BOSTON COLLEGE, GEORGETOWN, AND NOTRE DAME

BOSTON COLLEGE

On this campus of 14,300 students (9,100 under-graduates), the Jesuit identity shows through in the prominent statue of St. Ignatius of Loyola, the required core courses in philosophy, and the PULSE Program for Service Learning. PULSE at BC combines courses in philosophy and theology with community service placements in soup kitchens, domestic violence shelters, and schools. Students are drawn to BC for its high-quality academics and location on the edge of America's top college town (Boston). BC is a fun and social place where students ooze school pride, especially when cheering on the national championship-winning ice hockey team or the basketball and football teams that play in the Atlantic Coast Conference (ACC). In addition to its largest academic unit, the College of Arts and Sciences, BC has schools of education, law, nursing, social work, theology/ministry, and a management school (Carroll) that is frequently rated as one of twenty best for undergraduate business. Admission to BC is highly selective. Generally only 25 percent of the twenty-five to thirty thousand applicants get admitted. The Presidential Scholars program at BC funds full tuition and provides special opportunities for internships, service learning, and study abroad. Prominent alumni of BC include television host Elizabeth Hasselbeck, sportswriter Mike Lupica, Connecticut Governor Dan Malloy, actress Amy Poehler, and Atlanta Falcons quarterback Matt Ryan.

GEORGETOWN UNIVERSITY

Founded in 1789 and located in the District of Columbia, Georgetown is the oldest of the Jesuit/Catholic colleges in the United States. Among the 17,100 students at Georgetown, 7,600 are undergraduates while the rest are enrolled in graduate and professional programs (including Georgetown's highly ranked law school on Capitol Hill). Beyond DC, Georgetown has impressive study abroad facilities in Fiesole, Italy, and Alanya, Turkey. Many government leaders have taught at Georgetown's top-ranked Walsh School of Foreign Service, including Madeleine Albright (former secretary of state), Anthony Lake (former National Security Adviser), and George Tenet (former director of the CIA). One of the most selective colleges in the United States, Georgetown receives more than 20,000 applications for 1,600 freshman spaces. The Jesuit emphasis on serving others shows through in the all-volunteer, student-run Georgetown Emergency Response Medical Service that serves the campus and its surrounding neighborhoods. Unlike many Catholic colleges, Georgetown has Greek letter organizations, although none of them require members to live in a fraternity or sorority house. Since 2001, Georgetown has been led by a lay president. Prominent Georgetown alumni include Arizona Cardinals owner Bill Bidwell, Bill Clinton, actor Bradley Cooper, Alaska Senator Lisa Murkowski, MSNBC correspondent Norah O'Donnell, former Illinois Governor Pat Quinn, Supreme Court Justice Antonin Scalia, and former NFL Commissioner Paul Tagliabue.

UNIVERSITY OF NOTRE DAME

High-achieving students come to the ornate Notre Dame campus in the small city of South Bend, Indiana, for the quality of the education and the traditions and history. Notre Dame is famous for its signature golden-domed building, excellent academic programs, and storied football program, which has been portrayed in popular movies such as *Knute Rockne, All American* and *Rudy*. With more than 80 percent of the students at Notre Dame identifying as Catholic, the University's Catholic heritage is evident all across campus. For example, the Main Building's golden dome is topped by a statue of the Blessed Virgin Mary; the Basilica of the Sacred Heart has forty-four stained-glass windows designed by the Vatican painter Luigi Gregori; and one side of the Hesburgh Library (near the football stadium) is a mosaic showing Christ with upraised arms that is commonly referred to as Touchdown Jesus. On the academic side, Notre Dame's schools of architecture and business are rated among the nation's best. Notre Dame also has strong programs in the arts and sciences (especially philosophy and religion), education, engineering, and law. Supporting students and faculty are financial resources that put Notre Dame on par with several Ivy League universities. Getting admitted to Notre Dame is not easy. Nearly eighteen thousand students apply for two thousand spaces and nearly 75 percent of the entering students were ranked in the top 5 percent of their high school class. Perhaps because so many students have relatives who were golden domers before them, the Notre Dame alumni network functions like a close family. Prominent alumni of Notre Dame include sportscaster Mike Golic, television personality Regis Philbin, novelist Nicholas Sparks, football coaches Skip Holtz and Charlie Weis, and NFL Hall of Fame football players Nick Buoniconti, Dave Casper, Paul Horning, Joe Montana, and Alan Page.

HOLY CROSS, MARQUETTE, UNIVERSITY OF SAN DIEGO, SANTA CLARA, AND VILLANOVA

COLLEGE OF THE HOLY CROSS

Holy Cross is an academically rigorous Jesuit liberal arts college set on a hilltop in Worcester, Massachusetts, where all students are undergraduates. For a small liberal arts college, Holy Cross is unusual in having NCAA Division I athletics. With the likes of Bucknell, Colgate, and Fordham, Holy Cross is a member of the Patriot League. The academic experience at Holy Cross features the distinctive Montserrat Program, with its interdisciplinary seminar-style courses that are integrated into first-year residence clusters. The most popular majors at Holy Cross are economics, English, psychology, political science, and sociology. More than 90 percent of the students live on campus, students graduate at a 93 percent rate, and Holy Cross students have acceptance rates above 80 percent to law school and medical school. The student community at Holy Cross is close-knit and relatively homogeneous, meaning predominantly from the Northeast, Catholic, and white. Community service organizations, responding to the Jesuit call to be Men and Women for Others, have a strong tradition at Holy Cross, and it is often the top school by the percentage of graduates who join the Jesuit Volunteer Corps. Because it counts among its alumni noted 1960s figures central to the antiwar and antipoverty movements (Philip Berrigan and Michael Harrington) and because it has been more willing than many of its peers to host events like the *Vagina Monologues* and groups like Planned Parenthood, Holy Cross has at times been called the "cradle of the Catholic left." That does not mean Holy Cross is a hotbed of liberal activism. One of its best-known graduates is conservative US Supreme Court Justice Clarence Thomas. Other notable Holy Cross alumni include former US poet laureate Billy Collins, MSNBC *Hardball* host Chris Matthews, sportswriter Dan Shaughnessy, and ESPN columnist Bill Simmons.

MARQUETTE UNIVERSITY

Located near downtown Milwaukee, Marquette is a Jesuit institution of 12,000 students (8,400 undergraduates) named for the seventeenth-century missionary and explorer Father Jacques Marquette. One distinctive feature of the Marquette campus is the Saint Joan of Arc Chapel, which was reconstructed using the stones and architectural plans from an actual fifteenth-century chapel that was originally located near Lyon, France. Marquette is a comprehensive urban university with schools of arts and sciences, business, communications, dentistry, engineering, health sciences, law, and nursing. Highly ranked academic programs include accounting, biomedical engineering, and physical therapy. Catholic students looking for ways to put their faith into action will find more than twenty student organizations engaging in service projects in Milwaukee neighborhoods. Marquette's men's basketball team is a focus of student and alumni pride. Miami Heat star Dwayne Wade played for Marquette, and a sports facility is named for Al McGuire, who coached the 1977 NCAA championship–winning team. Students at Marquette are predominantly from the Midwest. Roughly 10 percent of the students belong to one of the twenty-three campus Greek organizations. Prominent Marquette alumni include *New York Times* columnist Gail Collins, the late actor/comedian Chris Farley, dean of the Annenberg School of Communications at the University of Pennsylvania Kathleen Hall Jamieson, and actor Danny Pudi (*Community*).

UNIVERSITY OF SAN DIEGO

Since opening in 1952, the University of San Diego has grown into a full-fledged university with 8,000 students (5,500 undergraduates) and six schools, including arts and sciences, business, leadership and education, law, nursing, and peace studies. The beautiful USD campus is comprised of ornate Spanish Renaissance buildings. Although USD has Catholic roots, it has a lay board of trustees, a lay president, and is no longer run by the Diocese of San Diego. USD is a place on the rise that is increasingly more selective in admissions and lauded for the high percentage of its students who study abroad. In the last decade, a $75 million gift established the Joan B. Kroc Institute for Peace and Justice Studies that intends "to not only teach peace, but make peace." The Kroc Institute is for graduate study, but USD undergraduates looking for ways to explore ethics, social justice, and spirituality have resources such as the Center for Community Service Learning, Center for Latina/o Catholicism, Center for Christian Spirituality, the Character Development Center, and the Values Institute. USD is more ethnically diverse than many prominent Catholic universities. Over one-third of the students at USD are students of color, the largest share of that population being Hispanic/Latino. USD's location in a major city makes for vibrant campus life that includes NCAA Division I sports and twelve Greek organizations (drawing roughly 25 percent of USD's students). Notable USD alumni include Oakland's Bishop Salvatore Cordileone, reality TV star Andrew Firestone (*The Bachelor*), and former NBA head coaches Bernie Bickerstaff, Mike Brown, and Eric Musselman.

SANTA CLARA UNIVERSITY

Billed as Silicon Valley's Jesuit university, Santa Clara (founded in 1851) is the oldest college in California. SCU has 8,800 students (5,400 undergraduates). SCU's Jesuit For Others ethos is expressed through several social justice programs that offer service and immersion opportunities in disadvantaged communities. As part of a required core curriculum, all undergraduates at SCU take three religious studies classes. Students who attend SCU tend to have a strong preprofessional orientation. SCU's business and engineering schools stand out among those found at undergraduate-focused, medium-sized universities, and many students remain for an MBA or a law degree. An up and comer in the Catholic university realm, Santa Clara's admissions selectivity has been on the rise. SCU is also often ranked the top regional university in the western United States. Prominent Santa Clara alumni include Dee Dee Myers, press secretary for President Clinton; NBA star Steve Nash; former Secretary of Homeland Security Janet Napolitano; California Lieutenant Governor Gavin Newsom; former Secretary of Defense Leon Panetta; and *That 70s Show* actor Kurtwood Smith.

VILLANOVA UNIVERSITY

With a pleasant suburban Philadelphia campus of happy students, Villanova has become a popular choice, especially for Catholic kids looking for a less selective alternative to Boston College, Georgetown, and Notre Dame. There are 6,400 undergraduates at Villanova amid a total student population of 10,400. Although Villanova has a law school and other graduate programs, undergraduates are the focus in the schools of arts and sciences, business, engineering, and nursing. Founded by Augustinians on the grounds of a former arboretum, Villanova has a Catholic heritage that is evident immediately to visitors. The most prominent campus building is the Gothic Revival St. Thomas of Villanova Chapel. Villanova's chemical engineering building is named for Gregor Mendel, the pioneering geneticist who was also an Augustinian monk. Another building at Villanova is called the St. Augustine Center for Liberal Arts. Students looking for ways to put their Catholic faith into practice will find an active campus ministry, the student-run Rays of Sunshine community service group, one of the largest chapters of Habitat for Humanity at a US college, and a student-run ambulance service. Greek life is more prominent at Villanova than at many other Catholic universities. Approximately 30 percent of Villanova students belong to fraternities or sororities, although there are no houses on campus. Notable alumni of Villanova include actress Maria Bello, Stanford University President John Hennessy, NFL Hall of Famer Howie Long, and the late singer Jim Croce.

CHRISTIAN COLLEGES AND UNIVERSITIES

Most of the conservative fundamentalist Christian colleges are regional in character. The state of Virginia has three such examples: Liberty University in Lynchburg, Patrick Henry College in Purcellville, and Regent University in Virginia Beach. Other colleges where the overwhelming majority of students are fundamentalist or conservative Christians include Bob Jones University in South Carolina, Calvin College in Michigan, Gordon College in Massachusetts, Grove City College in Pennsylvania, Oral Roberts University in Oklahoma, and Seattle Pacific University in Washington.

A number of small liberal arts colleges retain a Christian character without being fundamentalist. This group includes Augsburg College in Minnesota, Austin College in Texas, Bridgewater College in Virginia, Centenary College in Louisiana, Concordia College in Minnesota, Furman University in South Carolina, Goshen College in Indiana, Gustavus Adolphus and Saint Olaf in Minnesota, Hendrix College in Arkansas, Hope College in Michigan, Houghton College in New York, Luther College in Iowa, Millsaps College in Mississippi, and Moravian College, Thiel College, and Westminster College in Pennsylvania.

Christians of the Protestant stripe can also find active fellowship organizations on many campuses, including at public universities, particularly those located in the Bible Belt.

Saint Olaf College in Northfield, Minnesota, bills itself as a college of the church, a place where conversations about matters of faith are part of campus life. With roughly 40 percent of its students belonging to the Lutheran Church, the St. Olaf community embraces and lives its Christian heritage. St. Olaf still holds daily chapel services that often feature visiting speakers. But St. Olaf is also a pluralistic place that celebrates interfaith activity and exposes students to non-Christian religious beliefs and practices. All St. Olaf students must take two religion courses: one from the Christian tradition and one that provides perspectives into other religions. In addition, the good works aspect of faith and religion is very prominent at St. Olaf—with thirty-five community service programs to which students give roughly fourteen thousand hours of volunteer time annually.

The Principia (also known as Principia College) in Elsah, Illinois, located on the banks of the Mississippi River, is America's only college for Christian Scientists. A small liberal arts college of 526 students, the Principia has a high school on its campus and an endowment of nearly $300 million, which places its financial resources (on a per capita basis) in the upper tier of national liberal arts colleges. Located just over an hour north of St. Louis, the Principia is a quiet college in a small town far from the madding crowd. The backgrounds of its faculty, staff, and students tend overwhelmingly toward Christian Science. For students whose faith heritage is Christian Science, the Principia is a fitting choice. For all others, the Principia might seem like an alien world. Prospective students should be sure to visit to see if there is a fit. Studying there worked out for Robert Duvall, who went on to become an Oscar-winning actor.

At the following institutions, Christian faith is prominent.

Abilene Christian University—Abilene, TX (Churches of Christ)

Azusa Pacific University—Azusa, CA (interdenominational evangelical)

Baylor University—Waco, TX (Baptist)

Belmont University—Nashville, Tennessee (nondenominational Christian)

Berea College—Berea, KY (nonsectarian Christian)

Berry College—Rome, Georgia (Christian)

Bob Jones University—Greenville, SC (nondenominational Protestant)

Brigham Young University—Provo, UT (Latter Day Saints)

California Lutheran University—Thousand Oaks, CA (Evangelical Lutheran Church of America)

Calvin College—Grand Rapids, MI (Christian Reformed Church)

Carson-Newman College—Jefferson City, TN (Baptist)

College of the Ozarks—Point Lookout, MO (Christian)

Colorado Christian University—Lakewood, CO (Evangelical Christian)

George Fox University—Newberg, OR (Northwest Yearly Meeting of Friends)

Gordon College—Wenham, MA (nondenominational Christian)

Goshen College—Goshen, IN (Mennonite Church)

Grove City College, Grove City, PA (Presbyterian Church)

Harding University—Searcy, AR (Churches of Christ)

Hardin-Simmons University—Abilene, TX (Baptist General Convention of Texas)

Houghton College—Houghton, NY (Wesleyan Church)

Liberty University—Lynchburg, VA (Southern Baptist Conservatives of Virginia)

Mercer University—Macon, GA (Cooperative Baptist Fellowship)

Messiah College—Grantham, PA (nondenominational, but historically Brethren in Christ)

Mississippi College—Clinton, MS (Mississippi Baptist Convention)

Moravian College—Bethlehem, PA (historically Moravian but no longer officially affiliated)

Oral Roberts University—Tulsa, OK (interdenominational Christian)

Pacific Lutheran University—Tacoma, WA (Evangelical Lutheran Church of America)

Pepperdine University—Malibu, CA (Churches of Christ)

Point Loma Nazarene University—San Diego, CA (Nazarene)

Regent University—Virginia Beach, VA (interdenominational Christian)

Roberts Wesleyan College—Rochester, NY (Free Methodist Church)

Salem College—Winston Salem, NC (Moravian)

Seattle Pacific University—Seattle, WA (Free Methodist Church)

Texas Christian University—Fort Worth, TX (Disciples of Christ)

Westmont College—Santa Barbara, CA (Christian)

Wheaton College—Wheaton, IL (nondenominational Christian)

Whitworth University—Spokane, WA (Presbyterian)

A few institutions that are heavily Christian in character are also nationally prominent and draw students from around the world, such as Baylor University, Brigham Young University, Pepperdine University, Texas Christian University, and Wheaton College in Illinois.

BAYLOR UNIVERSITY—WACO, TEXAS

16,232 students—13,859 undergraduates

Baylor's Baptist roots are very evident to undergraduates who venture to the central Texas city of Waco, made infamous by the Branch Davidian compound, which was the site of a federal raid in 1993. Baylor's seal states the university's motto: *Pro ecclesia, pro Texana*, which translates to For Church, for Texas. In its mission statement, Baylor states that its pursuit of knowledge as a research university "is strengthened by the conviction that truth has its ultimate source in God." Like other research universities, Baylor aims to advance the frontiers of knowledge. Like other faith-based schools, Baylor seeks to cultivate a Christian worldview.

Although Baylor has Christian underpinnings, it has adapted as it has pursued progress. For example, Baylor changed its charter in 1991 to be less dependent on the Baptist General Convention of Texas. Led by Kenneth Starr, who came to prominence as the prosecutor of former President Clinton and later led Pepperdine University's law school, Baylor is an ambitious institution, committed to breaking into the top fifty of national universities in America. Even though the charter change has insulated it from denominational struggles, Baylor's aspirations to emerge as a top-tier research university have at times come into conflict with its strict Baptist foundation.

On the cusp between medium and large sized, Baylor has 16,232 students. While on an arc of progress, Baylor has enrolled a more diverse student body (36 percent students of color), attracted more top-quality students (71 percent in the top 20 percent of their high school class), and provided more scholarship support (90 percent of students receive financial assistance). In the last decade, Baylor has also achieved athletic prominence, winning the 2005 NCAA championship in women's basketball and the 2004 NCAA championship in men's tennis.

Baylor operates more than 150 undergraduate academic programs through its seven schools and nearly thirty academic centers and institutes. Reflecting Baylor's Christian character, there are centers for Christian education; Christian ethics; Christian music studies; effective preaching; family and community ministries; religion, politics, and society; biblical and related languages; faith and learning; and church-state relations. There are other academic centers and institutes at Baylor that are secular or religiously pluralistic, such as the centers for analytical spectroscopy; astrophysics, space physics, and engineering research; drug discovery; Jewish studies; and the Institute of Biomedical Studies.

Rankings place Baylor among the nation's top one hundred research universities. Top twenty-five programs at Baylor include accounting; apparel merchandising, design, and product development; engineering; entrepreneurship; philosophy; and religion. With eighty faculty members and four hundred students, the music school at Baylor has standout strength in church music and music education.

BELMONT UNIVERSITY— NASHVILLE, TN

7,244 students—5,837 undergraduates

Through the prominence of its alumni in the country music and Christian pop and rock industries, Belmont's brand has become more emblematic of its home city of Nashville than any of the other colleges located there. For example, the well-known country singers Brad Paisley, Lee Ann Womack, and Trisha Yearwood all studied at Belmont as did legendary Grand Ole Opry performer Minnie Pearl. In addition, a significant number of the key figures in the Christian pop and rock music industry are alumni of Belmont.

With academic offerings that span more than seventy-five areas of study, Belmont blends liberal arts and professional education. Belmont has seven schools and colleges, including a school of religion. Two standout academic units at Belmont are the Mike Curb College of Entertainment and Music Business and the School of Music (see the business and music chapters). Through its Inman College of Health Sciences, Belmont offers programs in nursing and social work. The School of Social Sciences has degree programs in audio and video production as well as organizational and corporate communication; the School of Sciences offers a major in science and engineering management; and the College of Visual and Performing Arts offers a major in design communications.

Belmont's goal is to "set the standard for what it means to be a great Christian university." Belmont's Christian character shows through in a number of substantial ways. A vice president for spiritual development oversees all of Belmont's faith-based programs, working to create a "Christian community of learning and service." All Belmont students are required to take courses focused on the Old Testament and the New Testament. Students attend Christian faith development convocations and are invited to participate in weekly on-campus worship services. On every floor of Belmont's residence halls, spiritual life assistants offer Bible study sessions and promote Christian mission and service opportunities. In addition, Belmont operates ten faith development organizations and maintains more than a dozen Christian community development groups.

BRIGHAM YOUNG UNIVERSITY— PROVO, UTAH

34,150 students, 30,745 undergraduates

Brigham Young University was founded by and is now guided and supported by the Church of Jesus Christ of Latter-Day Saints (LDS). Located just outside Salt Lake City, BYU is a large, multicampus university with more than 34,000 students on its main campus in Provo, Utah, and with an additional 18,000 students on its satellite campuses in Hawaii (2,800) and Idaho (15,600). BYU draws one-third of its students from Utah. California, at 13 percent, is the next most represented state. Although western states where there are significant LDS communities account for 68 percent of BYU's student population, nearly all fifty states are represented, and 6 percent of BYU students are from foreign countries.

BYU students are oriented toward professional success and in many ways resemble their counterparts at other large universities such as USC and Texas. In other key aspects, BYU students are very different. Due to rules prohibiting alcohol, drugs, and premarital sex, students at BYU do not experience the stereotypical college party and hookup scene. Faith is central to BYU. Nearly all (98 percent) of BYU's students are LDS, otherwise known as Mormons. BYU seeks to assist students in their quest for perfection and eternal life; in its mission statement, the development of a student's faith and character is given equal billing with the development of the student's intellect. BYU hopes that its students will graduate with a strengthened sense of character and spirituality, an enlarged intellect, and an interest in lifelong learning and service. BYU

is sometimes referred to by LDS leaders as the Lord's university and maintains a dual role as university and symbol/ambassador to the world for the LDS Church.

All LDS students at BYU are required to be religiously active. Virtually all of BYU's male students and nearly one-third of the female students interrupt their studies to serve as LDS missionaries. Men can go on mission after turning eighteen, while women must wait until they turn nineteen. BYU is often described as having a marriage culture because by the time graduation day arrives approximately 50 percent of students are married. Students sign a commitment to live by the Honor Code while they are at BYU. The BYU Honor Code states that students will

- Use clean language.
- Respect others.
- Abstain from alcoholic beverages, tobacco, tea, coffee, and substance abuse.
- Participate regularly in church services.
- Observe the Dress and Grooming Standards.
- Encourage others in their commitment to comply with the Honor Code.

With more than a dozen schools and colleges and nearly two hundred degree programs, BYU, in its size and scope, parallels many flagship state universities. BYU's most popular majors are (in order): exercise science, management, psychology, English, accounting, communications, computer science, economics, political science, and public health. There are more than sixty different languages taught at BYU, and (every semester) more than one-third of its students are enrolled in foreign language classes. Study abroad opportunities are so extensive that BYU sometimes gets ranked the number one university in the United States for study abroad. In addition to satellite campus centers in London, Jerusalem, and Paris, BYU has twenty other study abroad sites. Several other rankings smile on BYU. The Marriott School of Management is often ranked in the top ten, and the accounting program ranks in the top five. BYU's standout Museum of Paleontology holds a significant collection of fossils from the Jurassic period. BYU is also a top-ten school by the number of students who go to dental school, law school, medical school, and PhD programs.

BYU stands out in other ways. The BYU Creamery, an on-campus grocery store that was the first of its kind in the United States, has branches in several residence halls. The BYU Ballroom Dance Company, one of the best in the world, has won national competitions every year since 1982. BYU has a jazz group called Synthesis that has performed all around the world at music festivals, and the Men's Chorus is the largest all-male collegiate choir in the United States.

BYU attracts a highly self-selecting applicant pool. Of those admitted, nearly 80 percent (78 percent) choose to enroll at BYU. That yield rate of 78 percent is frequently the highest of any college in the United States. Applicants start the BYU admissions process by securing an endorsement from an ecclesiastical leader who states whether the student is worthy to attend BYU, ready to live by the Honor Code, and willing to follow the Dress and Grooming Standards. Non-LDS applicants must be interviewed by an LDS bishop. Other key admission factors include academic record (GPA and SAT or ACT scores), seminary attendance, service, personal essays, and demonstrated leadership qualities. Nearly all BYU freshmen held senior officer positions in their high schools.

Compared to other private universities, the price of BYU is a bargain. For LDS students, the annual comprehensive charge (2015 data) is a mere $17,778, an amount that is competitive with in-state rates at many public universities. Non-LDS students at BYU pay annual charges of $22,928. The relatively low price of a BYU education contributes to its ranking among the top fifteen universities whose graduates leave with the lowest amount of loan debt.

More than twenty-one BYU alumni have served in either the US Senate or US House of Representatives. Notable alumni include Aaron Eckhart (actor); Kim Clark (former dean of Harvard Business School); Ken Jennings (all-time leading *Jeopardy* champion); Mitt Romney; Stephanie Meyer (author of the *Twilight* novels); the Super Bowl–winning quarterbacks Jim McMahon and Steve Young; major league baseball stars Rick Aquilara, Wally Joyner, and Jack Morris; and NBA executive and former star Danny Ainge.

PEPPERDINE UNIVERSITY—MALIBU, CALIFORNIA

7,768 students—3,474 undergraduates

Despite its proximity to hedonistic Hollywood, Pepperdine maintains a strong focus on faith. Pepperdine calls itself a "Christian university committed to the highest standards of academic excellence and Christian values." Although Pepperdine draws students from more than eighty countries, roughly 54 percent of its undergraduate students come from California, and the majority describe themselves as Christian. At Pepperdine, Christianity and conservative politics are close companions. Since the 1980s, Pepperdine has become a prominent center for conservative political thought. Pepperdine faculty members have included right-wing thinkers and personalities such as Arthur Laffer, Daniel Pipes, Kenneth Starr, and Ben Stein.

One of the draws of Pepperdine is the location of its campus in the star-studded town of Malibu. Rising from the Pacific Coast Highway to overlook the ocean, Pepperdine's campus setting is nothing short of breathtaking. From campus, students can see Catalina Island and the Palos Verdes Peninsula. Famous beaches and surfing spots are just minutes away. In addition to its main campus in Malibu, Pepperdine has study abroad facilities in Argentina, China, England, Germany, Italy, and Switzerland. More than 60 percent of Pepperdine students study abroad.

The undergraduate school at Pepperdine is called Seaver College. The vast majority of Pepperdine's undergraduates study in Seaver, although there is an undergraduate track in the Graziado School of Business and Management. Pepperdine's other three schools (education and psychology, law, and public policy) are graduate schools whose students are more representative of the diversity of beliefs and backgrounds found in metro Los Angeles. Undergraduates at Pepperdine have more than forty different major choices. The five most popular majors are in order: business administration, psychology, political science, biology, and advertising. Within business administration, students can pursue specialized majors in accounting, computer science for business, finance, or international business, or they can complete the five-year BS/MBA option. The Washington, DC, internship program is another popular option.

Roughly two-thirds of Pepperdine students live on campus. The rest commute from home or rent apartments within driving distance. In addition to all the opportunities found in the Los Angeles area, there are numerous community service activities sponsored by Pepperdine's Student Volunteer Center. For students seeking a community of faith, Pepperdine has an active campus ministry, a Center for Faith and Learning, and the on-campus University Church of Christ.

The NCAA Division I athletic program at Pepperdine consistently fields teams that compete for championships in baseball, men's water polo, men's volleyball, men's and women's golf, and men's and women's tennis. Pepperdine has produced Olympic athletes and professional baseball and basketball players, such as former

NBA stars Doug Christie and Dennis Johnson. Other notable Pepperdine alumni include *Gossip Girl* actor Chace Crawford, US Representative Janice Hahn, Major League Baseball pitcher Dan Haren, actress Kelly Hu, actresses Tia and Tamera Mowry, and eHarmony cofounder Neil Clark Warren.

TEXAS CHRISTIAN UNIVERSITY— FORT WORTH, TEXAS

10,033 students—8,647 undergraduates

Nearly winning college football national championships in the last decade has put a spotlight on Texas Christian University (TCU). An up-and-coming university, TCU has capitalized on the publicity from football success and its location in the Dallas metropolitan area. The goal at TCU is to become a national institution like Rice and Texas. TCU is less conspicuously Christian in character than Baylor, but its reputation beyond the state of Texas is still tied, for better and for worse, to its prominent middle name.

TCU's stated mission is to be a values-centered university that educates its students to be ethical leaders and responsible citizens in the global community. The *Christian* in Texas Christian University reflects the institution's association with the Disciples of Christ, a denomination that professes a commitment to true community, deep Christian spirituality and a passion for justice. On one hand, TCU strives to maintain a community consistent with the values of the Disciples of Christ. On the other hand, TCU is a pluralistic community with more than sixty religious groups including organizations for Jewish and Muslim students.

TCU combines the resources of a larger institution with a small-college learning environment. Undergraduates there can choose from 118 programs of study distributed across eight colleges, including an honors college. TCU has numerous standout academic programs.

The Schieffer School of Journalism is named for Bob Schieffer, a 1959 graduate. The Film-Television-Digital Media Department has produced programs for national networks such as TBS. College of Liberal Arts students can get Washington, DC, internships. The Harris College of Nursing and Health Sciences offers leading programs related to speech and hearing. TCU education students have a nearly 100 percent pass rate on certification exams and a 100 percent placement rate as teachers. TCU is the only school in the nation with two special education laboratory schools. The John V. Roach Honors College at TCU has a focus on world cultures. And Neeley School of Business students can major in accounting, business information systems, entrepreneurial management, finance and real estate, and marketing and supply chain management.

Several programs in TCU's College of Fine Arts are outstanding. TCU's School of Classical and Contemporary Dance has one of the nation's top-ranked programs in ballet. TCU's choirs and jazz ensemble perform internationally. The art history department offers study programs at Fort Worth's world-renowned trio of art museums (the Kimbrell, Amon Carter, and Modern Art museums). The College of Fine Arts also has a leading program in design, merchandising, and textiles. Within its College of Science and Engineering, the TCU Energy Institute trains future geologists, engineers, and land managers to work in the energy industry. TCU's Department of Nutritional Sciences has a top-ranked dietetics program whose graduates have a first-time pass rate of 92 percent on the dietitian exam. And TCU has one of the finest meteorite collections in the world.

Texas Christian University is Texan in more than its name. Over 70 percent of TCU students are from Texas, and they come to campus knowing that in their state football is practically its own religion. Devotion to TCU football

has always been fervent, but pride in the Horned Frogs has grown beyond Texas as stars like LaDainian Tomlinson and Andy Dalton put the team on the national stage before starring in the NFL.

A number of events and programs work to create bonds among TCU students. Summer Frog Camp, which operates in conjunction with academic orientation, introduces new students to their classmates as well as to university history and traditions. At the Chancellor's Assembly, incoming students are applauded by faculty clad in academic regalia before being passed the Torch of Knowledge. Special first-year seminars foster affiliation and develop skills needed for academic success. TCU's Leadership Center offers programs and classes for sophomores, juniors, and seniors. And as seniors, students receive a TCU class ring at a special ceremony.

WHEATON COLLEGE—WHEATON, ILLINOIS

2,880 students (2,400 undergraduates)

Wheaton College in Illinois (not to be confused with the former women's college in Massachusetts) is an evangelical liberal arts college located twenty-five miles west of Chicago. Students from around the world come to Wheaton, drawn by its historic prominence in Christian education. With its high-quality academics, Wheaton resembles many top-fifty national liberal arts colleges. The difference at Wheaton is the strong Christian orientation of both the students and the faculty. Written in large letters on the sign marking the entrance to Wheaton is the phrase "For Christ and His Kingdom." Students and professors who are agnostic, atheist, or from non-Christian faith traditions must adjust their beliefs and attitudes to Wheaton's emphasis on Christianity, not the other way around.

The mission of Wheaton is to provide an excellent education within an atmosphere of deep faith. Chapel services are an active part of the Wheaton experience. All members of the campus community are required to sign the Wheaton Community Covenant, a set of guidelines and principles spelling out that Wheaton is "an educational community centered around the Lord Jesus Christ." The Community Covenant affirms biblical standards, emphasizes the Christian lifestyle, and allows for the exercise of responsible freedom. The Community Covenant condemns or disallows certain actions and attitudes, such as the consumption of alcohol and tobacco, sexual immorality (including homosexuality and premarital sex), vulgar language, immodesty in dress, lying, stealing, plagiarism, and gossip. Guests of the opposite gender are never permitted in Wheaton dormitories. Oddly, traffic or construction signage is also strictly forbidden as décor in dorm rooms, but that decision doesn't seem to be dictated by biblical teachings.

With an endowment of more than $405 million, Wheaton has impressive campus facilities. Notable buildings include the Todd Beamer Student Center, named for a Wheaton alumnus who resisted hijackers aboard United Flight 93 on September 11, 2001. The building housing evangelical scholarship institutes and archives is called the Billy Graham Center in recognition of the legendary evangelical Christian leader, who is perhaps Wheaton's best-known graduate. Wheaton's off-campus academic programs include a center in Washington, DC, a facility in London, a science station in the Black Hills of South Dakota, and a campus for leadership training and youth programs in Three Lakes, Wisconsin.

There are forty majors at Wheaton—from applied health science and biblical archaeology to engineering and nursing—the latter two taught with a liberal arts focus. Wheaton is a rare small college with a Conservatory of Music. Students in the conservatory pursue BM degree programs in music composition, music education, music history and literature, and music performance. Rankings tend to place Wheaton consistently among the top fifty liberal arts colleges in the United States and among the top ten colleges whose graduates join Teach for America. Nearly 90 percent of Wheaton students live on campus. Other prominent Wheaton alumni include Dan Coats (US senator, Indiana) and Wes Craven (horror film director).

COLLEGES WITH A JEWISH HERITAGE

The two most prominent colleges in the United States that tie their identity to the Jewish culture and faith are Brandeis University in Massachusetts and Yeshiva University in New York. Both have developed world-class programs while maintaining an ethos and atmosphere grounded in Judaism. In the case of Yeshiva, the emphasis is more on Conservative and Orthodox Judaism, while at Brandeis the Reformed (and even secular and pluralistic) approach to Judaism and faith predominates. Another emerging institution that puts Judaism front and center is Touro College in New York.

YESHIVA UNIVERSITY—NEW YORK, NEW YORK

6,513 students (3,017 undergraduates)

Orthodox Jewish students are right at home at Yeshiva, the oldest higher education institution in the United States under Jewish auspices. Yeshiva's heritage is rooted in a mission to teach the traditional Jewish texts and ideas to the children of New York's Orthodox Jewish community. More than perhaps any other college in the United States, students choose Yeshiva en route to rabbinical training or to stay within their Orthodox community. Yeshiva students are predominantly from New York's five boroughs or the surrounding suburbs. As it has developed, Yeshiva has become a research university of 6,513 students and four campuses. Yeshiva has three undergraduate programs: the Stern College for Women, the Syms School of Business, and Yeshiva College, a coeducational arts and sciences division. Yeshiva also has graduate and professional programs (such as the Albert Einstein College of Medicine and the Benjamin Cardozo School of Law) that have more cultural and religious diversity than the undergraduate divisions.

Yeshiva aspires to be a premier center of Jewish and worldly learning. Yeshiva expects its professors to inspire students to engage in the continuing pursuit of knowledge and wisdom. On the undergraduate level, the curriculum at Yeshiva joins contemporary academic education with the timeless teachings of the Torah. This approach integrates Jewish scholarship with secular studies in the arts and sciences, business, education, law, medicine, psychology, and social work. Students can major in academic disciplines found at other universities while also getting a firm grounding in traditional Jewish texts, a broad exposure to Orthodox ideas, and opportunities to study in Israel. Through Yeshiva's Abraham Israeli Program, approximately six hundred students study in Israel each year. Yeshiva also operates several research centers, including ones for Jewish law and contemporary civilization, Israel studies, Torah and Western thought, and the Jewish future. Supplementing the university are two high schools in New York City: the Marsha Stern Talmudical Academy for Boys and the Samuel H. Wang High School for Girls. Notable alumni of Yeshiva include the author Chaim Potok.

BRANDEIS UNIVERSITY—WALTHAM, MASSACHUSETTS

5,808 students—3,588 undergraduates

The only nonsectarian Jewish-sponsored-university in the United States, Brandeis is part world-class research institution and part small liberal arts college. Brandeis has emerged as a prominent university in a relatively short time frame. Within two decades of its founding, Brandeis had established a Phi Beta Kappa chapter, and before turning forty it had been invited into the prestigious Association of American Universities (AAU). Today, students come to Brandeis to attend a university that emphasizes academic excellence, interdisciplinary learning, and social justice. Undergraduates at Brandeis have access to excellent facilities and get taught by faculty who are path-breaking scholars.

Brandeis is more culturally than religiously Jewish. A high percentage of the students at Brandeis grew up in Jewish households. That means both Reformed and Orthodox Jewish students will feel at home on the Brandeis campus. On the other hand, due to its strong institutional commitment to social justice, students from a diverse spectrum of cultural and religious backgrounds fit in at Brandeis. Approximately 12 percent of the students are from outside the United States—with sixty-one countries represented across campus. As a result, the atmosphere on campus is pluralistic and welcoming of all viewpoints and backgrounds.

Two-thirds of the undergraduate students at Brandeis are enrolled in the College of Arts and Sciences. Undergraduate education at Brandeis connects theory to practice by providing experiential learning opportunities, such as fieldwork and internships. Knowledge at Brandeis is sought in the service of social justice and in the solution of real-world problems. Brandeis's roughly two thousand graduate students are enrolled in master's degree and doctoral programs in the arts and sciences, the Brandeis International Business School, and the Heller School for Social Policy and Management.

Brandeis's location just nine miles west of Boston provides students easy access to the artistic, cultural, and intellectual resources of what is arguably America's best city for college students. Through a consortium arrangement, Brandeis students can take courses at nearby Babson College, the F. W. Olin College of Engineering, and Wellesley College.

Brandeis has an impressive roster of alumni, including one Nobel laureate, three winners of the Pulitzer Prize, and several Emmy-award winners in acting, broadcasting, and production. Notable Brandeis alumni include actress Debra Messing, writers Mitch Albom and Thomas Friedman, columnist Joe Conason, *New Republic* editor Martin Peretz, CNN political analyst Bill Schneider, and Philadelphia Eagles owner Jeffrey Lurie.

TOURO COLLEGE—NEW YORK, NEW YORK

19,000 students (7,478 undergraduates)

Touro College is an institution of nineteen thousand students with campuses distributed around the world. The mission of Touro is to enrich the Jewish heritage. With campuses in California, New York, Florida, Nevada, Berlin, Jerusalem, and Moscow, Touro enrolls undergraduate and graduate students in full-time and part-time programs that range from the liberal arts to law and health sciences. Touro's original home base in New York City is where most of its undergraduates study. With separate divisions for men and women, Touro has undergraduate campuses in Brooklyn, Manhattan, and Queens. In the Flatbush neighborhood of Brooklyn, Touro operates Lander College of Arts and Sciences. In Manhattan, Touro operates Lander College for Women. In the Kew Garden Hills section

of Queens, Touro has Lander College for Men. Touro's School of Health Sciences offers undergraduate degree programs at several sites in and around New York City.

Touro's Lander College of Arts and Sciences (approximately one thousand students) has separate divisions for men and women. In both divisions, the goal is to provide a supportive Jewish environment. Virtually all the men enrolled at Lander have a deep background in Gemara study, including time spent studying in Israel following high school. At the heart of the women's division is a Judaic Studies Program that aims to develop each student's pride in her Jewish heritage. Women at Lander College acquire a thorough education in the Torah while pursuing a degree in a field of academic or professional interest. For its students Lander College provides mentors for academic guidance and assistance in finding internships or gaining entry into graduate and professional schools.

Some of the undergraduate degree programs at Touro have achieved national distinction. Touro's accounting graduates consistently outperform others on the business law section of the national CPA exam—leading major accounting firms to seek them out. Other distinctive offerings at Touro include undergraduate programs in actuarial studies, health-care administration, speech and communications, and web design and desktop publishing. Through the Touro College network of schools and campuses, undergraduates can get preferential admission into graduate programs in the health sciences, international business, and law. Touro graduates frequently gain admission to highly respected institutions, such as George Washington University Medical School, New York University's schools of dentistry and medicine, Tufts University School of Dental Medicine, and the law schools at Columbia, Georgetown, Harvard, and the University of Pennsylvania.

COLLEGES WHERE BUDDHISM IS PROMINENT

Students seeking to immerse themselves in Eastern spirituality or stay close to their Buddhist heritage should consider two colleges where Buddhism is central: Naropa University in Colorado and Soka University in California.

SOKA UNIVERSITY—ALISA VIEJO, CALIFORNIA

412 students (all undergraduates)

Located not far from the ocean and surrounded by a 4,000-acre wilderness park, Soka University in Orange County, California, is small, international in focus, and governed by the Buddhist principles of peace, human rights, and the sanctity of life. Although Buddhist ideas are central to Soka's mission, the campus is open to students of every nationality and belief. By design and demographics, Soka has a global focus. Half of Soka's students are from the United States, and the other half come from forty countries around the world. At Soka, every student has an international experience because tuition charges include the cost of one semester abroad.

Soka is a liberal arts university that emphasizes mentoring of students by professors. Classes at Soka are small, averaging thirteen students. Soka wants its students to become active and informed global citizens and lifelong learners. Through Soka's learning clusters program, special seminar classes capped at twelve students meet in three- to five-week blocks to investigate, research, propose, and model solutions to issues or problems. Learning cluster program classes frequently involve field research or service learning.

Soka offers the BA in liberal arts in one of four academic concentration options: environmental studies, humanities, international studies, and social and behavioral sciences. A core curriculum provides multiple perspectives and diverse cultural viewpoints. Like the great books colleges, Soka believes that students should study the great works of the human mind. Through its fusion of Eastern and Western thought and practice, Soka courses delve into the literature, art, and culture of the Pacific Basin. All students at Soka must take a minimum of four language classes before studying abroad during junior year. The languages offered at Soka are Chinese, Japanese, and Spanish. To graduate, all Soka students must complete a capstone experience course in the senior year. The capstone develops from the student's concentration and builds on accumulated academic skills, learning experiences, and research projects.

With an endowment exceeding $1 billion, Soka's per capita financial resources put it on par with America's wealthiest institutions. As a result, scholarship aid is generous. Students from families earning $60,000 or less annually can qualify for tuition-free attendance.

NAROPA UNIVERSITY—BOULDER, COLORADO

945 students (386 undergraduates)

Located in Boulder, Colorado, which is sometimes described as the Athens of the New Age, Naropa was founded in 1974 by a Tibetan Buddhist seeking to combine contemplative studies with traditional Western scholastic and artistic disciplines. Naropa's founder believed that acquisition of knowledge was not the primary way to wisdom and wanted Naropa to merge the educational traditions of classical Greece and classical India. The result is a campus where Eastern and Western ideas, insights, and perspectives meet. At Naropa, learning is infused with awareness and compassion for self and others and refined through the practice of sitting, meditating, and deep inward observation. A Naropa education starts with the belief that traditional Western liberal education neglects the inward look into the nature of mind, self, and other.

Naropa has evolved from an institute for intellectuals interested in taking workshops in Buddhist thought and practice into a university with undergraduate and graduate programs.

Naropa has a small number of full-time undergraduate students and a variety of part-time programs. Naropa is not for the typical high school student but rather for those who seek a different path, one that blends educational approaches from the East and West. Naropa offers undergraduate and graduate degree programs in the arts, education, environmental studies, psychology, religious studies, and writing.

QUAKER COLLEGES

There are several colleges with roots in the Quaker educational tradition, but three (Earlham College in Indiana, Guilford College in North Carolina, and Haverford College in Pennsylvania) stand out for their adherence to Quaker principles and national (even international) renown.

EARLHAM COLLEGE

Despite its location in a small Indiana city, Earlham is a globally focused liberal arts college of 1,064 students from around the world. To augment their learning, nearly 75 percent of Earlham students leave campus for programs in foreign countries, Chicago, New York, and Washington, DC. Although Earlham is open to students of all faiths, the community is united around Quaker values. The principles and practices that serve as guidelines for life on the Earlham campus emphasize inclusivity, equality, mutual support and respect, and cooperative learning. The result is a campus that feels like a family. Classes are small, averaging fifteen students. The curriculum encourages service to society, and nearly a third of Earlham graduates pursue careers related to social change. Each year Earlham students, faculty, and staff contribute more than thirty-five thousand hours of community service to the greater Richmond, Indiana, area.

GUILFORD COLLEGE

Central to the Guilford community are engaged learning and ethical behavior. In the last two decades, Guilford has evolved from a small Quaker college in Greensboro, North Carolina, to a more comprehensive arts and sciences institution that serves 2,056 full-time students and 406 part-time students. With fifty-four majors and thirty-eight minors, Guilford offers programs in liberal arts subjects, such as English and psychology, and specialized areas, such as business management, criminal justice, and forensic biology. Guilford's Quaker ethos shows through in the high percentage of students involved in community service.

HAVERFORD COLLEGE

In many respects, Haverford (located just outside Philadelphia) is the exemplar of the classic liberal arts college. Of the nearly 1,200 students at Haverford, 99 percent live on campus, half of the faculty members live on campus, the student-to-faculty ratio is eight to one, and classes are predominantly discussion based. But Haverford is by no means a generic prestigious liberal arts college. Campus life is decidedly Quaker in character. There is a palpable emphasis on community, consensus, and diversity (one-third of the students are multicultural). A high percentage of Haverford students participate in off-campus study and give community service to metro Philadelphia. From their first day on campus, Haverford students are given a greater amount of responsibility than most freshmen, through one of the oldest college honor codes in the United States. The Haverford Honor Code pervades all aspects of campus life and creates an environment where students are collegial and collaborative rather than adversarial. *Nice* is a word often used to describe the overall tone of the Haverford campus. Haverford is an apt choice for students drawn to the Quaker ideals of letting one's life speak and behaving in ways that preclude any discrepancy between word and deed.

Part 2

AREAS OF STUDY

The worldwide movement toward greater environmental consciousness has emerged on college campuses in a big way. Increased attention to sustainability has driven greater student interest in environmentally focused majors. Virtually every college now offers degree programs such as environmental studies, environmental science, and environmental engineering. A handful of colleges have gone further, designing their mission and academic programs around an environmental focus. At these colleges, ecological sustainability is at the core of their being. These colleges function as laboratories of environmentally sustainable living and learning. Four such colleges are the College of the Atlantic in Bar Harbor, Maine; Northland College in Ashland, Wisconsin; the State University of New York College of Environmental Science and Forestry (SUNY-ESF) in Syracuse, New York; and Unity College in Unity, Maine.

▶ COLLEGES WHERE IT'S ALL ABOUT THE ENVIRONMENT

Each of the four eco-focused colleges makes the claim that it is the premier place to study the environment. Northland says it is the environmental liberal arts college. Unity bills itself as America's environmental college. The College of the Atlantic has human ecology as its main focus. SUNY-ESF's vision is to create a better world through environmental discovery.

COLLEGE OF THE ATLANTIC— BAR HARBOR, MAINE

364 students from forty-two states and thirty-five countries

Only 10 percent of classes have more than twenty students.

65 percent of students study abroad; 55 percent go on to graduate school.

Study partnerships with the Eco League, University of Maine, F. W. Olin College of Engineering, SALT Institute for Documentary Studies, and the National Outdoor Leadership School (NOLS)

Average high school GPA: 3.6/4.0

Middle 50 percent on SAT: 1180–1330; ACT: 25–33

73 percent of applicants admitted:

Founded in 1969 as an alternative to the traditional liberal arts college, the College of the Atlantic (COA) is for questioners who want to learn from experience and push for change. Students choose COA because they want to be at a place where environmental sustainability is the focus. The education students get at COA promotes creativity, imaginative and critical thinking, community engagement, and interdisciplinary study. COA lives its ideals. It was the first college in the United States to reduce its greenhouse gas emissions to zero. Campus dining facilities serve food grown at COA's organic farm or procured from other local, organic, and free-range (for meat) suppliers. Low-flow renewable hydropower supplies COA's campus with its electricity needs.

Although it is a small college, COA has a handful of campuses. The main campus is in Bar Harbor adjacent to Acadia National Park. COA also utilizes two research stations, an organic farm, and a museum of natural history. Hands-on learning about sustainable agriculture and forestry occurs at COA's eighty-one-acre Beech Hill Farm and Forest, where the work of students provides the campus dining hall with organic produce. Students and faculty also conduct field research at COA's Mount Desert Rock and Great Duck Island offshore research stations; the latter has the only campus-operated lighthouse in the United States. In addition, COA operates the George B. Dorr Museum of Natural History.

Prospective students should not dismiss the College of the Atlantic on the grounds that the only degree program it offers is in human ecology. Human ecology at COA branches into three academic concentration areas: arts and design, environmental science, and human studies. COA's arts and design area encompasses courses in ceramics, drawing, film and video, graphic arts, landscape architecture and design, museum studies, music, painting, photography, and sculpture. COA's human studies program integrates perspectives from anthropology, economics, education, history, law, literature, philosophy, political science, and psychology. COA's environmental science program employs the scientific method to trace ecological and evolutionary patterns, examine natural communities, and explore the interactions of people and nature. Students at COA also have the freedom to design a program of study with a specialty area.

NORTHLAND COLLEGE—ASHLAND, WISCONSIN

600 students from forty-two states and a dozen foreign countries

120-acre Lake Superior environmental preserve

33 percent of classes have fewer than ten students

Average high school GPA: 3.3/4.0

Middle 50 percent on SAT: 970–1240; ACT: 21–27

59 percent admitted

Students who go to Northland meet the wilderness face-to-face. While walking across the Northland campus, students may see a bear or a moose crossing the athletic fields. Northland's hometown of Ashland, Wisconsin, is situated on the far northern border of the United States along the shores of Lake Superior. Making use of its rural location, Northland operates an environmental institute in the wilderness alongside America's largest lake. Northland aspires to become the leading environmental liberal arts college in the United States. Meaningful lives, according to Northland's mission statement, depend on cultivating awe, wonder, and humility toward the natural world.

Day-to-day, Northland operates according to environmental principles. Northland has two wind towers, relies on geothermal heat for its campus center and library, uses furniture made from recycled materials, and generates power from solar panels on campus buildings. Students maintain a campus garden that provides fresh produce for the cafeteria; they recycle thousands of pounds of food waste into a composting system; they operate a reuse room for nonperishable goods; they manage a renewable energy fund that promotes geothermal and solar projects on campus; and they have built an off-the-grid campus facility out of locally produced materials. Northland's efforts have been recognized by rankings that have called it one of the ten greenest colleges in America and one of the nation's most bike-friendly campuses.

The curriculum at Northland encourages integrated learning around three types of connections that express a distinctive focus on environmental education. Natural Connections emphasize the importance of the natural world. Superior Connections foster learning opportunities (such as a one-month field trip around the lake) using the Lake Superior ecosystem. In Growing Connections, students work with regional farmers to develop sustainable food systems. In fostering its three core connections, Northland blends classroom learning and hands-on experiences. The environmental majors and minors offered at Northland include environmental chemistry, environmental education, environmental humanities, environmental geosciences, geographic information systems, natural resources, humanity and nature studies, outdoor education, sustainable community development, and water science. Non-environmental majors at Northland include art, biology, business, education, humanities, math, Native American studies, sociology and social justice, and writing and English.

STATE UNIVERSITY OF NEW YORK COLLEGE OF ENVIRONMENTAL SCIENCE AND FORESTRY— SYRACUSE, NEW YORK

2,318 students—1,718 undergraduates

Ranger School in the Adirondacks offers associate degree programs.

Cross registration at Syracuse University

Average high school GPA: 3.7/4.0

Middle 50 percent on SAT: 1140–1260; ACT: 26–29

51 percent of applicants admitted

SUNY-ESF offers its 2,318 students a concentrated and comprehensive education focused on sustainability at a state university price. For students interested in careers related to the environment and the outdoors, SUNY-ESF provides unsurpassed opportunities on its main campus in Syracuse, at its 25,000-acre field stations, and at its Ranger School in the Adirondacks, where students can pursue applied associate degree programs in Upstate New York's Adirondack Park.

Students who choose SUNY-ESF are doers interested in learning the technologies on which a sustainable future will be founded. For example, students in bioprocess engineering and biotechnology learn about alternative and renewable energy, environmental engineering, bioremediation, and conservation of endangered plant species. Similarly, the construction management program emphasizes sustainable practices and the integration of environmental perspectives into building and design. Other environmental majors and minors offered at SUNY-ESF include aquatic and fisheries science, conservation biology, environmental biology, environmental chemistry, environmental and natural resources conservation, environmental resources engineering, environmental science, environmental studies, environmental writing, forest ecosystem science, forest health, forest resources management, forest technology, landscape architecture, natural history, natural resources management, renewable energy, and wildlife science. SUNY-ESF also offers programs in chemistry, paper engineering, and paper science. SUNY-ESF students are able to take classes, use library and recreation facilities, eat in dining halls, and join student clubs at Syracuse University.

UNITY COLLEGE—UNITY, MAINE

554 students

Internship sites in forty-plus states

Average high school GPA: 3.25/4.0

SAT/ACT: not required

89 percent admitted

Unity College seeks to create a community of adventurous learners focused on the environment. Unity is proud that its students get their hands dirty in an active learning experience, using Maine as a learning laboratory. Students who might like Unity are those who would be excited about swapping classrooms full of desks and chairs for on-site learning in rural Maine's bogs, barrens, forests, lakes, mountains, rivers, and parks. The central goal of a Unity education is to provide students with the intellectual tools and real-world perspectives needed to create a sustainable planet. Everything that occurs at Unity is focused on sustainability. Unity students and faculty seek to develop human-scale models of environmental sustainability that can be replicated by real people around the world. Unity's curriculum provides students with a mix of theory and practice through an underlying liberal arts foundation supplemented by more specialized courses that prepare students for careers in forestry, conservation law, fisheries, and landscape design and horticulture. Students with a passion for creating a more sustainable world will find ample access to fieldwork opportunities, service-learning experiences, and programs focused on environmental leadership.

Degree programs offered at Unity include adventure education leadership; adventure therapy; agriculture, food, and sustainability; aquaculture and fisheries; captive wildlife care and education; conservation law enforcement; ecology; environmental analysis; environmental biology; environmental policy and law; environmental science; environmental writing; forestry; landscape horticulture; marine biology; parks, recreation, and ecotourism; sustainable design and technology; teaching and learning; wildlife; wildlife biology; and wildlife conservation.

STANDOUT ENVIRONMENTAL PROGRAMS

A handful of other colleges have exceptional programs and facilities for studies related to environmental sustainability and a campus culture that supports environmental awareness at practically every turn. Focus on the environment is a significant part of the mission at these colleges, but it is not the totality of it as these colleges also offer nonenvironmental majors. Three small colleges prominent in this category are Green Mountain College in Vermont, Paul Smith's College in Upstate New York, and Warren Wilson College in North Carolina. At Warren Wilson, environmental responsibility is a core value articulated in the mission statement. The curriculum at Green Mountain College is built around a thirty-seven-credit required core program in environmental liberal arts. Paul Smith's College prepares students for careers as outdoor recreation outfitters, fisheries and wildlife scientists, surveyors, arborists, foresters, and backcountry guides.

For those looking for larger student populations, Humboldt State and the University of Montana have several programs to appeal to the environmentally minded. The natural beauty of Humboldt State University's setting in Arcata, California, and the campus's distance from major urban areas makes it an attractive option for those who want to get away from it all. Humboldt's College of Natural Resources and Sciences offers several environmental programs, such as majors in fire ecology, fisheries biology, and oceanography. Located not far from two of the largest wilderness areas in America's lower forty-eight states—Glacier National Park and Yellowstone—the University of Montana has developed strong programs in wildlife biology. Montana is *the* place to study grizzly bears. In fact, the grizzly is Montana's mascot. Montana's College of Forestry and Conservation operates a wilderness institute in addition to offering degree programs in parks, tourism, and recreation management; resource conservation; and wildlife restoration.

GREEN MOUNTAIN COLLEGE— POULTNEY, VERMONT

841 students—591 undergraduates

Special programs and facilities: Eco League, Farm and Food Project, Design Your Own Major Program, Service Learning

Average high school GPA: 2.7/4.0

Middle 50 percent on SAT: 920–1200; ACT: 20–27

76 percent admitted

The heart of the academic experience at Green Mountain is the required thirty-seven-credit sequence in the environmental liberal arts, which ensures that every graduate departs campus aware of the importance of sustainability. Green Mountain shows its commitment to environmental education in other ways. The college has its own farm and gardens, operates a solar harvest center, and provides block courses that enable in-depth field research opportunities.

Environmentally oriented majors and minors at Green Mountain include adventure education, environmental studies, environmental management, natural resources management, sustainable agriculture and food production, recreation management, renewable energy and eco-design, and therapeutic adventure. Within its environmentally focused study programs, Green Mountain encourages hands-on experience through internships and service learning. Sophomores in the adventure education program go on a field semester that includes a ten-day rock-climbing instruction course, five-day raft-guide training, a seven-day canoe expedition, a six-day mountain-bike management course, and a seven-day backpacking course. As juniors, adventure education majors plan and manage a twenty-one-day expedition.

HUMBOLDT STATE UNIVERSITY— ARCATA, CALIFORNIA

8,485 students—7,962 undergraduates

Average high school GPA: 3.2/4.0

Middle 50 percent on SAT: 870–1170; ACT: 18–24

76 percent admitted

Imagine a college located next to a rain forest in the redwoods amid the unspoiled natural beauty of the Northern California coast, a place where bicycling, camping, climbing, fishing, hiking, kayaking, and surfing opportunities are just minutes away and a place where students explore the Pacific Ocean in their own research vessel, take seismic readings along fault lines, photograph wildlife, maintain an on-campus fish hatchery, and learn captive fish husbandry. That place is Humboldt State University. Few universities offer more environmental programs of study than Humboldt or have a location and a campus community that so strongly supports sustainability.

Humboldt abounds with immersive learning opportunities. Undergraduates in Humboldt's College of Natural Resources have access to marine laboratories, ocean-going research vessels, fish hatcheries, a tree farm, a marine wildlife care center, a herbarium, a wildlife museum, greenhouses, nearby parks, nature preserves, forests, and wildlife sanctuaries. Students interested in environmental careers and the outdoors have options at Humboldt usually found only at much larger research universities. And as part of the California State University system, Humboldt is a reasonably priced option for students on a tight budget.

Humboldt's College of Natural Resources is divided into five divisions: biological sciences, environmental science and engineering, natural resources, marine sciences, and physical sciences. Environmental degree programs at

Humboldt include conservation biology, ecology, energy and climate, environmental biology, environmental education and interpretation, environmental ethics, environmental management and protection, environmental and natural resources recreation, environmental and natural resources planning, environmental policy, environmental resources engineering, ecological restoration, environmental science and management, environmental toxicology, fire ecology, fisheries biology, forest hydrology, forest operations, forest resource conservation, forest soils, freshwater fisheries, marine biology, oceanography, outdoor adventure recreation, rangeland resources, water resource policy, watershed management, wildlife, wild land fire management, wildlife management and conservation, and wildlife soil science.

UNIVERSITY OF MONTANA— MISSOULA, MONTANA

14,964 students—12,656 undergraduates

Special facilities: Bandy Ranch, Flathead Lake Biological Station, Lubrecht Experimental Forest, Theodore Roosevelt Memorial Ranch

Average high school GPA: 3.3/4.0

Middle 50 percent on SAT: 950–1200; ACT: 21–26

94 percent admitted

Students attracted to the outdoors will not find many locations that surpass Missoula, Montana, the home of the University of Montana. The Montana campus is located two hours from Glacier National Park, four hours from Yellowstone National Park, and less than an hour from ski and snowboard trails and hundreds of miles of rivers for kayaking and rafting. Montana's College of Forestry and Conservation enrolls nearly six hundred undergraduates and offers leading programs related to the study and preservation of forest and wildlife resources. A standout feature of Montana's forestry and conservation program is its extensive array of field stations, such as a 28,000-acre experimental forest thirty miles north of Missoula, a biological research station on Flathead Lake, and a 6,000-acre ranch along the east face of the Rocky Mountains.

There is impressive breadth to the environmental programs at Montana. Options to focus on the environment exist beyond the College of Forestry and Conservation. For example, Montana's College of Arts and Sciences offers a major in environmental studies with concentrations in environmental justice, environmental science, environmental writing and literature, and environmental prelaw. The concentration in sustainability has sub-concentrations in sustainable business, energy, food and farming, and water resources. Montana's biology department offers a field ecology specialty, and the geography department offers a concentration in environmental planning and a minor in mountain studies. To tie the environmental studies program to its home region, Montana requires all majors to take courses in Native American studies and also provides courses in Rocky Mountain ecology. Other environmental areas of study at Montana include ecosystem and conservation studies; forest management; geosciences; resource conservation; society and conservation; wilderness studies; wild land restoration; wildlife biology; and parks, tourism, and recreation management.

PAUL SMITH'S COLLEGE— BRIGHTON, NEW YORK

1,000 students

Average high school GPA: 2.9/4.0

Middle 50 percent on SAT: 880–1060; ACT: 20–25

75 percent admitted

The only college within New York's six-million-acre Adirondack Park, Paul Smith's provides its students a wilderness laboratory. Right outside their classrooms and residence halls, students will find forests, lakes, and streams. The Paul Smith's experience is largely defined by the environmental programs in its Division of Forestry, Natural Resources, and Recreation, where students are taught to be stewards of the earth. Paul Smith's graduates go on to manage fisheries and forests, work as professional surveyors, and lead expeditions as backcountry guides. Several magazines have named Paul Smith's one of the top colleges for outdoor activities and recreation. The sports offerings and student clubs at Paul Smith's reflect its wilderness location. Paul Smith's fields coed woodmen's teams, competes in sports like snowshoe racing and canoe racing, has a thirty-two-foot high climbing wall, has a whitewater kayaking club, and dedicates part of its recreational center to log birling. One of the more popular and unique sports at the college is lumberjacking.

Environmental study programs at Paul Smith's College include biology and environmental science; environmental studies; forestry; fisheries and wildlife science; natural resources management and policy; natural resources sustainability; arboriculture and landscape management; forest technology; surveying; geographic information systems; and recreation, adventure travel, and ecotourism. There is also a Division of Sciences, Liberal Arts, and Business.

The Paul Smith's campus started out as a hotel and, reflecting that heritage, provides degrees in hospitality, resort, and culinary management. But rather surprisingly, hospitality students are not involved in dining services, which seems like a missed opportunity for creativity, farm-to-table practices, and overall sustainability. Instead, the college contracts with Sodexo, a large-scale food service company that claims to have its own standards for sustainability.

WARREN WILSON COLLEGE— ASHEVILLE, NORTH CAROLINA

920 students—850 undergraduates

Three-hundred-acre farm and organic garden, six hundred acres of forest, twenty-five miles of hiking trails

Average high school GPA: 3.5/4.0

Middle 50 percent on SAT: 910–1250; ACT: 23–27

70 percent admitted

Founded in 1894 on principles of sustainability, Warren Wilson College is a learning-by-doing kind of place. The community is united by what Warren Wilson calls the triad of academics for the mind, work for the hands, and service from the heart. Through its triad approach to education, Warren Wilson teaches students how environmental awareness, responsibility, and sustainability relate to the future of life on earth. Students help operate a working farm, cultivate an organic garden that raises produce for the dining hall, and run a horse crew for logging and plowing.

Through its curriculum, Warren Wilson lives up to its intention to instill in students a sense of harmony with the environment. For example, there is a sustainable economic development track in the business and economics major. The environmental studies program offers concentrations in conservation biology, environmental education, and sustainable farming and forestry. The outdoor leadership major draws on the resources of Outward Bound and other adventure programs in western North Carolina. There are also concentrations in environmental chemistry and environmental policy.

Fieldwork is interwoven into the academic part of the Warren Wilson triad. Students have ample opportunities to analyze the water quality of local rivers, manage the composting system for the college farm, present outdoor education programs to local elementary schools, and evaluate the effectiveness of unmechanized logging and plowing. An Environmental Leadership Center brings in prominent sustainability practitioners and researchers for lectures, seminars, and connections to internships and jobs. Beyond the classroom, the work aspect of the Warren Wilson triad requires fifteen hours per week in jobs around the campus, while the service-learning part of the triad requires one hundred hours of service to the community over four years.

TOP ENVIRONMENTAL PROGRAMS AT PUBLIC UNIVERSITIES

The state of Colorado attracts students who want to commune with the environment. The University of Colorado is known for its location in the eco-conscious, tree-hugging people's republic of Boulder. Colorado students, regardless of major, tend to have a high environmental consciousness, and Colorado has plenty of options for the eco-friendly student. Often overshadowed by CU–Boulder, but arguably more of a hub for environmental study is Colorado State University (CSU) in Fort Collins. Students interested in the environment have many choices at Colorado State. They can study in Colorado State's School of Global Environmental Sustainability, or they can find programs of interest in the Warner College of Natural Resources.

For those looking to attend college in the Northeast, the University of Vermont (UVM) has been a perennial favorite for the environmentally conscious. UVM takes its environmental cue from its location in Burlington, the largest city in a state whose residents go to great lengths to preserve the natural world. Burlington is considered one of those people's republics and an epicenter for environmental awareness. Vermont's Rubenstein School of Environment and Natural Resources offers numerous majors and programs for the eco-oriented student, as does UVM's school of agriculture.

Historically, Oregon and Washington have depended on the fishing and timber industries.

The earliest inhabitants of Oregon and Washington learned to respect the environment because they lived off its bounty. Sustainability as a core value informs life in the Pacific Northwest, which is often described as the greenest, both literally and figuratively, region of the United States. Thus, not surprisingly, two universities in the Pacific Northwest—Oregon State University and the University of Washington—offer standout environmental programs. Other appealing venues for studying environmental issues include Arizona State, with its School of Sustainability; the University of Florida, with its numerous LEED (Leadership in Energy and Environmental Design)-certified buildings and environmental majors; and Montana State University, which has rangelands and wilderness areas within minutes of campus.

ARIZONA STATE UNIVERSITY—TEMPE AND PHOENIX, ARIZONA

83,301 students—67,507 undergraduates

Schools of Sustainability and Sustainable Engineering and the Built Environment

Global Institute of Sustainability

Average high school GPA: 3.5/4.0

Middle 50 percent on SAT: 1020–1270; ACT: 22–28

80 percent admitted

Arizona State University warrants a close look from students interested in sustainability. ASU's Global Institute of Sustainability works to create sustainability-related courses and programs across the curriculum. The School of Sustainability offers interdisciplinary, hands-on, research-based BA and BS programs as well as graduate degrees. The goal of ASU's School of Sustainability is to develop graduates equipped to tackle future challenges related to the natural environment. Students in ASU's sustainability studies BA program take a social science approach, concentrating on issues related to environmental economics, environmental design, human geography, and environmental politics and resources, while students in the BS program take a scientific approach, focusing on areas such as earth systems management, ecology, environmental biology, chemistry, engineering, and hydrology.

Beyond the School of Sustainability, there are degree programs in the College of Technology and Innovation—for example, environmental technology management, urban horticulture, and wildlife restoration ecology. In ASU's College of Liberal Arts and Sciences, the departments of biology, chemistry, and geology offer specialized tracks for students interested in sustainability and the environment. Within its engineering program, ASU operates the School of Sustainable Engineering and the Built Environment, where students and faculty focus on subjects such as air and water quality, environmental biotechnology, renewable technology, and sustainable materials. Other environmental areas of study at ASU include sustainable business; conservation biology and ecological sustainability; environmental chemistry; environmental humanities; meteorology and climatology; sustainability; and civil, environmental, and sustainable engineering.

COLORADO STATE UNIVERSITY— FORT COLLINS, COLORADO

31,256 students—23,798 undergraduates

Average high school GPA: 3.6/4.0

Middle 50 percent on SAT: 1020–1250; ACT: 22–27

77 percent admitted

Colorado State's commitment to environmental education can be felt all around the university. Students can find an in-depth focus on the environment at CSU in the Warner College of Natural Resources, the School of Global Environmental Sustainability, and the College of Engineering. The Warner College of Natural Resources at CSU offers seven majors and eighteen concentrations, making it one of the most comprehensive programs in the United States. Major programs in Warner include fish, wildlife, and conservation biology; forestry; geology; natural resource recreation and tourism; natural resources management; rangeland ecology; and watershed science. Environmentally focused students interested in engineering at CSU can concentrate on atmospheric science or civil and environmental engineering.

To stimulate research and curricular initiatives across its eight colleges, Colorado State established a School of Global Environmental Sustainability (SGES). Although SGES does not directly offer degree programs, it encourages course work and research related to biodiversity and conservation, climate change and energy, environmental institutions and governance, global food security, geospatial science, industrial ecology, land and water resources, sustainable engineering, and sustainable communities. SGES aims to train the new green workforce as well as the next generation of researchers, engineers, entrepreneurs, and big thinkers who will construct a future of long-term environmental sustainability for the Earth.

UNIVERSITY OF COLORADO— BOULDER, COLORADO

31,702 students—25,981 undergraduates

Average high school GPA: 3.6/4.0

Middle 50 percent on SAT: 1060–1280; ACT: 24–29

88 percent admitted

By putting the emphasis on environmental design, Colorado's College of Architecture and Planning stands apart from most architecture schools. Colorado aims to train architects and community planners who think about environmental sustainability and understand the ecological, cultural, historical, physical, and social factors that influence designed environments. Environmental design students at Colorado learn to design buildings, cities, gardens, and neighborhoods that are healthy and sustainable places. Other environmental degree programs at Colorado include ecology and evolutionary biology, environmental engineering, and environmental studies.

Students interested in the environment have a special beyond-the-classroom option at Colorado: the Baker Residential Academic Program (BRAP) creates a small, close-knit living-learning community focused on sustainability courses and activities. Classes in BRAP average twenty students and are taught by dedicated faculty who love teaching undergraduates. On the extracurricular side, BRAP students participate in outdoor activities such as backpacking, mountain climbing, rafting, and rock climbing. BRAP students get to take field trips to geological/paleontological sites, the Denver Zoo and Aquarium, working mines, and the Caribbean to study tropical marine ecology and oceanography.

UNIVERSITY OF FLORIDA— GAINESVILLE, FLORIDA

49,878 students—33,168 undergraduates

Average high school GPA: 3.9/4.0

Middle 50 percent on SAT: 1170–1360; ACT: 26–31

47 percent admitted

One of the largest universities in the United States, the University of Florida has a commitment to sustainability that matches its size. Majors and courses related to environmental sustainability can be found across the curriculum. At UF there are numerous centers for environmental research, conservation, and policy. UF is home to the Energy Technology Incubator, the Water Institute, and the Florida Institute of Sustainable Energy (FISE). Facilities such as FISE—where students and faculty expand the boundaries of research related to biofuels, fuel cells, and solar cells—have helped UF become a leading center for alternative energy research.

Sustainability efforts at Florida extend to architecture, construction, and design, as exemplified by the sustainability in the built environment major in UF's College of Design, Construction, and Planning. To show its commitment to sustainable campus facilities, UF built the state of Florida's first LEED Platinum–certified building, and the campus now has seventeen LEED-certified buildings. UF was also among the first universities to sign the American College and University Presidents Climate Commitment and intends to be a carbon-neutral campus by 2025.

Environmental areas of study at UF include environmental economics and policy; environmental engineering; environmental horticulture operations; environmental management in agriculture and natural resources; environmental science; food and resource economics; forest resources and conservation; forest resource management; horticultural science; land and water resources engineering; landscape and nursery horticulture; landscape architecture; organic crop production; natural resources conservation; protected areas management; recreation, parks, and tourism; recreation resource management; restoration horticulture; soil and water science; sustainability and the built environment; urban forestry; watershed science and management; and wildlife ecology and conservation.

MONTANA STATE UNIVERSITY— BOZEMAN, MONTANA

15,294 students—13,264 undergraduates

Average high school GPA: 3.3/4.0

Middle 50 percent on SAT: 1010–1260; ACT: 21–27

85 percent admitted

With its promotional slogan of Mountains and Minds, Montana State signals its distinctive strengths at the intersection of intellectual pursuits and outdoor endeavors. Students interested in the environment will find an array of degree programs across Montana State's curriculum as well as opportunities to do field research in places like Yellowstone National Park. Over the last two decades, Bozeman, Montana, has emerged as a choice destination for outdoor adventurers and artists inspired by the wide open spaces and natural beauty of the Mountain West. As a result, Bozeman and its leading institution, Montana State, have become known for environmental sustainability.

Like its counterpart in Missoula, MSU's curriculum draws upon its location. MSU, for example, is one of the few colleges offering undergraduate degree options in rangeland ecology and management of wildlife ecology and habitats. MSU's Department of Land Resources and Environmental Sciences offers study options in land rehabilitation and sustainable food and bioenergy systems. Areas of special focus include environmental biology, soil and water science, land resource management, and geospatial and environmental analysis. Students in the plant sciences and plant pathology division

at MSU can pursue concentrations in environmental horticulture science, landscape design, or sustainable crop production. MSU also offers degree programs in agroecology, bioresources engineering, earth sciences, ecology and evolution, environmental design, environmental health, environmental horticulture, environmental microbiology, environmental science, environmental studies, fish and wildlife management, geohydrology, land resource sciences, land resources analysis and management, landscape design, sustainable crop production, sustainable food systems, and water resources.

OREGON STATE UNIVERSITY— CORVALLIS, OREGON

27,925 students—23,161 undergraduates

Colleges of forestry and oceanic and atmospheric sciences

Marine and Freshwater Biomedical Research Center

Average high school GPA: 3.6/4.0

Middle 50 percent on SAT: 970–1220; ACT: 21–27

79 percent admitted

Oregon State's niche is in science-based programs that prepare students to understand and solve environmental challenges. Ways to study the environment are sprinkled across the curriculum at Oregon State. Students looking to learn how to build and engineer a more sustainable world will find options such as biological, ecological, and environmental engineering in OSU's College of Engineering and forest engineering and wood science and engineering in the College of Forestry. Also within the College of Forestry are programs in forest ecosystems and society, renewable materials, and recreation resource management. OSU's Food Science and Technology program applies chemistry and engineering in developing and delivering food products from farm to market. Horticulture students at OSU concentrate on environmental landscape in preparation for positions managing the plantings and ecosystems of golf courses, parks, gardens, and playing fields.

The numerous additional environmental programs at OSU include crop and soil science; ecosystems analysis and policy; environmental chemistry; environmental economics, policy, and management; environmental geosciences; environmental science; environmental science, resources, and management; fisheries and wildlife science; food quality; natural resources; rangeland ecology and management; sustainable ecosystems; and water resources. Students at Oregon State benefit from a number of research facilities such as the Environmental Health Sciences Center, the Hatfield Marine Science Center, the Institute for Water and Watersheds, the Linus Pauling Institute (dedicated to the study of micronutrients and phytochemicals), and the Oregon Forest Research Laboratory. Oregon State also operates a campus (called OSU Cascades) near Bend, Oregon—a town that has become a magnet for outdoor enthusiasts. OSU Cascades provides field learning opportunities and courses for students majoring in tourism and outdoor leadership.

UNIVERSITY OF VERMONT— BURLINGTON, VERMONT

12,723 students—10,912 undergraduates

Rubinstein School of Environmental and Natural Resources

Four research farms, nine natural areas, including on Mount Mansfield and Lake Champlain

Average high school GPA: 3.5/4.0

Middle 50 percent on SAT: 1080–1290; 24–29

78 percent admitted

From the University of Vermont (UVM) campus in Burlington, there are picturesque views of Lake Champlain and Mount Mansfield. Within minutes of their classrooms, students at UVM can find wetlands, forests, nature preserves, and some of the best hiking, skiing, and kayaking on the East Coast. Thus, it is fitting that Vermont's Rubenstein School of Environment and Natural Resources offers some of the nation's best academic programs focused on the environment.

Through its facilities and programs, the Rubenstein School makes good use of its location in one of America's greenest states. Rubenstein School faculty and students like to say that the whole state of Vermont serves as their outdoor laboratory. Hands-on and experiential learning opportunities abound for the approximately six hundred students working on degrees at Rubenstein. Special facilities utilized by the Rubenstein School include an aquatic research vessel, a lakeside ecosystem science center, a spatial analysis laboratory, an institute for ecological economics, and laboratories for the study of tree physiology, forest carbon dynamics, fisheries, watershed science, and the natural systems found in parks and preserves. The office of experiential learning in UVM's career services department is an especially useful resource for students seeking internships and jobs in environmental fields.

Beyond the Rubenstein School, UVM offers environmentally focused study programs in the colleges of agriculture, arts and sciences, business, and engineering. Environmentally oriented majors at UVM include ecological agriculture; environmental engineering; environmental sciences; environmental studies; forestry; geospatial technologies; green building and community design; management and the environment; natural resources; parks, recreation, and tourism; sustainable landscape horticulture; and wildlife and fisheries biology.

UNIVERSITY OF WASHINGTON—SEATTLE, WASHINGTON

44,786 students—29.468 undergraduates

Colleges and schools: built environments; environment; aquatic and fishery sciences; forest resources; marine affairs; oceanography

Center for Conservation Biology, Friday Harbor Laboratories, Joint Institute for the Study of the Atmosphere and Ocean

Average high school GPA: 3.8/4.0

Middle 50 percent: SAT: 1100–1360; ACT 25–30

55 percent admitted

Widely considered the leading research university north of Berkeley, California, UW (U-Dub, as the locals call it) combines the dynamism of the Pacific Northwest's leading urban center (Seattle) with proximity to the salmon-breeding waterways of Puget Sound, the rain forests on the Olympic Peninsula, and the mountain peaks and wilderness of the Cascades. UW is the leading academic light in a region of the United States that gave birth to visions of a nation (Cascadia or Ecotopia) founded on principles of environmental sustainability.

UW has environmental programs across the curriculum as well as two schools devoted to the environment—the College of Built Environments and the College of the Environment. The College of the Environment has programs in aquatic and fisheries science, atmospheric sciences, earth and space studies, environmental studies, forest resources, and oceanography. The College of Arts and Sciences has programs in ecology, evolution, and conservation biology and a geography track in environment, economy, and sustainability. Engineering offers majors in bioresources science and engineering (where students work on the green technologies of the future, such as biofuels, natural-products chemistry, and production of materials from renewable natural resources) and environmental engineering, where students can concentrate on water resources or sustainable construction. The College of Built Environment's programs in architectural studies, community and environmental planning, and landscape architecture have a strong emphasis on sustainable design. UW's School of Public Health offers an undergraduate major in environmental health.

HONORABLE MENTION ENVIRONMENTAL PROGRAMS

University of California at Berkeley. Frequently called the top public university in the United States and one of the leading universities in the world, Berkeley has much to offer students interested in issues of environmental sustainability. Berkeley's College of Environmental Design has an undergraduate program in landscape architecture. The College of Natural Resources has study options in conservation of resources, ecosystem management, environmental economics and policy, environmental sciences, forestry, and molecular environmental biology. Berkeley also offers programs in atmospheric science, environmental earth science, environmental engineering, and marine science.

University of California at Davis. Among the UC campuses, Davis stands out for its programs in agriculture, environmental sciences, and natural sciences. Davis has leading programs in avian (bird) sciences, plant biology, and viticulture and enology (the agriculture and science of wine making). Students looking for environmental study programs will find many options, especially in Davis's College of Agricultural and Environmental Sciences. Environmental major options include atmospheric science; biological systems engineering; ecological management and restoration; environmental education; environmental horticulture and urban forestry; environmental policy analysis and planning; environmental science and management; environmental toxicology; evolution, ecology, and biodiversity; hydrology; landscape architecture; and wildlife, fish, and conservation biology.

California Polytechnic State University at San Luis Obispo. Located along the Pacific Coast midway between Los Angeles and San Francisco, Cal Poly's spectacular surroundings remind students that inspiration can be drawn from the natural world. Students who want to solve environmental challenges using science and technology will find many programs of interest at Cal Poly, especially in its colleges of agriculture, environmental sciences, architecture, and environmental design. Major options include climate change studies, environmental engineering, environmental management, environmental planning, environmental protection, field and wildlife biology, landscape architecture, land and water resources, marine and fisheries biology, water engineering, and wild land fire management. Cal Poly also offers an outdoor, adventure, and resource recreation concentration within its Department of Recreation, Parks, and Tourism Administration.

Cornell University. The Cornell campus sits on a hill overlooking Cayuga Lake (one of the Finger Lakes) in a western New York region known for its gorges. Students can find environmental programs of study in Cornell's colleges of human ecology, agricultural and life sciences, and engineering. Majors include atmospheric science, design and environmental analysis, landscape architecture, natural and environmental systems, and environmental engineering.

Cornell's world-renowned ornithology lab for the study of birds includes a 230-acre campus sanctuary called Sapsucker Woods. Cornell also runs research institutes focused on fuel cells, waste management, and water resources.

Evergreen State College. Puget Sound waterways and shadows from Cascade peaks straddle Evergreen's hometown of Olympia, Washington. Evergreen attracts students who want to be within a short drive of the rain forests of the Olympic Peninsula or the hiking and camping opportunities in the national forestland around Mount Rainier and Mount St. Helens. Living up to its name, Evergreen is located within a forest that seems far removed from the sprawling Seattle metropolitan area. Within its highly individualized curriculum, Evergreen offers programs in ecology, environmental studies, field studies, marine science, natural history, outdoor leadership and education, and sustainability studies.

University of Georgia. At Georgia, there are six colleges or schools where students can find majors focused on the environment: the colleges of agricultural and environmental sciences, arts and sciences, environment and design, engineering, the Odum School of Ecology, and the Warnell School of Forestry and Natural Resources. Major programs include agriscience and environmental systems, biological engineering, ecology, environmental chemistry, environmental economics and management, environmental engineering, environmental sciences, fisheries and wildlife, forestry, landscape architecture, natural resources recreation and tourism, plant biology (one of the top programs in the United States), and water and soil resources. Georgia's forestry school maintains twenty-three thousand acres of land for research and teaching. Students in the wildlife sciences concentration can work toward becoming certified wildlife biologists, and Georgia's aquatic sciences concentration meets the professional certification requirements of the American Fisheries Society.

University of Maine. Woods, lakes, rivers, and streams surround the University of Maine's hometown of Orono. Not far away are the Atlantic Ocean and the Appalachian Trail. Maine's location and programs attract students interested in outdoor adventure and environmental education. Maine has five colleges and schools where students can study different aspects of the natural environment. The largest is the College of Natural Sciences, Forestry, and Agriculture, but Maine also operates a School of Biology and Ecology, a School of Forest Resources, and a School of Marine Sciences. Major options include aquaculture; earth sciences; ecology; environmental science; forest ecosystem science; forest resources; international conservation; land use planning; marine sciences; natural resource management; parks, recreation, and tourism; sustainable agriculture; wetland aquatic ecology; and wildlife ecology. Field research opportunities are available through the Aquaculture Research Center and the Darling Marine Center.

Middlebury College. Middlebury's commitment to sustainability shows across the campus. For over a decade, all buildings have been designed and constructed following energy efficient and eco-friendly processes. Middlebury's dining hall has a green roof and the Franklin Environmental Center is LEED Platinum certified. Middlebury boasts the nation's oldest major in environmental studies—established in 1965—with ten core professors and forty affiliated faculty members across twenty-four academic departments. Middlebury may be the only small liberal arts college with a dean of environmental affairs. Opportunities for field research in Vermont's mountains, streams, lakes, and wildlife preserves are just minutes away. Skiers and snowboarders can hit the slopes at the college-owned Middlebury Snow Bowl.

University of Minnesota. Minnesota's flagship campus in Minneapolis-St. Paul offers environmental programs across the curriculum. Within the College of Food, Agricultural, and Natural Resource Sciences, there are undergraduate majors and minors in bioproducts marketing and management; climatology; corporate environmental management; environmental sciences, policy, and management; fisheries and wildlife; forest and natural resource management; horticulture; Native American environmental knowledge; park and protected area management; recreation resource management; sustainable agriculture; sustainability studies; urban and community forestry; and water science. The College of Science and Engineering has programs in bioproducts and biosystems engineering, earth sciences, and geoengineering; the College of Biological Sciences offers a major in ecology, evolution, and behavior; and the College of Design has a program in landscape design and planning.

Oberlin College. Starting when it became America's first college to admit women and African Americans (in the 1830s), Oberlin has been a leader in progressive social change. When Oberlin opened the Lewis Center for Environmental Studies (in 1999), it became the trailblazer in green buildings on American college campuses. The Lewis Center transformed Oberlin both architecturally and pedagogically. Through its design and facilities, the Lewis Center serves as a teaching tool and demonstration project. Ecological processes and technologies utilized by the Lewis Center include solar panels on the roof, geothermal wells, plantings native to northern Ohio, storm water management, and the Living Machine that uses plants to purify wastewater. Students and faculty also monitor the 150 environmental sensors in and around the Lewis Center to determine energy flows and reuse of resources like water.

Pitzer College. Arguably, Pitzer is the greenest of the Claremont Colleges, Southern California's answer to Oxford. Pitzer looks and feels like an eco-friendly community. Resources include the John R. Rodman Arboretum for native ecosystems, the Ecology Center in Grove House that coordinates internships for students in environmental fields, the Pitzer Outdoor Adventure student club, an affiliation with the Firestone Center for Restoration Ecology in Costa Rica, and a handful of LEED-certified buildings. Eco-oriented students will find major options in environmental analysis at Pitzer and in environmental science through the joint science department shared by Pitzer, Claremont McKenna, and Scripps.

Wesleyan University. Students interested in sustainability issues can pursue either environmental studies or earth and environmental science at this liberal arts university in Middletown, Connecticut. Wesleyan also has a College of the Environment that infuses ecologically oriented courses and programs across the curriculum.

Western Washington University. Equidistant between Vancouver, British Columbia, and Seattle and set on a hill looking out toward Bellingham Bay and the San Juan Islands, the campus of WWU provides a perch for glimpsing the natural beauty of the Pacific Northwest. Dry in the summers but wet in other seasons, Bellingham is one of the rainiest towns in the United States, which means that it tends to be literally and figuratively green on WWU's campus. Students who attend Western Washington are drawn to the outdoors and have a high degree of environmental consciousness. Among Western Washington's academic units is the Huxley College of the Environment, which offers programs in environmental science and environmental studies. In those majors, students can concentrate on areas such as freshwater, marine, and terrestrial ecology; environmental chemistry and toxicology; environmental education; environmental journalism; planning and environmental policy; and environmental and resource management.

University of Wisconsin. There is a long heritage of environmental study at Wisconsin's flagship campus in Madison. Under the guidance of famed naturalist Aldo Leopold, Wisconsin in 1933 established the first wildlife studies program in the United States. Today, Wisconsin's Nelson Institute for Environmental Studies is the focal point for the study of sustainability, climate change, biodiversity, energy, environmental culture and history, global environmental sustainability, land resources, and environmental justice. Academic programs at Wisconsin include atmospheric and oceanic sciences, biological aspects of conservation, community and environmental sociology, forest science, landscape architecture, and wildlife ecology. Within landscape architecture, Wisconsin students can concentrate on natural resource planning and management. Engineering at Wisconsin offers study options in food and bioprocess engineering and in natural resources and environmental engineering.

STRONG ENVIRONMENTAL STUDY OPTIONS NORTH OF THE BORDER

UNIVERSITY OF BRITISH COLUMBIA— VANCOUVER, CANADA

The University of British Columbia (UBC) campus has a breathtaking setting that overlooks the Pacific Ocean and borders nearly eight hundred acres of forested parkland. More so than at most urban universities, students at UBC are reminded of nature and its long-standing importance in the Pacific Northwest. Although courses and degree programs related to sustainability are offered across the many schools of this large university, most of UBC's environmental majors are found in the schools or faculties of applied science, forestry, land and food systems, and science.

Students in the land and food systems program work to find solutions to the environmental challenges posed by the need to feed an ever-expanding global population. UBC environmental engineering students use engineering principles to safeguard scarce natural resources and improve the quality of air, land, and water systems. The School of Architecture and Landscape Architecture offers an undergraduate program in environmental design. Other environmentally related majors at UBC include atmospheric science, conservation biology, earth and ocean sciences, environmental design, environmental engineering, environmental sciences, food and environment, forest operations, forest resources management, forest sciences, geographical biogeosciences, environment and sustainability, global resource systems, natural resources conservation, and oceanography.

Supplementing UBC's academic programs are research centers that focus on applied conservation biology, biodiversity, clean energy, food and resource economics, sustainable food systems, and sustainability in BC's Okanagan region. UBC's Institute for Resources, Environment, and Sustainability focuses on eco-risk, forest economics and policy, sustainable development, and the waters of western North America. UBC has a Fisheries Centre that studies marine mammals and the ecosystems and economics of fisheries. UBC's Centre for Applied Conservation Research investigates forest gene conservation, international forest policy, Pacific salmon ecology and conservation, soil biodiversity, and sustainable business management. In addition, UBC maintains a botanical garden and a farm, where students learn sustainable food production methods.

MCGILL UNIVERSITY—MONTREAL, CANADA

Students at McGill have multiple avenues for studying the environment. Many of McGill's environmental science programs make use of the waterfront MacDonald campus (located in a suburb of Montreal) as well as several field research facilities, including an arboretum, two nature reserves, an avian science conservation center, a working farm, a horticulture research facility, and a water resources management center. McGill also offers field study semesters in East Africa; Barbados; Panama; and the deserts of Arizona, California, and Texas.

Designed to prepare students to tackle the pressing environmental problems facing the world, McGill's School of the Environment offers interdisciplinary programs that knit together perspectives from agriculture, arts, environmental sciences, law, and the natural sciences. Major options in the School of the Environment include atmospheric environment and air quality; biodiversity and conservation; ecological determinants of health; economics and the earth's environment; environment and development; food production and environment; land surface processes and environmental change; renewable resource management; and water environments and ecosystems. McGill's Faculty of Agricultural and Environmental Sciences offers courses of study to prepare its approximately 1,100 students to protect the environment and feed the planet. Faculty of Science students majoring in atmospheric sciences can concentrate on atmospheric chemistry or the atmosphere and the environment. McGill's bioresource engineering program offers tracks in agricultural engineering, bioenvironmental engineering, ecological engineering, food and bioprocess engineering, and soil and water engineering.

OUTDOORSY COLLEGES

Some colleges, due to their location and campus atmosphere, attract students interested in outdoor adventure activities, such as rock climbing, camping, hiking, white-water rafting, kayaking, mountain biking, sailing, and skiing. Students at outdoorsy colleges tend to be hearty types who can't wait to go outside for the next nature-oriented activity. Outdoorsy colleges are frequently located close to national parks, wilderness areas, and ski resorts. Some of the nation's best ski teams are found at outdoorsy colleges, and a few, such as Middlebury, operate their own ski area. Some outdoorsy colleges have special off-campus facilities and programs that get students out into the wilds. Colorado College, for example, has a mountain campus. During orientation, Bowdoin College introduces new students to the coast of Maine. Bowdoin also offers a concentration in arctic studies that provides field research opportunities in latitudes even further north than Brunswick, Maine. Dartmouth College's orientation program takes new students into New Hampshire's White Mountain National Forest, and Dartmouth operates an Institute of Arctic Studies that offers courses and sponsors research and travel projects.

► LIST OF OUTDOORSY COLLEGES

Bates College—Lewiston, Maine

Bowdoin College—Brunswick, Maine

Colby College—Waterville, Maine

College of the Atlantic—Bar Harbor, Maine

Colorado College—Colorado Springs, Colorado

Colorado State University—Fort Collins, Colorado

University of Colorado—Boulder, Colorado

Dartmouth College—Hanover, New Hampshire

Fort Lewis College—Durango, Colorado

Humboldt State University—Arcata, California

Lewis and Clark College—Portland, Oregon

University of Maine—Orono, Maine

Middlebury College—Middlebury, Vermont

University of Montana—Missoula, Montana

Montana State University—Bozeman, Montana

University of New Hampshire—Durham, New Hampshire

Paul Smith's College—Brighton, New York

University of Puget Sound—Tacoma, Washington

St. Lawrence University—Canton, New York

SUNY-ESF—Syracuse, New York

University of Vermont—Burlington, Vermont

Whitman College—Walla Walla, Washington

MARINE SCIENCE AND OCEANOGRAPHY

A number of the colleges already profiled in this chapter are excellent places to study marine biology or oceanography. Examples include **Humboldt State**, **Oregon State**, **University of British Columbia**, **University of Maine**, and **University of Washington**. Students interested in marine biology or oceanography will also find excellent programs or special marine semester options at the institutions listed (and in selected cases profiled) on the following page.

➤ COLLEGES THAT OFFER MARINE BIOLOGY OR OCEANOGRAPHY

Boston University—marine program

University of California at San Diego— Scripps Institute of Oceanography

University of California at Santa Barbara—marine biology

Coastal Carolina University—marine science

College of Charleston—marine biology

Dauphin Island Sea Lab—Dauphin Island, Alabama

Duke University Marine Lab—Beaufort, North Carolina

Eckerd College—marine science

Florida Institute of Technology—marine biology, marine and environmental systems

University of Georgia—Marine Institute at Sapelo Island

University of Hawaii at Hilo—marine science

Massachusetts Institute of Technology— ocean engineering

University of Massachusetts at Dartmouth—marine biology

University of Miami—Rosenstiel School of Marine and Atmospheric Science

University of New England—aquaculture and aquarium science

University of New Hampshire—oceanography

University of North Carolina at Wilmington—marine biology and physical oceanography

Northeastern University—Marine Science Center

University of Rhode Island—marine biology

Rutgers University—Institute of Marine and Coastal Sciences

San Diego State University—Coastal and Marine Institute

Sea Education Association (SEA) Semester—Woods Hole, Massachusetts

University of South Carolina—marine science

University of Southern California— Wrigley Institute for Environmental Studies

Stony Brook University (SUNY)—School of Marine and Atmospheric Sciences

University of West Florida—marine biology

Boston University. Study in the BU Marine Program (BUMP) takes an interdisciplinary approach that integrates marine biology, biogeochemistry, physical oceanography, and marine geology. Every degree-seeking student in BUMP completes a marine semester. During the marine semester, which typically occurs during a student's junior or senior year, courses are taught in four eighteen- to twenty-day blocks that weave in hands-on experiments, fieldwork, and sea travel. BUMP partner institutions include the New England Aquarium in Boston, the Stellwagon Bank Marine Sanctuary in Scituate, Massachusetts, and the Sea Education Association in Woods Hole, Massachusetts. Through its partnership with the Sea Education Association, BUMP students study the tropical oceanography of the Caribbean while living at sea and exploring from St. Croix to Key West. To supplement the academic programs, the student-run Marine Science Association sponsors lectures, field trips, and activities, such as whale watches and tours of the Boston Harbor Islands.

College of Charleston. The marine biology program at the College of Charleston takes full advantage of the campus's coastal location. Three facilities located within easy distance of campus expand the field and laboratory research opportunities available to C of C students: the Grice Marine Laboratory, the Hollings Marine Laboratory, and the 800-acre Dixie Plantation. Grice Laboratory has an aquarium and DNA sequencing facilities. The Hollings Laboratory focuses on applying biotechnology to the restoration of coastal ecosystems. And the Dixie Plantation includes a salt marsh, an estuarine habitat, and a maritime forest.

Duke University. Students from Duke and thirty-five other colleges in the Marine Science Education Consortium (MSEC) can spend a semester or summer at the Duke Marine Lab, a residential campus located in the coastal North Carolina town of Beaufort approximately three hours from Duke's main campus. MSEC member schools include Amherst, Brown, Bucknell, Davidson, Kenyon, Notre Dame, Oberlin, and Washington and Lee.

Facilities at the Marine Lab include an ocean conservation center, a research vessel, numerous laboratories and classrooms, a student center, a dining hall, residence halls, and a library. Duke Marine Lab students can take travel courses to study sea turtles in Puerto Rico, the marine ecology of the Pacific in San Francisco, the urban tropical ecology of Singapore, and the marine coastal reserves of Brittany, France.

University of Miami. Miami's Rosenstiel School of Marine and Atmospheric Science is a leader in marine education. Although it is a part of the University of Miami, the Rosenstiel School's main campus is a sixty-five-acre marine research and education park located in nearby Virginia Key, Florida. In addition to the Virginia Key facilities, the Rosenstiel School operates a seventy-eight-acre satellite reception and analysis center in Miami-Dade County. Rosenstiel School students have six study options: chemical oceanography, geological oceanography, marine affairs and policy, marine biology, meteorology, and physical oceanography. Rosenstiel students research areas such as air quality monitoring, coral reef conservation, the study of sea grass in Biscayne Bay, the biology of larval fish, ocean physics, and the study of sharks. Students conduct their marine science investigations using an advanced catamaran designed for tropical oceanography. Rosenstiel also operates a scientific diving program that takes students to the Florida Keys, the Galapagos Islands, and Panama. Another special feature of the Rosenstiel School is its affiliation with marine science programs at four Australian universities: James Cook University, Flinders University, the University of Melbourne, and Murdoch University.

Sea Education Association. Woods Hole, Massachusetts, is North America's epicenter for students and scientists interested in studying the ocean. Woods Hole is home to the eponymous Oceanographic Institute, the Marine Biological Laboratory, the National Marine Fisheries Service, and the Sea Education Association (SEA). SEA brings together students from different academic disciplines to study the science and culture of the ocean. Using its two 135-foot research vessels as both classroom and campus, SEA students study ocean ecosystems, marine life, and sea culture in the Atlantic, the Caribbean, and the Pacific. Since 1971, SEA has educated more than seven thousand students and sailed more than one million nautical miles. SEA's ocean exploration programs focus on energy and the ocean environment, oceans, and climate, documenting change in the Caribbean, sustainability in Polynesian island cultures and ecosystems, and marine biodiversity and conservation. SEA also offers courses in maritime studies, nautical science, and marine environmental history. Students come to SEA from the hundreds of colleges across North America that grant credit for SEA Semester or SEA Summer Session courses. Examples include Carnegie Mellon, Colorado State, Cornell, Georgia Tech, Harvard, McGill, MIT, Northwestern, Stanford, USC, and Vassar.

Stony Brook University (SUNY). Stony Brook's location on Long Island makes it a natural fit for students interested in studying the ocean. With ninety faculty and five hundred students, the School of Marine and Atmospheric Sciences at Stony Brook offers BS degree programs in atmospheric and oceanic sciences, coastal environmental studies, marine sciences, and marine vertebrate biology. Through its main campus and its Southampton campus (located in an ocean-side town fifty miles to the west), Stony Brook operates a number of research facilities, including the Flax Pond Marine Lab and Southampton Marine Station. At the Southampton campus, Stony Brook also offers a Semester by the Sea program for students interested in an intensive focus on ocean and marine sciences.

University of South Carolina—South Carolina's Marine Science Program has a national reputation for academic excellence. South Carolina's undergraduate program in marine science takes an interdisciplinary focus on the study of oceans and coastal regions. Marine science students have the option to specialize in coastal resource management or marine affairs, or in biological, chemical, geological, or physical oceanography. Courses offered in the program include aquatic chemistry, ecology of coral reefs, marine botany, and ocean data analysis. Field research opportunities are available through South Carolina's Baruch Institute for Marine and Coastal Sciences.

BUSINESS

Many students approach their college search looking for a place to study business. For students interested in business, there are thousands of choices. Just about every college offers business degree programs. Amid all the choices, how to pick the right school? This chapter aims to help cut through the thicket of possibilities by sorting and categorizing business programs according to characteristics and features that may make one school more appealing to certain students and another school more interesting to others. All of the schools highlighted offer strong preparation for first jobs and successful careers in the business world.

The first part of the chapter discusses colleges where business is either the most popular major or the central focus of the curriculum. The following sections highlight the best undergraduate business programs, including ones where students can get a world-class education at a state-school price. Another section examines business education at Catholic institutions. Next, the chapter discusses the options available for business-oriented students at small liberal arts colleges. And finally, the chapter concludes by highlighting some specialty options related to business and management in fields such as entertainment and sports.

COLLEGES WHERE BUSINESS IS THEIR BUSINESS

There are a handful of colleges in the United States that started out with a single focus on business-related degree programs, such as accounting, finance, marketing, or general management. As these institutions developed, their academic focus broadened to encompass programs in the arts and sciences and other specialized areas such as communications and media, criminal justice, education, health sciences, information technology, and law. Still, the job of preparing students for success in the world of business and commerce remains a key thrust at the institutions listed below.

- Babson College
- Bentley University
- Bryant University
- Menlo College

Rather than major in business at a comprehensive university, some students prefer colleges, such as Babson and Bentley, where the focus is primarily on business. At Babson and Bentley—both of which are located in suburban Boston—nearly every student majors in some area related to business management. Arts and sciences courses at Babson and Bentley are minimally woven into the curriculum or offered as minor options that attach to business specialties. Students at Babson and Bentley may take courses or (even minor) in areas such as American studies, gender studies, global studies, history, and philosophy, but those programs are not the draw. Students choose to attend Babson and Bentley to acquire the tools necessary for success in business specialty areas such as accounting, actuarial sciences, corporate communication, finance, international business, managerial strategy, marketing, and supply-chain management.

Are there advantages to attending a college primarily focused on business? The answer depends on what students want from the college experience. One advantage is the opportunity to get experience through internships, which are often required by business-oriented colleges. Bentley University, for example, boasts that nearly all of its students have internships before graduation. A specialized focus on business may also mean more concentrations that provide greater depth to the degree options offered. For example, in the area of finance, Bentley offers programs in corporate finance and accounting, economics-finance, and finance. In the area of information systems management, Bentley offers programs in computer information systems, information design and corporate communication, and information systems audit and control.

Some business-oriented colleges stand out for areas of emphasis that are not offered or emphasized elsewhere. Babson College, for example, has carved out a niche in entrepreneurship, becoming one of a small number of institutions (perhaps the leading one) where entrepreneurship is central to the business curriculum. Through its flagship course, Foundations of Management and Entrepreneurship, Babson tries to create a learning environment that fosters entrepreneurial ways of thinking and working. Students at Babson can concentrate on general entrepreneurship or tech entrepreneurship and design, the latter in collaboration with neighboring F. W. Olin College of Engineering. Babson also offers innovative concentrations in computational finance, global business management, leadership, planning and control, real estate, retail supply-chain management, and strategic management.

Due to their more specialized nature, Babson and Bentley are well-known and respected in the business world. In fact, Babson and Bentley host more corporate recruiters than many universities that are bigger household names. The networks established by Babson, for example, through programs offered by its Center for Executive Education and Arthur M. Blank Center

for Entrepreneurship bring business leaders to the campus from around the globe, increasing the possibility that visiting executives return to their companies eager to establish recruiting and internship connections with Babson.

Another way in which the colleges rooted in business, like Babson and Bentley, boost their students is in having established, over many years, a reputation for graduating work-ready students. The focus on applied learning, small, team-oriented classes, and internships helps distinguish places like Babson and Bentley from larger university business schools, where the real strength is often in the master's programs or in training doctoral students to be researchers and theorists rather than business practitioners. Schools like Babson and Bentley promote the benefits derived from small classes, a curriculum built around business, and access to world-class faculty with expertise as consultants, entrepreneurs, and executives.

BABSON COLLEGE—WELLESLEY, MASSACHUSETTS

2,844 students—2,106 undergraduates

25 percent international students

Arthur Blank Center for Entrepreneurship; Steven Cutler Center for Investments and Finance

Cross registration with F. W. Olin College of Engineering and Wellesley College

95 percent of graduates have jobs or are in graduate school within six months of graduation.

Notable alumni: Arthur Blank (cofounder of Home Depot and owner of the Atlanta Falcons), Terrell Braly (founder of Quiznos), Roger Enrico (former chairman of PepsiCo, current chairman of DreamWorks Animation), Daniel Gerber (founder of Gerber Baby Foods), and William Green (CEO of Accenture)

Average high school GPA: 3.6/4.0

Middle 50 percent on SAT: 1160–1350; ACT: 26–30

28 percent admitted

BENTLEY UNIVERSITY—WALTHAM, MASSACHUSETTS

5,658 students—4,247 undergraduates

90 percent of students complete internships

16 percent international students

Center for Business Ethics; Howard A. Winer Accounting Center for Electronic Learning and Business Management

95 percent of graduates have jobs or are in graduate school within six months of graduation.

Notable alumni: Edward King (governor of Massachusetts, 1979–83), Robert Smith (former chairman and CEO of American Express), Daniel Welbeck (chief operation officer and board member at Radio Shack), and Richard Zannino (former CEO of Dow Jones)

Average high school GPA: 3.5/4.0

Middle 50 percent on SAT: 1140–1310; ACT: 26–30

44 percent admitted

Business schools at professionally oriented institutions, such as Bryant and Menlo, offer programs and specialties not typically found elsewhere. Due to their central focus on job preparation, these schools are often quick to establish new majors that meet the needs of emerging industries. Menlo College, for example, has majors in management information systems and sports business, while students at Bryant University can select programs in actuarial mathematics, industry studies, and risk management.

BRYANT UNIVERSITY—SMITHFIELD, RHODE ISLAND.

Bryant enrolls 3,370 undergraduates in its schools of arts and sciences and business. Business-related majors at Bryant include accounting, actuarial mathematics, advertising and public relations, applied economics, applied mathematics and statistics, banking, computer information systems, entrepreneurship, finance, financial services, global supply-chain management, human resource management, industry studies, information technology, international business, international finance, investments, management, marketing, mathematics of finance, and risk management.

MENLO COLLEGE—ATHERTON, CALIFORNIA

Menlo bills itself as Silicon Valley's business school. Eleven of the thirteen majors at this 735-student college are oriented toward business: accounting; business entrepreneurship; finance; human resources management; international management; management; management information systems; marketing; real estate; and sports management. Menlo's internship office helps place students in Silicon Valley companies.

The other side of the debate about where to study business has its own set of counter arguments. Not every student is cut out for the business-centric college. Some students may prefer studying business at a more comprehensive university, where they can take classes alongside future architects, engineers, lawyers, physicians, and scientists. Business at such schools is just one among hundreds of different major options. Business students at large and well-known institutions such as Georgetown, Michigan, Notre Dame, Penn State, and USC also get to experience many of the features that help create the proverbial classic collegiate environment, such as the opportunity to cheer on big-time sports teams, enjoy an expansive social scene that includes fraternities and sororities, and gain vast alumni networks.

In the end, the decision about where to study business—at a smaller business-oriented college or at a business school embedded in a large university—is up to the student. For some, taking the more specialized route to Babson or Bentley will be the better fit, while for others studying business at a place like the Stern School at New York University or the Fisher School at Ohio State is the best choice.

Certain business schools (listed below) stand out consistently in the rankings of the top programs.

➤ TOP RANKED BUSINESS SCHOOLS

Boston College—Carroll School of Business

Boston University—Questrom School of Business

Brigham Young University—Marriott School of Business

University of California at Berkeley—Haas School of Business

Carnegie Mellon University—Tepper School of Business

University of Delaware—Lerner College of Business and Economics

University of Denver—Daniels College of Business

Emory University—Goizueta School of Business

Fordham University –Gabelli School of Business

Georgetown University—McDonough School of Business

George Washington University

University of Illinois

Indiana University—Kelley School of Business

University of Iowa—Tippie College of Business

Lehigh University

University of Maryland—Smith School of Business

Massachusetts Institute of Technology—Sloan School of Business

Miami University—Farmer School of Business

University of Miami

University of Michigan—Ross School of Business

Northeastern University—D'Amore-McKim School of Business

New York University—Stern School of Business

University of North Carolina—Kenan Flagler School of Business

University of Notre Dame—Mendoza School of Business

Ohio State University—Fisher School of Business

Penn State University—Smeal School of Business

University of Pennsylvania—Wharton School of Business

Purdue University—Krannert School of Management

University of Richmond—Robins School of Business

University of San Diego

Santa Clara University

University of Southern California—Marshall School of Business

Southern Methodist University—Cox School of Business

University of Texas—McCombs School of Business

Texas Christian University—Neeley School of Business

University of Virginia—McIntire School of Commerce

University of Wisconsin, Madison

Villanova University

Wake Forest University

Washington University—Olin School of Business

University of Washington—Foster School of Business

College of William and Mary—Mason School of Business

TOP-RANKED BUSINESS SCHOOLS AT PRIVATE UNIVERSITIES

BOSTON UNIVERSITY

The two thousand undergraduates majoring in business at BU are taught to view management as a system. BU's Questrom School of Business recognizes that markets are global and students must learn to compete and cooperate across cultures. The students in BU's Questrom School comprise a global learning laboratory, with 20 percent of its population coming from outside the United States. Business classes at BU emphasize team learning, collaboration, and entrepreneurial thinking in small groups that address challenges faced by real-world clients. To gain an understanding of business within an ethical, historical, international, and political context and develop critical thinking and writing skills, management students take more than one-third of their courses in BU's College of Arts and Sciences. The heart of BU's system-oriented approach is the cross functional core curriculum that stresses interconnections and culminates in a team project where student work groups develop a business plan for a new product. Students can specialize in one of ten areas of management. A select number of incoming students get invited into an Honors Program, which provides small seminar-style classes and monthly dinner meetings with faculty and alumni. Business students can also pursue dual degrees with BU's six other undergraduate schools and colleges; one popular option is the advertising major offered in BU's College of Communication. BU has programs in more than thirty cities and twenty countries, including internships in London and Los Angeles and programs at business schools in Auckland, Copenhagen, Dublin, Madrid, Paris, and Sydney.

EMORY UNIVERSITY

Emory University's Goizueta Business School consistently ranks near the top of surveys of the best undergraduate business schools, and employers from around the world make it a perennial recruiting stop. Nearly 20 percent of the students at Goizueta add a major from arts and sciences or carve out a special area of focus, such as environmental management. Students at Goizueta may choose a depth area for their

primary concentration/major from the following options: accounting, finance, marketing, strategy and management consulting, and information systems and operations management. Students may also combine two depth areas or add—to their primary depth area—one or more of the following specialties: analytic consulting, business and society, international business, marketing analytics, real estate, or an individually designed area. Like other top business schools, Goizueta places strong emphasis on developing leadership skills. Goizueta's BBA Leadership Academy sponsors group activities, seminars, and a 360-degree assessment that includes coaching and a follow-up a year afterward. Through a network of more than thirty partner business schools, approximately 35 percent of Goizueta students study abroad at places like the University of New South Wales in Sydney; the University of Economics in Prague; Copenhagen Business School; Trinity College of Dublin; Bocconi University in Milan, Italy; Singapore Management University; and the Stockholm School of Economics.

UNIVERSITY OF MIAMI

At every turn, it is evident that the business curriculum at Miami aims to be innovative and forward thinking. Recognizing that its location in a diverse and international city is a competitive advantage, the school of business at Miami aspires to develop global leaders at the crossroads of the Americas. All freshman take FIRST Step, a course that introduces them to the case-study method, develops critical analysis skills, and emphasizes ethical decision making. A critical part of FIRST Step is the freshman team experience, which brings students together to solve real-world business challenges facing Miami-area firms. Business students at Miami can major in accounting, computer information systems, economics, entrepreneurship, finance, health-sector management and policy, human resource management, international finance and marketing, legal studies, management, management science, marketing, or real estate.

NEW YORK UNIVERSITY

Many students looking for the best place to study business as an undergraduate look no further than the Stern School at NYU. Stern has all the elements of a top-notch business school: bright students, exceptional faculty, innovative programs, and outstanding career placement. Topping all that, Stern is in the world's capital city for business: New York. Global learning is a cornerstone of the Stern School. Every student participates in a semester-long program that features an overseas trip during spring break. The first course freshmen take at Stern stresses the interconnections among business, society, markets, politics, art, culture, and life. As sophomores, Stern students take a course called the Economics of Global Business. As juniors, students take a strategy-based course that includes a week visiting with executives in Asia, Europe, or Latin America to learn how to position a company in the context of its industry and country. The majority of Stern students pursue what the school calls its Core Business Program, which entails a major in business with a concentration chosen from eight different areas: accounting, actuarial science, economics, finance, information systems, management and organizations, marketing, and statistics. Students may also major in business and political economy (BPE), a program that offers the option to spend semesters studying at NYU's London, Shanghai, or Washington, DC, campuses. Frequently at Stern, visiting CEOs, entrepreneurs, politicians, writers, activists, and artists enrich classes as lecturers. With ninety thousand alumni in more than one hundred countries, Stern has one of the largest networks of any business school in the United States, which means students need not search too hard when seeking internships or first jobs. Stern students looking for jobs closer to campus are highly sought after by the thousands of companies located in the New York area.

NORTHEASTERN UNIVERSITY

One competitive advantage students at the D'Amore-McKim School of Business have is the world-renowned Northeastern co-op program. Through a global network of six hundred co-op employers, Northeastern places its business students in job settings, so they will be job ready when they graduate. Students can opt for a four-year degree sequence with two co-op placements or a five-year sequence with three co-op placements. The BS in business administration program at Northeastern offers concentration options in accounting; entrepreneurship and innovation; finance; management; management information systems; marketing; and supply-chain management. Students can also choose the four-and-a-half-year BS in international business that requires intensive language study (through Northeastern's World Languages Center) and includes one semester at a partner university abroad and one semester in an international co-op placement. Northeastern has international university partners in England, France, Germany, Ireland, Italy, Mexico, and Spain.

UNIVERSITY OF SOUTHERN CALIFORNIA

USC's Marshall School of Business aims to prepare graduates who are capable of crossing cultural and geographic boundaries with ease and becoming entrepreneurial, innovative, and socially responsible business leaders. USC students can pursue a BS in business administration (concentrations are available in finance and business economics; information and operations management; marketing; management and organization; management communication; and entrepreneurship) from Marshall or a BS in accounting from the Leventhal School of Accounting. Marshall also offers minors in business law, human resources management, management consulting, business technology fusion, consumer behavior, and operations and supply-chain management. Marshall's World Bachelor in Business program lets students spend at least one year studying at the Hong Kong University of Science and Technology and at the Universita Bocconi in Italy. To cultivate an atmosphere where new ventures develop, Marshall operates the Lloyd Greif Center for Entrepreneurial Studies. Marshall's numerous centers of excellence—including the Center for Effective Organizations, the Institute for Communication Technology Management, the Center for Global Innovation, the Society and Business Lab, the Center for Technology Commercialization, the Global Branding Center, the Sports Business Institute, the Center for Investment Studies, and the Center for Business Education and Research—extend the reach of USC's business brand and open doors into industries around the globe. Marshall also offers programs for students to link their business studies to cinematic arts, international relations, or computer science. Marshall's location in one of the world's most creative and multicultural cities (Los Angeles) provides vast opportunities for internship experiences. So tight are the bonds to alma mater that the USC alumni network is referred to as the Trojan family. Few universities rival the Trojan family's collective assistance to fellow graduates.

SOUTHERN METHODIST UNIVERSITY

That the Cox School of Business is located in Dallas is a strategic asset. Business school guidebooks frequently point out that Cox is the favored school of the Dallas business and professional elite. One example of this is the Business Associates Program (BAP) that connects students to leaders in companies such as Accenture, Archon Capital, Comerica Bank, the Dallas Mavericks, and Eagle

Oil and Gas. Through BAP, students can shadow an executive, attend meetings of professional societies, and see how business theory translates into on-the-job situations. Cox's relatively small size ensures an interactive and personal learning environment that revolves around team-oriented classroom work. Cox students find easy access to professors, academic advising, career assistance, and networking opportunities. Cox students can major in accounting, finance, general business, management, marketing, risk management and insurance, or three innovative specialty areas: alternative asset management, financial consulting, and real estate finance. Graduates of the latter programs become oil and gas investment managers, hedge-fund managers, venture capitalists, financial analysts, commercial lenders, and real estate managers and developers. A select number of Cox students participate in honors and scholars programs that provide merit scholarships and activities introducing them to different business sectors. Cox's BBA Leadership Institute joins academic theory to real-world experiences, helping students understand the difference between those who lead and those who manage. Rankings consistently cite the strength of the SMU and Cox alumni networks.

WAKE FOREST UNIVERSITY

The undergraduate business program at Wake Forest is often ranked among the top twenty in the United States. Wake Forest has particular strength in accounting, frequently ranking number one in the United States in the pass rate of its graduates on the CPA exam. Wake Forest runs a business incubator and a center for the study of capitalism. Within the BS in business program, Wake Forest students can major in accountancy, business and enterprise management, finance, and mathematical business. There are also interdisciplinary minor options in entrepreneurship and social enterprise, global trade and commerce, and international studies.

WASHINGTON UNIVERSITY IN ST. LOUIS

Washington University's Olin Business School prides itself on collaborative learning and a mission to turn out graduates who are analytical thinkers, innovators, and problem solvers. Olin courses combine business topics and case analysis with an emphasis on effective communication and ethical decision making. Olin's Management Communication Lab, for example, works with students on interview, presentation, and writing skills. The Olin Center for Experiential Learning (CEL) coordinates a hatchery for start-ups, sponsors business plan competitions, enables students to manage a $1.5 million fund, and provides opportunities for students to serve as pro bono consultants for nonprofit agencies and advisers to local, national, and international companies such as Anheuser Busch InBev, Boeing, Emerson, MasterCard, and Monsanto. Olin's flexible curriculum lets students add a major or minor from another school or customize a program of study. Olin students must take at least 40 percent of their courses outside of business, thus ensuring a broad education. Olin provides nine major options: accounting, finance, healthcare management, entrepreneurship, marketing, operations and supply-chain management, organization and human resources, economics and strategy, and international business. Through combined study options, Olin students can earn an MBA degree in five years or stay on to earn a master's in finance, supply-chain management, or accounting. Olin offers a semester in Washington, DC, for students seeking internships in businesses, government agencies, law firms, or nonprofit organizations. More than one-third of Olin undergraduates have a study abroad experience at partner business schools in countries that include Australia, England, France, Germany, Hong Kong, Israel, Italy, and Spain. Olin's excellent career center helps graduates find jobs with well-known companies such as Anheuser Busch InBev, AT&T, Bain and Company, Bank of America, Boeing, Boston Scientific, Deloitte and Touche, Deutsche Bank, Eli Lilly, General Electric, Google, Hewlett Packard, Miller Coors, Samsung, Turner Broadcasting, and Yahoo!

A WORLD-CLASS BUSINESS EDUCATION AT A STATE-SCHOOL PRICE

Many of the best business programs in the United States are found at flagship state universities, where tuition charges can be a bargain—especially for residents of that state. Large state schools such as the University of North Carolina's Kenan-Flagler School of Business tend to have big worldwide networks of alumni who are eager to hire one of their own. Large state schools also offer a wide array of major options in business. At Kenan-Flagler, for example, students can major in ten different areas of specialty, and at Indiana University's Kelley School of Business, students have a dozen business-focused study abroad options. The bottom line is clear: students interested in studying business should look at state schools because in most cases the quality of the program is high and the price is right. Most rankings of the top business schools in the United States include the following public universities (some of which are described in more detail).

- Arizona State University
- University of Arizona

- Binghamton University (SUNY)
- University of California at Berkeley
- University of Delaware
- University of Florida
- University of Georgia
- Georgia Institute of Technology
- University of Illinois
- Indiana University
- University of Iowa
- James Madison University
- University of Maryland
- Miami University
- Michigan State University
- University of Michigan
- University of Minnesota
- University of North Carolina
- Ohio State University
- Penn State University
- Purdue University
- Texas A&M University
- University of Texas
- University of Virginia
- University of Washington
- College of William and Mary
- University of Wisconsin

UNIVERSITY OF CALIFORNIA AT BERKELEY

Berkeley's Haas School of Business is ranked as a top-five program in most of the surveys of the best undergraduate business schools in the United States. Students at Haas experience a concentrated focus on business while studying at one of the world's best universities for the arts, engineering, humanities, sciences, and social sciences. At Berkeley (or Cal to the natives), every academic program strives to be the best in the world—and many are. Within the business curriculum are opportunities to concentrate and focus on specialized areas such as accounting, business communication, finance, marketing, and organizational behavior in preparation for future careers in brand management, consulting, corporate finance, public accounting, and technology management. The Cal alumni network (which includes the founders of Apple Computer, Intel, the Gap, LSI Logic, and Power Bar) exceeds twenty-five thousand graduates worldwide and comes in handy when students are looking for summer internships and entry-level jobs.

INDIANA UNIVERSITY

Nearly five thousand undergraduates are enrolled at Indiana's Kelley School of Business. The Kelley School does not just seek to prepare students for careers, its overriding goal is to provide an education that transforms lives and develops ethical understanding and global competency. Students at Kelley must take six credit hours of courses that provide a perspective on global business and policy. For students interested in venturing beyond the United States, Kelley offers summer or semester-long study programs in Austria, Australia, Brazil, China, Denmark, England, France, Germany, Italy, Mexico, the Netherlands, and Spain. Kelley students have eight major options to choose from: accounting, business communication, business economics and public policy, business law and ethics, finance, management and entrepreneurship, marketing, and operations and decision technologies. Kelley offers an honors program that provides students the benefit of smaller class sizes, leadership development, an honors adviser, and special networking opportunities with its ninety-two thousand alumni. Kelley School students can also apply to participate in consulting and investment banking workshops; graduates of those workshops have 100 percent job placement at attractive starting salaries.

UNIVERSITY OF MARYLAND

Over the past two decades, Maryland's Smith School of Business has established itself as a top-twenty program. Three of Smith's areas of study rank in the top ten: accounting, management information systems, and supply-chain management and logistics. Nearly three thousand undergraduates study at Smith. The size of the Smith School's alumni base (forty-five thousand worldwide) and its location in the heart of the Baltimore-Washington corridor make it a vibrant place to prepare for a business career. The Smith School connects students to the business and policy organizations of the nation's capital, provides a cutting-edge curriculum, introduces students to real-world challenges, and grows global citizens. All new Smith students stay in a cohort group throughout their first year—an approach that creates lasting bonds and makes a large university feel more personal. Students at Smith have eight majors to choose from: accounting, finance, general business, information systems, international business, marketing, operations management, and supply-chain management. Smith's innovative Hinman CEO's Program selects ninety students to live in an on-campus residential community focused on entrepreneurship. The Hinman CEO's Program provides a start-up company boot-camp experience, operates a business plan competition, provides coaching and mentoring, connects students to entrepreneurial internships, and furnishes a $250,000 seed fund for launching new businesses. Approximately 25 percent of the students who go through the program start companies by graduation.

MIAMI UNIVERSITY

Oxford, Ohio, is home to one of the top undergraduate business schools in the United States. The Farmer School of Business provides a broad-based liberal arts education in addition to specialized training in accounting, finance, and management. The high quality of the Farmer School's programs is matched by its expansive, attractive, and state-of-the-art buildings. Miami University also boasts one of the most beautiful campuses in America. Farmer offers eight majors: accounting, business economics, finance, interdisciplinary business management, management leadership, management information systems, marketing, and supply-chain and operations management. A select group of Farmer students participate in an honors program that guarantees smaller class sizes, provides a mentorship program, keeps each honors cohort together for four years, and culminates in a special capstone project or thesis. To help students be business ready by graduation, the Center for Entrepreneurial Studies operates the Red Hawk Hatchery for new businesses, arranges internships in start-up companies, and enables project work for real-world clients. The Center for Social Entrepreneurship encourages students to use their business education to make a difference in the developing world. Leading companies from around the world travel to Oxford to hire Miami students. As a result, nearly all Farmer School students have jobs or graduate school plans by graduation day.

UNIVERSITY OF MICHIGAN

Michigan's Ross School of Business consistently ranks among the top ten for undergraduate study. More than most business schools, Ross gives students the freedom to customize their curriculum and pursue dual-degree programs. Students at Ross can earn a bachelor of business administration (BBA) degree and combine it with degrees from five other colleges at Michigan: College of Literature, Science, and the Arts; College of Engineering; School of Art and Design; School of Music, Theatre, and Dance; and School of Kinesiology (Sports Management). Supporting the courses and programs at Ross are numerous centers that sponsor conferences, business plan competitions, consulting projects, and global research initiatives. Michigan has centers focused on business and society, entrepreneurship, emerging economies, sustainable enterprise, and venture capital and private equity. The approximately 1,500 undergraduates at Ross are on their way to joining forty thousand alumni in more than eighty countries. The strong reputation of Ross and its extensive alumni network form the foundation of Michigan's formidable job placement record. Beyond the business majors found at Ross, Michigan offers math department tracks in actuarial mathematics and the mathematics of finance and risk management.

UNIVERSITY OF NORTH CAROLINA AT CHAPEL HILL

The Kenan-Flagler School of Business places great emphasis on leadership, hands-on experience, and sustainable strategy. The culture at Kenan-Flagler stresses teamwork, and the curriculum develops problem-solving skills while providing opportunities for experiential leadership. Kenan-Flagler students have the opportunity to focus their BS in business administration studies in one of ten specific areas: consulting, corporate finance, entrepreneurial studies, finance, international business, investments, marketing management, operations, real estate, and sales. Kenan-Flagler stands out in more than just the rankings. It led the way in establishing a curriculum in sustainable business, it was the first top business school to require an ethics course, it annually hosts the country's top case competition, and it is a rare business school that runs a live trading room (the Capital Markets Lab).

OHIO STATE UNIVERSITY

The Fisher School of Business offers a wider range of specialty areas than most business schools. Business majors at Fisher get to choose from twelve specializations, including the standard specialty areas of accounting, economics, finance, human resources, information systems, international business, and marketing. But Fisher also offers less common but potentially valuable, specialties such as aviation management, logistics, operations, real estate, and risk management. Fisher's Wheeler Entrepreneurial Program provides internships in areas ranging from private equity and technology commercialization to new venture development. Study abroad opportunities abound for students looking to get a global perspective. Fisher has exchange partnerships with more than thirty leading business programs around the world, including the University of Dublin, the Swiss Banking Institute of the University of Zurich, Keio University (Japan), Hong Kong University of Science and Technology, Curtin University of Technology (Australia), Copenhagen Business School, Singapore Management University, and the Indian Institute of Management.

PENN STATE UNIVERSITY

The Smeal School of Business at Penn State offers majors in accounting, finance, management, management information systems, marketing, risk management, and supply-chain and information systems. Students in the risk management major can choose specialty options in actuarial science, real estate, or enterprise risk management. For its highest-achieving students, Smeal has the Sapphire Leadership Program. Benefits of the program include a special adviser, priority housing in PSU's Business and Society House (located close to the business building), workshops and seminars with business leaders, small class course sections, and a multiyear capstone leadership project.

UNIVERSITY OF TEXAS AT AUSTIN

With nearly 6,000 students, the McCombs School of Business is one of the largest schools at the University of Texas. Approximately 4,400 of McCombs's students are undergraduates. The McCombs alumni network is also vast—numbering 88,000 worldwide. McCombs offers nine major programs in business: accounting, business honors, finance, international business, management, management information systems, marketing, supply-chain management, and the engineering route to business, which seeks to produce technologically savvy graduates with training in engineering and business. The Business Honors Program (BHP) enrolls a select number of exceptional students—usually close to five hundred. BHP courses are modeled after the MBA program's courses, are taught by many of McCombs's most eminent faculty, and are smaller, more discussion based, and more case oriented than the typical business class at Texas. Finance, marketing, and business honors are the most popular majors at McCombs. McCombs consistently ranks among the top fifteen business programs in the United States—with accounting, international business, marketing, general management, and management information systems garnering top five rankings.

UNIVERSITY OF VIRGINIA

Tradition is important at UVA. People still refer to it as Mr. Jefferson's University, as if he continues to walk the grounds of the campus. Owing to the legacy of Thomas Jefferson, Virginia's McIntire School of Commerce considers integrity, citizenship, and leadership central to the learning environment. The highly ranked McIntire School prepares students for leadership in a global business environment, following a curriculum that emphasizes group work and simulations of real-world challenges. McIntire offers a two-year business program that students enter in their third year at UVA. In year one at McIntire, students complete an integrated core experience (ICE) that emphasizes teamwork and develops leadership skills. In year two, McIntire students can concentrate on one (or more) of six specialty fields: accounting, finance, information technology, international business, management, and marketing. Beyond the six core specialties, McIntire offers courses in creating and managing growth enterprises, global business, investments, and strategic consulting. Multidisciplinary study tracks are also available in entrepreneurship, global commerce, and real estate. A leadership minor, consisting of courses and student projects, is available to complement the core concentrations. Due to its academic excellence and consistent ranking near the top of every survey of undergraduate business programs, McIntire is a favorite stop of corporate recruiters.

COLLEGE OF WILLIAM AND MARY

In addition to its reputation as perhaps America's top public liberal arts college, William and Mary is an excellent place to study business. Rankings place the Mason School of Business in the top twenty-five, and its programs in accounting and marketing often chart out near the very top. With 450 undergraduates, Mason is relatively small and provides an environment that feels more individual in scale than the typical public university business school. Mason's human-scale approach shows through in the close mentoring by faculty, access to internships, and opportunities for guided research. Mason's individualized program enables students to concentrate in more than one area of business, combine a business major with one from arts and sciences, or pursue an international emphasis. The curriculum at Mason is built around four majors (accounting, finance, marketing, and process management and consulting) and three concentration areas (international business, entrepreneurship, or management and organizational leadership). Mason also encourages its students to take leadership positions in student organizations, to study abroad to better understand global business, and to view business in a framework that encompasses sustainability and social responsibility.

UNIVERSITY OF WISCONSIN AT MADISON

Perennially, Wisconsin ranks among the top fifteen schools in the United States for undergraduate business. Wisconsin gives its 1,500 business students the resources of one of the world's leading universities and the personal contact of a relatively small business school. Wisconsin's business program provides a comprehensive curriculum and ten major options: accounting; actuarial science; finance, investment and banking; information systems; international business; management and human resources; marketing; operations and technology management; real estate; and risk management and insurance. Business students seeking international exposure can choose from a half-dozen summer experiences and twenty semester-long study abroad programs. Through its workshops, Wisconsin's Accenture Leadership Center (ALC) helps students learn how to manage change, lead with integrity, build high-performing teams, and create a vision and bring it to reality. Wisconsin's Burrill Technology Business Plan Competition, which fields cross functional teams of students who work on creating companies, has resulted in the launching of several businesses. Wisconsin has a large network of business school alumni (35,000 worldwide) for new graduates to tap into when they are looking for an internship or a referral en route to their first job.

LEADING BUSINESS SCHOOLS AT CATHOLIC COLLEGES

BOSTON COLLEGE

BC's Carroll School of Management believes that broad knowledge, rather than specialized training, is the best preparation for career success in an ever-changing and increasingly more globally connected world. Before digging deep into business courses, Carroll students complete BC's core curriculum, consisting of courses in the arts, cultural diversity, history, literature, mathematics, natural sciences, philosophy, social science, theology, and writing. BC's management curriculum begins with an introductory course on business and ethics called Portico. Ethics are important at Carroll because BC is a Jesuit institution founded on the core value of service to others. The first-year Portico course places the study of business in a global and historical context and develops the capacity to recognize and respond to the kinds of ethical challenges business leaders face. Students at Carroll are also taught to create value for organizations in ways that serve local and global communities. Carroll students choose from twelve different concentrations: accounting, accounting information systems, corporate reporting and analysis, computer science, economics, finance, general management, human resources management, information systems, management and leadership, marketing, and operations management. Carroll has standout strength in accounting, as exemplified by the special concentrations in accounting information systems and corporate reporting and analysis. Carroll operates research centers (focused on asset management, corporate citizenship, retirement research, leadership and ethics, and work and family) that connect students and their faculty mentors to community leaders, global companies, and venture capitalists. Through its centers and executive programs, Carroll supplements its large, devoted alumni network with an additional network of business professionals available to hire graduates.

GEORGETOWN UNIVERSITY

Values matter at Georgetown's McDonough School of Business. Working from the core Jesuit belief in service to others, McDonough seeks to create a collaborative learning community that emphasizes ethics, social responsibility, academic excellence, integrity, interreligious understanding, and a multicultural and global context. McDonough students are trained to be ethically responsible leaders interested in raising global standards of living and morally responsible managers focused on serving all relevant stakeholders and the natural environment. During their freshman and sophomore years, McDonough students complete core liberal arts courses in order to get a broad-based education. A first-year seminar program introduces students to perspectives on business from international affairs and public policy. Juniors and seniors turn their focus to one of the six major areas: accounting, finance, international business, marketing, management, and operations and information management. McDonough's Entrepreneurial Fellows Program provides course work and activities designed to develop entrepreneurial aptitude. Nearly half of all McDonough students study abroad through partnerships with more than seventy universities in thirty-five countries. Popular programs include a full year of study at the London School of Economics and summer semesters at Oxford University and Fudan University in Shanghai. Outside the classroom, McDonough students can help run the Georgetown Alumni and Student Federal Credit Union (assets of $16 million), which is the oldest and largest student-run credit union in the United States. An Alumni Mentor Program helps students make connections in New York and Washington that can lead to internships. Student teams at McDonough also have numerous case competition opportunities, including an annual trip to Copenhagen for an international case competition. McDonough students benefit from studying in the nation's capital, both from the exposure to the many historic and cultural institutions and from the policy expertise of the people and organizations in Washington.

UNIVERSITY OF NOTRE DAME

Many surveys rank the Mendoza College of Business the top school for undergraduate business and near the top for corporate social responsibility. Values matter at Notre Dame, which is why Mendoza seeks to educate future leaders who will address difficult problems with integrity and devise value-based solutions, to create a better future for all. Notre Dame puts its Catholic heritage front and center in Mendoza's mission statement:

> To build a premier Catholic business school that fosters academic excellence, professional effectiveness and personal accountability in a context that strives to be faithful to the ideals of community, human development and individual integrity.

Students at Notre Dame complete a year-long liberal arts program called First Year of Studies before specializing in business. The Mendoza BBA program is built around four core majors: accountancy, finance, management, and marketing. Students who select management can major in management consulting, entrepreneurship, or information technology. Mendoza's academic centers support joint student–faculty research projects related to entrepreneurship, ethical business practices, business communication, accounting education, and financial regulation. The 1,200 undergraduate students at Mendoza have extensive opportunities for internships, study abroad, business plan competitions, leadership activities, and alumni networking. Collectively, Notre Dame's alumni network is legendary for functioning like a family that looks out for its own. That means Mendoza graduates will have doors to job opportunities opened to them around the world by fellow Golden Domers.

SANTA CLARA UNIVERSITY

The Leavey School of Business at Santa Clara draws energy and inspiration from the innovation and entrepreneurial collaboration that occurs in Silicon Valley. Studying within the Silicon Valley provides Leavey students a front-row seat to glimpse the future of commerce and technology. Owing to its Jesuit heritage, Leavey integrates values such as service to society and ethical reflection into its programs. Santa Clara views the liberal arts as the cornerstone of a sound education in business. As freshmen and sophomores, Leavey students begin to take some business courses but concentrate primarily on exploration and discovery as they fulfill core requirements in arts and sciences. Leavey students work toward a bachelor of commerce (BSC) degree, with seven majors available: accounting, accounting/management information systems, economics, finance, management, marketing, and operations and management information systems. Students may add a minor in international business or retail studies. Santa Clara's most outstanding business students get tapped to participate in the Leavey Scholars Program, which offers special honors sections in core business classes. Leavey's Senior Leadership Academy brings groups of seniors together to explore a leadership topic in depth. The Accelerated Cooperative Education (ACE) program connects students to alumni (twenty thousand worldwide) and business partners in an effort to link classroom learning with hands-on practice. The Contemplative Leadership and Sustainability program introduces students to organizations and firms engaged in sustainable enterprises. Another program takes twelve to fifteen Leavey students to El Salvador for one week to explore business practices and economic development.

UNIVERSITY OF SAN DIEGO

USD was an original member of a United Nations initiative to embed issues of social responsibility and sustainability into the study of business. The mission of USD's business school is to develop socially responsible leaders who bring a global mind-set to their work. In collaboration with the Kroc School of Peace Studies, USD's business school seeks to educate students to be change catalysts who will integrate innovative thinking and action into business management strategies to alleviate poverty and bring about peace. As a result, USD incorporates community service into its business curriculum. Students in courses on project management, for example, devise and execute plans to renovate homes for residents of disadvantaged neighborhoods, and USD's Burnham Moores Center for Real Estate seeks to be Southern California's leader for socially responsible real estate practices. Similar to other Catholic business schools, USD requires students to complete a core of arts and sciences courses. The business curriculum—built around a blend of innovative and interactive classroom learning and applied research—provides eight different major options: accountancy, business administration, business economics, economics, finance, international business, marketing, and real estate. Certificates in global strategy and management are available from the Ahlers Center for International Business, which links USD students to executives and scholars in residence. The School of Business Alumni Council provides career mentorship, internship opportunities, job placement connections, and perspectives on different industries. A USD education in business can open doors and lead down unexpected paths. One notable USD business graduate, Mike Brown (class of 1993), coached the Cleveland Cavaliers and the Los Angeles Lakers in the National Basketball Association.

VILLANOVA UNIVERSITY

Villanova's undergraduate business program often garners top-ten rankings due to the extensive resources it makes available to its 1,600 students. Villanova seeks to develop business leaders who will make positive contributions as global citizens. Villanova infuses the values of community, caring, service, and truth throughout the business curriculum while also emphasizing applied learning, hands-on education, ethics, and integrity. Villanova offers degrees in accountancy and business administration. The business administration program has majors in economics, finance, management, management information systems, marketing, and international business and minors in business analytics, entrepreneurship, real estate, and business law and corporate governance. Business is taught at Villanova in an interdisciplinary manner that builds on a foundation of liberal arts courses. For example, the Read to Lead Program organizes learning around a book that has relevance to the study of business. Villanova operates project-spawning research centers focused on marketing, public policy, global leadership, real estate, church management, entrepreneurship, and advanced financial technology. Just about half of all Villanova business students study or have internships abroad in places such as Beijing, Belfast, Geneva, Madrid, Milan, Moscow, Paris, Rome, Shanghai, Tokyo, and Warsaw. Students also get to manage a socially responsible investment fund (that has outperformed the S&P 500) and benefit from the Applied Finance Lab's simulated trading room, where students use the same technology and real-time information systems found on Wall Street. Students in Villanova's Business Honors Program often receive merit scholarships and have special opportunities, such as trips to New York, Philadelphia, and Washington to explore industries in those cities.

TWO EMERGING SCHOOLS TO CONSIDER

CHAMPLAIN COLLEGE
Champlain, located in Burlington, Vermont, stands out for specialized business programs not commonly found elsewhere. For example, Champlain students can major in management of creative media, event management, game production, business law, and communication in business. Champlain offers additional majors in accounting, financial accounting, human resources management, international business, managerial accounting, marketing, public relations, self-designed specialization in business, and small business and entrepreneurship.

QUINNIPIAC UNIVERSITY
At this emerging university of 8,400 students (6,000 undergraduates) in Hamden and North Haven, Connecticut, students benefit from a primary focus on job preparation. Quinnipiac started as a business school but has been on a remarkable upward trajectory of academic growth and program quality over the last three decades. There is much more than business at Quinnipiac. Still, Quinnipiac deserves mention among leading business schools for its distinctive specialty areas such as biomedical marketing, entrepreneurship and small business management, and European Union business studies. Other business tracks include accounting, advertising, computer information systems, finance, international business, legal studies, management, and marketing.

BUSINESS AT LIBERAL ARTS COLLEGES

Students often overlook liberal arts colleges as places to study business. This is understandable because the classic liberal arts approach is to focus on educating students in traditional arts and science subjects (art/art history, biology, English, history, languages, mathematics, philosophy, physics, etc.) believing that an education that develops critical reading, thinking, and writing skills and sharpens analytical and quantitative reasoning will best prepare students for any field (including business). Many of the best-known and most highly respected liberal arts colleges do not offer business as a major or minor: for example, Amherst, Bowdoin, Carleton, Colgate, Davidson, Haverford, Middlebury, Oberlin, Pomona, Swarthmore, Vassar, or Wellesley. Business courses, majors, and minors do exist, however, at a surprising number of high-quality liberal arts colleges, such as Claremont McKenna, the University of Richmond, Sewanee (the University of the South), Skidmore, and Washington and Lee. In fact, at some liberal arts colleges (such as DePauw University and Rhodes College), business is one of the most popular majors.

At many small liberal arts colleges, the economics major serves as a proxy for business, attracting future investment bankers and MBAs. Certain small colleges, such as Trinity (CT) and Williams, stand out as breeding grounds for future entrants into the worlds of finance and management, even though neither college offers a business major. The economics programs at Trinity and Williams are the most popular majors at those colleges and offer a large array of courses, including some more commonly found in business departments. Trinity College, for example, offers courses in accounting, cost-benefit analysis, financial markets, corporate and international finance, and business and entrepreneurial history.

Perennially ranked as one of America's top five small liberal arts colleges, Williams turns out large numbers of graduates who become successful in business and commerce. Williams alumni include Edgar Bronfman (CEO of Seagram's), Steve Case (founder of America Online), Neil Fiske (CEO of Eddie Bauer), Andreas Halvorsen (founder of Viking Global Investors), Willem Humes (founder of Greylock Capital), Robert Lipp (CEO of Travelers Property Casualty), John McCoy (former CEO of Bank One), Robert Nutting (owner of the Pittsburgh Pirates), Bob Scott (former president of Morgan Stanley), Walter Shipley (former president of Chemical Bank), and George Steinbrenner (famed owner of the New York Yankees). How does this happen at a college that has no business major? First of all, the Williams Economics Department is frequently cited as one of the best in the country. Numerous economics graduates find their first jobs through Williams's extensive network in the financial world. Still, the Williams curriculum helps develop business leaders in a more overt way through the Leadership Studies Program. Leadership studies is not a major at Williams but rather a track that students can choose if they are interested in taking courses such as Leadership and Management.

At Lafayette College, there is no mention of a business major but students interested in business are often drawn to Lafayette's program in international economics and commerce, which offers courses in accounting, finance, investments, and marketing. Union College in Schenectady, New York, offers two programs that might be of interest to business-oriented students: a major in managerial economics and a minor in entrepreneurship. The managerial economics curriculum aims to give Union students the tools and techniques of quantitative analysis that are essential to success as a manager. Embedded in its economics major, Colby College offers a minor in administrative science that has courses in accounting, finance, and management plus a track in financial markets. Mount Holyoke College offers a minor in global business as part of a program that encourages students to link their liberal arts education to their career goals.

At the University of the South (Sewanee), there is much support for the view that a liberal arts education is the best preparation for a career in business. Students in any major at Sewanee can minor in finance, international business, or managerial business. Sewanee's Babson Center for Global Commerce supplements the business minors by providing support for student internships in business and entrepreneurship and by offering summer scholarships for students who want to study at leading business schools. Through Sewanee's Wm. Polk Carey Pre-Business Program, students receive special scholarships, participate in an honors program, complete a paid internship, and meet business leaders brought to campus for lectures and seminars. Sewanee's active and intensely loyal alumni network is another resource for students looking for internships and first jobs in the business world. Listed (and in a handful of cases profiled) below are liberal arts colleges with business as a study option.

➤ LIBERAL ARTS COLLEGES WITH BUSINESS AS A STUDY OPTION

Agnes Scott College—economics and organizational management

Bard College—economics and finance (five-year BS/BA program)

Beloit College—business administration

Berea College—business administration

Bucknell University—business administration

Centre College—financial economics

Colby College—economics of financial markets

Colorado College—economics and business

Cornell College—economics and business

DePauw University—economics and management

Dickinson College—international business and management

Drew University—business

Eckerd College—business administration and management

Franklin and Marshall College—business, organizations, and society

Furman University—business

Gettysburg College—organization and management studies

Goucher College—business management

Hendrix College—economics and business

College of the Holy Cross—economics and accounting

Kalamazoo College—economics and business

McDaniel College—business administration

Mills College—business economics

Millsaps College—business administration

Morehouse College—business administration

Mount Holyoke College—global business (minor)

Muhlenberg College—business administration

Pitzer College—science and management

University of Puget Sound—School of Business and Leadership

Randolph Macon College- accounting, economics/business

Rhodes College—business

University of Richmond—Robins School of Business

Rollins College—international business

Saint Olaf College—management studies (concentration)

Skidmore College—management and business

Trinity University—business administration

Washington College—business management

Washington and Lee University—Williams School of Commerce, Economics, and Politics

Wheaton College (IL)—business/economics

Wheaton College (MA)—management (minor)

Williams College—leadership studies (track added to any major)

College of Wooster—business economics

BUCKNELL UNIVERSITY

Bucknell in Lewisburg, Pennsylvania, offers programs in the arts and sciences, business, and engineering. Students in Bucknell's School of Management start out with a class (Introduction to Organizational Management) in which they design and build companies and explore how organizations work. In their senior year, Bucknell management students can take a two-semester course in which they manage nearly $1 million of the university's endowment fund. Management students at Bucknell earn a BS in business administration (BSBA). Bucknell takes an interdisciplinary approach to management, offering majors in accounting and financial management; global management; managing for sustainability; markets, innovation, and design; and a five-year joint degree program, the bachelor of management for engineers (BME). Supporting the BME program is Bucknell's Institute for Leadership in Technology Management (ILTM). ILTM students visit industrial sites and companies, work with businesses on the management of technological projects, and have internships focused on the management of technology.

CLAREMONT MCKENNA COLLEGE

Southern California's CMC has a whole school devoted to business programs. The Robert Day School of Economics and Finance offers majors and course work in accounting, financial economics, and leadership studies. CMC's Robert Day Scholars get generous scholarship support, opportunities to participate in leadership development workshops, and the chance to work on thesis-culminating research projects with faculty. Day School students also have the opportunity to add a fifth year of study to earn a master's degree in finance. Whether in the Day School or another program at CMC, students can participate in leadership courses, internship programs, and the annual sophomore leadership experience sponsored by the Kravis Leadership Institute, named for CMC alumnus and pioneer of the leveraged buyout, Henry Kravis. CMC also offers a major in science and management. For a small school (1,200 students), CMC has a remarkable record for preparing future business leaders. In addition to Henry Kravis (class of 1967), CMC alumni standouts in business and commerce include Don Hall (CEO of Hallmark Cards), Michael Jeffries (CEO of Abercrombie & Fitch), Augie Nieto (founder of Life Fitness), Thomas Pritzker (chairman of Hyatt Corporation), and George Roberts (founding partner of Kohlberg, Kravis, and Roberts).

UNIVERSITY OF RICHMOND

Richmond is one of those liberal arts colleges with a business program that attracts a large segment of the student body. Although business occupies its own school at Richmond, students who earn their degrees in the Robins School get a solid grounding in liberal arts courses. Robins School of Business students must take at least a year's worth of liberal arts credits before declaring a major in accounting, business administration, or economics. Students seeking to specialize further can add a concentration in finance, management, or marketing. Richmond also operates the Jepsen School of Leadership Studies (offering a major and minor in leadership studies) that infuses leadership courses and leadership development throughout the curriculum.

TRINITY UNIVERSITY

Trinity University in San Antonio, Texas, offers students a business administration major with five choices for in-depth concentration: accounting, finance, management, marketing, and international business. Business students can also take a course focused on managing $1 million of Trinity's endowment. In addition, Trinity offers minors in communication management, information systems, and sport management.

WASHINGTON AND LEE UNIVERSITY

At W&L in Lexington, Virginia, roughly 40 percent of the students pursue majors in the Williams School of Commerce, Economics, and Politics. The Williams School offers degrees in commerce, business administration, accounting, and public accounting.

BUSINESS IN THE IVY LEAGUE

Many successful business leaders have degrees from one of the eight Ivy League schools: Brown, Columbia, Cornell, Dartmouth, Harvard, University of Pennsylvania, Princeton, and Yale. But only two of the Ivy League institutions (Penn and Cornell) offer undergraduate majors in business. The Wharton School of Business at the University of Pennsylvania is one of the world's best places to study business. At Cornell University, the business program (the Dyson School of Applied Economics and Management) is lodged inside the College of Agriculture and Life Sciences. Cornell also operates two schools that attract business-oriented students: the School of Hotel Administration (otherwise known as the Hotel School) and the Industrial and Labor Relations (ILR) School. Columbia University offers a special concentration in business management, and the Commerce, Organizations, and Entrepreneurship Program at Brown University draws students interested in the business world. The rest of the business schools in the Ivy League are graduate schools for MBA or PhD degrees. Excellent graduate business schools are found at Columbia, Cornell (Johnson), Dartmouth (Tuck), Harvard, Penn (Wharton) and Yale.

UNIVERSITY OF PENNSYLVANIA

Founded in 1881, the Wharton School was the world's first collegiate school of business. Today the Wharton School of Business vies with Harvard in terms of worldwide fame and consistently gets ranked at or near the top of lists of the best business schools. Wharton's 2,600 undergraduate students are taught by globally renowned experts in their fields, often the authors of the books and articles used in classes at Penn and elsewhere. With 250-plus business professors and nearly 500 affiliated faculty members, Wharton's teaching and research resources are unparalleled. The Wharton brand for excellence in business education is respected around the world. Wharton's 88,000 alumni hold leadership positions in over 140 countries and are eager to assist new graduates seeking jobs.

Still, there is an interesting paradox at the core of the Wharton School. The degree Wharton awards undergraduates is not in business but is rather a BS in economics. Although the degree is in economics, the concentrations available to undergraduates are all business. Wharton uses the term concentration, not major, to designate the areas students may choose as specialties. With twenty business concentrations available, Wharton has something for everyone and stands out for offering specialty areas found at few other business schools. Because a concentration at Wharton requires four courses, it is easy for students to complete more than one, and it is possible to work with professors to create unique concentrations. The business concentrations offered at Wharton are accounting, actuarial science, business and public policy, environmental policy and management, finance, global analysis, health-care management and policy, insurance and risk management, legal studies and business ethics, management, managing electronic commerce, marketing, marketing and communications, marketing and operations management, operations and information management, real estate, retailing, social impact and responsibility, statistics, and transportation. There are also specialized sub-concentrations in entrepreneurship and innovation, multinational management, organizational effectiveness, and strategic management.

Despite its many specialized offerings, Wharton takes a liberal arts approach to teaching business. Students must take at least 40 percent of their courses outside of Wharton, and they have ample opportunities to earn dual degrees with Penn's other academic units, including the graduate schools. Like other top business schools, Wharton educates its students for success in a global community. Students can study abroad through Wharton's twenty-plus different international programs, choose from the more than one hundred College of Arts and Sciences programs, or go on a Wharton International Program ten-day, travel-based business course. Beyond the classroom, Wharton students have access to twenty-five research centers and curricular programs focused on areas such as leadership, entrepreneurship, and adaptive, risk-tolerant management styles. Students at Wharton get the best that a business school can offer, crowned by an Ivy League degree.

CORNELL UNIVERSITY

Students seeking to major in business at Cornell have the Dyson School of Applied Economics and Management, embedded within the College of Agriculture and Life Sciences, a New York State–supported college that provides an Ivy League education for a state-school price. Applied economics and management is one of the ten most popular majors at Cornell. Students at the Dyson School learn to apply practical management

tools to solve pressing global business and social issues. The approximately seven hundred students in Cornell's Dyson School can choose from ten specializations: accounting, agribusiness management, applied economics, entrepreneurship, environmental and resource economics, finance, food industry management, international trade and development, and marketing strategy.

Cornell's School of Industrial and Labor Relations (ILR) is more public policy school than business school. The courses offered in ILR are an interdisciplinary blend of economics, history, sociology, psychology, and political science. The ILR School is organized into six academic departments: human resource studies; international and comparative labor; labor economics; labor relations, law, and history; organizational behavior; and social statistics. ILR is arguably more of a prelaw major than a prebusiness major—a reality reflected in the high percentage of ILR graduates who end up in law school. Through its worldwide connections—aided by the fact that 30 percent of ILR graduates live and work outside the United States—Cornell's ILR School provides students with internship and study abroad experiences in places ranging from California to New York and from Washington, DC, to Africa, England, Ireland, and Switzerland.

BROWN UNIVERSITY

The interdisciplinary commerce, organizations, and entrepreneurship major at Brown—sponsored by the departments of economics and sociology and the School of Engineering—focuses on the study of financial markets, management and organizational theory, innovation in the marketplace, the formation of new ventures, and the global economy. Students in the major can select specialization tracks in business economics, organizational studies, or technology management and entrepreneurship.

COLUMBIA UNIVERSITY

A special concentration in business management links Columbia College (Columbia's undergraduate arts and sciences unit) to the Columbia Business School (a graduate school). Columbia's business management curriculum covers finance, marketing, organizational leadership, strategic management, labor markets, entrepreneurship, monetary theory, and accounting. Benefits of the program include a lecture series, research with faculty members, and networking opportunities with MBA students, alumni, and executives from different industries. Students apply to the business management concentration as sophomores and need to have at least a B-plus average in their Columbia courses.

> ### ➤ MASTER OF BUSINESS ADMINISTRATION (MBA) PROGRAMS IN THE IVY LEAGUE
>
> Brown University—Executive MBA program with Instituto Empresa (IE) in Spain
>
> Cornell University—Johnson School of Management
>
> Columbia University—Columbia Business School
>
> Dartmouth College—Tuck School of Business
>
> Harvard University—Harvard Business School
>
> University of Pennsylvania—Wharton School of Business
>
> Yale University—School of Management

SPECIALIZED BUSINESS MAJORS AND CONCENTRATIONS

AGRIBUSINESS

Producing, distributing, and safeguarding the world's food supply represents an area of increasing significance. Students at the Mays Business School at **Texas A&M University** have the option to prepare for management positions in businesses that grow, harvest, and sell food products. The major in agribusiness is offered in cooperation with A&M's College of Agriculture and Life Sciences. Agribusiness majors supplement the core A&M business curriculum with an in-depth focus on the economics, ethics, logistics, and the managerial strategies of the agribusiness industry. The vast and loyal Texas A&M alumni body is an asset for agribusiness students seeking summer internships or first jobs in the industry.

AVIATION MANAGEMENT

Students seeking to enter the aviation industry have study options beyond those offered by specialized colleges. At least two prominent universities (Auburn and Ohio State) offer aviation management programs. Aviation management, one of the specializations open to students in the Fisher School of Business at **Ohio State University**, trains students in the economics and logistics of flight operations and transportation. The Fisher School's program is complemented by the BS in aviation management offered through Ohio State's College of Engineering. Students interested in learning about the global development of the aviation industry have access to the OSU's vast network of international exchange programs. The aviation management concentration offered by the College of Business at **Auburn University** provides an education focused on the operational aspects of the aviation industry. Graduates of Auburn's program land positions in airport management or in aviation-related businesses, such as airlines and airplane manufacturing companies.

CONSTRUCTION MANAGEMENT

Construction management and real estate are standout specialties at the Daniels College of Business at the **University of Denver**. In the Burns School of Real Estate and Construction Management (within Daniels), students can major in construction management, real estate, or real estate and construction management. Construction management majors take a foundation of business courses followed by specialized courses focused on construction codes and documents, construction estimating, project scheduling, real estate finance, and residential and commercial construction. In one class, students form a home-building company, choose a site, bid the project, get permits, manage construction, and market and sell the property. In another class, students have a hands-on introduction to the strategies and analysis involved in managing an actual real estate portfolio (DU's Mueller Real Estate Investment Fund). Students also can travel to other countries to meet with builders, government officials, and experts in real estate development. Such trips have taken Burns School students to Australia, Central America, Cuba, Eastern Europe, Great Britain, India, the Middle East, New Zealand, Scandinavia, South America, Southeast Asia, and Russia. Denver's Daniels College also offers specialties in accountancy; business information technology; economics; finance; general business; hotel, restaurant, and tourism management; international business; management; marketing; and statistics.

ENERGY MANAGEMENT

The **University of Tulsa** is one of a handful of institutions offering a major in energy management. The energy management major in Tulsa's Collins College of Business is limited to thirty new students per year, but the program's relatively small size belies its prominence in the energy business. Tulsa's energy management program draws strong support (through scholarships, internships, adjunct faculty, mentoring, and job placement) from the energy industry in Oklahoma and Texas. Energy management students at Tulsa have two concentration options: they can focus on the energy midstream (energy commodities trading) or on the energy upstream (exploration and production). Business students at Tulsa who major in energy management have the opportunity for summer or semester-long internships within the industry. Students looking for a global perspective on energy may choose to attend energy-oriented exchange programs at Robert Gordon University in Aberdeen, Scotland, or the China University of Petroleum in Beijing.

Established in 1958, the bachelor of business administration (BBA) program in energy management at **University of Oklahoma** is the oldest and one of the largest programs in the United States. The program's curriculum is interdisciplinary and innovative. Students majoring in this interdisciplinary program take courses in business, geology, law, meteorology, and petroleum engineering. Graduates are sought after by the energy industry and also find positions in commodities marketing and trading, energy finance, and land management.

FOOD INDUSTRY MANAGEMENT

Students in the Dyson School of Applied Economics and Management at **Cornell University** can pursue a specialization in food industry management. Food industry management courses cover food merchandising, agricultural finance, dairy markets and policies, food industry strategic issues, and food marketing.

GRAPHIC MEDIA MANAGEMENT

The Tepper School of Business at **Carnegie Mellon University** offers its students a specialty track in graphic media management. The graphic media management program draws upon CMU's strengths in art and design, technical communication, and emerging technologies. The program aims to develop graphic literacy and media management savvy through courses in desktop publishing, graphic communications, interactive media design, marketing research, and web publishing. Graphic media management majors leave CMU ready to present business plans and promote products in technologically sophisticated ways.

HEALTH-CARE MANAGEMENT

The School of Business at the **University of Connecticut** houses New England's leading undergraduate program in health-care management. Through cross state agreements, students from other New England states may study health-care management at UConn and qualify for the New England tuition rate, which is lower than the out-of-state rate but higher than the in-state rate. A key feature of the UConn program is a required internship, providing students with clinical experience at health-care organizations located in Connecticut, other northeastern states, or overseas. Supporting the program is UConn's Center for Programs in Health Care and Insurance Studies, a research think tank that works on solutions to pressing health-care industry challenges. Because UConn has one of the few business schools offering a major in health-care management, its graduates are in high demand by hospitals, clinics, government agencies, health maintenance organizations, hospital associations, consulting firms, health insurance companies, and manufacturers of hospital equipment. Health-care management programs are also found at the Wharton School at the **University of Pennsylvania**, the Olin School at **Washington University in St. Louis**, and the business school at **University of Miami** (health-sector management and policy).

INDUSTRIAL MANAGEMENT

The Krannert School of Management at **Purdue University** offers an industrial management major that draws upon Purdue's strength in engineering and science. Industrial management majors take a core of business classes at Krannert, supplemented by technical courses from the schools of engineering and science. Due to their strong technical training and sophisticated analytical and quantitative skills, industrial management majors are highly sought after by technology companies and other businesses.

MANUFACTURING MANAGEMENT AND CONSULTING

Fittingly at a place known for strong engineering programs in a city built on the manufacturing of steel, **Carnegie Mellon University** in Pittsburgh offers students a business track in manufacturing management and consulting. This specialty track within CMU's Tepper School of Business is for students interested in the design and production of goods and services. Manufacturing management students take courses in systems analysis and design, logistics and supply-chain management, manufacturing sciences, industrial design, quality principles, and cost-benefit analysis. In 2012, President Obama declared Carnegie Mellon a national site of importance for advanced manufacturing programs and research. Students in CMU's manufacturing management and consulting program have the opportunity to lead the United States—and the rest of the world—toward new models for an old industry (manufacturing) in the twenty-first century.

MUSIC BUSINESS

Many students with a passion for music would like to enter the music business but not major in music as an undergraduate. For those students, there is **Belmont University**'s Mike Curb College of Entertainment and Music Business in Nashville, Tennessee. Founded in 1971, the Curb College at Belmont has become, in the estimation of *Rolling Stone* and *Time* magazine, one of the top music business schools in the United

States. Classes at Curb are led by faculty who are academic scholars and authors, entrepreneurs, songwriters, producers, and sound engineers. Although Curb offers degrees in audio engineering technology, entertainment industry studies, and songwriting, students dreaming of management positions in the music industry might be most interested in the BBA in music business degree. The music business major offers two emphasis options: a business emphasis for managerial and marketing careers in the entertainment and music industry, and a production emphasis on developing and producing music. Due to Curb's location and reputation, music business students have success at finding internships and positions in artist management, music marketing, entertainment public relations, merchandising, music publishing and production, and record company operations. Due to Belmont's extensive network in the music industry, the demand for Curb students far exceeds the supply of available interns. Most of the internships occur in Nashville, but Belmont has built relationships around the globe, leading to steady placements in Australia, London, Los Angeles, and New York.

American University provides a route into the music industry through its Kogod School of Business, which offers a BS in business and music (BAM). Students in the BAM program complete a core of theoretical and hands-on courses in both the business school and in the music department. On the business side of their studies, BAM students take courses in accounting, finance, international business, information technology, operations management, global corporate citizenship, marketing, organizational theory, and business policy and strategy. On the music side, BAM students take courses in harmony, musicianship, and music history, then finish with a music business capstone. Elective courses are available for deeper exploration of music performance, music production,

or business and economics. In addition, BAM students complete internships in business and music. Music business programs are also found at the **University of Michigan** (Ross School of Business) and **University of Puget Sound**.

PUBLIC AND NONPROFIT MANAGEMENT

A few aspects of the Carlson School of Management at the **University of Minnesota** set it apart from other business schools. The Carlson School requires every business student to have an international experience, and Carlson offers an undergraduate major in public and nonprofit management. The public and nonprofit management major blends business-focused course work taken at the Carlson School with nonprofit- and public-policy–oriented courses taken through Minnesota's Humphrey Institute of Public Affairs. Students majoring in public and nonprofit management must complete another major at Carlson (chosen from accounting, entrepreneurial management, finance, finance and risk management insurance, human resources and industrial relations, international business, management information systems, marketing, and supply-chain and operations management), thus acquiring a range of management tools and skills to bring to the nonprofit sector. Students also take courses geared toward developing proficiency in budgeting, governance, community leadership, strategic planning, philanthropy, managerial psychology, negotiation strategies, and the management of innovation and change. Graduates of the program find jobs in government and nonprofit organizations focused on areas ranging from education and the environment to civil rights and health care.

RETAIL MANAGEMENT

Programs in retailing and retail management are usually found at specialized institutions such as New York's **Fashion Institute of Technology** or in textile departments in agriculture schools. **Syracuse University** is rare in offering a retail management major in its business school. The retail management and fashion-merchandising program in Syracuse's Whitman School of Management focuses on the global retail marketplace and on merchandise distribution networks. Courses in the program introduce students to retailing fundamentals, sales and strategic partnerships, product development, consumer law, strategic merchandise management, and electronic retailing and marketing. A supervised internship places retail management students in companies as buyers, product developers, store managers, and marketing personnel. Program guidance and internships come from well-known firms such as Ann Taylor, Bloomingdale's, Crate and Barrel, Donna Karan, and Macy's. In addition, the Leavey School of Business at the **University of Santa Clara** offers a minor in retail studies, and the Wharton School of Business at the **University of Pennsylvania** offers a concentration in retailing.

SPORTS MANAGEMENT

Two of the most respected programs in sports business and management are found at the **University of Oregon** and at the **University of Massachusetts**. Oregon's Lundquist College of Business is home to the nation's oldest sports business program, and in recent years, ESPN called it the nation's best. The approach at Oregon emphasizes the sports industry first and the principles and strategies of business second. Students pursuing the sports business concentration at Oregon learn about finance, marketing, management, and organizational operations in the context of the sports industry. In the classroom, Oregon's sports business students learn from faculty who are leaders in the field. Outside the classroom, Oregon's Warsaw Sports Marketing Center sponsors events, such as field trips, symposia, visiting speakers, and alumni

networking, that provide students with insight into the sports business. Sports business students also have opportunities to gain experience through internships at sports organizations, such as Adidas, Nike (founded by Oregon alumnus Phil Knight), and the Portland Trailblazers.

The McCormack Sport Management Program in the Isenberg School of Management at the **University of Massachusetts** has been called a world leader by publications such as *Sports Business Journal* and the *Chronicle of Higher Education*. Named for Mark H. McCormack, the founder and CEO of IMG (the world's largest sports management firm), the UMass program has three thousand alumni worldwide working in the sports industry. McCormack alumni frequently return to campus to make presentations, mentor undergraduates, and help students connect to internships across the sports industry. The McCormack program provides an experiential course of study taught by industry-focused faculty, while fusing three areas of emphasis: the theoretical perspectives of the sociology and the history of sport, the foundational methods and analytical tools of economics and business, and the application of a management framework to the sports industry. The program trains students for positions in sports marketing and public relations, sports law, financial and business operations for sports organizations, event management, media relations, broadcasting, and college athletic administration.

Students at **Ohio University** can prepare for sports business careers in two different ways. Within Ohio's College of Business, there is a BBA degree program in sports administration, whose students take courses in the history of the sports industry, marketing and risk management for sports, athletic facility management, finance of sports, sports promotion, and issues of ethics and governance in sports. All students in the major must have a practicum experience. The

Center for Sports Administration links current students to alumni, fosters student-faculty research projects, and forges connections to the global sports industry. The other route to a sports business degree at Ohio is through the Department of Recreation and Sport Sciences, where students can earn a major in sport management. Whichever sports management option students choose at Ohio, they prepare to enter a network of more than a thousand alumni who hold jobs in professional sports, sports media and entertainment, intercollegiate athletics, sports tours, and corporate sports organizations.

The Ross School of Business at the **University of Michigan** offers a sport management dual major in cooperation with the School of Kinesiology. Course work in the Michigan program encompasses promotion and marketing, legal and ethical issues, organizational strategy and behavior, fundraising, facilities management, media relations, finance, economics, and research methods. Sport management majors get internships or fieldwork placements with professional teams such as the New York Jets, companies such as Adidas, and sports organizations such as the Professional Golf Association (PGA). Sport management students at Michigan can complete the BA program through the School of Kinesiology or earn a dual degree with the Ross School of Business.

The Lerner College of Business and Economics at the **University of Delaware** offers a major in sport management. Students in the program examine sports industry issues related to events management, ethics, finance, human resources, marketing, media relations, law, facilities administration, and regulatory authorities. All sport management majors at Delaware must complete a nine-credit internship during their senior year. Delaware also encourages sport management students to get additional experience through volunteer positions with the UD athletic department or other campus sports organizations.

There are numerous other programs in sport management (some listed below) found in schools or departments of education, health, hospitality and tourism, kinesiology, exercise science, sport and leisure studies, or recreation and tourism.

- Ball State University
- Bowling Green University
- California Polytechnic University at San Luis Obispo
- Drexel University
- Florida State University
- George Mason University
- George Washington University
- Indiana University
- Indiana State University
- Louisiana State University
- University of Miami
- University of New Hampshire
- North Carolina State University
- Old Dominion University
- Rutgers University
- San Jose State University
- Temple University
- University of Texas at Austin

While this chapter focuses on business degree programs, students interested in business as a career need to know that there are many ways to get to the executive suite or to Wall Street. Large numbers of successful corporate leaders did not major in business as undergraduates in college. Some majored in liberal arts subjects, such as economics, history, mathematics, or political science and after graduating joined companies or fields where they acquired the specialized skills and knowledge necessary for success. Others went to a graduate business school to get a master of business administration (MBA) degree or a specialized master's degree in an area such as accounting or finance.

At the top-ranked graduate business schools (such as Harvard, Northwestern, and Stanford), the admissions offices actually favor applicants who did not major in business as undergraduates. Those programs look for analytical and quantitative skills, evidence of leadership, and success on the job. Many graduate admissions committees and employers see varsity athletics, ROTC programs or military academies, and student government as leadership laboratories. A candidate's demonstrated capacity for leadership can be as important (or more important) than the candidate's major field of study and grades earned in college. Students interested in business careers should be sure to pursue extracurricular activities that provide them with leadership opportunities to show on a résumé and discuss in an interview.

INTERNATIONAL RELATIONS AND PUBLIC POLICY

TOP INTERNATIONAL RELATIONS PROGRAMS

Students with an interest in other cultures and languages are often drawn to international relations. Many of the best-known schools for international relations are restricted to graduate students. Examples include the School of International and Public Affairs (SIPA) at Columbia University, the School of Advanced International Studies (SAIS) at Johns Hopkins University, and the Fletcher School of Law and Diplomacy at Tufts University. Some of the universities strong on the graduate level offer undergraduate programs in foreign affairs—for example Columbia, Johns Hopkins, and Tufts—but those programs are not part of the prestigious SIPA, SAIS, or Fletcher.

Perhaps the best-known undergraduate program in the international studies arena is Georgetown University's Walsh School of Foreign Service. The Walsh School at Georgetown stands atop just about every ranking of international relations programs. The Walsh School and other top international relations programs are listed and profiled below.

- American University
- Boston University
- University of British Columbia
- Brown University
- University of Chicago
- Columbia University
- Dartmouth College
- Emory University
- Georgetown University
- George Washington University
- Georgia Institute of Technology
- University of Georgia
- Johns Hopkins University
- Middlebury College
- New York University
- University of Pennsylvania
- Princeton University
- University of Southern California
- Stanford University
- University of Toronto
- Tufts University
- Washington University
- University of Washington
- College of William and Mary
- Yale University

American University. The School of International Service (SIS) at American is large and comprehensive. Housed in a LEED Gold–certified green building, SIS at AU enrolls 1,600 undergraduates. With more than one hundred study abroad choices, it is not surprising that more than half of AU's students have a first-hand global experience while enrolled. The cornerstone of SIS at American is its BA in international studies program. Each year AU admits fifty exceptional students into another program called global studies, which offers a three-year track to a BA in international studies and a four-year BA/MA option. Other international-related programs at AU include French/Europe area studies, German/Europe area studies, Jewish studies, Russian area studies, Spanish/Latin American studies, and certificate programs in Arab studies and Asian studies. In addition, AU's Center for Israel Studies runs exchange programs with Ben Gurion University, the University of Haifa, Hebrew University, and Tel Aviv University.

Boston University. BU's program in international relations offers specialization tracks in Africa and the Middle East, Asia, environment and development, Europe, foreign policy and security studies, international economics and business, international political economy, international systems and world order, Latin America, and regional politics and cultural anthropology. BU's area studies program offers degree options in East Asian studies, European studies, and Latin American studies. BU also operates an African Studies Center and an Institute for the Study of Muslim Societies and Civilizations.

University of British Columbia. The interdisciplinary international relations major at UBC is focused on global perspectives from areas such as anthropology, economics, geography, history, and political science. Specialization options include international diplomacy, security and peace studies; international economy and development; area studies; Canada and the Americas; or Europe and Eurasia. Additional international majors at UBC include Asian area studies, global resource systems, international business, Latin American studies, and modern European studies. UBC also operates the Liu Institute for Global Issues.

Brown University. With 125 to 135 graduates per year, the international relations concentration at Brown draws on the academic resources of more than twenty-five departments. Brown's interdisciplinary international relations concentration emphasizes the subthemes of security and political economy. Other internationally oriented concentrations at Brown include Africana studies, development studies, East Asian studies, French studies, German studies, Hispanic studies, Italian studies, Judaic studies, Latin American studies, Middle East studies, and Portuguese and Brazilian studies. Brown offers study abroad programs in Brazil, Cuba, France, Germany, Hong Kong, India, Italy, Japan, Spain,

and the United Kingdom. The innovative Brown Plus One program enables students to add a fifth year of study in Scotland (at the University of Edinburgh) or Asia (at the Chinese University of Hong Kong) and emerge with a bachelor's degree from Brown and a master's degree from the partner school.

University of Chicago. Chicago's undergraduate major in international studies has three tracks: political economy, transnational processes, and regional studies. Students in the program must take courses in each track and demonstrate proficiency in a foreign language. Chicago's vast language offerings include Arabic, Armenian, Bengali, Bosnian/Croatian/Serbian, Czech, Catalan, Hindi, Italian, Kazakh, Korean, Malayalam, Marathi, Pali, Persian, Polish, Portuguese, Sanskrit, Swahili, Tamil, Telugu, Tibetan, Turkish, Urdu, and Uzbek. Chicago also has majors in East Asian languages and civilizations, Germanic studies, Jewish studies, Latin American studies, Near Eastern languages and civilizations, Russian studies, and South Asian languages and civilizations.

Columbia University. Among graduate schools, Columbia's School of International and Public Affairs (SIPA) is frequently ranked in the top ten. But, as SIPA does not offer an undergraduate major, the closest equivalent at Columbia is regional studies, a program concentrated on the history and culture of a particular part of the world. Regional studies majors can concentrate on African studies, Brazilian studies, East Asia, East Central Europe, Europe, Iranian studies, Latin America, the Middle East, Russia and the former Soviet states, and South Asia. Through its centers and institutes, Columbia offers a vast array of languages. For example, the East Central European Center provides courses in Czech, Hungarian, Polish, Romanian, Russian, Serbian/Croatian/Bosnian, and Ukrainian. Additionally, there are internationally focused majors at Columbia in African studies, comparative ethnic studies, East Asian languages and cultures, French and Francophone studies, Latin American and Caribbean studies, and Middle Eastern and Asian languages and cultures. Columbia operates its own study abroad programs in Amman, Barcelona, Beijing, Berlin, Kyoto, Paris, Rio, Shanghai, and Venice.

Dartmouth College. At Dartmouth, international relations is a major offered by the Department of Government. Dartmouth international relations majors have numerous study abroad options, including a London School of Economics program focused on world affairs and comparative politics. Dartmouth also has internationally focused majors in Asian and Middle Eastern studies; French studies; Hispanic studies; Italian studies; Latin American, Latino and Caribbean studies; and Russian area studies. Dartmouth's Dickey Center for International Understanding gets students internships in organizations focused on global issues.

Emory University. The international studies major at Emory, embedded within political science, offers three concentration options: conflict and security, political economy, and state and society. For students interested in specific countries or regions, Emory has majors in African studies, French studies, German studies, Italian studies, Jewish studies, Latin American and Caribbean studies, Middle Eastern and South Asian studies, Russian and East European studies and minors in development studies, global health, culture and society, and Irish studies. Through the interdisciplinary studies in culture and society major, students can devise their own course of study around particular regions of the world or thematic areas.

Georgetown University. Arguably, Georgetown's Edwin A. Walsh School of Foreign Service (SFS) offers the nation's best undergraduate program. All SFS students at Georgetown must demonstrate proficiency in a foreign language and take courses in philosophy, theology, humanities, writing, history, and economics. Students at SFS have seven major options: culture and politics; international economics; international history; international politics; international political economy; regional and comparative studies; and science, technology, and international affairs. SFS students can also earn an interdisciplinary certificate focused on a theme or world region; examples include African studies; Arab studies; Asian studies; Australian and New Zealand studies; classical studies; European studies; international business diplomacy; international development; Islam and Muslim-Christian understanding; Jewish civilization; justice and peace studies; Latin American studies; medieval studies; religion, ethics, and world affairs; Russian and East European studies; social and political thought; and women's and gender studies. A special program enables selected SFS students to gain early admission to the Fletcher School of Law and Diplomacy at Tufts University.

George Washington University. The Elliott School of International Affairs at George Washington has highly ranked undergraduate and graduate programs. Undergraduates can major in international affairs, Asian studies, Latin American and hemispheric studies, or Middle Eastern studies in the Elliott School, or they can major in Africana studies or Judaic studies in GW's Columbian College of Arts and Sciences. Study abroad is central to the Elliott School experience. Through partnerships with scores of universities in Africa, Asia, Australia, Europe, and Latin America, GW ensures that its students have research, exchange, and study opportunities around the globe. Students may go on GW-managed programs in England, Latin America, Madrid, or Paris, or they can choose from 250 other approved programs.

Georgia Institute of Technology. For an institute of technology, Georgia Tech has surprisingly robust offerings in international studies. Through its Sam Nunn School for International Affairs and School of Modern Languages, Georgia Tech teaches Chinese, French, German, Japanese, and Spanish courses and offers BS programs in international affairs, applied language and intercultural studies, international affairs and modern language, economics and international affairs, and global economics and modern languages. Georgia Tech students get global experiences through summer study options focused on the European Union (Brussels), East Asia (China, Japan, Taiwan), Latin America (Argentina and Brazil), and Iberia (Portugal and Spain). Georgia Tech also encourages internships, cooperative experiences, and research projects in international settings.

University of Georgia. The School of Public and International Affairs at Georgia has approximately 800 students, nearly 750 of whom are undergraduates working toward a BA in international affairs. Within international affairs, students can focus on comparative politics, international relations, political economy, or security. Georgia offers many study abroad options in locations such as China, Croatia, Ecuador, Italy, Kyoto, Oxford, Paris, and South Africa. Georgia also has a major in Latin American and Caribbean studies and an international business track within its Terry College of Business.

Johns Hopkins University. The School of Advanced International Studies (SAIS) at Johns Hopkins is one of the leading international affairs graduate schools in the world. In addition to its main campus located in Washington, DC (DuPont Circle), SAIS has satellite campuses in Bologna (Italy) and Nanjing (China). Undergraduates at Hopkins can pursue a BA in international studies at the Krieger School of Arts and Sciences or a five-year BA/MA program that

combines three years of study in Baltimore with two years of study at SAIS. Other internationally focused majors at Hopkins include Africana studies, East Asian studies, Latin American studies, and Near Eastern studies. Among the many study abroad options are programs at SAIS Bologna and at Sciences Po Paris, where Hopkins students can earn a five-year BA/MA.

Middlebury College. Middlebury is arguably the most internationally focused small college in the United States. Renowned for its language programs, Middlebury offers Arabic, Chinese, classical Hebrew, French, German, Greek, Italian, Japanese, modern Hebrew, Portuguese, Russian, and Spanish. Specializations available through Middlebury's international studies major include African studies, East Asian studies, European studies, Latin American studies, Middle East studies, Russian and East European studies, and South Asian studies. Middlebury also offers a major in Jewish studies. In addition to its main campus in Vermont, Middlebury operates the Monterey Institute of International Studies in California, where Middlebury students can take study semesters or earn a BA and MA in five years. The integrated BA at Middlebury and MA at Monterey offerings include international environmental policy, international policy studies, nonproliferation and terrorism studies, teaching of foreign languages, and teaching English to speakers of other languages.

New York University. NYU has the bold aspiration of being the world's leading global university. Through its global network, NYU has established campuses and study abroad opportunities in ten different locations: Abu Dhabi; Accra, Ghana; Berlin; Buenos Aires; Florence; London; Madrid; Paris; Prague; Shanghai; Sydney; and Tel Aviv. NYU offers major options in international relations, Africana studies, East Asian studies, European and Mediterranean studies, Hellenic studies, Iberian studies,

Italian studies, Jewish history and civilization, Latin American studies, Middle Eastern and Islamic studies, and Russian and Slavic studies. Each year a group of freshmen is selected for a program called global liberal studies, which means they begin their NYU experience at the Florence, London, or Paris campuses.

University of Pennsylvania. Ranked among the top ten in the United States, the interdisciplinary international relations program at Penn includes courses in economics, history, politics, languages, and world religions. For students interested in global commerce, Penn offers the innovative Huntsman Program in International Studies and Business, which leads to a BS in economics from the Wharton School of Business and a BA in international studies from the College of Arts and Sciences. In addition, Penn offers majors in African studies, East Asian area studies, East Asian languages and civilizations, French studies, German studies, Hispanic studies, Italian studies, Jewish studies, Latin American and Latino studies, modern Middle East studies, Near Eastern languages and civilizations, and South Asia studies. Few universities offer as many languages as Penn. Complementing the standard languages (such as Chinese, French, and Spanish) are Arabic, Bengali, Gujarati, Hebrew, Hindi, Italian, Korean, Malayalam, Persian, Punjabi, Turkish, and twelve different African languages.

Princeton University. Princeton's Wilson School is a leader in training students for careers in international relations and public policy. While the Woodrow Wilson School of Public and International Affairs is largely a graduate school, it offers an undergraduate major that graduates eighty to ninety students annually. Students have the flexibility to shape whether their major in public and international affairs focuses more on public policy or on international studies. The Wilson School sponsors at least three study abroad programs annually. Students have gone to the Bogazici University in Istanbul, Turkey, the University of Cape Town in South Africa, the Chinese University of Hong Kong, the University of Havana in Cuba, Hertford College of Oxford University, and the Institute of Political Studies in Paris. Beyond the Wilson School, Princeton offers major programs in East Asian studies, Near Eastern studies, and Spanish and Portuguese languages and cultures.

University of Southern California. Students majoring in international relations at USC can choose an emphasis in global business or a regional studies concentration focused on Europe, Latin America, the Middle East and Africa, the Pacific Rim, or Russia, Eastern Europe, and Eurasia. Additional international relations concentration options include culture, gender, and global society; foreign policy analysis; international political economy; and international politics and security studies. The School of International Relations at USC sponsors numerous study abroad programs as well as summer internships in places such as Brussels (Belgium) and Geneva. Through its College of Arts and Sciences, USC also offers majors in Middle East studies and East Asian area studies.

Stanford University. Through its Division of International, Comparative, and Asian Studies, Stanford offers more than forty languages, operates leading research centers, and provides extensive study abroad resources. Stanford has undergraduate programs in East Asian studies, Iberian and Latin American cultures, and international relations. One of Stanford's most popular majors, international relations, encompasses the study of culture, economics, history, politics, and world affairs. Students majoring in international relations can specialize in comparative international governance, economic development/ world economy, international security, social development and human well-being, Africa,

East and South Asia, Europe and Russia, Latin American and Iberian studies, or Middle East and Central Asia. Among the vast language offerings at Stanford are Catalan, French, German, Hebrew, Italian, Persian, Portuguese, Russian, Spanish, Turkish, and Yiddish. In addition to a satellite campus in Washington, DC, near Embassy Row, Stanford has centers in Berlin and Moscow and programs in Amsterdam, Arusha (Tanzania), Australia, Barcelona, Beijing, Cape Town, Florence, Istanbul, Kyoto, Madrid, Mumbai, New Delhi, Oxford, Paris, Rio de Janeiro, and Santiago (Chile). Stanford also offers fellowships and internships in specific study areas such as Canadian studies, countries such as China and Guatemala, and placements at organizations like the Taiwan Foundation for Democracy.

University of Toronto. The Munk School of Global Affairs at Toronto is primarily a graduate school, but in cooperation with Toronto's residential, undergraduate-focused Trinity College, the Faculty of Arts and Sciences offers a degree program in international relations. Toronto also has undergraduate degree programs in European studies, Hungarian studies, Latin American studies, and South Asian studies. Within political science, Toronto offers concentrations in African studies, Asia-Pacific studies, European studies, and Russian and East European studies. Supporting the internationally focused majors at Toronto are study abroad opportunities in regions such as Central Europe, Ecuador, England, France, Germany, Hong Kong, India, Italy, Japan, Jordan, Kenya, Shanghai, southeastern Europe, and the United Arab Emirates. In addition, Toronto operates research centers focused on topics such as international history, global security, global journalism, global cities, and the global environment.

Tufts University. The Fletcher School of Law and Diplomacy at Tufts is one of the top-ranked places in the world to study international relations. The Fletcher School does not offer undergraduate degree programs, but Tufts does offer a major in international relations through its School of Arts and Sciences. International relations majors must select a thematic concentration, chosen from regional and comparative analysis; international economics; global health, nutrition and the environment; international security; the United States in world affairs; and ideas and ideologies in international relations. Within the regional and comparative analysis concentration, students can pursue subconcentrations focused on Europe and the former Soviet Union, East and Southeast Asia, Africa, the Middle East and South Asia, or Latin America. Those interested in international economics can focus on international trade, international finance, international environmental economics, or international development economics. The concentration in ideas and identity in international relations offers a subconcentration in ideologies and empires/colonialism/globalization. Tufts also has majors in Asian studies, German studies, Italian studies, Judaic studies, Latin American studies, Middle Eastern studies, and Russian and East European studies. Tufts has many study abroad programs in places such as Chile, China, Ghana, Hong Kong, Japan, London, Madrid, Oxford, Paris, and Tubingen.

Washington University. Students majoring in international and area studies at Washington University in St. Louis must demonstrate depth in at least one area of the world, chosen from Africa, East Asia, Europe, Latin America, the Middle East, and South Asia. The international and area studies major offers concentration options in development studies, global futures, and global cultural studies. Students interested in specific regions and cultures can major in African and African American studies; East Asian studies; European studies; Jewish, Islamic and

Near Eastern studies; or Latin American studies, or they can minor in Russian studies or South Asian languages and culture. Washington University offers more than ten languages, including Arabic, Chinese, French, German, Hebrew, Hindi, Italian, Japanese, Korean, Persian, Russian, and Spanish. Study abroad programs include summer language institutes in France, Italy, and Spain. Students learn Spanish in Madrid, study French at a chateau in the Loire Valley, and study Italian in Castelraimondo, Italy, while living in a sixteenth-century poolside villa.

University of Washington. Named for the legendary Senator Henry Jackson, the University of Washington's Jackson School of International Studies is one of the most comprehensive in the United States. For undergraduates, the Jackson School offers seven majors: Asian studies, Canadian studies, comparative religion, European studies, international studies, Jewish studies, and Latin American studies. International studies majors at Washington can choose from twenty-plus concentrations that focus on every region of the world and offer interdisciplinary themes such as development; environmental studies; ethnicity and nationalities; global health; international communication; international human rights law, state, and society; international political economy; and foreign policy, diplomacy, peace, and security. The Jackson School has particular strength in the countries of the Pacific Rim. Within the Asian studies major, there are specialized concentrations on China, Japan, Korea, South Asia, and Southeast Asia. The Jackson School also offers minors in African studies and comparative Islamic studies.

College of William and Mary. William and Mary offers some exciting international study options, which include joint degree programs with the University of St. Andrews in Scotland. The international relations major at William and Mary can be completed jointly with the University of St. Andrews through two years of study in Scotland. Economics and history majors also have the option to earn a joint St. Andrews degree. The global studies major at William and Mary is interdisciplinary and provides concentration options in Asian and Middle Eastern studies, European studies, Latin American studies, and Russian and post–Soviet studies. There are additional major options in Africana studies, Chinese language and culture, and French and Francophone studies.

Yale University. Through the Jackson Institute for Global Affairs, Yale students have major options in international studies and global affairs. International studies is frequently chosen as a second major to complement programs in a foreign language or a social science, such as economics. The major in global affairs offers two specialization tracks: international development and international security. For students interested in focusing on a region or culture, Yale offers majors in African studies, East Asian studies, Latin American studies, modern Middle Eastern studies, Russian and East European studies, and South Asian studies. Yale has unsurpassed academic resources, including the capacity to offer numerous foreign languages such as Arabic, Czech, Hebrew, Hindi, Igbo, isiZulu, Kiswahili, Persian, Polish, Sanskrit, Tamil, Turkish, and Yoruba.

OTHER NOTEWORTHY INTERNATIONAL STUDIES PROGRAMS

- University of California at Berkeley
- University of California at Davis
- University of California at Los Angeles
- University of California at San Diego
- College of Charleston
- University of Colorado Boulder
- University of Denver
- University of Florida
- George Mason University
- Indiana University
- University of Miami
- University of Michigan
- University of North Carolina at Chapel Hill
- Northwestern University
- Ohio State University
- University of Texas at Austin
- Vanderbilt University
- University of Vermont

Hand in hand with careers in international relations is training in languages and study experiences in foreign countries. A number of small liberal arts colleges (listed below) offer numerous foreign languages, encourage all students to study abroad, and focus on preparing global citizens.

- Bryn Mawr College
- Claremont McKenna College
- Connecticut College
- Dickinson College
- Kalamazoo College
- Lewis and Clark College
- Macalester College
- Occidental College
- Smith College

TOP PUBLIC POLICY PROGRAMS

Preparation for careers in government and policy can occur in a number of ways. There is the traditional route of majoring in political science or government, or there is the option to study in a specialized public policy program. A number of the highest-rated government and public policy programs are restricted to graduate students; for example, the Kennedy School of Government at Harvard, the Maxwell School at Syracuse, the Johnson School of Public Affairs at Texas, the Humphrey School of Public Affairs at Minnesota, and the Goldman School of Public Policy at Berkeley. Still, there are a number of prominent options (listed and profiled below) for undergraduates interested in public policy studies and public administration.

- American University
- Brown University
- University of Chicago
- Duke University
- George Mason University
- Georgetown University
- Harvard University
- Indiana University
- James Madison University
- University of Michigan
- Michigan State University
- State University of New York at Albany
- Princeton University

- Rice University
- Rutgers University
- University of Southern California
- Stanford University
- Syracuse University
- University of Toronto
- Vanderbilt University
- University of Virginia
- College of William and Mary
- Yale University

American University. Although American does not offer an undergraduate major in public policy, it does offer combined bachelor's and master's degree programs in public administration (BA/MPA) and public policy (BA/MPP). For their undergraduate studies, students in the combined degree program can major in any related field (typically in the social sciences).

Brown University. For students interested in shaping the future of public education, health care, criminal justice, and urban centers, Brown offers a concentration in public policy and American institutions. Through its Taubman Center for Public Policy and American Institutions, Brown brings in speakers, runs workshops, and provides career connections and internships at organizations such as the Children's Action Alliance, the Legal Aid Society of New York, the National Parental Information Center, the New England Small Farm Institute, the White House, the Washington Public Defender's Office, and in governors' offices in several states.

University of Chicago. The public policy BA program at Chicago has several areas for specialization, including economics, education, health policy, human rights, organizations, quantitative public policy, science and policy, urban studies, and work and family. Chicago's public policy department runs a winter quarter study abroad program in Paris whose participants can elect a specialization in comparative political economy.

Duke University. On the undergraduate level, the Sanford School of Public Policy at Duke offers a major in public policy studies that requires its students to complete an internship and encourages them to engage in undergraduate research or service learning. Public policy studies majors at Duke can narrow their focus by choosing one of five individual specialization pathways: economic policy, global policy, health policy, policy journalism, and social policy.

Georgetown University. Georgetown has leading graduate programs, but no undergraduate major, in public policy. The government major at Georgetown, on the other hand, is more focused on putting policy into practice than most. A government degree from Georgetown provides entrée into the world of political organizations and the university's top-rated graduate programs in foreign affairs, law, and public policy.

Harvard University. The Kennedy School of Government at Harvard is a world pacesetter in graduate and professional education, but it does not offer undergraduate degrees. Undergraduates with a government concentration (Harvard's term for a major) can take up to two Kennedy School courses. Students concentrating on government can pursue secondary field specializations in American politics, comparative politics, or political economy.

Indiana University. Students in the School of Public and Environmental Affairs (SPEA) at Indiana can select majors in environmental management, legal studies, management, policy analysis, public financial management, or public nonprofit management. For students seeking an immersion into policy, including an internship, Indiana offers the Washington (DC) Leadership Program.

James Madison University. JMU's BS program in public policy and administration requires a capstone seminar in public management as well as an internship. JMU encourages PPA majors to choose a minor from areas such as environmental management, nonprofit studies, political communication, public health, and urban and regional studies. JMU also offers a Washington Semester and the opportunity to stay on for a fifth year and earn an MPA degree.

University of Michigan. Although primarily a graduate school, the Gerald R. Ford School of Public Policy at Michigan enrolls approximately one hundred undergraduates. Students enter the BA in public policy program at Michigan as juniors. Students can pursue a focus area such as economic perspectives on policy, energy policy, health-care policy, historical perspectives on policy, or Middle Eastern policy.

Michigan State University. Through its residential colleges, Michigan State tries to create a more personal and interdisciplinary environment within a university of forty-seven thousand students. James Madison College at MSU is a social sciences–focused residential college that offers majors in social relations and policy, comparative cultures and politics, political theory and constitutional democracy, and international relations. Through its College of Social Science, MSU offers BA and BS degrees in interdisciplinary studies in social science—with concentration options in community governance and advocacy, health and society, and human capital and society.

State University of New York at Albany. Across town from Albany's Rockefeller College of Public Affairs and Policy are New York State's capital building, legislative offices, and public agencies. Rockefeller students frequently serve as interns in New York State's capital or in Washington, DC. Rockefeller offers a BA in public policy and management as well as BA/MA (political science) and BA/MPA (master of public administration)

programs. Public policy students can choose concentrations in economics, education policy, environment and society, international policy, local government, public administration, study of society, gender and policy, or urban issues and women.

Princeton University. The Woodrow Wilson School of Public and International Affairs at Princeton annually admits ninety rising juniors into an undergraduate major designed to interest students in public service. As juniors, Wilson School students take policy seminar classes either on campus or at an overseas location. As seniors, students complete a thesis on a domestic or international policy issue.

Rice University. Through its required internship, the policy studies major at Rice aims to give students real-world knowledge and experience. Policy studies majors must choose an area of specialization from energy policy studies, environmental policy, government policy and management, health-care management, international affairs, law and justice, managerial and business policy, and urban and social change. Internships are offered through the Rice Policy Studies in London program, the Social Sciences Gateway Internship Program, the Jesse Jones Leadership Center Summer in Washington, DC, the Lesotho (Africa) Sustainability Assessment Project, or the Baker Institute, which offers a special internship in energy.

Rutgers University. Students looking for a school strong in areas such as smart growth, transportation planning, workforce development, and environmental health may want to consider the Edward J. Bloustein School of Planning and Public Policy at Rutgers. The Bloustein School offers two undergraduate majors: a BA in planning and public policy and a BS in public health.

University of Southern California. The Sol Price School of Public Policy at USC capitalizes on its

Los Angeles location by connecting students to city leaders, nonprofit managers, state legislators, and health-policy advocates. The Price School offers one undergraduate major: the BS in policy, planning, and development (PPD), with concentration options in health policy and management, nonprofits and social innovation, public policy and law, real estate development, and sustainable planning. PPD majors frequently participate in USC's Washington (DC) Semester program.

Stanford University. Public policy majors at Stanford must choose a concentration and complete a senior capstone course in which they do a research project for an outside client or write a senior thesis. Concentration options in the public policy major include advanced methods of policy analysis; design of public institutions; development and growth policies; education; health care; international policies and national security; law and the legal system; science and technology policy; social policy (discrimination, crime, and poverty); urban and regional policy; and environment, resources, and population. Public policy majors frequently study for a quarter at the Stanford in Washington campus.

Syracuse University. The Maxwell School of Citizenship and Public Affairs at Syracuse is frequently ranked the top graduate policy school in the United States—ahead of Harvard's Kennedy School of Government and Princeton's Woodrow Wilson School. Maxwell has one undergraduate program, a major in policy studies, which requires students to complete a topical specialization, chosen from environment; health, education, and human services; government and business; or society and the legal system. Students in Syracuse's schools of management, human ecology, and visual and performing arts can add policy studies as a double major.

University of Toronto. Toronto's School of Public Policy and Governance is highly respected across North America for its graduate programs.

Undergraduates looking for a public policy major at Toronto will find a program offered jointly by the School of Public Policy and Governance and the departments of economics and political science. Toronto's public policy program (which students apply to in their first or second year of studies) develops theoretical and applied skills in policy analysis related to areas such as education, health care, and financial regulation.

Vanderbilt University. Within the College of Arts and Sciences, Vanderbilt students can choose the interdisciplinary major in public policy studies that is built around core courses in economics, ethics, government, research methods and statistics, and society and culture. Students in public policy studies individually design a specialty track; examples include crime and justice, health policy, and labor market policy.

University of Virginia. The Frank Batten School of Leadership and Public Policy offers a global, multidisciplinary major that integrates perspectives from economics, political science, psychology, and sociology. Undergraduate students at the Batten School can work toward a BA in public policy and leadership or add a fifth year to earn the joint BA/master of public policy (MPP). UVA's public policy and leadership graduates tend to find positions in consulting, government, think tanks, nonprofits, and NGOs. Virginia also offers a major in political philosophy, policy, and law.

College of William and Mary. As befits the alma mater of Thomas Jefferson, William and Mary offers an undergraduate degree in public policy. The curriculum for the public policy major is drawn from economics, government, history, business, psychology, and sociology. For majors in public policy, internships are encouraged but not required. Through the special Thomas Jefferson Program in Public Policy, William and Mary students can earn a BA and a master of public policy (MPP) in five years.

Yale University. There is no undergraduate public policy major at Yale. But within political science, Yale offers several policy-oriented concentrations, including child social policy; environmental politics; global health; and health, politics, and policy.

OTHER GOOD PUBLIC POLICY PROGRAMS

- Cornell University
- Carnegie Mellon University (ethics, history, and public policy)
- University of California at Riverside
- University of California at San Diego
- University of California at Santa Barbara
- University of Denver
- George Mason University
- Georgia Institute of Technology
- University of Iowa (ethics and public policy)
- Miami University
- University of North Carolina at Chapel Hill
- Ohio State University (John Glenn School of Public Affairs)
- University of Oklahoma
- University of Oregon
- Southern Methodist University
- University of Tulsa (environmental policy)
- Vanderbilt University
- Washington University

THE WRITTEN WORD

JOURNALISM, COMMUNICATIONS, AND NEWS MEDIA PROGRAMS

There are two ways that undergraduates typically prepare for a career in journalism and communications, and both involve real-world experience. One approach is to study journalism or communications and supplement course work with participation in a campus media organization and/or summer internships with a professional media company. Writing for a well-known college paper, such as the *Columbia Missourian*, the *Daily Cal*, or *Michigan Daily*, is another way to gain invaluable experience and determine if a media career fits. Students can gain similar indispensable experience by working for a campus television or radio station, especially at a large university such as Boston University or the University of Maryland. At such institutions, the campus papers and stations resemble professional news organizations and provide on-the-job training respected by media professionals. Studying journalism or communications and working for a big campus paper or radio or television station can also help students develop a professional network that opens doors into real-world job opportunities. In much of the United States, major local newspapers, such as the *Oregonian* or the *Indianapolis Star*, are full of graduates of the journalism and communications programs at the local flagship public university (in those cases Oregon and Indiana).

National newspapers, magazines, websites, and broadcast companies are populated by people with a wider range of backgrounds.

Besides journalism and communications graduates, there are reporters and editors with liberal arts degrees in fields such as English, history, or political science. Liberal arts entrants into the media world tend to have worked at the campus newspaper or radio/television station or gone to a graduate program in journalism or communications. Increasingly, there are newspaper and television reporters whose coverage of a specialized area depends on their expertise in law, international relations, or science. Still, in virtually every case, these media professionals started out working for a campus newspaper, television station, or radio station and/or had a summer internship in a media organization.

When aspiring journalists hear names of top programs bandied about, the Columbia Journalism School is often mentioned as a great place to prepare for a media career. While Columbia does have a journalism program that is often regarded as the best in the United States, students need to know that Columbia is a graduate journalism school with no undergraduate program. Another highly regarded journalism school limited to graduate study is the one at the University of California, Berkeley. Students seeking a graduate degree in journalism or communications will be well served by Berkeley, Columbia, or any of the other institutions listed and described below. The difference is that the schools below also have undergraduate programs in journalism and/or communications.

STANDOUT UNDERGRADUATE PROGRAMS IN JOURNALISM AND COMMUNICATIONS

- Ball State University
- Boston University
- University of Florida
- University of Georgia
- University of Illinois
- Indiana University
- University of Maryland
- University of Miami
- University of Missouri
- New York University
- University of North Carolina
- Northwestern University
- Ohio University
- University of Southern California
- Syracuse University
- University of Texas
- University of Wisconsin

Ball State University. The success of David Letterman has put a spotlight on his alma mater, the College of Communication, Information, and Media (CCIM) at Ball State. The nerve center of CCIM is the Letterman Communication and Media Building—a facility not unlike the studios and production houses in Hollywood, London, and New York. The cutting edge, environmentally friendly Letterman Building contains two recording studios, two control rooms, two isolation rooms, and five editing suites. Future media professionals at Ball State can major in advertising, journalism, or public relations. The journalism major at Ball State offers tracks in magazine, news, journalism graphics, and photojournalism. Ball State's program in advertising is one of the largest in the Midwest. Advertising majors run an advertising agency (called AAF) that works on projects for real clients. Likewise, students in Ball State's highly rated public

relations program tackle real-world projects through the student-run Cardinal Communications PR agency. Although Ball State's total enrollment tops twenty-two thousand, the average class size at CCIM is a reasonable twenty to twenty-five students. Besides David Letterman, other prominent media-related Ball State alumni include *Garfield* creator Jim Davis and sportswriters Mike Lopresti and Jason Whitlock.

Boston University. BU has one of the largest and most distinguished communications programs in the United States. There are nearly 2,300 students in the College of Communication, or COM as it is called at BU. BU offers BS degrees in communication, journalism, and film and television. There are specialized concentration options available in advertising, broadcast journalism, communication studies, film, photojournalism, public relations, and television. COM students can also pursue dual degrees in international relations and communications, mass communications and law, and media ventures. COM provides its students an extraordinary array of hands-on experiences. The student-run AdLab, PR lab, and Hothouse Productions work with real clients on advertising and public-relations projects. The Los Angeles Internship Program puts students in the heart of the film and television industry while they pursue study tracks in advertising and public relations, film and television, or entertainment management. Through BU's Washington Journalism Center, students spend a semester reporting on and studying public affairs. The BU State House Program gives student correspondents a front-row seat to view Massachusetts politics. BU's on-campus television and radio stations are run by students and serve as significant media outlets in the Boston metropolitan area. WBUR, Boston's National

Public Radio affiliate, is located on campus and gives students part-time jobs and internships. The COM alumni network is vast (21,000 members) and includes Mike Barnicle (MSNBC), Bud Collins (*Boston Globe*), Jerry Crasnick (ESPN), Tyler Hicks and Joe Nocera (*New York Times*), Randi Kaye (CNN), Howard Stern ("King of all Media"), and Nina Totenberg (NPR).

University of Florida. The College of Journalism and Communications at Florida offers top-ranked programs in advertising and journalism, not to mention exciting study abroad opportunities, such as the photojournalism program in Berlin, Germany. At Florida, students can major in advertising, journalism, public relations, or telecommunications, which offers four concentration options: management, media and society, news, and production. Selected journalism students can pursue an accelerated combined bachelor's/master's degree program. With four working newsrooms, two television stations, eleven satellite ground stations, four radio stations, and an interactive media lab, Florida's journalism and communications facilities are among the best in the nation. For students interested in getting media experience, Florida has one of the largest campus daily newspapers in the United States (the *Independent Florida Alligator*), a public radio station, a sports radio station, a country music station, a magazine, and two television stations. Florida media alumni include Erin Andrews (ESPN), Red Barber (legendary baseball announcer), Chris Collinsworth (NBC sportscaster), Carl Hiaasen (columnist/novelist), and Forrest Sawyer (ABC News).

University of Georgia. Among US schools that prepare students for media careers, Georgia's Grady College of Journalism and Mass Communication is one of the oldest and most respected. Grady College is the home of the Peabody Awards for excellence in electronic media and the site of several research centers that are focused on international mass communication, newspaper management, new media, and broadcast management. Georgia offers majors in advertising, journalism, public relations, and telecommunications. Journalism students can choose among four emphasis areas: magazine journalism, public affairs journalism, publication management, and visual journalism. The telecommunications program offers concentrations in digital and broadcast journalism and mass media arts. Students at Grady College gain hands-on experience as writers and editors for the *Red and Black* student newspaper and have access to extensive career services that include a job fair that attracts approximately fifty companies and connections to alumni in media-based fields. The latter is significant because Georgia is legendary for strong bonds within its alumni network. Prominent Bulldogs in media include Brooke Anderson (*The Insider*), Jack Davis (*Mad* magazine), Lewis Grizzard (longtime syndicated columnist), Charlayne Hunter-Gault (PBS), Tom Johnson (former president of CNN), Pat Mitchell (former president of PBS), Deborah Norville (host of *Inside Edition*), Amy Robach (coanchor of *Weekend Today*), and Mark Schlabach (ESPN).

University of Illinois. The College of Media at Illinois offers BS programs in advertising, broadcast journalism, news-editorial journalism, and media and cinema studies. Teaching faculty in the College of Media are experienced professionals who have won Clio and Emmy Awards, Pulitzer Prizes, and honors at film festivals such as Sundance. Illinois was one of the originators of public broadcasting. The broadcast journalism and news-editorial journalism programs at Illinois have sent graduates to work for numerous media organizations such as the Associated Press, MSNBC, and the *New York Times*. Established in 1949, the advertising department at Illinois is the oldest and one of the highest ranked in the United States. Illinois prepares its advertising students for jobs by connecting them with alumni networks and by sponsoring trips to agencies in Chicago, Detroit, Los Angeles, and New York. Through a partnership with the College of Agriculture, Consumer and Environmental Sciences, Illinois also offers a BS degree in agricultural communications. Prominent Illinois graduates in the media world include Dan Balz (national editor for the *Washington Post*), Roger Ebert (film critic), Hugh Hefner (*Playboy* founder), Suze Orman (host of television programs on personal finance), Dan Savage (syndicated columnist), and Gene Shalit (film critic).

Indiana University. At Indiana's Media School, students major in journalism en route to a bachelor of arts in journalism (BAJ) degree while pursuing concentrated study in one of eleven specializations. Journalism students work as reporters and editors for the *Indiana Daily Student* and get broadcast experience helping run Indiana University Student Television and WIUX, the campus radio station. A program called Journalism Experiences provides opportunities for international travel, special scholarships, honors programs, on-campus media jobs, and a speaker series that brings top journalism professionals to campus. To give students global perspective, IU's Media School operates an eight-week summer program in London and sponsors annual travel courses that have taken students to Australia, China, Japan, and Latin America. Through an arrangement with the acclaimed National Sports Journalism Center (and graduate program) at Indiana University-Purdue University Indianapolis, IU students can earn a concentration in sports journalism. IU's Media School has its own career services office that helps students get summer internships, find jobs with media organizations, and make connections within the school's extensive alumni network. IU graduates include Dick Enberg (sportscaster), Jane Pauley (host of several news shows), Tavis Smiley (radio host), and Sherri Sylvester (CNN).

University of Maryland. At Maryland's Merrill College of Journalism, students benefit from the proximity to the nation's capital. Students at Maryland operate a cable television station and the Capital News Service, a daily wire service with bureaus in Annapolis, College Park, and Washington, DC. Maryland is also the home of the renowned *American Journalism Review*. Maryland offers a BA in journalism with concentration options in broadcast news, news/editorial, and online journalism. Broadcast news students learn from professors who have worked as producers and correspondents for CBS News and CNN. News/editorial students have classes and workshops taught by distinguished professionals such as former *Philadelphia Inquirer* editor Gene Roberts. Online journalism students produce *Maryland Newsline*, an online news magazine. The media, self, and society program provides a living/learning opportunity, including numerous trips to broadcast studios and major newspapers, such as the *Washington Post*. The program also produces an entertainment and arts magazine called *Unwind*. One of the strengths of journalism at Maryland is its career placement record. Merrill graduates have been hired by the Associated Press, the BBC, *Black Enterprise*, *Chicago Tribune*, CNN, *Dallas Morning News*, *Los Angeles Times*, *Money*, *National Geographic*, National Public Radio, NBC News, *New York Times*, *Politico*, and the *Wall Street Journal*. Prominent Maryland graduates include Bonnie Bernstein (sportscaster), Carl Bernstein (Watergate journalist), Connie Chung (groundbreaking news anchor), Tim Kurkjian (ESPN), Bert Sugar (legendary boxing writer), Scott Van Pelt (ESPN), and Pam Ward (ESPN).

University of Miami. Miami's School of Communication offers a wide range of majors for students interested in media-related fields. At Miami, students can earn a BS in advertising, broadcast journalism, communication studies, electronic media, journalism, media management, motion pictures, public relations, and visual journalism. Advertising and public relations students run an agency (PRADUM) that takes clients from inside and outside the university and regularly have internships at major firms, such as Alma DDB, Ogilvy and Mather, Leo Burnett, and Young and Rubicam, as well as with magazines and television shows. Miami's broadcast journalism students produce a weekly half-hour newscast called *NewsVision*. Electronic media students gain experience at the university's television and radio stations. Journalism students can work for the student-run newspaper (*Miami Hurricane*), a quarterly magazine, or an online newspaper. Motion pictures majors can study directing, editing, new media, and production through special summer programs in Greece and Los Angeles. Visual journalism students learn tools for digital photography, computer imaging, postproduction, sound, and multimedia production. Facilities at Miami include two digital television studios and control rooms, editing suites, a film sound stage, and studios for animation, digital photography, and digital news. Miami alumni include Jill Arrington (Fox Sports), Roy Firestone (Emmy Award-winning sports journalist), and Pedro Gomez, Suzy Kolber, and Dan LeBatard (ESPN).

University of Missouri. Along with Columbia and Northwestern, the University of Missouri is the other giant in the journalism school world. Many leading figures in the history of US media have studied at Missouri, which in 1908 became the world's first school of journalism. A distinguishing feature of the program is the so-called Missouri Method, where students work as reporters and get experience in strategic communications agencies. Journalism students can work for a daily paper/news site (*Columbia Missourian*), the second citizen journalism site founded in the United States (MyMissourian.com), and a hyperlocal news site (Missourian

Neighborhood News). Students can also get experience working for a university-owned commercial television station (KOMM), a student-staffed ad agency (MOJO Ad), a digital news organization that covers state political stories (Missouri Digital News), two magazines, and a campus radio station (KBIA 91.3 FM).

Missouri's Journalism School offers two undergraduate major options: journalism or strategic communication. For future science reporters, Missouri also offers the interdisciplinary BS in science and agricultural journalism, which is jointly run by the Journalism School and the College of Agriculture, Food, and Natural Resources. The multifaceted curriculum at Missouri makes it possible for students to concentrate on their specific interests. In recent years, journalism students have pursued more than twenty areas of focus, including emerging media; magazine design; photojournalism; radio-television reporting; anchoring and producing; visual editing; watchdog journalism; and reporting focused on arts and culture, entrepreneurship, international affairs, science and health, or sports. Strategic communications majors have pursued interests in account management, art direction, copywriting, media planning, public relations, and interactive communication. Students at Missouri can also design an individually focused specialty within journalism or strategic communication.

The prominence of Missouri is exemplified by the many significant professional organizations and research centers housed in the Journalism School—including the Association of Health Care Journalists; Center for the Study of Conflict, Law, and the Media; Center for Excellence in Health Care Journalism; Center on Religion and the Professions; Committee of Concerned Journalists; National Freedom of Information Coalition; National Institute of Computer-Assisted Reporting; and Investigative Reporters and Editors. Truly outstanding students at Missouri become

Walter Williams Scholars or Journalism Scholars, giving them entry into the MU Honors College, study abroad stipends, early entry into master's programs, and a dedicated residence hall.

The effectiveness of the Missouri Method shows in the scores of alumni who have won Pulitzer Prizes or have led newspapers and broadcasting companies. Missouri journalism alumni include John Anderson (ESPN), Gerald Boyd (former *New York Times* metropolitan editor), Jann Carl (*Entertainment Tonight*), Sophia Choi (CNN), Pat Forde (Yahoo! Sports), Major Garrett (*National Journal*), Juliet Huddy (Fox News), James J. Kilpatrick (longtime columnist), Michael Kim (ESPN), Jim Lehrer (PBS news anchor), Joel Meyers (sportscaster), Lisa Myers (NBC News), Ken Paulsen (former editor in chief of *USA Today*), Chuck Roberts (longtime CNN anchor), Jon Scott (Fox News), and Elizabeth Vargas (ABC's *20/20* coanchor). Also, three actors of note studied journalism at Missouri: Tom Berenger, Robert Loggia, and Brad Pitt.

New York University. The Arthur L. Carter Journalism Institute at NYU includes an undergraduate major in journalism with additional options to pursue specialized concentrations in computational and digital journalism or media criticism. NYU believes that future media professionals should get a broad education, so every journalism student must fulfill a double major in an academic area offered in the College of Arts and Sciences. Through the Journalism Abroad program, NYU juniors and seniors can spend a semester taking classes and pursuing internships in international sites such as Accra (Ghana), Buenos Aires, London, Madrid, Prague, and Shanghai, where NYU has a full campus. Through its location in America's media capital, NYU offers journalism students access to internships, part-time jobs, and an extensive alumni network. Media luminaries frequently come to NYU's Journalism Institute for readings, lectures, and classroom appearances. Prominent journalism alumni of NYU include CNBC host Maria Bartiromo and film critic Leonard Maltin.

University of North Carolina at Chapel Hill. The School of Journalism and Mass Communications at North Carolina offers undergraduate programs in advertising/public relations and journalism. Within the advertising/public relations major, students can specialize in strategic communications. Within the journalism major, UNC offers specializations in editing and graphic design, electronic communication, multimedia, photojournalism, and reporting. Other special programs enable students to major in business journalism, take courses and pursue internships in sports communication, or earn a certificate in Latino journalism and media studies. Notable UNC journalism graduates include Howie Carr (radio talk show host), Rick Dees (radio personality), Jason Kilar (CEO of Hulu), Walter Hussman (publisher of the *Arkansas Democrat-Gazette*), Charles Kuralt (longtime host of *CBS News Sunday Morning*), Jim Lampley (sportscaster), Stuart Scott (ESPN sportscaster), Tom Wicker (longtime *New York Times* reporter), and Jonathan Yardley (longtime *Washington Post* book critic).

Northwestern University. The Medill School at Northwestern is one of the top journalism schools in the world—often ranked alongside Columbia. Students at Medill learn by doing through residencies in media organizations and by operating storefront newsrooms in Chicago neighborhoods. Every student spends a full quarter in a journalism residency, getting professional experience with media partners (many of which hire Medill graduates) that include Atlantic Media, *Bloomberg News*, Bravo, *Business Week*, *Chicago Tribune*, CNN, Comcast Sportsnet, Gannett Newspapers, *Glamour*, *Houston Chronicle*, *Marie Claire*, *Menshealth*, NBC, *New York Post*, *Newsday*, National Public Radio, Ogilvy Public Relations, PBS *NewsHour*, *Playboy*, *Rolling Stone*, *Slate*, the Associated Press, *The Ellen Degeneres*

Show, *Chronicle of Higher Education*, *Huffington Post*, *Wall Street Journal*, *Washington Post*, *Time* magazine, and *US News and World Report*. Journalism residencies are also available in Latin America, Qatar (where Northwestern has a campus), and South Africa. Medill is a professional school, where students receive a bachelor of science in journalism (BSJ) degree. Through the accelerated master's program (AMP), students can earn joint BSJ/MSJ degrees in less than five years. Prominent alumni of Medill include political writer/commentator David Sirota and sports writers and broadcasters J. A. Adande, Christine Brennan, Mike Greenberg, Brent Musburger, Darren Rovell, and Michael Wilbon.

Ohio University. Ohio's Scripps College of Communication is one of the leading media schools in the United States. Among the five schools in Scripps College are the Scripps School of Journalism and the School of Communication Studies. Undergraduate journalism students at Ohio can concentrate in one of six areas: advertising, broadcast news, magazine journalism, news writing and editing, online journalism, and public relations. The broadcast resources at Ohio are vast. Scripps is home to the WOUB Center for Public Media, which includes five public radio stations, two public television stations, and one cable television station. Each year more than 250 students get hands-on experience working for WOUB stations. Students can also write for the campus daily, the *Post*. Students pursuing the communication studies major can select concentrations in communication and public advocacy, health communication, or organizational communication. For students interested in publication design, photojournalism, or documentary journalism, Ohio offers the BS in visual communication. Ohio alumni prominent in media-related fields include Thom Brennaman (sportscaster), Laurie David (*Huffington Post*), Adam Hochberg (NPR), Peter King (*Sports Illustrated*), Matt Lauer (*Today*), Jay Mariotti (sports writer), Clarence

Page (syndicated columnist), Martin Savidge (CNN), and Brian Unger (History Channel).

University of Southern California. USC's Annenberg School of Communication and Journalism boasts that its location in Los Angeles puts it at the crossroads of media, entertainment, technology and globalization. Annenberg offers undergraduate degree programs in communication, journalism (with specializations in printed digital journalism or broadcast and digital journalism), and public relations. Annenberg students operate campus-based radio and television news programs, edit and report for the *Daily Trojan*, and produce a publication that covers South Los Angeles. For public relations students seeking to gain practical experience, Annenberg runs its own PR firm called Insight Communications. The Annenberg School's extensive study abroad offerings include internships and study opportunities in Amsterdam, Australia, Buenos Aires, China, Dublin, Hong Kong, London, New Zealand, and South Africa. Due to USC's prominence in the media and entertainment industry, Annenberg students make internship and job connections easily. Graduates work for ABC News, Burston Marsteller, CBS, CNN, *Entertainment Weekly*, Fox Searchlight, Lionsgate Entertainment, *Los Angeles Times*, Nielson Entertainment, *People* magazine, Saatchi & Saatchi, Turner Sports, and Warner Bros. One graduate even found work as a publicist for Los Angeles Lakers star Kobe Bryant. Other successful USC media alumni include Art Buchwald (legendary columnist), Julie Chen (*The Talk*), Joe Sheehan (sportswriter), and Lindsey Soto (NFL Network).

Syracuse University. The Newhouse School of Public Communications at Syracuse is a recognized leader. Scores of its graduates hold prominent positions. Examples include Michael Barkann (Comcast Sportsnet), Contessa Brewer (MSNBC), Bob Costas (NBC), Craig Carton (WFAN), Steve Kroft (*60 Minutes*), Jeanne Moos

(CNN), Fred Silverman (former president of ABC television), Robin Toner (*New York Times*), and ESPN sportscasters Sean McDonough, Jayson Stark, and Mike Tirico. Of the 2,040 students at Newhouse, the vast majority (1,800) are undergraduates pursuing BS degrees in advertising; broadcast and digital journalism; graphic design; magazine, newspaper and online journalism; photography; public relations; and television-radio-film. Newhouse draws renowned scholars and media attention through its special centers and programs related to television and popular culture, legal reporting, religion and media, digital literacy, and political reporting. Numerous advertising agencies, broadcast and print media organizations, and public relations firms send recruiters to Newhouse. The 250,000- square-foot, three-building complex at Newhouse (a campus unto itself) includes darkrooms, photo printing studios, more than two dozen video and audio editing booths, three music recording and sound production studios, a master control room, and two television studios (including one that has a set where students produce newscasts). Due to its prominence, Newhouse is one of the more difficult schools to gain admission to at Syracuse. Each year Newhouse receives approximately 4,000 applications for a first-year class of 350 students.

University of Texas. The large and diverse College of Communication at Texas offers top-rated programs and a location in the creative city of Austin. Students at Texas can earn degrees in advertising, communication studies, journalism, public relations, or radio-television-film. Advertising and public relations are especially popular programs at Texas. Within advertising, students can specialize in creative or media. Communication studies students can specialize in corporate communication, human relations (interpersonal communication), or political communication. A two-week New York City seminar enables students to connect to leading professionals (including alumni) in advertising, media, and public relations firms. Radio-television-film students have internship opportunities through the UT in Los Angeles Program. The College of Communication also offers study away programs in Austria, China, and the Czech Republic. College of Communication facilities include news and broadcast studios, advertising labs, and centers for brand research, interactive advertising, and new media. Future reporters and producers can work on the campus radio and television stations and the *Daily Texan*. Numerous Texas alumni are legends in the history of media including news anchor Walter Cronkite, *Frontline* host Bill Moyers, gossip columnist Liz Smith, and political pundit Paul Begala.

University of Wisconsin at Madison. Wisconsin's School of Journalism and Mass Communication is one of the oldest and most respected schools of its kind in the United States. To ensure small classes and individualized learning, Wisconsin limits entrance to 105 students per year, chosen from roughly 250 applicants. Students at Wisconsin work toward either a BA or BS in journalism or strategic communication. Journalism-track students focus on writing, reporting, editing, and design for print, broadcast media, and new media. Strategic-communication majors focus on advertising, integrated communications, and public relations. Wisconsin also offers a certificate in Japanese professional communication for students interested in Japanese media. To make sure its students have success breaking into the media profession, Wisconsin encourages internships, hosts recruiters, and helps students make connections to alumni networks. Students at Wisconsin can get practical experience writing for the *Daily Cardinal* or *Badger Herald* or working for WSUM, the campus radio station. Wisconsin alumni include Tim Cahill (founder of *Outside* magazine), Jeff Greenfield (political commentator), Arthur Nielson (founder of AC Nielson ratings), Edwin Newman (longtime

NBC reporter), Michelle Norris (National Public Radio), Anthony Shadid (Pulitzer Prize–winning *New York Times* reporter), and Greta Van Susteren (Fox News host).

OTHER NOTEWORTHY JOURNALISM AND COMMUNICATIONS PROGRAMS

- Arizona State University
- University of Colorado, Boulder
- Emerson College
- University of Houston
- Temple University
- Washington and Lee University
- Washington State University

Arizona State University. ASU's Walter Cronkite School of Journalism and Mass Communication requires students to get a broad-based education by taking two-thirds of their courses in liberal arts subjects. Students must also study cultural diversity, ethics, media law, and online media. The Cronkite School offers undergraduate degree programs in broadcast journalism, digital media, print journalism, and public relations. Journalism specializations include business journalism, reporting on Latino communities and culture, sports journalism, and a minor in geography for students interested in broadcast meteorology. Cronkite emphasizes learning by doing through student media, broadcast production, and internships. For example, in 2012, the Cronkite School sent eighteen student correspondents to the Summer Olympics. Sports journalism students cover Major League Baseball spring training, produce radio and television coverage of ASU sporting events, and report on national sports through a daily half-hour television newscast. To give students front-row access to reporting in one of the largest cities in the United States, the Cronkite School is based in downtown Phoenix on a state-of-the-art campus (which houses the university-run public television station and a 744-bed residence hall) located steps away from the *Arizona Republic*, Fox Sports Net, CBS Radio, the *Phoenix Business Journal*, three television stations, and a leading Spanish-language newspaper. Cronkite School students frequently get internships at the *Arizona Republic*, *Bloomberg News*, CNBC, *Houston Chronicle*, *Los Angeles Times*, *MarketWatch*, MSNBC, and Thomson Reuters.

University of Colorado. Students interested in reporting on environmental issues may want to look at the University of Colorado at Boulder's School of Journalism and Mass Communication (JMC). Housed within the JMC at Colorado is the Center for Environmental Journalism (CEJ), which helps journalists deepen their knowledge about the economic, political, and societal aspects of environmental issues. The CEJ also offers a master's degree focused on environmental journalism. On the undergraduate level, the JMC at Colorado offers specialization tracks in advertising, broadcast news, broadcast production, media studies, and news/editorial.

Emerson College Students interested in media fields have an array of choices at Emerson in Boston. Budding journalists can pursue a BS degree in journalism, broadcast journalism, or print and multimedia journalism. With a prime location near the Massachusetts statehouse, Emerson provides ample opportunities to get hands-on media experience. For example, a student group called Emerson Independent Video (EIV) produces a program called *EIV News @ 9* that has won a regional Emmy Award. Emerson's BS degree program in marketing communications offers specialized concentrations in advertising, public relations, data-driven marketing, digital marketing, marketing methods and insights, managing marketing campaigns, marketing campaign practices (creative), and marketing campaign practices (media). For future chiefs of staff and press secretaries to governors and legislators, there is a BS program in political communication. One prominent graduate of Emerson's broadcast journalism program is Maria Menounos of *Access Hollywood*.

University of Houston. Houston's Jack Valenti School of Communication has a large number of specialization options and internships built into its curriculum. Included in the BA degree in communication offerings are concentrations in advertising, corporate communications, health communication, integrated communication, interpersonal communication, journalism, media production, media studies, and public relations.

Temple University. With 3,900 students and eighty full-time professors, Temple has one of the nation's largest schools of communications. Temple offers programs in advertising; broadcasting, telecommunications, and mass media; communication studies; film and media arts; journalism; and strategic communication. Within the broadcasting, telecommunications, and mass media division, students can concentrate on media production, media business and entrepreneurship, media analysis, or emergent media. Advertising students can specialize in art direction, copywriting, management, or advertising research. Strategic communication specialties include organizational leadership, public communication, or public relations. Communications students can study abroad in a Tokyo program focused on Japanese contemporary media and culture, in Dublin to examine the Irish media professions, or for a semester or summer at Temple's London program.

Washington and Lee University. Washington and Lee is a rare small liberal arts college (2,200 students) with a major in journalism and mass communications. Drawing upon the strengths of its School of Commerce, Economics, and Policy, W&L offers a specialization in business journalism and a speaker series that brings reporters to campus from news organizations such as *Consumer Reports*, *Fortune*, Fox Business Network, *Newsweek*, the *New York Times*, and the *Washington Post*. Through the support of the Reynolds Foundation, W&L students get paid summer internships at news organizations such as the *Charlotte Observer*, Dow Jones Newswires, *Forbes*, the *Miami Herald*, and the *Seattle Times*.

Washington State University. The Edward R. Murrow College of Communication at Washington State offers programs in advertising, applied intercultural communication, broadcast news/production, communication and society, journalism, journalism and media production, organizational communication, public relations, and strategic communication. Washington State's communications students get experience working for campus-based radio and television stations, including a public radio affiliate.

COLLEGES FOR ASPIRING WRITERS

The prestige degree for future novelists and poets is the master of fine arts (MFA) in creative writing. The leading MFA program is the Iowa Writer's Workshop at the University of Iowa. Excellent MFA programs are also found at Columbia, Cornell, Indiana, Johns Hopkins, Massachusetts, Michigan, New Hampshire, Oregon, Syracuse, Texas, and Virginia. Strong low-residency MFA programs exist at Bennington, Hollins, Vermont College, and Warren Wilson. But aspiring writers do not have to wait for graduate school to study writing. A number of colleges offer an undergraduate major in creative writing or writing. Among the many options out there, several offer a creative thesis or capstone project, meaning that the student may write a novel, collection of short stories, or a play for credit. Most of the creative writing and writing majors are part of (or closely linked to) an English Department. There are some writing programs (seemingly modeled after MFA programs) that offer a BFA degree (for example, Bowling Green) and stand-alone BA programs, such as the creative writing major at Oberlin.

Still, getting into a creative writing program can pose a challenge. Because most creative writing departments are small and built on high levels of personal attention, entry into them is often competitive, and available slots are usually capped. Applicants with an interest in creative writing need to understand that there is no guarantee that a program will accept them once they enroll at the college. Entry into the creative writing major generally requires the submission of writing samples. Many colleges require completion of one or two creative writing classes as the basis for selection into the program. In such cases, only the most promising students in those prerequisite classes are chosen to be majors in creative writing. This gets to the essential paradox that plagues creative writing programs. Entry into courses, even the introductory ones, tends to be capped, which means that students may get shut out of the very classes they need for selection into the creative writing major. This issue is something that potential creative writing students need to investigate closely when looking at colleges.

➤ WHERE TO MAJOR IN CREATIVE WRITING OR WRITING

Agnes Scott College	Drury University	Purdue University
University of Arizona	Eckerd College	Pratt Institute
Ball State University	Emerson College (BA and BFA)	Princeton University
Beloit College	Emory University	Purchase College—SUNY
Bowling Green University (BFA)	George Washington University	University of Redlands
Brandeis University	Hamilton College	Roger Williams University (BFA)
University of British Columbia (BFA)	Hamline University (BFA)	Saint Mary's College (Indiana)
Brooklyn College (BFA)	College of Idaho	Saint Olaf College
University of California at Riverside	University of Illinois	Savannah College of Art and Design
Carnegie Mellon University	Ithaca College	Southern Methodist University
Chapman University (BFA)	Johns Hopkins University	Southern Oregon University
Chatham University (BFA)	Knox College	Stephens College (BFA)
Coe College	University of Maine at Farmington (BFA)	Steven F. Austin University (BFA)
Colby Sawyer College	Miami University	Susquehanna University
Columbia College of Chicago	Minnesota State University (BA, BFA, BS)	Sweet Briar College
Columbia University (School of the Arts)	Murray State University (BA/BFA)	Truman State University (BFA)
Converse College (BA and BFA)	Oberlin College	Valparaiso University
DePauw University	Ohio University	Wayne State University
Drake University	Pepperdine University	

University of Arizona. The creative writing major at Arizona is in the English Department. Along the way to developing their own individual voices, creative writing students at Arizona take classes and workshops in fiction writing, poetry, and nonfiction. Arizona also runs a Poetry Center and a respected MFA program.

Bowling Green State University. Every student in the creative writing program at Bowling Green in Ohio completes a BFA thesis that gets presented through a graduation readings series. Creative writing majors at BGSU have the option to live on campus in a special living/learning community (the residential Arts Village) for students pursuing art, dance, music, and theater. Adding to the literary atmosphere and prestige of Bowling Green's creative writing program is the *Mid-American Review*, a forum for fiction, nonfiction, and poetry, published by the English Department. The website describing BGSU's creative writing program has several pages listing the published writers who have graduated from the program.

University of British Columbia. UBC is a rare public institution that offers the BFA in creative writing. Students do not enter the program as freshmen but rather as juniors after two years of study. With fifty students and fifteen faculty members, the creative writing program at UBC has a student-faculty ratio that enables guided study and workshop classes throughout. Each student must take intensive workshops in three of the nine genre areas: creative nonfiction, fiction, libretto, poetry, screenwriting or song lyrics, stage play, translation, writing for children, and writing for radio. Admission to the program requires a portfolio.

Carnegie Mellon University. Home to one of the nation's oldest and most established creative writing majors, Carnegie Mellon also gives students the opportunity to earn a BA in professional writing or a BS in technical writing. The technical and professional writing programs draw on CMU's prominence in the arts and technology and strong record in career preparation. The capstone project at CMU gives creative writing majors an opportunity to complete a novel, book of poems, screenplay, or short story collection. Other writing opportunities are available through numerous student publications, such as the *Tartan* and the *Oakland Review*.

Chapman University. The BFA program in creative writing at Chapman combines a foundation in literature with writing workshops that develop each student's talent. That Chapman has the highly ranked Dodge College of Film and Media Arts (offering a BFA in screenwriting) makes it an excellent place for students interested in exploring potential careers writing for stage and screen.

Coe College. For aspiring writers, Coe offers two pathways: a major in creative writing through the English Department or a major in writing in the Rhetoric Department. The creative writing major (which includes courses in fiction, poetry, and playwriting) must be taken in conjunction with another major offered at Coe. The writing major offers concentrations in nonfiction (including creative nonfiction), journalism, or technical writing. Coe helps students arrange writing and publishing internships in Chicago, New York, and Washington, DC. There are five publications on campus that publish student writing. Because the famed Iowa Writer's Workshop is located just twenty-five miles away, Coe draws numerous visiting writers to campus annually.

Columbia College of Chicago. The Fiction Writing Department at Chicago's Columbia College is something of a misnomer. Although the major at Columbia is called fiction writing, students in the department can also specialize in nonfiction writing or playwriting. Students at Columbia run a widely admired Publishing Lab whose motto is "Where Stories Find Homes." The department also operates an award-winning anthology (*Hair Trigger*), a science-fiction journal (*Spec-Lit*), and a journal devoted to novels in progress (*F Magazine*). For students interested in writing for the film industry, Columbia College offers a semester in Los Angeles.

Columbia University. The undergraduate creative writing major at Columbia is a rarity for an Ivy League university. Students in Columbia's program can focus their work on fiction, nonfiction, or poetry. As seniors, creative writing students get to take workshop seminars taught by graduate program faculty members.

Emerson College. At Emerson in Boston, students can major in writing, literature, and publishing (WLP). With six hundred students, Emerson's WLP program is expansive enough to meet the needs of students intending to pursue fields related to writing, publishing, or teaching.

Emory University. Emory offers a major and a minor in creative writing as well as a double major in creative writing and playwriting. Students apply to the program after taking at least one writing course at Emory. Once in the program, all creative writing majors must complete five writing workshops before focusing their individual interests on genres such as creative nonfiction, fiction, playwriting, poetry, and screenwriting. Emory's Creative Writing Honors Program enables senior projects, such as a collection of stories, poetry, essays, a novella, a play, or a screenplay.

Ithaca College. The writing program at Ithaca is broad and flexible. On their way to a BA in writing, students at Ithaca can concentrate on creative writing, feature writing, nonfiction, or professional writing. Ithaca's writing program runs monthly faculty-student readings and helps students get internships in publishing, journalism, and public relations.

Johns Hopkins University. For more than sixty years, Hopkins has offered an undergraduate degree in writing through its Writing Seminars Program. Over the years, numerous literary luminaries have taught in the program, including Russell Baker, John Barth (alumnus), J. M. Coetzee, Howard Nemerov, Edna O'Brien, Robert Stone, and Gary Wills. Students in the writing seminars major at Hopkins can concentrate on fiction, poetry, or generalist writing en route to a BA degree.

Knox College. In the west Illinois town of Galesburg, a small liberal arts college (Knox) is becoming a giant in the literary world. Graduates of the Knox Creative Writing Program have won the Pulitzer Prize, the American Book Award, and Tony and Emmy awards. There are a number of on-campus outlets for student work, including an award-winning literary journal and online journals for science fiction and fantasy, children's literature, and general fiction and nonfiction. Among the dozen members of the Associated Colleges of the Midwest (ACM), Knox leads in the number of student winners of the ACM's Nick Adams Short Story Contest.

Oberlin College. Since 1975 the Creative Writing Program at Oberlin has graduated roughly five hundred students, many of whom have entered leading graduate writing programs at places such as Brown, Columbia, Iowa, Texas, and Virginia. The twenty to thirty creative writing majors in each graduating class have six genres open to them: fiction, poetry, drama, nonfiction, translation, and screenwriting. Poetry is a particular strength at Oberlin. Faculty and students in the creative writing and English departments operate the poetry journal *Field* and the Oberlin College Press, which publishes collections by emerging and established poets. For a small school, Oberlin has graduated an unusually large number of respected writers, including Ishmael Beah, Tracy Chevalier, Myla

Goldberg, William Goldman, James McBride, Peggy Orenstein, Domenica Ruta, and Gary Shteyngart.

Princeton University. There are two ways to study creative writing at Princeton: the concentration in creative writing (through the English Department) or (for non-English majors) the certificate in creative writing. Whichever route students choose, with fifteen practicing writers teaching the courses, the resources at Princeton are vast. Current and past writing instructors at Princeton have included Chang-Rae Lee, Toni Morrison, Joyce Carol Oates, Philip Roth, and Edmund White. Princeton creative writing classes follow the workshop format and average

eight to ten students. Seniors work individually with a mentor professor on a creative thesis, which may consist of a novel, collection of short stories or poetry, or translations.

Purdue University. Aspiring writers should not overlook Purdue simply because it is best known for science and engineering. Purdue, some might be surprised to discover, offers majors in creative writing and in professional writing. Creative writing majors can focus on poetry, fiction, or drama. Purdue's professional writing major, with tracks in technical writing or writing and publishing, is particularly strong at preparing students for work in digital publishing, multimedia, and emerging communications technologies.

➤ COLLEGES WITH A CONCENTRATION OR TRACK IN WRITING

Some of the colleges with a concentration, track, or an emphasis in creative writing (often through the English Department) are listed and profiled below.

Boston College	Franklin and Marshall College	University of Pittsburgh
Brown University	Goucher College	Reed College
Bucknell University	Hollins University	University of Rochester
University of California at Los Angeles (UCLA)	Indiana University	San Francisco State University
University of California at Santa Cruz	University of Iowa	University of Southern California
Case Western Reserve University	James Madison University	Stanford University
College of Charleston	University of Kansas	Swarthmore College
University of Cincinnati	Kenyon College	Tufts University
Clemson University	Lewis and Clark College	Tulane University
Colgate University	Macalester College	Trinity College (CT)
University of Colorado Boulder	University of Massachusetts	Vanderbilt University
Connecticut College	University of Miami	University of Virginia
Denison University	University of Michigan	University of Washington
University of Denver	Michigan State University	Wesleyan University
DePaul University	University of Nebraska at Lincoln	University of Wisconsin
Elon University	North Carolina State University	Yale University
Florida State University	University of Pennsylvania	
	Penn State University	

Brown University. At Brown, students complete concentrations rather than majors. Within its highly rated English Department, Brown offers selected students the option to pursue a track in nonfiction writing. The nonfiction writing offerings at Brown include journalism, creative nonfiction, criticism, and essay writing. With permission, students can take fiction and poetry writing classes through Brown's graduate creative writing program.

University of California at Santa Cruz. At Santa Cruz, the creative writing program is a concentration housed in the literature major. Students apply to the creative writing concentration after taking one lower-division creative writing workshop. Graduates of the UCSC creative writing concentration have strong track records at gaining admission to prestigious graduate programs at Arizona, Brown, Columbia, and Iowa.

Clemson University. Although well-known for its programs in agriculture, engineering, and science, Clemson offers an impressive breadth of writing options within its English Department. English majors at Clemson can concentrate on creative writing and pursue a specialized focus on drama, fiction, or poetry. The English major also offers concentrations in film and screenwriting and professional writing through a program called Writing and Publication Studies. Each April, the Clemson Literary Festival draws acclaimed writers to campus for readings, discussions, and seminars.

Colgate University. Colgate English majors can choose an emphasis in creative writing. The writing courses at Colgate are workshop oriented, and selected high-achieving students can spend part of their senior year working on a creative writing honors project.

Goucher College. Students looking for a small college with a strong writing program may want to consider Goucher's creative writing concentration under the English major. Goucher's Kratz Center for Creative Writing, codirected by acclaimed novelist Madison Smartt Bell, annually brings well-known writers—such as Sherman Alexie, the late Seamus Heaney, and David Guterson—to campus for lectures, semester-long residencies, readings, and classroom consultations with student writers. The Kratz Center also provides summer writing fellowships to students. Goucher alumni who have been published include Jenn Crowell, John McManus, Darcey Steinke, and Eleanor Wilner.

Hollins University. Hollins offers extraordinary resources to aspiring writers. With a leading MFA program and an undergraduate creative writing concentration in its English Department, Hollins has produced scores of published writers, including Margaret Wise Brown, Annie Dillard, and Lee Smith. Through Hollins's Jackson Center for Creative Writing, a select group of English majors can pursue a concentration in creative writing. Student writers can publish their fiction or poetry in the student literary journal (*Cargoes*) or a student periodical called *The Album*. In addition, Hollins students can spend a semester (the Rubin Writing Semester) focused intensively on their writing.

University of Iowa. The University of Iowa is home to America's most heralded graduate program in writing. From Raymond Carver and Jane Smiley to Wallace Stegner and John Edgar Wideman, countless acclaimed writers have studied at the Iowa Writer's Workshop. For undergraduates at Iowa, there are two routes for the study of writing. The first is through the English Department's track in creative writing, which enables a selected group of students to take classes in fiction, poetry, nonfiction, playwriting, and translation. Students apply to the creative writing track not as high school seniors but after enrolling and taking freshman and sophomore courses at Iowa. Getting in requires an application, including a writing sample. The less formal route to studying creative writing involves selecting among the seven to eight Writer's Workshop courses made available to Iowa undergraduates.

Kenyon College. In the last century, the small town of Gambier, Ohio, has had an outsized impact on the literary world through the accomplishments of Kenyon graduates and the influence of the *Kenyon Review*. Literary alumni of Kenyon include E. L. Doctorow, William Gass, Randall Jarrell, Robert Lowell, and Peter Taylor. Students at Kenyon can choose a creative writing emphasis within the English major; take courses in fiction, poetry, and creative nonfiction writing; and attend the vigorous visiting writer series. In addition, students can get internships with the *Kenyon Review* and have their work published in several campus literary journals.

University of Massachusetts. The English Department at the University of Massachusetts at Amherst offers specializations in creative writing, nonfiction writing, and professional writing and technical communication. The nonfiction writing classes at UMass encompass article and essay writing, creative nonfiction, commercial publishing, and writing for emerging technologies. Professional writing and technical communication students at UMass have a 100 percent job placement rate due to a strong co-op and internship program that provides professional experience along the way to graduation. UMass also has an acclaimed MFA Program for Poets and Writers.

University of Pennsylvania. At Penn, aspiring writers have an array of options and resources. English majors can choose an emphasis on creative writing or a minor in journalistic writing. The ninety to one hundred students concentrating on writing at Penn can take classes and workshops in fiction, poetry, nonfiction, screenwriting, playwriting, journalism, review writing, and writing for children. Supporting Penn's creative writing and journalistic writing programs is the Kelly Writer's House, where students take seminar classes with and attend readings by eminent writers. Penn also sponsors a number of writing contests and prizes open to undergraduate work in poetry, fiction, playwriting, translation, journalism, nonfiction, and review writing. Penn alumni include Jennifer Egan, Joe Klein, Lisa Scottoline, Martin Cruz Smith, and William Carlos Williams.

San Francisco State University. Within its English Department, San Francisco State offers a concentration in creative writing, with courses in fiction, playwriting, and poetry. San Francisco State also offers the MFA in creative writing.

Stanford University. In the writing world, Stanford commands respect for its Stegner Fellowship and its graduate program in creative writing. The presence of Stegner Fellows, graduate writing students, and frequent visiting writers creates a dynamic literary atmosphere at Stanford. Undergraduates with an interest in writing can elect a creative writing emphasis within the English major or pursue creative writing as a minor. Stanford offers courses in fiction writing, creative nonfiction, short story writing, the graphic novel, and the process of adapting fiction into film.

University of Virginia. Virginia is home to a top-ranked MFA in creative writing program and one of the best English departments in the United States. Although there is no undergraduate creative writing major at UVA, students majoring in English can elect a specialization in poetry writing. To gain entry into UVA's area program in poetry writing, students apply as rising juniors. In the program, students take poetry-writing seminars and are encouraged to create—through a senior capstone course—a collection of original poems.

Yale University. Yale is known as one of the top places in the world to study English and as a school that graduates strong writers. Yale students have won national writing competitions at a rate higher than any other college in the United States. Each year some of the world's most acclaimed writers come to Yale for readings, classroom visits, and seminars. English majors at Yale can choose a writing concentration but must apply (as juniors or seniors) for entry into the program. Students in the writing concentration get to work on a senior project in which they produce a collection of stories, novellas, a novel, or a play.

MUSIC

For the student seeking a degree in music performance, two considerations stand above all others: (1) the quality of instruction in the student's chosen instrument; and (2) the audition. Unlike most students who assemble a list of college choices weighing a combination of factors, music students zero in on one: the expertise and prestige of the teachers in the student's instrument or academic discipline. Studying music is like an apprenticeship, where the apprentice learns from the master. Evidence of this is on display in programs for classical concerts, in which the thumbnail biographies list the teachers under whom the musicians studied and the colleges where they earned their degrees. In the music school world, it is not unusual for students to pick up and follow a teacher from one music school to another.

The most talented and serious students who want to major in music performance tend to apply to music schools where the linchpin of the evaluation process is the audition. In music, high school grades, standardized test scores, and essays take a back seat to the audition. Auditions typically occur on campus, often under the evaluative eye of the professor whose studio the applicant is seeking to enter. Auditions are sometimes available in the city where the student lives, in a nearby city, or remotely via video or audio.

When planning their auditions, music applicants need to know something conservatory insiders know: it is best to audition in person on campus. The authors know this from their experience working in admissions at Oberlin College alongside staff familiar with the music application processes at the Oberlin Conservatory and other leading music schools such as Eastman, Indiana, Lawrence, and Northwestern. That experience made it clear that music schools tend to give an edge to applicants who audition on campus. Why? Because music schools (even in this technological age) still emphasize live performance skills, which are best seen in person. When music teachers see and hear extraordinarily talented students at auditions, they frequently begin recruiting them for their particular studio. In contrast, at most regional auditions, the student performs for an admission staffer and whichever faculty member has come along. There is no guarantee that the professor the student seeks to study under will be at the regional audition. Thus, for a student whose heart is set on attending a particular music school and studying under a particular teacher, the on-campus audition is a must.

Students whose interest in music schools is primarily driven by the strength of a particular program or performance area follow a relatively straightforward process. They look for suitable faculty in their area of interest, audition for each one, and choose the best studio to which they gain entry. At the point of choosing between music schools, another variable can play a significant role: finances. Many music students choose the best studio that gives them an attractive scholarship. Music schools compete strenuously to land the best students, and scholarship dollars are a key weapon in that competition. Music schools tend to offer the largest scholarships to the applicants they most want to enroll. The applicant talent pool varies from school to school. A student who earns an average audition score at Juilliard might be deemed exceptional by a good, but less competitive, music school like the Manhattan School of Music. As a result, Manhattan may offer that student an attractive scholarship, while Juilliard might not even offer admission.

MUSIC SCHOOLS: IS IT ALL ABOUT THE RANKINGS?

There is a definite pecking order in the music school world. Virtually everyone teaching in college music departments knows of the top twenty to twenty-five music schools and has either studied at or applied to one or more of them. The rank within the pecking order fluctuates slightly, but the names of the top twenty to twenty-five music programs remain relatively constant. Topping most lists are two institutions: Curtis and Juilliard. The Curtis Institute of Music in Philadelphia is very small. Few are chosen to enter Curtis, and those called rarely refuse. Turning down Curtis is rare not just because it represents the gold standard among conservatories but also because every student at Curtis gets a full scholarship, regardless of financial need. The yearly value of the scholarship is $36,500. Right next to Curtis in quality—and perhaps better known beyond music insiders—is the Juilliard School of Music in New York City. As with Curtis, few offered admission to Juilliard turn it down. Those who spurn Juilliard tend to do so for a full scholarship elsewhere or to study with a particular teacher in a performance area that is deemed equally outstanding elsewhere.

CURTIS INSTITUTE OF MUSIC

At Curtis, 165 exceptionally gifted young musicians get personalized attention from faculty members who themselves are distinguished musicians. Curtis takes a learn-by-doing approach. In addition to private lesson study, repertoire classes, and chamber music coaching, all Curtis students take courses in musical studies, career development, and liberal arts. Located in the arts district of Philadelphia, the Curtis campus is a cluster of historic mansions right next door to the Kimmel Center (home of the Philadelphia Orchestra) and the Academy of Music. Recent construction expanded the residence facilities, rehearsal areas, instrument storage space, commons areas, and technology available to Curtis students and faculty.

The bachelor of music (BM) program at Curtis offers majors in composition, conducting, keyboards, guitar, orchestral instruments, and voice. Admission to Curtis is based more on evidence of talent than on the degree of proficiency already attained. Curtis seeks to enroll students whose inherent musical gift shows promise of development to a point of exceptional professional quality. All applicants to Curtis must audition in person. Neither video nor audio recordings will be accepted—except for vocal studies applicants intending to concentrate on voice or opera. Prospective composition students must submit original compositions. Annual audition days are held at Curtis, and prospective students must make one of those days work with their schedule.

Students at Curtis do not pay tuition. Everyone admitted receives a full tuition scholarship (estimated at $37,600 annually). But Curtis is not free. Curtis students are expected to pay for fees and living expenses, which total approximately $23,000 annually. Curtis has a generous financial-aid program that makes it possible for lower-income students to attend. Once financial aid is factored in, the net annual price of Curtis tends to be much lower than $23,000.

THE JUILLIARD SCHOOL

Although its name is synonymous with music, Juilliard is more than a music school. Juilliard is a performing arts school of approximately 2,500 students, with programs in dance, drama, and music. Juilliard aims to enroll the most talented budding performing artists from around the world and shape the future of performing arts. Juilliard alumni have received hundreds of the most prestigious accolades in the performing arts including 105 Grammy Awards, sixty-two Tony Awards, forty-seven Emmy Awards, twenty-six Bessie Awards, twenty-four Academy Awards, sixteen Pulitzer Prizes, and twelve National Medals for the Arts.

The extraordinary facilities at Juilliard include 253 Steinway pianos (the largest such collection at any institution in the world), 200 stringed instruments available to students (including two Stradivari violins and a cello), four performance spaces with seating for 100 or more, and extensive special collections that include 73,000 scores, 25,000 sound recordings, and 138 composer autographs and annotated first editions. The numerous ensembles in residence, such as the Juilliard String Quartet, the American Brass Quintet, the New York Woodwind Quintet, and the Juilliard Baroque are complemented by the music community in New York City.

The Music Division at Juilliard enrolls six hundred students from more than forty countries. Undergraduate music students can pursue study in nineteen different (but primarily classical) musical areas. Juilliard also offers jazz and electronic music. Juilliard jazz students perform all over the world—including at Italy's Spoleto Festival and at the New Orleans Jazz and Heritage Festival. For its music technology students, Juilliard offers the Electric Ensemble student group, an annual electronic music and multimedia festival called Beyond the Machine, and a Music Technology Center that includes recording, rehearsal, and composition studios, and spaces for interdisciplinary collaborations with the dance and drama departments.

Admission to Juilliard is ultraselective. Fewer than 8 percent of applicants get admitted. All applicants to undergraduate programs must submit a prescreening CD or cassette tape. Composition majors must also pass an on-campus exam and interview. Applicants who successfully pass the prescreening are selected for on-campus auditions. Note: Juilliard does not accept video auditions in lieu of a live audition. Each year, Juilliard schedules a week when auditions take place. Dates for auditions and details regarding the prescreening and the required audition repertoire are spelled out on Juilliard's admissions website.

OUTSTANDING CHOICES BEYOND CURTIS AND JUILLIARD

Beyond Curtis and Juilliard are ten to twenty-five other excellent music schools and conservatories that offer strength across music performance, music theory, and music history. Some departments at these schools rank among the best in the country. In alphabetic order, the following music programs are consistently ranked in the top twenty to twenty-five by people in the know.

- Berklee College of Music
- Carnegie Mellon University School of Music
- University of Cincinnati Conservatory of Music

- Cleveland Institute of Music
- University of Hartford (Hartt School of Music)
- Indiana University (Jacobs School of Music)
- Johns Hopkins University (Peabody Conservatory of Music)
- Manhattan School of Music
- University of Michigan School of Music
- New England Conservatory of Music
- Northwestern University (Bienen School of Music)

- Oberlin College (Oberlin Conservatory of Music)
- Rice University (Shepherd School of Music)
- University of Rochester (Eastman School of Music)

CARNEGIE MELLON UNIVERSITY

Carnegie Mellon is a rare university that strives for excellence in technology and the arts. The School of Music at CMU balances classical with contemporary music styles and blends traditional performance with modern technologies. CMU's music school provides a relatively small number of students (350) with extensive degree offerings and facilities, and its intimate size makes it possible for every student to perform in an orchestra, chorus, wind ensemble, or chamber group.

Carnegie Mellon offers BFA degrees in composition and performance (in every orchestral instrument plus guitar, euphonium, saxophone, and bagpipes), BS degrees in music and technology, and innovative intercollegiate BXA programs in music technology and musicology. As seniors, CMU composition majors compose an orchestral piece for recording and performance by the Carnegie Mellon Philharmonic. Annually, the Pittsburgh Symphony Orchestra presents a public reading of orchestral pieces composed by CMU students. Vocal performance at CMU is geared toward solo classical performance and opera. Each year there are two fully staged operas with an orchestra. Musical theater is offered in the School of Drama. The BS program in music and technology is jointly offered by the School of Music, the School of Computer Science, and the Carnegie Institute of Technology. Music facilities at CMU include seventy-eight Steinway pianos, ten performance spaces/rehearsal halls, five recording and electronic music studios, and webcasting facilities.

All candidates for degrees in performance must complete an audition. Applicants to the programs in composition, flute, music and technology, piano, violin, and voice must also undergo a prescreening. Live auditions (offered on campus and in New York and Asia) are preferred over video and audio auditions. Some programs not requiring an audition or a prescreening require an interview or portfolio review.

UNIVERSITY OF CINCINNATI

Cincinnati's College Conservatory of Music (CCM) is a distinguished school of international acclaim. CCM offers students a professional conservatory education within a public research university of 35,000 students. CCM's voice, conducting, composition, orchestral, and musical theater programs are ranked among the best in the United States. Roughly 800 of the 1,500 music students at Cincinnati are undergraduates getting one-on-one instruction from faculty members respected for their talents as teachers and performers.

Cincinnati's comprehensive array of undergraduate programs in music is organized into eight specialty areas: electronic media; ensembles and conducting; keyboard studies; music education; opera, musical theater, drama, and arts administration; performance studies; and composition, musicology, and theory. Students in Cincinnati's highly acclaimed voice program have access to master classes with visiting artists and opera scene workshops. In addition to mounting six full-length opera productions annually, CCM collaborates with the Cincinnati Opera through a new works initiative. With twelve jazz faculty members as well as numerous visiting artists, CCM offers jazz performance as a concentration plus the option to pursue a double major in music education and jazz.

Musical productions at CCM make use of an 8,500-square-foot scene shop and a 3,000-square-foot costume shop. CCM students learn in so-called smart classrooms and create musical and artistic works in a sound design studio, a computer music studio, recording and digital editing studios, a vocal music laboratory, and a lighting laboratory. There are also two hundred pianos, eight harpsichords, and seven pipe organs. CCM's dozen-plus musical groups offer nearly one thousand recitals, concerts, and musical performances annually. The Student Artist Program helps CCM students find solo and chamber music performance opportunities in metro Cincinnati.

Applicants to CCM do not have to apply separately to the University of Cincinnati, but they must audition either on campus or at regional sites. Prescreening recordings must be completed by applicants to certain programs, such as flute and voice. Cincinnati does accept recorded auditions, but applicants should make sure their intended area of study accepts them. Scholarships at CCM are talent based and made according to faculty recommendations.

CLEVELAND INSTITUTE OF MUSIC

The Cleveland Institute of Music (CIM) is a top-tier conservatory located in an arts and culture district called University Circle. Within walking distance of CIM are Case Western Reserve University, the Cleveland Institute of Art and Museum of Art, and Severance Hall, home of the Cleveland Orchestra. CIM's location provides resources and opportunities normally found at larger schools. CIM is a classically based, performance-oriented conservatory with no programs in jazz or music education. Nearly forty members of the Cleveland Orchestra teach at CIM. With just 450 college division students (60 percent of them undergraduates), CIM is an intimate place. Despite its small size, CIM has large reach. International students comprise 25 percent of the students.

Facilities at CIM reflect its top-tier status. Two concert halls seat more than 250, including 500-seat Kulas Hall. Other facilities include studios for digital recording and CD production.

Annually, CIM presents more than one hundred concerts and recitals, including two fully staged and costumed operas and five performances in Cleveland's Severance Hall.

CIM offers two undergraduate degree programs: a BM and the five-year dual degree (BM/BA or BM/BS) in cooperation with Case Western Reserve University. Applicants to the dual degree program apply solely to CIM. CIM students interested in participating in exchange programs may study in Canada at the University of Montreal, in Paris at the Conservatoire de Paris, or in England at the Royal Academy of Music or at the Royal Northern College of Music.

CIM accepts recorded auditions, but students who audition on campus have higher acceptance rates. CIM does not offer regional auditions. Applicants to the composition and audio programs must submit a video recording that demonstrates proficiency on an instrument. CIM requires standardized test scores (either ACT or SAT) and a high school transcript. All applicants are considered for talent-based scholarships.

UNIVERSITY OF HARTFORD

The Hartt School of Music is a division of the University of Hartford, a school with 7,300 students. Hartt, which enrolls 645 undergraduate students in music, dance, and theater, devotes considerable financial resources to attracting students. Performing Arts Scholarships, held by nearly 90 percent of the students, range from $6,000 to full tuition.

At Hartt 80 percent of the courses are taken within the student's specific major while the other 20 percent are electives. In addition to performance degrees in voice, orchestral instruments, jazz, and organ, Hartt offers programs in composition, music education, music history, music theater, and music theory. The Hartt curriculum ranges further than most music schools, giving students the option to concentrate in music management, music production and technology, and acoustical engineering. Hartt has performance venues in three different campus buildings—the largest seats 750—as well as a recording studio, music production and technology facilities, and scene and costume labs. Hartt's more than twenty performance ensembles annually stage more than four hundred recitals, productions, and instrumental and vocal concerts. Hartt students also have opportunities to perform with the Hartford Symphony Orchestra.

Hartt applicants must meet minimum academic qualifications: B average in high school and 19 ACT, or 920 (CR plus M) SAT. The crux of the application to Hartt is the audition. All music applicants must audition and interview. On their audition day, applicants take three tests: (1) the undergraduate music theory placement test; (2) the music aptitude profile test; and (3) the musicianship test for vocal applicants. Applicants who live three hundred miles or more from Hartford can submit recorded auditions.

INDIANA UNIVERSITY

One of the largest music schools in the United States, the Jacobs School of Music enrolls 1,600 students, half of whom are undergraduates. Students at Jacobs study privately with 180 resident faculty members who are renowned performers, scholars, and teachers. Historically, the Jacobs School has been a place of significance. In 1942 the Metropolitan Opera of New York began fifteen consecutive years of presenting two operas per year on the Indiana campus. In 1980, the School of Music began the Music from Indiana series, now nationally syndicated on American Public Radio. In 1982 Leonard Bernstein wrote his final opera during a residency at Indiana. Subsequently, the Bernstein family donated the entire contents of his recording studio to the Jacobs School.

Located in the heart of the picturesque Indiana campus, the Jacobs School has a complex of five buildings housing two hundred practice rooms, three large performance halls, seven recording studios, and two electronic labs. With nearly twenty BM degree programs and a handful of BS programs, Jacobs offers specialized study in music performance, composition, music education, and recording arts. Jacobs is a recognized world leader for opera, voice, and orchestral conducting. Indiana's strength in opera owes to excellent faculty, talented students, and superb facilities for performance. The Musical Arts Center at Indiana houses an opera theater with European-style seating for 1,460 and has room for a hundred-piece orchestra. The Musical Arts Center's opera stage is often compared to the Metropolitan Opera House in New York. Top musicians and scholars visit Jacobs annually to give master classes, deliver guest lectures, and conduct operas and orchestras. Alumni of the Jacobs School include the renowned violinist Joshua Bell and conductor Leonard Slatkin.

The two dozen performance ensembles at Indiana span a broad range of musical styles from classical to jazz to new music to Latin American pop music. Jacobs School ensembles include thirteen choirs, eight bands (including four for jazz), and six orchestras. The number of performances at Indiana is extraordinary—nearly 1,100 annually, including seven fully staged operas.

The audition is central to the Jacobs admission process. Jacobs offers several on-campus audition weekends and accepts recorded auditions from applicants who cannot get to campus. All applicants must also meet Indiana's academic requirements for freshman admission. Jacobs provides merit scholarships based on a combination of talent, academic achievement, and departmental need.

JOHNS HOPKINS UNIVERSITY

For nearly thirty-five years, the Peabody Institute has been a division of Johns Hopkins University.

Students at Peabody have access to virtually all the opportunities and activities on JHU's campus and receive a Hopkins degree. Peabody offers BM degrees in performance, composition, and music education. Special programs include a double degree in performance recording and electrical engineering as well as a five-year BM/MM option. Peabody is a focused rather than a comprehensive school, which means there are no undergraduate degree programs in accompanying, church music, conducting, early music, ethnomusicology, music industry/arts administration, musical theater, music therapy, or pedagogy.

One distinctive program at Peabody, called recording arts and sciences, gives students an applied performance education along with technical instruction in recording technology. Students in the program complete an internship with recording studios, local radio or television stations, or recording companies. The Peabody jazz program is performance oriented and involves weekly one-on-one tutorials, improvisation workshops, and master classes with renowned visiting artists. Music education students get a four-part education that includes courses in the liberal arts, experience on several musical instruments, instruction related to child development, and a supervised teaching practicum. The music ensembles at Peabody have a distinguished history. The Peabody Symphony Orchestra has premiered countless new works and has performed at the Kennedy Center in Washington, Lincoln Center in New York, and Tchaikovsky Hall in Moscow. Notable Peabody alumni include pianist Andre Watts.

Peabody applicants who audition in person (either on campus or at a regional site) have a slight advantage over those who send in recordings. Peabody accepts recorded auditions from applicants who live outside the continental United States, more than three hundred miles west of campus, or more than 150 miles north or south of campus. Composition applicants must submit a portfolio for prescreening, and voice applicants must submit a recording for prescreening. Peabody strongly prefers applicants with at minimum a 3.0 high school grade average and 530 in critical reading and 480 in math on the SAT. Merit scholarships are offered to the most talented applicants.

MANHATTAN SCHOOL OF MUSIC

Located on New York's Upper West Side, the Manhattan School of Music (MSM) is rooted in excellence and access. MSM's original mission, when it opened in 1917, was to provide high-quality musical training to New York's immigrant communities. As it has developed, MSM has become one of America's premier music schools. A special strength of MSM is its faculty—many perform with famed musical institutions such as the New York Philharmonic, the Metropolitan Opera, the New York City Opera, the Chamber Music Society of Lincoln Center, the Orpheus Chamber Orchestra, and the Lincoln Center Jazz Orchestra.

MSM offers performance-based BM degree programs, twenty in classical and twelve in jazz. Among the approximately four hundred undergraduates at MSM, the majority study classical music. MSM does not offer double majors or degree programs in audio recording, electronic music, or musical theater. Students at MSM may cross register for classes at nearby Barnard College. At the master's level, MSM offers a joint degree in music education with Teachers College of Columbia University. One standout feature of MSM is its Center for Music Entrepreneurship (CME). The CME brings in panels of music industry professionals for presentations, helps students get internships, provides recording services, and runs seminars that connect students with professional career mentors.

The MSM campus includes a residence hall for 550 students, a dining hall, practice and performance spaces, a jewel-box theater, a recording studio, and four large recital halls, including an auditorium for full-scale opera and orchestral productions. Annually at MSM there are approximately seven hundred performances, including fully staged operas, orchestral concerts, recitals, master classes, and jazz concerts. MSM's student orchestras routinely perform at New York's most venerable concert spaces, such as Carnegie Hall, Lincoln Center, and Merkin Concert Hall, and its Jazz Orchestra frequently plays at jazz festivals around the United States.

Applicants to MSM must audition and provide evidence of satisfactory high school performance. Standardized test scores are not required. Except for composition (whose applicants must audition live and take an entrance exam), applicants may audition regionally (in Asia), or via a recording.

UNIVERSITY OF MICHIGAN

In the past two decades, the School of Music at Michigan has emerged as an innovative and excellent place to study. Several of Michigan's programs are top rated, and Michigan alumni perform with the Metropolitan Opera, play for the Boston and San Francisco symphony orchestras, win performance competitions, and teach at top music schools such as Eastman and Oberlin. The opera program at Michigan is one of the best in the United States. Each year opera students put on two main-stage and two studio-workshop productions. Opera students can also study abroad in Florence, Italy. Michigan's musical theater program is also strong. Each May senior musical theater students showcase their work in Ann Arbor and New York City.

Michigan's music department, housed within a school that includes dance and theater, has programs in voice, composition, theory, musicology, jazz, and all the orchestral instruments, plus innovative programs at the intersection of music and technology, such as sound engineering. Michigan offers four different undergraduate

degree programs in music: BM, BFA (jazz, musical theater, and performing arts technology), BS (sound engineering), and the bachelor of musical arts (BMA) for students who want to develop secondary areas of interest unrelated to careers in performance. The BM program in music education offers concentrations in choral music or instrumental music, and the music theory and musicology programs have BM and BMA tracks.

Michigan has a variety of performance venues, including a 1,300-seat theater. Michigan's nearly thirty musical performance groups stage more than 450 concerts and recitals annually. Performance ensembles at Michigan are open to any student, including nonmajors. Master classes enable students to work with performers from major orchestras, such as the Chicago Symphony, the Cleveland Orchestra, and the Berlin Philharmonic. Resources are vast at Michigan. The music library, for example, houses one of North America's most complete resources on the history of music.

The high academic standards Michigan is known for also apply to prospective music students. Music applicants must present strong enough academic credentials to get admitted to the University of Michigan. All students whose applications are judged promising are invited to audition on campus. In-person auditions are strongly recommended. All music performance degree programs at Michigan also require a résumé. The programs in composition and performing arts technology require a portfolio. Music scholarships are based on talent and financial need.

NEW ENGLAND CONSERVATORY OF MUSIC

The New England Conservatory (NEC) is located in the heart of Boston, within walking distance of the Boston Symphony Orchestra and the Boston Pops. Nearby are the campuses of the Berklee College of Music, Boston Conservatory,

Boston University, Emerson College, and Northeastern University. It is a short train ride to the Museum of Fine Arts, Isabella Stewart Gardner Museum, and Fenway Park, home of the Boston Red Sox. Total enrollment at NEC approaches 2,500 students, including 750 undergraduates. Nearly half of the musicians playing in the Boston Symphony are faculty at or graduates of NEC. The largest of NEC's five concert halls, Jordan Hall, is a National Historic Landmark acclaimed worldwide for its acoustics.

The BM program at NEC includes all orchestral instruments, jazz, vocal performance, historical performance, composition, and music education. Because it is a conservatory, the education at NEC is specialized, but not all required courses are in music—20 percent of courses must be in the liberal arts. A small number of students attend NEC through five-year (BA/MM or BS/MM) double degree programs with Harvard University and Tufts University. All Tufts majors, except engineering, are open to the NEC double degree option. Double degree aspirants must file separate applications and be admitted to both NEC and Harvard or Tufts.

The audition is the critical part of NEC's admission review. Applicants to all majors at NEC (except composition, music theory, and musicology) must audition on campus, unless the applicant lives more than five hundred miles from Boston. Some programs require a recording for prescreening—including cello, contemporary improvisation, flute, jazz studies, percussion, piano, viola, violin, and vocal performance. Composition applicants must have their portfolios prescreened to determine eligibility for an interview.

NORTHWESTERN UNIVERSITY
Twelve miles north of downtown Chicago, the Bienen School of Music at Northwestern provides superb facilities and robust resources for training excellent musicians. The 410

undergraduate students at Bienen have the opportunity to study with 125 eminent professors, attend the more than 300 annual concerts, participate in sixteen performance ensembles (several of which are open to nonmajors), and select from more than a dozen programs, including music performance, dual degrees, a self-designed major, and a BA in music.

Bienen offers BMus degrees in composition, jazz, musicology, performance, and theory. Musically inclined students who are not intending to pursue a performance career gravitate toward the BA program in music. Although the BA is a nonperformance degree, students applying to the program must audition. Dual degrees (BMus/BA with the Weinberg College of Arts and Sciences, BMus/BS with the McCormick School of Engineering and Applied Science, or BMus/BSJ with the Medill School of Journalism) take five years to complete. Double majors within Bienen are possible in any two areas except two performance majors. Double majors connecting Bienen students to the Weinberg College of Arts and Sciences generally can be completed in four years.

Facilities at Bienen encompass ninety-seven practice rooms, six performance spaces, digital studios for composition and multimedia, and a music library that contains an internationally renowned collection of post-1945 music. Performance spaces at Bienen include the 1,003-seat auditorium in Pick-Staiger Concert Hall (considered one of the finest performance venues in the Midwest) and a four-hundred-seat recital hall in a LEED-certified building that sits beside Lake Michigan and faces the Chicago skyline.

All applicants to Bienen must complete an audition, either on campus or through a video recording. A number of performance areas require prescreening recordings. Jazz studies and voice and opera applicants must submit a video (not an audio) recording to meet prescreening requirements. Scholarship support is generous at Northwestern especially for students who qualify for need-based financial aid. Northwestern meets the full need of all admitted students. In addition, a small number of exceptionally talented applicants receive merit scholarships.

OBERLIN CONSERVATORY OF MUSIC

Oberlin is America's oldest continuously operating conservatory of music. The conservatory enrolls 615 of the 2,900 students at Oberlin College, and nearly one-third (175) of those students are enrolled in a five-year BA/BM double degree program. Oberlin's remarkable facilities include 207 Steinway pianos, 150 practice rooms, five concert halls, a music library, a collection of 1,500 musical instruments, recording and music technology studios, a vocal arts laboratory, and fourteen practice organs. The arts environment at Oberlin is active and vibrant, providing opportunities typically only found in large cities. Between the twenty-five student ensembles and the recitals put on by students, faculty, and visiting artists (including an Artist Recital Series that brings internationally acclaimed soloists, orchestras, and musical groups to Oberlin), there are 500 concerts on campus annually.

Oberlin offers eight BM degree programs: performance, composition, electronic and computer music, historical performance, jazz studies, music theory, music history, and the technology in music and related arts (TIMARA) program that fuses music, technology, and other art forms. Private study is offered in thirty-one applied areas, and there are combined BM/MM programs in opera, conducting, and historical performance. Oberlin is one of the world's leading schools for organ study. Many church organists, university organists, and organ performance award winners have studied at Oberlin. Vocal studies majors at Oberlin, while concentrating in voice or opera, can make use of the Otto B. Schoepfle Vocal Arts Laboratory, which applies audio and computer technology to assist singers in maximizing their vocal skills. The jazz studies program offers majors in jazz performance and jazz composition. The Kohl Building housing Oberlin's jazz program was the first LEED Gold–certified music facility in the world.

Auditions are essential for admission to the Oberlin Conservatory. Live auditions are required of applicants who live within six hundred miles of campus and/or within two hundred miles of a regional audition site. Each year Oberlin hosts five on-campus audition weekends. Regional auditions are offered in Asia and across the United States. Students unable to have a campus or regional audition can submit a video recording. Some programs (including voice, jazz, TIMARA, and piano) require a screening recording.

RICE UNIVERSITY

In less than forty years, the excellent track record of its graduates and the expansive resources of Rice have propelled the Shepherd School of Music to the upper ranks in the music world. Numerous Shepherd alumni perform with the world's best orchestras, and Shepherd is also developing into a leading site for opera training.

Shepherd is home to 120 undergraduates and 165 graduate students studying at a medium-sized university of 5,663 students. The Shepherd School's small size enables a high degree of personal attention from faculty and unparalleled access to performance opportunities with high-quality ensembles. BM degree programs are available in performance, composition, and music history. All students in the BM program must take twenty-seven credit hours of courses in humanities, social sciences, and natural/physical sciences. Once enrolled, exceptional music students can apply to the Shepherd School's five-year BM/MM honors program. The BA in music option at Shepherd is only open to students after they enroll at Rice.

For a small music school, Shepherd stages

an extraordinary number of performances. Between students, faculty, alumni, and the dozen or so performance ensembles, the Shepherd School presents more than four hundred free concerts and recitals annually. Facilities are top notch at Shepherd. Music students have access to several recital halls, ample practice rooms, stages for opera, and two beautiful courtyards for creative contemplation.

All programs at Shepherd require an audition, and some require a preliminary (prescreening) recording. While it is possible to submit a recorded audition in lieu of a live audition, most of the studios at Shepherd prefer (or even require) an in-person audition. Shepherd does not conduct regional auditions because it wants prospective students to visit and get acquainted with its faculty, students, and facilities. Some majors have additional requirements. For example, applicants to music history must submit a writing sample (preferably a paper on a musical topic). Composition applicants must submit a portfolio of music they have composed. Because Rice University has high academic standards, Shepherd applicants must demonstrate strong academic preparation. Rice offers generous need-based financial aid and a limited number of merit-based scholarships.

UNIVERSITY OF ROCHESTER

The Eastman School of Music at Rochester is a famous conservatory with many notable graduates, including soprano Renee Fleming, jazz musicians Ron Carter and Chuck Mangione, and legendary arranger and producer Mitch Miller. Eastman boasts that it is the only major music school in America whose home city orchestra (the Rochester Philharmonic) resides on campus. Because Eastman's five hundred undergraduates are part of the University of Rochester, they

have the option to pursue a double degree—a BA or a BS at Rochester and a BM at Eastman. Approximately 10 percent of Eastman students pursue the double degree, which usually takes five years to complete.

Eastman provides some innovative training options beyond music, such as the Institute for Music Leadership, which teaches students about arts leadership and entrepreneurship. Eastman students can participate in Take Five, a program where students stay for one or two additional tuition-free terms at Rochester in order to broaden themselves intellectually by pursuing an academic interest beyond their major.

Opportunities to perform with ensembles are not lacking at Eastman. In addition to three orchestras, Eastman offers four choral groups, four jazz ensembles, two world music and new music groups, and opera productions. The jazz studies program at Eastman is for students interested in jazz performance, writing, and arranging but does not include vocal jazz. Students in Eastman's music education major, many of whom complete a double major in a performance area, have a 100 percent placement rate. Under Eastman's Forte Program, a few selected music education majors can stay for a tuition-free ninth semester to complete requirements for student teaching.

Eastman offers students several exchange opportunities with distinguished music schools in London, Milan, Paris, and Vienna. Admission to Eastman requires an audition. Certain programs require prescreening video recordings. Students who pass the prescreening must then audition on campus or at a regional site. Some programs, such as composition and jazz studies, do not accept regional auditions, and other programs, such as clarinet, flute, guitar, harp, organ, percussion, saxophone, and trumpet, will accept a video recording in lieu of an audition.

HONOR ROLL MUSIC SCHOOLS

BARD COLLEGE

Bard College has one of the newest conservatories of music in the United States. With its brash Frank Gehry building and recent affiliation with the Longy School of Music in Cambridge, Massachusetts, Bard has signaled its intentions to be a major player in music education. Enrolling just eighty students, the Bard Conservatory offers an intimate learning environment and the distinctive feature that all students complete a five-year (BA/BM) double degree program. Bard also offers a BA in music that can be completed in four years.

The emphasis at Bard tends toward classical. The professors teaching at Bard are musicians who have performed in the world's great concert halls. Making time amid their performance schedules, Bard's music professors are on campus weekly to give lessons, lead rehearsals, coach ensembles, and conduct master classes. Graduates of the Bard Conservatory's first classes have gone on to attend graduate programs at Yale, Juilliard, Rice, and the New England Conservatory.

Applicants must be accepted by both the Bard Conservatory and Bard College. The process starts with a prescreening recording for performance applicants or a recording of written works for composition applicants. Those who pass the prescreening must audition on the Bard campus. Students unable to travel to campus may audition by DVD. All students admitted to the Bard Conservatory are eligible for need-based financial aid and merit scholarships, including the Distinguished Musician Scholar Award that covers full tuition.

BOSTON UNIVERSITY

BU stands out in the history of higher education as the first degree-granting music school in the United States. Since then, BU has developed a music program that rivals leading conservatories. Music professors at BU include thirty members of the Boston Symphony Orchestra and scores of other distinguished musicians. BU's prominence in the music world is exemplified by its Tanglewood Institute, which is recognized as one of the world's top summer training programs for high-school-age musicians.

BU offers BM degree programs in composition and theory, music education, musicology, and performance, plus a five-year combined BM in performance/MM in music education option. Music students interested in taking their studies beyond Boston can go to the Royal College of Music in London for a semester. All music applicants must file a BU application and have an audition.

BUTLER UNIVERSITY

Among the nearly 4,700 students at Butler are 175 studying in the School of Music. For a small music school, Butler offers an unusually wide range of study options—including degrees in performance, composition, music education, piano pedagogy, arts administration, and music as a liberal art. Students interested in teaching music will find an extensive K–12-certified program that prepares future instructors of choral and instrumental music, keyboards, and voice.

The performance degree options at Butler include piano, voice, and the major orchestral instruments. There is a separate BM program for students interested in composition. Musicians interested in careers in arts management gravitate toward Butler's BS in arts administration program. For students drawn to music less as a career choice, Butler offers the BA in music. Music students at Butler have access to resources of professional quality, such as the multisensory learning facility, the electronic music studio, and the 2,200-seat Clowes Memorial Hall. The approximately fifteen performance ensembles at Butler offer opportunities for singers, jazz players, classical musicians, drummers, and marching band enthusiasts. Applicants must audition and fill out a supplemental application to Butler's School of Music. Butler offers need-based and merit-based scholarships.

CALIFORNIA INSTITUTE OF THE ARTS

Just thirty miles north of Los Angeles, Cal Arts is a hub of artistic activity and creative risk taking. The approach at Cal Arts is an integrative one, where collaboration across arts disciplines naturally develops. Cal Arts student musicians study alongside friends and classmates training in the fine arts, dance, film/video, and theater.

The Herb Alpert School of Music at Cal Arts offers degrees in composition, jazz, performance, musical arts, music technology, and world music. To a greater degree than at most music schools, the student ensembles (numbering more than thirty) at Cal Arts feature world music. For example, there are gamelan ensembles, Balinese flute and monkey chant ensembles, world percussion ensembles, a Persian ensemble, a salsa band, and ensembles for North Indian and African music. In addition, there is an opera theater performance group and multiple jazz ensembles. Complementing the several performance venues on campus, including the extraordinarily flexible indoor-outdoor music pavilion (called the Wild Beast), Cal Arts has a downtown Los Angeles center for student productions. Within the music building on campus, Cal Arts has more than twenty-five practice rooms, fifty pianos, two harpsichords, and two harps.

Music at Cal Arts requires an audition (either live or a recording). The programs in composition, jazz, and music technology require a portfolio.

DEPAUW UNIVERSITY

Located forty-five minutes from Indianapolis, the School of Music at DePauw offers undergraduate study in performance, education, and a BA/BM double degree program. Over its 130-year history, DePauw's School of Music has hosted legends like the composer Aaron Copland, who in 1971 directed the orchestra and held workshops, and has sent students and faculty groups to perform internationally.

The 150 to 175 music students at DePauw have four degree options. The BM in performance track offers concentrations in voice, piano, organ, strings, winds, brass, and percussion. The bachelor of musical arts (BMA) is a general music track students can follow to combine music with business or another major. The bachelor of music education (BME) can be earned with a choral, instrumental, or general emphasis. The BA in music (BAM) is for students with a general academic interest in music. The double degree (BM/BA) program combines performance with an arts and sciences subject.

The chance to perform or hear music at DePauw is never far away. There are numerous concerts, recitals, and performances by the DePauw Opera, University Jazz Ensemble, University Orchestra, five large ensembles, and more than twenty smaller ensembles. DePauw's Green Center for the Performing Arts (located in the heart of campus) has soundproof and environmentally controlled practice rooms and rehearsal halls, a music technology center, and a coffee shop. Performance venues include an auditorium that seats 1,250 and a 400-seat theater with a wraparound stage and pit orchestra.

Music applicants must complete DePauw's application and have an audition, preferably on campus. DePauw has a generous scholarship program and is a rare college that allows incoming students to combine or stack aid awards up to the level of full tuition.

FLORIDA STATE UNIVERSITY

Florida State has one of the largest and most comprehensive music programs in the United States. Music professors at Florida State include Grammy Award winners, Pulitzer Prize–winning composers, recipients of Guggenheim Fellowships, a former tenor for the Metropolitan Opera, and a former concert master for the New York Philharmonic. Rankings place FSU among the top dozen music schools in the United States, and the opera program is perennially ranked in the top five. Between the opera program, the nine world music ensembles, and the numerous orchestras, chamber groups, jazz bands, choral ensembles, and early music and baroque ensembles, there are more than five hundred concerts staged annually on campus. The outstanding facilities at FSU include some of the best acoustics to be found in university concert halls. Acclaimed for its world-class sound quality, Ruby Diamond Concert Hall, for example, seats nearly 1,200 and has a proscenium stage and a movable orchestra shell.

Florida State offers several degree tracks in music. Students can pursue the BM in performance in ten instruments or work toward a BM in composition, music theory, or music therapy. The BA in music degree has tracks in commercial music, jazz, and sacred music. The music education program offers specialties in choral, instrumental, and general music instruction. Few music schools offer the vocal performance opportunities found at Florida State. The highly ranked opera program presents fully staged productions each term and offers an opera workshop that trains students in the full gamut of operatic techniques. All applicants to FSU's College of Music must audition. The audition is a key factor in selecting applicants to receive merit scholarships.

GETTYSBURG COLLEGE

Set within a small liberal arts college, Gettysburg's Sunderman Conservatory of Music provides opportunities normally only found at larger and more prestigious music schools. For example, Sunderman opera students have toured in Europe, and the Jazz Ensemble has opened for noted performers such as Ray Brown and Phil Woods.

Sunderman offers study in classical orchestral instruments, jazz, and voice (including opera). Students at Sunderman have three degree options: BM in performance, BS in music education (which leads to K–12 certification), and BA in music. The course requirements Sunderman students must fulfill make it apparent that Gettysburg is a liberal arts college. Specifically, BM in performance students must take one-third of their courses in arts and sciences subjects outside of music. BA in music and BS in music education students take 35 percent of their courses in music and the rest in arts and sciences subjects.

All applicants to Sunderman must interview with a faculty member and audition. In-person auditions are best, but Sunderman allows auditions by DVD (preferred) or CD. Merit scholarship awards range up to $10,000 per year.

ITHACA COLLEGE

The School of Music at Ithaca resides within a college that offers two thousand courses and one hundred majors overall. The spectrum of musical styles covered at Ithaca is wide, ranging from classical, to jazz, to contemporary, and the reputation of the school is growing. Ithaca recently doubled the size of its music facilities, giving students access to three recording studios, three large recital and rehearsal halls, labs for jazz and electronic keyboards, and a music education suite.

Study options at Ithaca include music performance, music education, sound recording technology, and music in collaboration with an outside field. The School of Music has eight BM degree options and a BA in music for students with a less specialized focus. Performance opportunities in jazz, orchestral, and choral music are available in the more than two dozen ensembles. Annually, there are three hundred on-campus concerts and recitals. Student musical groups frequently have opportunities to perform around the world. For example, Ithaca performance ensembles have played at Lincoln Center in New York as well as in Dublin, London, and St. Petersburg, Russia. All Ithaca music applicants must audition, either on a major performance instrument or by voice. The percussion and sound recording technology programs require a prescreening audition. Ithaca offers scholarships based on musical merit (talent) and financial need.

UNIVERSITY OF ILLINOIS

Illinois has one of the top music schools located within a renowned research university. The eight hundred music students at Illinois have access to eminent faculty members, outstanding facilities, and vast performance opportunities. Illinois music alumni are found in prominent positions throughout the music world, and few music schools have a facility quite like its Krannert Center for the Performing Arts. The acoustics in Krannert's Great Hall are of such high quality that the Chicago Symphony has used it to make commercial recordings. Krannert also houses four theaters, costume shops, rehearsal rooms, and a restaurant. Facilities beyond Krannert include experimental music studios, recording facilities, and John Philip Sousa's music library.

Illinois offers two undergraduate degrees (the BM and BA) and three study tracks. For students interested in performance or composition, Illinois offers the BM track in orchestral, jazz, and vocal music. Music education students can specialize in band, choral, general, or orchestra. The extensive performance opportunities at Illinois include seven orchestras, nine bands, eleven jazz ensembles, six choirs, four percussion ensembles, seven chamber groups, four world music ensembles, and fully staged operas. Bands range from symphonic and sports bands to one that performs twilight summer concerts on the Illinois quadrangle. The Illinois trombone choir has a distinguished history of winning competitions. Over the years, Illinois jazz groups have recorded more than twenty albums and toured throughout the world. Illinois also stands apart for its strong emphasis on world music and features ensembles that perform African, Andean, Balkan, and gamelan music. All BM in music applicants must audition, either on campus or in New York City. Live auditions are strongly recommended, but applicants may submit recorded auditions.

LAWRENCE UNIVERSITY

Embedded within this small liberal arts college (1,500 students) in Wisconsin, the Lawrence Conservatory is a rare top-ranked music school solely focused on undergraduates. Typically, half of Lawrence's 350 music students pursue the dual BA/BMus degree, and more so than at most conservatories, Lawrence's numerous orchestras and ensembles are open to nonconservatory students. Although Lawrence built its reputation on orchestral music, *DownBeat* magazine has named Lawrence's jazz ensemble the best college big band several times.

Lawrence offers three music degree tracks. BMus students can specialize in performance, music education, or theory/composition while also taking one-third of their classes in arts and sciences subjects. Students who major in theory/composition can add an emphasis in jazz and improvisational music. Music education majors can concentrate on general music, choral, or instrumental. BA in music students tend to have a general, rather than a specialized, interest in music. Students who want to combine music with another major, such as math, enroll in the five-year (BA/BMus) double degree program. All

Lawrence Conservatory applicants must submit a music résumé and have an audition. Lawrence offers on-campus and regional auditions, but does not require prescreening recordings.

UNIVERSITY OF PUGET SOUND

Among the approximately 125 music majors at Puget Sound, typically 50 of them choose the BM in performance option, 50 select the BA in music track, and the rest head toward music education or music business. Puget Sound provides an intimate learning environment with a four to one student-faculty ratio. Students looking for performance opportunities will find nearly ten ensembles. Music facilities at Puget Sound include four performance halls, a percussion studio, keyboard lab, and an electronic music lab.

Puget Sound offers three bachelor's in music tracks: performance (in voice or an orchestral instrument), music education, and music with elective studies in business for students interested in careers in the recording industry, concert promotion, music publishing, and arts management. Music education students can choose to stay on for a master of arts in teaching (MAT) degree. BA in music students frequently add a double major or minor in an arts and sciences subject. Music applicants must audition, preferably in person, but students may submit recorded auditions in a video format.

SAINT OLAF COLLEGE

Many students pass up offers from prestigious conservatories to study music at this small Lutheran college located thirty-five miles south of Minnesota's Twin Cities. Although the music program at St. Olaf is strong overall, it is a recognized leader in vocal music. The St. Olaf Choir is a big reason for that. Internationally known, the St. Olaf Choir has taken fourteen world tours, issued twenty-seven discs (including one that sold 270,000 copies), performed at the White House, and for more than thirty-five years

staged the St. Olaf Christmas Festival, broadcast internationally on television and radio. Each year the St. Olaf Choir performs at prestigious music festivals, generating coverage by the *Wall Street Journal*, *Los Angeles Times*, and *TV Guide*. Members of the St. Olaf Choir are full-time undergraduate students who dedicate five days per week to rehearsals while also maintaining a full schedule of classes.

There is more to the music program at St. Olaf than its famous choir, however. There are approximately twenty musical performance ensembles, including jazz ensembles, orchestras, chamber groups, and handbell ensembles. Music degree options include the BM or BA in music, the five-year double degree (BA/BM) program, and majors in performance, composition, church music, and music education. St. Olaf requires an audition, a separate music application, and a screening recording. Double degree applicants must meet admission requirements for liberal arts and music. Merit-based scholarships go to applicants with exceptional musical talent.

VANDERBILT UNIVERSITY

The Blair School of Music at Vanderbilt is a rare acclaimed music school that is housed within a top-twenty research university. Blair is also unusual in its sole focus on undergraduates. Of the nearly 7,000 undergraduates at Vanderbilt, the 211 of them studying music at Blair enjoy a student-faculty ratio of four to one and have access to nearly 130 music professors when adjunct instructors are included. Blair students also find themselves living within the musical hub of Nashville.

All students at Blair complete a core of liberal arts courses while pursuing a specialized area of concentration. Blair has four degree programs: performance, composition/theory, musical arts (for students interested in music but not as a career), and a five-year BM/master of education. Blair students can also add a double major from another of Vanderbilt's three schools. Because Blair is small and undergraduate focused, its students are virtually guaranteed spots in the ensemble of their choice. There are fifteen performance ensembles sponsored by Blair and three community ensembles available to, but not exclusively for, music students. Blair alumni routinely go on to graduate study at top conservatories such as Eastman, Juilliard, Peabody, and the Royal Academy in London.

In addition to filing the required materials to gain admission to Vanderbilt, Blair applicants must submit a music profile and audition in person or by DVD. Blair offers need-based financial aid and talent-based scholarships.

THE INNOVATORS: BERKLEE, MIAMI, AND USC

BERKLEE COLLEGE OF MUSIC

For music students whose interests range beyond classical, there is Boston's Berklee College of Music. Music styles taught at Berklee range from jazz to rhythm and blues, pop, rock, gospel, and even classical music. With its long-standing excellence and scores of famous alumni, Berklee—now that it is a four-year institution—is arguably contemporary music's equivalent to Curtis/Juilliard in classical music.

Berklee began in 1945 as the vision of Lawrence Berk, an engineer and musical arranger, who saw the need for a school that taught contemporary music and provided career preparation for working musicians. While most of the music schools in the United States held to the European classical conservatory model, Berklee was the first music school to teach popular music. As it has developed into an influential and respected music school, Berklee has stayed true to its mission to teach the music of the time.

The 4,100 students at Berklee develop as musicians by performing. There are 375 student ensembles and a thousand annual concerts at Berklee. Students run two record labels and operate five Internet radio channels. Facilities at Berklee include 306 practice rooms, twenty-two recording and production studios, five facilities for film and video scoring and editing, 275 pianos, sixty-one ensemble lab rooms, and the Stan Getz Library with more than 100,000 musical items. In recent decades, Berklee has expanded its campus to encompass twenty-one buildings including residence halls for eight hundred students. Most of the rest of Berklee's students live a short distance from a campus straddled by two T stops and Boston's Back Bay commuter rail station.

Berklee offers a four-year BM degree program and a professional diploma program that is often pursued by students with degrees from other schools. Berklee has twelve majors: composition, contemporary writing and production, electronic production and design, film scoring, jazz composition, music business management, music education, music production and engineering, music therapy, performance (in twenty-nine instruments), professional music, and songwriting. All Berklee students take perspective-broadening liberal arts courses.

One of the strengths of Berklee is its alumni network of thirty thousand, 80 percent of whom work in the music industry. More than two hundred Berklee alumni have won Grammy Awards. Berklee students and alumni are frequent winners or runner-ups in the annual Thelonius Monk Institute of Jazz competition. Performers who attended Berklee include Gary Burton, Bruce Cockburn, Paula Cole, Rivers

Cuomo (Weezer), Gavin DeGraw, Al Di Meola, Melissa Etheridge, Donald Fagen, Bill Frissell, Keith Jarrett, Quincy Jones, Diana Krall, Patty Larkin, Natalie Maines (The Dixie Chicks), Aimee Mann, Branford Marsalis, John Mayer, Pat Metheny, Susan Tedeschi, Sadao Watanabe, and Gillian Welch.

All Berklee applicants must audition on campus and complete an interview. No standardized test scores are required. Annually, Berklee dispenses more than $30 million in merit-based scholarships and need-based aid.

UNIVERSITY OF MIAMI

Innovative is an apt word to describe Miami's Frost School of Music. Frost is a dynamic place that prides itself on breaking down the walls between the music disciplines. Frost's 710 students (taught by 114 professors) can get a traditional conservatory education or select from BM and BA programs in music business, studio music, music engineering, music therapy, contemporary music performance, and liberal arts and music.

Frost offers two dozen academic programs and fifty-four degree options. Like Berklee, Frost has embraced contemporary music, offering concentrations in contemporary bass, contemporary drum set, contemporary guitar, contemporary keyboard, and contemporary voice. Two institutes at Frost illustrate this commitment: the Bruce Hornsby (Miami alumnus) Creative American Music Program and the Henry Mancini Institute, named for the composer/arranger of some of the most recognizable television and movie theme songs of the twentieth century. Frost's excellent facilities include a music technology center, a music engineering lab, an electronic music lab, five rehearsal halls and the six-hundred-seat Maurice Gusman Concert Hall. Through corporate partnerships, Frost gets thirty new pianos annually from Steinway and Yamaha along with equipment from Sony, Fender, Roland, IBM, Dolby Laboratories, Cirrus Logic, Shure, Motorola, and Texas Instruments.

Learning by doing drives the Frost School. The more than thirty student music ensembles account for more than four hundred performances annually. Through its experiential music curriculum, Frost has been a groundbreaker in establishing study opportunities related to the entertainment industry and music engineering. More than most music schools, Frost recognizes the need to prepare students for careers in music. Beyond the classrooms and performance spaces, Frost students get hands-on training by running a record label called Cane Records and a music publishing company called Category Five. Frost's Weeks Center for Recording and Performance (where music engineering students maintain, install, design, and modify all the systems) is among the world's best university recording studios.

Music applicants must complete a University of Miami application and submit a Frost School of Music essay. Most Frost programs require applicants to pass a prescreening audition before their live audition. The composition and music engineering technology programs require a portfolio, and the music education and music therapy programs require an interview.

UNIVERSITY OF SOUTHERN CALIFORNIA

USC's Thornton School of Music has many connections with the vast arts community in Los Angeles. Thornton is the collegiate partner of choice for the Los Angeles Philharmonic, Los Angeles Chamber Orchestra, Los Angeles Opera, GRAMMY Foundation, and the Recording Academy. The Thornton Symphony works regularly with world-renowned conductors and composers such as Esa-Pekka Salonen, Michael Tilson Thomas, and Yo-Yo Ma. Thornton's student vocal groups and instrumental ensembles perform with the Los Angeles Chamber Orchestra, the Los Angeles Philharmonic, and at the J. Paul Getty Summer Music Festival. In addition, Thornton has a weekly radio show, *Thornton Center Stage*, broadcast in the Los Angeles media market.

Over the years, Thornton has become one of the top music schools for jazz. Its jazz studies program has four jazz ensembles and twenty faculty members, including trumpeter and pianist Arturo Sandoval and composer/producer/arranger Vince Mendoza. USC is one of the top places in the world to study jazz guitar. Alumni of Thornton's jazz guitar studio include Lee Ritenour and Paul Jackson Jr. Other jazz guitar graduates have gone on to perform with the Backstreet Boys, Michael Buble, Ray Charles, Enrique Inglesias, Ricky Martin, and Mel Tormé.

USC is one of the few global research universities offering a major in popular music. The BM degree in popular music is designed for instrumentalists, vocalists, and songwriters geared toward pop/rock, folk, R&B/urban, Latin/salsa, and other popular music styles. The popular music major enrolls approximately twenty-five freshmen per year, which enables it to maintain an intimate learning atmosphere. USC's program in scoring for motion pictures and television, arguably the premier program in the world, benefits from its location at a prominent film school in Los Angeles.

Thornton's eleven performing ensembles account for five hundred or more musical events annually. USC has outstanding performance spaces, including Bovard Auditorium, which seats 1,200, and Bing Theater, which seats 600. Applicants to the Thornton School who pass a pre-screening round must complete a live audition.

TOP SCHOOLS FOR JAZZ

Over the past quarter century, most of the leading music schools (including the standouts described below) have integrated jazz into the curriculum.

UNIVERSITY OF NORTHERN COLORADO

Professionals who tour and record internationally comprise the jazz studies teaching faculty at Northern Colorado. Jazz studies students at Northern Colorado have won ninety *DownBeat* magazine music awards, received nominations for Grammy Awards, toured worldwide, and released numerous albums. The strength of the jazz program at Northern Colorado is further exemplified by the campus-based UNC Jazz Press and an annual festival that brings notable jazz performers to Greeley.

En route to a BM degree, jazz students at Northern Colorado can specialize in piano, trumpet, bass, percussion, composition, saxophone, guitar, brass instruments, drums, or trombone. Northern Colorado also offers degree programs in music education, composition, piano, vocal performance, performance (classical), and business for music.

Jazz students at Northern Colorado have an extensive array of performance opportunities, including five big bands that have a history of distinction. In recent years, the UNC Jazz Lab Band has been named the best college big band by *DownBeat* magazine. There are also numerous jazz combos that tour throughout the United States, a jazz guitar ensemble, a Latin jazz ensemble, and vocal groups, such as the award-winning Northern Colorado Voices. Students get to perform in a 1,600-seat theater as well as at the annual UNC/Greeley Jazz Festival.

Applicants to the music program at Northern Colorado must complete the university's application and have an audition. Some programs at Northern Colorado also require an interview. The quality of the audition determines eligibility for talent scholarships.

NORTHERN ILLINOIS UNIVERSITY

Northern Illinois is nationally known for the quality of its jazz program and the performance credentials of its faculty. Several of NIU's jazz professors are renowned performers on the national and international scene. Ron Carter, the director of the jazz studies program, for example, has toured with famous musicians such as Clark Terry, Lou Rawls, and Jimmy Dorsey. Other NIU jazz professors have recorded with Blue Note Records or have worked with jazz legends such as Maynard Ferguson, Tito Puente, and Buddy Rich.

As they work toward a BM degree in performance, NIU jazz students can elect specialized concentrations in trumpet, saxophone, piano, percussion, trombone, guitar, and Latin percussion. NIU has five different jazz ensembles as well as two groups that feature world music. In addition to jazz studies, NIU offers BM degree programs in music education, classical performance, and composition. For students less interested in performing or teaching, there are BA and bachelor of general studies in music tracks.

Once applicants gain admission to NIU, they are offered an audition and asked to complete a School of Music application. The quality of the audition determines scholarship eligibility.

UNIVERSITY OF NORTH TEXAS

The College of Music at UNT is one of the largest and most comprehensive in the United States. UNT has trained award-winning jazz performers, nearly two thousand music teachers, the well-known pop musicians Don Henley, Norah Jones, and Meatloaf, and two members of the *Saturday Night Live* and Blues Brothers bands. The list of national music competitions where UNT students have won awards or made the finals is long. UNT students do especially well in brass and jazz competitions. Although UNT is a state university, 40 percent of its students come from outside Texas.

In 1947, UNT established the first jazz degree program in the United States. Since then, the BM in jazz studies program at UNT has earned international acclaim. The nearly four hundred jazz students at UNT study under eleven faculty members who are renowned and respected teachers, performers, and Grammy nominees. Jazz students at UNT can study vocal jazz, composition/arranging, or instrumental performance in saxophone, trumpet, trombone, piano, guitar, bass, or drums. One of the strengths of UNT's jazz program is its extensive range of performance ensembles. UNT has nine jazz lab bands, three jazz singing groups, a jazz repertory ensemble, two electric guitar ensembles, the Grammy-nominated One o'Clock Lab Band, and ensembles for Latin jazz, jazz trombone, and contemporary music. An annual lecture series brings acclaimed musicians to campus such as Dave Brubeck, Billy Hart, John Abercrombie, and Wycliffe Gordon.

There is more to music at UNT than jazz. UNT offers BM degrees in music performance, composition, music education, music history, and music theory as well as a BA degree in music. The composition program is one of the largest in the nation, enrolling seventy-five majors who study a wide variety of aesthetics and approaches under seven composition professors. Music education, also a large program, has produced teachers found in the music departments at hundreds of schools and colleges across the United States. There are more than forty groups not focused on jazz, including ensembles for choral music, wind instruments, new music, early music, and orchestral music. UNT also has unique research and performance centers focused on early adolescent vocal music, chamber music, experimental music, music and medicine, and mountain music.

Music facilities at UNT are housed in a

six-building complex located in the heart of the campus. The five major performance spaces at UNT enable nearly a thousand concerts annually. The largest is Winspear Performance Hall, which seats one thousand. Additional resources include three hundred practice rooms, a 400-seat theater, a 380-seat concert hall, the Stan Kenton collection, and the Maynard Ferguson Music Library.

Getting into the jazz program at UNT requires three steps: (1) admission to UNT; (2) admission to the College of Music; and (3) admission to the jazz studies program. The audition (either on campus or through audio submission) is the linchpin of the admission and merit scholarship selection process.

UNIVERSITY OF THE PACIFIC

The 180 music students at Pacific attend a distinguished conservatory known for graduating the legendary jazz pianist Dave Brubeck. Pacific offers a range of BA and BM majors in music performance, music education, music management, music therapy, composition, and jazz studies. While jazz is a small program (limited to twenty students), it is arguably the one that has put Pacific on the map in the music world. One reason for Pacific's prominence is the Dave Brubeck Institute, which operates a prestigious fellowship program for outstanding young jazz musicians. The Brubeck Fellowship provides full scholarships to three to five recent high school graduates for one to two years of jazz study at Pacific. Students who complete the Brubeck Fellowship Program get a certificate and the offer to stay at Pacific to earn a degree.

Brubeck fellows have extraordinary opportunities to get individual instruction from leading musicians such as Jimmy Heath, Wynton Marsalis, Christian McBride, Randy Jones, and Cleo Laine. The Brubeck Institute Jazz Quintet (comprised of Brubeck fellows) is as close as it gets on a college campus to a professional-level jazz group. The Brubeck Institute Jazz Quintet records and performs at prestigious jazz festivals (such as Monterey) and plays at concerts and clubs around the world. Four out of five years between 2007 and 2011, the Brubeck Quintet won the *DownBeat* magazine award for best collegiate jazz group in the United States.

Jazz students at Pacific have many other opportunities to play in combos and ensembles, such as the Pacific Jazz Ensemble, a big band that has performed at venues such as the Next Generation Jazz Festival in Monterey and the Reno Jazz Festival. Jazz masters in residence, such as Christian McBride and Joshua Redman, frequently spend a week on campus as guest directors of the Pacific Jazz Ensemble while giving clinics and master classes. Music resources at Pacific range from a music technology laboratory, to a recording studio, to a handful of concert and recital halls. There is much attention at Pacific on the quality of the pianos. Pacific is working toward a goal of becoming an all-Steinway institution.

All jazz applicants must complete Pacific's admission application and submit to a classical audition and a jazz audition. Pacific offers a number of talent-based conservatory scholarships, focused primarily on the audition.

OTHER GOOD MUSIC SCHOOLS

Students can get an excellent education at the music schools listed (and in some cases described) below.

- Baldwin Wallace University
- Ball State University
- Chapman University
- University of Colorado

- Crane School of Music—State University of New York College at Potsdam
- University of Iowa
- James Madison University
- Longy School of Music (affiliated with Bard College)
- Mannes College of Music (New School University)
- University of North Carolina School of the Arts
- San Francisco Conservatory of Music
- Southern Methodist University
- SUNY-Fredonia
- SUNY-Purchase
- Westminster Choir College of Rider University

Baldwin Wallace University. Baldwin Wallace (BW), a liberal arts institution of 4,300 students in Berea, Ohio (just south of Cleveland), has a full-fledged Conservatory of Music that enrolls 260 students. BW is distinguished by its renowned Bach Festival and a music theater program that maintains a professional collaboration with Playhouse Square, Cleveland's leading theater. BW offers BM degrees in keyboard performance, music theater, music therapy, composition, music theory, vocal performance and opera, and music history and literature, plus minors in jazz or arts management. Students can also earn a bachelor of music education degree (in vocal or instrumental teaching), or a BA in music.

Crane School of Music. Part of SUNY College at Potsdam in Upstate New York, the Crane School was one of the first music schools in the United States to offer programs to train public school music teachers. In addition to the BM degree program in music education, Crane offers BM degrees in music, music performance, musical studies, and the business of music; the latter is for students interested in the recording industry, arts administration, and music production.

Southern Methodist University. Within its Meadows School of the Arts, SMU has an up-and-coming music program. Many of the music professors at SMU perform with the Dallas Symphony Orchestra. On campus, there are eight ensembles, including a jazz orchestra, opera theater, symphony orchestra, and world music ensemble that put on upward of two hundred performances annually. SMU music students can pursue a BM with a performance focus in brass, composition, guitar, percussion, piano, strings, voice, or woodwinds; the BA in Music; or BM degree in music education, composition, or music therapy.

Westminster Choir College. Westminster Choir College enrolls 350 undergraduates and has its own campus in Princeton, New Jersey, not far from the main Rider University campus in Lawrenceville. Westminster is renowned for its outstanding choral program that includes nine vocal ensembles and one of the top programs in sacred music. The Westminster Choir has been the chorus in residence at the Spoleto Festival USA in Charleston, South Carolina, since 1977. Degree programs at Westminster include music education, organ performance, piano, sacred music, theory and composition, and voice performance.

MUSIC AT LIBERAL ARTS COLLEGES

The following liberal arts colleges have quality music programs and performance opportunities for majors and non-majors.

Coe College. Students at Coe in Cedar Rapids, Iowa, can choose a liberal arts approach to music and earn a BA or have a conservatory-type experience and earn a BM in one of four areas: keyboard or instrumental performance, vocal performance, theory and composition, or music education. For a college of 1,400 students, the size of the music department (twenty-seven professors) and the range of the facilities (including a $1.5 million E. M. Skinner organ, electronic music and recording studios, and an auditorium that seats 1,000) are impressive. Recent tours have taken Coe student musicians to Asia, Central America, and Europe.

Marlboro College. This rural college with 350 undergraduates in Vermont is famous for the summer Marlboro Music Festival that for more than sixty years has played a transformative role in the world of chamber music. Following Marlboro's unique self-designed Plan of Concentration, music students can focus on electronic music, historical musicology, music composition, music performance, or the history, philosophy, and culture of music.

Wheaton College. At this Christian college of three thousand students in metro Chicago, there is a full-fledged Conservatory of Music. Wheaton Conservatory students can choose among BM degree tracks in performance (with concentration options in organ, piano, voice, or an orchestral instrument), composition, music history and literature, or music education. BM students can add an elective concentration in another field of music or in an outside field. There is also a BA degree track offered by the music department of Wheaton's liberal arts college.

PREPARING FOR THE MUSIC INDUSTRY

The program in commercial music at Nashville's **Belmont University** is emblematic of an institution that wants its students to be well prepared for success in the music industry. Belmont has a whole school (the Mike Curb College of Entertainment and Music Business) devoted to preparing students for jobs in the music industry. In addition, Belmont's School of Music offers a commercial music specialty option with five tracks: composition and arranging, music business, music technology, music performance, and song writing. Performance ensembles at Belmont span a wide range of musical styles. For example, there are six jazz ensembles, a rock ensemble, a world percussion ensemble, and, reflecting its home region, a bluegrass ensemble.

At **Florida State University**, the commercial music major (leading to a BA in music) combines courses in music history and theory with courses in audio production, film scoring, economics, and management.

James Madison University in Virginia offers a program called music industry. Students in the program take a core of business, music, and music industry courses. Music industry graduates work for major and independent record labels, music journals and magazines, radio stations, recording studios, and television stations. Because the music industry major is part of JMU's music school, all students in the program must audition in instrumental or vocal performance.

New York University offers music business as a major under the BM degree program in its Steinhardt School of Culture, Education, and Human Development. The music business major at NYU is embedded in a music department acclaimed for film scoring, music for theater, and music technology. The program's location in the world's capital for music business augments courses, internships, and alumni networks. The interactive learning environment of NYU's music business program is designed to teach students about the systems and practices of the music industry. For example, students help run NYU's record company, Village Records. Alumni of the

NYU program have success in landing leadership positions in the global music industry.

The **University of the Pacific**'s music management program teaches students about the financial, marketing, organizational, and legal issues of the global music industry. Students at Pacific can select the BM in music management or the BA in music with an emphasis in music management. There are specialized tracks in record company operations, music products management, arts administration, and recording technology. The program provides internship opportunities in concert production, record company operations, recording technology, and artist management. Pacific also has a program in the city famous for launching the Beatles at the University of Liverpool's Institute of Popular Music. Music management graduates have found positions with companies such as Warner Music Group, Dolby Laboratories, Clear Channel Radio, Universal Music Publishing, Warner-Chappell Music Publishing, and the CW television network. Music management applicants must audition and have an interview with the department.

The **University of Southern California**'s program in music industry prepares students for careers in the recording, concert promotion, music publishing, artist management, music production, and music technology fields. The music industry program at USC's Thornton School of Music offers two tracks: the BM track for students with the skills to complete all the requirements for a major in music performance and the BS track with concentrations in music industry or music technology. Students in either program are required to complete an internship. USC's location in Los Angeles is a definite door opener to internships and first jobs.

MUSIC TECHNOLOGY

Students drawn to careers in audio engineering, sound design, and electronic and computer music, should investigate the following schools.

- Berklee College of Music
- Carnegie Mellon University
- University of Cincinnati
- University of Hartford
- Indiana University
- University of Miami
- University of Michigan
- Oberlin Conservatory of Music
- University of Southern California

STRONG MUSIC EDUCATION PROGRAMS

The music education major can be found at just about any university that has a school of music and a department or school of education. Some schools with standout programs are listed below.

- Ball State University
- Boston University
- Crane School of Music (SUNY-Potsdam)
- University of Illinois
- Indiana University
- University of Iowa
- Ithaca College
- James Madison University
- University of Michigan
- University of North Texas
- Oberlin College
- SUNY-Fredonia

THE PERFORMING ARTS

For some, life is a stage. All the high school actors, dancers, singers, or triple threats looking to perfect their craft (or just have fun performing) have many options at the collegiate level. Both the recreational performer and the classically trained aspiring star can find their niche. College performing arts programs vary in intensity and exclusivity. Some maintain a specialized, audition-based, conservatory type of environment, whereas others are open to those who have just caught the acting/dancing/singing bug. Starting with theater, this chapter provides a guide for navigating the many study options in the performing arts.

COLLEGES FOR THEATER

Drama or theater departments are found at just about every college in the United States. Students interested in acting, costume and stage design, lighting, and other theater arts can go to a liberal arts institution and get involved in stage productions, which was the route taken by Jennifer Garner and Steve Carell (both Denison University); Bradley Cooper (Georgetown); Lena Dunham and Ed Helms (Oberlin); Susan Sarandon and John Slattery (Catholic University); Hope Davis, Lisa Kudrow, and Meryl Streep (Vassar); and Dana Delany and Bradley Whitford (Wesleyan University).

Alternatively, students can go to a specialized, conservatory-style theater program. Conservatory-style programs usually offer the bachelor of fine arts (BFA) degree and boast numerous alumni in Hollywood or on Broadway. Some examples include **Boston University** (Jason Alexander, Emily Deschanel, Ginnifer Goodwin, Julianne Moore), **California Institute of the Arts** (Alison Brie, Don Cheadle, Ed Harris, David Hasselhoff), **UCLA** (Carol Burnett, Mariska Hargitay, Kal Penn, Tim Robbins, Dax Shepard), **Carnegie Mellon University** (Ted Danson, Holly Hunter, Jack Klugman, Megan Hilty, Zachary Quinto), **DePaul University** (Gillian Anderson, Joe Mantegna, John C. Reilly), **Emerson College** (Gina Gershon, Spalding Gray, Norman Lear, Dennis Leary, Jay Leno, Steven Wright), **Juilliard** (Jessica Chastain, Kelsey Grammer, Patti LuPone, Kevin Spacey), **University of North Carolina School of the Arts** (Jennifer Ehle, Tom Hulce, Mary Louise Parker, Jada Pinkett Smith), **Northwestern University** (Zach Braff, Steven Colbert, Julia Louis Dreyfus, Cloris Leachman, Megan Mullally, Dermot Mulroney, David Schwimmer, Warren Beatty), **NYU** (Alec Baldwin, Kristen Bell, Alexis Bledel, Billy Crystal, Philip Seymour Hoffmann, Idina Menzel, Adam Sandler), **Southern Methodist University** (Kathy Bates, Aaron Spelling), and the **University of Texas** (Marcia Gay Harden, Matthew McConaughey, Tommy Tune, Eli Wallach, Renee Zellweger).

► TOP THEATER PROGRAMS

Ball State University	University of California at Los Angeles	DePaul University
Boston University	Carnegie Mellon University	Emerson College
California Institute of the Arts	Catholic University	Florida State University

➤ TOP THEATER PROGRAMS *(CONT.)*

Ithaca College	New York University	Rutgers University
Juilliard School	North Carolina School of the Arts	Southern Methodist University
University of Miami	Northwestern University	Syracuse University
University of Minnesota	Purchase College—State University of New York	University of Texas
Muhlenberg College		Vassar College

BEST OF THE BEST

BOSTON UNIVERSITY

Each year the School of Theatre at BU enrolls sixty to seventy new undergraduate students. After completing the freshman core curriculum, students can choose among five concentrations: acting, design, production, stage management, or theater arts. Theater majors also have the option to pursue dual degree programs in conjunction with another school at BU. Nearly all BU theater students study abroad. BU's London Internship Program enables students interested in design, production, and stage management to get real-world experiences in one of the world's greatest and most historic cities for theater. BU operates semester-long exchange programs with the London Academy of Music and Dramatic Art and with the Accademia dell'Arte in Avezzo, Italy. BU has additional theater internship connections in Auckland, Dublin, Madrid, Paris, Quito, Sydney, and Tel Aviv.

The opportunities for theater performance at BU are vast. The ten performance venues at BU include a nine-hundred-seat Broadway-style proscenium stage and a sixty-seat black box studio. All of the twenty-five to thirty-five annual productions are performed, designed, and built by School of Theatre students. At BU there is a guaranteed casting policy that means all eligible theater majors will be cast in a production every quarter.

One of the strengths of the theater program at BU is its connections to the profession. BU's Professional Theatre Initiative links the school to numerous theater companies and festivals with national reputations, such as the Williamstown (MA) Theatre Festival. Since 1982, BU has had the professional Huntington Theatre Company in residence. Having the Huntington mount seven productions each season enables students to gain experience in lighting, costuming, scenic design, directing, stage management, and production. Similarly, the BU New Play Initiative gives students the opportunity to develop plays and present them through workshop productions.

CALIFORNIA INSTITUTE OF THE ARTS

Production is the core experience of theater students at Cal Arts. Central to the learning atmosphere is the cross-pollination between arts areas. Students collaborate with aspiring artists, writers, musicians, composers, choreographers, filmmakers, video artists, animators, graphic designers, and painters. The vast Roy and Edna Disney Cal Arts Theater (REDCAT) provides an interdisciplinary venue for innovative performance projects, and the student-faculty ratio of eight to one enables small classes and close mentoring by teachers whose professional backgrounds help connect students to theater companies and television and film production firms.

Cal Arts offers BFA programs in acting, costume design, lighting design, scene design, sound design, technical direction, and stage management. Versatility is a hallmark at Cal Arts. The goal is to prepare actors for all forms, styles, and settings so that graduates will be equally adept in theater, film, television, and emerging media. The Cal Arts Interim Session (during the first two weeks of the spring semester) enables students to immerse themselves in a study project or activity beyond regular course work. Interim projects tend to involve exploration of new and unfamiliar topics and encompass self-directed and interdisciplinary work between schools and departments. The final semester of the acting program at Cal Arts culminates with a showcase, where graduating students perform for film and theater professionals.

Several programs and facilities at Cal Arts provide exceptional opportunities. The Center for New Performance fosters the creation of adventurous new and interdisciplinary works in theater, dance, and music. The Cotsen Center for Puppetry and the Arts provides a laboratory for studying and creating puppets for theater, film, dance, and art. A nationally recognized and award-winning program enables students to provide free after-school arts training for youth. Giving students exposure to the global arts community is a key focus of the education at Cal Arts. There are study programs and class trips to Barcelona, Hong Kong, India, Japan, Singapore, and Tel Aviv. Cal Arts students also frequently perform in key international venues such as the Edinburgh Fringe Festival.

CARNEGIE MELLON UNIVERSITY

The oldest drama-degree–granting program in the United States, the Carnegie Mellon School of Drama from its inception has set the standard in conservatory training for performing arts professionals. Prominent alumni of CMU include the actors James Cromwell, Blair Underwood, and Patrick Wilson as well as television director/producer Steven Bochco. Drama at CMU is one of five schools within the College of Fine Arts. The core of the drama school is its BFA programs in design; acting and music theater; dramaturgy; directing; and production, technology, and management. Within the program in design, students can concentrate on costume design, lighting design, scenic design, or sound design. Acting and music theater students pursue a core curriculum of classes in acting, voice and speech, and movement. Dramaturgy students benefit from a wide-ranging curriculum that encompasses new play development, production support, critical writing, audience outreach, play season development, and play translation and adaptation.

The directing program at Carnegie Mellon trains students in techniques for stage and camera. The program in production, technology, and management offers specialized training in technical direction, production, and stage management. In addition to the BFA tracks in drama, CMU students can pursue intercollege degree programs involving computer science, humanities, and sciences. Numerous CMU facilities are designed to lead students into future frontiers. For example, there are voice and speech rooms, several large theaters, a sound lab, dance and movement studios, scene and costume shops, design and video studios, a light lab, a production and technology classroom, and a renovated warehouse with fifteen thousand square feet of space for scenography, media and visual design, and interdisciplinary study.

DEPAUL UNIVERSITY

Located in the heart of a world-class theater city (Chicago), DePaul's Theatre School is one of the oldest and most respected performing arts conservatories in the United States. The Theatre School at DePaul is a specialized conservatory that offers twelve BFA degree programs. All theater students at DePaul receive individual attention, study in a highly structured atmosphere, and learn by doing. With more than forty productions per year, students at DePaul have ample opportunities to act, direct, and design plays and musicals. DePaul's eighty theater faculty members bring a wealth of experience acquired in the Chicago and international theater communities.

DePaul's BFA programs are organized into departments for performance, design and technical, and theater studies. Within performance, DePaul offers a specialization in acting. Within the Design and Technical Department, students can specialize in costume design, costume technology, lighting design, scenic design, sound design, stage management, or theater technology. Within the theater studies program, students can specialize in dramaturgy/criticism, playwriting, theater arts, or theater management.

Seniors in DePaul's Theatre School transition into the professional world through performance showcases held in Chicago, Los Angeles, and New York. The annual Wrights of Spring festival features the work of DePaul's playwriting students. DePaul's theater facility, located on its Lincoln Park campus (within walking distance of Chicago's theater district) houses a 250-seat studio theater; a 100-seat flexible theater; spaces for set, prop, and costume shops; rehearsal studios; lighting laboratories; and new media workshop spaces. The specialized technical areas in the building are integrated with informal spaces, like lounges, in order to encourage creative interaction. In addition to the prominent actors mentioned already, notable DePaul theater graduates include Tony Award–winning designers and Broadway directors.

THE JUILLIARD SCHOOL

In training for theater, the name Juilliard is arguably the gold standard. Scores of prominent performers have studied for a BFA or MFA in acting at Juilliard. Part of the Drama Division, acting at Juilliard is a four-year conservatory training program that provides intensive instruction in acting, movement, voice, and liberal arts subjects. Juilliard's Drama Division accepts just eight to ten BFA candidates each year. To enter the program, applicants must audition. Juilliard also has a highly ranked MFA in acting program, limited to eight to ten students.

Theater at Juilliard is taught as a collaborative art that requires nurturing the body, mind, and imagination. The four-year acting curriculum is structured in a way that distinguishes the program from others. Year one in acting is the discovery year, when students acquire tools and practice techniques related to voice, movement, improvisation, and scene study. Through four rehearsal projects in year two, students immerse themselves in the works and world created by Chekhov, Shakespeare, and prominent American playwrights. In year three, students integrate all they have learned. Much of year three revolves around learning and performing Shakespeare, including two fully staged productions performed in repertory in a modern version of the Globe Theater. During year three, acting students also train intensively in singing, attend master classes taught by guest artists, and perform a naturalistic play and a cabaret.

Year four in the Juilliard BFA program serves as the bridge to the acting profession. Acting students are very busy rehearsing and performing in workshops, readings, and main-stage productions. Students are learning audition techniques for stage, film, and television, while also performing mock auditions for casting directors, agents, and other stage and screen professionals. In addition to getting a sense of the life of a working actor, students go on a three-day silent retreat for artistic reflection and renewal. After returning from their retreat, acting students present their unique talents and skills—in a series of scenes—to industry representatives in Los Angeles and New York.

Aspiring writers at Juilliard can study in the Lila Acheson Playwrights Program directed by Marsha Norman and Christopher Durang. Through play laboratories, staged readings, and workshop productions, the American Playwrights Program serves as an incubator for new works and collaborations between writers and actors. Students begin acting and rehearsing Durang and Norman plays as early as freshman year.

NEW YORK UNIVERSITY

NYU is famous for its programs in theater, and the Tisch School of the Arts contributes hugely to that fame. Tisch is regarded as one of the world's best places to get theater training; studying there can be a ticket to stage and screen success. Tisch's unique advantage is combining the vast offerings of a leading university (NYU) with the artistic resources of North America's (if not the world's) best city for theater.

Tisch's BFA drama programs stress performance and production. Drama at Tisch is one of seven undergraduate departments, the others being film and television production, photography and imaging, recorded music, dance, dramatic writing, and cinema studies. Drama students at Tisch get an education that combines intensive conservatory training and comprehensive theater study. Instruction in drama at Tisch is organized around a studio system comprised of small classes and intensive hands-on training. Tisch's drama studios provide training in acting, music theater, directing, and production and design. In the acting studios, students receive foundational training in scene study, improvisation, acting technique, vocal technique, dance and movement, script analysis, singing, directing, stage management, design, production, and music theater. The seven studios at Tisch are as follows:

- Atlantic Acting School
- Experimental Theatre Wing
- Meisner Studio
- New Studio on Broadway: Music Theatre and Acting
- Playwrights Horizons Theatre School
- Production and Design Studio
- Stella Adler Studio of Acting

Prospective Tisch students do not designate a studio at the point of application. Studio placement is determined by Tisch after students enroll, and students remain in their studio for four of their eight semesters at NYU. Tisch requires all drama students to be enrolled in the program for a year before auditioning for departmental or studio productions. By year two, Tisch believes, students will have embraced the techniques they have learned, adjusted to living in New York City, and established themselves academically. Drama students at Tisch have an extraordinary number of performance opportunities (more than two hundred annually). Students with initiative can get stage and screen internships in New York.

Students interested in teaching theater may want to pursue the BS in educational theater degree program offered through NYU's Steinhardt School of Culture, Education, and Human Development. The Steinhardt BS program prepares students for K–12 teacher certification.

NORTHWESTERN UNIVERSITY

Northwestern has one of the top undergraduate theater programs in the United States. Northwestern theater students learn from more than thirty faculty members who have expertise in acting, children's theater, choreography, costume design, dance, directing, light design, music theater, playwriting, set design, stage management, storytelling, theater history, and theater criticism. Northwestern offers major and minor programs in theater and dance as well as a certificate in music theater. The theater curriculum at Northwestern provides instruction and training in acting, dance, design, directing, dramaturgy, movement, playwriting, stage production, and voice as well as theater history, literature, and criticism. Theater facilities at Northwestern are extensive and encompass multiple performance and rehearsal spaces, dance studios, a digital media studio, a film sound stage, a digital media lab, and halls for fully staged productions. In addition to its leading undergraduate theater program, Northwestern offers standout MFA programs in directing, stage design, and writing for the screen and stage. There is also an interdisciplinary PhD program in theater and dance.

Annually, Northwestern students put on approximately forty stage productions. Each year a select group of Northwestern theater students participates in the New York Showcase, an opportunity to perform before an invited group of Big Apple talent agents and casting directors. Graduating seniors also perform in the Chicago Showcase for casting directors, agents, and others in the stage profession. Supplementing the opportunities in theater is a Senior Dance Concert choreographed, produced, and performed by students. For theater-interested applicants to Northwestern, there is no admissions audition process. Instead, students apply to the School of Communication and designate theater as the intended major.

PURCHASE COLLEGE

Purchase College of the State University of New York has a highly regarded Conservatory of Theatre Arts that offers BA, BFA, and MFA degrees. The BFA programs are in acting, dramatic writing, and theater design and technology. The BA programs are in playwriting and screenwriting as well as in theater and performance. Because Purchase is located just thirty minutes north of New York City, its Conservatory of Theatre Arts students have access to outstanding professional opportunities. Purchase has an excellent performing arts center, which includes theaters, design studios, and spaces for dance productions.

The BFA program in acting at Purchase has an enrollment of seventy students, which enables it to be individualized. The program requires an intensive commitment of time and effort from its students. Alumni of the Purchase acting program include Edie Falco, Melissa Leo, Parker Posey, and Stanley Tucci. The BFA in dramatic writing program trains students to write for stage, film, television, and emerging media. As seniors, dramatic writing students complete a required eight-credit project focused on producing works of professional caliber. Students in the BA in playwriting and screenwriting program are taught by industry professionals and have access to theater, film, and television production facilities. The BFA in theater design and technology program offers concentrations in scenic design, costume design, lighting design, costume technology, stage management, and technical direction/production management. The BA in theater and performance program is self-designed, enabling students to explore individual interests. Theater students at Purchase are encouraged to study abroad and explore interdisciplinary connections between writing, directing, and acting.

SYRACUSE UNIVERSITY

Within Syracuse's College of Visual and Performing Arts, the Department of Drama offers BFA programs in acting, musical theater, stage management, and theater design and technology. Acting students at Syracuse start with a foundation year where they learn the Stanislavski system and the Strasburg method, both of which stress the actor's psychological, emotional, and sensory development. As they progress through the curriculum, acting students have the opportunity to take additional courses in theater history, directing, voice, playwriting, and technical theater. The BFA programs in drama at Syracuse require an audition.

Musical theater students at Syracuse get training in acting, voice, singing, and dance, while also taking courses in the history of musical theater and in liberal arts subjects. The theater design and technology curriculum combines training in set design, costume design, lighting design, scenery, sound, and drafting/rendering for the theater with hands-on production support experiences. Students get opportunities to work with a professional company called Syracuse Stage, serve as assistants to guest designers, or pursue technical production internships. Stage management students learn through a combination of classes and experiences that simulate professional stage management. Students supplement their courses by working behind the scenes as production assistants, assistant stage managers, and stage managers for campus productions and Syracuse Stage productions.

Syracuse also offers a broader BS in drama program that enables students to tailor their studies to match their interests. BS in drama students can sample courses from or build a concentration in areas such as directing, playwriting, theater management, and community-based theater. Alumni of the drama program at Syracuse include the actors Taye Diggs, Vera Farmiga, Frank Langella, Tom Everett Scott, and Vanessa Williams as well as screenwriter/producer Aaron Sorkin.

UNIVERSITY OF TEXAS

The old cliché that everything is bigger in Texas actually does apply to theater at UT. The Department of Theatre and Dance at UT is one of the largest in the United States. Students have at their disposal more than 150 courses taught by more than fifty faculty members who are professionally active directors, performers, designers, choreographers, and scholars. The theater program at UT is professional in focus, giving students ample opportunities to learn and practice their craft.

Theater students at UT can earn either a BA or BFA degree. The lone BFA program—in theater studies—is for students seeking teacher certification in the theater arts. Within the BA in theater program, there are numerous specialty areas for students to explore and turn into a concentration, including acting, directing, playwriting, performance as public practice, lighting design and technology, costume design and technology, set design and technology, stage management, and creative drama.

Productions abound at UT. In addition to an annual slate of six to eight departmental productions, there are twenty to thirty laboratory shows and readings and a biennial new works festival. UT's top-notch facilities include three fully equipped theaters, a lab theater, two costume shops, two scenic studios, a properties shop, a robotic lighting lab, and a computer design lab. Theater students at UT benefit from a number of special facilities, including the Harry Ransom Center, which houses the papers of famous performers and playwrights such as Stella Adler, David Hare, Lillian Hellman, Harry Houdini, Doris Lessing, Steve Martin, Arthur Miller, Harold Pinter, and Tennessee Williams. Theater students at UT also have access to study abroad programs in places like Florence, where students work side by side with professionals from the Global Theatre Project.

BEST OF THE REST

BALL STATE UNIVERSITY

Steadily over the years, Ball State has developed one of the top theater programs in the Midwest— and that is saying something because Ball State's regional neighbors are the outstanding programs at DePaul, Minnesota, and Northwestern. One indication of Ball State's strength is that acting and musical theater students get to perform annually in Chicago, Los Angeles, and New York for stage and screen professionals looking to discover new talent. At Ball State there are BFA degree tracks in acting and in musical theater and BA or BS tracks in design and technology, production, theatrical studies, and theatrical education. There is a clear professional focus at Ball State. Acting students take courses in voice, movement, acting for the camera, and acting styles. Students in the design and technology track can concentrate on scenery, lighting, costuming, or sound design. The production degree is for students interested in directing or in stage management. Theatrical studies students pursue interests in playwriting; stage management; dramaturgy; or theory, history, and criticism. The program in theatrical education prepares students for secondary education licensure to teach high school drama. Regardless of the theater degree program chosen at Ball State, students receive a firm grounding in liberal arts courses.

UNIVERSITY OF CALIFORNIA AT LOS ANGELES

The offerings in theater at UCLA are extensive. Students can choose BA degree specializations in acting, design/production, musical theater, playwriting, general theater studies, and the teaching of theater. Competition for admission is fierce, with 1,100 applicants for one hundred spaces. The Theatre Department at UCLA is part of the renowned School of Theatre, Film, and Television. Undergraduates benefit from studying with the faculty and the graduate students drawn to the strength of UCLA's MFA programs in acting, design for theater, directing, and playwriting. Being located right next to Hollywood is an obvious plus as well.

CATHOLIC UNIVERSITY

Due to the inspiration and efforts of its founder, Father Gilbert V. Hartke, who became known in Washington, DC (including at the White House), as the "showbiz priest," the Drama Department at Catholic University grew into prominence in the latter half of the twentieth century. Honoring Father Hartke's legacy is CU's professional-quality Hartke Theatre. In addition to its BA degree program in drama, CU offers renowned MFA degree programs in acting, directing, and playwriting. At the undergraduate level, CU believes that aspiring actors, directors, playwrights, and technical theater professionals will benefit most from a broad-based liberal arts approach to the dramatic arts rather than from a more specialized conservatory-type program.

EMERSON COLLEGE

Located beside Boston's theater district, Emerson offers six undergraduate programs in theater. Four of the theater programs lead to a BFA degree, and the other two lead to a BA degree. Emerson's BFA tracks are in acting, musical theater, stage and production management, and theater design/technology. The BA tracks in theater studies and theater education are offered with or without acting components. Theater education students have the option to earn teaching licensure in Massachusetts.

On-campus production and performance opportunities are extensive at Emerson. The centerpiece is a program called Emerson Stage that mounts eight to ten annual productions.

The Emerson Playwrights Festival presents productions, workshops, and staged readings of new works written by students and directed by faculty and guest professionals. Through Arts Emerson, legendary and pioneering performers come to campus to present their work.

Theater facilities at Emerson are professional quality. Emerson's Cutler Majestic Theatre has 1,200 seats and a proscenium stage. The Paramount Center has a 590-seat theater, a 125-seat black box theater, a scene shop, rehearsal studios, practice rooms, a state-of-the-art screening room, and a residence hall. The Tufte Performance and Production Center has 218 seats, a thrust stage, a 108-seat end-stage theater, a makeup studio, a design technology studio, and costume design labs. Emerson has a strong track record at helping its theater students get internships and jobs in areas such as casting, lighting, and stage management. Emerson theater graduates find acting, technical, and stage management positions across the United States.

FLORIDA STATE UNIVERSITY

Florida State has a leading theater program with a good record at preparing future actors for Broadway and screen roles. For undergraduate students, Florida State offers specialized BFA programs in acting and musical theater as well as a more general program leading to a BA in theater. Through a focus on production, theater students at Florida State get extensive experience in performance, design, and technical work. FSU's theater program encourages students to collaborate on imaginative projects with faculty, guest artists, and graduate students. Acting students take a sequence of courses in acting, movement, and voice and participate in specialized workshops. FSU seniors perform a BFA Showcase each spring in Los Angeles. Theater facilities at FSU include two proscenium stages and two flexible black box spaces as well as studios, shops, and classrooms. Florida State also offers a London Theatre Program, where students attend theater performances several times per week and visit other countries during breaks. Florida State's BA program in theater offers students a flexible liberal arts curriculum that includes courses in performance, directing, design, technical theater, theater history, performance studies, dramaturgy, theater management, playwriting, play analysis, and makeup for the stage. BA program students can audition for roles in productions, get experience as stage managers, and work on technical and design crews. Admission to the acting BFA program at FSU is competitive and requires an audition. Alumni include Megan Boone, and Alan Ball (screenwriter).

ITHACA COLLEGE

There are approximately three hundred students in the five undergraduate theater programs at Ithaca. Ithaca offers BFA programs in acting, musical theater, and theatrical production arts; a BA program in theater studies; and a BS in theater arts management. The acting BFA program is performance oriented and built around individualized instruction. Students have opportunities to act and direct in classes, workshops, and productions. Majors in theatrical production arts can concentrate on theatrical design or theater technology; the latter is for students interested in scenic carpentry, sound technology, lighting technology, and technical direction. The theatrical design concentration is for students interested in scenic design, costume design, or lighting design. The theater arts management program teaches students about marketing, personnel management, publicity, accounting, and development, while connecting students to internships. The theater studies major is a liberal arts–oriented program offering students the opportunity to explore acting, directing, theater history, stagecraft, design management, dramaturgy, and theater arts management.

Ithaca operates two professional theater companies on its campus and a London Center focused on British drama and culture at the National Theater Institute. Seniors at Ithaca spend a week on a field studies trip to New York City to network with theater alumni and practice their audition skills in a workshop setting. Ithaca's Dillingham Hall includes two acting studios, design and sound studios, dressing rooms, a costume shop, and extensive student lounge spaces. Ithaca also has state-of-the-art lighting, sound, scene automation, and rigging systems.

UNIVERSITY OF MIAMI

Miami theater students can choose a conservatory-type track of study or a more general track. The conservatory track leads to a BFA degree in one of five specialty options: acting, design/production, musical theater, stage management, and theater management. The more general track leads to a BA in theater arts. Acting students at Miami get intensive training in acting, voice/speech, movement, singing, and dance. Musical theater at Miami is completely focused on undergraduates. Design/production students can specialize in scenic design, lighting, costuming, sound design, or technical production management. Stage management students get to observe professional stage managers on Broadway, off Broadway, dance and opera productions, and touring companies. Students in the theater management program acquire hands-on experience at Miami's Ring Theatre in areas such as house management, box-office sales, marketing, and business operations.

The BA in theater arts track at Miami fits students interested in theater but not yet ready to specialize in one area. Students in the BA program take five core courses that introduce them to acting, stagecraft, scenery, costumes, lighting, prop construction, and theater history. Some BA students see the program as good liberal arts degree preparation for many possible careers, while others go on to more specialized MFA study. Actors Dwayne "the Rock" Johnson and Ray Liotta studied at Miami.

UNIVERSITY OF MINNESOTA

The Twin Cities of Minneapolis and St. Paul have one of the most vibrant theater communities in the United States. Undergraduate theater students at Minnesota have two degree options, the BA in theater arts and the BFA Actor Training program. For more than forty years, Minnesota has offered its Actor Training Program in partnership with the Guthrie Theater, one of the leading professional theaters in the United States and the longtime venue for *Prairie Home Companion*. Acting students take liberal arts courses at Minnesota and receive professional training at the Guthrie. The theater arts BA degree track enables students to explore acting, directing, design, dramatic history, theater criticism, and theater technology. All students in theater arts participate in productions staged by the University Theatre, the Minnesota Centennial Showboat, or the Creative Collaboration Series. Theater faculty members at Minnesota are active producers, directors, and technical professionals with national and regional reputations. The late actor Peter Graves is one of Minnesota's most notable theater alumni.

Students applying for the BFA program are required to audition. Students who are seeking the BA in theater apply as general applicants to the university and can declare theater as a major or minor.

MUHLENBERG COLLEGE

The Theatre and Dance Department at Muhlenberg College (2,125 students) in Allentown, Pennsylvania, combines professional-quality studio training with liberal arts education. Students at this liberal arts college have extensive opportunities to act, choreograph, design, stage manage, and direct productions. Muhlenberg operates an ambitious production schedule that includes musical theater performances, student plays, dramas, comedies, world premieres, classic pieces, and experimental plays. Theater majors at Muhlenberg have five different concentration options: acting, directing, performance studies, production design, and stage management. Students can also choose a double major in theater and dance or pursue multidisciplinary study in areas such as arts administration, dance medicine/dance therapy, arts education, playwriting, and literary and dramatic studies. Theater and dance students at Muhlenberg can study drama at the University of London or have an intensive cultural immersion in Tuscany, where they share meals with their teaching faculty and fellow students.

UNIVERSITY OF NORTH CAROLINA SCHOOL OF THE ARTS

The drama program at UNCSA in Winston-Salem takes a conservatory approach to training future performance professionals. Within UNCSA's School of Drama, there are two BFA degree programs: actor training and directing. In the actor training program, students focus on voice, movement, and acting and get acquainted with mask work, stage fighting, verse speaking, and period singing styles. In mastering technique, acting students focus on classical and twentieth-century works. The directing program is open to a limited number of students who have completed two years of actor training. Aspiring directors study under directors-in-residence, take acting and movement classes, learn design and production, create production books for plays, and direct long scenes, one-act plays, and Shakespeare scenes. In addition, UNCSA offers several degree programs in its School of Design and Production of potential interest to future theater professionals, such as costume design and technology, lighting design, scene design, scene painting, scenic technology, sound design, stage management, stage properties, and wig and makeup design.

Facilities at UNCSA reflect that performance is central to the student experience. UNCSA's main venue (aptly named Performance Place) includes two state-of-the-art theaters, a 300-seat theater with a proscenium thrust stage, a 200-seat flexible arena, dressing rooms, performers' lounges, classrooms, rehearsal spaces, and a lobby that doubles as a gallery. UNCSA also mounts musical productions in the other key performance venue, called the Stevens Center, which has a 1,380-seat neoclassical theater and a 188-seat theater.

RUTGERS UNIVERSITY

Within the Mason Gross School of the Arts at Rutgers is an excellent theater department where students learn from master teachers and stage professionals. Rutgers offers BFA conservatory-style training in acting, design, and stage management and technical direction. Within the design major, for example, students focus on set, costume, and lighting design and explore costume technology. Applicants to the acting BFA program must audition and submit a résumé with a headshot. Applicants to the design and production BFA program are required to submit a résumé and sit for an interview in which they present a design portfolio or examples of theater productions they have staged. Students interested in a less specialized approach to theater can choose the BA in theater major offered in Rutgers's School of Arts and Sciences.

The theatrical performance schedule at Rutgers is vibrant, with fifteen to eighteen plays staged annually, not to mention BFA senior project performances, class scenes, workshops, and salons. Theater facilities at Rutgers include two stages for full productions, a studio theater, an extensive scene shop, two costume shops, two large studios for casting workshops, a movement studio, and state-of-the-art lighting technology. BFA students in theater can participate in a program that connects Rutgers to the famous Globe Theater used by Shakespeare in the sixteenth century. Students in the Rutgers Globe Theater program study acting, design, and stage management under master teachers and scholars from around the United Kingdom. While enrolled in the Globe program, students see countless productions throughout the United Kingdom and take guided tours of London's major museums and art collections. Students in the London Globe program also study Shakespeare's plays in context and get introduced to British art and culture. Rutgers theater alumni include Calista Flockhart and James Gandolfini.

SOUTHERN METHODIST UNIVERSITY

Each year the Division of Theatre at SMU's Meadows School of the Arts enrolls twenty to twenty-five new freshmen, selected from over three hundred applicants, all of whom must audition. SMU offers BFA specializations in theater studies and acting. On the graduate level, SMU offers MFA programs in acting and in design. Through its BFA and MFA programs, SMU runs a top-ranked actor training program. The acting specialization at Meadows combines liberal arts courses with professional training in acting, voice, and movement. Students also learn about the backstage and business aspects of theater. The specialization in theater studies gives students a broad exposure to theater by requiring focused study in directing, playwriting, stage management, critical studies, and design.

Theater facilities at SMU are top notch, including two theaters named for famous actors who made contributions to SMU: the 400-seat Bob Hope proscenium-stage theater and the Greer Garson 380-seat classical thrust-stage theater. There is also a 125-seat black box facility. Special residency programs have brought theater luminaries (such as Angela Lansbury, Arthur Miller, and Stephen Sondheim) to campus to work with students. To provide a bridge into the profession, SMU's Meadows School partners with theaters and acting companies in Dallas to give its students professional experience.

VASSAR COLLEGE

Vassar was one of the first small liberal arts colleges to offer drama as a major. An early drama faculty member at Vassar was Hallie Flanagan Davis, who went on to direct the Federal Theatre Project for the Works Progress Administration (WPA) under President Franklin Delano Roosevelt. Vassar has always taken a liberal arts approach to the study of drama and encouraged experimental work. Since 1985, Vassar has presented an eight-week summer program of new works in theater and film called the Powerhouse Theatre program, which has earned Vassar a national reputation in the world of stage and screen. The facilities at Vassar are exceptional for a college of its size. They include a Center for Drama and Film, a 330-seat proscenium theater, a black box theater, studio theaters, a 1,600-square-foot scene shop, and technologically advanced light and sound systems. Course work in drama at Vassar encompasses acting, design, directing, dramaturgy, and playwriting.

LEADING MUSICAL THEATER PROGRAMS

- Baldwin Wallace University
- Ball State University
- Boston Conservatory at Berklee
- Carnegie Mellon University
- University of Cincinnati
- Emerson College
- Florida State University
- Indiana University
- James Madison University
- University of Miami
- University of Michigan
- Muhlenberg College
- New York University (Steinhardt)
- Northwestern University
- Oklahoma City University
- Penn State University
- Purchase College—State University of New York
- University of Utah

One of the top programs in musical theater is found at a small college south of Cleveland, Ohio. No, not Oberlin, but **Baldwin Wallace University** in Berea, Ohio. The music theater program at BW is restricted to undergraduates and is run by faculty with professional backgrounds and connections. Those connections have led to an annual senior showcase in which BW music theater students perform in front of two hundred stage and screen professionals. Many BW seniors get signed by agents after the showcase. Music theater students at BW are part of the Conservatory of Music, which means that students in the program receive a bachelor of music (BM) degree, as opposed to the more general BA in music. In training students for professional work on stage and screen, BW's music theater curriculum includes instruction in music, theater, and dance. Performance classes in voice make up the core of the program. Students are also required to study ballet, modern, jazz, and tap dance as well as take classes in theater literature, stagecraft, acting, makeup, and dance for theater. BW music theater alumni have appeared in major motion pictures, such as *How Do You Know*, and in national productions of *Billy Elliott, Chicago, Godspell, Hair, Jersey Boys, Legally Blonde, Mamma Mia, Memphis, Phantom of the Opera, Rent, The Scottsboro Boys*, and *Spider Man*.

At the **Boston Conservatory**, a specialized school within the Berklee College of Music, a central strength is vocal performance. With many degree programs related to voice, including opera, vocal pedagogy, and musical theater, the Boston Conservatory aims to prepare professional singers. The theater program at the Boston Conservatory is organized around musical theater and offers a BFA program that is comprehensive, with course work in voice, speech, theater, dance (modern, ballet, jazz, and tap), stagecraft, directing, and liberal arts courses such as Shakespeare and the History of Musical Theatre. Musical theater students at the Boston Conservatory study in a performance-oriented environment. There are more than 250 performances each year, including fully staged musicals, main-stage productions, operas, orchestral productions, and dance concerts. As seniors, musical theater students perform in a New York showcase for professional agents and casting directors. Alumni of the Boston Conservatory have appeared on Broadway as well as in television and film and have also worked at many prestigious performance organizations, such as the Boston Symphony and Chicago Lyric Opera.

The music theater BFA degree program at **Carnegie Mellon University** provides conservatory-style training in acting, voice, speech, and movement. The twenty-eight music theater students who enter the program annually learn in small classes, averaging ten to twelve students, led by teachers with professional theater backgrounds. Students at CMU have extraordinary opportunities to develop professional skills and connections without ever leaving the campus. Partnering with the Pittsburgh Light Opera and the American Society of Composers and Publishers (ASCAP), CMU has a special program (the New Works Series) that enables music theater students to work with professionals, such as School of Drama alumnus Stephen Schwartz (of *Godspell*, *Pippin*, and *Wicked* fame) to create and perform new musical works. Student work gets produced each year through the Playground Festival and Dance/Light series. In addition, CMU's annual senior showcase gives music theater students the opportunity to perform for industry professionals in Los Angeles, New York, and Pittsburgh. Music theater students are eligible to participate in study abroad programs at institutions in China, France, South Africa, and South Korea as well as at the National Institute of Dramatic Art in Sydney, the Moscow Art Theatre, and London's Drama Centre. The required audition is the most important aspect of the CMU music theater admission process.

Among the 1,200 students attending the College Conservatory of Music (CCM) at the **University of Cincinnati** are undergraduate students majoring in musical theater. Majoring in musical theater at Cincinnati (because the program is housed in the CCM) leads to a BM degree. The aim at Cincinnati is to turn out musical theater graduates who are triple threats, that is, students who can sing, dance, and act. Facilities for Cincinnati's musical theater productions are top of the line, including dance studios, rehearsal halls, a scene shop, a costume shop, a makeup lab, dozens of practice rooms, teaching studios, a proscenium theater, a thrust stage, a new vocal arts center, a black box studio

theater, and an acoustically world-class concert hall. Graduates of the CCM musical theater program have consistent success getting roles on Broadway, in television, and in international and national touring productions, such as *Billy Elliot*, *The Book of Mormon*, *Chicago*, *Les Miserables*, *Mamma Mia*, *Sister Act*, and *Shrek*.

Emerson College stands out as a training ground for future performers. In the Boston area, Emerson is synonymous with musical theater because for many years its radio station (WERS, 88.9 FM) has run popular programs featuring show tunes. Faculty at Emerson nurture students in the development of their acting, singing, and dancing talents. Course work in Emerson's BFA in musical theater program encompasses the history and development of the American musical as well as instruction in voice, movement, stagecraft, acting, and dance. Emerson's proximity to Boston's theater district enhances student opportunities to see productions and make connections to the professional stage scene.

Drawing on the strength of its offerings in vocal performance, **Florida State University** has one of the best music theater programs in the United States. The music theater major at FSU is part of the College of Music, which means that applicants must present music conservatory–level credentials for admission. The program leads to a BM degree in music theater. All students in the program perform recitals and participate in the senior showcase, which is held on campus and in New York City. Music theater students at FSU also have opportunities to perform in numerous operas and musical revues.

Currently directed by a choreographer with an Emmy Award and a Tony nomination to his credit, the BFA program in musical theater at **Indiana University** is limited to ten to fourteen new students per year. The small and personal program provides training in acting, singing, and dancing. There are at least a dozen plays and musicals staged annually in the professional-quality theater facilities on campus. The world-class voice and opera program in the Jacobs School of Music at Indiana provides further instructional and performance resources. Seniors in musical theater perform an annual showcase in New York City for agents, casting directors, and other stage and theater professionals. Graduates of IU's musical theater program have toured internationally and have gone on to Broadway and television careers. Getting admitted to musical theater at Indiana requires an audition. Talent-based scholarships are available for incoming freshmen and continuing students with distinguished records.

The musical theater (BFA) program at **Ithaca College** is a performance-oriented major designed to offer professional training in singing, acting, and dance. The goal of Ithaca's musical theater program is to prepare students to perform on Broadway, in films, and on television. Course work includes voice lessons, scene study, voice and movement for the stage, musical theater styles, stagecraft, ballet, modern, tap, and jazz dance. With, on average, fourteen campus shows per year, musical theater students at Ithaca get extensive performance experience.

Nestled in Virginia's Blue Ridge Mountains far from the lights of Broadway, **James Madison University** operates a powerhouse musical theater program. JMU offers two distinct routes to earning a degree in musical theater. Through the School of Theatre and Dance, students can earn a BA in musical theater, or through the School of Music, students can earn a BM in musical theater. Each degree program holds separate auditions. Annually, there is at least one large-scale musical at JMU and one studio musical. JMU students have consistent success at getting summer theater performance opportunities. In recent years, JMU musical theater students have performed in theater festivals in the Midwest, Northeast, South, and Southwest.

JMU graduates have gone on to perform in Broadway, national, and international productions of *Beauty and the Beast*, *A Chorus Line*, *Fame*, *Grease*, *Jersey Boys*, *Les Miserables*, *The Lion King*, *The Producers*, *Riverdance*, and *Shrek*.

The musical theater program at the **University of Miami** takes a conservatory approach to training students to be singing actors who will be ready, upon graduation, for performance careers on the musical and nonmusical stage. Students at Miami get intensive instruction in acting, dance, movement, singing, and voice/speech. There is no MFA program in musical theater at Miami, which means all the attention and performance opportunities go to BFA students.

The **University of Michigan** has one of the nation's top-ranked programs in musical theater. The program resides in Michigan's School of Music, Theatre, and Dance, leads to a BFA degree, and includes intensive course work in dance, theater, voice, performance history, composition, stage direction, choreography, lyric and libretto writing, and technical theater. Michigan musical theater students get a comprehensive education by taking 25 percent of their classes in liberal arts subjects. Students at Michigan can also pursue a dual degree, adding either a BA or BS to the BFA in musical theater. One distinguishing feature of Michigan's musical theater program is the high number of performance opportunities available. Students frequently stage revues, Broadway musicals, operettas, new and experimental works, and workshops. Graduates of the program are highly valued by professional casting directors, agents, and producers. Alumni have gone on to television and Broadway and off-Broadway performance careers, appearing in productions such as *The Full Monty*, *Little Women*, *The Scarlet Pimpernel*, and *Urinetown*. Michigan (which requires auditions) recommends that applicants be able to sight read and have previous experience and training in musical theater and ballet.

Musical theater is one of the strengths of the Theatre and Dance Department at **Muhlenberg College**. Muhlenberg is an appealing option for those seeking a high-quality musical theater program within a small school. The program at Muhlenberg is highly collaborative, with strong linkages to the dance and music departments. Each year Muhlenberg students mount at least one large-scale musical, such as the world premiere of *An American Tragedy*. A student-run theater association offers students additional production and leadership experiences. Muhlenberg's Summer Music Theatre program connects students with guest artists, professional directors, and designers and gives them experience working on full orchestral productions.

Within its Steinhardt School of Culture, Education, and Human Development, **New York University** offers an undergraduate degree in vocal performance with a specialization in music theater. Students in the program take private lessons and studio/workshop classes and get experience mounting fully staged productions. Teaching in the program are directors, choreographers, conductors, and designers from Broadway and professional theater companies. In their last semester at NYU, music theater students present a revue (called the Graduation Showcase) in front of talent agents, casting directors, producers, and directors. NYU also offers musical theater training through the BFA in drama program located in the Tisch School's New Studio on Broadway. Students interested in getting a specialized degree in musical theater from Tisch can pursue one on the graduate level.

Northwestern University has outstanding programs in both music and theater. Its annual student show has been a training ground for future stars such as Craig Beirko, Tony Randall, and Charlotte Rae. Although there are major programs in music and in theater at Northwestern, there is no music theater major. Instead, music theater is a certificate program that is highly sought after and widely respected. Each year thirty students are admitted to the program on the basis of their vocal, monologue, and dance auditions. Many alumni of Northwestern's music theater certificate program end up on Broadway and in national tours.

Good things often come in small packages, as petite powerhouse performer Kristen Chenoweth often says. She could very well be referring to her alma mater, **Oklahoma City University**, a private, Methodist-affiliated college that has a mere 1,750 undergraduates. Since 1930, Oklahoma City University has been dedicated to musical theater. In 2006, the Wanda L. Bass School of Music doubled its size with the addition of the $38.5 million, 113,000-square-foot Bass Music Center. Students at this school have reaped the benefits of the state-of-the-art facilities, and many have stayed on to pursue a master of music in musical theater. Broadway star Kelli O'Hara is also a graduate of Oklahoma City University.

Numerous Broadway-bound students find their way to State College, Pennsylvania, where **Penn State University** has the country's largest corps of musical theater faculty. The goal of the program at Penn State is to produce versatile singers who can act and dance. Voice classes cover a range of styles from classical to cabaret, and students get diagnostic voice sessions. All musical theater students at Penn State also get intensive dance training in ballet, jazz, and tap. Annually, there are dozens of musical theater performances on the PSU campus, giving students multiple opportunities to showcase their talents. To assist its musical theater students in breaking into performance careers, Penn State has a special fund called the NEXT STEP endowment. Enrollment in Penn State's BFA in musical theater program is limited. Entry into the program occurs via auditions held in the fall and spring.

Musical theater students at **Syracuse University** draw upon the strength and resources of the Department of Drama and the School of Music. Musical theater students undergo rigorous performance-based training that includes revues, operettas, musical comedies, and experimental works. Musical theater students get production experience in faculty-directed and student-sponsored productions as well as with the professional Syracuse Stage company.

Training in musical theater at the **University of Utah** involves intensive instruction in acting, singing, and dancing by faculty who are working professionals and guest artists. The BFA in musical theater program benefits from its close association with Utah's highly ranked dance programs. All musical theater students at Utah study ballet, jazz, modern, and tap dance. The performance seasons at Utah are extensive, with more than a dozen theater and dance productions each year. Admission to Utah's musical theater program requires an audition that assesses abilities in dance, acting, and singing. Although applicants may audition in cities such as Chicago, Las Vegas, Los Angeles, and New York, Utah strongly encourages on-campus auditions.

COLLEGES FOR DANCE

Some students want to major in dance, while others want to continue to take dance courses and keep performing. Stand-alone dance departments that offer a major are numerous but not ubiquitous. Frequently, dance as a program area is embedded within the theater department and offered either as a joint dance-theater major or as a dance minor. Those types of programs are often too small to interest potential dance majors with professional aspirations. For that reason, prospective dance students are advised to look most closely at dance programs that are offered as a major in a stand-alone dance department.

A key issue for prospective dance students is the quality of training in the student's particular area of interest. Students tend to want to specialize in ballet, modern dance, jazz and tap, or ethnic/cultural dance. Departments vary in their strengths. A small number of dance departments are strong across the board, while in other cases the strength is found in just one or two specialty areas. The following institutions (some of which are described briefly) have strong dance departments.

➤ COLLEGES WITH STRONG DANCE DEPARTMENTS

University of the Arts
Ball State University
Barnard College
Bennington College
California Institute of the Arts
University of California at Irvine
University of Cincinnati
University of Colorado
Columbia College (Chicago)
Connecticut College
Eugene Lang College of the New School University

Goucher College
University of Illinois
Indiana University
University of Iowa
James Madison University
Loyola Marymount University
University of Michigan
Muhlenberg College
New York University
University of North Carolina at Greensboro

University of North Carolina School of the Arts
Northwestern University
Rutgers University
Sarah Lawrence College
Southern Methodist University
University of Texas at Austin
Texas Christian University
University of Utah
Virginia Commonwealth University
Washington University
Wesleyan University

The **University of the Arts** in Philadelphia has one of the largest undergraduate dance programs in the United States. The three hundred students in dance at UA learn from resident faculty and guest artists who are professionally accomplished. Located next door to art museums, theaters, and the Kimmel Center, where the Philadelphia Orchestra performs, UA provides students with an education in a dynamic creative urban setting. The dance curriculum has a conservatory environment that reflects the professional world of dance that graduates will enter. Performance is at the core of the program. In the first two foundation years of study, dance students undertake intensive studio training in ballet, jazz, and modern techniques plus emerging styles, such as hip-hop and improvisation. Dance training culminates in a senior project that is critiqued. Facilities include fourteen practice rooms and a 1,800-seat theater.

Due to its professional focus, the **University of the Arts** encourages its dance students to have internship and apprentice experiences. Guest choreographers frequently are in residence to work with students. Students have performed on the television programs *So You Think You Can Dance* and *Live to Dance*. Alumni have performed in numerous Broadway productions or have been members of prestigious companies such as the Joffrey Ballet, Pilobolus, Martha Graham Dance Company, and Cirque de Soleil.

En route to a BA or BS degree, dance majors at **Ball State University** study the techniques of ballet, modern, ethnic, jazz and tap dance while also taking courses in theater, musical theater, and the liberal arts. A campus-based company (Ball State Dance Theatre) gives dance majors experience in performing and choreographing productions. Each year Ball State Dance Theatre presents at least two major performances in the 410-seat University Theatre. The dance production schedule at Ball State is vigorous. Every semester features junior and senior choreography showcases, numerous student and faculty dance projects, and student-led choreography and production workshops.

On the **Barnard College** campus in New York, there are on average thirty students majoring in dance and 1,200 students taking dance classes. The facilities and performance opportunities at Barnard provide professional-level training, and Barnard's location in Manhattan puts its dance students in America's epicenter for the performing arts. Between full-time and part-time teaching faculty, there are forty dance instructors at Barnard. Barnard's comprehensive dance curriculum ranges across ballet, modern dance, movement, choreography, dance history, and dance theory. Dance classes at Barnard include students from neighboring Columbia University. Barnard dance alumnae include the renowned choreographer Twyla Tharp.

The Sharon Disney Lund School of Dance at the **California Institute of the Arts**, located forty-five minutes north of Los Angeles, offers BFA and MFA programs built around dance composition, performance, and choreography. Students learn from faculty mentors and guest artists who are working professionals. The BFA program in dance at Cal Arts includes instruction in ballet, modern dance, and world styles, such as African and Balinese dance. The curriculum grounds students in dance production areas such as stagecraft, lighting design, costume design, and audio and video production. A travel/study partnership connects Cal Arts with the London Contemporary Dance School in England. Cal Arts offers stipends to a selected number of summer study program students, enabling them to get experience with dance companies or in dance festivals. Cal Arts maintains a vigorous performance schedule of eight to ten dance concerts per year and has its own residence company called the Next Dance Company.

Dance at **University of California at Irvine** (UCI) is part of the Claire Trevor School of the

Arts, which also includes the departments of drama, music, and studio art. Among the 220 dance students at UCI are 200 undergraduates, studying for either a BFA or a BA degree, and twenty MFA students. All dance students at UCI start out as BA candidates. As sophomores, students who want to undertake more specialized study in dance can begin pursuing the conservatory-style BFA in performance or the BFA in choreography. The BA in dance option provides a general liberal arts approach to the field, while also providing instruction in ballet, modern, jazz, tap, world dance, and dance technology. Technique classes average twenty to thirty students. Each year there are at least five fully staged productions.

For thirty years (1948–78), **Connecticut College** hosted the American Dance Festival. During that period, Connecticut built one of the top dance departments at a liberal arts college. That legacy continues. In addition to hosting a resident company (David Dorfman Dance), Conn's Dance Department attracts frequent guest artists who teach classes and perform works and has hosted national college dance festivals. Taught from an interdisciplinary perspective, the dance major at Conn focuses on movement technique, dance studies, dance history, dance theory, choreography, and improvisation. Conn encourages dance majors to have internship experiences, often arranged through alumni, in cities like New York.

The Dance Department at the **University of Illinois** garners consistent top-ten rankings from *Dance Teacher* magazine. Each year twenty new freshmen enter the dance program at Illinois, having been chosen from sixty to seventy-five auditioning applicants. Dance students are taught by practicing professionals and guest artists in a more individualized atmosphere than is typically associated with a university that enrolls forty thousand students. The student-faculty ratio of seven to one makes it possible for Illinois

dance students to experience a nurturing education within a large, dynamic research university. The BFA program offers specialized concentrations in technique, improvisation, composition, and performance. The performance facilities at Illinois stand out in the Midwest. Dancers have access to five studio spaces and get to perform in a 674-seat theater. Illinois also encourages its dance students to study abroad.

Indiana University is a place known for excellence in the performing arts, and dance at Indiana is no exception. Although its BS program in dance encompasses classical and contemporary styles, Indiana is a standout for ballet. IU Ballet Theater is recognized as one of the top college dance performance groups in the United States. Since dance at IU is a degree program housed within the Jacobs School of Music, dancers have the opportunity to perform in musicals and operas and with orchestral accompaniment.

Students in the BA program in dance at **James Madison University** get to create, perform, and produce works while devising an individualized path toward a performing arts career. The dance curriculum at JMU encompasses technique courses in ballet, modern, jazz, tap, ballroom, improvisational, and international dance styles. Students also study dance composition, dance history, and stage production and management. Dance students become members of one of the performance groups, such as the Contemporary Dance Ensemble and the preprofessional Virginia Repertory Dance Company. JMU's ensembles are frequent performers at the American College Dance Festival. Many famous dance companies have come to JMU for guest residencies during which students take master classes and perform. JMU dance alumni go on to join dance companies, teach dance, or work in the performing arts. Admission to JMU's dance program requires an audition.

Dance at the **University of Michigan** is taught in an interdisciplinary context. The Dance

Department is part of a school at Michigan that includes music and theater. Michigan offers BFA and MFA degrees in dance and makes it relatively easy for students to add another major. The dance curriculum gears students toward performance and choreography in classical and contemporary forms. Performance opportunities begin in the first year with the Freshman Touring Company and branch out to include choreography and production experience with the Dance Repertory and the University Dancers. Michigan dance alumni have gone on to perform with leading companies founded by luminaries such as Merce Cunningham, Martha Graham, Bill T. Jones, Mark Morris, Paul Taylor, and Twyla Tharp. One former Michigan dance student established a successful singing career as Madonna.

The dance program at **New York University** offers a BFA degree that is earned in three intensive years plus two summers. Dance at NYU is part of the Tisch School of the Arts. Students in the NYU dance program focus on technical training, choreography, and performance. Training at NYU includes workshops and master classes in dance technique and composition supplemented by approximately thirty-five annual productions. The Second Avenue Dance Company provides a laboratory for student choreography. Dancers are trained broadly within a curriculum that includes acting, improvisation, music theory, and music literature. Dancers are also instructed in the kinesthetics of anatomy (including yoga and Pilates) in order to learn how to dance in the most efficient and healthy way.

The dance major at **Northwestern University** sits alongside the famous theater program in the School of Communications. Northwestern's dance curriculum spans composition, choreography, dance theory and analysis and includes instruction in ballet, jazz, modern, tap, and improvisational dance. Students learn from resident faculty, who are award-winning professional choreographers and from guest artists who

lead master classes. Students at Northwestern get extensive performance experience through campus-based dance troupes that perform frequently at the American College Dance Festival and in theater productions. Graduates of the BA program in dance become performers, dance critics, dance teachers, choreographers, dance therapists, and arts administrators.

Sarah Lawrence College has an outsized impact on the dance profession. Numerous graduates of its BA and MFA programs lead dance companies, perform in prestigious venues, and work as dance faculty at colleges. Dance at SLC is taught broadly within a liberal arts context. Students can select classes in modern and postmodern styles, classical ballet, African dance, belly dance, composition, improvisation, music for dancers, lighting design and stagecraft, and dance history. Other classes address the health and wellness aspect of dance, bringing perspectives from yoga, Feldenkreis, and awareness through movement. SLC's Dance Department encourages interdisciplinary linkages to theater, music, and the visual arts and lets students create individualized programs around their special interests and needs. The Schinberg Dance Theatre and DeCarlo Performing Arts Center provide students with professional quality performance spaces. Annually, there are more than a dozen dance performances that include students, guest artists, and guest choreographers.

The dance program at **Southern Methodist University** is part of the Meadows School of the Arts. More than half of the credits students earn in SMU's BFA in dance program are in studio classes. Dance students at SMU get comprehensive training in ballet, modern dance, and jazz techniques. The curriculum requires students to perform in productions, provides opportunities to create and choreograph works, and gears graduates toward professional careers. SMU dance alumni have performed with prestigious organizations such as Alvin Ailey American Dance Theater, Ballet Hispanico, Dance Theatre of Harlem, Martha Graham Dance Company, and Paul Taylor Dance Company. The excellent dance facilities at SMU include the spacious Bob Hope Theatre and three major studios that have sprung dance floors, mirrors, barres, pianos, and sound systems. Every studio class in dance at Meadows includes live musical accompaniment.

At **Texas Christian University** in Fort Worth, there is a whole school dedicated to dance. TCU has become prominent in the dance world through the accomplishments of its alumni, who have danced in Broadway productions and performed with professional companies such as the Atlanta Ballet, Boston Ballet, Mark Morris Dance Group, Paul Taylor Dance Company, Pilobolus, Texas Ballet Theatre, and the American Dance Festival. The School for Classical and Contemporary Dance at TCU prides itself on its close-knit community, where undergraduates are mentored by faculty and graduate students. The dance curriculum at TCU is both thorough and specific, enabling exploration of dance technique, choreography, improvisation, dance history, aesthetics, music and lighting for dance, jazz dance, kinesiology, and international dance forms. TCU dance students can pursue a BFA in ballet, a BFA in modern dance, a double major combining the two, or a double degree that pairs dance with another field of study. TCU also offers the MFA degree in dance. Based on an audition, students are accepted into either ballet or modern dance for a one-year trial period, during which they have their progress and potential evaluated. The School for Dance at TCU encourages every student to have an international experience and provides a number of options. Students and faculty have traveled in groups to international destinations such as England, Germany, Japan, and Scotland for master classes and performances. TCU also operates a program with the Universidad de las Americas-Puebla in Mexico. Fort Worth, in combination with Dallas, provides exceptional artistic resources, including some of the nation's best museums, orchestras, and performance groups. TCU offers a number of talent-based scholarships in addition to need-based financial aid.

At the **University of Texas** flagship campus in Austin, all dance majors (in the BFA program) automatically become members of the student dance company. Admission to the BFA program in dance requires an audition, either on campus or by video. The departments of dance and theater at Texas are closely connected, so in addition to the BFA in dance, students can elect to pursue a combined theater and dance BA degree.

The College of Fine Arts at the **University of Utah** is nationally recognized for its programs in dance. One indication of the prominence of dance at Utah is that there are separate departments for ballet and modern dance, both of which offer BFA and MFA degrees. At Utah, there are ninety undergraduates and twenty to twenty-five graduate students specializing in modern dance. Within modern dance, there are two areas of emphasis: performance and teaching, with the latter leading to certification to teach dance in schools. Regardless of the emphasis, all modern dance majors at Utah get intensive training in improvisation, choreography, and performance. The close working relationship between the modern dance and ballet departments makes Utah a uniquely vibrant dance community. Student dance groups, including the nationally recognized Performing Dance Company, showcase their talents in a 333-seat state-of-the-art theater.

The BFA in Ballet program at **Utah** emphasizes performance, teaching, and character dance. Among the performance opportunities are Utah Ballet, a campus-based, preprofessional dance company, and the Character Dance Ensemble that has given more than 250 performances since 1995 in cities such as Athens, Beijing, and St. Petersburg. Alumni of Utah's ballet program dance worldwide in companies, pursue solo careers, or work in high-level arts management positions. Prominent ballet alumni include Jiang Qi, who has danced with leading companies around the world and teaches at the University of Cincinnati. Another Utah ballet alumnus, Douglas Sonntag, is director of dance for the National Endowment for the Arts.

Washington University's reputation for medicine and science sometimes overshadows its strong arts programs. Students who take a close look at WashU will find an excellent and comprehensive dance program that has courses in modern, ballet, jazz, and African dance.

Seminar and studio classes are limited in size and taught by faculty experienced as professional dancers and choreographers. A residence program enables distinguished guest artists to visit the campus to teach master classes and preview new work with WashU students as the performers. The student-based Washington University Dance Theatre often enters works into the American College Dance Conference. Dance students at WashU have access to special study abroad programs (such as MADE in France) that offer an interactive historical survey of European art, dance, and design. One MADE in France program, held in Burgundy, encouraged multidisciplinary performance involving choreographers, actors, musicians, artists, and dancers.

ART, ARCHITECTURE, DESIGN, AND FILM

ART SCHOOLS

Art schools are specialized places where students concentrate on creating art and developing artistic skill. Because they offer few courses in subjects outside of art, art schools can be a perfect choice for the student who found English, math, and social studies courses in high school a tedious distraction away from the art room.

Art schools base admissions decisions largely on an assessment of the prospective student's talent and promise, which is why a central part of applying to an art school is the portfolio. Typically, art schools require applicants to submit a portfolio of work, such as drawings, paintings, photographs, and other examples of artistic talent. Portfolio requirements (usually explained on the art school's website) vary depending on the medium the student intends to study. Special on-campus or national or regional portfolio days introduce students to the art school approach to education and admissions. At National Portfolio Days (held between September and March), students can meet for ten to fifteen minutes with an art school representative and get an evaluation of their skill and future potential. High school grades and standardized test scores matter very little in the art school admissions process, especially if an applicant's portfolio is strong.

Several of the top art schools in the United States are located in urban areas where large concentrations of artists and diverse communities give rise to the creative ferment that inspires art making. A number of the top art schools are attached to or located near leading museums and art galleries. The top arts schools tend to have comprehensive course offerings and extensive facilities, resulting in strength across the curriculum. Many art schools, especially those that are not world renowned, stand out in one or two areas rather than across the board.

Although there are many excellent places to study art, two institutions are names that everyone in the art world knows and respects. **The School of the Art Institute of Chicago** shows up on virtually every list of top art schools. Students at this institution experience a great city, attend a campus in a prime location, and walk the halls of an museum where many of the world's most famous works of art are on display. A degree from the School of the Art Institute of Chicago, while no guarantee that a graduate's artworks will end up in galleries and museums, signifies impressive artistic talent.

Another art school synonymous with high quality is the **Rhode Island School of Design** (RISD). RISD, pronounced riz-dee, is a fertile training ground for future art faculty and influential artists. Located in a gentrified hillside neighborhood overlooking downtown Providence, RISD offers cross registration opportunities for students to take classes at an Ivy League university (Brown). The artistic power of RISD is not just apparent in the studios and galleries on its campus. In the past two decades, RISD students and graduates have also invigorated the neighborhoods of Providence, spurring a renaissance that has transformed a formerly rundown and crime-ridden city into a vibrant place to live and study.

THE SCHOOL OF THE ART INSTITUTE OF CHICAGO—CHICAGO, ILLINOIS

Since 1866, the School of the Art Institute of Chicago has been a world leader. For as long as it has existed, a unifying goal of the Art Institute has been to graduate artists whose work pushes boundaries. The respected artists and scholars teaching at the Art Institute impart a multidisciplinary approach to art and design and encourage students to be provocative thinkers and makers of art. In addition to its world-renowned art collection, the Art Institute facilities include the Gene Siskel Film Center, a video data bank, a Poetry Center, and a visiting artists program.

All freshmen at the Art Institute take a required set of courses called contemporary practices that introduce them to a range of approaches to art. After that first year, students have more freedom to follow an individualized plan of study. All students pursuing bachelor of fine arts (BFA) programs must also take liberal arts courses that develop competence in writing; provide perspectives from the humanities, social sciences, and natural sciences; and develop familiarity with art history, theory, and criticism. Major options in art include interior architecture and designed objects; art education; art history, theory, and criticism; ceramics; fashion design; fiber and material studies; film, video, new media, and animation; painting and drawing; photography; print media; sculpture; sound; visual communication design; and visual and creative studies.

Not all Art Institute students train for careers as working artists. The Art Institute offers excellent programs in art history, art education, fashion design, interior architecture, sound, and writing. Graduates of the fashion-design program have launched their own fashion lines or taken senior design positions at firms such as Jones New York, Nike, Tommy Hilfiger, Calvin Klein, Alexander McQueen, and Zac Posen. Students in the sound program leave prepared for work in audio recording, audio installation, live performance, software design, and distributed technologies such as radio and the Internet.

Applicants must submit a portfolio of ten to fifteen examples of artwork and have a minimum composite ACT score of 20 or at least 500 on the SAT critical reading exam. On Immediate Decision Days, students whose applications are complete come to campus for a portfolio review and receive an admission decision. There is no separate application for the merit scholarships given to the most talented applicants.

RHODE ISLAND SCHOOL OF DESIGN— PROVIDENCE, RHODE ISLAND

Despite its name, the Rhode Island School of Design (RISD) is not a public institution. One of the world's preeminent art schools, RISD is a relatively small private college for talented people who thrive in a creative culture. Students at RISD develop expertise in a specific field while getting an education that goes beyond mere practical training. A RISD education combines discipline-based, immersive art and design instruction with a cross disciplinary core of liberal arts classes. Applicants who think that art schools provide an impractical and ornamental education might be surprised to learn that 96 percent of RISD alumni find employment or enter graduate school within one year of graduation.

RISD students start with a first-year common studio curriculum, move on to selecting and completing a major field of concentration, and supplement their intensive study and training with liberal arts courses that emphasize critical thinking and creative problem solving. The liberal arts requirement ensures that students leave RISD having studied art history, architectural history, English, history, philosophy, social sciences, culture and film, theater, science, and math. The common studio curriculum focuses on drawing, design, and special dynamics in classes of approximately twenty students. RISD has three academic divisions and seventeen undergraduate major options. The most popular majors are illustration, industrial design, graphic design, and architecture.

The Division of Architecture and Design at RISD has six major options. Architecture offers a four-year BFA degree and a five-year bachelor of architecture (BArch) degree that prepares students for professional licensure. Complementing architecture is an industrial design major that perennially ranks as one of the top programs in the United States. Industrial design graduates earn a bachelor of industrial design (BID) and a BFA. RISD's Division of Architecture and Design also offers majors in apparel design, furniture design, graphic design, and interior design. Within its Fine Arts Division, RISD has ten BFA programs: ceramics, film/animation/video, glass, illustration, jewelry and metalsmithing, painting, photography, printmaking, sculpture, and textiles. RISD fine arts students commonly have internships at places such as Google, Disney, the Cartoon Network, the Museum of Modern Art, and Martha Stewart Living Omnimedia.

The more than five hundred RISD professors are expert practitioners and scholars as well as dedicated teachers. The quality of the instruction and the overall satisfaction students have with the RISD experience translates into a 90 percent graduation rate. RISD takes pride in stating that more students transfer into the school than transfer out. In addition to its leading-edge facilities for making art, RISD has other education-enhancing resources including a Museum of Art with more than eighty-six thousand works, a nature lab with more than eighty thousand natural history objects and live specimens, and the Fleet Library with impressive collections in architecture, art, design, and photography.

Right next door to RISD is Brown University. RISD students can take courses at Brown at no extra cost, plus they can cross the street to attend lectures, concerts, and theatrical productions and to use library and athletic facilities. Since 2007, RISD and Brown have teamed up to offer a dual BA (Brown)/BFA (RISD) degree program. RISD's international exchange program offers students opportunities to study in twenty-two different countries, including a European honors program in Rome.

Applying to RISD is an involved process requiring high school transcripts, test scores, recommendations, two drawings, a portfolio of twelve to twenty examples of artwork, and two writing samples (one addressing the anticipated effect of a RISD education). Early decision applicants who are selecting RISD as their first choice must apply by November 1. Getting into RISD is far from assured: just one-third of applicants get admitted.

BEYOND RISD AND THE ART INSTITUTE OF CHICAGO

Talent is the driver of success in the art world. Although a degree from RISD or the Art Institute of Chicago may open some doors, what really matters is artistic ability. An excellent education can occur at just about any art school as long as there are inspirational teachers, accessible facilities, and a spirit of innovation. A number of excellent art schools are listed (and in selected cases described) below.

- Art Center College of Design
- California College of the Arts
- California Institute of the Arts
- Cleveland Institute of Art
- Kansas City Art Institute
- Maryland Institute College of Art
- Minneapolis College of Art and Design
- Otis College of Art and Design
- Parsons School of Design at the New School University
- Pratt Institute
- Ringling School of Art and Design
- Savannah College of Art and Design
- School of Visual Arts
- University of the Arts

ART CENTER COLLEGE OF DESIGN—PASADENA, CALIFORNIA

The 1,554 undergraduates at the Art Center College of Design get an education that anticipates future changes in art and creative commerce. From the first course, students learn by doing in small studio classes led by professors who are practicing artists and designers. Because there is no introductory foundation year, Art Center students take courses in their major from day one. This approach gives students a head start on acquiring the level of specialization needed for professional success and may account for the 84 percent employment rate Art Center graduates have one year after earning their degree. The Art Center College also fosters transdisciplinary education, as exemplified by the recent Beautiful Networks studio that explored how systems in culture and the natural world inspired artists, designers, filmmakers, and photographers.

The Art Center's innovative Designmatters Department focuses on the social impact of design and how design can help shape a better future. In Designmatters courses, students collaborate across disciplines and explore art and design's role in addressing social and humanitarian needs. Programs at the Art Center (leading to BFA or BS degrees) include advertising, entertainment design, environmental design, film, fine art, graphic design, illustration (with four tracks), interaction design, photography and imaging, product design, and transportation design. The five most popular majors, in order, are illustration, graphic design, transportation design, product design, and photography. The product design and transportation design majors are consistently ranked among the best in the United States. The interaction design major teaches students to develop new product ecologies and use technology creatively.

While the Art Center strives for excellence in all of its programs, certain majors stand out. The advertising program is the oldest in the United States and is taught by faculty who are leading art directors and copywriters. Entertainment design students go on to careers in animation, video game design, film, and television. The film program has a close relationship with Hollywood studios, partly because its faculty members are accomplished film industry professionals. For more than sixty years, the Art Center's transportation design major has prepared graduates for careers in automotive, motorcycle, marine, aircraft, and public transit design. Transportation design students have access to the twenty-plus professional automotive design studios located in Southern California. Art Center students in product design have at their disposal a state-of-the-art Color, Materials, and Trends Exploration Laboratory for research projects. In addition, the Art Center has a partnership with INSEAD, one of the world's top business schools.

Applying to the Art Center requires high school transcripts, ACT or SAT results, and a portfolio of work. The portfolio is the most important component of the application.

CALIFORNIA INSTITUTE OF THE ARTS—VALENCIA, CALIFORNIA

Thirty miles north of Los Angeles, 1,400 students attend a world-renowned arts institution established fifty years ago by Walt and Roy Disney. Cal Arts offers leading programs in art, dance, film/video, music, and theater to a student body that comes from numerous countries and every state in the United States. Cal Arts garners consistent high ratings for its fine arts programs but especially for digital imaging, graphic design, multimedia/visual communication, sculpture, and photography. Faculty members at Cal Arts are innovative art practitioners leading a curriculum that embraces and anticipates new currents in art and design.

The program in art leads to a BFA degree and enables Cal Arts students to explore a range of media, including painting, drawing, print-making, photography, digital imaging, sculpture, installation, video, film, writing, and performance. Graphic design students at Cal Arts work in communal studios (grouped by year level), creating a body of work to present when seeking jobs at design firms. Photography and media students can concentrate on traditional photography, digital media, or the integration of the two. One of the strengths of Cal Arts is its collaborative environment. Amidst the extensive studio spaces in the 500,000-square-foot Cal Arts complex, art students work alongside filmmakers, actors, composers, musicians, set designers, and choreographers. A centerpiece of the campus is REDCAT, the Roy and Edna Disney Cal Arts Theater, which provides a space for innovative visual media and performing arts. Fine arts facilities include media, photo, print, and video labs and a Super Shop for woodworking, metalworking, machining, mold making, spraying, and sandblasting.

Applicants to the fine arts programs at Cal Arts must submit a portfolio that represents their best work completed in the last twelve months. Also central to the admission review is a required artist's statement.

MARYLAND INSTITUTE COLLEGE OF ART—BALTIMORE, MARYLAND

The Maryland Institute College of Art (MICA) dates back to 1826, making it the oldest continuous degree-granting college of art in the United States. In numerous rankings, MICA shows up among the nation's top dozen art/design schools, especially in graphic design. The 1,900 undergraduate students at MICA get a globally focused education, which helps explain why it stands out among art schools for producing Fulbright Scholars.

All freshmen at MICA take an identical core of foundation skills courses. When students turn toward a specialized major, they find sixteen choices, including animation, fiber, interaction design and art, and video and film arts. Studio concentrations are available in book arts, curatorial studies, experimental fashion, game arts, sound art, and sustainability and social practice. MICA also offers a five-year BFA/MAT in art education as well as the opportunity to remain for a fifth year and earn a master's degree in the business of art and design, community arts, or social design.

The environmental design program at MICA enables studio work related to furniture, interiors, architecture, and urban spaces. MICA's environmental design students frequently place high in international design competitions. Interaction design and art—an interdisciplinary program focused on the user experience and the interactions between websites, electronics, objects, and systems—prepares students to enter fields such as game design, mobile technology, and social networking. Students in the program can pursue a studio concentration in sound art. MICA's graphic design program, which often gets ranked in the top ten, offers a special concentration in book arts. MICA students can prepare for the fashion world with the fiber major (which has both a fine art and an applied art emphasis) or through the more avant-garde studio concentration in experimental fashion.

The global orientation of MICA shows through in its extensive study abroad offerings, which include programs and direct exchanges with art schools in Australia, Chile, the Czech Republic, France, Germany, Israel, Italy, Japan, Korea, the Netherlands, Poland, Singapore, Spain, Sweden, Switzerland, and the United Kingdom. MICA also offers summer travel trips—involving eight to twelve students per trip—to New York City and several foreign countries. Beyond the portfolio, MICA applicants must submit a standard college application, including test scores and an essay. MICA offers need-based financial aid and merit-based scholarships (some of which are reserved for residents of Maryland).

OTIS COLLEGE OF ART AND DESIGN— LOS ANGELES, CALIFORNIA

The Otis College of Art and Design is both a fine arts and an applied arts school. The 1,200 undergraduates at Otis can study illustration, painting, photography, and sculpture, but they can also train for careers in advertising, digital media, graphic design, architecture, fashion design, product design, and toy design. The curriculum at Otis capitalizes on its location in the heart of the film industry. Among the alumni of Otis are the artists who sculpted the Oscar statue and the illustrator who drew Bambi.

Otis has standout strength in the area of design, offering a full range of programs from advertising design to interior design and product design. But Otis has one design program rarely found elsewhere, the major in toy design—an integrated curriculum that grounds students in the art, imagination, engineering, and marketing involved in designing toys. The toy design program at Otis is frequently called the best such program in the world. Toy design graduates hold leading positions in the toy industry.

All students at Otis start their education with a studio-focused foundation program supplemented with liberal arts courses. In year two, students can begin to pursue more specialized majors, choosing among ten BFA options: advertising design, architecture/landscape/ interiors, digital media, fashion design, graphic design, illustration, painting, photography, sculpture/new genres, product design, and toy design. Otis students also have the opportunity to elect minors in sustainability, cultural studies, art history, creative writing, community arts engagement, and preparation for teaching credentials. Applying to Otis requires an essay, high school transcript, standardized test scores (ACT or SAT), and a portfolio of ten to twenty examples of the applicant's best and most recent artwork (drawn from any medium).

PARSONS SCHOOL OF DESIGN (AT THE NEW SCHOOL UNIVERSITY)— NEW YORK, NEW YORK

One of the nation's top schools for art and design, Parsons is embedded within the New School University, a New York institution that has pioneered interdisciplinary study since its founding. One of Parsons's strengths is its location within a university that has a liberal arts college (Eugene Lang), a school for jazz and contemporary music, and dozens of graduate programs, including options for Parsons students to elect a five-year dual degree program and graduate with two bachelor's degrees. Students at Parsons begin with a foundation year program that introduces the tools needed for creative areas of study. Then, alongside a specialty in art, they take a required liberal arts core to get a broader context for specialized studio practice and careers that involve cross disciplinary collaboration and creative experimentation. Most of the more than seven hundred professors teaching at Parsons are artists and designers with active practices in New York.

Parsons is organized into schools for art and design history and theory; art, media, and technology; constructed environments; design strategies; and fashion. The School of Art, Media, and Technology offers BFA degrees in communication design, design and technology, illustration, photography, and fine arts (including concentrations in drawing, painting, sculpture, video, visual culture, design, printing, photography, and illustration). The School of Constructed Environments offers BFA degrees in interior design, product design, and architectural design—a flexible program, enabling preparation for graduate study or careers in architecture, interior design, landscape architecture, urban design, and environmental design. The School of Design Strategies offers degree programs in design and management, environmental studies, integrated design, and urban design. Integrated design students can concentrate in fashion, service design, sustainability, or urban design. Fashion is the oldest school at Parsons and has become a world leader due to the expertise of its teaching faculty, the stature of its alumni, and its location in North America's fashion epicenter.

In addition to a completed application (including results of standardized tests), all applicants must submit and describe an original work in response to the Parsons challenge. How an applicant responds to the Parsons Challenge helps the admissions committee understand how that applicant structures and conveys ideas. Majors that require a portfolio include architectural design, communication design, design and technology, fashion design, fine arts, illustration, integrated design, interior design, photography, and product design. Applicants may also submit an optional five-hundred-word artist's statement.

PRATT INSTITUTE—NEW YORK, NEW YORK

Pratt offers twenty-two undergraduate programs, including concurrent bachelor and master's degree options, in an educational environment that emphasizes theory and practice. With locations in Brooklyn and Manhattan, Pratt has six schools: architecture; art; design; information and library science; liberal arts and sciences; and continuing and professional studies. No matter the degree program, all undergraduates at Pratt must take at least 25 percent of their classes from the School of Liberal Arts and Sciences in areas such as English, cultural history, science, mathematics, social sciences, and philosophy.

Pratt's bachelor's and dual degree (BFA/MS) options include art and design education; art history; communications design; digital arts; fashion design; film; fine arts; industrial design; interior design; photography; theory, criticism,

and history of art; design; and architecture. The School of Architecture offers undergraduate degree programs in construction management, building and construction, and architecture (BArch). Pratt also offers a BA degree in critical and visual studies, a BFA in writing, and two-year associate degrees in graphic design, illustration, painting/drawing, and digital design and interactive media. Pratt's location in America's fashion capital (New York City) is an asset for its fashion-design program, which prepares students to enter the global design community with both a technical and a creative grounding. Students in Pratt's interior design program—a recognized leader in the field—can spend a semester at the Danish International School (DIS) in Copenhagen, immersing themselves in the Scandinavian region and its design heritage.

Pratt requires applicants to submit high school transcripts, standardized test scores (ACT or SAT), and a portfolio (except for the construction management program).

RINGLING COLLEGE OF ART AND DESIGN—SARASOTA, FLORIDA

The Ringling School of Art and Design is frequently heralded as one of the most innovative arts colleges in the United States—especially for its use of technology. Rankings and guidebooks have rated Ringling's digital arts and computer animation programs among the best in the world. Ringling students routinely win Student Academy Awards for computer animation as well as ADDY awards and Society of Illustration awards. Whatever the criteria, rankings tend to place Ringling among America's top ten art schools.

Unlike city art schools, Ringling has a verdant forty-eight-acre campus with almost one hundred buildings. Nearly two-thirds of Ringling's 1,400 students (all of them undergraduates) live on campus. Although Florida residents comprise half of the student body,

Ringling is international in scope with students from forty-six states and forty-eight countries. More so than most art schools, Ringling attracts companies seeking to hire its graduates, such as Apple Computer, Cartoon Network, CNN, Disney, DreamWorks, Electronic Arts, ESPN, General Motors, Lucas Arts Entertainment, Ogilvy and Mather, Sony Pictures, Universal Studios, and Warner Bros. Some Ringling students get on-the-job skills by staffing a design center that provides free services to nonprofit organizations in the Sarasota area.

The BFA programs at Ringling are built around studio, liberal arts, and art history courses. Freshmen take Core Studios Program courses in drawing, figure, color, and design, plus a course or two in their intended major. Beginning in year two, studio courses are in a student's major area. Classes are small and taught by mentor-teachers who are practicing artists. The four most popular majors are (in order) illustration, computer animation, game art and design, and graphic and interactive communication. Ringling offers one BA program—in the business of art and design—and thirteen BFA programs: advertising design, computer animation, digital filmmaking, fine arts, game art and design, graphic and interactive communication, interior design, illustration, motion design, painting, photography and digital imaging, printmaking, and sculpture.

Getting admitted to Ringling requires a completed Common Application (but not test scores) plus a portfolio for all programs except business of art and design. Admission is rolling for all programs, except computer animation (January 15 deadline). To be considered for a merit-based scholarship, students must apply by March 1.

SAVANNAH COLLEGE OF ART AND DESIGN—SAVANNAH, GEORGIA

In the last twenty-five years, the Savannah College of Art and Design (SCAD) has become one of the largest and most influential art schools in the world. More than ten thousand students from all fifty states and a hundred-plus countries attend SCAD on its main campus in Savannah, Georgia, and through off-campus programs in Atlanta, Hong Kong, and France. As it has grown, SCAD has revitalized the city of Savannah, converting formerly run-down houses into campus buildings. For its efforts, SCAD has won numerous historic preservation awards.

Art, architecture, and design programs form the heart of the curricular offerings available through SCAD's eight schools. Students have over thirty majors to choose from, ranging from advertising and animation, to fashion and furniture design, to industrial design and sound design. Future video game developers, writers, production designers, and historic preservation professionals will also find programs of interest. The five most popular majors at SCAD are graphic design, animation, photography, fashion, and illustration. In addition to its BFA programs, SCAD offers BA options in advertising, graphic design, illustration, interactive design and game development, photography, sequential art, and television producing.

SCAD enables its students to get global perspectives on art, architecture, and design through programs offered in Atlanta, Hong Kong, and LaCoste, France. Resources at SCAD include eight galleries in Savannah, four galleries in Atlanta, and two galleries in both Hong Kong and LaCoste. Based in a rural medieval village, the LaCoste program offers courses in painting, drawing, sculpture, printmaking, film, photography, historic preservation, interior design, art history, architecture, illustration, graphic design, industrial design, performing arts, and fashion. SCAD's Atlanta campus enrolls two thousand students and includes two residence halls, fitness facilities, a dining hall, a 60,000-square-foot digital media center, and a 312,000-square-foot art and design center that houses classrooms, galleries, and a library. SCAD Atlanta offers twenty academic programs including one (television producing) not available elsewhere. With its fourteen bachelor's and master's programs, SCAD's Hong Kong campus (housed in a historic building), has become the leading site in Asia for the study of digital media.

Undergraduate students may enter SCAD in the fall, winter, spring, or summer terms. Applying to SCAD requires a high school diploma, standardized test scores (either ACT or SAT), and supplementary materials. Portfolios are not required but are encouraged, especially for students seeking a scholarship.

SCHOOL OF VISUAL ARTS—NEW YORK, NEW YORK

There are 3,300 undergraduates at the School of Visual Arts in New York City learning from nine hundred faculty members who have won Academy Awards, Emmys, and Caldecott Book Awards and who are members of the advertising and graphic design halls of fame. Students come to SVA from forty-seven states and forty-five countries to work on BFA degrees in advertising, animation, cartooning, computer art, film and video, fine arts, graphic design, illustration, interior design, photography, and visual and critical studies.

SVA has strength across the curriculum, but a few areas stand out. With more than one hundred professors, the SVA Photography Department is one of the largest in the United States. SVA's advertising program is widely regarded as the best one in New York—a powerful statement, given that New York is the advertising capital of the world. SVA students and graduates consistently win Art Director's Club awards and perennially dominate the Graphic New Talent Design competition. A pioneer in the study of cartooning, SVA's program, which began in 1947, was the first to offer a degree in the field. SVA's cartooning faculty—considered the largest and best of any arts college—includes a MacArthur genius grant winner and the creator of the first *Batgirl* comics. The cartooning curriculum has stayed at the leading edge by ranging into areas such as the graphic novel and manga/anime.

By taking a production-based focus, SVA's programs in computer art, computer animation, and visual effects enable students to produce portfolio-quality work. Students get instruction in 3-D animation, broadcast design, compositing, and visual effects. Facilities include four production labs, a professional sound room, and a dedicated green-screen studio with high-definition video capture. Students at SVA have twenty-four-hour unlimited access to modeling labs and learn how to work in teams. Animation students at SVA work with the same equipment found in the leading professional firms, including a stop-motion studio for Claymation and miniature set construction and design. SVA's animation program is a primary source of talent for studios at Disney, Pixar, DreamWorks, Blue Sky, and Nickelodeon.

Many top graphic and industrial design firms view SVA as a pioneer in the use of techniques such as 3-D graphics and modeling. More than one hundred leading professionals teach in SVA's graphic design program, and each graphic design student develops a professional portfolio and network (through SVA's strong connections in the field). The interior design faculty at SVA is second to none—including luminaries (Neville Lewis and Theodore H. M. Prudon) and former associates at leading design firms, such as Gensler and Skidmore, Owings, and Merrill. SVA requires a portfolio of fifteen to twenty pieces of recent work to assess an applicant's talent in composition, spatial relations, and the use of light and form.

EXCELLENT OPTIONS BEYOND ART SCHOOLS

For students interested in art but not quite ready to specialize as an undergraduate, pursuing an art major at a college or university might be the best choice. Studying art beyond art schools entails taking a well-rounded curriculum in the arts and sciences rather than a specialized arts-centric course of study. Students at college or university art programs major in art but also fulfill the general education requirements expected of all students. There is always the opportunity to concentrate solely on art as a graduate student in a master of fine arts (MFA) program. In the art world, the MFA is the terminal degree. Most specialized art schools, and many university art departments, offer MFA programs. Some universities, such as Yale, offer excellent MFA programs, but no BFA program. Others, such as UCLA, are best known for their graduate art programs but also offer undergraduate art options.

A number of colleges and universities have highly ranked art departments. There are excellent programs in the studio arts at Alfred University, Arizona State, Boston University, UCLA, UC–San Diego, Carnegie Mellon, Columbia University, Cornell University, University of Georgia, Indiana University, University of Iowa, University of Michigan, University of North Carolina at Greensboro, University of North Carolina School of the Arts, Ohio State, Rochester Institute of Technology, USC, Temple University, University of Texas, Virginia Commonwealth University, and Washington University. One indicator of a strong college art department is whether it offers BFA degrees. Below are brief descriptions of some of the top art programs located within universities.

Alfred University. With its New York State (SUNY) College of Ceramics, Alfred is the leading place in the United States to study ceramic and glass art and engineering. The history of ceramic/glass art and technology in America (as exemplified by famed New York State institutions like Corning and Steuben Glass) is tied closely to Alfred. Standout facilities at Alfred include the International Museum of Ceramic Art, the National Casting Center, the Paul Vickers Gardner Glass Center, and a metal foundry with an induction furnace for melting high-temperature metals such as stainless steel. In addition to ceramic art, BFA and MFA students at Alfred can also concentrate in sculpture and dimensional studies (which includes work in cast glass, fabricated metal, mixed media and paper, blown glass, wood, light and glass, cast metal, and stone), expanded media (which encompasses design, print media, sonic art, video art, and digital interactive arts), drawing, and art history. Students majoring in art at Alfred can participate in honors programs, study abroad, and minor in another academic area. Although Alfred is a private university, students in the College of Ceramics pay in-state rates if they are residents of New York.

Arizona State University. Among public research universities, the art and design programs at Arizona State stand out for the many choices students have across the campus. In the Herberger Institute for Design and the Arts at ASU, there is, for example, a School of Art; a School of Arts, Media, and Engineering; and a School of Design. The School of Art offers undergraduate degree programs in art education, art history, art studies, ceramics, drawing, fibers, intermedia, metals, museum studies, painting, photography, printmaking, sculpture, and wood. With the exception of the BA in art studies program, art study at ASU leads to the BFA degree. Students can major in art studies in ASU's School of Art directly out of high school. The other School of

Art programs become available to students in their sophomore year, following a year as an art exploratory major. Entry to ASU's BFA programs requires a portfolio. Through ASU's School of Arts, Media, and Engineering, undergraduates can earn a BA in digital culture, with concentration options in design, art, film, media processing, interdisciplinary arts and performance, or art and design studies. The School of Design at ASU offers a BA program in design studies and BS programs in architectural studies, housing and community development, industrial design, interior design, graphic (visual communication) design, and landscape design.

University of California at Los Angeles. With its faculty of internationally respected artists, UCLA has one of the top graduate (MFA) programs in art. Undergraduates at UCLA also benefit. There are BA degree programs in the following areas: art theory, ceramics, painting and drawing, photography, sculpture, and new genres (encompassing installation, performance art, and video).

Carnegie Mellon University. Carnegie Mellon is a leader in design. CMU's School of Design offers BFA programs in communication design and industrial design. Renowned as well is CMU's School of Art, which has BFA offerings in drawing, painting, printmaking, photography, sculpture, and installation. Consistent with the future-directed and technologically oriented core of the institution, CMU has dynamic programs in emerging and interdisciplinary areas of the arts. Examples include a BFA program in electronic and time-based media, which encompasses specializations in animation, bioart, computational and interactive art, game arts, tactical media, tangible media, and video and performance. CMU's BFA program in contextual practice provides a trailblazing opportunity for students to explore and produce socially engaged art projects, such as street art, participatory art, urban intervention, interactive social media, and public installations.

Art students at CMU can also link to special programs in computer science and arts, humanities and arts, and science and arts.

Cornell University. Within its College of Art, Architecture, and Planning, Cornell offers a BFA program in studio art with specialized concentrations in combined media, electronic imaging, painting, photography, and printmaking. For studio art majors, Cornell operates semester-long programs in Rome and New York City. Cornell's College of Human Ecology offers concentrations in apparel design, fiber science, fashion-design management, and interior design.

University of Iowa. Iowa's BFA program in printmaking is often ranked in the top five, and its program in painting and drawing garners top-ten ratings. Undergraduate classes for printmaking majors are small, averaging ten to fifteen students, and enriched by workshops and lectures led by visiting artists. Painting and drawing classes average twelve to sixteen students and are taught by professors whose own work is exhibited in galleries around the world.

Iowa State University. Students at Iowa State can pursue a BA degree in biological/premedical illustration. Limited to forty-five students, the program prepares graduates for careers as illustrators for publishing companies, medical centers, pharmaceutical companies, advertising agencies, and research organizations.

University of New Mexico. With resources such as the world-renowned Tamarind Institute Printer Training Program, New Mexico has become a leader in printmaking. New Mexico also offers a unique program in art and ecology, focused on the environments and communities of the southwestern United States. Students learn to understand the ecological impacts of art, land use, and land art in the region.

Ohio State University. The art-related offerings at Ohio State are comprehensive, including specialized training in fine arts, design, and architecture. The key to finding the right program at Ohio State requires knowing where it is located within the university's vast academic resources. In its Art Department (part of the College of Arts and Sciences), Ohio State has one of the most comprehensive studio glass facilities in the United States and top-ranked BFA programs in glass and ceramics. Ohio State also offers BFA degrees in art and technology, painting and drawing, photography, printmaking, and sculpture. For students with a more general focus, there is the BA in art. OSU's Department of Design (also located in the College of Arts and Sciences) offers bachelor of science in design (BSD) degrees in industrial design, interior design, and visual communication design and operates active internship and study abroad programs. Within its Knowlton School of Architecture (in the College of Engineering), Ohio State has four-year BS degree programs in architecture and landscape architecture that prepare students for preprofessional positions or graduate study.

Rochester Institute of Technology. The array of arts programs offered at RIT is impressive. The College of Imaging Arts and Sciences includes the School for American Crafts and individual schools for art, design, film and animation, photographic arts and sciences, and print media. Within the School for American Crafts, RIT offers BFA programs in ceramics and ceramic sculpture, glass, metal crafts and jewelry design, and woodworking design. Many of the BFA programs at RIT are geared toward training students for jobs in applied and commercial arts. For example, the School of Art has a program in medical illustration. The design program at RIT spans BFA offerings in 3-D digital graphics, graphic design, industrial design, interior design, and new media design and imaging. RIT is one of the few institutions with separate schools for film and photography. The School of Film and Animation offers BFA and BS programs in animation, motion picture science, and production. For the photo enthusiast, RIT has a School of Photographic Arts and Sciences where students can earn a BFA in areas such as advertising photography, fine art photography, photojournalism, and visual media or pursue a BS degree in biomedical photographic communications or imaging and photographic technology. There is also a School of Print Media that offers a BS degree in media arts and technology.

Syracuse University. Syracuse was the first university in the United States to offer the BFA degree. Within its College of Visual and Performing Arts, Syracuse has two art-related departments: the Department of Art and the Department of Art, Design, and Transmedia. The art department offers BFA programs in art education, ceramics, fiber and textile arts, history of art, illustration, jewelry and metalsmithing, painting, printmaking, and sculpture. The Department of Design offers BFA programs in communications design, environmental and interior design, and fashion design. Students can also pursue a five-year bachelor of industrial design (BID) program in industrial and interaction design. The Department of Transmedia offers a highly ranked BFA program in film as well as BFA programs in art photography, art video, and computer art and animation. Students majoring in art, design, and transmedia have opportunities to take their studies to far-flung places, through off-campus programs in New York, Los Angeles, London, Florence, and Berlin. Syracuse also gives its students a leg up on job preparation through its Professional Practice in the Arts course that addresses issues such as copyrights, contracts, grant writing, and résumé preparation.

Temple University. On its main campus in Philadelphia, Temple has highly ranked art programs in the Tyler School of Art. On its Ambler, Pennsylvania, campus just north of Philadelphia, Temple has a School of Environmental Design that offers a

BS degree in landscape architecture. Tyler School of Art students can earn BA or BS degrees in architecture, architectural preservation, facilities management, art education, visual studies, or art history. Tyler also has nine BFA options: ceramics, fibers and material studies, glass, graphic and interactive design, metals/jewelry, CAD-CAM, painting, photography, printmaking, and sculpture. The Tyler School boasts a 255,000-square-foot, state-of-the-art building that was designed by world-renowned architect Carlos Jimenez and contains creative studios, galleries, workshop facilities, and exhibition spaces.

Virginia Commonwealth University. The School of the Arts at VCU in Richmond, Virginia, has numerous programs—including sculpture, graphic design, ceramics, fiber arts, glass, metals/jewelry, multimedia, painting, and printmaking—that are ranked in the top twenty in the United States. VCU art alumni and faculty have won three MacArthur genius awards, have been recognized by the American Academy of Arts and Letters, and have also won prestigious fellowships from the Guggenheim Foundation, Getty Foundation, and Dedalus Foundation. VCU's art programs attract three thousand undergraduate students from thirty-four states and seven foreign countries to earn degrees in the following areas: art education, art history, cinema/film, communication arts, craft and material studies, fashion design and merchandising, graphic design, interior design, kinetic imaging, painting and printmaking, photography and film, and sculpture and extended media. International programs available to VCU art students include opportunities to study weaving and embroidery in Guatemala, attend an international design conference in Qatar, study communication arts in Florence, or study at the Glasgow School of the Arts in Scotland.

University of Wisconsin. Few universities have as many art-related programs as Wisconsin. Through its Art Department, Wisconsin offers BS programs in art and art education and BFA programs in numerous studio art specialties. Known for strength in ceramics and glass, Wisconsin established the first glass art program in the United States in 1961. Glass art at Wisconsin includes work in the medium of neon, and ceramics. Facilities include a 3,500-square-foot glaze studio and six electric kilns. Other BFA studio programs include graphic design and typography, book arts, photography, printmaking (including digital printmaking, etching and intaglio, lithography, relief printing, and serigraphy), painting and drawing (including concepts of figuration, life drawing, and abstraction), digital modeling, jewelry and metalsmithing, sculpture, video and performance, and wood and furniture (with a 5,000-square-foot wood studio). Students in Wisconsin's Design Studies Department (in the School of Human Ecology) can earn degrees in textile and apparel design and interior design. Wisconsin's College of Agricultural and Life Sciences offers a major in landscape architecture.

STRONG ART PROGRAMS AT LIBERAL ARTS COLLEGES

The better art departments at small liberal arts colleges have extensive studio space, a variety of courses, and an affiliated museum or gallery. Outstanding art museums/galleries are found at Oberlin, Smith, Vassar, and Williams.

Bard College. Bard offers concentrations in studio arts, photography, and film and electronic arts. Bard's Avery Arts Center—one of the more impressive arts facilities on a small college campus—provides individual studio spaces for senior projects as well as a welding shop and a forge.

Bennington College. The visual arts at Bennington encompass architecture, art history, ceramics, digital arts, drawing, film and video, media arts, painting, photography, printmaking, and sculpture. Bennington's studio art facilities rival those found at many art schools—especially the 120,000-square-foot Visual and Performing Arts Center (VAPA), where studios are open to students twenty-four/seven. During fieldwork term, Bennington students can get internships in the art world.

Denison University. Denison is a rare liberal arts college that has a BFA degree in studio art. Studio courses at Denison are offered in ceramics, painting, photography, sculpture, video, animation, mixed media, and electronic arts. A studio art fund pays for group trips by students to art museums in cities such as Cincinnati and New York.

Oberlin College. Within an art building designed by Robert Venturi, Oberlin offers concentrations in studio art and visual art and has studio spaces for drawing, digital media, painting, photography, silk-screening, and sculpture. Oberlin is perhaps the only college in America that allows students to rent paintings from its acclaimed art museum. Oberlin dorm rooms have been known to be decorated with an actual Picasso, Giacometti, Arp, or Haring.

Sarah Lawrence College. Art facilities at Sarah Lawrence are housed in a LEED-certified green building (Heimbold Visual Arts Center) that provides its interior spaces with natural light, circulates air through special venting systems, and has walls coated with nontoxic materials. Studios in Heimbold are equipped with digital technology, and there are spaces for welding, woodworking, clay and mold making, not to mention a darkroom, digital imaging lab, sound studio, and screening room. Sarah Lawrence offers instruction in letter-press printing, metal working, web design, drawing, painting, woodworking, sculpture, bookmaking, and photography.

Skidmore College. Skidmore offers a studio art major with specialties in ceramics, communication design, digital media, drawing, fibers, metals, painting, photography, printmaking, and sculpture. For course credit, students can get a professional internship in artists' studios, advertising agencies, graphic design firms, printing houses, galleries, museums, and artist cooperatives.

Smith College. Alongside its renowned museum of art, Smith offers concentrations in art history, studio art, and architecture as well as a minor in graphic arts. Printmaking is one of Smith's strengths. Prominent artists and master printers come to campus for specialized workshops in areas such as typography, lithography, and woodcut printing.

Wesleyan University. Wesleyan's studio art program offers concentrations in architecture, drawing, painting, photography, printmaking, sculpture, and typography. All Wesleyan studio art majors complete a thesis project, resulting in a solo exhibition of their work.

➤ TOP-RANKED GRAPHIC DESIGN PROGRAMS

California College of the Arts	University of Delaware	Rhode Island School of Design
California Institute of the Arts	Maryland Institute College of Art	School of Visual Arts
Carnegie Mellon University	Pratt Institute	Virginia Commonwealth University

► OTHER STRONG GRAPHIC DESIGN PROGRAMS

Arizona State University

School of the Art Institute of Chicago

University of the Arts

Boston University

University of Cincinnati

Cleveland Institute of Art

Columbus College of Art and Design

Drexel University

University of Illinois at Chicago

Iowa State University

Minneapolis College of Art and Design

North Carolina State University

Ohio State University

Otis College of Art and Design

Parsons, the New School for Design

Penn State University

Rochester Institute of Technology

► TOP-RATED INDUSTRIAL AND PRODUCT DESIGN PROGRAMS

Arizona State University

Art Center College of Design

California College of the Arts

Carnegie Mellon University

University of Cincinnati

Cleveland Institute of Art

University of Illinois (Urbana/
    Champaign)

North Carolina State University

University of Notre Dame

Ohio State University

Parsons, the New School for Design

Pratt Institute

Rhode Island School of Design

Rochester Institute of Technology

Savannah College of Art and Design

Syracuse University

► TOP-RATED ANIMATION PROGRAMS

Art Institute of Boston at Lesley
    University

University of the Arts

Brigham Young University

California Institute of the Arts

Carnegie Mellon University

University of Central Florida

Pratt Institute

Rhode Island School of Design

Ringling College of Art and Design

Rochester Institute of Technology

Savannah College of Art and Design

School of Visual Arts

University of Southern California

ARCHITECTURE

Architecture blends art with science. Architects are designers and problem solvers whose training is necessarily interdisciplinary. Mastery of architecture requires knowledge and facility related to art and design, civil engineering, environmental science, botany, geology, and geography. Due to the growing prominence of sustainable living, architecture has taken a renewed interest in designing structures and landscapes that use the earth's limited natural resources as efficiently as possible. As fields like green building, landscaping, and city planning have become growth areas, architecture programs have connected with departments of environmental studies, environmental engineering, and sustainability.

Like art schools, architecture schools tend to consider a portfolio in the admissions evaluation. Because architecture departments believe that they can teach a student how to be an architect, the portfolio is less central to the admissions process than it is for art schools. Still, the portfolio enables schools to gauge an applicant's aptitude in drawing, creativity, visual facility, and spatial intelligence. Unlike art schools, architecture schools pay very close attention to the courses and grades on an applicant's high school transcript as well as to scores on standardized tests.

There are two ways to enter architecture. The shortest route is by studying in a professional architecture program as an undergraduate. Professional architecture programs commonly take five years to complete and result in a bachelor of architecture (BArch) degree. Architecture is a profession that requires no more than a bachelor's degree and a passing grade on the professional licensure exam. Still, students can find it confusing to sort through the undergraduate degree options (such as BArch, BA, BFA, or BS) in architecture. Here is a helpful general rule to follow: undergraduate preparation for professional licensure occurs only through BArch programs. BA, BFA, and BS programs in architecture are preprofessional programs that require additional study (usually on the master's level) for licensure.

The other route to an architecture career is by earning a master's degree in the field. There are master's programs for students seeking their first degree in architecture, and there are master's programs for students who majored in architecture as undergraduates.

Getting a second degree in architecture enables the acquisition of a specialty such as acoustics, landscape design, historic preservation, lighting design, or urban planning. Typically, the student getting a first degree in architecture will study for two or three years beyond the bachelor's degree. Students from prearchitecture programs (such as BA or BS programs in architectural studies) usually need less than three years to earn a master's degree in architecture. The master's in architecture route is a good choice for students who enter college interested in keeping their options open while exploring architecture, perhaps through a major in art history, a concentration in architectural studies, or an internship with an architectural firm.

Studying architecture at a university with a large array of academic programs can provide aspiring architects with numerous career routes to pursue. For example, the chance to take courses in city and regional planning is essential for students interested in real estate development. Similarly, architecture students at universities with business schools often have the opportunity to learn about construction management or the business skills needed to run their own architecture firm. At tech schools, architecture students have the opportunity to take courses in civil engineering and environmental engineering, providing them with a deeper knowledge of the role engineers play in building and landscaping projects. At tech schools, such as Carnegie Mellon University, the architecture programs are often on the leading edge of the applications of computation, modeling, and nanotechnology to architecture. Students at such schools have an easier route to pursuing design specialties such as aerospace architecture, industrial architecture, and lighting and acoustics.

➤ TOP UNDERGRADUATE PROGRAMS FOR PROFESSIONAL TRAINING

California Polytechnic State University at San Luis Obispo

Carnegie Mellon University

Cooper Union

Cornell University

Iowa State University

University of Notre Dame

Penn State University

Pratt Institute

Rhode Island School of Design

Rice University

Southern California Institute of Architecture

University of Southern California

Syracuse University

University of Texas at Austin

Virginia Polytechnic Institute and State University

CALIFORNIA POLYTECHNIC STATE UNIVERSITY—SAN LUIS OBISPO, CALIFORNIA

The BArch program at Cal Poly is part of the College of Architecture and Environmental Design, which also offers programs in architectural engineering, city and regional planning, construction management, and landscape architecture. Perennially ranked in the top ten, Cal Poly's BArch program is a five-year course of study that prepares students for professional licensure and practice. BArch students at Cal Poly can add a minor in architectural engineering, city and regional planning, construction management, integrated project delivery, real property development, or sustainable environments. Facilities supporting the architecture program include a digital fabrication laboratory and construction shops.

Studying architecture from a global or urban perspective is an integral part of the education at Cal Poly. In their fourth year, Cal Poly architecture students have off-campus study options in Alexandria, Virginia; Copenhagen; Florence; and San Francisco. Another standout feature of Cal Poly's architecture program is the internship possibilities it provides. Students frequently get summer internships with federal agencies in Washington, DC, or with firms in places such as Honolulu, London, Los Angeles, Seattle, and Singapore. Architecture applicants must file a Cal State application and submit a portfolio.

CARNEGIE MELLON UNIVERSITY— PITTSBURGH, PENNSYLVANIA

Carnegie Mellon's architecture programs are consistently ranked in the top ten. Carnegie Mellon aims to produce architects skilled in the design tools of the future, focused on sustainable urbanism, and attuned to environmental, social, and technological innovations. One standout feature of the program at CMU is the Urban Design Build Studio—a collaborative that brings together students and professors, community organizers, local citizens, building contractors, and grant makers to produce positive architectural solutions for communities in need. The Urban Design Build Studio projects help to give architecture students real-world experience in implementing design in an urban context.

CMU's undergraduate architecture program takes five years to complete and leads to a BArch degree. Graduates of the program are prepared to sit for professional licensing exams. CMU also offers intercollege degree programs that link architecture with areas such as computer science, the physical sciences, and the arts and humanities. Through such linkages, architecture students can explore game design, computer animation, robotic art, and emerging media. CMU architecture students have ample opportunities for study abroad. Summer studio programs have taken CMU architecture students to Barcelona, Hong Kong, India, Japan, Prague, Rome, Singapore, and Venice. Fourth-year architecture students can participate in semester or year-long exchanges at universities in Belgium, Mexico, Singapore, and Switzerland.

Carnegie Mellon's architecture admissions process assesses how prepared applicants are to study the subject in a rigorous environment. A portfolio is required and having an interview is optional. Admissions decisions are made in an aid-blind context, removing from consideration an applicant's ability to pay.

COOPER UNION—NEW YORK, NEW YORK

Cooper Union's undergraduate program in architecture is often ranked in the top twenty. Students at Cooper Union study in a city (New York) that provides an unparalleled urban laboratory. The small and highly interactive Cooper Union program—with its five-to-one student to faculty ratio—revolves around design studios, which are team taught by multiple faculty members. Cooper Union wants its architecture graduates to take a multidisciplinary view of the built environment. For that reason, the study sequence integrates construction, form, space, and architecture's relationship to other creative disciplines. The five-year BArch program at Cooper Union prepares students for professional licensure. Cooper Union also has a highly ranked MArch program.

In addition to submitting transcripts and standardized test score results, architecture applicants must complete a home test in January of the year in which they are applying. No portfolio is required. Although it was historically tuition free, Cooper Union now charges tuition.

CORNELL UNIVERSITY—ITHACA, NEW YORK

To its highly ranked architecture program, Cornell attracts two types of students: those interested in training for professional careers (through the five-year BArch degree) and students interested in architecture as an area of study rather than a career path. For the latter type of student, Cornell offers a BS degree in the history of architecture.

Within an Ivy League research university of 20,000 students, the undergraduate architecture program at Cornell resembles a small college, one that enrolls 275 students taught by twenty-four full-time and ten visiting professors in an interactive studio environment of small classes. Students must take ten terms of design courses, which underscores that design is central to Cornell's BArch program. Students also get grounding in the historical and global context of architecture through the required semester in Rome during the third year. Additionally, architecture students have the flexibility to take one-quarter of their courses in other colleges at Cornell and can take classes at Cornell facilities in New York City.

The other undergraduate architecture degree Cornell offers is a BS in the history of architecture. The BS program is focused on history, theory, and criticism rather than the actual practice of architecture. Students enter the BS program after two years of undergraduate study at Cornell or after transferring from another institution. Gaining admission to Cornell's BArch program requires submission of a portfolio. At Cornell, although the architecture school makes admission decisions, applicants must still meet the overall quality standard for admission to the university in order to have their portfolio receive serious consideration. Cornell offers need-based financial aid and meets full need.

IOWA STATE UNIVERSITY—AMES, IOWA

The undergraduate and graduate architecture and design programs at Iowa State are consistently ranked among the finest in the nation and as the best in the Midwest. Each fall approximately eighty students enter the five-year, professional BArch program (in the College of Design) that prepares students to become licensed, registered architects. Iowa State also offers highly ranked programs in community and regional planning, graphic design, industrial design, interior design, and landscape architecture. *DesignIntelligence* magazine, for example, ranks Iowa State's architecture, industrial design, interior design, and landscape architecture programs in the top ten.

For all students in Iowa State's College of Design, the first year consists of a core design sequence that prepares them to apply to any of the professional degree options in the second semester of their freshman year. Admission to architecture is 85 percent determined by freshman grades in the core design courses, the portfolio, and the required essay. Through the Core Design Program, first-year students can participate in a residential learning community that sponsors trips to museums, design firms, and commercial developments in Minneapolis–St. Paul. Students not enrolled in the Design Exchange Community must participate in a one-semester, nonresidential community called the Design Collaborative that provides insights into design disciplines, career options, portfolio development, and internships. College of Design students have study abroad options in China or Rome or through the Summer Academy Berlin (Germany) focused on design and architecture for a low-carbon lifestyle.

Iowa State's College of Design also offers a standout landscape architecture (BLA) program that provides professional training for licensure and practice. The highly ranked interior design program follows a four-year (BFA) professional training sequence, and there is a BS program in community and regional planning.

UNIVERSITY OF NOTRE DAME— SOUTH BEND, INDIANA

Architecture at Notre Dame is a five-year program that prepares students for professional licensure and practice. One distinguishing feature of Notre Dame's top-ranked architecture program is its global focus. For example, juniors at Notre Dame can spend the year in Rome studying urbanism and classical architecture, while taking field trips to historic sites around Italy, including Umbria, Tuscany, and Sicily. Notre Dame also operates summer programs that take architecture students to China, Cuba, Greece, Italy, Japan, and Portugal.

Specialized concentrations (open to fourth-year students) and hands-on projects enable students to explore furniture design, preservation and restoration, architectural practice and enterprise, building arts, and a minor in sustainability. Building arts students work on projects such as researching a historically significant building and then constructing a detailed scale model of it. They also get to build a traditional architectural element, such as a mantel piece, stair, or balustrade assembly. Students concentrating on preservation and restoration can work on revitalizing historic buildings in South Bend. Those in the architectural practice and enterprise concentration take courses in accounting, finance, and management in the Mendoza College of Business. And furniture design students use Notre Dame's woodshop to construct furniture of original design.

Admission to the architecture program at Notre Dame requires completion of a university application. Submission of a portfolio of artwork (that demonstrates facility with multiple subjects and media) is encouraged but not required.

PENN STATE UNIVERSITY—STATE COLLEGE, PENNSYLVANIA

The architecture programs at Penn State are housed in a LEED Gold–certified facility. Rankings frequently list Penn State's architecture and landscape architecture programs among the best in the United States. Penn State offers four undergraduate degree programs in architecture: the professional, five-year BArch; the preprofessional, four-year BS in architecture; the professional, five-year bachelor of landscape architecture (BLA); and the integrated BArch/MArch.

International study is central to the architecture curriculum at Penn State. A program in Rome (required of all BS students) offers students the opportunity to spend their fourth year taking courses in design, urban studies, cartography, and architectural analysis at the Pantheon Institute. Through the integrated BArch/MArch program, outstanding architecture students can start taking graduate-level courses in their fourth year of study and are usually able to complete both degrees in six years. Penn State's highly rated landscape architecture program requires all students to study abroad, either at the school's program in Bonn, Germany, or at approved programs in other countries. Applicants to all architecture programs must meet Penn State's admissions requirements.

PRATT INSTITUTE—NEW YORK, NEW YORK

Frequently ranked among the top places to study architecture in the United States, Pratt Institute seeks to educate architects who will become future leaders in urban design, city planning, environmental management, historic preservation, and ecological design. Pratt's BArch program culminates in a fifth-year degree project that focuses on design, preservation, building technology, planning, and/or urban design. In addition, Pratt offers a minor in construction management, which is the only program that does not require a portfolio for admission.

Through research partnerships with industry and government, Pratt stays connected to practice in architecture and helps its students secure internships and jobs. The research partnerships enable Pratt faculty and students to share their skills and expertise and make professional connections. Areas where Pratt has partners include lighting research, fabric

architecture, industrial construction, sustainable surfaces, coastal infrastructure, nanoarchitecture, experimental structures, carbon neutral design, and the redevelopment of the Ninth Ward of New Orleans. Pratt has a special focus on Latin America. A program called Latin Pratt brings new technologies to architecture, design, and urban planning projects in Central America, Mexico, and South America. Through Latin Pratt, there are university partners for study abroad and exchange programs in Bogota (Colombia) and Argentina.

RHODE ISLAND SCHOOL OF DESIGN—PROVIDENCE, RHODE ISLAND

Architecture at RISD is taught within the context of a world-leading school of art and design. RISD takes a studio approach to architecture that integrates perspectives from the liberal arts, architectural history, and construction technologies. This approach enables students to understand the technical demands of building design as well as the imaginative and artistic processes that lead to socially responsible and sustainable buildings and landscapes. Of RISD's two undergraduate degree options in architecture, the five-year track (leading to a BArch degree) is for students interested in professional practice. The other track (leading to a BFA) is for students who are interested in architecture but unsure it is their calling. The four-year BFA program requires at least forty-two credits of courses in liberal arts subjects and provides excellent preparation for graduate study in many fields, such as architecture, city and urban planning, environmental studies, and landscape or interior design.

In choosing among applicants, RISD looks for a diversity of intelligences. The required portfolio helps provide evidence of ability to communicate through visual means, a critical eye, and spatial cognitive ability.

RICE UNIVERSITY—HOUSTON, TEXAS

The architecture program at Rice is small (200 students, 125 undergraduates) and intensive by design. To get a Rice BArch degree and be prepared for professional licensure requires six years of study. Students who decide that they are not committed to architecture as a profession may opt out of the six-year track and depart Rice after four years with a BA in architectural studies.

The students who complete the six-year program at Rice are well equipped to enter the world of architecture. In fact, certain features of Rice's architecture program make it a superb choice for students who are serious about the profession. For example, fifth-year Rice students complete a nine-month preceptorship that provides placements in the world's top architecture firms. While serving as preceptors, students get to work on long-term design projects and experience life in the architecture profession. Upon returning from their preceptorship, students may spend their sixth year taking graduate-level courses, studying abroad for a semester in Paris, getting hands-on experience through the Rice Building Workshop, or taking studio courses with visiting professors from around the world. Students who complete the six-year sequence of study at Rice graduate with two degrees: a BA and a BArch. In addition to the courses required to complete the architecture degree, Rice students can select from a broad range of arts and sciences courses.

Getting into the architecture program requires a completed Rice admission application and a portfolio of creative work. While not required, Rice strongly recommends that applicants interview on campus with an architecture professor.

UNIVERSITY OF SOUTHERN CALIFORNIA—LOS ANGELES, CALIFORNIA

The School of Architecture at USC, like other leading schools, encourages its students to get a global perspective. USC makes this possible through architecture-focused study abroad programs in Europe (Barcelona and Milan, Italy) and Asia (China and Malaysia). Undergraduate students at USC have two choices for architecture degrees: a five-year professional BArch and a four-year, preprofessional BS in architectural studies. Students in USC's BArch program take design studio courses and integrative seminars in preparation for a fifth-year comprehensive project that simulates the work of professional architects. USC also gives its BArch students the latitude to add a minor or complete a dual degree in areas such as business, fine arts, history, and urban planning. The BS in architectural studies program provides an option for students who determine that the BArch program is too professionally focused for their interests. Some students complete the BS degree as a preprofessional stop on the way to graduate study in architecture, design, or urban planning. Applicants interested in studying architecture must submit all the materials required for admission to USC, plus (if applying to the BArch program) a portfolio.

SYRACUSE UNIVERSITY—SYRACUSE, NEW YORK

DesignIntelligence magazine consistently ranks Syracuse's BArch program as one of the top five in the United States. Syracuse's architecture program encourages students to broaden their perspective beyond the school's campus in Upstate New York. A study program in Florence, focused on Renaissance architectural treasures, takes students on sketching trips to Venice, Milan, Rome, Lucca, and Pisa. Study at Syracuse's London Center, located in the historic Bloomsbury district—not far from Covent Garden and the British Museum—features field trips to sites outside the city such as Bath, Cambridge, Edinburgh, and Oxford. Syracuse's studio program in New York provides a semester-long focus on urban theory, history, planning, and real estate development in the largest US city. There are also short-term travel programs to countries such as Austria, China, Germany, Ghana, Greece, Japan, Russia, and Spain.

The architecture curriculum at Syracuse is built around a design studio sequence that stresses creativity, modeling, problem solving, communication, and research. Syracuse takes a broad approach to architecture education, drawing upon its strengths as a comprehensive research university. One-quarter of the credits students earn in the five-year BArch program are in arts and sciences courses and free electives chosen from any of Syracuse's colleges and schools. Getting into the architecture program at Syracuse requires a portfolio consisting of an opening statement explaining the applicant's interests and aspirations related to architecture, and twelve to fourteen examples of original artwork, such as drawings, paintings, 3-D designs, sculpture, or photography. Mechanical or architectural drawings are discouraged.

UNIVERSITY OF TEXAS—AUSTIN, TEXAS

One of the largest and strongest architecture programs in the United States, Texas offers students interested in architecture five undergraduate degree options. For students interested in licensure and practice, Texas has the five-year BArch professional degree program. For students who want to combine architecture with engineering, Texas offers a six-year dual degree: BArch/BS (engineering). Architecture students interested in Texas's Plan II Honors Program can pursue a joint BArch/BA degree that takes five years plus summers to complete. For students less certain of their commitment to architecture, Texas offers the four-year, preprofessional BS in architectural studies.

The Professional Residency Program at Texas enables upper-level students to supplement their education with work experience. While in residence, students spend six months working with an architecture firm. Since its inception in 1974, the Professional Residency Program has placed students in nearly three hundred different firms in twenty-nine countries. Students can also study architecture abroad in Italy, Mexico, and Western Europe—experiencing a semester-long tour of buildings, cities, and artifacts in Austria, England, France, Germany, Italy, the Netherlands, Spain, and Switzerland. Supporting the course work at Texas are some extraordinary facilities, including an architecture conservation lab, a thermal lab for designing energy-efficient building technologies, the Center for American Architecture and Design, and the Charles Moore Center for the Study of Place. Freshman applicants to architecture at Texas do not have to submit a portfolio.

VIRGINIA POLYTECHNIC INSTITUTE AND STATE UNIVERSITY—BLACKSBURG, VIRGINIA

The architecture, interior design, industrial design, and landscape architecture programs at Virginia Tech perennially show up on lists of the most admired programs in the United States. Undergraduates in Virginia Tech's College of Architecture and Urban Studies (CAUS) have four degree options: BArch, BS in Industrial Design, BS in Interior Design, and bachelor of landscape architecture (BLA). The BArch and BLA programs take five years to complete and prepare students for professional licensure and practice. The industrial design and interior design BS programs at Virginia Tech take four years to complete.

All students at CAUS take foundation courses, meaning that freshmen in architecture, industrial design, interior design, and landscape architecture learn together before embarking on their specific major tracks in year two. This approach enables CAUS students to see the interconnections among the different design disciplines. Because CAUS teaches the foundations of design to first-year students, freshman applicants are not required to submit a portfolio.

Fourth-year architecture students can participate in off-campus programs, including study abroad and externships that provide on-the-job-preparation. During spring or fall, architecture majors can spend a semester at Virginia Tech's Center for European Studies and Architecture, located in Switzerland on Lake Lugano. Another program takes students to Europe for nine weeks of travel and courses focused on the design and history of cities and buildings. In addition to its studio programs in Egypt and Germany, CAUS has exchange programs with architecture schools in Australia, Chile, China, Estonia, Finland, Japan, Russia, and Switzerland (at Accademia di Architettura in Medndrisio, one of the world's foremost schools of architecture). Virginia Tech also operates off-campus studio programs in Chicago and at a satellite campus in historic Old Town Alexandria, Virginia. The CAUS Community Design Assistance Center helps neighborhood groups and nonprofit organizations improve their natural and built environments.

STAND-ALONE ARCHITECTURE SCHOOLS

There are two respected stand-alone architecture schools where everything revolves around the study of the built environment. The East Coast has Boston Architectural College (BAC), and the West Coast has the Southern California Institute of Architecture in Los Angeles.

BOSTON ARCHITECTURAL COLLEGE— BOSTON, MASSACHUSETTS

Nearly 1,100 students attend the BAC, a professional training school located in the heart of Boston's Back Bay. Most students attending BAC are combining part-time study with full- or part-time work. Roughly 600 of the students at BAC are studying toward their first design degree, while the remaining approximately 500 are in master's programs. BAC's distinguishing feature is the blending of practical experience with academic study. No matter the degree program, experiential learning is the cornerstone of a BAC education.

There are six undergraduate programs at BAC that lead to a bachelor's degree. Three are professional training programs: architecture (BArch), interior design (BID), and landscape architecture (BLA). All students in the BArch and BLA programs (which are geared toward professional licensure and practice) complete a two-semester design project that proposes an architectural solution to a real-world challenge. BAC's professionally-accredited interior design program unites academic course work and on-the-job experience. Similarly, BAC's landscape architecture graduates enter the job market with portfolios, professional networks, and résumés showing professional accomplishments.

BAC also offers bachelor of design studies (BDS) programs in architectural technology, historic preservation, and sustainable design. Architectural technology students focus on how buildings are constructed and how they work, thus learning about building codes and regulations as well as how mechanical and structural systems can be designed to conserve energy and natural resources. Historic preservation students learn about the design, policy, finance, law, and planning issues surrounding preservation, restoration, and adaptive reuse of historic buildings and neighborhoods. The program in sustainable design, which can be tailored to each student's interest and career objectives, emphasizes high-performance building design, ecologically responsible urban planning, and natural-resource conservation. Admission to BAC requires a portfolio.

SOUTHERN CALIFORNIA INSTITUTE OF ARCHITECTURE—LOS ANGELES, CALIFORNIA

One of the nation's top design schools, SCI-Arc is a center of innovation focused on shaping the future of its home region. Often ranked as the top architecture program on the West Coast and in the top ten nationally, SCI-Arc enrolls five hundred students who engage in collaborative study with eighty faculty members, many of whom are distinguished practicing architects. Rankings often highlight SCI-Arc's curricular strength in design, computer applications, analysis and planning, and cross disciplinary teamwork.

SCI-Arc offers professional architecture degrees on the undergraduate and graduate level. The BArch program at SCI-Arc (requiring a portfolio for admission) is built around design studios; interdisciplinary seminars in arts, sciences, and the humanities; and courses in visual studies, media, technology, history, and theory. SCI-Arc also offers two MArch options and a master of design research (MDesR) degree with concentration options in city design, planning and policy, and emerging systems and technologies/media.

Located in a quarter-mile-long former freight depot, SCI-Arc is part of an urban arts district in downtown LA. Students and faculty at SCI-Arc view the surrounding city as an extended campus and living studio space. Within SCI-Arc's campus buildings are state-of-the-art design facilities, including a 5,000-square-foot fabrication shop for hands-on experimentation with materials and construction. SCI-Arc is committed to applying its design expertise to improve its home region, including efforts to reimagine downtown LA. One example is the Los Angeles Cleantech Corridor and Green District Competition sponsored by SCI-Arc. Awarding the Cleantech prize is a way for SCI-Arc to encourage a future downtown LA where products are designed and made using clean technologies.

OTHER QUALITY PROFESSIONAL ARCHITECTURE TRAINING PROGRAMS

Students can also find quality undergraduate professional training programs at the University of Arizona, Auburn University, City College of New York, Louisiana State University, University of Miami, North Carolina State University, Oklahoma State University, University of Oklahoma, University of Oregon, Rensselaer Polytechnic Institute, and University of Tennessee. Kansas State University and Montana State University have five-and-one-half-year programs (open to high school applicants) that lead to a master of architecture degree.

▶ BEST PREPROFESSIONAL ARCHITECTURE PROGRAMS

University of California at Berkeley	Massachusetts Institute of Technology	Stanford University
University of California at Los Angeles	University of Michigan	University of Virginia
University of Cincinnati	University of Pennsylvania	Washington University
Columbia University	Princeton University	Yale University

University of California at Berkeley. The Department of Architecture at Berkeley (part of the College of Environmental Design) offers bachelor's, master's, and doctoral programs. Berkeley's MArch program is considered one of the best in the world. Berkeley's BA in architecture program is a preprofessional course of study that prepares students for entry-level jobs or graduate study. In addition to getting a foundation in environmental design and architecture, BA in architecture students can follow an individualized path suited to their particular interests—including specializations and minors in environmental design and urbanism in developing countries, history of the built environment, social and cultural factors in environmental design, sustainable design, landscape architecture, city and regional planning, or structural engineering. Graduates of Berkeley's BA program are well positioned for entry into MArch programs.

University of California at Los Angeles. Architecture at UCLA is best known for its professionally oriented graduate degree programs. The undergraduate program at UCLA is the preprofessional BA in architectural studies, offered by the Department of Architecture and Urban Design within UCLA's School of Arts and Architecture. Students cannot enter the architectural studies major until their junior year. Students must complete two years of course work at UCLA before the department deems them eligible.

University of Cincinnati. The College of Design, Architecture, Art, and Planning at Cincinnati ranks as one of the top design schools in the world. Perennially situated in the top ten are Cincinnati's MArch program and its departments of industrial design and interior design. Cincinnati's BS in architecture option provides excellent preparation for graduate study in a professional MArch program. Design and architecture students at Cincinnati have the opportunity to get professional experience through a highly regarded cooperative program that connects students to paid co-op placements with regional, national, and international clients.

Columbia University. Columbia's Graduate School of Architecture, Preservati.on, and Planning (GSAPP) has highly ranked programs leading to MArch and PhD degrees. Through its arts and sciences division, undergraduates at Columbia can pursue the four-year, preprofessional BA in architecture program offered jointly with nearby Barnard College. Students in the BA program develop technical skills, design excellence, and a critical understanding of architecture's relationship to history, culture, and society. Program graduates have high rates of success at gaining admission to the world's leading architecture graduate schools, including GSAPP at Columbia.

Massachusetts Institute of Technology. MIT has one of the top-ranked graduate programs in architecture. For that reason, and for its strength in urban and regional planning, MIT is always listed among the best places to study architecture. For undergraduates, MIT offers a four-year, preprofessional BS in architecture program that features a specialty in architectural design. While the MIT BS program does not lead to licensure, it offers several courses related to building systems, environmental design, and structural systems. Upon graduation, students are well prepared to intern with architects and find positions in construction management.

University of Michigan. .Undergraduates studying architecture at Michigan are doing so at one of the country's best training grounds for the professional MArch degree and PhD in architecture. Undergraduate architecture at Michigan is a four-year program (leading to the BS degree) that provides excellent preparation for graduate study. Students at Michigan spend their first two years in prearchitecture study, after which they apply to enter the BS program. A number of BS in architecture graduates stay on at Michigan to earn a MArch degree, while others find work in fields related to architecture.

University of Pennsylvania. The School of Design at Penn offers top-ranked architecture programs. But the Design School at Penn—including its professional training programs in architecture—is for graduate study only. Penn's undergraduate major in architecture is part of the College of Arts and Sciences and provides an interdisciplinary liberal arts–based education leading to a BA degree. Penn's BA in architecture program offers concentrations in design; history, theory, and criticism; and the six-year intensive BA/MArch option. Students pursuing the BA/MArch begin taking graduate-level courses in the School of Design in their fourth year.

Princeton University. Programs in Princeton's School of Architecture give students a broad cultural context that encompasses urban planning, building technology, architectural history, landscape design, and building sites. Architecture is taught at Princeton in an interdisciplinary liberal arts context addressing social and practical issues and considerations of the natural environment and sustainability. Princeton's BA program (with a concentration in architecture) is a liberal arts course of study that prepares students for graduate study in architecture or related areas such as landscape design, civil engineering, urban planning, art history, and the visual arts. Princeton also offers a bachelor of science in engineering (BSE) program that combines architecture and engineering. Students interested in professional licensure and practice in architecture need to complete Princeton's MArch program.

Stanford University. Through its department of civil and environmental engineering, Stanford offers a BS degree with a specialty in architectural design. The emphasis of the program is on the ways architectural design intersects with engineering technologies. Architectural design majors study construction management, structural engineering, and fine arts in addition to taking architectural design studio classes. The four-year architectural design major is a prearchitecture program, not one that leads to professional licensure. Some architectural design students go on to graduate school in architecture or engineering, while others enter fields such as construction management and structural engineering.

University of Virginia. Virginia offers leading graduate programs in architecture, landscape architecture, and urban and environmental planning. Virginia's School of Architecture has three undergraduate study options (architecture, architectural history, and urban and environmental planning) that prepare students for top-ranked graduate programs or work alongside professional architects. The BS in architecture program is a preprofessional, four-year course of study that offers the option to minor in landscape architecture or pursue interdisciplinary concentrations that connect architecture to business, archaeology, or materials science. For students interested in preserving the built environment, Virginia offers the bachelor of architectural history. Students interested in sustainable community development and the environmental impacts of buildings have the option to work toward a bachelor's degree in urban and environmental planning. Architecture, landscape architecture, and urban and environmental planning students at Virginia can study abroad in Barcelona, Beijing, Copenhagen, London, Germany, Jamaica, and Italy. Virginia's program in Beijing introduces students to Chinese architecture and often leads to internships with American firms operating there. The semester program in Germany takes students to the Architecture School at Brandenburg Technical University, where classes taught in English focus on architectural design, conservation, planning, and theory. Architectural history students can go to Jamaica to study building design and preservation in a Caribbean context.

Washington University. The Sam Fox School of Architecture at Washington University in St. Louis offers tracks that lead to the BA, BS, or bachelor of design in architecture (BDES) degree. No matter the track, architecture at WUSTL combines a rigorous education in design with arts and sciences courses that prepare students to be flexible thinkers. As respected as the Fox School is, none of its undergraduate architecture programs qualify graduates for professional licensure without additional training. Because there are only fifty architecture students in every freshmen class at WUSTL, studio classes are small and interactive, typically enrolling fifteen students. Students who complete one of the undergraduate programs in architecture are well prepared to enter graduate or professional study. For prospective students who are intent on entering the architecture profession, there is a six-year four-two BS/MArch option. The architecture program also offers numerous international study options, including semesters in Buenos Aires, Copenhagen, Florence, and a program called the European Tour. Fox School applicants seeking a merit scholarship must submit a portfolio consisting of twelve to fifteen examples of recently completed artwork, such as drawings, two- or three-dimensional pieces, or photographs. There are portfolio days offered on campus and through the National Portfolio Days held across the United States. Washington University has the financial capacity to offer generous need-based aid and merit scholarships. Awards range up to the full cost of attendance.

Yale University. Yale's School of Architecture is headed by world-renowned architect Robert A. M. Stern. Stern's firm devised the plan for the town of Celebration, Florida, and designed the George W. Bush Library at Southern Methodist University. Yale is often ranked among the best places in the world to study architecture at the graduate level. Yale offers a full array of architecture degrees, including the professional MArch, the master of environmental design, and the PhD. Yale's undergraduate architecture program is a liberal arts course of study that leads to a BA degree. Architecture majors at Yale can choose to concentrate on architecture and design; history, theory, and criticism; or architecture and urban studies.

OTHER PREPROFESSIONAL ARCHITECTURE PROGRAMS

Through its highly ranked art history department, **New York University** offers a major in urban design and architectural studies taught in a historical and critical context. **Connecticut College** offers a major in architectural studies that provides preparation for entry-level jobs or graduate study in the design professions. **Bryn Mawr College** has an interdisciplinary major focused on architectural design in cities.

Students at **Amherst College**, **Hampshire College**, **Mount Holyoke College**, and **Smith College** can major in architecture through the **Five College Architectural Studies Program**. Hampshire College also offers a concentration in architecture and environmental design featuring a semester at the New York Institute for Architecture and Urban Studies. The Department of Civil and Environmental Engineering at

Northwestern University offers a certificate program in architectural design and engineering. The architectural studies major at the **University of Pittsburgh** has tracks in design and historic preservation and sponsors annual field trips to study the architecture of places like Ann Arbor, Charlottesville, Chicago, Detroit, New Haven, New York, and Washington, DC. Other colleges that offer undergraduate architecture-related majors include Arizona State University, Brown University, University at Buffalo (SUNY), Case Western Reserve University, Clemson University, University of Florida, Harvard University, University of Illinois, University of Kansas, Lawrence Technological University, Lehigh University, University of Maryland, University of Massachusetts-Amherst, Miami University (Ohio), Middlebury College, University of Minnesota, University of Missouri, Northeastern University, Ohio State University, Parsons School of Design at the New School University, University of San Diego, Savannah College of Art and Design, and Tufts University.

➤ STANDOUT UNDERGRADUATE LANDSCAPE ARCHITECTURE PROGRAMS

Ball State University

University of California at Davis

California Polytechnic State University at San Luis Obispo

Colorado State University

Cornell University

University of Florida

University of Georgia

Iowa State University

Kansas State University

Louisiana State University

Michigan State University

North Carolina State University

Ohio State University

Penn State University

Purdue University

SUNY College of Environmental Science and Forestry

Texas A&M University

West Virginia University

Virginia Polytechnic Institute and State University

➤ TOP UNDERGRADUATE PROGRAMS IN INTERIOR DESIGN

Arizona State University

University of Cincinnati

Cornell University

Florida State University

University of Florida

Kansas State University

Miami University

University of Oregon

Pratt Institute

Radford University

Rhode Island School of Design

Savannah College of Art and Design

Suffolk University (New England School of Art and Design)

Syracuse University

University of Texas at Austin

Virginia Commonwealth University

Virginia Polytechnic Institute and State University

University of Wisconsin at Madison

UNDERGRADUATE FILM PROGRAMS

While many of the top film programs in the United States are for graduate students only, there are a number of colleges that offer undergraduate degrees in film. The leading undergraduate film programs are listed and profiled below.

- California Institute of the Arts
- University of California at Los Angeles
- Chapman University
- Emerson College
- Florida State University
- Loyola Marymount University
- New York University
- North Carolina School of the Arts
- Northwestern University
- Rhode Island School of Design
- Ringling College of Art and Design
- University of Southern California
- Syracuse University
- University of Texas at Austin
- Wesleyan University
- University of Wisconsin at Milwaukee

California Institute of the Arts. Known primarily for its strength in animation, Cal Arts offers BFA programs in character animation and film, video, and experimental animation. The atmosphere at Cal Arts verges on the experimental. Cal Arts is the alma mater of award-winning directors Tim Burton and Sofia Coppola, Stephen Hillenburg (creator of *SpongeBob SquarePants*), John Lasseter (chief creative officer at Pixar), and Andrew Stanton (*Finding Nemo*).

University of California at Los Angeles. UCLA offers a BA degree in film and television distinguished by its liberal arts base and indie vibe. UCLA film students can specialize in film production and directing, producing, documentary film, screenwriting, animation, digital media, or critical studies. Students benefit from studying alongside students in UCLA's top-rated graduate programs. Notable alumni include Francis Ford Coppola (MFA), Alexander Payne (MFA), and Tim Robbins. UCLA also has a film and television archive with holdings only surpassed by the Library of Congress.

Chapman University. Younger than the film programs at UCLA and USC, Chapman's Dodge College of Film and Media Arts is a dynamic place with thirty-five full-time and seventy adjunct faculty members with ties to the film industry. Located in Orange County, California, Chapman is within easy driving distance of Hollywood. The Dodge College operates like a studio, and for the 1,300 students studying film and media there, the focus is on storytelling. That does not mean Chapman lacks technical sophistication. In fact, the Dodge School's home base is a 76,000-square-foot building called Marion Knott Studios that is equipped with two sounds stages, cinematography and directing insert stages, Foley and motion capture stages, a hair and makeup studio and green room, two audition rooms, a set design shop, a production design studio, a production management office, thirty-six editing suites, three mixing rooms, plus a 500-seat theater with Kinoton 35 mm projectors, Dolby digital surround sound, and a Barco 2k digital projector. Chapman offers BA and BFA programs in screenwriting, creative producing, digital arts, film production, screen acting, film studies, and television and broadcast journalism. Chapman alumni include Ben York Jones (*Like Crazy*).

Emerson College. Boston's Emerson College runs a semester-long program in Los Angeles. Students in the Emerson in LA program take courses and learn about the film industry through internships with film editors, casting directors, set designers, screenwriters, film and television producers, talent managers, and publicity directors. A new Emerson in LA campus, designed by Thom Mayne, is under construction in Hollywood. In addition to its degree programs in film, the Emerson Department of Media and Visual Arts offers BA and BFA majors in animation and motion media, cinematography and videography, directing narrative fiction, documentary production, experimental media production, interactive media, postproduction, producing, sound design and audio, studio television production, and writing for film and television. Notable Emerson alumni include Norman Lear, Dennis Leary, and Henry Winkler.

Florida State University. The College of Motion Picture Arts at FSU offers BFA degree programs in animation and digital arts, production, and a minor in film studies. FSU instructors have won two Academy Awards and received twelve nominations. FSU students are perennial winners of College Television Awards and Student Oscars. The Torchlight program at FSU procures work opportunities for students on feature films shot in Florida. Facilities include postproduction studios, a back lot, a suite for screening dailies, sound stages, a visual effects lab, and mix theaters. FSU alumni include Alan Ball (*American Beauty*) and Melissa Carter (MFA, *Little Black Book*).

Loyola Marymount University. The School of Film and Television at LMU has BA degree programs in animation; film and television production; film, television, and media studies; recording arts; and screenwriting. Through its incubator lab that connects new graduates with mentors in the film industry and a vigorous internship program, LMU has a strong focus on getting its students into film. LMU students also have the option to go to Bonn, Germany, for an intensive, hands-on workshop related to documentary filmmaking and European media and culture. LMU alumni include David M. Evans (*Beethoven's 3rd & 4th*), Brian Helgeland (MA, *Mystic River*), Francis Lawrence (*Water for Elephants*), Sean McNamara (*Soul Surfer*), and Alexandra Pelosi (documentary filmmaker).

New York University. NYU is considered one of the best places to prepare for a career in film. Within NYU's Tisch School of the Arts, students can pursue a BFA in film and television. For the less specialized film enthusiast, NYU's Skirball Center for New Media offers a BA degree in cinema studies. Prominent alumni of NYU's BFA or MFA film programs include Joel Coen, Chris Columbus, Jim Jarmusch, Charlie Kaufman, Ang Lee, Spike Lee, Brett Ratner, Morgan Spurlock, Oliver Stone, Martin Scorsese, and M. Night Shyamalan.

University of North Carolina School of the Arts. UNCSA emphasizes practical skills in its BFA programs in animation, art direction, cinematography, directing, editing, sound, producing, and screenwriting. UNCSA also offers a concentration in music composition for film. Alumni of the program include David Gordon Green (*Pineapple Express*), Jody Hill (*Observe and Report*), and Danny McBride (*Eastbound and Down*).

Northwestern University. At this university known for leading programs in theater and music, students can earn a BA or BS in radio, television, and film; minors in sound design and film and media studies; and a certificate in creative writing for the media. Course work enables students to focus on directing, cinematography, editing, and postproduction. Northwestern alumni include Greg Berlanti (*Green Lantern*), Zach Braff (*Garden State*), and Garry Marshall (*Pretty Woman*).

Rhode Island School of Design. Students at RISD can earn a BFA in film, animation, and video (FAV). Facilities supporting the FAV program include animation software, a production suite, and studios for stop-action animation, green screen, and blackout shooting. Alumni of RISD include Gus Van Sant (*Milk*), Seth McFarlane (*Family Guy*), and David Byrne (musician/filmmaker).

Ringling School of Art and Design. Ringling has highly ranked and innovative BFA programs in digital filmmaking, computer animation, and motion design. Because Ringling emphasizes learning by doing, students direct commercials as freshmen, documentaries as sophomores, narratives as juniors, and then create, direct, and produce a film for a senior thesis project. In a short time, Ringling has developed strong connections to the film and animation industries. Ringling alumni have worked on each of the ten all-time highest grossing animated films.

University of Southern California. Along with NYU, USC is the place most often spoken of as the best film school in the United States, especially for technical training. The USC School of Cinematic Arts (SCA) offers bachelor's and master's degree programs in film and television production, film and television writing, film studies, and producing. Graduates say that USC's SCA is run like a studio that simulates the professional working environment. Filmmaking facilities at USC include the Robert Zemeckis Center for Digital Arts, the Steven Spielberg Music Scoring Stage, and the Marcia Lucas Post-Production Center. With more than ten thousand SCA alumni, USC has the largest network in the film industry. The accomplishments of SCA alumni are extraordinary. For example, every year since 1973, SCA alumni have been nominated for an Academy Award—for a total of 256 nominations and 78 wins. Since the early 1970s, 119 SCA alumni have won Emmy Awards and 473 have been nominated. The top seventeen grossing films of all time have alumni connections to USC's SCA. Filmmaking alumni of SCA include Judd Apatow, Ron Howard, Jon Landau, Doug Liman, George Lucas, Shonda Rimes, Jay

Roach, John Singleton, Matthew Weiner, Robert Zemeckis, and Laura Ziskin.

Syracuse University. Through the Department of Transmedia, students at Syracuse can focus on filmmaking, computer art (animation and visual effects), and video art. Because enrollment in the program is limited to forty, BFA students get an individualized, not an assembly-line, education. Syracuse also runs the Sorkin in LA Learning Practicum, a week-long program (named for alumnus Aaron Sorkin) that gives drama and film students a sampling of life in the entertainment industry. Other Syracuse alumni in the film industry include Peter Guber (producer of *Rain Man*) and Chris Renaud (*Despicable Me*).

University of Texas at Austin. The success of filmmaker Richard Linklater and the South by Southwest arts festival have put Texas (and its hometown of Austin) on the map in the film world. Linklater is not an alumnus of the film program at UT–Austin, but Robert Rodriguez (*Machete*) and Bruce Hendricks (*Pirates of the Caribbean*) are. Texas offers a BS degree program in radio, television, and film and MFA degrees in film and media production and screenwriting. More than half of the undergraduate students in the radio, television, and film school get internships. Facilities at Texas include a professional television studio, two sound stages, and post-production suites for digital, audio, and editing.

Wesleyan University. This Connecticut liberal arts college of three thousand students located far from Hollywood has made an outsized mark on the world of film and television. Students in Wesleyan's BA in film studies program are required to write, direct, and edit their own movie. The program is equipped with digital facilities as well as an archive that includes the papers of noted filmmakers Frank Capra, Clint Eastwood, Federico Fellini, and Martin Scorsese. Wesleyan alumni in Hollywood include Miguel Arteta (*Chuck & Buck, Cedar Rapids*), Michael

Bay (*Transformers*), Akiva Goldsman (*A Beautiful Mind*), Matthew Weiner (*Mad Men*), and Joss Whedon (*Buffy the Vampire Slayer*).

University of Wisconsin at Milwaukee. Within its Peck School of the Arts, UWM offers a BFA program in film, video, and new genres. One of the strengths of UWM's film program is its extensive facilities. Film students have at their disposal film and video studios; animation and lighting studios; and film, sound, video, digital, postproduction, and film processing labs. UWM's Documentary Media Center gives students opportunities to work on professional productions. In addition UWM runs film and video festivals for student works and works by and about members of the lesbian, gay, bisexual, and transgender community. UWM alumni in the film industry include Chris Smith (*The Yes Men*), actor Willem Dafoe (studied drama), and comedian/impressionist Frank Caliendo (studied mass communications).

OTHER INTERESTING OPTIONS FOR ASPIRING FILMMAKERS

Boston University. BU's College of Communication (COM) offers a BS degree in film and television. Students in the program explore film, television, and new media and have the opportunity to specialize in screenwriting, production, or management and producing. They can also get experience through Hothouse Production, a video production company run by COM students; BU TV, the student-produced and -managed television station; and a Los Angeles Internship Program that connects students to Hollywood.

Colorado Film School. This stand-alone film school in Denver offers BFA, associate of applied science, and certificate programs in writing and directing, writing and producing, postproduction, cinematography, and acting for the screen. The BFA degree programs at CFS are offered in partnership with Regis University in Denver. One of the attractions of CFS is its low tuition. Four years at CFS costs approximately $25,000 for Colorado residents, $55,000 for nonresidents, and $33,000 for students in the Western University Exchange.

Oberlin College. The closest thing to a film program at this Ohio liberal arts college is the major in cinema studies. Oberlin cinema studies students can spend a semester studying film production at NYU's Tisch School of the Arts. Still, something is happening at Oberlin to have spawned alumni like Julie Taymor (*Frida* and *Across the Universe*), Mark Boal (*The Hurt Locker* and *Zero Dark Thirty*), Lena Dunham (the HBO series *Girls*), and Ry Russo-Young (*Nobody Walks* and *You Won't Miss Me*).

Temple University. The BA program in media production and theory at Temple provides students with technical skills in film, video, audio, and new media. Temple gives students exposure to the film industry through its Los Angeles internship program and its semester in London focused on British film and television. Temple also has a summer study program that immerses students in the media culture of Dublin, Ireland.

Sarah Lawrence College. The intimate, interdisciplinary nature of Sarah Lawrence's Filmmaking, Screenwriting and Media Arts Program (FSMA) serves as an excellent jumping off point for budding industry professionals. In addition to connections the program has in nearby NYC, FSMA students can broaden their horizons by studying animation, through participating in an exchange program with Cal Arts, or through studying abroad in Paris, Cuba, or Prague (at the Film and TV School of the Academy of Performing Arts). Film industry veterans J. J. Abrams, John Avnet, and Debra Zane studied at Sarah Lawrence.

THE HEALTH PROFESSIONS

Students seeking to enter the health professions can take many different routes, and this chapter tries to illuminate the numerous paths available. Starting off the chapter is a discussion of the ways students can enter the nursing profession. Next up is a focus on pharmacy programs, especially those offering direct-entry pathways to applicants from high schools. The chapter then moves to a brief discussion of programs that offer high school applicants early entry into medical, dental, and podiatry schools. How to prepare for veterinary school (along with descriptions of the few early-entry DVM programs) next takes the spotlight. Following that is a section on optometry programs, including early-entry options. The next section discusses programs in physical therapy and occupational therapy, including accelerated pathways directly from high school. The chapter then shifts to physician assistant programs, noting accelerated options for high school applicants and the top graduate programs. Following that is a brief description of undergraduate and graduate public health programs. Closing out the chapter is a section on kinesiology, exercise science, and athletic training programs.

NURSING

Aspiring nurses have numerous options, some of which require just one or two years of study. A student can become a Licensed Practical Nurse (LPN)—called Licensed Vocational Nurse (LVN) in California and Texas—following one year of training in a hospital, vocational school, or community college, and passage of the local state licensing examination. For licensure, many states require prospective LPNs to pass the National Council Licensure Examination-Practical Nurse (NCLEX-PN). Many LPNs go on to become registered nurses (RNs). Work as a registered nurse usually requires at least an associate degree in nursing or a diploma from a state-certified nursing program. To obtain the RN license, students must pass the National Council Licensure Examination-Registered Nurse (NCLEX-RN) and fulfill any other certification requirements stipulated by their state.

Although students can enter the nursing profession through a hospital-sponsored LPN or RN track, better paying jobs and greater career advancement opportunities tend to come to nurses holding at least a bachelor's degree. For that reason, our discussion of nursing programs concentrates on the schools that offer a bachelor of science in nursing (BSN) degree.

Sorting out the myriad ways to prepare for BSN programs can be confusing. When searching for options, students should look beyond the name and ranking of the nursing school to make sure that the school has the entry track they seek. For example, Johns Hopkins University is a prestigious name in health sciences education, but the nursing school at Hopkins does not admit students directly from high school.

One route to nursing is straight from high school. Students who apply to BSN programs from high school are called direct-entry students. Many nursing programs reserve spots for direct-entry students, while others require applicants to have already earned an associate degree in nursing or to have taken two or three years of prenursing courses, either at that university or elsewhere. Some students decide to apply to BSN programs after earning a degree in a subject other than nursing, such as biology or chemistry. Still, others find their way to BSN programs after working in the nursing field for a number of years. For those working nurses who have achieved RN status but have never earned a bachelor's degree, a number of nursing schools have what are called RN to BSN degree tracks.

The lists and descriptions of nursing schools below are not exhaustive or encyclopedic. Nursing schools are found near almost any hospital, at just about every university with a medical center, and even at branch or satellite campuses of colleges and universities. The nursing schools listed (and in a number of cases profiled) below are divided into two groups: those at universities with medical schools and those at schools with no medical center or school. Good programs can be found at both types of venues.

➤ NURSING PROGRAMS AT UNIVERSITIES WITH MEDICAL SCHOOLS

University of Alabama at Birmingham	University of Iowa	Oregon Health and Science University
University of Arizona	Johns Hopkins University	University of Pennsylvania
Baylor University	University of Kansas at Kansas City	University of Pittsburgh
University at Buffalo (SUNY)	University of Kentucky	University of Rochester
University of California at Los Angeles	Louisiana State University (New Orleans campus)	Rutgers University
Case Western Reserve University		St. Louis University
University of Cincinnati	University of Louisville	Stony Brook University (SUNY)
University of Colorado at Denver	Loyola University Chicago	University of Southern California
Columbia University	University of Maryland	University of South Carolina
University of Connecticut	University of Miami	Temple University
Creighton University	Michigan State University	University of Tennessee
Drexel University	University of Michigan	Texas A&M University
Duke University	University of Minnesota—Twin Cities and Rochester	University of Texas at Austin
Emory University		University of Vermont
Florida State University	University of Missouri at Columbia	Virginia Commonwealth University
University of Florida	University of Nebraska at Omaha	University of Virginia
Georgetown University	University of New Mexico	University of Washington
Howard University	New York University	Wayne State University
Indiana University-Purdue University Indianapolis (IUPUI)	University of North Carolina at Chapel Hill	West Virginia University
	Ohio State University	University of Wisconsin

Case Western Reserve University. The Frances Payne Bolton School of Nursing at Case accepts freshman directly from high school as well as transfers from other majors at CWRU or from other colleges. The emphasis of Case's BSN program is on clinical learning, which occurs in more than two hundred partner health-care centers in the Cleveland area.

Emory University. The Woodruff School of Nursing at Emory has BSN programs for students who enter as freshmen or as bachelor's degree holders seeking a nursing degree. Freshman BSN students begin at Emory's Oxford College campus (located forty-five minutes east of Emory's Atlanta campus) and apply to enter the Woodruff School after two years of study.

Johns Hopkins University. Hopkins is frequently ranked as the top US school for nursing. JHU's BS program in nursing enrolls four hundred and is limited to students who already have a bachelor's degree in another subject.

University of Miami. Miami's School of Nursing and Health Studies has leading-edge clinical simulation facilities. Students enter the BSN program directly from high school or as transfers from within Miami or from other colleges. Miami also offers a RN to BSN program, BS degrees in health sciences and public health, and graduate nursing programs focused on acute care, anesthesia, family health, and midwifery.

University of Minnesota. Minnesota's nursing program (founded in 1909) is the oldest one that has been continuously housed on a university campus. Minnesota offers BSN programs at its main campus (UMN-TC) in the Twin Cities as well as at the branch campus (UMN-R) in Rochester, home of the famed Mayo Clinic. Minnesota's nursing programs have clinical connections (for student rotations) at forty-five hospitals. There are 128 freshmen slots available for entering BSN students: 96 at UMN-TC and 32 at UMN-R.

University of North Carolina at Chapel Hill. UNC's nursing programs (BSN, MSN, and PhD) rank in the top five in the United States. UNC is especially strong in mental health and psychiatric nursing. Students gain admission to UNC's approximately four hundred undergraduate nursing slots as college sophomores or as degree holders seeking a BSN.

Ohio State University. The approximately 1,500 students in Ohio State's highly ranked nursing school are enrolled in BSN through PhD programs. Students can enter Ohio State's BSN program directly from high school, through OSU's prenursing sequence, or as an experienced RN seeking a BSN. The nursing program at Ohio State operates an innovative Center for Transdisciplinary Evidence-Based Practice.

University of Pennsylvania. Penn's top-ranked BSN program offers students double major connections to its renowned schools of arts and sciences, business, and engineering. Nursing students have clinical rotation opportunities at Penn's hospitals and at other nearby health facilities such as the Children's Hospital of Philadelphia. Students can enter Penn's BSN program after earning another bachelor's degree at Penn or elsewhere. There is also a combined BSN/MSN program.

Stony Brook University (SUNY). At Stony Brook, there are BSN options for first degree seekers from high school, students with bachelor's degrees in another subject, and RNs. Applicants from high school take two years of prenursing and general education courses at Stony Brook before entering the BSN program. The RN to BSN program is open to students with either a diploma or an associate degree in nursing. A small number of outstanding RN to BSN students are invited to stay on for a MS degree in a nursing specialty. There is also a twelve-month accelerated BSN program for students holding a BA or a BS degree in another subject.

University of Texas at Austin. Students can enter UT's highly selective BSN program directly from high school, from other majors at UT, as transfers from another college, or after completing an associate degree in nursing elsewhere. UT has a Nursing Honors Program for students achieving a GPA of at least 3.45/4.0.

University of Virginia. A special focus at UVA's top-ranked nursing program is the Compassionate Care Initiative that trains students in end-of-life care for patients with chronic and terminal illnesses. Students can enter UVA's BSN program directly from high school, as transfers following two years of study at Virginia, as transfers from another college, or as RNs seeking a BSN degree.

➤ NURSING PROGRAMS WHERE THERE IS NO MEDICAL SCHOOL

Arizona State University
  (Phoenix campus)

Auburn University

Binghamton University (SUNY)

Boise State University

Boston College

Brigham Young University

Catholic University

Clemson University

University of Delaware

Fairfield University

University of Illinois at Chicago

University of Maine

Marquette University

University of Massachusetts at Amherst

Miami University

Montana State University

University of New Hampshire

The College of New Jersey

University of North Carolina at
  Greensboro

Northeastern University

Penn State University

University of Portland

Purdue University

University of Rhode Island

San Diego State University

Seattle University

University of San Francisco

SUNY-Brockport

SUNY-Plattsburgh

Villanova University

Washington State University

University of Wyoming

Boston College. The BSN program at BC's Connell School of Nursing provides training in adult and child health and community, maternity, and psychiatric nursing. BC encourages its nursing students (most enter from high school) to study abroad and engage in research. Outstanding students can earn early entrance into BC's master's program in nursing. BC nursing graduates have a 95 percent pass rate on the national licensing exam.

Clemson University. Clemson's clinically focused BSN program enrolls forty freshmen each year directly from high school. Clemson also offers a BS program for experienced nurses.

University of Delaware. Each year of Delaware's BSN program revolves around a clinical immersion experience. Routes into nursing at Delaware include direct entry from high school, internal transfer from another university program, and an accelerated BSN track for students who already have a bachelor's degree.

Miami University. At Miami of Ohio, nursing is part of the School of Engineering and Applied Science. Direct entry from high school into Miami's BSN program requires an ACT of at least 23, a high school GPA of at least 3.0/4.0, plus a 3.0/4.0 average in science courses. Miami also offers RN to BSN and school nursing licensure tracks.

University of North Carolina at Greensboro. UNCG has an impressive legacy in nursing education. There are three BSN tracks at UNCG. From high school, students follow a two-year pre-BSN track, leading to entry into the nursing major as a junior. UNCG also has an RN to BSN program for experienced nurses, a three-year BSN program for students with a bachelor's degree in another field, and MSN, PhD, and doctor of nursing practice programs.

San Diego State University. Students can enter San Diego State's BSN program as freshmen or transfers. A unique feature of SDSU's BSN program is its requirement that all students have an international experience. SDSU also offers a BS degree for experienced nurses, the school nurse credential, and an MS program with concentrations in elderly care and women's health.

Villanova University. The College of Nursing at Villanova enrolls six hundred BSN students in a program that has many clinical connections in metro Philadelphia. Villanova also has an exchange program with the Department of Nursing at the University of Manchester in England. Students can enter Villanova's BSN program from high school or through transfer.

Washington State University. WSU offers direct-entry BSN and RN to BSN programs at its main campus in Pullman. Following two years in Pullman, BSN students finish at the WSU College of Nursing, which is located in Spokane but also has satellite campuses in Yakima and the Tri-Cities (Kennewick-Pasco-Richland).

PHARMACY

Students interested in pharmacy have three degree pathways open to them. For students exploring the field of pharmacy without committing to the professional path necessary to become a pharmacist, there is the bachelor of science (BS) degree in pharmaceutical sciences. This track prepares students to work as pharmacy technicians either in drug companies or in pharmacies, while also providing the prerequisite courses needed to enter graduate and professional pharmacy programs. For students focused on becoming a licensed pharmacist, the required degree is the doctor of pharmacy (PharmD). Students have two routes to earning the PharmD. The first is direct entry from high school into six-year or seven-year PharmD programs. Many pharmacy schools (but not all) offer direct-entry PharmD admission from high school. The other route to PharmD programs is through pre-pharmacy study at college. Typically, pre-pharmacy students take two to three years of core courses, after which they apply to PharmD programs. PharmD programs normally require four years of additional study beyond the pre-pharmacy track. Below are lists and brief descriptions of standout pharmacy programs.

SPECIALIZED PHARMACY SCHOOLS

Albany College of Pharmacy and Health Sciences. Albany offers direct entry from high school into its six-year PharmD program. Albany also has a BS program in pharmaceutical sciences and a satellite campus near Burlington, Vermont.

Massachusetts College of Pharmacy and Health Sciences. High school students can apply for direct entry into MCPHS's six-year PharmD program. This Boston-based school also offers BS programs in pharmaceutical sciences, pharmacology and toxicology, and pharmaceutical and health-care business.

St. Louis College of Pharmacy. STLCOP offers applicants from high schools the option of direct entry into its seven-year PharmD program. En route to the PharmD degree, students receive a BS.

University of the Sciences. Formerly called the Philadelphia College of Pharmacy, this specialized health sciences school offers direct entry from high school into its six-year PharmD program as well as BS degrees in pharmaceutical chemistry, pharmaceutical and health-care business, pharmaceutical sciences, and pharmacology and toxicology.

UNIVERSITY PHARMACY PROGRAMS

University of Arizona. Arizona's College of Pharmacy offers a pre-pharmacy track that requires two to three years to complete. The PharmD degree at Arizona takes an additional four years to complete.

University at Buffalo (SUNY). There are two ways to enter the PharmD program at Buffalo: either through the early assurance program for high school applicants or by completing the two-year pre-pharmacy core curriculum.

University of Connecticut. UConn offers a BS in pharmaceutical studies for high school applicants. Entrance to the PharmD program requires two years of high achievement in pre-pharmacy courses.

Duquesne University. Duquesne offers early entry (from high school) into its PharmD program.

University of Georgia. Before advancing into Georgia's PharmD program, students must complete the pre-pharmacy core. Georgia does not offer direct entry from high school.

Hampton University. Students enter Hampton's pre-pharmacy program directly from high school. After two years of successful pre-pharmacy study, students move into the PharmD program.

University of Houston. Students interested in the PharmD program must complete two years of pre-pharmacy courses.

University of Michigan. The BS in pharmaceutical sciences program at Michigan prepares students for work as pharmacy technicians, not licensed pharmacists. After earning their BS, students can apply to stay on for their PharmD or apply to Michigan's innovative master of pharmaceutical engineering program.

Northeastern University. Northeastern has a six-year program in which applicants from high schools are admitted to the PharmD program.

Ohio Northern University. ONU has a direct-entry 0–6 PharmD program for applicants from high school.

Ohio State University. Through the Early Admissions Pathway (EAP), a limited number of students enter OSU's PharmD program from high school. OSU also offers a BS in pharmaceutical sciences as well as a pre-pharmacy track.

Oregon State University. Oregon State offers direct entry from high school into its PharmD program.

Purdue University. Purdue offers a BS in pharmaceutical sciences. To enter Purdue's PharmD program, students must complete the BS degree or pre-pharmacy course work.

University of Rhode Island. Pharmacy students at URI can pursue a BS in pharmaceutical sciences or a 0–6 PharmD program that offers direct entry from high school.

Rutgers University. The Mario School of Pharmacy at Rutgers admits selected high school students to its PharmD program.

Shenandoah University. Shenandoah admits a small number of applicants from high school as pre-pharmacy students. Success in the pre-pharmacy track qualifies students for entry into the PharmD program.

St. John's University. St. John's offers direct entry (from high school) into its PharmD program.

University of Toledo. Toledo offers direct entry from high school into its PharmD program and a BS in pharmaceutical sciences.

University of Wisconsin. Wisconsin has a BS program in pharmacology and toxicology that can be pursued in preparation for a PharmD but does not offer direct entry from high school.

EARLY ENTRY TO MD AND DO PROGRAMS

Some universities that have medical schools admit a small number of students into BA/BS/MD or BA/BS/DO (doctor of osteopathic medicine) programs directly from high school. Direct-entry programs typically take six or seven years to complete and require that applicants present exceptional credentials, that is, very high standardized test scores, strong preparation in math and science courses, stellar grades, and a rank at or near the top of their high school class. Listed below are the universities offering direct entry into their medical of osteopathic schools. Admission requirements vary, so prospective students need to look closely at the particulars of each program.

► UNIVERSITIES OFFERING DIRECT ENTRY INTO THEIR MEDICAL AND OSTEOPATHIC SCHOOLS

University of Alabama at Birmingham

Baylor University

Boston University

Brown University

University of California at San Diego

Case Western Reserve University

University of Cincinnati

University of Colorado at Denver

University of Connecticut
(Connecticut residents preferred)

Drexel University

East Carolina University

Florida State University

University of Florida
(Florida residents only)

George Washington University

University of Hawaii
(Hawaii residents only)

Howard University

University of Illinois at Chicago

Indiana State University

University of Kentucky

University of Louisville

Loyola University Chicago

University of Miami

University of Missouri at Kansas City
(Missouri residents preferred)

University of Nevada at Reno
(Nevada residents only)

University of New England

University of New Mexico
(New Mexico residents only)

University of North Texas

Northwestern University

Nova Southeastern University

University of Pittsburgh

University of Rochester

St. Louis University

University of South Alabama

University of South Florida

Sophie Davis School of Biomedical
Education of the City College of
New York

Stony Brook University (SUNY)

Temple University

Texas A&M University

Texas Tech University
(Texas residents only)

University of Toledo

Touro College

Tulane University

Virginia Commonwealth University

Wayne State University

Washington University

West Virginia University

There are additional programs (listed below) leading to a BS or BA in conjunction with an MD or DO degree offered by medical or osteopathic schools through partnerships with one or more undergraduate institutions. Students interested in these programs must apply through the admissions office at the partner undergraduate institution. In most cases, applicants that make the cut will get a final review by the medical or osteopathic school's admissions office.

Albany Medical College—Rensselaer Polytechnic Institute, Siena College, Union College

Baylor College of Medicine—Rice University

University of California at Los Angeles School of Medicine—University of California at Riverside

University of California at San Diego School of Medicine—California Institute of Technology

Chicago College of Osteopathic Medicine—Illinois Institute of Technology

Drexel University College of Medicine—Kean University, Lehigh University, Monmouth University, Muhlenberg College, Robert Morris University, Rosemont College, Ursinus College, Villanova University, West Chester University, Wilkes University

Eastern Virginia Medical School—Christopher Newport University, Hampden Sydney College, Hampton University, Old Dominion University, Randolph Macon College

George Washington University School of Medicine—Claremont McKenna College, Colgate University, Franklin and Marshall College, George Mason University, Hampden Sydney College, Knox College, University of Maryland, Randolph Macon College, Rhodes College, Rowan University, St. Bonaventure University, Scripps College

Jefferson Medical College of Thomas Jefferson University—Penn State University

Kansas City University of Medicine and Biosciences College of Osteopathic Medicine—Avila University, Central Methodist University, Missouri Western State College, Pittsburg State University, Rockhurst University, William Jewell College

Kirksville College of Osteopathic Medicine—Massachusetts College of Pharmacy and Health Sciences

Lake Erie College of Osteopathic Medicine—Fairleigh Dickinson University, Gannon University, Juniata College, Niagara University, St. Bonaventure University, Seton Hill University, Utica College

Meharry Medical College—Fisk University, Grambling State University

University of Nebraska College of Medicine—Chadron State College, Wayne State College

University of Nevada School of Medicine—University of Nevada at Las Vegas

University of New England College of Osteopathic Medicine—University of Hartford, Utica College

New York College of Osteopathic Medicine—Geneseo College of SUNY, New York Institute of Technology, SUNY-New Paltz

State University of New York Downstate Medical Center College of Medicine—Brooklyn College of CUNY, NYU Polytechnic, College of Staten Island

State University of New York Upstate College of Medicine—Clarkson University, Colgate University, Geneseo College of SUNY, Hobart and William Smith Colleges, St. Bonaventure University, St. Lawrence University, Wilkes University

Northeastern Ohio Universities College of Medicine—University of Akron, Kent State University, Youngstown State University (Ohio residents preferred)

University of North Texas, Texas College of Osteopathic Medicine—University of Texas at Dallas

Nova Southeastern University College of Osteopathic Medicine—Florida International University

University of Oklahoma College of Medicine (Oklahoma City)—University of Oklahoma (Norman)

Philadelphia College of Osteopathic Medicine—Gannon University, University of the Sciences-Philadelphia, Widener University, Wilkes University

Rutgers School of Biomedical and Health Sciences—Caldwell College, Drew University, Montclair State University, College of New Jersey, New Jersey Institute of Technology, Ramapo College, Richard Stockton College, Rutgers University-Newark, Stevens Institute of Technology

University of South Florida College of Medicine—Florida Gulf Coast University, Florida Southern College, University of West Florida

Temple University School of Medicine—Duquesne University, Washington and Jefferson College, Widener University

Texas A&M Health Sciences Center College of Medicine—Prairie View A&M University, South Texas College, Tarleton State University, Texas A&M International University, Texas A&M University-Commerce, Texas A&M University-Corpus Christi, Texas A&M University-Kingsville, West Texas A&M University

University of Texas Medical Branch School of Medicine—Prairie View A&M University, Texas International University, Texas Southern University, University of Texas at Brownsville, University of Texas at El Paso, University of Texas Pan American

University of Texas School of Medicine at San Antonio—St. Mary's University, Texas A&M International University, University of Texas Pan American

Tufts University School of Medicine—Boston College, Brandeis University, College of the Holy Cross, Northeastern University, and special program to develop physicians for Maine with Bates College, Bowdoin College, Colby College, and the University of Maine campuses

Wayne State University School of Medicine—Michigan Technological University, Northern Michigan University

Western University of Health Sciences College of Osteopathic Medicine of the **Pacific**—Pitzer College

West Virginia University—Shepherd University

EARLY ENTRY TO DENTAL SCHOOLS

A number of dental schools offer early-entry BA/BS/DDS programs. The first list below includes universities that offer BA/BS/DDS programs to their own undergraduates, either as applicants from high school or following one or two years of college course work.

- Boston University
- University at Buffalo (SUNY)
- Case Western Reserve University
- University of Connecticut
- University of Detroit Mercy
- Howard University
- University of Illinois
- Marquette University
- New York University
- University of the Pacific
- University of Pennsylvania

- Southern Illinois University
- Temple University
- Virginia Commonwealth University

The following list includes dental schools and their early-entry partners.

University at Buffalo (SUNY) School of Dental Medicine—Canisius College, Geneseo College (SUNY), LeMoyne College, Niagara University, SUNY College at Fredonia, St. Bonaventure University, St. Lawrence University, Siena College, Utica College

New York University School of Dentistry—Adelphi University, Caldwell College, Fairleigh Dickinson University, University of Hartford, Iona College, Manhattanville College, Wagner College, Yeshiva University

University of Pennsylvania School of Dental Medicine—Hampton University, Lehigh University, Muhlenberg College, Villanova University

Rutgers School of Biomedical and Health Sciences—Fairleigh Dickinson University, New Jersey Institute of Technology, St. Peter's College, Stevens Institute of Technology

Temple University School of Dentistry—Moravian College, Penn State Erie at Behrend, Wilkes University

EARLY ENTRY TO PODIATRY SCHOOLS

An often overlooked medical specialty is podiatry. Podiatrists are doctors whose work is somewhat similar to the bone and joint doctors (orthopedists) who work on knees, hips, ligaments, and cartilages. But podiatry is even more specialized, focusing on the diagnosis and treatment of the feet and ankles. Students interested in this specialty may want to investigate the small number of accredited schools of podiatric medicine located in the United States (listed below) that offer seven- to eight-year BA/BS/ DPM programs.

Kent State University College of Podiatric Medicine. Located in the Cleveland suburb of Independence, Ohio, and formerly called the Ohio College of Podiatric Medicine, KSUCPM's partners are Cleveland State University, Elmira College, Cuyahoga Community College, Gannon University, Juniata College, Lewis University, Lorain County Community College, Marshall University, Maryville University, Mercyhurst College, Ursuline College, and Viterbo University.

New York College of Podiatric Medicine. The partners for this Manhattan-based podiatry school include Brooklyn College, Clarkson University, Fairleigh Dickinson University, University of Hartford, Manhattan College, Marist College, Quinnipiac University, Roger Williams University, St. Johns University, and Springfield College.

Scholl College of Podiatric Medicine at Rosalind Frank University of Medicine and Science. This specialized medical university north of Chicago has partnerships with Carthage College, Carroll University, and Lewis University.

Temple University College of Podiatric Medicine. Temple's more than forty partners include University at Buffalo (SUNY), Cabrini College, Delaware Valley College, Gannon University, Hampton University, Howard University, Indiana University of Pennsylvania, Lycoming College, North Carolina A&T University, Rensselaer Polytechnic Institute, Rowan University, Salisbury University, University of Scranton, Siena College, and Washington and Jefferson College.

PREPARING FOR VETERINARY SCHOOL

There are twenty-eight accredited veterinary schools in the United States and one scheduled to open in 2016. Admission to veterinary schools is very competitive. Students generally need to follow a premedical curriculum, which includes required courses in calculus, chemistry (organic), and physics and highly recommended courses such as physical chemistry and statistics. Among the veterinary schools, there are at least five (Colorado State, Kansas State, Mississippi State, Missouri, and Purdue) that have early-entry programs available to high school applicants. These early-entry programs (all at public universities) give preference to applicants who are residents of that state. In some cases, these programs specifically state how many students get early admission and what criteria can sway the admissions committee. For example, Colorado State University enrolls five high school graduates annually in its Vet Start Program, giving special consideration to Colorado residents from disadvantaged backgrounds.

A few other schools (listed below) offer early-entry opportunities for students in their freshman or sophomore year. The early-entry program at Tufts' veterinary school is also open to sophomore applicants from the University of Massachusetts at Amherst, the University of Vermont, and Worcester Polytechnic Institute.

- Cornell University—sophomore year
- Oklahoma State University—freshman year
- Tufts University—sophomore year
- Washington State University—freshman year

The following veterinary schools only admit students who have earned (or nearly completed) a bachelor's degree.

- University of Arizona (opening in 2016)
- Auburn University
- University of California at Davis
- University of Florida
- University of Georgia
- University of Illinois
- Iowa State University
- Louisiana State University
- Michigan State University
- University of Minnesota
- North Carolina State University
- Ohio State University
- Oregon State University
- University of Pennsylvania
- University of Tennessee at Knoxville
- Texas A&M University
- Tuskegee University
- Virginia Polytechnic and State University (Virginia-Maryland Regional College of Veterinary Medicine)
- Western University of Health Sciences
- University of Wisconsin

OPTOMETRY SCHOOL

Jobs as an optometrist require a Doctor of Optometry (OD) degree. Most OD programs require that applicants have earned at least a bachelor's degree. Optometry schools do not expect applicants to have majored in a particular field, such as biology, but they do expect strong preparation in laboratory science and quantitative subjects, such as mathematics and physics.

There are twenty-two optometry schools (listed below) in the United States and Canada.

➤ OPTOMETRY SCHOOLS IN THE UNITED STATES AND CANADA

University of Alabama at Birmingham

University of California at Berkeley

Ferris State University

University of Houston

Illinois College of Optometry

University of the Incarnate Word

Indiana University

Massachusetts College of Pharmacy and Health Sciences

Midwestern University Arizona College of Optometry

University of Missouri at St. Louis

University of Montreal

New England College of Optometry

State University of New York (SUNY) College of Optometry

Northeastern State University

Nova Southeastern University

Ohio State University

Pacific University

Pennsylvania College of Optometry

Southern California College of Optometry

Southern College of Optometry

University of Waterloo

Western University of Health Sciences

A few optometry schools offer early entry to their OD program. Some of the programs listed below reserve early-entry slots for students applying from high school, but in most of those cases, students still must later apply (after successful completion of prerequisite courses) for entry into OD study.

Ferris State University. The Michigan College of Optometry at Ferris State has a 3-plus-4 option that accepts highly qualified third-year students.

Illinois College of Optometry. Located in Chicago, ICO has 3-plus-4 programs with Augustana College (IL), Knox College, and Illinois Institute of Technology.

Massachusetts College of Pharmacy and Health Sciences. MCPHS offers several premed pathways, including the BS/OD.

University of Missouri in St. Louis. UMSL offers a seven-year BS/OD program through its Laclede Honors College.

New England College of Optometry. From high school, applicants can get conditionally accepted into a partner college's seven-year BA/BS/OD

arrangement with NECO. Official entry into OD study at NECO occurs following three years of strong academic work at a partner college. NECO's partners include Assumption College, University of Hartford, University of Maine, Providence College, and Wheaton College (MA).

Ohio State University. Exceptionally strong students can apply to the OD program as juniors, but preference is given to applicants who have already earned a bachelor's degree.

Pennsylvania College of Optometry. Students can apply from high school to PCO's seven-year BA/BS/OD program. In year three at one of the partner colleges, students must gain official entry to OD study. PCO's many partners include Arcadia University, Bennett College, Caldwell College, Delaware Valley College, Elizabethtown College, Gannon University, Gettysburg College, Grove City College, Indiana University of Pennsylvania, Ithaca College, Johnson C. Smith University, Juniata College, LeMoyne College, Millersville University, Old Dominion University, University of Pittsburgh at Bradford, University of Pittsburgh at Johnstown, St. John Fisher College, St. Joseph's College (Maine),

Salisbury State University, Siena College, Rowan University, University of the Sciences, Seton Hall University, Villanova University, Washington and Jefferson College, Widener University, and Wilkes University.

SUNY College of Optometry. This New York City school has twenty-five affiliate colleges where students complete their first three years of study. Students are admitted to the seven-year BA/BS/OD program during their freshman year at a partner college or straight from high school.

Partners include Adelphi University, Canisius College, CUNY Brooklyn College, CUNY College of Staten Island, Ithaca College, Lehigh University, Muhlenberg College, New Jersey Institute of Technology, College of New Jersey, Pace University, Ramapo College of New Jersey, St. John's University, Siena College, SUNY Albany, SUNY Binghamton, SUNY Fredonia, SUNY Geneseo, SUNY New Paltz, SUNY Oneonta, SUNY Oswego, SUNY Plattsburgh, SUNY Potsdam, Utica College, Wagner College, and Yeshiva University.

PHYSICAL THERAPY

Less than a generation ago, students could earn a bachelor's degree in physical therapy and find employment as a physical therapist. Much has changed in the last twenty years. Now positions as a full-fledged physical therapist require a graduate degree, generally the doctor of physical therapy (DPT). At the undergraduate level, students now prepare for a career in physical therapy by following a curriculum heavily weighted with courses in the health or life sciences that are found in majors such as biology, exercise physiology, health science, athletic training, kinesiology, or nursing. In cases where students can enter an accelerated BS/DPT from high school, applicants need to have four years of course work in the sciences (preferably in biology, chemistry, and physics), four years of math, and four years of English. Listed and briefly described below are some of the schools with BS/DPT programs.

➤ SCHOOLS WITH BS/DPT PROGRAMS

Arcadia University

Boston University

University of Cincinnati

Drexel University

Duquesne University

Fairleigh Dickinson University

East Carolina University

University of Evansville

University of Hartford

Ithaca College

Marquette University

Misericordia University

New Jersey Institute of Technology (with Rutgers Biomedical and Health Sciences)

New York Institute of Technology

Northeastern University

Nova Southeastern University

Penn State University (with Thomas Jefferson University)

Quinnipiac University

Seton Hall University

St. Joseph's University (with Thomas Jefferson University)

St. Louis University

Shenandoah University

Simmons College

Springfield College

SUNY Brockport, ESF, Geneseo, Oneonta, Oswego (with SUNY Upstate Medical University)

Utica College

Villanova University

Boston University. BU's Sargent College of Health and Rehabilitation Sciences has a highly ranked physical therapy program that puts a strong emphasis on clinical training. Students get experience working in BU's centers for physical therapy and sports medicine. For applicants from high schools, BU offers an accelerated six-year program in which students earn a BS in health studies followed by a DPT.

University of Cincinnati. The seven-year BS/DPT program at Cincinnati is a pathway open to students admitted from high school into the College of Allied Health Sciences. Students major in health sciences and upon completion of that program begin their studies for a DPT degree.

Drexel University. Within its pathway to the health professions program, Drexel offers an accelerated BS/DPT option that students can complete in six years. Drexel's strong focus on cooperative education gives students ample opportunities to have internships and gain clinical training. Drexel admits applicants directly from high school.

Duquesne University. The Duquesne BS/DPT program takes six years to complete and is open to high school applicants. Duquesne's School of Health Sciences also offers students the option of earning a BS in athletic training en route to getting a DPT degree.

Northeastern University. Northeastern's Bouve College of Health Sciences offers an early-entry option for high school applicants into its six-year BS/DPT program. Students can pursue special concentrations in sports conditioning or in early intervention, a track that focuses on infants and toddlers with disabilities. Physical therapy students at Northeastern are required to have at least two six-month-long cooperative experiences in clinical settings.

Quinnipiac University. Quinnipiac offers early-entry options from high school into its two BS/DPT programs. Students can earn a BS in health sciences and a DPT degree in a program that normally takes seven years to complete. Students can complete the BS/DPT program in six years if they study for two summers. Quinnipiac also offers a seven-year BS (in athletic training)/DPT program. Applicants to either program need to have a minimum of twenty hours of observation in two different clinical settings.

St. Louis University. Within its Doisy College of Health Sciences, SLU offers a six-year BS/DPT program that students can enter directly from high school. Students earn a BS in exercise science and complete two summers of study en route to fulfilling requirements for the DPT. The physical therapy program at SLU has affiliations with more than three hundred clinical sites.

Seton Hall University. Seton Hall's seven-year BS/DPT program accepts applicants from high school. In their first three years, students complete a major in biology before moving on to four years of study in the School of Health and Medical Sciences. Clinical experiences and internships are an integral part of Seton Hall's DPT program.

Temple University. Temple's accelerated three-plus-three BA/DPT program is open to high school seniors applying to one of eight majors: biology, chemistry, computer science, information science and technology, kinesiology, math, natural sciences, or physics. Students apply for formal entry to the DPT program as sophomores at Temple.

➤ TOP-RANKED GRADUATE PHYSICAL THERAPY PROGRAMS

Boston University

University of California at San Francisco

University of Delaware

Duke University

Emory University

University of Iowa

Northwestern University

University of Miami

University of North Carolina at Chapel Hill

Marquette University

Ohio State University

University of Pittsburgh

University of Southern California

University of Utah

Washington University

OCCUPATIONAL THERAPY

Professional positions in occupational therapy require at least a master's degree. Higher levels of opportunity—including faculty positions—are available for holders of Doctor of Occupational Therapy (DOT) degrees. In most cases, admission to a graduate occupational therapy program requires a bachelor's degree in a science-related field, such as biology, health sciences, kinesiology, or nursing.

➤ TOP-RANKED DOCTOR OF OCCUPATIONAL THERAPY (DOT) PROGRAMS

Boston University

Colorado State University

Columbia University

Creighton University

University of Florida

University of Illinois at Chicago

Indiana University

University of Kansas

New York University

Ohio State University

University of Pittsburgh

University of Southern California

University of Texas Medical Branch Campus at Galveston

Texas Women's University

Thomas Jefferson University

Tufts University

Virginia Commonwealth University

Washington University in St. Louis

University of Washington

University of Wisconsin

A number of colleges (some listed and profiled below) offer accelerated BS/MS programs in occupational therapy, several of which are open to students applying from high school. Completion of accelerated BS/MS programs varies from five to six years, depending on the school.

- University at Buffalo (SUNY)
- Duquesne University
- Elizabethtown College
- Gannon University
- Ithaca College
- University of Kansas
- Long Island University
- University of New Hampshire
- New York Institute of Technology

- Nazareth College
- Philadelphia University
- University of the Sciences, Philadelphia
- University of Scranton
- Seton Hall University
- Springfield College
- Stony Brook University (SUNY)
- Towson University

University at Buffalo (SUNY). Students can enter Buffalo's five-year BS/MS program from high school. While completing a BS degree in occupational science, students in Buffalo's BS/MS program complete a two-year, pre-professional course sequence and get seventy hours of volunteer or work experience in an occupational therapy setting.

Duquesne University. At Duquesne, students can follow a five-year program, earning either a BA or BS in health sciences, followed by a MS in occupational therapy. Duquesne also offers a six-year BS (in athletic training)/MS program for students interested in therapy in sports settings.

Ithaca College. Ithaca admits students from high school into its five-year BS/MS program that awards a BS in occupational science and a MS in occupational therapy. The MS portion of the program requires two three-month-long fieldwork terms in one of the many affiliated treatment/therapy settings. Ithaca also operates an assistive teaching laboratory.

University of Kansas. Students start the BS program in occupational studies at the main KU campus in Lawrence. After completing a minimum of twenty-four prerequisite courses, students can apply to the master's in occupational therapy (MOT) program, housed at the Kansas University Medical Center in Kansas City, Kansas. Kansas does not offer an early-entry BS/MOT option for high school applicants.

University of New Hampshire. UNH offers two entry points into its five-year BS/MS program. Students can apply from high school or as juniors, following two years of study at UNH. Fieldwork in a clinical setting is an integral part of UNH's BS/MS program.

University of Scranton. Students in Scranton's five-year program work toward a BS in health sciences followed by a MS in occupational therapy. Admission into the BS/MS program is open to students applying from high school. All students in the program complete a faculty-mentored research internship.

Seton Hall University. The BA/MS program at Seton Hall takes five years to complete and admits students directly from high school. Students earn a BA in behavioral sciences en route to completing a MS degree in occupational therapy. The clinical internship in a treatment setting occurs during the MS portion of the program.

Stony Brook University (SUNY). Students apply from high school to enter the BS program in health sciences. Success in the BS program leads to entry into the MS program in occupational therapy.

PHYSICIAN ASSISTANT PROGRAMS

The physician assistant field has been growing. PAs—as physician assistants are often called—now handle many of the patient-care and consultation duties that were the exclusive domain of physicians just a generation ago. Becoming a PA does not require the number of years of education necessary to become a doctor of medicine (MD or DO). In most cases, to get a job as a PA requires a master's degree in physician assistant studies. There are two pathways for entering the physician assistant field. Students can enter a five- or six-year BS/MS PA program by applying directly from high school or after two years of undergraduate study. An alternative route is to earn a BA or BS degree in a science-related subject as an undergraduate and then apply to a master's program in physician assistant studies. This latter route is arguably the prestige route, because the highest-rated PA programs are almost exclusively at colleges that offer just the master's degree option, not the BS/MS option. Schools offering an undergraduate (BS/MS) route into the physician assistant field are listed (and in a few cases profiled) below.

➤ SCHOOLS OFFERING AN UNDERGRADUATE (BS/MS) ROUTE INTO THE PHYSICIAN ASSISTANT FIELD

University at Albany (SUNY) (through Albany Medical College)

Arcadia University

Butler University

Daemen College

University of Detroit Mercy

Drexel University

Duquesne University

D'Youville College

Felician College (through Rutgers School of Biomedical and Health Sciences)

Gannon University

Hofstra University

Kean University (through Rutgers)

LeMoyne College

Lock Haven University

Marquette University

Massachusetts College of Pharmacy and Health Sciences

Montclair State University (through Rutgers)

Misericordia University

University of New England

New Jersey Institute of Technology (through Rutgers)

New York Institute of Technology

Philadelphia University

Quinnipiac University

Ramapo College of New Jersey (through Rutgers)

Rochester Institute of Technology

Rutgers University

St. John's University

St. Peter's College (through Rutgers)

Seton Hall University

Seton Hill University

Springfield College

Touro College

Wagner College

William Patterson University (through Rutgers)

York College of the City University of New York (CUNY)

Arcadia University. Arcadia has a four-plus-two program in which students major in biology, chemistry, or psychology while taking prerequisite courses to help them gain entry into the master of medical science/physician assistant program.

Butler University. Butler annually admits thirty applicants from high school to a program that culminates in a master's degree in physician assistant sciences. Direct-entry applicants must meet the requirements of Butler's School of Pharmacy and Health Sciences.

Drexel University. Drexel offers a five-year BS/MHS program (open to applicants from high schools) for students interested in becoming a PA. Drexel's prominence in cooperative education assures high-quality clinical experiences for students in the program.

Duquesne University. Duquesne was the first college in the United States to develop a five-year direct-entry BS/MS program in physician assistant studies. BS/MS students follow a three-year preprofessional curriculum before transitioning into a PA program that stresses clinical experiences.

Hofstra University. Hofstra offers a direct-entry BS/MS option for high school applicants. Alternatively, students who have taken prerequisite courses or are following the BS in physician assistant studies curriculum can apply to the MS program during their junior year at Hofstra.

Marquette University. Marquette has a pre–physician assistant program open to students admitted to the biomedical sciences. After two years of successful study at Marquette, students can apply to the combined bachelor's/master's physician assistant program.

New York Institute of Technology. NYIT has a six-year BS/MS program that is open to applicants from high school. Students work on a BS in life sciences and then advance toward earning an MS in physician assistant studies.

Rochester Institute of Technology. RIT has a five-year BS/MS program that is open to high school applicants. RIT also accepts transfer students into its BS/MS program. A highlight of RIT's PA program is a clinical rotation through every major area of medical practice from emergency medicine to psychiatry.

Rutgers University. Students are not accepted into the BA/MS program directly from high school. Instead, they begin Rutgers's six-year (BA/MS) program in the School of Arts and Sciences, where they take prerequisite courses as freshmen. As sophomores, students apply to the School of Biomedical and Health Sciences' physician assistant MS program.

St. John's University. St. John's in New York City is a rare school that offers a PA program on the bachelor's degree level. High school applicants interested in the BS program apply through the College of Pharmacy and Health Sciences.

Springfield College. For high school applicants, Springfield offers a six-year BS/MS program. In the program's pre-professional phase, students work toward a BS degree in health science. The program's twenty-seven-month professional phase emphasizes clinical practice and culminates in a MS in physician assistant studies.

Wagner College. Wagner offers a BS/MS program consisting of a two-year pre–physician assistant phase followed by professional study toward the MS in advanced physician assistant studies. Applicants from high school apply to Wagner's pre–physician assistant program. After two years in the pre-PA curriculum, students present their grades and have an interview to determine whether they will be accepted into the MS program. The Wagner BS/MS program also accepts transfer students.

Students looking for physician assistant training at the graduate level have even more options than BS/MS aspirants. Below is a partial list of the top-ranked physician assistant graduate programs.

- University of Alabama at Birmingham
- Baylor College of Medicine
- University of Colorado at Denver
- Drexel University
- Duke University
- Emory University
- University of Florida
- George Washington University
- University of Iowa
- Northeastern University
- Oregon Health Sciences University
- Philadelphia University
- Quinnipiac University
- Rutgers University School of Health Related Professions
- Stony Brook University (SUNY)
- Tufts University
- University of Southern California
- University of Texas Southwestern Medical Center at Dallas
- University of Utah
- Wake Forest University
- University of Washington
- Yale University

PUBLIC HEALTH

To land a high-impact job in the field of public health, it helps to have a master's degree. Top-ranked master of public health (MPH) programs are generally found at universities with medical schools. In some cases, medical students pursue joint MD/MPH degree programs. Students interested in studying public health as an undergraduate will find that a number of universities offer BA or BS programs. Entry-level jobs in the public-health and health-care fields are open to students with bachelor of public health (BPH) degrees. Getting a bachelor's degree in public health can also provide potentially valuable preparation for medical school, graduate programs in public health, law school, and public policy graduate programs. Immediately below is a list of leading undergraduate programs in public health, a few of which are profiled.

➤ LEADING UNDERGRADUATE PROGRAMS IN PUBLIC HEALTH

University of Alabama at Birmingham (BS)

University at Albany (SUNY) (BS)

American University (BS)

University of Arizona (BS)

Boston University (BA/MPH or BS/MPH)

University of California at Berkeley (BA)

University of California at Irvine (BA or BS)

University of California at San Diego (BS)

University of Colorado at Denver (BA or BS)

University of Florida (BS/MPH)

George Washington University (BS and BS/MPH))

University of Hawaii at Manoa (BA)

University of Illinois at Chicago (BA)

Johns Hopkins University (BA)

University of Maryland (BS)

University of Miami (BS)

New York University (BA or BS)

University of North Carolina at Chapel Hill (BS)

St. Louis University (BS)

University of South Carolina (BA or BS)

Temple University (BS)

University of Texas at Austin (BS)

Tulane University (BS and BS/MPH))

University of Alabama at Birmingham. Students in UAB's BS program in public health can choose from the following specialties: environmental health science, global health studies, or public health preparedness. UAB also has a distinguished MPH program.

University of Arizona. Arizona's College of Public Health offers a BS program with concentrated study options in environmental and occupational health, health behavior, or health delivery.

Boston University. BU offers a five-year program in which students can earn either a BA/MPH or a BS/MPH. Students apply to the program in the second semester of their sophomore year.

University of California at Irvine. UC–Irvine operates one of the largest undergraduate public-health programs in the United States. Irvine students can pursue a BS in public health sciences or a BA in public health policy.

University of California at San Diego. UCSD began offering a BS program in public health in 2013 through its medical school. UCSD offers specializations in epidemiology and biostatistics, health policy and management, and social and behavioral sciences.

University of Florida. Florida offers a BS/MPH program that shaves a semester off the typical length of time to complete a BS and MPH separately. Students can begin the combined degree program in their senior year at UF.

George Washington University. At GW students can pursue a BS degree or a minor in public health. GW also has a BS/MPH program to which students apply during the spring semester of their sophomore year.

Johns Hopkins University. Through its Krieger School of Arts and Sciences, Hopkins offers a BA program in public health studies. Hopkins has one of the highest-rated MPH programs.

New York University. Housed in the Steinhardt School, NYU's undergraduate program in global public health requires students to have a combined major with another discipline. Students can link global public health to anthropology; applied psychology; food studies; history; media, culture, and communication; nursing; nutrition and dietetics; social work; sociology; or science.

University of North Carolina at Chapel Hill. UNC's Gillings School of Public Health is frequently rated among the best of the best. Students in UNC's BSPH program can specialize in biostatistics, environmental health sciences, health policy and management, or nutrition.

Temple University. A central feature of Temple's BS program in public health is the internship experience. Students spend two different semesters at health agency sites in the Philadelphia area.

University of Texas at Austin. Students in the BS program in public health at Texas have numerous specialties open to them, including biostatistics and public health informatics, environmental health sciences, health policy and management, infectious diseases and public health microbiology, nutrition, and social and behavioral sciences.

Tulane University. Students in Tulane's BS in public health (BSPH) program take a core curriculum of courses in biostatistics, environmental health, epidemiology, health systems, global health, and public health. As juniors, BSPH students can apply to a combined degree program, such as the master of public health (MPH), master of science in public health (MSPH), or master of health administration (MHA).

> ## ➤ TOP GRADUATE PROGRAMS IN PUBLIC HEALTH

University of Alabama at Birmingham	University of Illinois at Chicago	University of Pittsburgh
Boston University	University of Iowa	University of Texas—Houston Health Sciences Center
University of California at Berkeley	Johns Hopkins University	
University of California at Los Angeles	University of Michigan	Tulane University
Columbia University	University of Minnesota	University of Washington
Emory University	University of North Carolina at Chapel Hill	Yale University
George Washington University	Ohio State University	
Harvard University		

NUTRITION AND DIETETICS

Studying nutrition opens up a number of career pathways. Nutrition science programs can provide preparation for entry into dental or medical schools or public-health graduate programs. Dietetics programs prepare students to become licensed as a registered dietitian. And food-science majors can lead to positions in the food industry. Some of the colleges offering undergraduate programs in nutrition and dietetics are listed (and in a handful of cases profiled) below.

► COLLEGES OFFERING UNDERGRADUATE PROGRAMS IN NUTRITION AND DIETETICS

University of Alabama	University of Houston	Ohio University
Arizona State University	Howard University	Oklahoma State University
University of Arizona	University of Illinois	Oregon State University
University of Arkansas	Indiana University	Penn State University
Auburn University	Iowa State University	University of Pittsburgh
Baylor University	James Madison University	Purdue University
Boston University	Kansas State University	University of Rhode Island
Brigham Young University	University of Kentucky	Rutgers University
California Polytechnic State University at San Luis Obispo	Louisiana State University	Simmons College
University of California at Berkeley	University of Maine	SUNY-Oneonta
University of California at Davis	University of Maryland	SUNY-Plattsburgh
Case Western Reserve University	University of Massachusetts	Syracuse University
University of Cincinnati	Miami University	University of Tennessee
University of Connecticut	Michigan State University	University of Texas at Austin
Cornell University	University of Minnesota	Texas A&M University
CUNY: Brooklyn College, Hunter College	University of Missouri	Texas Christian University
University of Dayton	Montana State University	University of Vermont
Drexel University	University of Nebraska	Virginia Polytechnic and State University
Florida State University	University of New Hampshire	Washington State University
University of Florida	New York University	West Virginia University
University of Georgia	University of North Carolina at Greensboro	University of Wisconsin at Madison
University of Hawaii at Manoa	Ohio State University	University of Wyoming

University of California at Davis. UCD's clinical nutrition BS program prepares students for internships and eventual certification in dietetics, while the BS program in nutritional science offers students the option to concentrate on nutritional biology or nutrition in public health.

Iowa State University. Students at Iowa State

have three options. The BS in dietetics prepares students for an internship and licensure. The BS in nutritional science offers concentrations in wellness and pre–health professions and research. There is also a five-year BS/MS program in diet and exercise.

University of New Hampshire. UNH's BS in nutrition program offers major options in dietetics (preparing students to become registered dietitians), nutrition and wellness, and nutritional sciences (that can be pursued as a pre–health professions track). Nutrition frequently offers study modules in the UNH-in-Italy program.

New York University. Within its major in nutrition, NYU offers concentrations in food studies and nutrition and dietetics; the latter prepares students to become registered dietitians. Students can also study nutrition alongside public health: pursuing global public health and food studies or global public health and nutrition/dietetics.

Oregon State University. OSU's BS program in nutrition offers three major options: dietetics, nutrition and health sciences, and nutrition and food service systems. Students interested in dietetics must earn at least a 3.0 in their first two years to qualify for the internship required as a step toward licensure as a dietitian. One special feature of nutrition at Oregon State is the Moore Family Center for Whole Grain Foods, Nutrition, and Preventive Health.

Purdue University. Purdue's Department of Nutrition Science offers majors in dietetics (leading to internships and licensure); foods and nutrition in business, nutrition, and fitness; and health and nutrition science. Purdue's nutrition science department has its own honors program.

Simmons College. Simmons has extensive undergraduate and graduate study and internship options in nutrition. There are BS programs in nutrition and dietetics, nutrition and food science, and nutrition and food service management. There are also BS/MS programs linking nutrition to health promotion and exercise science.

Virginia Polytechnic and State University. Virginia Tech's Department of Human Nutrition, Foods, and Exercise offers BS programs in dietetics; exercise and health promotion; and the science of food, nutrition, and exercise. The didactic program in dietetics prepares students for internships and licensing.

KINESIOLOGY AND EXERCISE SCIENCE

Kinesiology—the scientific study of human movement and performance—attracts students interested in the physiological processes involved in sport, exercise, and fitness. The kinesiology field encompasses specialized areas such as exercise science, athletic training, exercise physiology, and sport science. The following schools listed (and in some instances profiled) below have respected undergraduate programs in kinesiology and its related areas.

➤ SCHOOLS WITH RESPECTED UNDERGRADUATE PROGRAMS IN KINESIOLOGY

Arizona State University	McGill University	Rice University
University of British Columbia	Miami University	Rutgers University
Colorado State University	University of Michigan	University of Southern California
University of Connecticut	Michigan State University	SUNY-Brockport
University of Delaware	University of Minnesota	SUNY-Cortland
University of Florida	University of North Carolina at Chapel Hill	Syracuse University
Florida State University	University of North Carolina at Greensboro	University of Texas at Austin
University of Illinois		University of Toronto
Indiana University	Ohio State University	University of Utah
Iowa State University	Oregon State University	University of Vermont
James Madison University	Penn State University	University of Virginia
University of Maryland	Purdue University	College of William and Mary
University of Massachusetts at Amherst	Queen's University	University of Wisconsin

Arizona State University. Through its School of Nutrition and Health Promotion, ASU offers BS programs in exercise and wellness, health promotion and health education, and health promotion and kinesiology. ASU also has a BS program focused on healthy lifestyle coaching.

University of Connecticut. UConn's Kinesiology Department (part of the Neag School of Education) is ranked among the best in the United States. Kinesiology students at UConn can earn BS degrees in athletic training, exercise science, and strength and conditioning. A special resource at UConn is the Korey Stringer Institute for the Prevention of Sudden Death in Sport.

University of Florida. Florida's College of Health and Human Performance (famous for developing Gatorade) offers a BS program in applied physiology and kinesiology that has two specialization tracks: exercise physiology and fitness and wellness. Florida also has BS programs in athletic training and health education. Special resources at Florida include a Center for Exercise Science that has laboratories for applied neuromechanics, muscle physiology, performance psychology, and sports medicine.

Michigan State University. MSU has one of the largest, oldest, and most respected kinesiology departments. Housed in the College of Education, Kinesiology at MSU offers BS programs in athletic training and kinesiology. Typically, there are 1,000 kinesiology majors and 170 athletic training majors enrolled at MSU. Michigan State's PhD program in kinesiology is one of the best in the country.

University of Michigan. Undergraduates in Michigan's School of Kinesiology have four major options (leading to a BS): athletic training, health and fitness, movement science, and sport management. The vast resources at Michigan for kinesiology students include laboratories for behavioral biomechanics, exercise endocrinology, human performance innovation, and neurosport research.

Rice University. The Department of Kinesiology at Rice offers BA programs in sports medicine and health sciences. Internships for kinesiology students are available at the nearby Texas Medical Center. Some Rice kinesiology graduates go on to get certified in athletic training, exercise science, or physical-fitness evaluation. Others pursue additional study to become physicians, occupational or physical therapists, or physician assistants.

University of Southern California. Kinesiology at USC is housed in the Department of Biological Sciences and offers undergraduates the choice of either a BA or a BS. The kinesiology program offers study abroad opportunities in the Department of Human Movement Studies at the University of Queensland in Australia and in the Department of Physical Education at the University of Otago in New Zealand.

University of Virginia. At UVA, kinesiology is part of the Curry School of Education. Undergraduates have two options: a BSEd program in kinesiology or a five-year program that leads to a BS degree in health and physical education and a master's degree in teaching. UVA also offers kinesiology graduate programs in areas such as athletic training, exercise physiology, and sports medicine.

College of William and Mary. Undergraduate research is a cornerstone feature of William and Mary's Department of Kinesiology and Health Sciences. William and Mary's kinesiology and health sciences program offers concentration options in health sciences (BS), premedical (BS), or health (BA).

University of Wisconsin. Housed in the School of Education, Wisconsin's kinesiology program has three BS degree options: athletic training, exercise and movement science, and physical education teacher education. The vast resources at Wisconsin include laboratories for studying biomechanics, exercise psychology, human sensor and motor control, and injury in sport.

ATHLETIC TRAINING

Students interested in becoming an athletic trainer have a wide variety of options. Many of the undergraduate degree programs in athletic training are found in schools or departments of kinesiology. Listed below are some of the standout undergraduate programs in athletic training, all of which are certified by the National Athletic Trainers' Association.

- University of Alabama
- Boston University
- College of Charleston
- University of Connecticut
- University of Delaware
- University of Georgia
- University of Florida
- Florida State University
- George Washington University
- University of Iowa
- Iowa State University
- Ithaca College
- University of Kansas
- Louisiana State University
- University of Maine
- Miami University
- University of Michigan

- Michigan State University
- University of New Hampshire
- Ohio State University
- University of Pittsburgh
- Purdue University
- San Diego State University

- University of South Carolina
- Stony Brook University (SUNY)
- University of Texas at Austin
- University of Tulsa
- University of Vermont
- University of Wisconsin

GERONTOLOGY

With advances in medicine and technology, people are living longer than ever before. As a result, there is a growing need to better understand the biological, sociological, political and medical issues of an aging society. The Davis School of Gerontology at **University of Southern California** has two study tracks, one focused on social sciences and one concentrating on health sciences. Students who are doing well in the program are eligible to start working (as undergraduates) toward a master's in gerontology. USC has the most established school of gerontology, but the schools listed below also offer opportunities for studying the field.

- Barton College
- Bethune-Cookman University
- Bowling Green State University
- California University of Pennsylvania
- California State University at Sacramento
- Miami University (Ohio)
- Missouri State University
- Mount St. Mary's College (Los Angeles)
- University of North Texas
- San Diego State University
- University of South Florida
- Winston Salem State University

EMERGENCY MEDICINE

Students in the **University of Pittsburgh**'s School of Health and Rehabilitation Sciences can choose a BS program in emergency medicine that provides the technical and clinical skills and administrative knowledge needed to succeed in the emergency medical services field. Numerous other colleges, such as Boston College, Duke, and Georgetown, offer training (but not degree) programs for students interested in serving as EMTs on campus.

OFFBEAT MAJORS AND SPECIALIZED PROGRAMS

UNUSUAL MAJORS

Every year articles and lists poke fun at colleges and universities for offering supposedly weird majors like turf management and fire prevention engineering. While unusual majors (global wine studies, anyone?) can provoke some eye rolling and head scratching, those programs often provide the training and connections for interesting and rewarding careers. This chapter focuses on some of the more surprising and specialized areas offered as majors and presents reasons why choosing the less commonplace or the more specialized path might be a worthwhile option.

TURF MANAGEMENT: WHERE THE GRASS IS ACTUALLY GREENER

First, we feel compelled to defend what is perhaps the most maligned major in the college universe: turf management. Along with its equally ridiculed cousin (golf course management), turf management is the metaphoric punching bag of majors. Leaving aside the snickering, turf management and golf course management are actually dynamic and useful majors that combine science, business, public policy, and landscape architecture. Anyone who has ever seen a golf course recognizes that it is a complex ecosystem. A great deal of science and technology goes into maintaining the glass-smooth greens and carpet-like fairways found on the United States Golf Association (USGA) tour. Students in turf management programs acquire the background in chemistry, biology, and environmental science necessary to understand the challenges posed to golf courses by issues related to climate and conservation of natural resources. Not just

golf enthusiasts may find turf and golf course management programs appealing. Design and environmental studies aficionados might be drawn to the training such programs provide in designing, developing, and managing facilities that are attractive, well-maintained, and challenging to golfers. As environmental awareness drives interest in sustainable landscaping, turf and golf-course management programs are becoming (literally and figuratively) places to learn green technologies.

Studying turf management can provide preparation for a growing industry. Country clubs and public golf courses are multilayered businesses. Golf is just one aspect of the turf-grass management industry. Turf-grass management programs also train students to maintain the athletic fields found in parks, at schools, and in stadiums. There is even a turf-grass management scholarship that enables the winner to get an internship with sports organizations such as the National Football League. Tell that to the writers of all those snarky articles about turf management. For students interested in turf management and its related industries, the schools listed below are options worth exploring.

- Auburn University
- Clemson University
- Colorado State University
- University of Connecticut
- University of Georgia
- Kansas State University
- Louisiana Tech University
- University of Nebraska
- New Mexico State University

- North Dakota State University
- Ohio State University
- Penn State University
- SUNY Cobleskill
- Texas A&M University

PACKAGING SCIENCE: BUILDING A BETTER SNACK-FOOD BAG

There are fewer than a dozen undergraduate degree programs in packaging in the United States. For students interested in the engineering side of packaging, **Rutgers University** arguably has the top program (described in more detail in the tech-school chapter). For students interested in the design and science of packaging, there are study options outside of engineering departments, such as the packaging science major at **Clemson University**. The BS in packaging science at Clemson is an interdisciplinary major built upon insights from biology, chemistry, and physics. Packaging science majors can specialize in such areas as distribution, transportation and engineering technology, food and health-care packaging, package design and graphics, and advanced materials. All packaging science students complete a four- to six-month co-op assignment in an industrial setting, and seniors have the option to begin work on a master's degree. Packaging science degrees are a sought-after credential. Nearly 90 percent of new BS recipients from Rutgers, Clemson, and the schools listed below get jobs or go immediately to graduate school.

- California Polytechnic State University at San Luis Obispo
- Fashion Institute of Technology (SUNY)
- University of Florida
- Indiana State University
- Michigan State University
- Missouri University of Science and Technology

- Rochester Institute of Technology
- University of Wisconsin at Stout

THE COLLEGE THAT CAR COLLECTORS LOVE

Finding the nation's only four-year degree program in automotive restoration requires travel to the small prairie town of McPherson, Kansas, located an hour north of Wichita. At **McPherson College**, a career-oriented liberal arts college of 620 students, the most popular major (enrolling 110 students) is the BS in automotive restoration—a program whose quality and renown has attracted donations and publicity from Mercedes Benz, the *New York Times*, *Popular Mechanics*, and the comedian and avid car collector Jay Leno. McPherson's program has become an important pipeline for training restoration technicians, shop managers, and restoration facility owners. Students at McPherson learn in a restoration facility that houses shops for painting, body repair, sheet metal fabrication, upholstery work, and engine and transmission rebuilding. McPherson connects students to internship opportunities in auto restoration shops across the United States and in museums such as America's Car Museum (ACM) in Tacoma, Washington. Through a partnership with ACM, McPherson students get internships, and the museum supplies cars to McPherson for students to restore. As McPherson's automotive restoration program has gained notice, it has begun to attract a number of non-traditional-age students with college degrees who are seeking second careers. Not only is a degree in automotive restoration from McPherson a conduit to jobs, it is also a good deal. With total annual charges of approximately $32,000, McPherson is less expensive than most private colleges, and nearly 100 percent of students receive some form of financial assistance.

VIDEO GAME DESIGN

Students who dream of working as a video game designer have many choices. There are options at tech schools, such as the programs at **Carnegie Mellon University** (computer science and arts), **Georgia Institute of Technology** (interactive games design), **Massachusetts Institute of Technology** (games and interactive media), **Rensselaer Polytechnic Institute** (games and simulation arts and sciences), **Rochester Institute of Technology** (interactive games and media), and **Worcester Polytechnic Institute** (interactive media and game development). There are game-design degree programs at many art schools, including the **Art Center College of Design** in Pasadena, California; **Cleveland Institute of Art**; **Parsons–The New School for Design** in New York City; **Savannah College of Art and Design**; and **Ringling College of Art and Design** in Florida. In addition to the list below, other standout programs are found at **University of California at Irvine** (computer game science), **Columbia College in Chicago** (game design and game programming), **University of Denver** (game development), **DePaul University** (computer game development), **George Mason University** (computer game design), **The College of New Jersey** (interactive multimedia), **University of Southern California** (interactive entertainment and computer science—games), **University of Texas at Austin** (game development), and **University of Utah** (game art and game engineering). Additional options for would-be game designers are listed below.

- Becker College
- Bradley University
- University of California at Santa Cruz
- University of Central Florida
- Champlain College
- University of Colorado at Colorado Springs
- Drexel University
- Lawrence Technological University
- Miami University
- Michigan State University
- North Carolina State University
- Northeastern University
- Quinnipiac University
- University of Texas at Dallas
- University of Wisconsin at Stout

POULTRY SCIENCE: DETERMINE ONCE AND FOR ALL WHETHER THE CHICKEN OR THE EGG CAME FIRST

The USDA has estimated that the average American eats about sixty-seven pounds of poultry a year, and that number is on the rise. For anyone who eats chicken and eggs or finds health issues like bird flu or the environmental effects of factory farming disturbing, poultry science is an important area of study. Farmers, researchers, agribusiness executives, and others who care about food sustainability, safety, and quality all can benefit from learning about bird science and production. Lack of proper knowledge about poultry care can lead to massive egg recalls, inhumane conditions for birds, and less-safe products for the consumer. Poultry science sets out to develop treatments for disease and better environmental stewardship practices for those who raise birds. Students interested in studying and improving the welfare of chickens, turkeys, and ducks will be more effective advocates if they have a background in poultry science. Careers for poultry science majors can range among farming, biochemistry, pharmaceuticals, business, veterinary science, genetics, natural resource conservation, and even animal rights law. There are a handful of good poultry science programs (listed below), but one of the biggest and best funded is the Department of Poultry Science at **Texas A&M**.

- University of Arkansas
- Auburn University
- University of Georgia
- Mississippi State University
- North Carolina State University
- Stephen F. Austin State University
- Texas A&M University

TEXTILE ENGINEERING: BECAUSE POLAR FLEECE MADE OUT OF OLD SODA BOTTLES IS AWESOME

Almost everybody wears clothes. Even the most enthusiastic nudists use textiles constantly. Towels, yoga mats, car interiors, upholstery, carpet, and wound dressings are just a few of the places where textiles are found in addition to the vast amounts of fabric used for clothes. Students who study textile engineering learn about the production, structure, and properties of natural and man-made fibers and figure out how to convert those fibers into textile structures. They also study coloring agents and finishes to improve the desirability and serviceability of a fabric. Increasingly, polymers (plastics) are incorporated into fiber production; thus, textile engineering is sometimes combined with polymer engineering. Textile engineers are the folks who figured out how to make Modal (a type of rayon) from the cellulose fibers of beech trees. Bamboo is another material frequently engineered into fiber and, subsequently, fabric. Although they are often criticized for producing artificial products, textile engineers have been instrumental in reducing the environmental impact of fabric production. Cotton fabrics, for example, can be produced with light or severe environmental impact based on the processes developed by textile engineers. Some textile engineers have a more chemistry-based background, while others take the mechanical route, focusing more on devising machinery to create fiber-based materials. For those rare students who have wondered how the cat fur on their sofa could possibly be transformed into a sweat-wicking sports bra, the schools listed below are worth a look.

- Auburn University (polymer and fiber engineering)
- Clemson University
- Georgia Tech (polymer and fiber engineering, within material science and engineering)
- University of Massachusetts at Dartmouth
- North Carolina State University (its teaching center includes a textile factory)
- Philadelphia University (formerly called the Philadelphia College of Textiles)

HISTORIC PRESERVATION

Interested in historic buildings and objects? Among the study options available are standout programs located in three cities famous for their historic neighborhoods and architectural grandeur. At the **College of Charleston** in South Carolina, **Salve Regina University** in Newport, Rhode Island, and **Savannah College of Art and Design** in Georgia, field study of historic structures requires but a short walk from campus. On the undergraduate level, the College of Charleston offers a BA in historic preservation and community planning. Salve Regina offers a BA in cultural and historic preservation. Savannah College of Art and Design, whose campus is a collection of restored buildings, provides a living laboratory for students in its BFA in historic preservation program. The **University of Mary Washington**, located in the prominent colonial and Civil War–era city of Fredericksburg, Virginia, also offers a degree in historic preservation. Listed below are other colleges that offer undergraduate programs in historic preservation:

- American College of the Building Arts (Charleston, South Carolina)
- Boston Architectural College
- Southeast Missouri State University (Cape Girardeau, Missouri)
- Roger Williams University (Bristol, Rhode Island)
- Ursuline College (Pepper Pike, Ohio)

NAVAL ARCHITECTURE

Webb Institute of Naval Architecture is a one-of-a-kind place. Located on Long Island Sound in Glen Cove, New York, the Webb campus is a twenty-six-acre former estate that has a private beach and many boats. Webb has just eighty students, all of them undergraduates enrolled in the lone degree program: BS in naval engineering and architecture—an interdisciplinary blend of ship design and systems plus marine, electrical, mechanical, civil, and structural engineering. Tuition is free at Webb; all students get paid work experiences, and the placement rate of graduates is 100 percent. Although tuition is free, Webb charges approximately $19,000 per year for room, board, books, and supplies. Financial aid is available to defray those charges for lower-income students. During Webb's Winter Work Term in January and February, students work in paid positions in the marine industry. Freshmen take jobs in shipyards, sophomores go to sea as cadets and observers, and juniors and seniors have internships in design and engineering firms. The four required Winter Work terms go a long way toward preparing Webb students to get jobs.

ART CONSERVATION

The **University of Delaware** offers a BA program in art conservation, an interdisciplinary field that draws upon anthropology, art, art history, and chemistry. Art conservation students at Delaware can get practical experience in the field through internships at art galleries, auction houses, and museums. Jobs as a professional art conservator require a master's degree. Delaware art conservation graduates have a strong track record at getting into one of the four options for master's degrees in the field, found at Buffalo State, Delaware, NYU, and UCLA.

WHAT'S WITH BAGPIPES?

Carnegie Mellon University offers a music performance degree in bagpipes through its School of Music, which means that not just any bagpipe player comes out of CMU. Carnegie Mellon bagpipers are of orchestral quality, that is, if orchestras featured bagpipes. For a number of years, Ohio's **College of Wooster** had a promotional brochure whose cover photo was of a bagpiper in a kilt. The attention-getting brochure, a nod to Wooster's Scottish heritage, explained somewhere in the fine print that the college has a special scholarship ($2,000 to $8,000) for applicants who play the bagpipes. Similarly, **Monmouth College**, a small liberal arts institution in Illinois, has Scottish tartan in its colors and a scholarship for students who play the bagpipes. **Alma College** in Michigan has an iconic bagpipe band and offers a Scottish Arts Scholarship to bagpipers. Tartan and bagpipe motifs also show up in promotional materials for **Macalester College** in Minnesota, which offers bagpipe lessons and has a bagpipe band.

MAJORING IN WINE

The best places to study the agriculture, business, and science of the wine industry are (no surprise) in regions where there are many vineyards. For students interested in the wine industry, the majors to investigate are oenology and viticulture (the agriculture and science of wine). Less than a dozen universities offer undergraduate degree programs in oenology and viticulture, and even fewer offer programs focused on the business of the wine industry. Perhaps the most comprehensive program is the global wine studies BS program at **Central Washington University**, which educates students about wine marketing and branding and the fundamentals of oenology and viticulture. Standout undergraduate programs focused on viticulture and oenology are found at **California Polytechnic State University at San Luis Obispo**, **University of California at Davis**, **California State University at Fresno**, **Cornell University**, **Oregon State University**, and **Washington State University**. Further afield from West Coast and East Coast wine country, the **University of Missouri's** flagship campus in Columbia offers an oenology track (and is planning a viticulture concentration) within the food science major.

For students seeking to work on the business side of wine making, there are a handful of options. At **Washington State University**, there is a wine business management concentration offered in the hospitality business major. En route to the wine business management degree, WSU students must complete an internship of four hundred to one thousand hours. **Sonoma State University**, located in one of the world's best wine regions, offers a concentration in wine business strategies through its School of Business and Economics. Within its Conrad Hilton College of Hotel and Restaurant Management, the **University of Houston** offers a specialized concentration in wine and spirits management.

AVIATION PROGRAMS

Often billed as "the best aviation and aerospace university in the world," **Embry-Riddle Aeronautical University** is undeniably the world's oldest and largest university specializing in aviation and aerospace. The instruction and training at Embry-Riddle encompasses the engineering, science, business, research, and practice of modern aircraft and their supporting systems. Embry-Riddle has two residential campuses. The oldest campus, and arguably its home base, is located in Daytona Beach, Florida. The other campus is in Prescott, Arizona. In addition, the university operates Embry-Riddle Worldwide through online learning and more than 150 satellite locations in the United States, Europe, Canada, and the Middle East.

Overall, Embry-Riddle enrolls 34,000 students in associate, bachelor's, master's, and doctoral degree programs. At Daytona Beach, there are 4,200 undergraduates and 4,800 graduate students. At Prescott, there are 1,535 undergraduates and 1,585 graduate students. Through its worldwide centers, Embry-Riddle enrolls 22,000 students: 20,200 in the United States and 1,800 in Europe. Through a $30 million contract with the US Department of Defense, Embry-Riddle is the sole provider of aviation and aeronautical degree programs to military service personnel stationed in Europe.

Embry-Riddle offers nearly forty undergraduate degree programs. Areas covered include aeronautical science, aeronautical systems maintenance, aeronautics, aerospace electronics, aerospace engineering, air traffic management, applied meteorology, aviation business administration, aviation environmental science, aviation maintenance science, aviation management, business administration, civil engineering, communication, computational mathematics, computer engineering, computer science, electrical engineering, engineering physics, global security and intelligence studies, homeland security, human factors psychology, mechanical engineering, safety science, software engineering, and space physics. The two most popular majors at Embry-Riddle are aerospace engineering (1,578 students) and aeronautical science (1,320 students).

Learning at Embry-Riddle is hands-on, using the latest equipment—including a fleet of ninety-two instructional aircraft and forty-one flight simulators. In a typical year, three to four hundred students supplement their studies with a co-op or internship. A degree from Embry-Riddle creates many opportunities, as nearly 100 percent of its graduates find jobs within a year. Alumni of Embry-Riddle include numerous astronauts, admirals, generals, and airline pilots.

A number of other schools offer degree programs in aviation-related areas. Within the College of Aeronautics at **Florida Institute of Technology**, for example, there are BS programs in aeronautical science, aviation computer science, aviation management, and aviation meteorology. Students interested in flight can make that the focus of FIT's degree programs in aeronautical science, aviation, management, or aviation meteorology. At **Ohio University** aviation students learn at a university-owned and -managed airport. **Baylor University** operates an Institute for Air Science. Students at **Louisiana Tech University** train using thirteen college-owned Cessna airplanes. **Saint Louis University** runs a flight school that offers BS programs in aviation management and flight science. Among the aviation degree programs at the **University of North Dakota** are specializations in commercial aviation (for students interested in piloting helicopters), unmanned aircraft systems operations, and airport management.

Listed below are additional schools that offer bachelor's degree programs in aviation.

- University of Alaska at Anchorage
- Arizona State University
- Bowling Green State University
- Daniel Webster College
- Dowling College
- Farmingdale State College of the State University of New York
- Indiana State University
- Kansas State University at Salina
- Kent State University
- Minnesota State University
- University of Nebraska at Omaha
- Ohio State University
- Purdue University
- San Jose State University
- South Dakota State University
- Southern Illinois University at Carbondale
- Vaughan College of Aeronautics and Technology
- York College of the City University of New York

CULINARY SCHOOLS

THE CULINARY INSTITUTE OF AMERICA

In the world of cooking education, the Culinary Institute of America (CIA) is the most prestigious place in the United States to get trained for leadership positions in the food industry. Nearly 2,800 students are enrolled at the CIA, most of them on its main campus in Hyde Park, New York, perched above the Hudson River two hours north of New York City. On its campuses, the CIA offers degrees and certificates as well as

short-term training programs. Students seeking a bachelor's degree and a residential experience are drawn to the historic Hyde Park campus, which is the only CIA site that offers bachelor's degrees and has residence halls. CIA Hyde Park students can pursue bachelor's degrees in culinary arts management or in baking and pastry arts management. The Hyde Park campus also offers associate degree programs in culinary arts, baking and pastry arts, and culinary arts for advanced career experience. At its St. Helena

(Napa Valley) and San Antonio campuses, the CIA offers associate degree programs in culinary arts and baking and pastry arts. In addition, the St. Helena campus offers a wine and beverage certificate and the San Antonio campus offers a Latin cuisines certificate.

The core of the student experience at the CIA is learning by doing. On each of its campuses, the CIA operates multiple restaurants that are staffed and run by students. At Hyde Park, the American Bounty Restaurant showcases the diversity of cuisines in the Americas; the Caterina de Medici features Italian food, and Bocuse Restaurant interprets classic French cuisine. At St. Helena, the CIA emphasizes farm-to-table cooking and operates the Wine Spectator Greystone Restaurant, which features local ingredients and wine. At its San Antonio campus (located in the landmark Pearl Brewery building), the CIA operates a café that showcases the cuisines of Latin America. In recent years, the CIA has expanded into Asia through collaboration with the Singapore Institute of Technology and Temasek Polytechnic, also in Singapore. Graduates of those two institutions may pursue a CIA bachelor's degree in culinary arts management.

CIA alumni occupy key positions around the world in the food industry. CIA grad celebrity chefs include John Best, Anthony Bourdain, Anne Burrell, Michael Chiarello, Cat Cora, Rocco DiSpirito, Amanda Freitag, Duff Goldman, Vikas Khanna, Sara Moulton, Charlie Palmer, Roy Yamaguchi, and Andrew Zimmern.

JOHNSON AND WALES UNIVERSITY

With four campuses and seventeen thousand students, Johnson and Wales is a career-focused institution that offers degree programs in business, culinary arts, education, hospitality, and technology. The original Johnson and Wales campus—in Providence, Rhode Island—started as a business school but soon gained notice for its culinary arts programs. Over the years, Johnson and Wales has added campus locations in Charlotte, Denver, and north Miami. Although Johnson and Wales offers fifty-plus degree programs (including graduate degree options), the school stands out primarily for its associate and bachelor's degree programs in culinary arts and hospitality. Notable JWU alumni include celebrity chefs Michelle Bernstein, Tyler Florence, Andy Husbands, Anna Olson, Aaron Sanchez, and Chris Santos.

Johnson and Wales teaches its culinary arts students to master both the art and the business of the food industry. At any of the four JWU campuses, students can work toward an associate degree in baking and pastry arts or culinary arts. At Providence (and at most of the other campuses), students can pursue a bachelor's degree in baking and pastry arts, culinary arts and food service management, culinary nutrition, food service entrepreneurship, or baking and pastry arts and food service management.

JWU encourages its students to have internship or study abroad experiences. Students can go to France to study baking and pastry arts at the legendary Ecole Nationale Supérieure de la Pâtisserie. Students can learn wine and food matching in Germany's wine country. Students can venture to Italy to study the Mediterranean diet and lifestyle. In Lima, Peru—sometimes described as the foodie capital of South America—students learn about Peruvian foods, beverages, and culture. A Switzerland-based program introduces students to hands-on work in five-star hotels and kitchens in Gstaad, Lucerne, and Zurich. And another program takes students to Singapore and Thailand to learn the secrets of Pan Asian cuisine.

TOP SCHOOLS FOR HOSPITALITY AND HOTEL MANAGEMENT

CORNELL UNIVERSITY

Cornell is the granddaddy of hospitality schools, the one widely regarded as the leader of the pack. Originating in 1922, the Cornell School of Hotel Administration (otherwise known as the Hotel School) runs the oldest collegiate hotel program in the United States. With sixty full-time faculty members, Cornell has the world's largest corps of teachers and scholars found at a single hospitality school. The Hotel School has 860 students enrolled in its bachelor's, master's, and doctoral programs. The eight hundred undergraduates come from thirty countries across the globe. New graduates join an alumni body of nearly thirteen thousand, many of whom are leaders in the hospitality industry.

Facilities at the Hotel School are extraordinary. Home base is Statler Hall, located in the heart of the Cornell campus. Statler Hall and its neighboring building, the Beck Center, house classrooms, auditoriums, computer labs, offices, study spaces, and student lounges. Nearby is the Hotel School's showcase building, the Statler Hotel, a 14,000-square-foot teaching building that has 153 guest rooms offering spectacular views of the campus and Cayuga Lake. Working at the Statler Hotel provides valuable career-related experience as well as connections to industry professionals who come to Cornell from around the world for seminars.

Undergraduate students in the Hotel School follow a business management course of study focused on preparing them for careers in the hospitality industry. En route to earning a BS in hotel administration, students at Cornell have three concentration options: (1) finance, accounting, and real estate; (2) hospitality leadership; and (3) service marketing and operations management. Along the way to graduation, Hotel School students must complete an internship or an externship in a hospitality-industry setting. Students find it easy to get such real-world experiences. Due to its prominence in the field, the Hotel School draws more than one hundred companies annually seeking to hire Cornell students for summer or full-time positions. For those interested in the hospitality industry beyond the United States, Cornell operates a robust study-away program. Each year roughly fifty Hotel School students study abroad.

MICHIGAN STATE UNIVERSITY

Founded in 1927, the School of Hospitality Business at Michigan State is one of the oldest and most distinguished in the United States. The hospitality school at Michigan State is a close community of students, faculty, and alumni mentors embedded within the Eli Broad College of Business. Students in the school have the option to major in hospitality business or pursue a more specialized program in hospitality business real estate and development. Career preparation is ever present throughout the student experience. For example, all students must complete two paid internships in the hospitality industry. Through the Spartan Sponsors Mentor Program, each hospitality student gets paired with an alumni mentor from freshman year until graduation. Numerous alumni of Michigan State's School of Hospitality hold prominent positions and seek to hire students as summer interns or as new graduates. Each year a career expo brings hundreds of companies to campus. Hospitality students have numerous study abroad options available at management schools in Australia, China, India, and Norway.

UNIVERSITY OF NEVADA, LAS VEGAS

With its larger than life casinos, shows, and hotels, Las Vegas is one of the top vacation destinations in the United States. So it is fitting that the University of Nevada, Las Vegas, operates one of the top hospitality schools in the country. Students at UNLV's Harrah College of Hotel Administration have abundant opportunities to get internship experience with casinos, hotels, and golf courses. A professional mentoring program connects students to leaders in the hospitality industry. Concentration options offered at Harrah include gaming management for those interested in learning the operation of casinos; meeting and events management for students interested in conventions, trade shows, and special events; and restaurant management. Another concentration—professional golf management—distinguishes UNLV's Harrah College from other hospitality schools. Students in golf management complete a sixteen-month internship at a golf facility. En route to their degree, golf management students complete the Professional Golf Association's Level 1, 2, and 3 examinations, making them eligible to become members of the PGA. Harrah also has a campus in Singapore and offers summer study programs in Jamaica.

OTHER STRONG HOSPITALITY AND HOTEL SCHOOLS

California State Polytechnic University at Pomona. The Collins College of Hospitality Management at Cal Poly Pomona emphasizes learning by doing. The BS in hospitality management at Collins has specializations in restaurant management, hotel and resort management, and club management. Students in the restaurant management program get hands-on experience working at Cal Poly's restaurant at Kellogg Ranch. There is also a minor in culinology, a hospitality discipline that blends culinary arts with the science of food.

University of Central Florida. With 3,500 students, UCF's Rosen School of Hospitality Management is the largest school of its kind in the United States. Due to the Rosen School's location in Orlando, its students have no trouble finding sites at which to complete the required three semesters of paid internships. Drawing upon the many nearby Disney facilities, the Rosen School offers a specialized concentration in theme park and attraction management. Other concentration tracks at UCF include event management, golf and club management, and restaurant and food service management. The $28.1 million, 159,000-square-foot Rosen School complex at UCF is one of the most advanced hospitality teaching facilities in the world. The complex includes eighteen classrooms, a 200-seat dining room and bar for teaching, a beer and wine lab, multiple test kitchens, and an executive education center. Beyond Orlando, the Rosen School offers exchange and study abroad experiences focused on international hospitality in Australia, Austria, France, Hong Kong, Italy, and the United Kingdom.

University of Denver. Within Denver's Daniels College of Business, the Fritz Knoebel School of Hospitality Management offers a BS in business administration (BSBA) in hospitality management and a minor in tourism. Course work covers areas such as the management of restaurant operations, hotels and resorts, hospitality services, human capital in hospitality, and revenue management. Students in the Knoebel School must choose an area of focus from three options: lodging and resort operations, hospitality sales and marketing, or restaurant and food and beverage management. All hospitality management students must study abroad for a semester and complete internships in the industry. A program called Backpacks to Briefcases helps students make the transition to the working world.

Drexel University. The hospitality management, culinary arts, and food science program at Drexel offers BS degree tracks in culinary arts, culinary science, hospitality management, and a five-year BS/MBA program. Students in the BS in hospitality management program can concentrate on food and beverage management, travel and tourism, hotel administration, or gaming and resort management. Drexel's culinary science program uniquely integrates culinary arts with chemistry and microbiology. All students at Drexel participate in co-op work programs for credit and experience. Special facilities and programs include a student-run restaurant and study abroad options in London.

Fairleigh Dickinson University. The International School of Hospitality and Tourism at Fairleigh Dickinson in northern New Jersey capitalizes on its proximity to Atlantic City and New York. Students in FDU's BS in hotel and restaurant management program can complete the required 1,200 hours of work experience at Atlantic City and New York City facilities affiliated with FDU or at the Wyndham International in Parsippany, New Jersey. In addition to its main campus in Florham Park, FDU has satellite locations in Teaneck/Hackensack, New Jersey; Vancouver, British Columbia; and Oxfordshire, England. A special program enables students to earn a BS/MS in hotel and restaurant management in five years.

Georgia State University. Its downtown-Atlanta location enhances the student experience at Georgia State's Cecil B. Day School of Hospitality, which is part of the J. Mack Robinson College of Business. Students get hands-on experience at Georgia State's culinary center housed across the street from campus in a major convention facility—Atlanta's Georgia World Congress Center. The Day School offers a bachelor of business administration in hospitality administration. Through its Maymester program,

Georgia State introduces students to European hospitality management and tourism sites in France, Germany, Italy, Monaco, and Switzerland. Georgia State also operates exchanges with universities in China and France.

University of Houston. Students at the Conrad Hilton College of Hotel and Restaurant Management run the on-campus Hilton hotel as a learning lab. Within the BS program in hotel and restaurant management, there are numerous options for specialized emphasis, such as catering management, country club management, event management, gaming and casino management, international hospitality management, lodging management, restaurant management, sales and marketing management, spa management, tourism management, and wine and spirits management. Students can also craft a customized area of emphasis or pursue a minor in beverage management. To give students work experience beyond the United States, UH offers internships at hotels in Abu Dhabi, Japan, Paris, Saigon, and Scotland. There are also exchange programs with universities in Australia, France, Hong Kong, and Mexico.

Iowa State University. The top-twenty hospitality and tourism program at Iowa State is part of the Department of Apparel, Events, and Hospitality Management in the College of Human Sciences. The two hundred students working on a BS in hospitality management get experience running the on-campus 105-seat dining facility. Hospitality management students can also belong to a special learning community called Directions that fosters peer mentorship and social connectivity.

Johnson and Wales University. In addition to its culinary programs, the Hospitality College at Johnson and Wales offers bachelor's degrees in seven areas—all available on the Providence campus, and some at it's Charlotte, Denver, and north Miami outposts. Hospitality degree areas include culinary arts and food service management; hotel and lodging management; international hotel and tourism management; baking and pastry arts and food service management; restaurant, food, and beverage management; sports, entertainment, and event management; and travel-tourism and hospitality management. Hospitality students have numerous internship opportunities at top companies such as Disney, ESPN, Marriott, and the Ritz-Carlton. JWU even set up internships for its students to coincide with the Democratic national conventions in Charlotte and Denver. Hospitality students at JWU have study abroad opportunities at hotels, resorts, and tourism businesses in Australia, Belgium, Costa Rica, South Africa, Spain, and Switzerland. JWU's study abroad programs are tailored toward particular industries. In Belgium students focus on operations management at resorts; in Costa Rica students focus on adventure tourism; in South Africa students focus on sports tourism, and in Australia students learn the ins and outs of managing sports and entertainment events in Melbourne and Sydney.

Kansas State University. Students in the Department of Hospitality Management and Dietetics—located within the College of Human Ecology—at Kansas State are required to get four hundred hours of industry work experience. Finding a job or internship is not difficult because K-State has many hospitality industry connections near campus as well as in Kansas City, Topeka, and Wichita. K-State's BS in hotel and restaurant management program offers specialization tracks in food service and restaurant management; convention, meeting, and event management; and lodging management.

University of Massachusetts at Amherst. The Isenberg School of Management offers a BS in hospitality and tourism management. Students can pursue specializations in casino management; club management; food and beverage

management; lodging management; or tourism, convention, and event management. The Marriott Center on the UMass campus provides jobs and internships, and there are a number of study and work programs available in Europe and Australia. UMass students can study at DCT Hospitality University in Vitznau, Switzerland, or participate in an exchange program in Australia, England, Lucerne, or Paris.

Northern Arizona University. Within its Franke College of Business, NAU operates a School of Hotel and Restaurant Management that offers BS programs in international hospitality management and restaurant management. In completing the required 1,200 hours of work in the hospitality industry, NAU students find opportunities in nearby Sedona (thirty miles away), the Grand Canyon National Park (seventy-five miles away), and Phoenix/Scottsdale (one hour away). NAU maintains internship partnerships with Disney, Four Seasons Resorts, Hyatt Hotels and Resorts, Marriott, Sodexo, and Starwood and has study abroad partnerships with schools in the Netherlands and Switzerland.

Oklahoma State University. The School of Hotel and Restaurant Administration at OSU has been ranked as high as eighth. OSU operates the Atherton Hotel and two restaurants (Taylor's Dining Room and the West Side Café) where students can complete the required eight hundred hours of work experience in the hospitality industry. Special facilities and programs include food production and research laboratories, a distinguished chef series, an international hospitality learning experience in Switzerland, and a dual degree program with several European university partners.

Penn State University. The School of Hospitality Management at Penn State offers a BS in hotel, restaurant, and institutional management as well as a concentration in dietetics that prepares graduates for jobs with health-care organizations. To graduate, all PSU hospitality management students must get a thousand hours of work experience. A standout feature of the Penn State program is the opportunity to get an international perspective on hospitality through study abroad agreements with the Chinese University of Hong Kong, Maastricht Hotel Management School in the Netherlands, and Universidad San Ignacio de Loyola (USIL) in Lima, Peru. University-sponsored spring break and summer programs have taken PSU hospitality management students to France, Italy, Greece, and Puerto Rico.

Purdue University. Purdue's BS program in hospitality and tourism management (HTM) has been ranked in the top five and draws hundreds of companies looking to hire its students. In fulfilling the four-hundred-hour internship requirement, HTM students at Purdue can get six-month placements at the Intercontinental Hotel in Nanjing, China, or at the Shangri-La in Tainan, Taiwan. Unpaid internships for credit are also available in London and Sydney. In addition, Purdue operates exchange programs with hospitality schools in Australia, Hong Kong, Ireland, Mexico, the Netherlands, Scotland, and Spain.

Virginia Polytechnic Institute and State University. Within its Pamplin College of Business, Virginia Tech offers a major in hospitality and tourism management. The approximately 450 undergraduates majoring in hospitality and tourism management can complete the four hundred hours of required work through internships at the Inn at Virginia Tech or at the university-owned Hotel Roanoke. Concentration options available include hospitality event management, hospitality operations management, global tourism management, and restaurant and food management. VPI also operates annual faculty-led summer study programs at hospitality schools in Austria, Costa Rica, France, Italy, and Switzerland.

Washington State University. WSU's School of Hospitality Business Management is widely respected for the quality of its career services. Nearly 90 percent of the students in the school have jobs lined up by graduation. Students interested in working in the wine industry will do well to consider WSU. The major in wine business management draws strength from the burgeoning Napa north wine country found in eastern Washington towns such as Paterson, Prosser, and Walla Walla. Students in the wine business major as well as those in the school's primary major—the BA in hospitality management—get career preparation through the thousand-hour work requirement. For students interested in adding a global dimension to their hospitality management education, the school operates study abroad programs in Italy, Switzerland, and Thailand.

LEADING FASHION-DESIGN AND FASHION-MERCHANDISING PROGRAMS

Auburn University. Within its College of Human Sciences, Auburn offers a BS in apparel merchandising, design, and production management. Students have two concentration options: apparel merchandising or product design and production management. The program sponsors a speaker series that brings industry leaders to campus. Students may also elect to go on study trips to Atlanta, New York, and Italy.

California College of the Arts. Between its campuses in Oakland and San Francisco, CCA has approximately sixty-five students in the BFA in fashion-design program. An annual fashion show provides a forum for student work, and internships are readily available. CCA fashion-design students have found internships or postgraduation jobs at DKNY, Gap, Gymboree, Hollister, J. Crew, and Williams-Sonoma.

School of the Art Institute of Chicago. Fashion-design students in the School of the Art Institute's BFA program get a strong foundation in the fine arts. Learning by doing occurs through the annual fashion show and internships. Notable SAIC fashion-industry alumni include Matthew Ames, Gary Graham, Halston, and Cynthia Rowley.

University of Cincinnati. Through its highly ranked School of Design, Cincinnati offers a BS degree in fashion design. The program includes a mandatory cooperative education experience (beginning in year two) during which students work full-time in the fashion industry.

Columbia College. Within its Department of Fashion Studies, Columbia College in Chicago has BA and BFA programs in fashion design and fashion business. Students get hands-on experience in a fashion lab as well as through internships. Students can also take a semester at Columbia's LA campus, which offers a program in costume design for television, film, and entertainment.

Columbus College of Art and Design. There are approximately 130 students enrolled in CCAD's BFA program in fashion design. Students in the program build their own collection, which they display at the annual Senior Fashion Show. CCAD alumni hold prominent positions with Tommy Hilfiger, Nautica, and Ann Taylor.

Cornell University. Within its School of Human Ecology, Cornell's Department of Fiber Science and Apparel Design offers concentrations in apparel design and fashion-design management.

Students in those concentrations frequently find summer or winter break internships in the fashion industry. The School of Human Ecology is state supported, which means that New York residents pay lower tuition.

University of Delaware. Within its Department of Fashion and Apparel Studies, Delaware has options for students interested in the design or the business aspects of fashion. Business-oriented students can concentrate on fashion merchandising, while design-oriented students can major in apparel design.

Drexel University. There are more than 350 students enrolled in Drexel's degree programs in fashion and fashion merchandising. Numerous students at this 23,500-student university in Philadelphia have won national and international fashion awards.

Fashion Institute of Technology. Located in New York City, FIT is part of the State University of New York (SUNY) system. Among FIT's ten thousand undergraduates are approximately four thousand studying art and design in programs areas such as fabric styling, fashion design, fashion merchandising, marketing for the fashion industries, menswear, jewelry design, textile and surface design, and textile development and marketing. FIT fashion notables include Carolina Herrera, Calvin Klein, and Michael Kors.

University of Georgia. The College of Family and Consumer Sciences at Georgia offers a major in fashion merchandising. Georgia's location in Athens, a cauldron of creative activity a little more than an hour from Atlanta, is a plus for fashion students.

Iowa State University. Among its respected design programs, Iowa State offers a major in apparel merchandising and design. Students in the program produce a fashion and lifestyle magazine.

Kent State University. This eighteen-thousand-student university in Ohio has two hundred students in fashion programs as well as a garment design studio in New York City. Degree programs at Kent State include fashion design and fashion merchandising.

Massachusetts College of Art. Located in Boston, this state-supported art college offers BFA programs in fashion design and jewelry making. MCA's learning-by-doing curriculum (culminating in an annual fashion show of student work) creates job opportunities for its graduates.

University of Minnesota. Within the College of Design at its flagship Minneapolis campus, Minnesota offers a BS in apparel design. Minnesota design students get internships and jobs at the headquarters of fashion and retailing giant Target as well as with places like Kohl's and Sears.

University of Missouri at Columbia. For students interested in the business side of fashion, Missouri's flagship campus offers a BS in textiles and apparel management. The program, housed within the School of Human Environmental Sciences, offers four study tracks: apparel marketing and merchandising, apparel product development, international apparel marketing and merchandising, and international apparel product development. One special feature at Missouri is the 5,500-artifact collection of historic clothing and textiles.

University of North Carolina at Greensboro. Within its Department of Consumer, Apparel, and Retail Studies, UNCG offers concentrations in apparel product design and global apparel and related industry studies. The internship program at UNCG has a strong track record at leading to jobs in the fashion industry.

North Carolina State University. Located in Raleigh, NC State's College of Textiles offers a BS in fashion and textile management. Students in the program have three concentration options: textile brand management and marketing, fashion development and product management, and retail and supply chain management in textiles.

Oklahoma State University. Within its Department of Design, Housing, and Merchandising, OSU offers degree programs in apparel design, apparel production, and apparel merchandising. Facilities at Oklahoma State include laboratories for design testing and design research. Students get internships with fashion firms such as BCBG, Lands' End, and Vera Wang.

Oregon State University. OSU's Department of Design and Human Environment offers two majors for fashion-oriented students: the BS in apparel design and the BS in merchandising management. An Apparel Research Center assists Oregon State students in developing new products and start-up fashion companies.

Otis College of Art and Design. Known as one of the very best design programs in the United States, Otis is located in Los Angeles. Fashion-design majors at Otis work with guest design mentors within a curriculum that simulates a design studio.

Parsons School of Design. Part of the New School University in New York City, Parsons is a fashion powerhouse that enrolls roughly 1,400 students in its fashion programs. Fashion students at Parsons can pursue degree programs in fashion design and fashion marketing. Notable alumni include Tom Ford, Marc Jacobs, and Donna Karan.

Philadelphia University. Philadelphia has a comprehensive program that offers majors in fashion design, fashion-industry management, and fashion merchandising. An alumnus of Philadelphia (Jay McCarroll) was the 2005 winner of *Project Runway*.

Pratt Institute. The BFA program in fashion design at Pratt is a leader in the field. Due to the prominence of the program as well as to its location in New York City, Pratt fashion students have opportunities to get internships at leading firms such as DKNY, Rag & Bone, and Ralph Lauren. Students also participate in annual design competitions sponsored by fashion firms.

Rhode Island School of Design. There are 220 students enrolled in the RISD division that offers degree programs in fashion, textiles, and jewelry. Students in RISD's BFA in apparel design program get experience through a six-week internship in New York City as well as through the annual student collection showcase that attracts industry leaders. Noted designer Nicole Miller is a RISD alumna.

Ryerson University. The emphasis in the School of Fashion at this Toronto-based university is on fashion as an art. Students can pursue bachelor of design degrees in fashion design or fashion communication. All fashion students at Ryerson must complete a four-hundred-hour internship in the fashion industry. Through its many connections to the Canadian fashion industry, Ryerson operates special programs, such as the Danier Design Challenge for third-year students. Ryerson alumni hold leading fashion positions in Canada and elsewhere.

Savannah College of Art and Design. With more than five hundred students pursuing fashion-related degree programs, SCAD has become a leading supplier of talent to the industry. One distinguishing feature SCAD offers is a collection of campuses around the globe. Students can pursue a BFA in fashion or a BFA in fashion marketing and management at SCAD's home base in Savannah or at its satellite campuses in Atlanta and Hong Kong.

University of South Carolina. At its flagship campus in Columbia, South Carolina operates a Department of Retailing that offers specializations in fashion merchandising and retail management.

EDUCATION PROGRAMS

Students interested in preparing for teaching careers have a number of options. At universities that have a school of education, students generally will find bachelor's degree programs that lead to teacher certification. Some of those programs have the option to add a fifth year and a master of arts in teaching (MAT) degree. In addition, a number of small liberal arts colleges offer education as a major or minor, with teacher certification and/or MAT degree tracks complemented by on-campus lab schools. Most commonly, teacher education programs prepare students for initial licensure in the home state of the college or university. In many cases, licensure can transfer from one state to another. Some of the many options in teacher education are listed and profiled on the next page.

➤ LEADING UNDERGRADUATE PROGRAMS IN EDUCATION

Albion College

American University

Amherst College

Arizona State University

University of Arizona

Bates College

Baylor University

Boston College

Boston University

Brigham Young University

Bryn Mawr College

Butler University

California State University campuses

College of Charleston

Colgate University

Colorado College

University of Colorado at Boulder

Connecticut College

University of Delaware

University of Denver (BA/MA)

Dickinson College

Drake University

Drew University

University of Florida

Furman University

University of Georgia

Grinnell College

Haverford College

College of the Holy Cross

University of Illinois

Indiana University

University of Iowa

University of Kansas

University of Kentucky

University of Louisville

Loyola Marymount University

University of Maryland

Miami University

University of Miami

Michigan State University

University of Michigan

Middlebury College

Millsaps College

University of Minnesota

Mount Holyoke College

Muhlenberg College

University of North Carolina at Chapel Hill

Ohio University

Ohio State University

Penn State University

University of San Diego

San Diego State University

University of San Francisco (BA/MAT)

Skidmore College

Smith College

Southern Methodist University

Stony Brook University (SUNY)

SUNY comprehensive colleges

Syracuse University

University of Texas at Austin

Trinity College

Tulane University

University of Tulsa

Vanderbilt University

Vassar College

Villanova University

University of Virginia (BA/MAT)

University of Vermont

Wake Forest University

Washington and Lee University

Wellesley College

Wheaton College (IL)

Wheaton College (MA)

College of William and Mary

College of Wooster

University of Wisconsin

Albion College. Education is a concentration at Albion that is joined to a student's primary major. Albion offers elementary, secondary, and K–12 certification (by the state of Michigan) in biology, chemistry, earth science and geology, English and language arts, French, German, history, integrated science, math, music, physics, political science, psychology, social studies, and Spanish. Albion's Fritz Shurmur Center for Teacher Development prepares aspiring teachers by providing mentorships, cocurricular activities, a speaker series, and other training workshops.

University of Arizona. Within Arizona's College of Education, students have BA options in cross-cultural special education, early childhood education, and elementary education (including with a bilingual emphasis). Arizona's College of Fine Arts offers a BFA in art education and a major in music education. Arizona's College of Science offers degrees in math education and science education.

Boston University. The School of Education at BU offers undergraduate majors in bilingual education, deaf studies, early childhood education, elementary education, English education, mathematics education, modern foreign language education, science education, social studies education, special education, and a double degree BS/BA program with the College of Arts and Sciences. The teacher certification programs at BU prepare students for initial licensure in Massachusetts.

Butler University. Located in Indianapolis, Butler offers three education tracks: elementary education, middle and secondary education, and all-grade education. Elementary education students can specialize in English as a new language, reading, or special education. Students in middle and secondary education have specialty options in English, foreign language (French, German, Spanish), math, science (biology, chemistry, physics), social studies, and English as a new language. All-grade education students can specialize in music education or physical education and health. Butler's teacher education programs lead to initial licensure in Indiana.

University of Colorado Boulder. Teacher education at CU–Boulder is not a major but rather a certificate program that leads to state of Colorado licensure to teach at the elementary or secondary level. Colorado offers music education as both an elementary and secondary specialization. Subject area specializations offered for prospective secondary school teachers are English, math, science, social studies, and several foreign languages (French, German, Italian, Japanese, Latin, Russian, and Spanish).

Furman University. Education is a major at this small university located in Greenville, South Carolina. State of South Carolina certification is available to students specializing in early childhood, English, English for speakers of other languages, French, Latin, Spanish, literacy (reading and writing), math, music, special education, social studies, and science (biology, chemistry, and physics).

University of Iowa. Iowa offers programs in elementary education and secondary education. Students can prepare for state of Iowa licensure in art, elementary education, English, foreign language, library, math, music, science, social studies, and special education. Iowa also offers endorsements for students interested in athletic coaching, hearing impairment, middle school, and talented and gifted.

University of Michigan. The programs in elementary teacher education and secondary teacher education at Michigan lead to a BA or a BS and state of Michigan certification. The many teaching specialties offered at Michigan include biology, chemistry, earth and space science, economics, English, French, German, history, integrated science, Latin, math, music education, physics, physical education, political science, social studies, and Spanish.

Middlebury College. Middlebury offers a minor in education studies that provides students with classroom experience and a track to become licensed to teach in Vermont. After taking prerequisite courses, students in education studies apply for the student teaching professional semester.

Vanderbilt University. Through its Peabody College of Education, Vanderbilt offers programs in early childhood education, elementary education, musical arts teacher education, secondary education, and special education. Musical arts teacher education is a five-year BM/MEd program. Students in secondary education can specialize in English, math, science, or social studies. Vanderbilt's teacher preparation programs are designed to lead to licensure in Tennessee and other states.

University of Vermont. UVM offers BS programs in art education, early childhood education, early childhood special education, elementary education, middle-level education, music education, physical education, and special education. UVM programs prepare students for licensure in Vermont.

College of William and Mary. At William and Mary, education is offered as a second major that gets paired with a primary major. The options in elementary education and secondary education lead to certification in Virginia. Specialized focus areas include English, foreign language (Chinese, French, German, Spanish, and Latin), math, science (biology, chemistry, earth science, and physics), and social studies (history and political science and government).

THE SADDLE CLUB: EQUINE AND RIDING PROGRAMS

For some, mucking out a stable and feeding a carrot to an equine friend is the high point of their day. For students who love horses and the accompanying barn and riding culture, college as a horse-free zone is not a viable option. For such students, being able to bring a horse to college, continue riding, and find a core of horse lovers matters a great deal. Students who want horses and riding to be part of their college experience have a particular set of needs and interests not usually addressed by the typical college guide. While there is a group of schools where horses are significant in the social and, in some cases, academic landscape, information on those options can be hard to find. As result this chapter was written for students looking to continue riding in college as well as for students seeking to take their interest in horses into the classroom.

This chapter focuses on colleges offering strong riding programs and on some of the standout equine-related academic programs available as major options. First, we will discuss equestrian riding as a college sport, including the various competitive riding options offered at US institutions. That discussion will highlight schools with particularly active riding teams. Following the section on riding is a look at colleges with academic programs focused on horses. Last of all, we provide information on prominent college polo teams.

RIDING AS A SPORT

Since 1998 the NCAA has classified riding as an emerging sport. The good side of the emerging sport classification means that colleges sponsoring NCAA riding can award athletic scholarships and fund teams. The downside of being an emerging sport is the recognition that there are not enough teams to have an official NCAA championship. Until there are at least forty Division I and II NCAA equestrian teams, competition for a national title cannot occur under the banner NCAA National Equestrian Championship. As a result, the twenty-three Division I and II NCAA equestrian teams compete for the National Collegiate Equestrian Association (NCEA) Championship. Teams cannot compete in both the NCAA and in the IHSA (Intercollegiate Horse Show Association). In 2006, the NCAA ruled that member equestrian teams can only compete for one national championship, not vie for both the NCEA and IHSA title.

Because of Title IX regulations requiring an equal number of male and female sports, riding is often considered a women's sport by the NCAA so that colleges can count it as one of their women's teams to balance out athletic offerings. Currently, several schools have NCAA Division I and Division II teams, but there are no Division III riding teams at the time of this publication. Some riders prefer to opt out of NCAA varsity riding because there are very strict rules about when and where a rider can compete and still maintain the necessary amateur status. For example, a NCAA rider cannot compete for monetary prizes. Also, like any potential NCAA athlete, riders must register in high school with the NCAA Clearinghouse in order to get recruited by coaches. The process for filling out the NCAA Clearinghouse is outlined on the NCAA website or available by calling 877-262-1492. Confusingly, information about NCAA riding is not on the general NCAA website.

A listing of current NCAA teams and other vital information on competitive riding can be found at varsityequestrian.com.

NCAA EQUESTRIAN TEAMS

- Auburn University
- Baylor University
- Brown University
- California State University at Fresno
- College of Charleston
- Cornell University
- Delaware State University
- University of Georgia
- Kansas State University
- University of Minnesota at Crookston
- New Mexico State University
- Oklahoma State University
- Pace University
- Sacred Heart University
- Seton Hill University
- University of South Carolina
- South Dakota State University
- Southern Methodist University
- Stonehill College
- University of Tennessee at Martin
- Texas A&M University
- Texas Christian University West Texas A&M University

NCEA EQUESTRIAN NATIONAL CHAMPIONS, 2004–15

- 2004—University of Georgia
- 2005—University of South Carolina
- 2006—Auburn University
- 2007—University of South Carolina
- 2008—University of Georgia
- 2009—University of Georgia
- 2010—University of Georgia
- 2011—Auburn University
- 2012—Texas A&M University
- 2013—Auburn University
- 2014—University of Georgia
- 2015—University of South Carolina

IHSA, ANRC, AND IDA

Another major outlet for competition occurs through the Intercollegiate Horse Show Association (IHSA). Since 1967 the IHSA has been a major player in collegiate riding. Eight levels of hunting/ English riding and six levels of western-style competitions occur through IHSA. The IHSA website (ihsainc.org) lists all college equestrian teams as well as information on competitions and IHSA scholarships. One gauge of a college's horse friendliness is its presence on IHSA competition rosters. It is a pretty sure bet that any IHSA college riding team has institutional support and resources. On the other hand, teams competing on the IHSA circuit often have to raise their own money to support their activities. In some cases riding clubs are funded through student activities monies designated by student government for particular clubs and organizations. Not surprisingly, the teams that receive more monetary support tend to comprise the leading places to ride. In English riding, for example, a small number of well-funded teams (Centenary, Mount Holyoke, and Skidmore) have dominated the national championship competitions over the last two decades. In IHSA western riding, the American Quarter Horse Association Trophy awarded to national champions has seen a handful of frequent winners in the last twenty years: University of Findlay, Ohio State, and Texas A&M.

The American National Riding Commission (ANRC) exists to promote the American System of Forward Riding. Each April, the ANRC holds its Intercollegiate Equitation Championship. In team competition, riders are judged and scored in four areas: (1) a ride that includes United States Equestrian Federation (USEF) hunter equitation tests; (2) performance on a hunter seat equitation course; (3) performance on a derby course; and (4) a written test assessing knowledge of riding theory and stable management. There are seventy-four collegiate members of the ANRC, many of which also compete in IHSA and IDA events. The ANRC has many prominent members, including Cornell, Duke, Georgetown, MIT, Stanford, Virginia, and William and Mary.

IHSA NATIONAL CHAMPIONS, 1994–2015—ENGLISH (HUNT SEAT)

- 1994—Colby-Sawyer College
- 1995—Skidmore College
- 1996—Skidmore College
- 1997—University of Delaware
- 1998—Hollins University
- 1999—Skidmore College
- 2000—Mount Holyoke College
- 2001—University of Findlay
- 2002—Ohio University

- 2003—Stonehill College
- 2004—Virginia Intermont College*
- 2005—Virginia Intermont College*
- 2006—Mount Holyoke College
- 2007—Virginia Intermont College*
- 2008—University of Kentucky
- 2009—Centenary College
- 2010—Skidmore College
- 2011—Centenary College
- 2012—St. Lawrence University
- 2013—Skidmore College and St. Lawrence University (tie)
- 2014—Centenary College
- 2015—Svannah College of Art and Design

*closed in 2014

IHSA NATIONAL CHAMPIONS, 1994–2015—WESTERN

- 1994—Colorado State University and Texas A&M University (tie)
- 1995—New Mexico State University
- 1996—Ohio State University
- 1997—Ohio State University
- 1998—New Mexico State University
- 1999—Ohio State University
- 2000—Oklahoma State University
- 2001—University of Findlay
- 2002—Texas A&M University and Ohio State University (tie)
- 2003—Texas A&M University and West Texas A&M University (tie)
- 2004—Texas A&M University
- 2005—University of Findlay
- 2006—Ohio State University
- 2007—University of Findlay

- 2008—Ohio State University
- 2009—University of Findlay
- 2010—University of Findlay
- 2011—Berry College
- 2012—Oregon State University
- 2013—West Texas A&M University
- 2014—Ohio State University
- 2015—Berry College

ANRC NATIONAL CHAMPIONS, 1994–2015

- 1994—University of Virginia
- 1995—University of Virginia
- 1996—St. Andrew's Presbyterian College
- 1997—St. Andrew's Presbyterian College
- 1998—St. Lawrence University
- 1999—Sweet Briar College
- 2000—St. Andrew's Presbyterian College
- 2001—St. Andrew's Presbyterian College
- 2002—St. Andrew's Presbyterian College
- 2003—Savannah College of Art and Design
- 2004—Virginia Intermont College*
- 2005—Savannah College of Art and Design
- 2006—Savannah College of Art and Design
- 2007—St. Andrew's Presbyterian College
- 2008—Savannah College of Art and Design
- 2009—Savannah College of Art and Design
- 2010—Savannah College of Art and Design
- 2011—Savannah College of Art and Design
- 2012—Savannah College of Art and Design
- 2013—Centenary College
- 2014—Savannah College of Art and Design
- 2015—Savannah College of Art and Design

*closed in 2014

Sometimes called horse ballet, dressage is understood among the horsey set as the highest expression of horse training. Dressage riders guide their horses through a sequence of movements that tests the horse's natural athletic ability and willingness to perform. Founded in 1995, the Intercollegiate Dressage Association (IDA) has adapted the principles of classical dressage to competition. It was actually a Mount Holyoke student rider (Michelle Hoffman) who originated the concept and drew up the first guidelines for IDA individual and team competitions. The first IDA Eastern Region Finals occurred in 2001 at Virginia Intermont College (now closed) and included teams from colleges and secondary schools. In 2003, the IDA became a collegiate-only organization. Now the IDA has fifty-eight member colleges and universities across North America. Competitions are held at the regional and national level. A few college teams have dominated the national championships over the years.

IDA NATIONAL CHAMPIONS, 2004–15

- 2004—Mount Holyoke College
- 2005—Lake Erie College
- 2006—Virginia Intermont College*
- 2007—Virginia Intermont College*
- 2008—Mount Holyoke College
- 2009—University of New Hampshire
- 2010—Virginia Intermont College*
- 2011—Lake Erie College
- 2012—Johnson and Wales University
- 2013—Mount Holyoke College
- 2014—Virginia Intermont College*
- 2015—Emory and Henry College

*closed in 2014

Beyond the competitive riding options, prospective students will want to check out the barn facility and the boarding options on each campus. Horse-related details are almost always neglected during the general campus tour or information session. So it is usually up to the student to conduct some research prior to and during the visit in order to evaluate if riding there will be a viable option. Obviously, a campus-owned barn, like at Albion or Skidmore, is a good sign, but what about colleges that utilize a private facility off campus? It is important to determine the logistics of getting to the barn, particularly if it requires having a car. For students who anticipate spending significant time at the barn with the people who work with the horses, the campus visit should include a stop at the college's riding facility and a chat with the staff there. Ask about the cost to board versus leasing a horse, the team or club's activities, and general accessibility to riding and competitions. The barn folks are a potentially rich source of information about the riding program and maybe even about the college as well. If you see students at the barn, ask how riding has been integrated into their college experience.

MAJORING IN HORSES?

Several colleges offer academic options related to horses. The two basic categories are equine science and equine business. There are other majors and concentrations, such as communications in the equine industry, but those programs all tend to derive from equine science and equine business. While some colleges, like Centenary in New Jersey and Otterbein in Ohio have well-defined equine departments, many colleges place their horse-related majors within a particular college or school. For example, since 1973 the University of Arizona has operated the Race Track Industries Program (RTIP) under the College of Agriculture and Life Science. RTIP at Arizona is all about horses, but it is not a program easily found through admissions media. Finding out about RTIP requires searching within animal sciences, a department embedded within the College of Agriculture and Life Science. Furthermore, within the RTIP program, there are two tracks; business and equine management. For someone interested in equine business, who would think that one of the best places to find a top program would be in the University of Arizona Ag School?

Since the point of this guide is to simplify the process and highlight interesting hidden opportunities, we have done the detective work for you—resulting in brief descriptions of what we believe are some of the best options for students looking for a horse-centric college experience. The schools listed and described below are known for their academic and/or extracurricular horse-related resources. These schools are highlighted because, in addition to standout horse-related offerings, they are a mix of public and private, academically competitive and highly accessible, and secular and church affiliated. The following is a comprehensive, but by no means exhaustive, list of options for the horse-loving student.

➤ STRONG EQUINE PROGRAMS

Albion College

Auburn University

Berry College

Brown University

University of California at Davis

California Polytechnic State University at San Luis Obispo

California State University at Fresno

Cazenovia College

Centenary College

Colby-Sawyer College

College of Charleston

Colorado State University

University of Connecticut

Cornell University

University of Delaware

Earlham College

University of Findlay

University of Florida

University of Georgia

Goucher College

Hollins University

Johnson and Wales University

Kansas State University

University of Kentucky

Lake Erie College

University of Louisville

University of Maryland

University of Mary Washington

University of Massachusetts

Miami University

Morrisville State College (SUNY)

Mount Holyoke College

University of New Hampshire

New Mexico State University

Ohio University

Ohio State University

Oklahoma State University

Otterbein University

Oregon State University

Randolph College

St. Andrew's Presbyterian College

St. Lawrence University

St. Mary-of-the-Woods College

Savannah College of Art and Design

Skidmore College

University of South Carolina

Southern Methodist University

Stanford University

Stephens College

Stonehill College

Texas A&M University

Texas Christian University

Albion College. The Nancy G. Held Equestrian Center on the Albion campus is arguably the finest college equine facility in the Midwest. The 340-acre Held Center is an approved British Horse Society facility that has barns with stalls for seventy-nine horses, thirty-seven turnout paddocks, an indoor arena, an outdoor sand arena, a grass jumping arena, and manicured trails. The Held Center is accessible to all Albion students, whether they are members of the IHSA hunt-seat and western riding teams, members of the IDA dressage team, or students who are either boarding their horse at the facility or taking beginning riding lessons. College-owned horses at the Held Center are available for group and private lessons.

Auburn University. Within Auburn's Department of Animal Sciences, there is an undergraduate degree option in equine science. Animal sciences also operates a horse center that serves as a teaching, research, and extension program resource for both the campus and the state of Alabama. The horse center, which sits on sixty acres near the campus, is the home of the Auburn Equestrian Team—winners of the 2006 and 2011 NCEA championship. The Auburn Horse Center has a main barn with ten stalls, three arenas, treatment areas for veterinarians and farriers, eleven pastures, four paddocks for turnouts, two tack rooms, laboratories, locker rooms, and offices.

Berry College. Within the animal science major at Berry, students can pursue an equine specialization by taking courses in stable management, equine health, horse systems and management, and equine evaluation. Berry also runs a small breeding program for quarter horses and sells horses. The nationally competitive Berry equestrian team won the 2011 and 2015 IHSA national championships in western. At the 2012 IHSA nationals, a Berry rider took home the title in novice equitation. The Berry team trains at the 185-acre Gunby Equine Center that has four barns with lighted stalls, 180 acres of pasture, two small round pens, an outdoor lighted arena, a covered arena with a judges stand, seating for four hundred, an attached classroom, and a tack room. Between the Gunby Center and the vast Berry campus, prospective riders have 23,000 acres of trails to explore.

Brown University. Riding is an NCAA sport at Brown and thus receives university funding through the athletic department. As an Ivy League school, Brown does not award athletic scholarships. Team tryouts occur in the first two weeks of school and little outside recruiting is done. Windswept Farms—located twelve miles from campus—has college horses and boarding facilities for student-owned horses. Riding students typically go to Windswept Farms twice a week via carpool.

University of California at Davis. Within its leading veterinary school, UC Davis conducts extensive equine-related research. Undergraduates also have many opportunities to get involved academically, primarily through animal science. In addition to the Center for Equine Health, UC Davis has a twenty-five-acre equestrian center equipped for English- and western-style riding. There are several horse-related clubs, three competitive teams (including a draft-horse driving team), and numerous riding events and dressage. The IHSA riding team is divided into hunt-seat and western units. Students may board their horses at the equestrian center or ride one of UCD's horses.

California Polytechnic State University at San Luis Obispo. In its Animal Science Department, Cal Poly offers a major in equine science. Cal Poly's equine science program attempts to expose students to the full range of the equine industry. Equine science students work with the university's two hundred horses to learn to breed and foal mares, train two year olds, and prepare horses for sale. For students interested in extracurricular competition, Cal Poly has dressage and equestrian teams. The dressage team is often ranked in the top ten nationally and has won several regional championships. The highly ranked Cal Poly Equestrian Team took top honors at the 2008 IHSA National Championship. Supporting the dressage and equestrian teams is the Cal Poly Horse Unit, which consists of a mare barn, a working horse barn, a five-hundred-ton hay barn, outside pipe corrals, over 150 acres of pasture, miles of trails, two arenas, and a round pen. The horse unit offers boarding for Cal Poly students who bring horses to campus.

California State University–Fresno. Despite Fresno's cowboy vibe, there are equal opportunities for English and western riders. The Equine Laboratory is a comprehensive center offering academic courses (under animal sciences) and riding opportunities. Fresno students can train colts and also help with the preservation of the endangered Hackney breed through the school's breeding and educational program. There is also an extensive quarter-horse program. Fresno competes in NCAA riding.

Cazenovia College. Located not far from Syracuse, New York, Cazenovia has just about everything a horse-oriented student would want in a college. The equine business major at Cazenovia prepares students for work in the commercial aspects of the equine industry as well as for fields such as horse breeding, advanced horse care, and stable management. Equine facilities at Cazenovia include a 243-acre horse farm located less than five miles from campus and a herd of seventy-two horses. In its herd Cazenovia has thoroughbreds, warmbloods, quarter horses, and numerous other breeds.

The Cazenovia horse farm has an indoor arena, a dressage arena, turnout paddocks, multiple outdoor riding areas and trails, and a wired classroom. Cazenovia fields several competitive teams, including IHSA hunter-seat and western riding teams, an (IDA) dressage team, and a horse-judging team. Over the last decade, Cazenovia's riding and dressage teams have placed in the top ten in several national and regional competitions.

Centenary College. Not to be confused with a college of the same name in Louisiana, this small New Jersey school could just as easily be called Equine U. Centenary has multiple equine majors, including communication for the equine industry, equine science, equine business management, riding instruction and training, and a certificate program in therapeutic riding. The equine department at Centenary has a large, well-trained faculty, and there is even a special admissions officer dedicated to serving prospective students interested in riding or equine studies. Unique to Centenary is a special equestrian-oriented open house in the fall for prospective students. The riding team is active and hosts IHSA events at Centenary's large facility.

College of Charleston. Equestrian teams at Charleston compete at the IHSA and NCAA level. The Charleston Equestrian Team, which consistently competes for regional championships in one of the toughest zones in the United States, has placed in the top ten at the IHSA nationals. Riders at Charleston train and compete at Storybrook Farm, which is a full service hunter and equitation barn located eleven miles from downtown Charleston. Storybrook Farm has a twenty-two-stall aisle barn, climate-controlled tack room, office and lounge with dressing room, two riding rings (one with lights for night riding), complete jump courses, and two outdoor stalls for washing horses.

Colby-Sawyer College. The equestrian program at Colby-Sawyer provides opportunities for female and male riders. The Colby-Sawyer team won the IHSA national championship in 1989 and 1994 and sends individual riders to the nationals nearly every year. The team trains twenty minutes from campus at Double Clear Farm in Warner, New Hampshire. Double Clear Farm has eighteen box stalls, an indoor arena, two outdoor riding rings, a jumper course, a stadium course, and a cross-country course.

Colorado State University. For riders and future horse industry professionals, Colorado State has vast resources. Within Colorado State's College of Agricultural Sciences, the BS program in equine science offers nearly thirty equine-specific courses and utilizes facilities such as the Equine Reproduction Lab. Equine science students can get hands-on experience through internships and an annual performance horse sale held on campus. Equine facilities at CSU include a 300-by-150-foot indoor arena with seating for two thousand, classrooms, faculty offices, thirty-six stalls, a veterinary treatment center, an outdoor arena, round pens, paddocks, tack and storage rooms, sheds, a farrier station, stables, and a grooming rack. Beyond its strong collegiate riding team, Colorado State has a horse-judging team, a polo club, a rodeo club, a ranch-horse club, an English riding club, a mountain rider's horse club, and a chapter of the Collegiate Horsemen's Association.

University of Connecticut. In addition to an equine focus in the animal science department, UConn offers some unusual opportunities related to horses, including the Morgan Drill Team. Comprised solely of Morgan horses bred at the campus barn, the drill team does synchronized routines with riders and horses. UConn fields men's and women's polo teams in addition to a competitive equestrian team. Although a western riding club was created in 2009, English remains the predominant riding style.

Cornell University. With strong schools of agriculture and veterinary medicine, Cornell has numerous resources for the study of horses. Undergraduates working on a degree in animal sciences can take courses such as equine biology and management and do research in the Brooks Equine Genetics Lab. Veterinary students at Cornell have access to an Equine Research Park. Beyond the classroom and lab, Cornell students can belong to the Block and Bridle Club and ride for an equestrian team that in recent years has won the Ivy League championship, qualified for the national finals, and had an individual rider finish eleventh in the country. Cornell's Oxley Equestrian Center has two barns, twenty-five horses, seventy-nine stalls, two outdoor arenas, a heated indoor arena, and IHSA regulation jumps.

University of Delaware. Winners of the 1997 IHSA National Championship in English (hunt seat) competition, Delaware's equestrian team is accomplished and popular. The roughly one hundred students who belong to the equestrian club team do not need to bring a horse to campus. Delaware has several livestock barns and training areas. The Department of Animal and Food Sciences at Delaware maintains the Webb Farm and an equine teaching facility. Students interested in careers in equine science might want to consider majoring in animal and food sciences at Delaware.

Earlham College. The equestrian program at Earlham is led by a student-run cooperative that cares for the horses, maintains the facilities, and provides riding lessons. Through the cooperative, Earlham students hold positions as barn manager, horse-care manager, barn director, barn correspondent, lesson coordinator, instructors, and assistants. Equestrian at Earlham is both a program and a team. The emphasis of the program is on making equine education and riding opportunities accessible to the campus and the surrounding Richmond, Indiana, community. Earlham's equestrian team competes on the club level in roughly ten IHSA meets per year. Facilities at Earlham's Suzanne Hoerner Jackson Equestrian Center include sixteen acres of rolling pastures, a holding pen, indoor and outdoor arenas utilizing recycled rubber and sand for better traction, a twenty-five-stall barn, three heated tack rooms, a classroom, and a feed room. Students can bring a horse to Earlham and board it at Hoerner.

University of Findley. Horses are a major component of life at Findley. In addition to multiple equine-related majors and excellent animal-science facilities, Findley stands out for its excellent preveterinary offerings. One of the few schools offering vaulting, Findley also fields English and western riding teams that have been consistent winners at IHSA tournaments. With separate facilities for English and western riders, Findley offers plenty of space and staff dedicated to riding. Findley also encourages horse-related internships as part of the academic experience.

University of Florida. For students looking for a big state university with extensive resources, both equine and nonequine related, Florida is an excellent option. Florida is one of the few schools offering doctoral programs (PhDs) in equine science, which means that exhausting the horse-related curriculum as an undergraduate will be a near impossibility. As for horse facilities, there is a separate riding barn apart from the horse health center. Florida offers western- and English-style riding as well as dressage. Note that although some people bring their own horses to UF, students are required to ride a school horse when competing in IHSA events.

University of Georgia. At Georgia there is a varsity equestrian team that competes in the NCAA and a club riding team that competes in the IHSA. With six NCEA championships to its credit, Georgia's varsity equestrian team is one of the best in the United States. The team prepares for competitions at a top-notch facility, located twelve miles south of campus, called the UGA Equestrian Complex (UGAEC). The UGAEC has served as a training site for the US Olympic dressage team. The IHSA club team at Georgia rides at Silverthorn Farm, which is located fifteen minutes from campus, and has two outdoor arenas, stalls, pastures, jumps, and trails.

Goucher College. Equestrian at Goucher is a varsity (IHSA) sport. Within its region, Goucher won seven overall or reserve championships between 2005 and 2011. Roughly sixty students participate in Goucher equestrian events each semester. The fee assessed for participation depends on the student's use of the facilities. In addition to stalls for student boarders, Goucher has more than ten horses, an outdoor hunter course, USEF approved jumps, miles of fields and wooded trails, and indoor and outdoor arenas that include a 100-by-175-foot indoor ring and a 160-by-180-foot sand ring.

Hollins University. Few schools rival Hollins for quality of equine facilities and prowess in riding competitions. Located in Roanoke, Virginia, Hollins has one of the nation's strongest riding programs. In 2012, two Hollins riders won national titles. For a record eight consecutive years (2005–12), Hollins teams and riders qualified for the IHSA National Championships. Hollins coaches have been named coach of the year more than a dozen times. When not on the national stage, the Hollins riding teams compete in the Old Dominion Athletic Conference, the home of several premier riding programs. On its campus Hollins annually hosts two open horse shows, two IHSA horse shows, and one in-house show. The impressive Hollins Riding Center is located within walking distance of the campus. Facilities include forty-three large box stalls, two large tack rooms, seven pastures and paddocks, a

200-by-110-foot indoor ring, a transport trailer, and air-conditioned rooms for instruction and events. Students can bring and board their own horses or use one of Hollins's thirty horses.

Johnson and Wales University. At the Providence, Rhode Island, campus of Johnson and Wales, students have two equine-related bachelor's degree options. There is the general equine business management major as well as the same degree with an emphasis on riding. Equine business management and riding students can also add the instructor/trainer concentration. Supporting JWU's equine programs are a thirty-one-acre horse farm located within thirty minutes of campus that has a thirty-two-stall barn, pastures and turnout paddocks, a round pen for schooling and training, and outdoor arenas that serve as jumping, dressage, and warm-up rings. The horses at Johnson and Wales represent many different breeds—including Dutch and Swedish warmblood, Hanoverian, Holsteiner, Morgan, quarter horse, thoroughbred, and Trakehner—and frequently become JWU horses following successful show careers in dressage, hunting and jumping, and eventing.

Kansas State University. Within its Department of Animal Sciences and Industry, Kansas State offers a certificate program in equine science. The equestrian team at K-State started as a club sport in 1999 and moved up to NCAA varsity status in 2000. In NCAA competition, K-State's equestrian team has won three reserve national championships, and individual riders have brought home five national titles. K-State riders train at Timbercreek Stables located four miles east of the campus. At Timbercreek, there are eighteen stalls, twenty-two runs, indoor and outdoor arenas, show and practice jumps, two round pens, a dressage arena, and pastures.

University of Kentucky. Horses have been central to the history and identity of the state of

Kentucky. At the University of Kentucky, there are opportunities to earn degrees and do research in equine science, some of the best academic and riding facilities in the United States, and an overall recognition that the state's economy depends on horses. Through the Equine Initiative, Kentucky's School of Agriculture integrates research, instruction, and projects that benefit the state. In its School of Agriculture, Kentucky offers an undergraduate degree in equine science and management that requires students to complete an internship in the equine industry. Given that Lexington is the horse capital of the world, internships are not hard to find. In the extracurricular realm, there are many teams at Kentucky for horse enthusiasts. In addition to the IHSA equestrian team and the horse-racing club, Kentucky has teams for dressage and eventing, polo, and saddle-seat riding. Kentucky teams won IHSA national championships in 2008 and 2009. As would be expected, equine facilities at Kentucky are vast. For riders there are one hundred horses, twenty-five pastures and paddocks, twenty-five box stalls, and a nutrition barn. In addition, an equine health research facility houses three hundred horses.

Lake Erie College. The major in equine studies at Lake Erie offers students the option to concentrate on therapeutic horsemanship or stud farm management. All equine studies majors at Lake Erie must complete a one-hundred-hour internship within the industry. Students find placements at horse farms, riding stables, equine clinics, feed companies, and therapeutic riding facilities. Located five miles from the campus, Lake Erie's eighty-six-acre Humphrey Equestrian Center has classrooms, offices, a student lounge, a computer lab, laboratories for equine studies classes, and stables for ninety-five horses in two barns—providing room for college horses and student and faculty boarders. In addition to turnout paddocks, the Humphrey Center has an indoor arena with seating for

seven hundred, an attached warm-up area, four outdoor riding rings—including an enclosed lighted arena—and a hunt field with cross-country jumps. The college provides six-day-a-week shuttle service to the Humphrey Center. Lake Erie frequently hosts professional clinics and several dressage and hunter and jumper horse shows at the Humphrey Center. A perennial championship contender, the Lake Erie equestrian team has approximately forty members and competes in IHSA hunt seat, IHSA western, IDA dressage, and United States Equestrian Foundation (USEF) jumper shows.

University of Louisville. The business school is the home of Louisville's equine programs. Students at Louisville can earn a bachelor of science degree in business administration with a concentration in equine industry. For nonbusiness majors, there is the option to earn a certificate in equine business. The College of Business's equine industry program also sponsors the Louisville equestrian team, which competes in saddle-seat and western riding.

University of Maryland, College Park. Maryland offers students two ways to prepare for careers in the equine field. The School of Agriculture's animal science major has a concentration option in equine studies, and the Department of Animal and Avian Sciences offers a certificate program in equine business management. For students interested in general riding, there is the University of Maryland Equestrian Club, which makes use of Waredaca Farm located thirty miles from the campus in Laytonville. The Maryland Equestrian Team also uses the facilities at Waredaca, which include a horse barn with eight stalls, four turnout paddocks, and a riding ring.

University of Mary Washington. Riding is a mixed sport at Mary Washington, which means that both men and women compete on the equestrian team. The Mary Washington riding teams compete in the same IHSA region as Goucher,

Maryland, and Richmond. At the national level, UMW riding teams have ranked in the top ten, and UMW riders have competed for individual championships. UMW riders train at Hazelwild Farm, located ten minutes from Mary Washington's Fredericksburg, Virginia, campus. Hazelwild Farm sits on five hundred acres of land, has stalls for sixty-two horses—including separate barns for UMW horses and boarder horses—two outdoor arenas, an indoor arena, and miles of trails

University of Massachusetts at Amherst. Students interested in equine studies and riding should consider UMass's Stockbridge School. A school-within-a-school, the Stockbridge School offers an equine studies major, runs the 131-acre farm adjacent to campus, and operates the Baystate Morgan Breeding Program. Internships are a required part of the curriculum for Stockbridge's associate and bachelor's degree programs of study. The equestrian team at UMass is more modest than some but is friendly and accessible. Students from neighboring New England states are often eligible for reduced tuition because the equine studies major qualifies as part of the New England regional tuition exchange.

Miami University. The 2011 regional champions, the Miami Equestrian Team is competitive every year in the IHSA and the IDA. Miami has more than sixty horses and fields a team of sixty-five to seventy-five riders who compete in dressage, hunt seat, jumping, and western riding. At Miami's Browne Equestrian Center, students can take classes in beginning, intermediate, and advanced horseback riding, jumping, and western riding. The Browne Equestrian Center has a barn, riding arenas, turnout areas, and trails for boarding, training, instruction, and horse shows. On the drawing board at Miami is an expanded equestrian center that will have indoor and outdoor riding arenas, turnout

paddocks, spectator seating, classrooms, locker rooms, and a tack room.

Mount Holyoke College. The equestrian center at Mount Holyoke is considered one of America's finest college facilities. The stable provides sixty-nine spacious, rubber-matted stalls, a large all-weather show arena, a permanent dressage arena, two indoor arenas, all-weather turnout paddocks, a hunt field, and a cross-country course through 120 acres of fields, woods, and streams. The Holyoke riding team frequently competes for IHSA national championships—taking home national titles in 2000 and 2006 and reserve championships in 2005 and 2007. Holyoke's dressage team has won three Intercollegiate Dressage Association (IDA) national championships. Mount Holyoke's equestrian center welcomes visits from prospective students.

University of New Hampshire. The equine offerings at UNH are comprehensive. On the academic side, students can choose either the associate of science degree in equine management or the BS degree in equine studies. The BS program offers three specialization options: equine industry management, therapeutic riding, and equine science. For students interested in riding, there are programs in dressage, eventing, and therapeutic riding. On the competitive level, UNH fields two highly decorated equestrian teams. One UNH team won the IDA national championship in 2009, while another team won the IHSA regional championship in 2011. The equine center at UNH houses laboratories, classrooms, conference spaces, and two apartments for students who work at the stables. UNH's Tirrell Horse Barn has fifty-two stalls, indoor and outdoor riding courses, an indoor arena, a lighted outdoor arena, space for students to board their horses, and three regulation-size dressage competition arenas.

New Mexico State University. New Mexico State's equestrian center has nearly four thousand square feet of facilities that house classrooms, locker rooms, offices, horse stalls, and a tack room. NMSU riders compete in the NCAA and are frequently in contention for regional and national championships. In addition, NMSU students operate a rodeo club, a therapeutic riding club, a horseman's association, and an annual campus horse sale. Within the BS program in animal science, NMSU students can specialize in equine science or minor in horse management.

Ohio State University. Over the years, Ohio State has been a powerhouse in IHSA western riding competitions, winning seven national championships since 1992. At its Griffith Equestrian Center, Ohio State has twenty-eight box stalls, two foaling stalls, two stallion stalls, a breeding lab, a classroom that seats fifty, a large outdoor arena, and turnout paddocks. In the classroom, Ohio State offers a minor in equine science within the animal science major. One standout feature of Ohio State's equine science program is the opportunity to get hands-on experiences in stable management, equine behavior and training, breeding management, and outreach through 4-H equine extension offices.

Ohio University. Ohio U is the home of nationally competitive IHSA hunt-seat and western equestrian teams. The hunt-seat team at Ohio won the IHSA national title in 2002. Training facilities for the English hunt-seat team are at Stonegate Farm in Coolville, Ohio, which is thirty minutes from the main Ohio University campus in Athens. Stonegate Farm has a barn with forty-seven stalls, a 225-by-116-foot heated indoor arena, and a 300-by-100-foot outdoor sand arena. Ohio's western riding team trains at a facility in Tupper Plains, which is thirty minutes from campus. Students interested in an equine-related degree can earn an associate degree in equine studies at Ohio University-Southern, located in Ironton, Ohio.

Oklahoma State University. At a university whose sports teams are called the Cowboys, it should not come as a surprise that OSU's horse-judging team has a national reputation and the equestrian team has won several IHSA reserve national championships in western riding. Just about every year, OSU riders win individual national championships. The on-campus, fifty-acre OSU equine center has facilities for research and equestrian training—including 120 acres of pasture, indoor and outdoor arenas, tack rooms, offices, and locker rooms. While there is no equine science major at OSU, there is a concentration in ranch operations offered within the Department of Animal Science.

Oregon State University. Oregon State has a 250-acre horse center that includes indoor and outdoor riding arenas, multiple barns, and a boarding program for student horses. Classes taught through the equine science program include, but are not limited to, riding, dressage, and laboratory classes such as equine marketing, equine nutrition, and stable management. Oregon State is home to the state's only veterinary program and has a strong reputation in animal sciences. The riding team competes primarily in the Pacific Northwest (including British Columbia) and has both English and western riders. The unique colts-in-training program enables students to train a two-year-old colt for saddle and cattle work.

Otterbein University. Resources for horses and those who love them got even better at Otterbein when its state-of-the-art equine science facility opened in the fall of 2009. The eighty-acre facility, located ten minutes from Otterbein's suburban Columbus, Ohio, campus, provides facilities for equine study as well as for individual riders, equestrian enthusiasts, and the dressage team. Otterbein offers three different horse-related majors, one minor, and an extensive pre-veterinary program. To supplement their academic programs, students are encouraged to have internship experiences. Otterbein's promotional admissions materials include loving descriptions of its campus family of horses.

Randolph College. At this small college in Lynchburg, Virginia, the riding program offers students two lessons per week, coaching for schooling and showing, and special clinics. Randolph riding teams belong to the competitive Old Dominion Athletic Conference. In regional and national IHSA competitions, Randolph riders and teams have achieved much success over the years. Randolph had individual qualifiers at the IHSA national championships in 2000, 2004, and 2007, and in 1996 and 1999 its equestrian team finished third nationally. Facilities at Randolph include one hundred acres of trails, two outdoor rings, a jumping amphitheater, a schooling ring, an indoor arena, a hunter course, a four-stall barn, more than thirty horses, and an outdoor schooling area for jumps.

St. Andrew's Presbyterian College. There are two undergraduate degree options for horse lovers at St. Andrew's: the (BA or BS) program in equine science and the first-of-its- kind BA in therapeutic horsemanship management, which is offered through the Department of Business Administration. The equestrian teams at St. Andrew's have won numerous national titles in ANRC, IDA, and IHSA competitions. For a college with fewer than seven hundred students, St. Andrew's has exceptional facilities for equine studies and riding. Just two miles from its campus in Laurinburg, North Carolina, the St. Andrew's Equestrian Center sits on three hundred acres with miles of riding trails and four barns that contain a total of 112 stalls. There is a separate barn for the therapeutic riding horses and another barn for the lessons horses. Among the riding facilities are two hunter trail courses, five outdoor show and teaching arenas, an indoor arena, a dressage arena with paddocks, two covered arenas, classrooms, viewing rooms, and offices.

St. Lawrence University. The winners of the 2012 IHSA national championship in hunter-seat competition, the St. Lawrence equestrian team also has a strong record at winning individual titles at the national level. Over the years, St. Lawrence riders have won twenty individual national championships. The on-campus St. Lawrence riding arena hosts several horse shows annually. Equestrian is a coed sport at St. Lawrence.

St. Mary-of-the-Woods College. This small (just 325 students) Catholic women's college in Indiana provides extensive academic and riding options through its Mari Hulman George School of Equine Studies. In addition, St. Mary-of-the-Woods participates in a study abroad program with the International Specialized Equestrian Training Centre in Dublin, Ireland, where students can participate in show jumping, breeding, eventing, racing, and fox hunting. As for riding, there are separate English and western teams, a therapy riding program, and other options for the recreational rider. Over 90 percent of the student body receives some form of financial aid.

Savannah College of Art and Design (SCAD). SCAD is unusual because it is an art school with an equestrian studies major. Because it is primarily an art college, the core classes (outside of the equine major) at SCAD are drawing, painting and other art fundamentals. In addition to coursés on riding, equine health, and business, the SCAD equestrian studies major has some classes that nod to the arts, such as barn and stable design. SCAD's equestrian team has been highly competitive on the IHSA riding circuit.

Skidmore College. What Skidmore lacks in equine-related classes, it more than makes up for in ambience. Located in Saratoga Springs,

New York, one of the most horse-oriented towns in the United States, Skidmore provides its students with access to the historic racetrack and the museums, shops, and restaurants that cater to the horse crowd. Skidmore combines excellent riding and barn work opportunities with a strong liberal arts college experience.

The riding center at Skidmore is less than one mile from campus. The equestrian team, which focuses on hunt seat, consistently wins at local and national shows. There are also polo fields nearby. The college's athletic teams are appropriately known as the Thoroughbreds.

University of South Carolina. In the relatively short history of NCAA equestrian sports, South Carolina has emerged as a powerhouse. South Carolina Equestrian won the NCEA national championship in 2005, 2007, and 2015 and routinely sends individual riders to compete for IHSA national titles. The team trains at its own equestrian center located fifteen minutes from campus. These facilities include fifteen acres of trails, twenty-two stables, and two riding arenas.

Southern Methodist University. At a school whose athletic teams are called the Mustangs, one would imagine that at least one sport involves horses. SMU meets those expectations with competitive equestrian and polo teams. The SMU equestrian team is a member of the NCAA and has been ranked in the top ten in national championship competition. The team trains at BuckBranch Farm, located thirty-five to forty minutes from campus on the southern edge of Dallas County. The 120-acre BuckBranch Farm has numerous trails, two dressage arenas, an outside jumping arena, a covered and lighted 100-by-200-foot arena, thirty-four stalls, a feed room, a tack room, an office, and showers. The SMU polo team won its region in 2012 and advanced to the national championship round.

Stanford University. Each summer at its Red Barn, Stanford operates two one-week sessions for high school students interested in riding on the collegiate level. The sessions include daily riding lessons with a coach from the Stanford equestrian team, presentations on IHSA and NCAA riding, discussions regarding riding and the college admission process, and afternoon fitness activities such as Pilates, running, swimming, weight training, and yoga. The impressive facilities at the Red Barn include ninety-nine stalls, thirty horses, a 120-by-260-foot show arena, an indoor arena, a 115-by-200-foot outdoor arena, a regulation-size dressage court, covered and uncovered lunging arenas, turnout paddocks, grooming stalls, wash racks, men's and women's locker rooms, and picnic areas. The Stanford equestrian team is a perennial competitor for IHSA national riding championships in western horsemanship, hunt-seat equitation, and dressage.

Stephens College. There are two equine degrees offered at Stephens: the BS in equestrian studies and the BS in equestrian science, a program closely allied with the crosstown University of Missouri School of Veterinary Medicine. Because the equestrian science program meets preveterinary course requirements, a number of students choose the major as a step toward vet school. Through their studies and cocurricular activities, students have the option to earn certification from the Professional Association of Therapeutic Horsemanship International. Two popular clubs at Stephens are the Prince of Wales Club (which is the oldest continually active riding club in the United States) and the Stephens Equine Therapeutic Association. Riding instruction and opportunities at Stephens include saddle seat, hunt seat, western, and reining. The Stephens Equestrian Center has two stable areas, a saddle-seat and western barn, a hunter and dressage barn, sixty-one stalls, two riding arenas (indoor and outdoor), and seven grass turnout areas (including three paddocks). Students can board their own horse at the Stephens Equestrian Center.

Stonehill College. The Stonehill equestrian team competes in the IHSA and the NCAA. In 2003, Stonehill's English (hunt seat) team won the IHSA national title. The Stonehill riding teams train at Dry Water Farm, a thirty-five-acre property located in nearby Stoughton, Massachusetts. Dry Water Farm has a 355-stall barn, 830 acres of conservation trails, indoor and outdoor arenas, group turnout areas, an outdoor dressage arena, and a cool-down perimeter trail.

Texas A&M University. Horses have been a part of this university since its beginnings in 1876. The 120-acre University Horse Center in College Station, located less than a mile from campus, provides ample academic and athletic opportunities. For nearly forty years, A&M has sponsored a horsemanship program that sends students out all over Texas to teach youngsters about horses and riding. In addition, academic programs in the animal science department, the Horseman's Association, Rodeo Club, judging team, and equestrian team fuel the horsepower on campus. A&M also boasts that 15 percent of the nation's horses are in Texas.

Texas Christian University. TCU competes in NCAA equestrian sports. At the 2012 NCEA championship, TCU's western team placed sixth. The team at TCU is comprised of fifty riders who compete in hunt seat and western. Riding facilities for TCU equestrian are at October Hill Farm, a facility twenty-five miles west of the Fort Worth campus. October Hill Farm has 28,800 square feet of equestrian space situated on two hundred acres. The farm has four barns, fourteen pastures, twenty stalls for TCU horses, a fully enclosed arena, two wash stalls, and multiple outdoor riding spaces.

► COLLEGES WITH POLO TEAMS

Brown University	University of Louisville	Southern Methodist University
California Polytechnic State University at San Luis Obispo	University of Massachusetts at Amherst	Texas A&M
University of California at Davis	University of Michigan	Texas Christian University
University of California at Santa Barbara	Michigan State University	University of Texas
Colorado State University	Montana State University	Texas Tech University
University of Connecticut	New Mexico State University	Vassar College
Cornell University	Oklahoma State University	University of Virginia
Emory University	Oregon State University	Washington State University
Harvard University	Purdue University	Westmont College
Johnson and Wales University	University of Richmond	University of Wyoming
University of Kentucky	Skidmore College	Yale University
	University of Southern California	

THE SCOOP ON SELECTED COLLEGE POLO TEAMS

Brown University. The polo club at Brown is a group of men and women who take polo lessons and compete in United States Polo Association (USPA) matches. Beginners are welcome. The team is coached by a member of Newport Polo and trains at a facility thirty minutes from campus in Portsmouth, Rhode Island.

University of California at Davis. One of the top teams in its region, the UC Davis Polo Club is managed by students. Prospective club members do not need to bring their own horse to campus. The polo club utilizes the facilities and resources of the UC Davis Equestrian Center.

Colorado State University. With forty-five players, the polo teams at Colorado State compete in a region that includes New Mexico State, Oklahoma State, Texas A&M, Texas Tech, and the University of Texas. In 2012 both the men's and women's teams ranked second in the country. CSU's men's team has won the national championship three times: 1990, 1991, and 1999.

University of Connecticut. Polo at UConn has a storied history. UConn polo teams have won the USPA national championship many times: the women in 1996, 1997, 1998, 2005, 2006, 2007, and 2008, and the men in 1972, 1973, 1974, 1982, and 1984. UConn's polo teams train and compete at the nearby Shallowbrook Equestrian Center.

Cornell University. Cornell fields men's and women's polo teams. Both teams compete in Ivy League polo and have been contenders for the USPA national championship. In 2012, the Cornell women's team lost in the national final to the University of Virginia.

Harvard University. Polo at Harvard traces its roots to 1883. Harvard fields men's and women's teams that practice at a facility forty-five minutes north of campus in Hamilton, Massachusetts. Annually, the Harvard polo teams travel to the United Kingdom to compete in matches with Cambridge, Oxford, and Yale and then ventures on to Chantilly, France; Geneva, Switzerland; and Rome, Italy, for additional matches. The polo team's most generous patron is the actor Tommy Lee Jones, who played at Harvard. Each year he invites the team to train at his ranch in Texas.

University of Richmond. Started by students in 2009, the polo club at Richmond is part of the recreational sports program. The team is small (about eight members) and fields men's and women's teams that compete in arena polo. The team practices at the expansive and prestigious Virginia Polo Center in Charlottesville, home of UVA Polo.

Skidmore College. Skidmore's men's and women's polo teams compete in a challenging region that includes Cornell, Harvard, UConn, and Yale. Generally, the Skidmore teams make it to the USPA regional finals, and at those competitions, the team often wins awards. The women's team won the national championship in 1989. Skidmore's polo teams train at an expansive facility located fifteen minutes from campus that includes an indoor arena, acres of turnouts, and spacious stables.

University of Southern California. Polo at USC has a long tradition, dating back to the 1930s. USC fields men's and women's teams that consistently compete for regional championships. The teams train at Fair Hills Farm located north of the USC campus in Topanga Canyon. The current coach of USC polo (Adeshir Radpour) played at USC and also served as Tommy Trojan, the horse-riding mascot, from 1995 to 2000.

Southern Methodist University. Started by a student in 2004, the SMU polo program is on the rise. The polo team at SMU has fifteen horses and competes at the USPA national championships.

Texas A&M University. A&M has one of the top intercollegiate polo programs in the United States. Team facilities include a riding center and twenty horses. The men's team won USPA national championships in 1996, 1997, 2007, 2008, and 2010. The women's team won the USPA national championship in 1994 and 1995 and was runner-up in 2010.

Texas Christian University. The TCU Polo Club practices and exercises its horses weekly at a facility forty-five minutes from the Fort Worth campus. TCU polo is part of a very competitive region that includes the likes of Colorado State, New Mexico State, Oklahoma, Oklahoma State, Texas A&M, Texas Tech, and the University of Texas.

University of Virginia. Established in 1951, the UVA Polo Club has a distinguished history. The men's team has won ten USPA national championships and the women's team has been USPA national champion five times, including in 2012. A signature event in collegiate polo, the Harriman Cup competition annually pits UVA against Yale.

Westmont College. This small college (1,300 students) located near Santa Barbara has built a strong polo tradition. Westmont won the 2014 national USPA championship.

University of Wyoming. Wyoming fields men's and women's teams that compete in the western region. Polo at Wyoming is a club that is affiliated with the College of Agriculture and Natural Resources.

Yale University. Founded in 1903, the Yale Polo Team is the oldest and most successful collegiate polo team in the United States. The Yale team is coed, but in USPA competitions the men and women compete separately. Annually, Yale plays UVA in a historic and prestigious competition called the Harriman Cup. Yale's polo team has sixteen horses and trains at a ranch located twenty-five minutes from campus. Yale is in the midst of planning and raising the funds for a new polo and equestrian center.

APPENDIX I:
ADMISSION ADVICE FOR SELECTED SPECIAL CASES

STUDENTS WITH LEARNING DIFFERENCES

For a number of students applying to college, success in high school came hand in hand with an individualized learning plan (ILP). Most commonly, students with ILPs receive accommodations related to attention deficit hyperactivity disorder (ADHD), dyslexia, Asperger's syndrome, or visual and spatial processing challenges. For such students, it is especially important to find a college that will be sensitive to their different learning styles and special needs. In some cases, students with learning differences (LD) will seek (and be best served by) specialized LD colleges, such as Beacon and Landmark. Other students are more interested in mainstream colleges and universities that have special LD centers or programs. In some cases,

participation in the LD program requires an additional fee. In other cases, the LD programs are coordinated through an office housed within student services or academic advising. Because LD issues are relatively well-known at all colleges and universities in the United States, students needing LD accommodation (such as extended time on exams) can find services on just about any campus. Still, LD services are more extensive at some colleges and less extensive at others. This appendix will focus primarily on the colleges with the most extensive LD services. All of the colleges listed and profiled below are known for their strong records of addressing the needs of and graduating students who enroll with LD concerns and issues.

LD SPECIALTY SCHOOLS

BEACON COLLEGE—LEESBURG, FLORIDA

Less than twenty-five years old, Beacon College started as the vision of a group of parents who believed that students with learning disabilities should have the opportunity to get a college education focused on critical thinking skills. Students come to Beacon, located in a small town fifty miles northwest of Orlando, from more than thirty states and a dozen foreign countries. The two hundred students at Beacon can choose associate of arts (AA) and BA degree programs in business management, computer information systems,

human services, interdisciplinary studies, and psychology.

Through highly personalized classes that average twelve students, Beacon serves students with ADHD, auditory and visual processing differences, dyslexia, expressive/receptive language deficits, language-based learning disabilities, reading/writing disabilities, and math disabilities. Educational support services at Beacon include a center for student success, a math lab, a peer mentoring program, and a writing center. Beacon also provides life coaches, who work one-on-one with students for at least ten weeks to help them set and work toward goals.

LANDMARK COLLEGE—PUTNEY, VERMONT

When founded in 1985, Landmark became the first college-level institution in the United States for students with dyslexia. Located in a rural Vermont town, Landmark is a highly personalized place, dedicated to helping students discover the learning style that works best for them. Landmark views each of its five hundred students as a partner in learning and strives to help all of them reach their potential. Landmark offers two degree tracks: the associate of science (AS) degree program, which offers majors in life sciences or computer science/gaming, and the BA in liberal studies degree, with tracks in general studies, liberal arts, business studies, and business administration.

To help its students succeed, Landmark provides comprehensive support—such as weekly sessions with an academic adviser—as well as regular workshops with a team consisting of fellow students, faculty, and advisers. Landmark provides coaching services for students with executive function challenges as well as centers focused on science and math support. Throughout its individualized learning environment, Landmark utilizes assistive technologies and innovative learning strategies to help students succeed.

For students with autism spectrum disorders (ASD), Landmark takes an integrated services approach that provides a structured living and learning environment in addition to social and programmatic support tailored to individual needs. For high school students, Landmark runs summer programs focused on helping LD students have greater success in high school and with the transition to college.

➤ COLLEGES KNOWN FOR STRONG LD PROGRAMS

Adelphi University	University of Hartford	New York Institute of Technology
University of Akron	Hofstra University	Northeastern University
Alfred University	Humboldt State University	Nova Southeastern University
American International College	Iona College	University of Pittsburgh
American University	University of Iowa	Regis University
University of Arizona	Ithaca College	Ripon College
Augsburg College	Kent State University	Rochester Institute of Technology
Barry University	Long Island University	Roosevelt University
Boston University	Loyola University of New Orleans	Schreiner University
Centre College	Lynchburg College	Southern Illinois University
University of Connecticut	Lynn University	Southern Oregon University
Curry College	Manhattanville College	SUNY-Cobleskill
Davis and Elkins College	Marist College	Syracuse University
Dean College	Marshall University	Texas State University at San Marcos
University of Denver	McDaniel College	Texas Tech University
DePaul University	University of Memphis	University of Toledo
Fairleigh Dickinson University	Menlo College	Towson State University
Florida A&M University	Mitchell College	University of Vermont
George Mason University	Muskingum College	Western Michigan University
University of Georgia	University of Nevada	West Virginia Wesleyan College
Georgia Southern University	University of New England	

Note: in the profiles below, all special LD program fees represent 2014 charges.

American University. Through its Academic Support and Access Center (ASAC), AU assists students with documented ADHD or learning disabilities. Services include letters of accommodation for courses and exams, sessions with ASAC counselors, assistance with writing, and workshops on study skills. For students seeking more extensive resources, AU offers the Learning Services Program (LSP) for a $3,000 one-time fee. The LSP helps first-year students transition to college by providing peer tutors, student mentors, weekly meetings with LSP counselors and writing mentors, a special section of the first-year writing course, and help using assistive learning technologies.

University of Arizona. Arizona is internationally renowned for providing resources for LD students. The Disability Resource Center (DRC) at UA works with students who need academic accommodations and with professors to help them structure courses and assignments in ways that are sensitive to differing learning styles. For a fee ($1,100 upper division and $2,600 lower division), students have access to the Strategic Alternative Learning Techniques (SALT) Center—a team of twenty-four full-time employees dedicated to helping students with learning and attention challenges succeed. The SALT Center provides individualized learning plans; tutoring and study sessions; seminars to develop math, science, and writing skills; programs to develop leadership and social skills; strategies for listening, reading, and note taking; psychological counseling; and assistive technologies, such as dictation software and applications. In addition, Arizona operates a policy, research, and education think tank called the Sonoran University Center for Excellence in Developmental Disabilities.

University of Connecticut. Through its Center for Students with Disabilities, UConn offers a program called Beyond Access. Students enrolled in Beyond Access work with an assigned counselor (called a Strategy Instructor) to create a plan for academic success tailored to the student's individual goals and learning style. Beyond Access offers tracks where students meet with Strategy Instructors for one or for three hours per week. The program helps students develop better time management, self-advocacy, organization, reading and writing, and study skills; improve their memory and concentration; and assist with stress management, career preparation, and health and wellness.

Curry College. A dedication to individualized learning characterizes this two-thousand-student college located in the Boston suburb of Milton, Massachusetts. Curry's Program for Advancement of Learning (PAL) is one of the oldest and most respected college programs for students with language-based learning disabilities, executive function disorders, and ADHD. PAL students, who comprise 20 percent of each entering class at Curry, are fully mainstreamed. PAL students have the opportunity to take special for-credit classes (fees range from $1,775 to $3,370 per semester, and scholarship assistance is available) that teach strategies and skills in reading comprehension, writing, speaking, listening, time management, and organization. PAL also operates an intensive two-and-a-half-week summer program designed to help students transition to college. The Education Diagnostic Center at Curry provides additional resources and expertise for the campus and the surrounding region.

University of Denver. With two programs for LD students, Denver is a recognized leader at helping students with learning differences succeed. All students at Denver can utilize the Disability Services Program (DSP) free of charge. DSP services include extended time on tests, note-taking services, and alternate format texts. For an additional fee of $1,100 per quarter, Denver students have access to the Learning Effectiveness Program (LEP). With eleven academic advisers and a handful of additional staff, the LEP goes beyond DSP to provide one-on-one academic counseling, individual tutoring in specific subjects, and assistance with organization and time management. Approximately 230 students sign up for LEP each quarter.

DePaul University. DePaul's Center for Students with Disabilities (CSD) provides a comprehensive program of services focused on student success. The Productive Learning Strategies (PLUS) program, operated by the CSD at DePaul, gives students access to services and accommodations such as real-time captioning, audio books readers and transcribers, adaptive technologies, note-taking services, and extended time on tests and assignments. Students can have one-on-one sessions with a CSD clinician for a per-quarter fee of $350 for one hour per week or $600 for two hours per week.

Florida Agricultural and Mechanical University. At Florida A&M, assistance for LD students begins with the admissions process. Applicants to FAMU can request special admission consideration that takes their learning difference into account. Incoming freshmen have the option to strengthen their study and technological skills through a summer transition program called the College Study Skills Institute. FAMU's Center for Disability Access and Resources (CEDAR) provides services to LD students such as assessment, academic advising, tutoring, an adaptive learning laboratory, innovative assistive technologies (including talking calculators), and accommodations for tests and courses.

Hofstra University. Through its Program for Academic Learning Skills (PALS), Hofstra makes learning specialists available for weekly one-on-one consultations from the first semester of freshman year through graduation. Hofstra's PALS learning specialists help students develop learning strategies for academic success, time management skills, and executive function abilities. Skills acquired through PALS are applied to regular Hofstra courses rather than to a special array of courses for LD students. Students in PALS pay a one-time fee of $11,550. Hofstra LD students not affiliated with PALS have access to free accommodations such as extended time for assignments and exams, note-taking services, and the latest in assistive technologies.

Marist College. The Learning Disabilities Support Program at Marist provides students with an individual learning specialist. Learning specialists help students establish a plan for academic accommodations that may include personal readers, note takers, scribes, adaptive testing, alternative text, and assistive technology. Students usually meet with their learning specialist for two sessions per week to focus on improving their skills in writing, note taking, personal organization, test taking, and time management. Services provided by learning specialists require a fee.

Marshall University. For more than thirty years, Marshall (located in Huntington, West Virginia) has operated the Higher Education for Learning Problems (HELP) Center. With a staff of eighty-five (including seventy-five tutors), the HELP Center provides educational support, mentoring, and academic success strategies for students with LD and ADHD. Students can go to the HELP Center to work on improving study and organizational skills, note taking, and memory. Roughly two hundred students use the HELP Center as a bridge between them and their classes.

McDaniel College. At this liberal arts college

near Baltimore (with an undergraduate enrollment of 1,600), the Student Academic Support Services (SASS) office provides accommodations and services such as extra time on tests, audio books tutors, and training in the use of assistive technologies,. McDaniel also offers three fee-based options (the Academic Skills Program, the Mentorship Advantage Program, and Providing Academic Support for Success) that offer weekly one-on-one sessions and workshops designed to improve time management, organization, and self-advocacy skills. In addition, the Mentorship Advantage Program provides interactive workshops on résumé writing and interviewing.

Mitchell College. The mission of this nine-hundred-student college in New London, Connecticut, is to provide a student-centered academic experience crafted to individual learning differences. To LD and ADHD students, the Bentsen Learning Center provides personalized academic support that encompasses accessible technologies, learning strategies, career readiness workshops, and peer mentoring. Mitchell also operates Thames Academy, a bridge program that enables LD students to have a postgraduate college preparatory experience (akin to attending a thirteenth grade before college) while at the same time earning college credit.

Northeastern University. Cited by the *Huffington Post* for its strong Learning Disabilities Program (LDP), Northeastern takes a comprehensive and individualized approach to helping LD students make their way at this 21,000-student school in Boston. For an annual fee of $5,300, students in the LDP meet with a learning specialist for two hours each week to focus on achieving success in their courses. The assigned learning specialists help individual students develop better skills in time management, organization, reading comprehension, writing, and research.

Rochester Institute of Technology. RIT's Disability Services Office provides many accommodations for LD and ADHD students, such as extended time for tests, assignments, projects, and labs; recorded lectures; alternative format texts; plus readers and scribes for exams. Through the Empower program, RIT students can meet with an academic support counselor up to twice per week each semester. Academic support counselors help students establish goals and create a plan for academic success that addresses issues such as time management, study strategies, and the need for tutoring. Per semester fees for the Empower program range from $660 (for a single weekly session) to $1,320 (for two weekly sessions).

Texas Tech University. Staffed by nine full-time professionals, the TECHniques Center at Texas Tech offers one-on-one tutoring, counseling, and academic support services for students with LD and ADHD. The goal of the TECHniques Center is to help students with learning differences succeed academically. Counselors and tutors at the TECHniques Center work with students individually to help them build self-esteem, self-confidence, and the ability to advocate for their learning needs as they transition into a college curriculum. Fees for the TECHniques Center range from $1,000 to $1,750 per semester, depending on the services utilized.

University of Vermont. Through its ACCESS program, UVM provides advising, test and assignment accommodations, and an array of educational support services to students with LD and ADHD. Professional disability specialists work individually with students to help them develop self-advocacy skills and make the best use of resources such as e-books, note-taking services, and adaptive and assistive technologies. There is no special fee for the ACCESS program.

HOMESCHOOLED STUDENTS

Homeschooled students can be highly successful in the college and university environment. But to get college doors to open to them, they must (more than most applicants) help admissions offices understand their readiness for collegiate-level academic success. On the one hand, colleges recognize that the learning experiences of most homeschooled applicants vary greatly from those of applicants who have followed the more traditional path to college. On the other hand, the burden falls on homeschooled applicants to show admissions offices that they have completed course work in the subjects typically required for high school graduation. To be competitive at selective colleges, it is best for homeschooled applicants to follow a curriculum that signals clearly to admissions offices that the student is ready to do college-level work. Because their schooling is likely to have been unconventional, homeschooled students must make efforts to provide documentation for (and explanations of) the precollege work they have completed. Doing so will make it possible for colleges to understand and evaluate the homeschooler's curriculum and performance in comparison with the rest of the applicant pool. Many homeschooled students have had phenomenal educational opportunities, so it is a shame when those experiences get misunderstood or devalued by an admissions office due to poor documentation. Below are tips to help homeschooled students make their best case to college admissions offices.

For homeschooled students, the key to establishing academic legitimacy is to present a clearly documented transcript, often incorporating respected outside sources that verify the student's performance. For example, homeschooled students who have taken courses through Stanford University's Online High School or through Brigham Young University's Independent Study program can show an official transcript from Stanford or BYU, verifying the work completed and the grade(s) earned. On the other hand, if the applicant's parent is the chief course instructor, it is harder for college admissions offices to ascertain and evaluate what the student learned. As a general practice, homeschooled applicants should provide a reading list or curriculum summary for all self-directed or parent-taught classes. Another way to validate classes not taken in a formal institutional setting, albeit one that some homeschoolers may find ironic (especially if they chose homeschooling to avoid an exam-based curriculum), is to take a standardized test (such as Advanced Placement or SAT II subject tests) to illustrate their learning. When Dad has taught the applicant American history, one way to document learning and comprehension (using a means that enables colleges to feel comfortable that the work done at home compares favorably to a similar class at a traditional high school) is through a high score on the AP or SAT II exam in US history.

For a number of students, homeschooling means a self-directed approach to learning that blends instruction at home, a sampling of online classes, and/or selected classes at community colleges. Regardless of the learning method, homeschooled applicants are more attractive to college admissions offices when they can show they have taken accredited courses. Thus, when selecting online courses, homeschooled students should err on the side of choosing programs or organizations that are accredited by the same authorities that accredit brick-and-mortar high schools and can supply the college admissions offices with a transcript. Applicants whose schooling has occurred through one-on-one instruction or self-directed home study may want to seek out a home-school accreditation agency to organize and translate their curriculum into a workable transcript to send to colleges. Similarly, applicants who take courses at community colleges or at accredited online high schools should make sure that the colleges to which they apply are sent those transcripts.

For reasons as varied as each individual making the decision, homeschooling can be the right educational choice. Still, homeschooled students need to know that when they apply to college, the burden falls on them to present their educational background in ways that are comprehensible and persuasive to admissions offices. When colleges provide guidelines for homeschooled applicants, students should pay close attention to and follow those guidelines. Remember, as well, that homeschooled students still account for a very small portion of the national college applicant pool, which means that familiarity with and sensitivity to homeschooled applicants varies from college to college. Although very few hard and fast rules apply to homeschooled applicants, it is a truism that accredited courses and high standardized test scores pull more weight in the admissions process and that small liberal arts colleges and Christian colleges are more familiar with (and perhaps more welcoming to) the concerns of homeschooled applicants.

There are numerous websites explaining and promoting online study for homeschoolers. Among the many options, two mentioned already (Stanford Online High School and BYU Independent Study) as well as George Washington University Online High School, Indiana University High School, UM Global Academy at the University of Miami, MU (University of Missouri) Online High School, University of Nebraska High School, and the University of Texas Online High School are known and respected among college admissions offices. Other accredited online homeschooling options offered by colleges include Liberty University Online High School and National University Virtual High School. A useful site that connects homeschoolers to a large number of resources, some of which may be helpful for establishing the legitimacy of an academic transcript, is the Home School Legal Defense Association (www.hslda.org).

EARLY ENTRANCE TO COLLEGE

Students interested in starting college early have an increasing array of options. For example, Bard College operates a network of early-college high schools in cities such as New York and New Orleans, where students can start earning college credits before receiving a high school diploma. Bard also has an early college in western Massachusetts (called Simon's Rock) that students can enter after their sophomore year of high school. Credits earned at Bard's early high schools or at Simon's Rock are transferrable to Bard College but are not transferrable everywhere—policies vary from college to college. Students interested in the Bard network but who are not planning to enroll at Bard College need to check whether the colleges that interest them will accept their credits.

A handful of states, such as Washington, provide a path for students to finish high school while enrolled at a community college. Washington State's Running Start Program enables students to earn a high school diploma concurrent with an associate degree. As with the Bard early-college high schools, students in Running Start (or similar programs offered in other states such as California, Minnesota and Oregon) need to be sure that their college credits will transfer to their preferred college destinations.

With Running Start (and its analogues in other states), credits will generally transfer to in-state public colleges but may not transfer to private colleges or public universities in other states. Students investigating such programs also need to determine whether their preferred colleges will consider them a freshman applicant or a transfer applicant. Policies vary. But most colleges will not award college credit for community college courses that counted toward a student's high school diploma requirements. As a result, it is common for early-start students to have a portion (but not all) of their credits recognized by out-of-state or private colleges.

TRANSFER ADMISSION

Transferring is a second-chance opportunity. Through the transfer process, students whose first choice was a mismatch have the chance to move to a college that will better meet their needs. Transfer applicants generally fall into three categories. One group consists of students transferring up to earn a higher degree, such as when a student moves from a community college to a four-year institution. Others transfer up from a college they settled for due to a weak high school record. Following strong academic work at the first college, this type of upward transfer involves movement to a more selective and higher profile institution. Transferring up is the most common type of transfer, due to the voluminous number of students who move from two-year colleges to four-year universities.

The second type of transfer is the lateral move to a different college, usually more for personal fit reasons. In some cases, lateral transfers are made from a single-sex college to a coeducational college, such as transferring from Smith College to Oberlin College. Lateral transfers may be made due to a mismatch in location, atmosphere, or size. A student desiring a clearer focus on undergraduates and a more classic collegiate environment might transfer from Columbia University to Williams College. Another student seeking a larger city atmosphere might transfer from Carleton College in the small town of Northfield, Minnesota, to the University of Chicago. Another student may decide on a more specialized major, such as engineering, that is not offered at a liberal arts college and might transfer from Pomona College to the University of California at Berkeley. In most lateral transfers, students move between colleges of similar academic quality and distinction. For example, a student may transfer from Duke University to Dartmouth College to be closer to family.

The third type of transfer is the unfortunate forced transfer, which is often the result of an unexpected problem that prevents the student from continuing at the first college. Typically, the unfortunate forced transfer occurs due to one of three issues: finances, a traumatic experience, or academic failure. For some students, the first college is just too expensive, resulting in withdrawal for financial reasons. For other students, an unfortunate incident (such as a sexual assault) spurs transfer to a new campus, where there are no reminders of trauma. For other students, continuing at the college is impossible due to failing grades in multiple classes, resulting in academic dismissal. Unfortunately, students facing this third kind of forced transfer are usually left with fewer college options (due to their poor academic records) than the students who are transferring due to a mismatch. Consequently, this chapter is written primarily for students aiming to transfer in order to correct an initial college choice that no longer fits.

NEED-TO-KNOW ITEMS FOR PROSPECTIVE TRANSFER STUDENTS

1) **Some colleges offer midyear transfer entry**. The good news here is standards may be lower for midyear transfers. The bad news is that entering midyear can be challenging if the institution enrolls only a handful of transfer students and treats them as an afterthought. Potential transfers need to know whether the college provides more than a cursory orientation program for the midyear entrants. Entering midyear, especially if orientation resources are scant, can feel a bit like walking into a party that is already in progress. Friendships have been made and many classes have been filled. In such cases, potential transfer students may do well to wait for fall entry.

2) **Financial aid can be limited or nonexistent for transfers.** At many private colleges (including some that are need-blind for freshmen), transfer admission is not need-blind. At institutions where financial aid is limited, only the very best of the needy transfer applicants will be admitted and offered aid. Odds are, not needing financial aid will enhance a transfer applicant's chances for admission. When investigating potential options, applicants need to find out whether needing aid factors into the transfer admission process.

3) **Be wary of colleges that have more than two hundred transfer applications for five to fifteen spaces.** Colleges that enroll just five to fifteen transfers per year and select them from an applicant pool of more than two hundred are likely places that view transfers as an afterthought and reserve the majority of transfer spaces for special case applicants. Those special-case applicants may find themselves at the head of the line because they are athletic recruits or legacies (sons and daughters of alumni) that did not get admitted as freshman but were encouraged to reapply as transfers. In other cases, a certain number of transfer slots may be set aside for applicants from community colleges that have special connections with the senior institution through course and credit transfer articulation agreements. For the applicants who do not fall into one of the special-case categories, those five to fifteen transfer slots (available to more than two hundred applicants) are actually more like a mirage. Perhaps only two to three of the transfer slots are actually open to the remaining 175-plus unaffiliated applicants. Obviously, those are not good odds. This hidden reality of reserved slots for special cases is another reason why transfers applicants should always try to ferret out the number of slots available and the ratio of those applying to those admitted. If the application to spaces available ratio is fifteen to one or higher (and there are fewer than twenty transfer spaces available), be wary of the mirage phenomenon.

4) **College grades matter more than any other factor in transfer admission.** In the evaluation of transfer applicants, the college transcript is the centerpiece. The quality of courses taken and grades earned in college trumps the high school record. In some cases, colleges do not even require an applicant to submit a high school transcript. On the other hand, having a strong high school record, especially one within the institution's middle 50 percent range for SAT/ACT and GPA, will put a transfer applicant in a more competitive position, particularly at the most selective colleges.

5) **Extracurricular activities rarely matter**

for transfer admission, unless the applicant is a recruited athlete (see number three above). Academic strength is the basis for most transfer admission decisions. While having an interesting personal profile might serve as a tie breaker between two equally qualified transfer candidates, the best predictor of admission success at the new college is grades earned at the previous college.

6) **The transfer application essay matters.** Applicants who can persuasively articulate their reasons for transfer get the most positive attention from admission committees. It is especially important for transfer applicants to explain why their hoped-for future college will be a better match than their current college. Also, essays tailored to the specific transfer institution boost an applicant's chances. If the reason for transfer is founded on an interest in a specific program at the desired college, then it is critical to point that out.

7) **Transfer applicants need a robust list of college options.** Follow this rule when targeting highly competitive colleges that enroll very few transfer students (see number three above) and there is no interest in staying put in the event of a pile of rejection letters. This rule is doubly important if the applicant's college and high school record are weaker than the requirements at the dream transfer destination.

8) **State universities often prefer community college students who have earned an associate's degree.** This is especially true if there is a credit transfer articulation agreement between the community college and the senior university. Through articulation agreements, universities set clear criteria for the grade point average, credit hours, and (in some instances) courses needed to satisfy admission requirements. Many public universities consider it part of their mission to give priority to transfer applicants from community colleges in their state.

9) **Transfer applicants rarely get admitted after just one semester of college.** Students applying for transfer during their first semester of college are usually at a disadvantage. Why? Because most colleges want to see a full year of courses and grades before making an admission decision. Colleges may also question if the quick impulse to transfer is due to the adjustment challenges that many first-semester freshmen encounter. Unless life is just unbearable, it is advisable to stay put, try to do well academically, and file transfer applications during the second semester.

10) **Transferring after one year, rather than two, tends to make it easier to graduate in four years.** Nearly every institution requires transfer students to complete at least two years of courses there to earn a degree. Transferring as a junior can be difficult because it requires that students be ready to declare a major and spend the next two years fulfilling departmental and overall graduation requirements. Unless all previously earned credits transfer and the applicant has completed all required prerequisites for the intended major (including core distribution requirements, where they exist), it may be impossible for a junior-level transfer to graduate in four semesters. Sophomore transfers have more time at their new institution to complete core distribution requirements and courses required to enter certain majors. In some cases, such as colleges that require a senior thesis, potential applicants are better off entering as sophomores than as juniors. Reed College, for example, advises prospective transfer students that it is uncommon for junior year entrants to have the academic preparation needed to complete the required junior qualifying exam and thesis proposal in their second semester there. Institutions like

Reed that have specific graduation requirements (such as a senior thesis or required internship and study abroad experiences) may be easiest to enter as a sophomore.

11) **Women's colleges are often transfer friendly.** In most cases—the exceptions being the extremely selective Barnard and Wellesley and the very small Scripps—women's colleges have room for significant transfer classes. First-year attrition at women's colleges is relatively high because not every eighteen-year-old woman can appreciate a single-sex environment. Women's colleges accept numerous transfer students for another reason: the appeal of a women's college can take time to germinate. For some students, the idea of a women's college becomes appealing after an unhappy year at a coeducational college. Many women's colleges also have programs for nontraditional-age women. Such programs are open only to transfer applicants and are focused toward degree completion for students whose college attendance got interrupted by family and life events.

12) **Some institutions may not admit any transfer students.** The most notable example was (until 2016) Princeton University.

13) **Some institutions do not transfer in credits from other colleges.** One example of this rare policy is St. John's College, the great books college with campuses in Annapolis (Maryland) and Santa Fe (New Mexico). Because every student at St. John's takes the same highly structured course curriculum in sequence, all new students (whether a transfer or freshman) must start from the beginning.

14) **A few colleges operate transfer-feeder campuses.** Examples include Oxford College of Emory University and Bard College at Simon's Rock. Students who finish two years at Emory's Oxford College campus transfer to Emory's Atlanta campus to complete their degree. Simon's Rock, which operates as an early college for precocious teens, lets students in good standing transfer to Bard to complete their BA degree.

➤ HIGHLY RANKED TRANSFER-FRIENDLY COLLEGES

The following colleges welcome significant numbers of transfers, offer financial aid to them, and admit transfers at rates similar to (or higher than) admissions rates for freshmen.

Boston University	Mount Holyoke College	SUNY colleges and university centers
Brandeis University	New York University	University of Texas at Austin
University of California campuses	University of North Carolina at Chapel Hill	Tufts University
Carnegie Mellon University	Northwestern University	Vanderbilt University
Case Western Reserve University	University of Notre Dame	University of Virginia
Cornell University	Oberlin College	Washington University
Emory University	Reed College	University of Washington
Georgia Institute of Technology	Rensselaer Polytechnic Institute	Wesleyan University
Georgetown University	University of Rochester	College of William and Mary
Grinnell College	Smith College	University of Wisconsin at Madison
University of Illinois	University of Southern California	
University of Michigan		

A TRANSFER-FRIENDLY IVY LEAGUE SCHOOL: CORNELL UNIVERSITY

More than its other Ivy League brethren, Cornell is friendly to transfer students. Typically, Cornell receives 3,000 transfer applications and admits upward of 750. The size of the Cornell incoming transfer class numbers in the hundreds and is distributed across all seven of the undergraduate colleges and schools. In fact, Cornell's admissions website makes clear that each of its seven colleges and schools welcomes transfers. Due to the decentralized nature of Cornell, prospective transfer applicants need to follow the procedures and requirements outlined by the university's central undergraduate admissions office while also working closely with the admissions officials housed in the college or school they hope to enter. Cornell has other programs and policies that signal its interest in transfer students. For example, it is well-known within the state of New York that Cornell admits and gives financial aid to the very best community college students. Also, each year Cornell encourages a select number of wait-listed applicants to reapply in a year as a transfer.

One thing homeschooled, LD, and transfer students have in common is that their concerns are addressed in special categories separate from the standard admissions process and academic program. Still, each of these formerly atypical groups is now moving toward the mainstream. For example, studies show that increasing numbers of college students finish their degree at a different college from where they started; homeschooling is becoming more common, and federal and state regulations have spurred the creation of offices for students with disabilities on virtually every college campus in the United States. The authors, both of whom were transfer students, know from experience that students who inhabit the special-case categories addressed in this chapter will be primed to thrive in college the more they are informed about the options and programs available to them.

APPENDIX II: PAYING FOR COLLEGE

Paying for college is a challenging prospect for most students and their parents. For at least a decade, the annual cost to attend public and private colleges and universities has been rising more rapidly than the consumer price index (CPI). The cost increases have been dramatic. For example, state universities that charged no tuition to their residents (or less than $1,500 annually) as recently as thirty years ago now charge upward of $15,000 to $25,000 per year. The average public university charges just under $23,000 on average for a full-time resident student. Private college costs now exceed $60,000 per year in many, but not all, cases, and the average private college bill comes to roughly $45,000 annually.

We hope that after reading this chapter, students will consider college as an investment rather than a product. The media frequently portrays college as a very expensive product that is getting pricier by the minute. While undoubtedly true, there is more to the story. Parents and students must also think of a college education as an extremely valuable investment that pays dividends throughout a degree holder's lifetime. Indeed, college is arguably the most important investment a student can make. Getting a bachelor's degree is the first critical step toward expanding career opportunities and earning capacity. The difference in annual earnings between college graduates and high school graduates is strikingly significant. Consistently, including as recently as 2014, studies have shown that bachelor's degree holders (over the course of their careers) earn nearly $1 million more than high school graduates. Studies also show that holders of graduate and professional degrees earn $1.3 million to $2.1 million more in their careers than high school graduates.

Considered chiefly as a product, a college education differs from most big-ticket items in a number of ways but perhaps most significantly in the way its price is discounted to every paying customer. First of all, the tuition charged by colleges generally covers only 50 percent to 75 percent of the actual cost to educate each student. Tuition represents one part of how non-profit colleges generate operating funds. For-profit colleges, such as University of Phoenix, are a different animal altogether and not discussed in this book. Whether a student attends Princeton or the University of North Carolina, his or her education is subsidized. Colleges and universities are able to offer students a subsidized (read lower than they could charge) cost because they have additional revenue sources. Those other revenue sources include donations from alumni, income from the accumulated investment pool (called an endowment), research grants that help support faculty and students, rental payments collected for use of campus facilities by outside groups during the summer, federal and state grants for financial aid, and (in the case of public universities) state appropriations.

The other way colleges discount their full cost is through need-based and merit-based financial aid. The discount provided through financial aid and merit scholarships is pretty extraordinary. How many product sellers offer the buyer a reduced price based on her/his ability to pay (need-based aid)? How many products or services entice some buyers (those with the strongest qualifications) with a scholarship offer? How many companies charge less than full price to as many as 95 percent of the consumers seeking their product? Indeed, many colleges give some form of scholarship aid to more than 75 percent of the enrolled students. Numerous college websites state prominently that nearly every student receives financial or scholarship aid. That few students pay the full cost of college is a reality often lost in the noisy public conversation about the rising cost of college.

Conversations about paying for college are often confusing to students and their parents. This confusion stems from the many terms associated with financial aid and the role it plays in the admission process. Terms such as need-blind admissions, expected family contribution, merit scholarship, work study, Pell Grant, FAFSA, and Perkins Loan can sound like a foreign language to students and families. Students and parents need to become educated consumers about costs and aid before they begin their college visits. Families who understand the key terms related to scholarship opportunities and financial-aid programs will be better equipped to negotiate the admissions process successfully. Below are some questions to ask in order to better understand the college affordability landscape.

ASK THESE QUESTIONS ABOUT FINANCIAL AID

Here are some critical questions for students and parents to ask when visiting college campuses and when speaking to officials in admissions and financial-aid offices.

- Is the admissions process at this college need blind? This matters because at need-blind colleges, requesting financial aid does not disadvantage the applicant.

- Does the college meet 100 percent of need for all admitted students? This matters because meeting 100 percent of need and making admissions decisions need blind is the gold standard—meaning no one gets denied admission due to having a low income, and everyone with need gets his or her need fully met. Sounds perfect, right? Unfortunately, not every college can do both. That means families will usually be looking at either a need-blind college that cannot meet 100 percent of need in every case, or a college that meets full need but does not make admissions decisions in a need-blind way. Which one is preferable depends on your perspective and, quite frankly, on your income. Many believe that meeting 100 percent of need is the best approach. Why? Because if college A is need blind in admission but does not meet full need, some students, especially the poorest ones, may not be able to come up with the gap in aid. College B, if it places some applicants on the admission waiting list simply because they need aid, will obviously disadvantage some needy applicants and invite charges of unfairness. But college B, if it meets 100 percent of need for all admitted students, is arguably no less generous in its financial-aid policies than college A. Families need to decide for themselves if it is better to pass through what is called a need-aware admissions sift, and, if successful, get a generous financial-aid package, or whether it is better to be offered admission solely on one's merits, even if the admission offer comes with no aid or an unsatisfactory aid amount. Families that have low or no need for financial aid may also want to decide if they should forego applying for aid— because at some need-aware colleges, it can be advantageous to be categorized as a full-pay student.

- If full need is not met, what is the average gap? This matters because any gap can be insurmountable for the lowest-income families. Gapping policies favor low-need families over high-need families—often by design. Families need to know what the average gap in aid is and how applicants are expected to make up the gap.

- If admission is not need blind, explain the process. This matters because it is helpful to know how many applicants are affected, whether there is a financial-aid waiting list, whether the college meets 100 percent of need for those it admits, and so on.

- Is the financial-aid award adjusted annually based on changes in family income? This matters because colleges can bait students with a large freshman-year award and adjust downward in subsequent years. Also, if you are getting need-based aid, it is best if the college reassesses your need each year in order to boost your award when tuition increases. Merit scholarships, on the other hand, may not get adjusted upward as tuition increases. Get these policies clarified.

- Do scholarships come with a GPA requirement? This matters because a GPA requirement is a string attached to your scholarship. If a student falls below the GPA requirement (often 3.0), that student's scholarship may get taken away. GPA requirements can also influence student course selection patterns. Students trying to stay above a certain GPA threshold may not take courses perceived to be harder ones, even if those courses appear attractive. As a general rule, it is a good idea to be suspicious of scholarships that have strings attached, whether those strings extend to GPA or on-campus living requirements. The attached strings may restrict choice.

- What forms need to be filed, and by when (deadlines)? Like the location, location, location mantra in real estate, the financial-aid mantra is "deadlines, deadlines, deadlines." There are two key financial-aid forms: the FAFSA and the CSS Profile. The FAFSA (Free Application for Federal Student Aid) has no fee and is required for eligibility for federal sources of financial aid, such as Pell Grants. Some colleges also require financial-aid applicants to submit the College Scholarship Service (CSS) Profile form, which delves deeper into a family's financial circumstances. Filing the CSS Profile costs $25 for the first school and $16 per school thereafter. Make sure you do not miss the filing deadlines for financial-aid eligibility. Missing deadlines almost always results in being out of the running for aid. Do not miss deadlines.

- What is Expected Family Contribution (EFC)? Perhaps the most important three letters in the financial-aid process are EFC. EFC is the annual amount that a family is expected to contribute toward the cost of college. EFC is determined by analyzing the data provided by the FAFSA and CSS Profile forms.

- What tuition payment plans does the college offer? Most colleges offer monthly or quarterly tuition payment plans, even for students receiving financial aid and scholarships. The financial-aid or bursar's office is usually able to provide this information to families. Be aware that payment plans often add surcharges.

- What is the percentage of students receiving financial aid, and what is the average aid award? It is important to know this because the percentage of students getting aid helps you determine if you will be in the minority or majority as a financial-aid recipient. Some students would rather blend in with the crowd than stand out as a scholarship student. The average financial-aid award can signal how generous the college is with aid, especially when coupled with the following very important statistics: the average percentage of financial need that the college meets and the average merit scholarship the college awards.

- What are the criteria and the process for getting a merit scholarship? This is important because you need to know if the college requires an interview, an essay, or a nomination to make you eligible. Such requirements will usually be spelled out in the admissions application. If no specifics are given, assume that simply applying (and being admitted) makes you eligible to receive a scholarship. Usually notification of a merit scholarship award accompanies the admission offer or follows quickly thereafter.

- What is the average loan indebtedness of graduates? Knowing this statistic can help you determine which colleges give generous grants rather than high loans. Average loan indebtedness after four years ranges from $20,000 to $60,000. One way to gauge loan expectations is to ask colleges to tell you the average amount that students are expected to borrow each year. Colleges with average loan expectations below $5,000 tend to be the most generous. In any case, owing $20,000 after four years is a figure lower than the cost of most used cars. Also, student loan payment structures tend to be accommodating, giving most people a manageable amount of time to pay down the amount.

- How are outside scholarships handled if a student is also getting aid from the college? Many colleges will apply the outside scholarship funds against the self-help aid (nongrant funds, such as loans). Once those self-help funds are reduced down to zero, the college may reduce their grant aid dollar for dollar or by fifty cents on the dollar. Although how colleges handle this varies, it always pays to win outside scholarships.

- If I do not get financial aid my freshman year, can I get it in subsequent years? It depends on the college. Some colleges have a rule that if no financial aid is provided to a student as a freshman that student will never have an opportunity to get aid. Make sure you ask this critical question.

- Should I negotiate for more financial aid? If you can show changed financial circumstances or important information that was overlooked, go ahead and appeal. But remember, more than one appeal may be futile—especially if your repeat appeal presents no new information (beyond wanting more aid). You do not want to become the family that the admission and financial-aid offices scurry to avoid.

- Is home equity factored into the expected family contribution? Check with each college. There are no uniform policies on home equity's treatment by financial-aid offices. In recent years, the wealthiest private colleges have begun excluding or adjusting home equity for families in regions where housing prices are well above the national average.

- Are there income levels under which no loans are expected? Yes, some colleges (listed later in the chapter) do not require loans for financial-aid recipients.

- Does financial-aid eligibility increase if more than one student in the family is attending college? Yes. For example, if the Expected Family Contribution (EFC) is $30,000 for one student attending college, it will most likely be halved to $15,000 when a sibling enters college. Conversely, students should plan for the EFC to increase once siblings graduate from college. Some colleges treat a parent in college the same way, but most do not.

- When calculating financial-aid eligibility, do colleges make allowances for families that are paying for private high school tuition? Generally, high school costs are not part of the financial-aid review. That is because free public education is widespread in America, and sending a child to private school is considered a choice. But, as with home equity, some of the wealthiest colleges now consider private school tuition an annual expense that will reduce the Expected Family Contribution (EFC).

► TUITION-FREE COLLEGES

Curtis Institute of Music—Pennsylvania

Deep Springs College—California

Webb Institute of Naval Architecture—New York

CUNY Teacher Academy—New York

► STUDENTS WORK IN EXCHANGE FOR FREE TUITION

Alice Lloyd College—Kentucky

Berea College—Kentucky

College of the Ozarks—Missouri

► STUDENTS WORK IN EXCHANGE FOR REDUCED TUITION

Berry College—Georgia

Blackburn College—Illinois

REGIONAL TUITION EXCHANGES

In some regions of the United States, agreements between states enable tuition reciprocity between public colleges and universities; thus, students who attend a participating university in another state do not pay the out-of-state tuition premium. In researching tuition exchange consortiums, students need to pay close attention to the terms and restrictions. Not all public universities in member states participate, and some limit the availability of specific academic programs.

Academic Common Market. Tuition reciprocity covers public universities in Alabama, Arkansas, Delaware, Georgia, Kentucky, Louisiana, Maryland, Mississippi, Oklahoma, South Carolina, Tennessee, Virginia, and West Virginia, but only for degree programs not offered in the student's home state.

Midwest Student Exchange Program. All members (public and some private colleges in Illinois, Indiana, Kansas, Michigan, Minnesota, Missouri, Nebraska, North Dakota, and Wisconsin) agree no to charge out-of-state students more than 150 percent of the in-state tuition rate. Some member institutions restrict the eligible academic programs.

New England Regional Student Program. Students who cross borders between Connecticut, Maine, Massachusetts, New Hampshire, Rhode Island, and Vermont cannot be charged more than 175 percent of the in-state tuition rate. The regional discount only covers degree programs not offered in the student's home state.

Western Undergraduate Exchange. The WUE has member institutions in Alaska, Arizona, California (several CSUs and only one UC, Merced), Colorado, Hawaii, Idaho, Montana, Nevada, New Mexico, North Dakota, Oregon, South Dakota, Utah, Washington, and Wyoming. Some member institutions restrict the majors available, but all agree to charge out-of-state students no more than 150 percent of the in-state tuition rate.

➤ COLLEGES OFFERING FULL SCHOLARSHIPS

The colleges listed below offer merit scholarships covering tuition plus room and board (in most cases) and, in some instances, special stipends for internships, research, or study abroad. Competition for these scholarships is stiff.

Boston College—Presidential Scholarship

Clemson University—National Scholars Program

University of Connecticut—Stamps Scholars and Nutmeg Scholarship

University of Delaware—Du Pont Scholars

Duke University—A. B. Duke Scholarship

Emory University—Robert Woodruff Scholarships

Fordham University—Presidential Scholarship

Georgia Institute of Technology—President's Scholarship

Indiana University—Wells Scholarship

Johns Hopkins University—Westgate Scholarship (engineering)

University of Maryland—Banneker Key Scholarship

University of Miami—Stamps and Jenkins Scholarships

Michigan State University—Alumni Distinguished Scholarship

University of North Carolina at Chapel Hill—Morehead/Cain Scholarship

Northeastern University—Torch Scholars

Ohio State University—Eminence Scholarship

University of Oklahoma—National Merit Scholars

Santa Clara University—Johnson Scholars

Seattle University—Sullivan Leadership Award

University of Southern California—Trustee and Stamps Leadership Scholarships

Southern Methodist University—President's Scholars

University of Texas at Austin—Forty Acres Scholarships

Tulane University—Stamps-Tulane Scholarship

University of Tulsa—National Merit/Presidential Scholars

Vanderbilt University—Chancellor's Scholars

Villanova University—Presidential Scholarship

University of Virginia—Thomas Jefferson Scholarship

Washington University—Danforth Scholars

College of William and Mary—1693 Scholars

➤ LOAN-FREE AID PACKAGES (SO STUDENTS GRADUATE WITH ZERO DEBT)

Amherst College

Bowdoin College

Colby College

Columbia University

Davidson College

Harvard University

Haverford College

Pomona College

Princeton University

Swarthmore College

Stanford University

Vanderbilt University

Yale University

ABOUT THE AUTHORS

Paul Marthers earned a BA from Oberlin College, masters' from Boston University and Reed College and his doctorate from University of Pennsylvania. His many years of experience working in higher education and college counseling include positions at Duke, Vassar, Phillips Academy, Boston College, Oberlin, Reed, RPI, Bennington, and the SUNY (State University of New York) system.

Janet Marthers earned a BA from Stanford University and a master's from Reed College. She is an independent college counselor, working with families on the college and prep school admission processes. She has worked in admissions at Oberlin College and Skidmore College. To learn about Janet's counseling services, please refer to JanetMarthers.com for more information.

CPSIA information can be obtained at www.ICGtesting.com
Printed in the USA
LVOW09s1806060916

503449LV00006B/514/P